Youth, Crime, and Society

| JOANNE C. MINAKER | BRYAN HOGEVEEN |
GRANT MACEWAN COLLEGE   UNIVERSITY OF ALBERTA

Youth, Crime, and Society

Issues of Power and Justice

PEARSON

Prentice
Hall

Toronto

Library and Archives Canada Cataloguing in Publication

Minaker, Joanne Cheryl, 1974–
    Youth, crime and society : issues of power and justice / Joanne C. Minaker,
Bryan Hogeveen. — 1st ed.

Includes bibliographical references and index.
ISBN 978-0-13-200127-4

    1. Juvenile delinquency—Canada—Textbooks. 2. Juvenile justice,
Administration of—Canada—Textbooks. I. Hogeveen, Bryan Richard, 1972–
II. Title.

HV9108.M55 2009   364.360971   C2007-905507-9

ISBN-13: 978-0-13-200127-4
ISBN-10: 0-13-200127-6

Vice President, Editorial Director: Gary Bennett
Senior Acquisitions Editor: Laura Paterson Forbes
Marketing Manager: Sally Aspinall
Senior Developmental Editor: Patti Altridge
Production Editor: Amanda Wesson
Proofreader: Sally Glover
Production Coordinator: Janis Raisen
Composition: Laserwords
Photo and Permissions Research: Cheryl Freedman
Art Director: Julia Hall
Cover Design: Anthony Leung
Cover Image: Masterfile

9 10 11 CP 13 12 11
Printed and bound in Canada.

For our children, Ayden and Taryk…

Brief Contents

Contents

Preface

In *Positive Discipline*, Jane Nelson asks rhetorically, "Where did we get the crazy idea that in order to make children do better, first we have to make them feel worse?" We might not have articulated it this way, but this is a question we have struggled with for years during our work with youth detention, throughout our graduate studies, and as we have embarked on our academic careers and parenthood. It was not one thing that inspired this book but many significant moments—from Bryan seeing the faces of Aboriginal youth stare back at him in custodial facilities or Joanne receiving a Valentine's Day card signed with a heart from a "notorious" female young offender to our continual search for an appropriate textbook to use in our own classrooms that would encourage, challenge, and inspire our students.

Our interest in the related topics of youth crime and youth justice stems from our passion for justice. From very different vantage points and travelling along somewhat dissimilar paths, we mutually came to the realization that criminalized youth were a prime example of the quintessential "other." We joined forces in more ways than one to create, inspire, and instill a different way of thinking about young people who engage in crime and deviance. We strongly believe that we each make choices every day that reflect our own attitudes, beliefs, and socialization in the cultural and historical context in which we live. These seemingly personal decisions, however, are conditioned and contoured by our social position and reflect power differentials in society. Youth as a group are all too often called upon to take responsibility for their "bad" choices without the opportunity to question the social and structural bases of their lives, which for many disenfranchised youth are characterized by violence, systemic discrimination, and marginalization.

Both of us were challenged early in our academic careers to think through what it means to be a scholar and how scholarship—research and teaching—can or should be about more than simply our own interests. We continue to engage with the challenges and contradictions involved in making ameliorative changes in our social world that offer hope instead of despair, compassion instead of intolerance, and justice instead of marginalization, exclusion, and silencing. Having children of our own fosters this desire.

In the summer of July 2007, when we were in the final stages of writing, I was watching my eldest son's swimming lessons at the local YMCA. Hanging from the ceiling was a banner of the Y's values in red, green, blue, and yellow letters that spelled caring, honesty, respect, and responsibility. It hit me: *that* is what we are trying to do in this book—instill in our students, who will become police officers, social workers, probation officers, lawyers, judges, business owners, and community members, a culture of sensitivity toward youth based on an ethic of care (rather than punishment); an approach to issues of youth crime and justice based on authentic or honest claims that do not silence youth; respect for young people and their concerns; and the inspiration for Canadians to take greater responsibility not for dealing with the problem of youth crime *per se*, but for tackling the problems underlying the choices that bring youth into the YCJS. That, for us, is *justice for youth*.

Organization of This Book

The book is distinct in several ways:

■ It is written from a *critical perspective*, recognizing issues of power that are systemic in the construction of youth crime and in responses to it.

■ It encourages readers to *think critically* about the issues confronting youth and the youth justice system in Canada.

■ It includes the most recent empirical and theoretical developments in the field, paying particular attention to the Canadian context.

■ The book's *philosophy* and *orientation* are consistent throughout and themes are developed across the chapters.

■ It encourages a process of critical reflection and social engagement called social justice praxis.

The primary market for the book is post-secondary instructors teaching third- or fourth-year courses in youth crime/youth justice issues at colleges or universities in Canada. Criminologists and socio-legal scholars undertaking research in the field should also find this book useful.

The text is organized into three sections:

■ Youth, Legislation, and History (Chapters 1–5)

■ Special Populations: Making Race/Class/Gender Connections (Chapters 6–9)

■ Recent and Future Directions: Responding to Youth, Crime, and Society (Chapters 10–12)

When the phrase "youth and crime" is uttered, many tend to ignore the *and*, focusing instead on "youth crime," and almost invariably the discussion revolves around youthful offenders. Our text challenges this assertion and begins with an introductory chapter intended to provide students with an overview of the complexities involved in the study of youth and crime. We outline the philosophical approach of the book and its various themes. Chapter 1, "Toward Understanding Youth and Crime," demonstrates that how a problem is defined has considerable implications for its control, a process that is informed by various discourses that construct the problem of youth crime—media, popular, governmental, and criminological discourses.

Chapter 2, "Practices of Governance and Control: Theoretical Underpinnings," exposes students to the sets of ideas and "ways of theorizing" that underlie various responses to youth crime. The chapter is not intended to review criminological theories, but to give students the tools to make sense of various issues raised throughout the book. Since we all have a "starting point" when it comes to understanding youth justice, the chapter begins by asking students to think about their own theories of youth crime (i.e. the set of claims they use to interpret it). Chapter 2 examines a wide range of knowledge claims, among them the traditional criminological perspective, feminist theory, and risk discourse.

In the third chapter, "Responding to Youth Crime: Historical Origins of Juvenile Justice Legislation," we explore the historical development of a separate juvenile justice system, including Canada's first legislation to govern young people, the *Juvenile Delinquents Act* . In particular, we outline the ruptures and shifts in the transition from classical legal governance (pre-*JDA*) to modern legal governance (*JDA* era). This historical perspective on conceptions and treatment of children will position students to better understand current attitudes about how we should deal with young people who break the law.

Chapter 4, "Legislating Youth Crime: From the YOA to the YCJA," explores the origins, development, and passage of the *Young Offenders Act (YOA)* and the *Youth Criminal Justice Act (YCJA)*. It provides a thorough explanation of the main tenets of each piece of legislation and compares the current act with previous legislation. As well, the chapter asks what it means to "legislate" the problem of youth crime.

Chapter 5, "The Operation of the Youth Criminal Justice System," takes students through the processes a young person may go through when they break the law, including formal criminal justice processing and alternatives (i.e. extra-judicial measures).

The four chapters in the "Special Populations" section each focus on one group of criminalized youth: female youth (Chapter 6), Aboriginal youth (Chapter 7), street-involved youth (Chapter 8), and violent youth (Chapter 9). In each chapter, we integrate issues of power and justice around age, class, race, and gender inequalities. Necessarily there is some overlap in these discussions.

Chapter 10, "What to do About Youth Crime?" begins the final section of the book. As is clear from the title, we explore various responses to youth and crime, which may fall under either a retributive or restorative justice paradigm. Students are challenged to consider the difference between "system-based" and "systemic" approaches to youth, crime, and society.

Chapter 11, "Youth Voices and Youth-Centred Innovations," directs attention to youthful perspectives on what to do about youth crime. Here we recognize youth as authorized knowers and attempt to listen to what they have to say. We follow this direction in the concluding section, Chapter 12, where we review the book's main claims and encourage students to articulate their own.

Pedagogical Features

- **Starting Point**: Each chapter begins with a unique Starting Point. Whether it is a poem, vignette, satirical cartoon, or Xhosa proverb, it immediately draws students into the chapter and sets the stage for the upcoming topic.

- **Reflective Questions:** Following the Starting Point, a set of reflective questions promotes critical thinking and suggests ideas for students to keep in mind while reading.

- **Learning Objectives:** These specify intended learning outcomes and help students stay on track in their reading and studying.

- **Bulleted Summary:** The end-of-chapter summary captures the key points of the chapter in a concise recapitulation.

- **Discussion Questions:** Following the summary, Discussion Questions stimulate critical thinking and/or guide classroom discussions.

- **Recommended Readings:** At the close of each chapter, additional readings are listed to enable students to study the issues developed in the chapters more fully.

- Throughout the book, additional features including tables, figures, box inserts, visuals, and student activities are intended to allow students to apply information to the "real world," aid in recall, give relevant examples, and so on.

Instructors' Supplements

- **Instructor's Manual:** This supplement can be downloaded by instructors from a password-protected link on Pearson Education Canada's online catalogue (vig.pearsoned.ca). Simply search for the text, then click on "Instructor" under "Resources" in the left-hand menu. Contact your local sales representative for further information.

- **Test Item File:** Also found in the online catalogue.

Acknowledgments

Support, encouragement, and guidance are three essential ingredients for any writing project to progress from an idea and plan into a finished product. Thanks are needed for all those individuals (too many to mention here) who gave a hug, a kind word, a listening ear, a much-needed "pep talk" or gentle reminder to push ahead.

We were very fortunate to be surrounded by a remarkable group of youth justice professionals, colleagues, friends and family, students and research assistants who helped bring this book into being. Our gratitude to Research Assistant *Extraordinare*, Rebecca Taylor. Thanks Becky for what you have done for the project and for who you are. You remind us of all that is special about young people today. Special thanks also goes to the entire production team at Pearson.

Above all else, I extend my appreciation to my co-author, Bryan Hogeveen. Thank you, Bryan, for your gifted mind and prolific writings on youth, crime, and justice issues. Your enthusiasm for the project inspired me (especially if my own began to wane). You continue to teach me about patience and perseverance and how to envision a more just world for the future. Thank you for the love and laughter and the zeal with which you approach every day. This work is dedicated to our children, Ayden and Taryk Hogeveen, who, along with my remarkable partner, have shown me sheer joy. Having children has shown me how significant relationships based on love, respect, and compassion can be.

Joanne Minaker

The impetus for this book goes back a long way. Its articulation should be linked, however, to the intelligence, generosity, critical thought, and demand for justice that is genuine to my co-author. It is her dedication to social justice and infinite responsibility to the call of the suffering other that made this work possible. It bears witness to her devotion to the power she locates in young people—a promise that will inspire readers to move beyond their own antipathy. What fixes me here in this book, in life, and above all, is the gift of my co-author. For the grace of a friendship in thought and love beyond all thought; I am forever grateful. For *our* children. . .

Bryan Hogeveen

The ability to act in and through love, to be non-violent, to be generous, and to respect the rights and needs of others comes from having been generously and gently loved and respected.

Rita Nakshima Brock, Christianity, Patriarchy, and Abuse

Chapter 1

Introduction: Toward Understanding Youth and Crime

STARTING POINT

Trouble(d) Youth
Troubling? A Menace
To Society, some say.
Drug Abuser, Thief, Gang-banger,
Or worse, murderer—they must pay!

What if we stopped to consider
The troubles that youth face,
The abuse, addictions, and poverty
That are too commonplace?

Could we look behind the exterior?
View something else inside?
Who wants to look, who fails to look?
Can we no longer hide?

Do we hear their voices?
Do we stop to care?
Can we look past the stereotypes,
And see a person there?

Troubled, a child, lost or in need
For society to mould,
To expand his or her life chances,
Or limit and withhold.

Youth crime and youth justice
Complex issues, real demands
Care and compassion
Is it as simple as *helping* hands?

Anonymous, 2003.

Are youth troubled? Are youth troubling? (Tanner, 2001) Take a few minutes to write your own reaction to the above poem before you read the rest of this chapter. We encourage you to revisit your initial response throughout your reading of the text. Perhaps your views on youth crime and youth justice will change. Start by considering these questions:

- What does it mean to refer to youth as "troubled" or "troubling?"
- What stereotypes about youth crime exist in North American culture?
- What role should members of society play in dealing with youth crime?

LEARNING OBJECTIVES

After reading this chapter, you should be able to

- Describe the relationships between media discourse, popular discourse, and official crime rates.
- Explain the difference between focusing on "youth crime" and focusing on the relationships between youth, crime, and society.
- Identify the two main elements of social justice praxis.
- Illustrate how the way a problem (e.g., youth crime) is constructed influences the responses to it (e.g., youth justice).
- Explain the disadvantages of overemphasizing the offending behaviours of youths.
- Describe the role of critical thinking in the study of youth crime and youth justice.

INTRODUCTION

Youth crime is a hot topic in Canadian society. It pervades **popular consciousness.** When the words *youth* and *crime* are uttered in the same sentence, the mind typically combines them so that we might hear youth crime but think young offenders. We have all witnessed or participated in discussions about the new youth "super-predator" and are familiar with the fear and outcry over groups of "terrifying teenagers" swarming through our "once safe" communities. The media is rife with examples of horrendous offences committed by young people. Newspaper headlines exposing youth offences such as "Young and Bloodied" (*The Edmonton Journal*, June 25, 2006) are much more common than those that highlight the positive efforts of youth, namely "Teens lead anti-violence march" (*The Edmonton Journal*, May 20, 2006). The accompanying articles usually draw attention to "bad" decisions made by "bad kids."

One horrific case, the murder of Barb Danelesko, is striking not only for its sensationalized media representations of youth **violence,** but also for its iconic status (at least in Western Canada). The press-reading and news-watching public could, and did, point to the event as evidence that today's young people are out-of-control.

On April 16, 1999, Barb Danelesko was murdered in the Edmonton suburb of Millwoods. Two young males, Sonny Head and David Larocque, were tried and convicted in adult court and found guilty of second-degree murder and manslaughter, respectively. Larocque was sentenced to four years in jail and Head to life imprisonment. A third (unidentified) youth was given a sentence of three years for manslaughter, the maximum allowable under the then-governing **Young Offenders Act (YOA)**. Shortly thereafter, then-premier Ralph Klein called for the death penalty for young offenders convicted of murder in adult court. He was not alone in arguing that if Head and Larocque had paid for their crimes with their lives, then other youth would have been sent a loud and deterrent message that youth crime would be punished severely. It was widely held that Edmonton streets could be made safer through such punitive reactive interventions.

The issue of youth crime and violence was insidiously saturated in the public imagination. It appeared that youth as a group were "out of control," that they could not be held accountable under the YOA, and that new youth justice legislation was required. Indeed, legislation "must be seen as a reflection of the attitudes and beliefs of society regarding the most appropriate means of dealing with young offenders" (Reid-MacNevin, 2001: 129).

Politicians and citizens seem to be caught in an ethos of punishment, believing that more austere methods of punishment will curb the tide of youth crime and violence. However, when it comes to the claim that there are more out-of-control youth today, the reality may lie more in our subjective sensitivity to youth violence than in its actual presence. The most significant shifts concerning youth crime have been in the way that problems have been constructed and responded to, rather than in youth behaviour itself.

Moreover, despite recent high-profile violent crimes by youth in Alberta and other Canadian provinces and reactionary political rhetoric and public opinion centred on the problem of out-of-control youth, the available facts and figures fail to provide a sound argument for a stronger, more punitive response. When critically examined, the nature and extent of youth crime presents a very different picture.

To develop an informed understanding of youth crime and youth justice, with all of its complexities, we will focus on three main arguments. First, we argue that the way a social problem is defined has profound implications for how individuals, groups, and social institutions react and respond to it. In the case of youth justice, various policies, processes, and practices—which involve the handling, regulation, management, or control of youth and youth crime—operate in conjunction with particular ways of knowing or **discourses** (ways of speaking) and sets of ideas. How the problem of youth crime is conceived, constructed, or otherwise conceptualized directly influences what happens to young people who defy the law and/or deviate from socio-cultural scripts of appropriate behaviour. The consequences are the most dramatic for those who most vehemently offend the values upheld by law and social institutions (i.e., those who commit the most serious offences or do so repeatedly). In short, discourses about youth crime dictate its governance through various youth justice practices. Later in this chapter we will investigate how media and popular discourses construct the problem of youth crime.

Second, we hold that the main issue to be addressed is not youth crime *per se*, but the relationships between youth, crime, and society. Our investigations in the book centre on a group called **youth**. The **Youth Criminal Justice Act (YCJA)** and its predecessor, the YOA, define youth as individuals between the ages of 12 and 17. Our definition is significantly broader. We include young people in their mid-twenties, many of whom are serving youth sentences and/or are affected by their experiences in the youth justice system. The problem we address is both political and theoretical; both concrete and abstract. Youth, crime, and society must be engaged at the level of ideas (theory) and in a material context (practice). We attempt to move beyond the level of ideas to the social situations, circumstances, and lives of individuals who most intimately experience the implications of both **practices of governance** (*what* is done in response to youth crime) and

rationalities of governance (*why* it is done). As such, we must attend to discourses related to youth crime and youth justice, being careful not to obscure the **social conditions**—the cultural, historical, political, and social context—under which youth make choices. Social conditions include, but are not limited to, age, race, class, and gender inequalities. What conditions contour and constrain the lives of youth involved in the youth justice system? How are age, race, class, and gender implicated in societal responses to youth crime?

Finally, what makes our approach unique is our view of praxis. Several scholars have adopted the **Marxian praxis** that knowledge should not simply exist for its own sake but should be used for social transformation. Paraphrasing social conflict theorist Karl Marx, a knowledge of the social world should not be reserved for academics and found only in books on library shelves. Rather, research done on humans, whom Marx considered social beings by nature, should be used to make change in society. In our view, praxis as it relates to youth and crime is not tied simply to social change. Dangerous and destructive claims of knowledge (from 19th century eugenics to the contemporary "war on terrorism") have been employed to ill effect, justifying reforms, practices, and policies that have irrevocably damaged the psyches, identities, and life chances of human beings. Our praxis is one of social justice—a process of critical reflection and social engagement. **Social justice praxis** is aimed at addressing the systemic conditions of **marginalization**, exclusion, and social inequality that lead to the involvement of youth in crime in the first place. It is about making meaningful changes to improve the life chances of young people. Examples of social justice praxis include addressing the affordable housing shortage in Edmonton, dealing with extreme child poverty in Winnipeg, reducing the over-13% unemployment rate in Prince Edward Island, connecting displaced youth who "squeegee" in the business district of Toronto to skills-building and employment agencies, and mentoring 14-year-old Aboriginal girls in Regina who are being sexually exploited and lured into prostitution.

We are not content to teach our students about the social world—to pass on knowledge claims about what *is*—without also encouraging a process of critical reflection and social engagement about what *could be*. Hogeveen and Woolford (2006) refer to this endeavour, which they define as the **"praxis of possibility,"** as an integral part of critical criminology. They argue that "our task is to attend to the suffering of those about us and to open up worlds of the possible beyond human misery" (Hogeveen and Woolford, 2007: 690). Youth are suffering—without a place to live, without food to eat, without a job, without positive role models. The youth crime problem is too often met with calls for more of the same (more "cops, courts, and corrections") and a stronger, harder "crack down" on recalcitrant youth.[1] Is this the most creative solution society can develop? It is very tempting to distance ourselves from the problem, to pass judgment on the "bad" choices of those who are marginalized by race, class, gender, and/or age. Alternatively, respect for difference has the potential to create meaningful new horizons and more just social spaces. We encourage our readers to think outside the current **socio-political climate**; that is, the social, economic, and political context in which we live. In so doing, we can **problematize** embedded assumptions and ideologies usually taken for granted, and then envision how alternative, more just, and humane social conditions are possible. This process involves questioning society; its practices (action); and the claims, discourses, and

---

[1] The phrase "cops, courts, and corrections" is uttered in public discourse, not coined by the authors. We refer to the professionals involved in law enforcement as police officers.

rationalities (ideas) that justify those practices. Without questioning the current political ethos, ideas and action tend to reinforce and re-create a **gendered, racialized, class-based,** and **adult-centred social order**. These terms, discussed at length later in the book, refer to the way society is structured along lines of gender, race/ethnicity, class, and age.

This process of critical engagement requires a **culture of sensitivity** toward youth, based on respect of differences and empathy toward needs. "Worlds of the possible beyond human misery" (Hogeveen and Woolford, 2006: 690) is not an idealistic idiom. Passionate individuals can be engaged in social justice praxis that goes far beyond the traditional discourses associated with youth crime; namely, law and order, punishment, and legislation. They start with the assumption that youth should be respected. What would a more "just" world for all youth (including youth who have been victimized or have a history of offences) look like? What else is possible?

Thus we take a **critical approach,** which we have defined as a social justice praxis, to examine the following issues:

- societal perceptions of youth, youth crime, and violence
- the prevalence of youth **victimization,** youthful offending, and violent behaviour
- how the youth justice system responds to youth and youth crime
- alienation, exclusion, and marginalization of youth
- the conditions of youth crime and the context of youth choices
- access to social support, services, and institutional assistance
- questions of **social (in)justice** as they relate to race, class, and gender inequalities[2]

  - gendering youth crime and youth justice
  - over-representation of Aboriginal youth in the YCJS
  - how race, class, and gender affect the lives of street-entrenched youth

- the implications, consequences, and effectiveness of the YCJS
- ways to respond to youth crime outside the traditional YCJS
- questions around silence and voice in relation to the role youths play in the youth justice process

THE POPULAR CONSCIOUSNESS OF YOUTH CRIME: MEDIA AND POPULAR DISCOURSE

Crime generally and youth crime specifically pervade public consciousness. As such, it is important to consider the knowledge claims about youth crime that are widely circulating in society. Much of what is done about youth crime is media and politically driven. Within what can be loosely referred to as the "popular consciousness of youth crime," there are two main discourses. As mentioned earlier, discourses are ways of speaking about a particular social issue or problem, representing "that-which-is-believed-to-be-reality" (Hamilton, 1999). If it is believed that "young people engaged in crime are inherently troubling," then

---

[2] We use the phrase (in)justice to denote that justice is not "all or nothing." Inequalities of race, class, and gender reinforce and perpetuate social *injustice*, but working to change the way such power relations condition peoples' lives is defined as social *justice*.

the systems set in place to deal with them take them as such—inherently troubling. Discourses, however, are not merely "talk," but talk that matters. In other words, discourses have social consequences. What is said, by whom, and who is listening all have implications for the group being discussed. As we will see in the next section, there is a significant relationship between how the media represents the issue of youth crime—media discourse—and how the general public perceives the problem—popular (or public) discourse.

Media Discourse

Media discourse on the subject of youth crime can be categorized into 1) news and information and 2) entertainment. However, the boundaries between the two are not always easily distinguished. Consider the vast number of television "entertainment" programs that have crime as a central or secondary concern (*Law and Order, CSI, Prison Break*, etc.). The focus on young people's involvement in crime figures prominently in the narratives of several frequently watched programs; youth crime is a dominant theme. Watch the news on any given night and you will hear about numerous criminal events. The same holds true for the front-page stories and headlines in your local paper, for instance: "Toll Keeps Mounting as Violent Youth Spawn an Epidemic of Violence" (*Calgary Herald*, June 29, 1992), "45 Gangs Plague York Schools, Malls: 'Know No Boundaries': Police Compiled Database with Gangsters' Profiles" (*National Post*, March 30, 2006), "Girl Gang Members on the Rise; Six Per Cent Are Female, say Police, Major Change in the Last Five Years" (*Toronto Star*, May 17, 2006), "Record Number of Manitoba Youths Facing Homicide Charges" (*Winnipeg Free Press*, July 4, 2007), and "Continuing Crime Wave Convinces Langdon to Bring in Teen Curfew" (*The Edmonton Journal*, September 3, 2002). More recently the headline "Two Sides of Killer Emerge from Medicine Hat Trial" (*The Star Phoenix*, July 11, 2007) and its accompanying article described the case of a 13-year-old girl convicted of murdering her parents and 8-year-old brother.

The use of the term "gang" to describe a group of youths involved in criminal activity and the increased attention on "school violence" in the media misrepresents youth crime as mostly "gang-related" and schools as increasingly unsafe. According to Hackler (2005: 197), "despite very low levels of lethal violence in schools, the media hype and the 'violence' crisis had led to cuts in after-school programs, police officers in schools, and the expulsion of students for minor acts of violence."

Media discourse presents a one-sided conversation filled with images and messages about youth crime. To varying degrees, members of the general public digest, interpret, and may call into question these accounts on the basis of their own experiences, depending on what alternative explanations they have access to. We are bombarded with a litany of images—often graphic—of violence by young people. As Christie Barron (2000: 67) puts it, the media

> often decontextualizes the acts of crime for public consumption. When youth crime is presented in a social, economic and political vacuum, it appears as if nothing else is occurring in a society except kids doing bad things . . . violent youths have become 'folk devils,' to whom are attributed characteristics that feed societal panic but clash with the youths' perceptions of self. Youth are pathologized within professional discourse and portrayed as unremorseful monsters in need of medical treatment.

We agree with Barron that "explaining youth crime as an individual problem [as media discourse puts it] denies the **structural and cultural barriers** that youths say contribute to their actions" (Barron, 2000: 67). For example, cultural barriers (feelings of hopelessness, lack of belonging, and lack of identity) and structural barriers (lack of recreational opportunities, being expelled from school, and growing up in an impoverished environment) may influence a young person's choices to engage in deviant or criminal activity.

To what extent does the representation of youth crime endemic to media discourse actually resemble its reality? Before answering this question, we will explore popular discourse.

Popular Discourse

Humans are not simply passive recipients of the world. We actively engage with images and messages from various sources. But without alternative sources of information about crime, the general public tends to rely heavily on the media when developing beliefs, attitudes, and opinions on the subject. The barrage of headlines and images presents a sensationalized, decontextualized, and individualized picture of youth crime that the general public uses to frame their own accounts of the problem. Popular discourse refers to all that is said about a topic by members of a particular culture and society at any given historical moment. In North America, popular "talk" on the subject of youth crime has been especially heightened since the 1980s. Popular discourse can be divided into two forms: gossip and urban legend. Popular perceptions of youth crime are formed through the circulation of stories—experiential narratives and media-informed personal tales—about young people's involvement in crime. This includes everything from *true* stories or "gossip" passed between friends, relatives, and neighbours to fictitious, captivating accounts or "urban legends," usually involving graphic details of youth violence (widely told as true stories). In contrast to media discourse, popular discourse involves informal, two-way, interactive conversations.

Stanley Cohen coined the term **"moral panic"** in *Folk Devils and Moral Panics*. Moral panic occurs when there is "exaggerated attention, exaggerated events, distortion, and stereotyping" (Cohen, 1972: 31). Like the "mods and rockers" in Cohen's study, youth today are largely viewed as a threat to law and order, especially when filtered through the lens of media discourse. In Cohen's terms, youth—and more specifically the violent young offender—have become "folk devils." A case in point is British toddler James Bulger, who was murdered by two children in the early 1990s. Bulger's story and the children accused of his death made headlines worldwide (see Bradley, 1994, for more). Cohen's concept highlights the role media plays in doing more than simply reflecting reality by actually constructing a "that-which-is-believed-to-be" reality.

Does North American culture predominately *celebrate*, *tolerate*, or *condemn* youth? Does it surprise you that when discussions of youth and crime take place, the tendency is to focus on "youth crime" and direct attention to youths as offenders rather than youths as victims or to the involvement of young people as agents of meaningful change? This is the case, even though victims of youth crime tend to be other young people (peers), not adults. Youth as a group are disproportionately represented as victims of crime. Given that youth comprise approximately 10% of the Canadian population, it is remarkable that they represent 20% of the victims of crime.

The Canadian public believes that crimes of violence form a much higher proportion of crime than they really do. In a Canadian Sentencing Commission study, 95% of respondents said their knowledge of crime came from the media (Canadian Sentencing

Commission, 1995). Furthermore, participants *overestimated* the amount of crime and *underestimated* the severity of penalties. Almost 80% of Canadians believe that the youth justice system is too lenient (Doob and Sprott, 1998). In short, there is a gap between our understanding of youth crime and our response to it.

THE NATURE AND EXTENT OF YOUTH CRIME

Does the popular consciousness of youth crime resemble statistical evidence? How do trends in youth crime rates compare to popular and media accounts of it? There is a substantial gap between the *rhetoric* and the *reality* of youth crime and justice (Hartnagel, 2002). Furthermore, statistics on youth crime (based on police and court data) do not adequately describe the criminal behaviour of youth. The *youth crime* rate refers to "all young persons aged 12 to 17 accused of committing a crime, whether they were formally charged by police or dealt with by other means such as a warning, caution, or referral to a diversionary program" (*The Daily, Juristat*, 2007). The youth crime rate, then, measures only those instances of youth crime that have come to the attention of police.

Are youth crime and violent youth crime on the rise? It all depends on how we look at the data. In 1999, the youth crime rate was down for the seventh consecutive year, its 7.2% drop bringing the rate to 21% lower than it had been a decade earlier. The violent youth crime rate also dropped by 5% in 1999—its fourth decline in a row. However, despite this downward trend, the youth violent crime rate was still 40% higher in 1999 than it had been in 1989.

The media has fuelled lay arguments that the behaviour of girls is getting worse. The "nasty girl" phenomenon has been at the centre of recent debate (Barron and Lacombe, 2001). Over the ten-year period 1989–1999, female youth violent crime increased by 81%. On the surface, such data appear to demonstrate that female youth crime is very much on the rise. However, this view obscures the fact that the real numbers are still relatively low and that the male rate has been declining more rapidly than the female rate. The male youth violent crime rate is still close to three times higher than that for females (*The Daily, Juristat*, 2000).

In 2000, the youth crime rate rose slightly (+1%) (see Table 1.1 on p. 10). Violent offences increased by 7%, but the rate of property offences decreased by 4%. For the most serious crime—homicide—41 youths were charged, four fewer than in 1999. Another slight increase occurred in 2001 (+1%). After decreases throughout the 1990s, it may have appeared that youth crime was on the rise. While the property crime rate continued to drop, the violent youth crime rate increased by 2%. For homicide, however, only 30 youths were accused in 2001, the lowest level in over 30 years (and 18 fewer than the average of 48 over the previous decade) (*The Daily, Juristat*, 2002).

In 2002, the rate of youths charged with crime dropped by 5%, bringing it to 33% lower than it had been in 1992. After increasing steadily throughout the 1980s and rising slowly during the 1990s, the youth violent crime rate dropped (but was still 7% higher than a decade before). Yet for property crime, the youth rate fell 5%, bringing it to the lowest it had been in over 25 years (Statistics Canada, *The Daily*, 2003).

According to the numbers, youth crime rose again in 2003. Violent crime among youth was up 3% and property crime was up 4% (The Daily, *Juristat*, 2004). In 2004, however, the overall youth crime rate declined 4%—with a 6% drop in youths charged and a

Table 1.1 Youth Crime Rate Trends

1999	Down 7%
2000	Up 11%
2001	Up 1%
2002	Down 5%
2003	Up 3%
2004	Down 4%
2005	Down 6%
2006	Up 3%

Source: Statistics Canada, *The Daily,* 1999–2006

2% drop in youths cleared by other means. The rate of violent crime among youth fell by 2% (The Daily, *Juristat*, 2005). Crimes committed by 12- to 17-year-olds decreased again in 2005 by 6%. Although the number of young people accused of homicide rose from 44 in 2004 to 65 in 2005—putting the youth-accused homicide rate at its highest point in more than a decade—violent crime among youth decreased by 2% and property crime dropped 12% (Statistics Canada, *The Daily*, 2006).

What do the latest statistics tell us? In 2006 the youth crime rate increased by 3%—its first increase since 2003. Although violent crime among youth was up 3%, property crime was 3% lower than the previous year. The biggest difference was in "other" Criminal Code offences (e.g., mischief and disturbing the peace), which were up 9%. The only province not to report an increase in youth crime was Quebec, where the youth crime rate fell 4%.

More youths came into contact with the police in 2006, but fewer were formally charged. "About 74 000 youths were charged with a criminal offence in 2006, and a further 104 000 were cleared by other means" (*The Daily, Juristat*, 2007). Since the YCJA was introduced in 2003, we have seen a reduction in the proportion of youths formally charged by police—from 56% in 2002 to 42% in 2006.

Put another way, the rate of youth who were not formally charged by the police was 25% higher in 2006 than in 2002. As well, since the implementation of the YCJA, fewer youth have appeared before a judge. During 2005–2006, the number of youth court cases tried totalled 56 271, down 2% from the previous year. Youth court case-loads dropped 26% compared to before the legislation was enacted. This was largely the result of fewer youth appearing in court for property crimes (i.e., theft, breaking and entering, fraud, and possession of stolen property). Yet property crime still accounted for 38% of youth court cases (compared to violent crime at 27%, offences against the administration of justice at 9%, and drug-related crimes at 6%, based on 2005–2006 data). In 2005–2006, 62% of youth court cases resulted in guilty findings. Shifting a trend evident in the 1990s, fewer are being sentenced to custody under the YCJA. Compared to 27% in 2002–2003 (before the act was implemented), 18% of all guilty cases resulted in custodial sentences in 2005–2006.[3]

---

[3] Source: Statistics Canada, "Youth Court Statistics, 2005 – 2006." *The Daily*, Tuesday, October 23, 2007.

The rate of youth accused of homicide has been on the rise and reached its highest point since 1961 (when data were first collected) in 2006. The highest provincial rate was seen in Manitoba, with Alberta close behind. Out of 605 homicides, youths were accused in 54—less than 1%. For 54 victims, 84 youths were accused, suggesting multiple offenders in several cases.

What are the implications of these statistics? First, media portrayals of youth crime are at odds with scientific evidence. Media discourse exaggerates, sensationalizes, and decontextualizes by presenting *atypical* cases as representative and constructing a *problematic image* of youth that does not always correspond to actual behaviour.

Second, we argue that many of the changes in youth-crime statistics over the past few decades reflect a more intrusive response to youth rather than changes in actual behaviour (See Figure 1.1). Approximately 31 700 youths aged 12 to 17 years were admitted to correctional services in 2004–2005. Of those, 15 900 (50%) were remanded in custody and 15 800 (50%) were committed to community supervision, with the majority (12 900 or 81%) of community supervision admissions being probationary (*Juristat*, 2006). Although the proportion of violent cases entering youth court is higher now than in previous decades, it does not imply that young people's behaviour has in fact become more violent. Violence has been redefined. In other words, how we perceive violence has shifted over time. For example, schoolyard fights once handled informally in a principal's office are now finding their way into the courts, and verbal bullying among girls (gossip, name calling, etc.) is being recognized as aggressive behaviour. We will return to questions of violence in Chapter 9.

Given that there *is* youth crime, you may argue that the general public *should* be focused on youthful offending. Typically, we think in terms of categories (e.g., young offender) and rely on the dominant discourses (e.g., punishment) of the day without question. Considerations of "youth crime" need not necessarily be solely focused on the offending behaviours of youth. When we think about the implications of overemphasizing youthful

Figure 1.1 Youth Crime Rate, 1986 to 2006

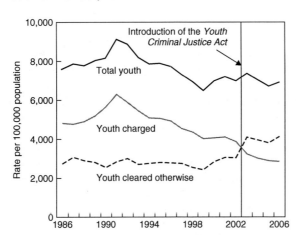

Source: Statistics Canada, CANSIM: Tables 252-0013 and 252-0014. "Crime Statistics in Canada," *Juristat*, 2006, Vol. 27, no. 5, (85-002-XIE).

offending, we can see how such a partial view distorts our thinking about the relationship between youth and crime. It obscures who is doing what to whom. Neglecting *victimization* deliberately avoids the social conditions that influence the choices that young people make and may contribute to their troubles. Interpreting "youth crime" to mean offending and not victimization or any other elements related to the behaviours or individuals involved allows for a narrow set of responses. Fears of youth crime are more easily intensified and situations become ripe for moral panic surrounding youth. Historically, fear has been accompanied by negative evaluations of the YCJS and a call for the legal system to better address the problem. In this context, there is often much support for more punitive crime-control policies. Of course, not all members of the general public are calling for a punishment-oriented youth justice system. However, given the tendency in our society to look to law as a panacea, efforts to do something about the problem have been largely directed at punitive reactionary measures rather than at remedial or preventive ones located outside the formal law and order process and inside the communities where young people live.

Processing young people through the YCJS can actually increase the likelihood of future offending (Doob and Cesaroni, 2004). Lee found that the more frequently youth were brought to court, the higher the likelihood of recidivism (Lee, 2002). As we will see in the following pages, the amount of crime in our society is not only an empirical issue; it is also a political one. We will raise the question: To what extent is the youth justice system the most appropriate place to deal with the problem of youth crime and youths' troubles? We will explore how the YCJS can exacerbate the problem and reproduce the inequalities that conditioned the choices that put youth in conflict with the law in the first place. Narrowly dealing with youth crime as a criminal justice issue avoids looking closely at the socio-economic, gender, racial, and ethno-cultural realities of youths' lives.

Take a look at Table 1.2 on p. 13. After reading this section, do you consider any of the "myths" to be accurate reflections of the realities of youth crime?

BOTH TROUBLING AND TROUBLED?

Youth crime is not simply a topic of private conversations, something that individuals hold their own beliefs and opinions about; it is a public issue and wider social problem. At the start of the chapter we asked you to consider whether youth are troubled and/or troubling. We hope you realize how complex a question this actually is. As you read the text you will notice that there is much overlap between victimization of youth and their offending behaviours.

Popular and media discourses frame public perceptions of youth crime in a way that is at odds with official youth crime rates. Most Canadians use the accounts given to them through media and popular discourses to form, justify, and otherwise articulate their own understandings of youth crime.

Youth crime stories, like news of crime more generally, favour violence. News coverage of particular events, such as the shootings at Virginia Tech or the murder of Jordan Manners in Toronto, often involves sensationalized stories, graphic images, and gruesome headlines, and reveals how closely media discourse and popular discourse are connected.[4] Watershed events concentrate public attention on the disposition and behaviour of young

---

[4] The tragedy at Virginia Tech captured the attention of North Americans when on April 16th, 2007, Seung-Hui Cho killed 32 people, wounded more than 20, and then killed himself. More recently, 15-year-old Jordan Manners was killed after being shot at C.W. Jefferys Collegiate Institute in Toronto, Ontario.

Table 1.2 Myths and Realities of Youth Crime

Myths	Realities
The good old days existed, a time when youth crime wasn't a problem.	Historically, adults have always been preoccupied with concerns about the behaviour of children and youth.
Youth crime rates, particularly violent crime, are rising.	Youth crime has been on the decline in recent years. Although it rose steadily throughout the mid-20th century, since the mid-1990s rates of youth crime, including violent crimes, have decreased.
Youth are responsible for most of the violence in society.	Youth are disproportionately represented as victims of violent crime. They are much more likely to be involved in property crime than violent crimes, and their crimes of violence are typically relatively minor.
Incarceration is *the* answer.	Harsher criminal sanctions have not been shown to systematically discourage youth crime and may have the reverse effect.
Young offenders are bad kids.	Youth involved in crime are multidimensional individuals, each with his or her own story. Their experiences are much more varied than the homogeneous label "young offender" captures.

people—acts of youth, on one hand, and what punishment they deserve on the other. In this way, the names "Columbine" and "Taber" have become synonymous with fear of contemporary youth.[5] For many people, such instances provide sufficient "evidence" that today's young people are *more* aggressive and violent than their predecessors. The case of the girl convicted in Medicine Hat, Alberta, of killing her parents and brother and the media frenzy surrounding it no doubt heightened fears of how dangerous youth can be. Compounding fears, the youth was 13 and female, and it isn't difficult to see how moral panic sets in.

Squarely focusing on the behaviour of youth in isolation from the social conditions in which they make their choices and thereby viewing young people as one dimensional (as only extensions of crime categories) tends to dehumanize them. A common refrain is that surely, there must be something dramatically wrong with *her* or *him* if they are capable of violence.

Is it possible to push our thinking past this troubled/troubling dichotomy? What alternative understandings are possible? What can and should be done about the problem of youth crime? What does youth justice mean? We will these address questions as we grapple with issues of power and justice as they relate to youth, crime, and society. There are no easy answers or quick fixes to the problems, challenges, and issues associated with youth and crime. However, theorizing about the interconnections between youth, crime,

---

[5] On April 20th 1999 two youths, Eric Harris and Dylan Klebold, were responsible for murdering 12 students, and a teacher, and wounding 24 others at Columbine High School in Littleton, Colorado. They then committed suicide. At W.R. Myers High School in Taber, Alberta on April 28th, 1999 student Jason Lang was killed and another student injured when a 14-year-old boy fired a rifle.

and society has much potential for developing more effective crime prevention, interventions, societal responses, and, ultimately, more humane relationships.

LOOKING FORWARD

The text is organized into three sections, each with a specific goal and contribution to the overriding theme—social justice for youth. In Section A, "Youth, Legislation, and History," we provide a historical backdrop to discussions of youth crime/justice and an overview of contemporary law and youth justice practices. The four chapters in this section examine the theoretical, historical, and legal issues of youth crime and youth justice. Understanding the history of juvenile justice models is particularly important in appreciating how and under what conditions the current Canadian youth justice system developed.

The chapters in Section B, "Special Populations: Making Race/Class/Gender Connections," highlight gender, race, class, and age, and pay particular attention to issues of marginalization, subordination, and exclusion. Taking this approach allows us to highlight three heterogeneous groups: female youth, Aboriginal youth, and street-involved youth. Particularly timely, in Chapter 9 we concentrate on the relationship between youth and violence. As the purpose of this section is to make race/class/gender connections rather than isolate one aspect of social position and identity, you will notice considerable overlap in our discussion.

Finally, Section C, "Recent and Future Directions: Responding to Youth, Crime, and Society," offers insight into the way in which Canadian society *does* and *could* respond to the problems and issues discussed throughout the book. By pushing the limits of traditional binaries, we attempt to reconcile seemingly opposite vantage points: youth as "troubling" or "trouble" versus youth as "troubled" or "having troubles." This requires problematizing many assumptions about youth, the YCJS, and Canadian society. Chapter 11 makes the silencing of youth its starting point and seeks to emphasize youth voices.

Underlying youth justice is "the paradoxical prescription that young people are *not* rational and responsible enough to be fully empowered, but *are* deemed fully rational and responsible *if they offend*" (Muncie and Hughes, 2002: 15, emphasis added). This is one of the contradictions with which we must grapple—youth are simultaneously empowered and disempowered; silenced and called to take action. Indeed, the history of youth justice is one of "conflict, contradictions, ambiguity, and compromise" (Muncie and Hughes, 2002: 1). In our concluding chapter we do not attempt to present a summary of what came before. We put forward ideas in response to the question: Where do we go from here? Table 1.3 on p. 15 provides a quick review of the trends in youth crime.

Table 1.3 Trends in Youth Crime: Quick Review
Most youth crime is property related and non-violent.
Males outnumber females in the youth justice system at all levels.
Youth crime rates have consistently decreased since the mid 1990s, with only yearly fluctuations.
Far fewer charges are being laid for less serious offences.
Youth are victims of crime in disproportionate numbers.

SUMMARY

■ A distorted view of youth crime pervades popular consciousness, largely as a result of the strong influence of media discourse. There is a substantial gap between the rhetoric and reality of youth crime and justice. Youth crime rates are not as high and youthful offending is not as violent as media discourse suggests.

■ How youth crime is understood directly influences how the problem is handled. It impacts most directly those youth who defy the law and/or deviate from socio-cultural scripts of appropriate behaviour.

■ The main issue to address is not youth crime *per se*, but how youth, crime, and society are interrelated. Critical thinking about systemic issues (e.g., poverty, racism, discrimination) is one way to approach controversies in youth justice.

■ Discourses and the social conditions under which youth make choices are inter-connected in our analysis of youth, crime, and society.

■ We encourage a process of critical reflection and social engagement called social justice praxis.

■ Overemphasizing youthful offending not only distorts our thinking about youth, crime, and society, but it neglects victimization of youth, intensifies fears about "youth crime," and is often accompanied by punitive reactionary measures focused squarely on the youth criminal justice system.

DISCUSSION QUESTIONS

1. What is the relationship between media discourse and popular **discourse** on youth crime?
2. How is it possible to create a culture of sensitivity toward youth, and how is it related to social justice praxis?
3. Discourses have social consequences. How might a discourse of social justice praxis be used against rather than for youth?

RECOMMENDED READINGS

Garland, D. and R. Sparks. (2001). "Criminology, sociology and the challenge of our times," In *Criminology and Social Theory*. London: Oxford

Hogeveen, B. (2007). "Is there justice for youth?" In G. Pavlich and M. Hird (eds.) *Questioning Sociology, Canadian Perspectives*. Don Mills, Ontario: Oxford.

Sacco, V. (1995). "Media constructions of crime." *Annals of the American Academy of Political and Social Science,* 539. p.141–154.

Chapter 2

Practices of Governance and Control: Theoretical Underpinnings

STARTING POINT

To listen to the current round of public discourse, we're not only going to hell in a hand basket, but that vehicle of society's demise is being woven by an entire generation of slack-jawed, sneering youths whose purpose in life is to flout the system . . .

(Excerpt from "Opinion" column. Catherine Ford, Calgary Herald, March 12, 1992).

Each of us has a starting point when it comes to understanding youth justice. Perhaps you have never considered yourself the author of a theory of youth crime. Put simply, a theory is a set of claims used to interpret reality. Supposing that reality is youth crime, ask yourself:

- What is my starting point?
- What is my theory of youth crime?
- On what are my claims about the problem based?

We suggest you attempt to summarize your position in your own words *before* you read this chapter and later revisit it after reading this chapter and throughout the course.

LEARNING OBJECTIVES

After reading this chapter, you should be able to

- Describe the meaning of theory as it relates to youth crime.

- Illustrate how the category of the "other" is useful in understanding youth crime.

- Differentiate between positivist and classical conceptions of juvenile delinquency.

- Identify the authorized knowers and their knowledge claims.

- Distinguish between the "reformable young offender" and the "punishable young offender" and the implications of each understanding.

- Discuss recent critical theorizing on youth crime and justice such as feminism, risk, and governmentality.

INTRODUCTION

The *types* of deviant and criminal conduct that bring young males—and some females—to the attention of the justice system have changed very little over time. How their conduct is *understood* and *governed*, however, has undergone significant variation. Indeed, as Nikolas Rose (1989: 121) argues, "childhood is the most intensively governed sector of personal existence." Issues of control and order are central to discussions of youth and crime. Discourses lie at the centre of various understandings of youth crime. Discussions oscillate between two competing discourses. Advocates of one consider youth vulnerable, in need of assistance and protection. For example, throughout the 19th and 20th centuries, prison reformers and justice officials (and, later, experts trained in the mental sciences) identified a particular group of youth (specifically, working-class male youth) as problematic. In so doing, they constructed a **reformable young offender**, one who required intervention and could be rehabilitated. More recently, child advocates concerned about youth involvement in prostitution have sought to intervene on behalf of child "victims" of sexual exploitation. Alternatively, the other discourse considers youth in need of discipline and punishment. Today this discourse is pervasive for at least four groups: violent youth, squeegee kids, Aboriginal youth, and (increasingly) female offenders.

The problem of violent and serious youth crime continually made headlines during the 1990s across Canada. With widely publicized cases of violent attacks by youth (mostly on other youth) presented as typical, it is no wonder many people began to fear the "violent young offender." As the understanding of an out-of-control youth population became firmly etched in the public mind, strategies to deal with the problem soon followed. The Canadian public demanded a law-and-order agenda that called for a more punitive justice system.

Indeed, throughout the late 1990s, debates about the problem of youth crime focused on the concept of a **punishable young offender** (Hogeveen, 2005b). The punishable young offender (unlike the reformable young offender) requires punishment first and foremost, leaving reform and rehabilitative interventions as secondary measures. Foremost in political rhetoric and public discussions was the claim that we (i.e., the government through law and legislation) must come down *tougher, stronger,* and *harder* on problematic youth. This ethic of punishment shuns "any pretence of compassion towards serious offenders" (Hogeveen, 2005b: 73). Instead, as M.P. John Williams's popular sentiments illustrated, the best way to govern young offenders was to punish them, with the creation new legislation that would effectively accomplish this:

> Somewhere along the way, through our soft and fuzzy and pat them on the head and ask them not to do it again concept, we have lost the notion that we have to teach our kids the difference between right and wrong . . . In the United States serious inroads into crime are being made. They are *tough on crime.* Perhaps this is a correlation there . . . If we are tough on crime, if we punish crime, then people get the message (John Williams, *Hansard Debates*, Canada, September 25, 2000. emphasis added).

Underlying this approach—"if we are tough on crime, if we punish crime, then [youth] get the message"—is an **intrusive punishment discourse** that holds young people accountable for their criminal actions and applies more punitive sanctions (Muncie and Hughes, 2002). This discourse of intrusive punishment was not the only one considered during the late 1990s, and is certainly not the only one around today. However, its pervasive mentality of coerciveness seems to resonate with voters, victims, and the voices of power. What is particularly troubling about viewing young offenders as "punishable" rather than "reformable" is the prejudiced impact this has on youth. Aboriginal youth are grossly over-represented in detention centres across Canada, especially in the Prairies. As Hogeveen (2005b: 74) argues, "As a group, native adolescents are among the most disadvantaged in Canadian society. They are also the most punishable." We will discuss the inequality of the label "punishable" in more detail in Chapters 6, 7, and 8.

The views of young offenders as punishable or as reformable are not inevitable. In this chapter, we explore the significant and continually shifting contours and discourses at work in the field of youth crime and youth justice studies. We cast a critical eye on historical, recent, and emerging literatures, rather than presenting an overview of traditional criminological theories on the causes of youth crime. The purpose of this chapter is to introduce students to the **theoretical underpinnings**—that is, the assumptions, discourses, concepts, and implications—of various responses to youth crime. Our efforts to theorize are geared toward making sense of how youth crime is understood and thereby governed.

TOWARD THEORIZING

In criminology, theories are used to predict, describe, and explain, as well as to develop a broader awareness of particular social issues as they relate to crime in society. Theories are knowledge claims that attempt to interpret a complex world and the events that take place therein (see Box 2.1 on p. 19). Academics, practitioners, politicians, program planners, and policy makers use theory. Theories provide a context in which to consider youthful conduct and attitudes, social policies, and legislative practices. Theories do not exist in a vacuum; they are a reflection of the larger society in which they are developed. Appreciating the theoretical underpinnings of any youth justice strategy will enable you to think critically about the strengths, limitations, and implications of any particular approach to youth crime.

We all interpret social reality. Every time we make a claim about a social problem, it is guided by the things we do not say. These are **assumptions**; preconceived understandings about how some aspect of the world works. All theories (lay or academic) are based on assumptions about human nature and society. Think back to your starting point or theory of youth crime and ask, "What assumptions did I make?" Remember, any theory is only as correct as the assumptions on which it is based.

In this section we consider the purpose of sociological theory. Sociology is a discipline about **debunking**—what Peter Berger (1963) described as looking beyond the obvious explanation, unpacking taken-for-granted assumptions, and searching for deeper meaning. Sociological knowledge moves us beyond common-sense understanding. Sociological theorizing requires what C. Wright Mills (1959) called the **sociological imagination**. Mills described the sociological imagination as the ability to see the relationships between individual experiences (biography) and the larger society (history). For Mills, the capacity to link biography with history implies recognition that private or personal troubles are related to larger public or social issues. Using your sociological imagination requires you to make connections between individual young people and the society in which they live;

What is a Theory Anyway?

A wide range of theorizing, or attempts to make meaning of our social world, exists—from academic, empirical, tested theories to informal, lay, exploratory models. But what is a theory anyway? A theory is a set of knowledge claims that attempt to interpret a complex world and the events that take place therin. Theories, like those of humour referred to in this cartoon, provide a vantage point and conceptual tools from which to view the world or some aspect of social life. They give us different interpretive frameworks for understanding empirical reality. Theories are diverse, complementary, and competing. For example, the theoretical statement, "We laugh because we are happy" is in opposition to, "We laugh to hide our sadness," but complements, "Laughter expresses emotions of joy."

"On the other hand, maybe humor shouldn't be analyzed."

www.CartoonStock.com.

that is, the social, cultural, political, economic, and historical context in which their lives are embedded.

Canadian society is organized along lines of **race, ethnicity, class, gender,** and **age**. The terms *race* and *ethnicity* are often used interchangeably, but sociologically they are distinct social constructions. Race refers to categorical divisions between groups of people based on physical characteristics that are deemed socially relevant, such as skin colour. Ethnicity is tied to cultural identity based on factors that include language, nationality, or religion. In capitalist societies, class relates to relative economic positioning (e.g., wealth), although this division can be based on other valued resources like power or prestige. Whereas sex is associated most commonly with the biological and anatomical differences between men and women, gender is the socially constructed meaning of those differences. Gender refers to the socio-cultural ideas (beliefs, values, and attitudes) and accompanying practices (behaviours, expressions, and characteristics) associated with being male—masculinity—and/or being female—femininity. Masculinity and femininity are social constructions.

There are two broad paradigms that underlie sociological explanations of crime and delinquency: consensus and conflict.

- A **consensus approach** is based on the assumption that agreement exists among members of society on matters related to youth crime and justice, which stems from shared beliefs, values, and goals.

- A **conflict approach** assumes that individuals and groups in society hold conflicting social, political, cultural, or economic interests, which often pit powerful groups against the marginalized.

Although mainstream criminological theories such as strain theory are consensus approaches, others such as Marxist and labelling theory represent conflict approaches.

Beginning in the 1970s with Carol Smart's (1976) ground-breaking work, *Women, Crime and Criminology*, a growing number of feminist scholars engaged in a massive critique of mainstream criminology. Their point of departure was criminology's **androcentric** nature; that is, its male-centredness. These scholars argued that women were excluded as subjects and producers of knowledge. Moreover, they pointed out that female offenders could no longer be considered "too few to count," and nor could women's victimization ignored (Adelberg and Currie, 1989). Various **feminist perspectives** (radical, liberal, socialist, anti-racist) have since paid close attention to the structural inequalities in women's lives and have examined the relationship between gender, crime, and deviance (Comack, 1996). Feminist discourses on gender and girls' and women's criminality have demonstrated the blurred boundaries between victimization and offending. More recently, feminist scholars have begun speaking about "criminalized women" rather than "criminal women," as it better underscores the processes that criminalize behaviours rather than individuals themselves who are "criminal" (Comack and Balfour, 2004).

Women of colour soon developed scholarship that contested the race blindness of previous analyses. Since these important critiques in the 1980s and 1990s, recognition of race and difference is now becoming a critical component in feminist discourse. According to Comack and Balfour (2004: 20)

> The character and meaning of gender, race, and class categories are given concrete expression by the specific social situations and historical contexts in which they are located.

The contributions of feminist scholars are particularly useful in theorizing about youth and crime. For example, that gender, race, and class are important is illustrated in the numbers of sex-trade workers in Winnipeg, Regina, and Saskatchewan who are poor young Aboriginal girls. Another place we see these concepts (class, race, and gender) visible in society is in the fact that the professionals employed in the criminal justice system are, by a vast majority, white, male, and middle-class.

Recall from your introductory criminology courses that men are the offenders in a disproportionate number of cases, which also holds true for youth crime. Not until relatively recently, however, has a small but growing segment of criminology focused on men "as men" and boys "as boys," exploring the ways masculinity is related to crime (Messerschmidt, 1997). This means looking at the gendered contexts in which boys and men live and are criminalized and governed. For example, research of this nature might examine how male children and adolescent youth are socialized to accept a violent masculinity and adopt this cultural script in their behaviour, identity, and beliefs. We will return to this issue in Chapter 9.

In large part owing to the **feminist critique** of mainstream scholarship, a diverse group of criminological and socio-legal scholars worldwide have, since the late 1980s, asked new kinds of questions about crime. This work focuses less attention on "causes" of crime. Instead the group examines **criminalization** (the process of making criminal) and the consequences of criminal justice intervention, and attempts to demystify law and legal practices (Comack and Balfour, 2004: 1). Our theoretical approach follows this emergent scholarship.

We take a critical view that directs attention to issues of *power, justice, and structural inequalities* and is informed by feminist, social constructionist, and critical criminological discourses that reject the traditional assumptions of mainstream criminological theory. Within society, we each occupy a gender, race, and class position. We are also differentiated by other social identities such as (dis)ability, sexual orientation, nationality, and age. In other words, we live in a gendered, racialized, class-based, and age-segregated society. These axes of power (or social relations) impact particular groups of people in different ways, largely depending on whether one's social position is one of privilege or marginalization. Marginalization is the partial exclusion of certain social groups from mainstream society.

You may have heard Canadian humorist Elvira Kurt imitate her mother talking to her friends and relatives with the refrain, "She is a comedian and a lesbian—*both* at the *same* time!" Our lives are complicated by the fact that we occupy a position of gender, race, ethnicity, class, age, etc. all at the same time. Consequently, it is important to make race, class, and gender connections in our analyses of youth, crime, and society rather than attempting to determine which one is *more* important.

THEORIZING YOUTH AND CRIME

There are divergent views as to the purpose of theories of youth crime. One common view holds that "understanding crime causation allows us to explain the frequency, perceived seriousness, and social impact of youth crime, which in turn allows us to better control, deter, or prevent" it (Winterdyk, 2000: 36; Campbell, 2005: 17). From this standpoint, most theoretical introductions in youth crime and justice texts respond to the question, "Why do young people commit delinquent acts?" This discussion requires that students review the mainstream theories of crime they learned in their introductory criminology courses. The three main theoretical perspectives often touted to explain juvenile delinquency are social control, social learning, and strain theories.

Social control theories begin with the presumption that the appropriate question is not why individuals commit crimes, but why most people conform to societal rules and norms. Travis Hirschi (1969), for example, argued that deviance stems from weak social bonds, which should act like glue holding a person to social expectations and a life of conventional values and norms. Attachment, one of Hirschi's key elements of the social bond, is described as the ties that a young person has to other people. In response to the question, "Why do young people commit delinquent acts?" a social-bond theorist might say, "The child had no connection with his mother, subsequently weakening his social bond."

Social learning and labelling theories take a more micro-level approach, guided by the category "**social construct**" or **social construction**. Sociologically speaking, a social construct is a label (the name and its meaning) given to a particular phenomenon in society. According to Berger and Luckmann (1967), only through language can we come to understand our society; that is, we make sense of the world around us by relying on symbols whose meaning is not innate, but emerges from culture and society. Tannenbaum

(1938) was the first to recognize how important societal reactions are to a young person's subsequent behaviour and identity. Several other scholars, most notably Edwin Lemert (1951) and later Howard Becker (1963), expanded on these insights in the context of the sociological school of thought called *symbolic interactionism*. They drew attention to the processes and affects of labelling in young people's lives. Canadian sociologist Erving Goffman (1963) is credited with highlighting the impact of **stigmatization** on behaviour and identity. Stigmatization is the process of applying a stigma—a negative evaluation of difference—to an individual or group. Labelling theory affected social policy in two main ways: it addressed the issue of stigmatization attached to incarcerated youth, and it encouraged community-based alternatives to custody. In response to the question, "Why do young people commit delinquent acts?" this view would place the blame on labels. Social constructivism continues to hold much influence today, yet as a micro-level approach it avoids discussion of socio-economic circumstances and political context.

Robert Merton (1938) elaborated on Emile Durkheim's (1893) concept of anomie (a state of normlessness) in his own strain theory. For Merton, strain exists when there is a gap between socially accepted *goals* or aspirations (e.g., nice car, good home, etc.) and the legitimate *means* or ways of accessing these goals. Deviance and crime are illegitimate means to reach societal goals encapsulated under the phrase the "North American dream," which is to achieve financial wealth and power through the acquisition of products and commodities. In their adaptation of strain, Cloward and Ohlin (1960) suggested that youth crime could be explained by youth's reaction to a lack of opportunity or what they called "differential opportunity structures." In response to the question, "Why do young people commit delinquent acts?" "strain" is a familiar answer provided by mainstream criminology.

An Alternative Standpoint

A different view is that there is more to theorizing about youth, crime, and society than exposing inherent causes of youthful misbehaviour. Instead, while crime prevention and control of youth crime remains relevant, an alternative standpoint would place more emphasis on the social, economic, political, and historic context in which youth crime and youth justice are situated. It asks different kinds of questions and rejects mono-causal explanations as incomplete and misleading (Smandych, 2001a).

Youth crime is multi-dimensional. As such, it is misleading to discuss isolated factors such as poverty, violence, or neglect as *causing* youth crime. No single event or life experience necessarily brings about a particular consequence. Even though decades of research have found a relationship between child neglect and troubles with the law, we cannot assume that every child who is mistreated by their parent or guardian will grow up to be a criminal. This is just not the case. Many adults who were child victims of abuse function today not only as productive citizens, but have dedicated their lives to helping others. In addition, non-social factors play a role in determining individual experiences. Our attitudes, behaviours, and dispositions are shaped by our social environment as well as genetics and biology. As sociologists, our concern in this book is with understanding the large and pivotal role of social forces in this process.

Rather than focusing on "youth crime" or "youth justice" in isolation, this **way of theorizing** adopts a more integrative approach to understanding the relationships between youth, crime, and society. A way of theorizing is an approach *to* theory, not knowledge claims. We do not present a theory on youth crime, nor do we adopt one theoretical perspective. We try to provide a more critical understanding (i.e., way of theorizing) of how criminalized youth are constructed and governed by the **authorized knowers** of their day. Authorized knowers are those key individuals and groups whose claims are heard, who are granted the status of "expert," and whose arguments are taken seriously and subsequently acted upon.

As discussed in Chapter 1, youth are disproportionate victims. In addition, the targets of most youthful offending are either other youth or property. Taking this critical approach allows us to recognize youthful victimization. Our discussion explores the assumptions underlying the claims that various groups (including government, community members, and academics) make about the delinquent or criminal behaviour of young people. How we respond to or govern youth crime is directly related to how we talk about or understand it. This is why a critical understanding of the processes by which offenders are understood and thereby governed is essential to making sense of youth crime and youth justice.

Our ideas about choice, constraint, and contradictions as they relate to issues of power and justice are informed by critical criminology, and feminist discourse in particular. A key concept in feminist theorizing, "**the other**," is illustrative in helping to make sense of the place that youthful offenders occupy in contemporary society. "The other" is the disenfranchised, marginalized individual or group in society and their systematic exclusion—especially those most disadvantaged in race, class, and gender terms. They are the voiceless; those whose claims are silenced, not heard, ignored, and not taken seriously by authorized knowers. In our view, theorizing youth crime and justice is a political project aimed at improving the circumstances that produce youth crime and challenging the processes involved in defining young people who offend as "others."

HISTORICAL CONCEPTIONS OF JUVENILE DELINQUENCY

It is important to recognize that theories of crime and deviance do not exist in isolation or in a social vacuum. They must be viewed in the context of 1) authorized knowers; 2) criminological knowledges; 3) forms of social control and/or punishment; and 4) societal patterns and changes. **Criminological knowledges** are those knowledge claims about youth and crime upon which forms of social control and/or punishment are based. They are not limited to the academic discipline of criminology. In the following section we explore historical conceptions of delinquency beginning with the classical perspective. Table 2.1 on p. 24 summarizes the history and concepts discussed.

Classical Theories of Crime, Deviance, and Control

Classical (or pre-modern) conceptions of youth crime dominated early criminology until the mid-19th century. **Classical theory** is considered the first formal school of criminology. Based on the Enlightenment philosophies of liberalism and utilitarianism, the classical school made no distinction between offenders. Classical theory offered a simple explanation for crime and focused more attention on finding ways to control it.

Classical thought did not differentiate between adult and youth offenders, but viewed all criminals as rational, calculating actors. Viewing human beings as hedonistic (pleasure seeking), classical scholars believed conduct was motivated by internal drives and needs (self-interest). It followed that the dominant mode of punishment was deterrence, not rehabilitation. If people rationally calculate the consequences of their behaviour, then punishments need to be applied to deter them by making the pain associated with the act greater than the pleasure gained from the act.

Classical scholars like Beccaria (1819) argued that the punishment should fit the crime and should be swift and certain. Reforms to the administration of justice and the prison system were largely attributed to the work of the classical school. Canada's Criminal Code and some aspects of our modern criminal justice system (e.g., due process) are a reflection of classical thinking (Caputo and Linden, 2005: 206). Despite its legacy, the classical school failed to question the injustices in the application of "rationally determined" punishment. A return to the search for causes came with the emergence of Lombrosian thought during the late 19th century, when classical theories fell out of favour among academics. As we will see in Chapter 3, in the late 19th-century, criminal justice system practices for young people based on these tenets were called into question in Canada.

Table 2.1 Historical and Conceptual Map

Historical Period	Criminological Knowledges	Authorized Knowers	Social Control and/or Punishment
Pre-Modern (up to 18th century)	classical theories of crime, deviance, and control	philosophers	adult-styled governance retribution deterrence
Positivist Theories of Crime (19th century)	philanthropic knowledges and eugenics-informed psychiatry	philanthropists psychiatrists	reformatories detention centres
JDA-era (turn of 20th century) [Positivism Continued]	environmental psychology and symbolic interactionism	medical authorities, psychologists, criminologists	juvenile court custody probation
Pre-YOA (to 1980s) [Critical Discourses]	labelling theories rights discourse/ feminism	psychologists criminologists	custody diversionary measures
YOA-YCJA [Contemporary Approaches]	risk, critical, and political discourses	public psychologists criminologists	youth justice court custody, risk assessment and community based

Source: Adapted from "Winning deviant youth over by friendly helpfulness: Transformations in the legal governance of deviant children, 1857-1908." In R. Smandych (Ed.) Youth Justice: History, Legislation and Reform. Toronto: Brace/Harcourt.

Positivist Theories

Modernist or positivist conceptions of youth crime took hold during the late 19th century. **Positivism**, the first scientific school of criminology, predominated from the late 1800s to the early 1900s. Positivism argues that criminality is determined—that there is a cause-and-effect sequence. The Positive School, led by Cesare Lombroso (1972[1876]), held the view that we can understand the world through investigation using methods of controlled observation, and was committed to the search for causes of crime.

This was a radical departure from the paradigm that preceded it. Five characteristics define positivism. First, as every offender is viewed as unique, positivism demands "facts" about individuals. Second, it assumes there are mind and body differences between "criminals" and "law-abiding" people. For example, Doctor P. Spohn, a physician at the Penetanguishene Reformatory, testified in 1891 that wayward boys were "different in physique" and "not so well developed as a rule" (Commissioners Appointed to Enquire into the Prison and Reformatory System of Ontario, 1891, p. 471).

Third, positivists believed that the punishment should fit the individual, not the crime. The fourth characteristic is that early positivists believed that criminals could be treated, rehabilitated, corrected, and reintegrated into society. Finally, late positivists saw a key role for professionals and believed that the criminal justice system should be guided by scientific experts.

How positivism influenced juvenile justice in Canada can be divided into three waves—which share some features but differ on others. These waves can be identified according to the types of knowledge that dominated and who the authorized knowers were. They are 1) **philanthropic elite**, 2) **eugenics-informed psychiatry**, and 3) **environmental psychology**.[1] These knowledges influenced how juvenile delinquency was understood and governed. The following section examines these types of knowledge, and Chapter 3 continues with the governing strategies employed.

Let's begin during the mid- to late 19th century when the seeds for the first wave were sown during a time of rapid social change.

Philanthropic Elite: The First Wave of Positivism Early Canadian reformers in the area of juvenile justice were mostly interested volunteers from the male political and business elite. In Toronto, for example, they included Toronto School Board trustee W.B. McMurrich and former mayor W.H. Howland. The philanthropic wave can be described with the acronym **PPP**—progressive, perfectibility, and products of the environment. First, philanthropists interested in the cause of juvenile justice wholeheartedly believed that they were part of a movement toward **social progress**. They had a forward-looking attitude toward social and personal betterment. As white, Anglo-Celtic, and elite members of society, they saw their place as at the top of the hierarchy of races. For society to move forward, crime, disorder, and social decay required intervention. The individuals responsible for crime—the lower, immigrant classes—needed their assistance.

---

[1] The following conceptualization is loosely based on Hogeveen's (2004) recent article, "The Evils with Which We are Called to Grapple." Please consult this article for a more detailed discussion of the three early positivist approaches to the understanding and governance of youth crime. This material originally appeared in Labour/Le Travail 55 (Spring/Printemps 2005). Used with appreciation to the journal.

Secondly, the philanthropic elite believed in the **perfectibility** of both society and human nature. Juvenile justice philanthropists believed that the human race could be perfected, or made better, through human attention, effort, and initiative. They saw their task as enabling juvenile delinquents to rise above their criminal lifestyles rather than their lower-class ranks. This belief is based on the final assumption—environmental influences. Juveniles were **products of** their **environment**. The philanthropic elite strongly believed that a child's environment, either positive or negative, would affect the direction of his or her life. If a child grew up in what they referred to as "depraved" social circumstances (neglectful parents, abuse, poverty, hunger, and maltreatment), a life of criminality would likely result. Moreover, corrupting role models were to blame. Delinquent characters were not born, but were made by a lack of schooling, disregard for religious influences, idleness, gangs, felonious peers, and parental neglect. However, if juveniles were products of their environment, it followed that negative influences could be reversed; that is, their lives were salvageable. If a child was exposed to a healthy environment and taught lessons in industry, good citizenship, piety, and morality, they could be reformed.

Recall that early positivists were not scientists or doctors trained in mind and body; they were concerned citizens, many of whom were lawyers. They lacked any formal training or education on these matters. Crime, to their collective mind, was a "social" problem. While many students of criminology today would not contest this, at that time the recognition of social influences on behaviour was a radical departure from the dominant classical views of human culpability and reason.

Early positivists saw youth crime as a symptom of an underlying problem, such as cumulative exposure to family or the street, or idleness, without the positive normalizing influences of the classroom and church. For example, they believed that truancy was a precursor to juvenile delinquency. A. Ainger (1890: 378), a teacher in Toronto during the late 19th century, argued that truancy was the "first step in the downward career of those who, at length, constituted the criminal class."

For first-wave positivists, the individual offender was the main subject of concern, rather than their "crimes" or deviant conduct. That is not to say that they paid little attention to behaviour, but rather that actual conduct became secondary to why offenders behaved that way in the first place. As one commentator lamented, youth have "no respect for adults as such. They feign none." He continued,

> When a group of boys were playing ball near your windows, and you, not wishing to spoil their sport, say to them: 'Boys watch those windows,' one of the boys was sure to retort, 'how long do you want me to look at them?' If a boy on his way to school was rebuked by an adult for abusing his younger brother, he would almost certainly turn and say: 'Aw, what's chewin' you?—mind your own business!' ("Boys and the Police," *Toronto Daily Star*, August 20, 1900).

Early positivists believed that behaviour was the result of environmental forces. First and foremost, they supported individualized treatment. However, such intervention strategies did not yet exist. Many philanthropists lobbied to create better environments for juveniles through welfare reforms and supervision of families. Underlying these strategies was a concern with *cause* and *cure*. To put it simply, they asked, "Why did they do it?" and, "What can we do to change them?" In summary, the first wave of positivism was reform-oriented and individualistic (recognized individual differences) and favoured non-institutional, community-based interventions.

Eugenics-Informed Psychiatry: The Second Wave By the late 1910s and early 1920s, Canadian juvenile justice had been influenced by medical psychology and psychiatry. As criminal justice, mental health, and child welfare systems developed, professionals played an increasingly important role. "Expert" knowledge came to challenge the judgment of non-trained philanthropists. Social scientific knowledge about causes and treatment justified new methods. During the 1900s, juvenile justice in Canada was influenced by the rise of the expert, and by the late 1910s, medical psychiatry had garnered a prominent place. Medical doctors and psychiatrists emerged on the juvenile justice scene and offered a controversial and alternative theory about the birth of youth deviance. For example, in Toronto, pioneering psychiatrists such as C.K. Clarke and Helen MacMurchy reinvented juvenile delinquency. Together they adhered to **eugenics discourse** (translated as "well born" or "good genes") and considered juvenile delinquents to be a product of inferior breeding and defective genes. Eugenics is based on the assumption that, like livestock, *some* human beings (white, Anglo-Saxon) possess "better" genes than *others* (non-white immigrants), and that interventions should prevent the latter from reproducing—in the same way that farmers remove sick cows from breeding herds (McLaren, 1990).

In the post-WWI economic boom and mood of social progress, perfectability took on new meaning and shape. Inspired by the growing discourse of eugenics, second-wave positivists were committed to progress through social and biological engineering. New language entered the fray to explain juvenile delinquency. Eugenicists believed that juvenile delinquents could not help but act as they did, given their lesser intelligence. They were products of improper breeding. In other words, the supposed cause of delinquency began to shift away from environment toward biology.

In place of environmental explanations, eugenicists and medial psychological experts deemed criminals (or the vast majority of them) to be **feeble-minded** or defective. As Hogeveen (2005b: 39) explains, "[w]hile class-related concerns were at the heart of white Anglo eugenicist discourse, its philosophy and practice were inherently racialized." Eugenics-inspired scholars such as H.H. Goddard perceived juvenile deviance very differently from first-wave positivists. Eugenicists argued that vast majority of juvenile delinquents were defective in mind. Goddard's (1912) famous study of the Kallikak family is indicative of this trend:

> . . . they [the Kallikaks] were feebleminded and no amount of education or good environment can change a feebleminded individual into a normal one, anymore than it can change a red-haired stock into a black-haired stock.

This called into question the solutions advocated by first-wave positivists. The problem with the argument that criminality stems from genetic make-up is that nothing can be done to change it. In other words, juvenile delinquents could not be reformed and therefore permanent solutions were needed.

Interestingly, to make their claims, eugenicists drew on the work of Cesare Lombroso and the idea of the born criminal. They advocated three main solutions: deportation of feeble-minded immigrants (and their families), incapacitation of feeble-minded criminals (adult and juvenile), and sterilization (especially for females) to prevent "transfer of

The Views of the Man Who Drafted the First Piece of Juvenile Justice Legislation

In 1913, W.L. Scott held true to his view that:

A child is like a lump of putty, soft at first and easily moulded, taking its shape from its surroundings. Despite the undoubtedly great influence which heredity exerts on the psychological make up of the individual, it has no direct effect in moulding his moral character. That is the work of the environment . . .

I am of course aware that the very reverse is taught by a certain school of criminologists, notable among whom are Lombroso, and others of what is known as the Italian School. These men speak of the "born criminal" and pretend to recognize him by certain "stigmata" or marks of crime. But leaving aside the exceptional cases of the mentally or physically defective, the children who are breaking the criminal law are just ordinary normal children and their moral condition is entirely the result of environment.

Source: Library and Archives Canada. W.L. Scott Papers. MG 30, C-27, vol. 1 (1905–10), vol. 2 (1911–15).

defect to progeny." This approach and its underlying assumptions totally contradicted the philosophy of the Juvenile Court. The beginning of the modern juvenile justice system was based on the view that juvenile offenders were malleable and could be reformed, yet the eugenics argument presumed that permanent solutions were the only method appropriate for feeble-minded delinquents.

The second wave—with its recognition of expert knowledge and claim that juveniles could not be reformed—did not entirely replace the first wave, nor were medical psychological knowledges more powerful than philanthropic knowledges during the entire period of their dominance (see Box 2.2).

Criticisms of the second wave's permanent approach paved the way for the third wave of positivism. Still scientific, still with experts as authorized knowers, the third wave shared much in common with the first wave.

The Third Wave: Environmental Psychology Eugenics was in decline as the boom of the 1920s was followed by the bust of the 1930s in Canada. Third-wave positivists were concerned with alleviating the causes of deviance, yet they disagreed that all juvenile offending resulted from feeble-mindedness. As a more benign mental hygiene perspective entered psychology, the period witnessed a return to environmental causes. Environmental psychology viewed the offender as malleable and therefore treatable. Although the concept of juveniles as "maladjusted" re-entered the scene, there was resistance to giving up on correctional treatment in carceral settings. Third-wave positivists advanced treatment-based solutions, but did not wholly accept the first wave's view that reform should take place within the community.

W.E. Blatz was the most influential scholar in the environmental psychology approach to Canadian juvenile justice. Having returned from the University of Chicago and learned from the Chicago or symbolic interactionist school of criminology, Blatz built on social psychological ideas. By the mid-1920s, juvenile offenders were reconsidered as deterministic subjects who were the product of social, psychological, and economic forces, situated in unique social milieus. Like their earlier philanthropic counterparts, Blatz and his colleagues encouraged thorough investigation of offenders' backgrounds. In contrast to the first wave, these investigations were performed by trained professionals rather than well-meaning citizens.

Although it may seem that the third wave was simply a return to the first wave, two important differences existed. First, juvenile justice in Canada had been influenced by the rise of the expert by the time of the third wave. Having concern for a problem or the financial ability to do something about it was no longer considered sufficient qualification to be accepted as an authority in juvenile justice. Second, the emphasis each group placed on the mind was distinct. The third wave relied on scientific expertise in determining mind differences, while the first wave viewed the mind as closely connected to a young person's morality, soul, or "character" rather than in scientific terms (like "brain").

During the mid-20th century, the discipline of criminology came into its own. Criminologists entered the scene as authorized knowers or "experts" about crime and its control. As the next section will show, different theoretical traditions attempted to explain youthful misbehaviour in distinct ways.

Interactionism

The Chicago School of Sociology, characterized by the tradition of symbolic **interactionism**, was in its heyday during the 1930s and 1940s. Interactionism "absorbed the notion of the social and converted it fully into a cause of crime, viewing the patterns and rates of crime as expressions of social disorganization" (Sumner, 2004: 7). Sumner continues (2004: 7): "[T]he definition of action as criminal was increasingly seen as related or relative to the standpoint of both the offending subject and the community, the legislator or the police officer, with their specific economic, political or cultural interests, needs and perceptions." Once again, the criminal conduct of young people was understood as reflective of their individual experiences and social circumstances. For example, "[b]ad boys were no longer failures evidencing personal deficiency," but had now become "social products and social responsibilities" (Sumner, 2004: 14).

However, interactionism did not view the offender or his or her background as linked to any objective or external factor. As Sumner (2004: 14) explains, it saw offences as "products of social interaction between lawbreakers and lawmakers." Tannenbaum (1979[1938]) argued that beyond adolescents themselves, society—parents, communities, legislators—was really to blame for juvenile delinquency.

While this approach highlighted micro-social processes involved in criminalization, it ignored social structural matters such as social inequality and conflict. Social influences were read primarily as cultural patterns of behaviour, not social structural conditions or constraints. Given this emphasis on the mind or culture, new programs aimed at "treatment," "social work," and "education and training" soon appeared across North America for adults and juveniles. Sumner argues that while the sociology of deviance was paying close attention to "social deviation" (individual expression of society's cultural failures) between the 1950s and 1970s, conventional criminology

> derided and dismissed most of these new sciences of the social, absorbing only those elements consistent with its acceptance of external causation driving weak individuals to

crime: that is, accepting only those forms of sociology and social administration which did not introduce choice, subjectivity, symbolism, cultural meaning, reflexivity, and interaction." (Sumner, 2004: 15)

Labelling Theories

Quantitative analysis of the "correlates" of crime and delinquency, based on official statistics, dominated criminology until the 1960s, when it was challenged by a new critical perspective called **labelling theory**. A growing contingent of scholars, among them Howard Becker, were sympathetic to the plight of offenders and questioned the wisdom and efficacy of criminal justice processing, especially its negative impact on disenfranchised groups like African Americans, women, and youth. Some focused on rights, others on labelling. Becker's (1963: 9) famous phrase "deviant behaviour is behaviour that people so label" held considerable significance for a time.

Between 1965 and 1975, this new perspective—which saw criminal and deviant acts as stemming from the labelling of social groups and institutions—led to a shift in understanding—from crime and deviance as characteristics of individuals to statuses constituted by social definitions. Becker and other labelling theorists attempted to engage in a critical discussion on the power of labelling and stigmatization and its effects. They saw the YCJS as responsible for youth crime in that it created criminals through the labels it invoked and the sanctions it employed against those so labelled. However, the critical edge of labelling theory was lost, largely because some labelling theorists tended to ignore the authorized knowers doing the labelling. Criticisms centred on the failure to contextualize micro-level processes of labelling in the societal context of social structures.

Rights Discourse

Various social processes that emerged during the 1960s and 1970s altered the shape of not only juvenile justice, but also state politics. It is important to note that the questions raised in this discussion are posed in light of the political, economic, and cultural challenges that coloured social life during the period from which they emerged (Garland and Sparks, 2000). The restructuring of social relations in the turbulent 1960s and 1970s, the fluidity of social relations, and notable cultural heterogeneity challenged youth justice scholars. Thus, changes in theories about youth crime must be understood in, and as a part of, the social context in which they materialized. The 1960s and 1970s witnessed the rise of a rights revolution that saw women, blacks, gays and lesbians, and other social groups fight for equality, which vastly changed the shape of academic theorizing on crime and criminals. **Rights discourse** became dominant during this period as various groups lobbied for legal and social recognition. Emergent theorizing about crime reflected a new respect for cultural, sexual, and other differences brought about through social protest and criticism of the state. No longer would the close relationship between state and capital go unrecognized by academics; they came to be seen as intertwined in a form reminiscent of the double helix. From the late 1960s to the present, socialist, feminist, and neo-Marxist criminologies (critical criminologies) have developed theoretical discourses that begin with the premise that society is hierarchically organized and, as such, the dominant elite (men) produce discourses that guide definitions of crime and practices of governance. **Counter-discourses**, they argue, must be developed to allow for more tolerant, respectful, and hospitable social relations. A counter-discourse challenges dominant paradigms.

With the emergence of "critical criminology" and a "critical sociology of law" came new topics (e.g., corporate crime, domestic violence) and new theories (including deconstruction, neo-Marxism, Foucaultian, feminisim), which exposed the inequities embedded in social structure and language (Beirne and Messerschmidt, 1991; Garland, 1990).

CONTEMPORARY CONCEPTIONS: RECENT CRITICAL THEORIZING

For much of the 20th century, social control was a key concept of North American sociology. In 1901, American sociologist Edward A. Ross (1969) described a planned, conscious, and scientifically based form of regulation called "**social control**." According to Colin Sumner (2004: 10), social control refers not to natural or pre-social regulation but to that which is "of the community by the community, of like-minded people by like-minded people." By the mid-1980s, however, critical criminologists had all but abandoned the concept. Stanley Cohen (1985: 2) dubbed social control a "Mickey Mouse concept" and claimed that it was like a hammer criminologists had *hit* everything with until it became analytically meaningless. Some scholars opted for other terms such as Sumner's (1990: 28–29) "**censure**"—"categories of denunciation or abuse lodged within very complex, historically loaded practical conflicts and moral debates." David Garland (2001) recently argued that Western society is a pervasive "cultural of control." If "social control" is more descriptive than analytical, then what alternative concepts can we use? Recent theorizing offers much in the way of conceptual tools to understand youth crime and youth justice. We begin this section with a discussion of the emergent youth-at-risk discourse.

Youth at Risk

It seems that in the 20th century, "generation X" has given way to "generation risk" as young people are frightened into conformity. The **youth-at-risk discourse** is a powerful truth claim. Youth, it seems, are particularly *at risk* for everything, including unwanted pregnancies, STDs, HIV/AIDS, motor vehicle injury and death, obesity, anorexia, drug addiction, and severe depression. The dissemination of risk discourse to the public is perhaps one of the most powerful elements of this trend. A recent example is the risk-based mental health and functioning assessments being used in schools in Medicine Hat, Alberta, to determine children's "risk" for violence toward their parents in the wake of the conviction of a 13-year-old girl for the 2005 killings of her parents and younger brother. Even the dangers associated with crossing the street have been calulated into a useable form for the average citizen. Our life, actions, and the choices we make are mediated by our understanding of risk. Decisions about when and where to buy or build a house, for example, are mediated by risk discourse. We are presumed to be aware of which neighbourhoods have the highest crime rates and thus should act accordingly. Throughout our lives, we continuously negotiate how we understand and react to the risks associated with various forms of conduct. Many people have quit smoking because of its associated risk of cancer. For others, the risk of second-hand smoke has compelled them to quit their jobs. Many pregnant mothers obsess about the risks to their unborn babies brought about by every manner of evil and doom. From caffeine to too much exercise, certain acts are shunned in an attempt to avoid any undue harm to the developing fetus.

Above all else, citizens are provoked into action and have the greatest concern about the risks that crime poses to their security and well-being. Risk discourse goes hand in hand with the rise of the security industry and the public's perceived insecurities about safety. The recent boom in the private security industry coincides with a *perceived* rise in crime. That is, the "escalating" violent crime rate of the mid-1990s was a boon to those who made and sold burglar alarms and anti-theft devices. "Crime" connotes harm to the individual; loss of private property; fear, violation of self; and blame, punishment, exclusion, and censure. Thus, as Anthony Giddens (1991) persuasively argues, what is "out there" in the sliding contours of risk discourse is "in here" in the sliding contours of worry, anxiety, resentment, and evasive manoeuvers. The public's increasing unease about the rising crime rate has transformed into anxiety about individual security.

Discerning the connections between individual and perceived risk(s) has produced some of the most innovative recent theorizing, especially as it relates to youth crime. The concept of a **risk society** is credited to Ulrich Beck (1992), who argues that a break with modernity has occurred, and the contours of the classical, industrial (modern) society are giving way to a new (advanced modern) risk society. Beck (1992: 19) explains that in our current "risk" society

> the social production of wealth is systematically accompanied by the social production of risks. Accordingly, the problems and conflicts relating to distribution in a society of scarcity overlap with the problems and conflicts that arise from the production, definition and distribution of techno-scientifically produced risks.

What does this mean? Risk is another means of producing social inequality and stratifying society along race, class, and gender lines. As a consequence, "institutionally structured risk environments have emerged with the capacity to reconfigure social relations" (Giddens, 1991). Risk, from this perspective, refers to external dangers, such as natural disasters (tornados, hail), technological catastrophe (the panic around "Y2K"), or menacing human conduct (violent attack) (Ericson and Haggerty, 1997). These factors clearly have real effects, whether spoken about in risk discourse or not, but the point is that any and all action is becoming calculable in terms of risk.

Failing to heed the warnings of the pervasive risk discourse invariably slides into blaming victims. For example, a homeowner whose property is burglarized can be blamed for failing to adequately equip the house with necessary risk-reducing hardware. More problematic is how this discourse can translate into making victims of sexual assault feel responsible for their own victimization. We need not push the analysis farther to get the picture. Why were you in that bar? Why did you wear those clothes? Why did you go home with him?[2] The problem is that such risk discourses conceal systemic problems and ideological effects that produce and legitimate crimes like sexual assault. Risk discourse permits fundamental elements of social inequality to masquerade as individual pathology.

---

[2] These are the kinds of questions asked of a woman's culpability in cases of sexual assault that feminist activists and academics have struggled to remove from courtrooms and public consciousness.

There is nothing inherent in sexual intercourse, buying a house, crossing the street, or being *in utero* that renders each harmful or somehow problematic. These "problems" are socially constructed. It is only when they are subject to accumulation and rendered in a form amenable to calculation that social factors become "risks." Thus, as Francois Ewald (1991: 199) argues, "[n]othing is a risk in itself; there is no risk in reality. But on the other hand, anything can be a risk; it all depends on how one analyses the danger, considers the event." Risk discourse orders reality in a way that makes it governable and controllable with particular techniques.

To say that risk is calculable suggests that seemingly random happenings can be determined in very specific ways and to very specific ends (Dean, 1999). Insurance agencies operate upon this premise. They make the *seemingly incalculable* calculable. Car accidents are, on the surface, completely random events that can strike anyone at any time. There is no way to accurately predict or prevent them. However, if we closely examine car accidents and translate our observations into a form amenable to calculation, then predictive measures can be assembled (insurance companies do this based on lifestyle factors and individual driver characteristics). Thus, age, sex, income, and occupation, for example, can be related to auto theft. On their own these demographic conditions hold little significance, but in combination they yield considerable predictive and preventative value. As such, an unemployed 21-year-old male is at a greater risk (and pays more insurance) than a 35-year-old female banker. This understanding of "risk-insurance-aegis" is not limited to the insurance industry, but has had a powerful impact on the YCJS, on the manner in which youth are governed, and on how individuals view their personal security. Feely and Simon (1994) refer to it as "actuarial justice." As we have seen, a search for *causes* has shifted to a focus on *risks*.

How does this relate to youth? For youth, "the practice of institutionalized reflexive monitoring of young people's behaviours and dispositions energizes the emergence of discourses of youth at-risk" (Kelly, 2001: 25). Although the search for the "cause" of youth crime has not been abandoned, there is heightened concern about youth at risk. At the level of risk management, however, risks are presumed to emerge from *individual* decision making, not from structural location. For example, a 15-year-old Aboriginal youth is "at risk" of becoming involved in a gang. His risk gets translated as an individual failing, rather than a systemic factor related to growing up Aboriginal in an urban centre with few appealing alternatives to crime and gang activity. Risk discourse has implications for the response to youth crime because changes with respect to political and social intervention that rely on a risk analysis are directed at personal rather than social structural factors.

With individualization comes **responsibilization**; that is, new forms of responsibility are placed upon youth and their families to *manage* their risks (Burchell, 1996). Through regulatory spheres like communities, schools, and law enforcement, individual youth and their families are "responsibilized." That is, they are held accountable for their own riskiness. Individuals themselves are categorized as "at risk." As Rose (1996) argues, identifying risk factors and certain populations (such as youth) as "at risk" can be understood as a technique mobilized to produce "rational, choice making, autonomous, responsible citizens within (neo)liberal projects of government" (as cited in Kelly, 2001: 23). In other words, risk discourse (rationality) and responsibilization strategies (practices) are increasingly common in the contemporary era of **neo-liberalism**.

Neo-liberalism is a social, political, and economic regulatory system characterized by policies and programs around security, privatization, and "risk." Since the mid-1980s, neo-liberal reforms have made it easier for capital to expand (i.e., corporations to make larger profits) and have contributed to the disappearance of the social welfare state. Protections such as employment insurance and social assistance have been increasingly difficult to access and even harder to rely upon to maintain even the most modest standard of living. Neo-liberalism is also exemplified in the strengthening of the penal state (Wacquant, 2000: 404). In this context, the discourse of **neo-conservatism**, cloaked in moralism, provides rationale for law and order and a crime control model based on harsher punishments for offenders.

Neo-liberalism assumes that citizens need to become more responsible and governments need to reduce the size and cost of their operations. The impact of neo-liberalism is greatest on marginalized peoples—those for whom heightened employment insecurity, reduction in social services, and precarious living situations are life altering. Living in a climate of neo-liberalism has tremendous social, economic, cultural, and political consequences for **criminalized youth**, especially the disenfranchised.[3]

The Collapse and Slippage Between Risk/Need Youth is an artifact of expertise, which constructs ways of thinking about a group comprised of neither children nor adults (Kelly, 2000a). Institutionalized expertise plays a role in the process of defining and categorizing youth. That is, authorized knowers make claims about which youths are at risk and what populations are targeted. As youth is a period of transition, young people are in the process of *becoming* (for instance, becoming an adult, a citizen, independent, etc.). At-risk discourse constructs youth as at risk of jeopardizing "desired futures" (Kelly, 2001: 30). However, not all youth live in social circumstances where the chance of a preferred adult future is available.

During the 21st century, psychologists have come to play a key role in the correctional field, especially in diagnostics. As Hannah-Moffat and Maurutto (2005) explain in "Youth Risk/Need Assessment: An Overview of Issues and Practices," in practice, risk factors are linked to identifying **criminogenic needs**—factors that play a role in preventing offending. Practitioners use actuarial tools to classify prisoners in terms of security risks and criminogenic needs. **Risk/need** classification, then, leads to a security classification as well as the allocation of a particular level of treatment and supervision. Recently, criminogenic needs have been divided into static factors (e.g., age, offence history) and dynamic factors (e.g., things that treatment programs can modify, such as antisocial attitudes, personality traits, or substance abuse). Static criminogenic needs evaluations produce a rigid knowledge of risk and a fixed risk subject (Hannah-Moffat, 2002), who is then designated into a particular risk category (high, medium, or low). The most recent version of the *Youth Level of Service/Case Management Inventory* (YLS/CMI) used in Canadian youth correctional facilities integrates both factors.

These tools are based on what Andrews and Bonta (1998: 245) refer to as the "four principles of risk, need, responsivity, and professional discretion." The *risk principle* says that criminal behaviour is predictable and treatment services must match the offender's level of risk. The *needs principle* implies that targeting criminogenic needs and providing treatment will reduce recidivism. Treatment is often cognitive and behavioural, to

---

[3] Neo-liberal politics are clearly evident in Alberta, the first province to make sweeping cuts to social welfare, according to the National Council of Welfare (1997). Beginning in 1993, the province made obtaining welfare increasingly difficult, cut maximum basic allowances by $26 per month, and stopped paying moving allowances and laundry costs for infants. Across-the-board cuts to welfare resulted in a drop in the number of welfare cases by 63% (NCW 1997).

teach more than to treat. The *responsivity principle* is the delivery of programs in a style and manner consistent with the ability and learning style of the offender. Finally, the *principle of professional discretion* "strategically reasserts the importance of retaining professional judgment, provided that it is not used irresponsibly and is systematically monitored" (Hannah-Moffat and Maurutto, 2005: 3). Little research has been conducted on the risk/need instruments used with young offender populations.

Hannah-Moffat and Maurutto (2005: 7) found that corrections officials and practitioners failed to conceptualize "the problems intrinsic to this kind of needs assessment and how a failure to distinguish between risk and need can result in increased surveillance of youth." Rather, participants saw risk and need as "part of the same issue." According to Hannah-Moffat (2000: 36), blending risks and needs into risk/need creates a paradox because it

> combines two quite different elements: traditional security concerns, which are generally associated with danger and the prevention of harm to others, and a more recent emphasis on need, which by contrast implies that a prisoner is lacking something and entitled to resources.

Significant variables requiring intervention not related to recidivism, such as poor health, are deemed "**non-criminogenic needs**." Such needs are lower in priority. Moreover, intervenable needs are not identified according to particular individuals, and only those characteristics an individual shares with a population that is statistically correlated with recidivism are addressed.

Risk discourse is gendered and racialized, but risk categories mask gender- and race-based realities. Concerns about the use of such tools for youth are magnified for female and non-white populations. Notably, "female offenders are more often deemed higher risk because of their risk to themselves, whereas high-risk male offenders are more likely to pose a risk to others" (Hannah-Moffat and Shaw, 2001). Gender and cultural variation in offending and recidivism have yet to be explored. For example, tests do not adequately capture the histories of physical, mental, or sexual abuse prevalent among female youth. The broader socio-cultural context of Aboriginal youth and their unique issues are also not adequately addressed by risk-assessment tools.

Risk assessments are premised on an insurance model. Probabilistic calculations produce a score, which is presumed to be indicative of the likelihood of an event occurring (in this case recidivism). Predicted risk of re-offending informs and justifies correctional practice. O'Malley (1992) refers to the "risk" that these assessments create as a **statistical artifact**. Indeed, the management of risk by the autonomous, responsible youthful self is a radical departure from positivism. Another shift in rationalities governing youth crime is seen in the work of Michel Foucault and his followers and discussed in the following section.

Governmentality and Power: Foucault and Criminology

Much of the literature that deconstructs risk society and risk discourse emerges from a growing body of work inspired by the writings of French theorist Michel Foucault. Nevertheless, Foucault is seldom regarded as a significant contributor to the discipline of criminology for his own work. On the rare occasion when he did comment, he referred to its "garrulous discourse" and "endless repetitions" as staggering and its only utility as justifying retribution (Foucault, 1980: 47). Foucault's most significant contribution to criminology can arguably be found in *Discipline and Punish*, his penological treatise on the "birth of the prison," and in his later work on power, which inspired fresh criminological theorizing. In particular, his ideas about how **power/knowledge** operates through the social construction of truth claims are significant.

Drawing on Foucault, Bernard Schissel (1997, as cited in Smandych, 1999: 88) explains, "[m]odern political discourse controls the way in which the news media speak about young offenders by restricting the debates to individual or family-based accounts of the origins of crime."

Foucault sees power as something that is produced and is only evident when it is exercised. It is not something held, accumulated, possessed, or monopolized by the state. Moreover, it is not negative in that it only oppresses or represses. Rather, a **Foucaultian conception of power** is a positive theory of power—not in terms of good or benefial, but rather productive. He argues that

> we must cease once and for all to describe the effects of power in negative terms: it 'excludes,' it 'represses,' it 'censures,' it 'abstracts,' it 'masks,' it 'conceals.' In fact power produces; it produces reality; it produces domains of object and rituals of truth. (Foucault 1979: 194)

One of the consequences of Foucault's steering clear of the negative or repressive view of power is that he insists on a move to the small powers that attend to details at the individual level. What he calls "the political anatomy of detail" and how it is manifest in his understanding of **discipline** is important. Discipline is found operating at the smallest level of detail, at the intricacies of human movements through surveillance (i.e., from holding a pen to firing a gun). It is the everyday and the mundane that are important for governing. Discipline functions to increase the efficiency and usefulness of human actions by coordinating them individually and bringing them together with others.

Meticulous, constant surveillance is required. As such, discipline demands that individuals be organized in space and time. Consider the timetables in public schools. They provides a general framework for activity and organize the day. They structure not only our *use* of time but also the *space* that we occupy at certain points in the day. The bell organizes behaviour. Thus time, space, and signals coexist to train the mind and body.

Foucault's analysis of discipline has been criticized for abandoning the state (e.g., centralized government) in its analysis, and for a supposed tendency to characterize human subjects as "docile" (inactive) bodies as opposed to active agents (Garland, 1997). Foucault's later work on governmentality and his 1982 essay "The Subject and Power" (Foucault, 1982) stress the importance of *active* subjects as the medium through which governance is exercised. Here, governmental power does not "objectify," but rather "subjectifies." It "constructs individuals who are capable of choice and action, shapes them as active subjects, and seeks to align their choices with the objects of governing authorities" (Garland, 1997: 175).

Foucault's understanding of governance and **governmentality** must not be reduced to its parliamentary forms (in other words, state government); it has a wider application. Governmentality is the "conduct of conduct" (Gordon 1991: 2). Conduct denotes leading, directing, or guiding with some form of calculation about how it may be accomplished (as opposed to forcing and repressing). Foucault argues that "government is not a matter of imposing laws on men (sic), but rather of disposing things, that is to say to employ tactics rather than laws, and if need be to use the laws themselves as tactics" (Foucault, 1991: 95). For Foucault (1982: 221) government

> must be allowed the very broad meaning which it had in the 16th century. Government did not refer only to political structures or the management of states; rather it designated the way in which the conduct of individuals or states might be directed; the government of children, of souls, of communities, of families, of the sick.

Therefore, the study of governmentality should cast its gaze widely and address such broad questions as "how to govern oneself, how to be governed, how to govern others, by whom the people will accept to be governed, and how to become the best possible governor" (Foucault, 1991: 45).

This way of thinking about government is embodied in a distinct set of objectives (ends) and the practices (means) used to realize them, all of which are situated within a material reality targeted by government. Summarizing our discussion of Foucault's writings, government(ality) entails "any attempt to shape with some degree of deliberation aspects of our behaviour according to particular sets of norms and for a variety of ends" (Dean, 1999: 10).

CONCLUSION: TOWARD JUSTICE FOR THE OTHER?

Unique questions emerge from recent theorizing—including governmentality, risk, and feminist discourses—each particularly relevant to youth justice discussions. Given our concern for social justice, we must not lose sight of those individuals to which various forms of governance, categories of risk, and "othering" processes are directed. During the late 1990s, the privileging of lay expertise accompanied the recognition of victims and (adult) community members as authorized knowers. Where are youth? Where are criminologists? Whereas youths have never been granted the status of authorized knowers, criminologists have become almost displaced as "experts" on matters of crime and delinquency. What significance does this hold for justice?

We deliberately leave this chapter without any firm conclusion on the question of justice for the other. Instead, we hope to challenge you to think about what justice for youth meant in various historical periods and what it could mean in the future. We hope the following questions will guide your thinking and stimulate your critical engagement with the material presented in the rest of the text.

- How have conceptions of youth and youth governance changed over time?
- How is it possible to discern the changes in the dominant character of the modern legal governance of deviant youth?
- What is the relationship between state, law, non-governmental control, communities, and the juvenile justice system?

In the next two chapters, we will explore the variety of paths in which youth justice has been directed.

SUMMARY

- Theorizing youth crime is essential because theories provide a context in which to place youthful conduct and attitudes, social policies, and legislative practices.
- Social relations of race, class, gender, and age figure prominently in the governance of youthful misbehaviour. Feminist discourse is informative in this regard.
- Viewing troubled youth as "the other" attends to the processes of criminalization, marginalization, and exclusion.
- Authorized knowers, or resident experts on youth crime who create dominant discourses, have varied along with their claims. Different understandings of youthful offending range from classical theory to the three forms of positivism, labelling to rights and risk, and more recently, theorizing from feminism to governmentality.
- Feminist discourse offers ways to theorize youthful offenders as criminalized youth. The category of "the other" presents way of analyzing the position of youthful offenders in the YCJS and the larger society.
- Youth-at-risk discourse individualizes systemic, socially structured events as well as processes and circumstances, and responsibilizes youth and their families rather than dealing with structural inequalities.
- Governmentality provides a unique window from which to view contemporary governing practices directed at youth.

DISCUSSION QUESTIONS

1. To what extent can the way the problem of youth crime is conceptualized be separated from the way it is governed?
2. What are the potential implications of the pervasiveness of youth-at-risk discourses?
3. How is youth justice full of "conflict, contradictions, ambiguity, and compromise"?

RECOMMENDED READINGS

Ericson, R. and K. Haggerty. (1997). *Policing the Risk Society*. Toronto: University of Toronto Press and Oxford: University of Oxford Press.

Foucault, Michel. (1977). *Discipline and Punish: The Birth of the Prison*. New York: Vintage.

Garland, D. and R. Sparks. (2001). "Criminology, sociology and the challenge of our times." In *Criminology and Social Theory*. London: Oxford.

Chapter 3

Responding to Youth Crime: Historical Origins of Juvenile Justice Legislation

STARTING POINT

A 13-year-old boy in Montreal was hanged for stealing a cow in 1818 (Carrigan, 1998).

In these days, when the value of a child to the State is just beginning to be recognized, attention has been directed to the comparative worth of the two methods of treatment— that of mere punishment, as the law punishes an adult criminal, or that of winning the youthful offender's confidence, teaching, moulding, guiding . . . The first method, that of punishment, is the first and only principle of penology applied by man and his fellows [sic]. Penal servitude has been a dismal and dreary failure. A newer and better way . . . has been discovered and applied to youthful delinquents, in a few modern communities. The reason for its remarkable success lies, perhaps, in the fact that punishment is subordinated altogether to the idea of child training (Toronto News, 19 March, 1907).

We explore the following ideas in this chapter and encourage you to keep them in mind as you read:

■ Why was a separate system for juvenile delinquents established around the turn of the 20th century?

■ Who were the authorized knowers behind this move away from generalized justice?

■ What is the relationship between actions and actors?

■ What claims did social reformers make about "juvenile delinquents" and "juvenile delinquency"?

■ What were the various strategies offered as an antidote to juvenile delinquency?

■ What precursors led to the creation of the *Juvenile Delinquents Act?*

LEARNING OBJECTIVES

After reading this chapter, you should be able to

■ Illustrate that juvenile delinquency is a social construction.

■ Differentiate between classical legal governance and modern legal governance.

- List and explain the factors and events that led to the creation of a separate system for the governance of juvenile delinquency.

- Identify the dominant players in the initial era of "juvenile justice" (late 19th and early 20th centuries) and their primary claims.

- Describe the key features of Canada's first separate system for governing juvenile delinquents, including the *Juvenile Delinquents Act*.

INTRODUCTION

Today we rarely question the importance of a separate juvenile justice system. In fact, a youth justice court, legislation, and contemporary responses to young offenders are largely taken for granted. However, Canada did not always differentiate between youthful deviance and adult criminality, nor did it always have **juvenile courts** (specialized courts hearing only youth cases).

From the early days of settlement in New France (now Quebec) to the present day, adult members of society have, to some degree, been troubled by antisocial behaviour or law-breaking by children and youth (Carrigan, 1998). During the pioneer period, many orphaned, abandoned, and neglected young people found themselves in circumstances that put them at a greater likelihood of getting into trouble. Little is known about this period, given the poor record keeping, inadequate law enforcement, and pioneer conditions, but young people certainly committed acts that went against social norms. What we have come to call "youth crime" is not new. Historical records of the pre- and post-Confederation periods are more complete, but by no means thorough.

In early Canada, "juvenile delinquents" and "juvenile delinquency" had not yet entered the public consciousness, but children of various ages still engaged in behaviour that was subjected to punishment. Youthful deviants, with a few limited exceptions, were governed in much the same manner as adult offenders. A young person came before the same judges, received the same punishments, and was sentenced to the same institutions as his or her adult counterparts. As the above statement by Carrigan (1998) illustrates, before the introduction of a separate system for governing juvenile delinquents, young people found guilty of criminal-code infractions suffered harsh and, at times, arbitrary penalties.

This chapter focuses on juvenile governance in Canadian society between the mid-19th century and the early decades of the 20th century. We trace the origins of the ***Juvenile Delinquents Act (JDA)*** and the discourse of **juvenile delinquency** that conditioned it. As we shall see, the wayward behaviour of recalcitrant young people came to be understood as "juvenile delinquency" around the turn of the 20th century. In this chapter, you will learn when, how, and why a separate system for governing young people's misbehaviour emerged. We pay particular attention to how this strategy was **gendered**—that is, inextricably linked to particular conceptions of masculinity and femininity. Youthful misbehaviour during the era of juvenile delinquency was cast in large part as a "boy problem." Although girls were also caught up with the law and in institutions designed for their care and control, the separate juvenile justice system as a whole was primarily conceived of, established by, and operated by men for boys. In other words, female young offenders were an afterthought.

Recall any history courses or classes you have taken. Although different in content and delivery, each journey most likely involved asking the question, "What happened?" What happened, however, involves more than a linear sequence of events. The historical origins of any phenomenon are rooted within an evolving society; changing attitudes, values, and modes of conduct—and can be understood from different perspectives. This is no less the case with the invention and treatment of juvenile delinquency. If, as Carrigan (1998) argues, "delinquency and its treatment are two sides of the same coin and frequently interact," then we need to ask in whose hands the coin lies at any particular historical moment. Reform movements and social reformers figure prominently in this history because they were among the authorized knowers—those key individuals and groups whose claims were heard, who were granted the status of "expert," and whose arguments were taken seriously and subsequently acted upon.

Understanding the evolution of Canada's separate youth criminal justice system involves making sense of more than the introduction of legislation dealing specifically with young people. It concerns the processes by which a traditional, generalized, punitive system of governance evolved into a modern, separate, juvenile justice system. We must also examine shifts in the political and economic organization of early Canada and the role of broader social, cultural, and historical factors. To this end, Chapter 3 is intended to provide an appreciation of both the historical origins of the *JDA* and how a distinct set of practices, policies, and ideas about the governance of juvenile delinquency came into being. Part One outlines governance and introduces the influence of social reformers in early juvenile justice practice and policy. Part Two provides a historical context for the social construction of childhood and juvenile delinquency. Part Three examines how youthful deviants were handled before the development of juvenile-specific practices. Part Four explores the circumstances under which interested, philanthropic reformers and the political elite argued for a response to the crimes and delinquency of young people.

SOCIAL REFORMERS AND GOVERNANCE STRATEGIES

During the 19th century, **social reformers**—primarily upper-middle-class business, political, and legal and male elites—began to question the wisdom of the dominant governance practice of adjudicating young people through a generalized system of punishment. Gradually, these prominent and interested citizens created a separate juvenile justice system fashioned on different principles and philosophies. The recognition that juvenile offenders should be treated differently and be subject to a distinct set of laws, institutions, and practices culminated in the implementation of the *Juvenile Delinquents Act* (*JDA*) in 1908.

Not only did the passage of the *JDA* signal Canada's first formalized juvenile justice system, but it also represented a break from **classical legal governance** (a generalized system of adjudication and punishment) and a move toward **modern legal governance** (a particularized system based on knowledge of the offender rather than his or her criminal conduct). It is important not to exaggerate change at the expense of continuity. Although often neglected in criminological studies, informal mechanisms of social control and customary laws, sometimes referred to as legal pluralism, continued to operate during this shift in juvenile justice (Smandych and Linden, 2005). **Informal governance** includes such forms of social control as church discipline, shaming, and other community-based strategies, and remains in existence today. Informal governance exerts control over youthful deviance at a distance, either from the city, the street, the rural countryside, the community, the state, or the formal legal system.

In rural areas, church governance was common during the mid- to late 19th century. In Ontario, for example, religious authorities governed spheres of life that many people today see as outside the church purview (Marks, 1998). Minor theft and disputes between neighbours or family members, including family violence, were dealt with through church officials and community members (Lethwaite, 1994). Shaming practices were evident in community rituals like the charivari (sliwaree), which involved the mocking of culprits by an entourage (at times violent) of masked serenaders (Palmer, 1978). The community expressed its disapproval of certain behaviours through public displays of shame. Communities intervened informally to bring about harmony and **normalize** deviant actions. Keep the economic and political context of these informal structures of governance in rural 19th-century Canadian society in mind as you learn about the creation of the first laws specifically geared toward juveniles.

A traditional reading of the history of juvenile delinquency would present delinquency as a problem simply because adolescents' antisocial behaviour and/or criminal conduct (i.e., harm to persons and/or property) became *dangerous* to the broader society at a particular historical moment (Tanner, 2001: 4). This is referred to as an **objectivist approach**, which is in contrast to our own approach. A **social constructionist perspective** holds that juvenile delinquency becomes a *problem* when it is defined as such by social reformers (be they prominent individuals or social groups). It becomes problematic when it is labelled as such by authorized knowers. As Best (1989, p. xviii, emphasis added) argues, "Our sense of what *is* or *is not* a social problem is a product, something that has been produced or constructed through social activities." While Best provides a basis from which to explore the social construction of juvenile delinquency, his account tends to ignore *who* is responsible. This chapter puts the introduction of a new response to the misbehaviour of young people in the context of both *activities* (actors and events) and *actors* (key players) evoking change in mid- to late 19th-century Canada.

To discuss the socially constructed nature of juvenile delinquency does *not* imply that there is nothing "real" about the problem of youth crime in Canada. Visit your local youth court and you will see young people cast as offenders being sentenced by judges for infractions against the criminal code. There is nothing more real to a mother who has lost her young son to gang violence than "youth crime." A famous W.I. Thomas (1925) statement is significant here; to paraphrase, if we define situations as real, they are real in their consequences. Victims of youth crime know too well the reality of their suffering. Adolescents serving time in detention centres across the country have experienced the real effects of the label "young offender" and the sanction of "6 months secure custody." However, taking terms and categories such as juvenile delinquency or youth crime as inevitable or as having an obvious, widely shared, and understood meaning obscures the processes involved in constructing youthful misbehaviour as a social problem in need of a solution. It ignores the key players at the table, as well as those left standing without chairs. More importantly, it does not require that we question our assumptions about our social world. It requires no sociological imagination (Mills, 1959). This is not to suggest that we fail to take into account the tangible or objective characteristics of youth crime and youth justice (e.g., kids in jail, lives lost). To the contrary, we argue that we can only fully appreciate such concrete matters if we recognize the claims made about them, by whom they are made, and to what ends. Juvenile delinquency, juvenile delinquents, and other related categories as social constructions are imbued with meaning, largely from authorized knowers' claims about particular individuals and certain kinds of conduct. We now turn our attention to early perspectives on juvenile deviance.

EARLY PERSPECTIVES: SURELY *THESE* ARE THE WORST OF TIMES?

Our Earth is degenerate . . . Children no longer obey their parents. (An Egyptian priest, 6000 B.C.E.)

There is widespread agreement among adult members of contemporary Canadian society that the group we commonly refer to as "youth" are somehow more poorly behaved and more problematic today than they were in the past. It *appears* this is the case; recall our discussion in Chapter 1 on media discourse and youth crime. However, a historical look at this issue presents a different perspective. In fact, the idea of the *good old days*, when young people actually listened to their parents, respected authority, and otherwise behaved properly, is a myth. Long ago the philosopher Socrates and the poet Hesiod commented that boys and girls were destructive and lacked discipline. As the above quotation from 6000 B.C.E. shows, thousands of years in the past, religious authorities claimed young people had lost their way. Of course, you are likely more familiar with more recent heightened concern—what Stanley Cohen (1972) calls moral panic—about youth crime. Moral panics are overreactions to forms of deviance or wrongdoing resulting from claims made about particular groups being a threat to the moral order and touch people's fears, gain momentum, and infiltrate public consciousness. During the late 1990s, Canadians received a daily dose of media images and stories about the growing tide of criminal activity of young people, and particularly its violent nature. As discussed in Chapter 1, youth violence today has become a symbol of all that is wrong with Canadian society.

Childhood and Juvenile Delinquency

It is a common misconception that there has always been a separate category for children or a stage of life called youth. Childhood was not always understood as a distinct status or period of life. Moreover, the meaning of childhood has changed over time (Empey, 1982). We will explore how the concept of "juvenile delinquency" materialized from the recognition of childhood as a distinct stage of development, with children having distinct needs. In this context, we can understand how a new response for dealing with the misdeeds of children came into being. The concept of "juvenile delinquency" reflected wideranging social change in the late 19th century. It represented a new way of thinking about, responding to, and treating young offenders.

Philippe Aries's (1962) famous book, *Centuries of Childhood*, questions the common assumption that childhood has always existed. Aries had a dual career as a writer on historical topics (although not as an academic) and as an information officer with an institute established to promote the production and consumption of tropical fruit (Macey, 2004). His arguments regarding the "invention of childhood" have led many historians to examine the numerous realms of childhood experience. Aries's detailed historical study of the treatment of children in Western Europe from the Middle Ages to the 19th century revealed that childhood was discovered in 17th-century Western Europe. Before that time, European society viewed children as **"little adults"** and made few social and cultural distinctions on the basis of age. Children were very much integrated into the work and recreation of family life. Aries pointed to the fact that children wore the same clothing as adults, were educated through apprenticeships, and learned trades or professions working alongside adults. The concept of "childhood" as we know it today did not exist. In addition, Aries claimed that a high infant-mortality rate discouraged parents from forming strong emotional attachments to their children, as reflected in the practices of wet-nursing (e.g., mothers hiring other lactating women to breastfeed their babies) and sending children away to boarding school or to work as servants or apprentices. An attitude of indifference may have been protection against the tragic loss parents would feel at the death of their children. Aries (1962: 329) argued that up until the 19th century, once a child

> had passed the age of five or seven, the child was immediately absorbed into the world of adults . . . thus adolescence, never clearly defined under the *ancien regime*, was distinguished in the nineteenth century and indeed already in the late eighteenth century by conscription and later by military service.

Although Aries's evidence has been criticized, his main claim that childhood is a **cultural artifact** rather than a biological imperative warrants our attention. As a cultural artifact, childhood is socially constructed and not biologically based. Aries's analysis suggests a need to rethink assumptions about youth and challenge the naturalness of a separation between children and adults. Despite his class bias, the ideological underpinnings of his analysis (he was a member of the ultra-conservative group Action Française), and the fact that his own positive memories of childhood may have clouded his analysis, Aries was the first to argue that childhood is socially constructed. His thesis suggests a connection between changing adult images of childhood and the development of modern thinking about juvenile delinquency and its treatment. The concept of childhood, as Empey (1982: 53) explains,

> grew and expanded, the meanings attached to it were significantly altered. The acts of children which in previous centuries were not seen as particularly deviant now became unique problems. New norms and expectations developed as childhood became a special phase in the life cycle.

In Canada throughout the 17th and 18th centuries, adults considered childhood a very short stop on a child's way to adulthood (Pinchbeck and Hewitt, 1969). As such, their behaviour was governed by much the same standards as adult conduct. If children were "little adults," then a juvenile delinquent was simply a miniature criminal. Russell Smandych (2001b) cautions that attitudes toward children were more ambivalent than they appear and suggests that the markers of where childhood ends and adulthood begins remain ambiguous today. Smandych (2001b: 9–10) offers the following lesson:

> If you approach the history of childhood with the hope of finding an earlier time when raising children was more simple, and when there were clear cut rules about how children were supposed to behave, you will be sadly disappointed.

Moreover, finding the emergence of a separate system of juvenile justice in the discovery of the concept of childhood or in changing images of childhood alone over-simplifies things. Smandych (2001b) argues that while changes that occurred at the turn of the 20th century appear to have had much to do with the "invention of childhood," a century later changes seem to be connected to a growing adult desire for the "disappearance of childhood," a symptom of a perceived crisis in youth crime (discussed in Chapter 4).

GENERALIZED JUSTICE: CLASSICAL LEGAL GOVERNANCE

The earliest form of youth regulation can be considered classical legal governance (Hogeveen, 2002: 46). This generalized approach made very little distinction between young and adult offenders and was primarily concerned with establishing guilt or innocence. For a crime to have occurred in a legal sense, two fundamental conditions must be met. First, an act that violates criminal law statutes must take place—*actus reus*. Second, the individual whose behaviour contravened the law must have the mental capacity (or criminal intent) to fully appreciate the consequence of his or her conduct. Before Confederation, Canadian criminal law handled young people over the age of seven in much the same manner as adult offenders, with one exception: *doli incapax*. Young people over the age of 14 were presumed mature enough to appreciate the consequences of their behaviour. However, given their immaturity, children and youth as a group could be not considered to comprehend the seriousness of their conduct the way adults could. To a limited degree, the English common-law doctrine *doli incapax*, which literally translated means incapable of wrongdoing, manifested this belief (Bala, 1988).

Doli incapax held that since children under the age of seven were presumed to be too immature to form the requisite intent for criminality, they were immune from prosecution. Children between the ages of 7 and 14 were thought to possess a diminished ability to appreciate the implications of their behaviour. Therefore, they were assumed to be *doli incapax* and, unless the Crown could prove otherwise, *mens rea*, and they could not be legally convicted (Griffiths and Verdun-Jones, 1994). For example, if the Crown could demonstrate that nine-year-old Sarah did, in fact, appreciate the consequences of her actions, then the presumption of *doli incapax* would be rebutted and she would be ordered to stand trial. Despite the sympathy and mercy sometimes extended to young offenders, their transgressions were often handled in very punitive ways (Hay, 1975; Langbein, 1978; Beattie, 1986; Smandych, 1991). Young people received only minimal consideration for their age, and the penalties for criminal conduct were notoriously harsh.

Were young people subject to the whim and fancy of magistrates? Were penalties such as hanging, whipping, servitude, exile, incarceration, iron collars, branding, or corporal punishment warranted for young offenders? Carrigan (1998) recounts the tale of a young female servant charged with the theft of two shirts from her merchant employer. She denied the accusation and was subjected to torture to illicit a confession. She was tied up by her wrists with her feet only barely touching a chair, which was subsequently removed. She hung for 15 minutes while the tips of her fingers were burned with a candle. With deep cuts on her arms she was finally let down, still protesting her innocence (Seguin, 1972).

Tender age was definitely not a mitigating factor in the case of the Montreal boy mentioned in the opening of this chapter. Guilty verdicts were almost solely based on a young person's aberrant behaviour, with little attention given to his or her life experiences, social position, mental state, or age. The classical legal approach reflected the twin goals of **retribution** (punishment deserved, "an eye for an eye") and **deterrence** (preventing crime through threat or fear of punishment). Punishments were applied generally to the population of "offenders" with very little consideration given to specific individual circumstances (Carrigan, 1991; Baehre, 1982). The liberal attitude guiding generalized justice was that offenders were hedonistic, rational, and calculating actors who weighed the benefits and consequences of conduct before engaging in unlawful behaviour.

Evidence that age was not a primary consideration can also be found in the routine housing of young people with adults in prison. This generalized treatment carried over into how children were dealt with while awaiting trial. Children suspected of, or serving time for, committing crimes were confined in facilities with adult offenders. With the growth of the colonial population, communities established local jails where children were frequently and indiscriminately mixed with "hardened criminals, prostitutes, drunkards, and the insane," with no regard for the child's special status. The Kingston Penitentiary, a notoriously punitive and draconian institution, counted children among its first inmates when it opened in 1835. Young boys were incarcerated alongside adult male prisoners, and young girls were housed in the female quarters. The sentencing of children as young as 10 to a prison for adult male offenders characterized the generalized mode of juvenile justice during the early to mid-19th century in Canada. For example, in 1852, 23 of the 138 inmates in Kingston (16%) were 18 years old or younger (Carrigan, 1998: 18). Imprisoned children were not immune from routine prison discipline, which included lashing and flogging (Brown Commission, 1849).

TOWARD A SEPARATE JUVENILE JUSTICE SYSTEM

No single reason can explain why the generalized approach began to unravel. Several factors and events came together during the mid- to late 19th century that eventually led to the development of a separate juvenile justice system. The following discussion examines four significant factors that help account for when, how, and why Canada moved toward a separate system. These are 1) socio-economic climate, 2) social reformers and movements, 3) social welfare penality, and 4) anti-institutional discourse (see Table 3.1).

In addition to these four factors, several legislative precursors and developments hold considerable relevance and will be considered below.

Table 3.1 Key Factors in the Emergence of a Separate Juvenile Justice System

Socio-Economic Climate	Social Reformers and Movements	Social-Welfare Penality	Anti-Institutional Discourse
immigration	reformatory and industrial schools	the Canadian state	dissatisfaction with institutionalization
urbanization	public schools and child welfare	the rise of social welfare	appeal of community strategies
industrialization	international influences	changes in punishment	probation

I. Socio-Economic Climate: Immigration, Urbanization, and Industrialization

During the early to mid-19th century, Canada was a predominantly agrarian nation. This began to change around Confederation (1867) as urbanization and industrialization reshaped the social, economic, and political climate. Between 1800 and 1900, the urban population more than doubled, rising from 14% to almost 40% of the population (Wallace, 1950). The Irish famine of the 1840s created a large group of orphans. Increasing numbers of immigrants from Europe searching for a better life on the Canadian frontier contributed to urbanization, with many forced to migrate to urban centres in central Canada. The population of Upper Canada doubled in size from 186 488 in 1828 to 374 099 in 1836 (Carrigan, 1998: 6). In Toronto, the population grew from 56 092 in 1881 to 208 040 in 1901. Other cities, such as Montreal and Hamilton, experienced similar growth (Census of Canada, 1871–1921; Careless, 1984). Massive migration from the rural countryside and immigration combined to establish cities and create new problems in the recently individualized and anonymous social milieu. By the turn of the 20th century, Canada was a growing centre of industry.

As these changes transformed the landscape of class and race relations between 1860 and 1930, the population of urban poor grew significantly (Noble, 1979). In a period of intense nation building—of a "white, Protestant" Canada—elite men and women targeted "dangerous working-class and immigrant parents" as detrimental (Valverde, 1991). In particular, reformers believed that such groups would transfer evil influences to their children, and sought intervention strategies to minimize the likelihood that the next generation would suffer a similar fate. Reformers increasingly saw the impoverished and working class as a threat to the emerging Canadian nation state, given their tenuous connection to the labour market. This reinforced the isolation of the working class and justified intrusive forms of governance aimed at them (Simon, 1993).

Thus the stage was set for officials to question the governance of young people. A new social problem was about to emerge—how to manage the great number of juvenile immigrants "flooding in from all over the world"—and would have significant effects on the governance of juvenile delinquency (Canada MG 30: Kelso Papers, vol 1).

Brown Commission Because of the oppressive conditions of the Kingston Penitentiary, interest in a **particularistic** (unique to the individual) knowledge concerning the special *legal* status of children began to grow. The **Brown Commission** of 1849 represented a move toward a new way of thinking about the legal governance of deviant children; that is, a new conceptualization of young people and their crimes and a corresponding shift in how to respond to them.

The commission's investigation of the Kingston Penitentiary found appalling conditions, including drunken staff, unsanitary conditions, dilapidated facilities, and excessive discipline. Most importantly, the commission recognized the problematic nature of housing young people alongside adults—particularly those hardened in a life of crime, whom George Brown referred to as "hoary-headed evil doers." When the investigation took place, there were three children under the age of 12 (including one 8-year-old boy) and 12 children under the age of 16 incarcerated alongside adults (Brown Commission,

1849: 10). Investigators criticized the practice of confining children in adult facilities as follows:

> It is distressing to think that no distinction is now made between the child who has strayed for the first time from the path of honesty, or who perhaps has never been taught the meaning of sin, and the hardened offender of mature years. All are consigned together to the unutterable contamination of the common gaol [jail]; and by the lessons there learnt, soon become inmates of the Penitentiary. (Brown Commission, 1849: 73)

The Brown Commission (1849: 576) argued for "immediate action . . . on behalf of the juvenile delinquent." As we will see, prison inspectors, philanthropists, and religious officials used the commission's report to push for the creation of separate reform institutions for juvenile offenders. They argued that facilities modelled after American and European reformatory institutions would have a positive impact on this population. For example, members of the Prisoners' Aid Society (PAA), the forerunner of the modern-day John Howard Society, were convinced that incarcerating young offenders with long-time recidivists had a disastrous impact.

Subsequently, in 1857, the Province of Canada passed two pieces of legislation that applied specifically to young persons: *An Act for the More Speedy Trial and Punishment of Young Persons,* which accelerated the trial process for deviant youth, and *An Act for Establishing Prisons for Young Persons,* which allowed for *reformatory* prisons in Upper and Lower Canada. For the first time, children could be "detained and corrected, and receive such instruction and be subject to such discipline as shall appear most conducive to their reformation and the repression of crime" (Canada 1857: 20 Vic, c28). Underlying these acts was a belief in the *special status* of children and the view that punishment must have a purpose greater than **incapacitation** (incarceration not for what people have done, but to prevent future harm), retribution, or deterrence.

Although it would be 60 years before the JDA came into being, the Brown Commission and the resulting legislation signalled the emergence of a new way of thinking about youth as a *separate category* of offender, and the recognition that juvenile offenders required *separate institutions* (Hogeveen, 2001). Controversy over this new sensibility continues to this day (Feld, 1999). Attitudes toward children were changing and a new paradigm was taking hold, one that rejected the view that children were miniature adults and recognized that they had special needs. This change in ideas was most evident among churches, benevolent and charitable societies, school officials, and reformers. The new way of thinking about the social problem of juvenile delinquency set the stage for the creation of alternate solutions and for modern developments in the treatment of juvenile delinquency. Special institutions for the incarceration of juveniles represented this shift in discursive rhetoric.

The first separate institutions were the Isle aux Noix, established in Quebec in October 1858 to serve Canada East, and the **Penetanguishene Reformatory** on Georgian Bay, which opened in August 1859 to serve Canada West. Only Isle aux Noix housed both girls and boys. The rise and fall of Penetanguishene will be discussed later.

In theory, young deviants were no longer considered criminal but were thought of as misguided children who were the products of their social environments. Proper intervention could reshape a child to lead a productive life in the community. In practice, however, the reformatory movement was successful only in removing children from adult facilities; it accomplished very little in the way of reform.

II. Social Reform Movements

The reformers who played a key role in the emergence of a unique juvenile justice system were economically and socially privileged. They called for changes to existing juvenile justice practices that would, to their minds, better reflect the unique conditions of youth. This upper-middle class reform movement put working-class parents at the centre of the youthful deviance problem. In the wake of the Brown Commission, they argued that delinquent parents were failing to raise law-abiding children by not viewing education as important and by allowing their children to wander aimlessly along city streets. From their white and privileged vantage point, the reformers saw immigration as central to the problem of juvenile deviance. Hogeveen (2005c) argues that overemphasizing the distress felt by the social and economic elite ignores the lived reality of working-class families and youth's love of adventure. Given that numerous working-class families were recent immigrants struggling to maintain a meagre existence, children's economic help was necessary for mere survival. Nevertheless, not all children were responsible. Some shirked their home and school responsibilities in favour of the excitement of the streets.

The Public School Movement and Child Welfare The move toward compulsory education extended the period of dependency, which, in effect, contributed to a more favourable climate for recognizing the special status of young people. In 1855, for example, the city of Toronto provided free schooling, although large numbers of children did not attend. Reverend Ryerson was one of the most influential school promoters and was later appointed chief superintendent of common schools for Canada West (Curtis, 1988; Burwash, 1906). Ryerson estimated that approximately 2500 school-age children were absent from the system in 1860. Nineteenth-century reformers believed that school attendance could not go unchecked and lobbied for measures to compel working-class children to attend (Houston, 1982). They believed that those most in need of educational instruction were absent. In Nova Scotia, school promoters were active as early as 1820, but in Ontario the movement occurred some 30 years later. Across the country, reformers mounted a campaign for free and compulsory schooling (Prentice, 1977; Curtis, 1988).

With attention to structure and economic-context, Anthony Platt (1969) argued that a "child-saving" movement emerged across American states in the late 19th century, led by middle-class Anglo-Saxon and Protestant social reformers who were concerned about controlling the largely Catholic immigrant lower classes. The benevolence of these reformers tended to disguise their paternalism and desire to control the behaviour of the working-classes. Indeed, as Platt argued, reform strategies directed at young people were racist and classist.

In the 1890s, the Children's Aid Society (CAS) of Ontario emerged, and an influential child-welfare inspired movement led by former journalist J.J. Kelso flourished. Kelso and his supporters directed their attention to the plight of newsboys, child immigrants, neglected children, and other "street urchins" in the city (Bullen, 1991; Jones and Rutman, 1981; Maynard, 1997) (see Box 3.1 on p. 50). Foreshadowing a discursive shift, Kelso opposed institutional care of children on the grounds that they would be exposed to the detrimental influences of hardened offenders. He placed much importance on family,

Box 3.1

Kelso Begins a New Career

A key event took place one afternoon as J.J. Kelso walked home from his position as a political columnist at the *Globe and Mail* and was approached by two homeless children begging for money. When asked where they lived, the older child replied that they could not return home empty-handed for fear of physical punishment. An outraged Kelso took them into his care immediately. He later tried to place them in an orphanage, without success. He used his newspaper column to express his displeasure that in all its affluence, Toronto was ill-equipped to deal with such emergency cases. There began Kelso's career as president of the Toronto chapter of the CAS, which he established in 1891, and as Ontario's first superintendent of Neglected and Dependent Children in 1893. Kelso (1911: 7) exercised the CAS's educational mission: to organize for "better laws, better methods, [and] the development of the humane spirit in all affairs of life."

Source: Hogeveen, B. (2003). *"Can't you be a man?" Rebuilding wayward masculinities and regulating juvenile deviance in Ontario, 1860-1930.* Unpublished doctoral thesis, University of Toronto.

which he saw as essential for instilling values of industry, honesty, thrift, modest behaviour, cleanliness, religious conviction, respect for law, and a benevolent attitude toward fellow human beings (Jones and Rutman, 1981). Kelso and other social reformers across the country used their influence and "powers of persuasion to bring about a wide variety of humanitarian developments at both the provincial and federal levels" (Carrigan, 1998: 66). As we will see, Kelso had much influence as an authorized knower because by the turn of the 20th century, an anti-institutional discourse was beginning to take hold.

Ontario was first to respond, with the *Act for the Protection and Reformation of Neglected Children* in 1888. Here again was a shift away from classical legal governance toward a more particularistic modern approach. Underlying the act was a new rationality of governing juveniles as a special, distinct group. Understanding the social and familial environment as being the "cause" of errant behaviour became essential to managing children's actions (Hogeveen, 2001: 52). Other legislative initiatives, such as the *Act Respecting the Custody of Juvenile Offenders* (1890) and the *Act Respecting the Commitment of Persons of Tender Years* (1890), came about through the work of the CAS.

Reformatories and Refuges While some reformers focused their attention on lobbying for formal schooling or greater state protection as means of keeping children from crime, others supported **reformatories** and other reform-oriented institutions to reverse the ill effects of children's home environments. These efforts were not mutually exclusive; they reinforced one another. Reformatories were based on the idea that **reformation** (corrective rehabilitation-oriented practices) rather than punishment was the best antidote to crime. These institutions were originally established to provide a "better environment" in which to detain juvenile offenders. Much enthusiasm for the potential of reformatories ensued. In 1863, a prison inspector stated that although sentencing "a child of 10 years to a reformatory for eight years for stealing a dollar's worth of stuff" may seem harsh, it would have been worse to sentence him to *less* time than was needed to truly reform (Ontario Legislative Assembly, 1883: 81).

As we will see, the reformatory ethos was gendered. Attention to the problem of juvenile delinquency was directed squarely at the behaviour of boys and was aimed at curbing what Hogeveen (2003) calls the "boy problem." However, as Carolyn Strange (1995) points out, an emerging "girl problem" was developing during the late 19th century. Until this time, legislators, juvenile justice officials, and social reformers had largely considered female juvenile delinquents "too few to count" (Adelberg and Currie, 1987). The problem of juvenile delinquency as a male issue largely defined it as a social problem in need of control. In contrast, as the 1800s came to a close, girls drew more attention and an emerging panic over female delinquency cast it as a sexual or pathological problem. Inappropriate femininity—as demonstrated by staying out late with boys, involvement in the sex trade, or otherwise errant sexuality—warranted institutionalization (Minaker, 2003). Boys required training in trades and farming to become better working-class men, and girls needed instruction in proper femininity and lessons in domesticity to become good working-class women.

In 1879, middle-class women, who believed their special maternal qualities fit them for saving the criminal and fallen of their sex, assisted Inspector Langmuir in establishing the Andrew Mercer Reformatory for Women. Mercer was the first prison for women in Canada. Strange (1985: 81) explains that in addition to the view that reformation was more powerful than punishment, Canada's first women's prison was based on the idea that "men's and women's natures—their sensibilities, their minds, their souls, and hence their 'proper' spheres—were distinct." This **ideology of separate spheres** was the logic behind Langmuir's efforts to establish a special reformatory for women. Mercer, modelled after American reformatories (first established in 1873 in Indianapolis, Indiana, then four years later in Massachusetts), did not have much public support. As Strange (1985: 83) explains

> The origins of Mercer Reformatory were thus not rooted in a popular protest or reform movement. Although Langmuir drew easily upon popular notions of femininity to portray the unique nature of women as both offenders and reformers, there was not yet a solid body of support for the reform ethos. Neither legislators, officials in the criminal justice system, nor the public felt any great commitment to the reformatory or the principles behind its founding.

Strange (1985: 87) argues that although the reformatory operated without scandal, it "floundered in terms of its loftier purpose of uplifting criminal women through motherly reform." A year later, the Reformatory for Girls opened for girls under fourteen. The young women who ended up in these institutions had been deemed "bad girls," doubly deviant as offenders and as women. They defied feminine prescriptions of domesticity, submissiveness, dependence, and piety. Instead, such females were often incarcerated for immorality—a euphemism for **errant female sexuality**. Superintendent M.J. O'Reilley explained that the "discipline is the discipline of the family; we try to rule by kindly admonition, and by appeals to their better nature, rather than by terror of punishment" (Report of the Superintendent, Andrew Mercer Reformatory, 1883: 111).

In addition to reformatories, another type of institution emerged called **refuges**. A refuge, supposedly, offered not punishment but protection; that is, a safe, home-like atmosphere where working-class females could develop their moral character through lessons in femininity and domesticity offered *voluntarily* by upper-middle class Protestant women. Little has been written about these institutions, such as the Toronto Industrial Refuge for Girls (opened 1853) or the Home of the Good Shepherd (opened in 1880).

Minaker (2003, 2006) found in her historical study of the Toronto Industrial Refuge that benevolent attempts on the part of upper-middle class Protestant women to save those they referred to as "fallen women" and "incorrigible girls" were tempered with punitive strategies designed to maintain their lower-class station in life. After spending months or years in the refuge, many women left to take up positions as domestic servants in upper-class homes. In 1917, the refuge came under Ontario's *Female Refuge's Act (FRA)*. The FRA, initially enacted in 1897 and revised in 1917, allowed any person who suspected that a female between the ages of 15 and 35 was leading an "idle and dissolute life," was "incorrigible," or "unmanageable" could take her before a magistrate to be sentenced to a period of five (soon amended to two) years in a refuge. Previously, some young women who had "voluntarily" (meaning under the direction of the police, parents, husbands, the CAS, or lured in by prison visitors) entered the Toronto Industrial Refuge in their teens would stay for decades.

The Pentanguishene Reformatory Let us turn our attention to a brief history of the Penetanguishene Reformatory, one of the first reformatories for boys in Canada. Although the Pentanguishine Reformatory got off to a better start than its sister institution (Isle aux Noix), it nevertheless had many difficulties. Pentanguishine admitted only boys to its poor facilities (built, in part, by the inmates themselves), which were on an old army barracks left over from the War of 1812.

David Rothman (1980) argues that the power of ideas and rhetoric played a huge role in juvenile justice reform in the United States. Similarly in Canada, alternatives to institutional confinement came about with new sensibilities about treating deviants. Despite the efforts of Penetanguishene officials and supporters to employ humane treatment methods, the implementation of specific reform programs came to serve bureaucratic and professional interests. Further, Rothman claims that smooth links between rhetoric and practice can hardly be found. The absence of education was among the most notable gaps that plagued Pentanguishene. The institution failed to include any programming directed toward reformation (with the exception of trade training programs introduced later). Instead, emphasis was placed on work, including building roads and improving the grounds. The institution was isolated, located far away from any city centres (i.e., 150 km from Toronto), which made contact with the boys' communities and families almost impossible. Moreover, there were no classification provisions that would require first-time offenders (more malleable boys) to be separated from hardened recidivists. In effect, it was less of a reformatory and more of a jail for young people. Fixed sentences failed to allow time for meaningful change in the boys' lives. Although politically touted as exemplar, soon after its doors opened it was subject to damaging criticism (Jones, 1978).

Pentanguishene's infrastructure mirrored that of a prison, and few staff actually made a practical distinction between the treatment of adult and juvenile offenders. They erred on the side of punishment, restraint, and exclusion. For example, inmates were locked in their cells behind doors with iron bars in the evening and for the majority of the day. A high fence locked the inmates inside. Although the official name of the institution was changed in 1880 from "reformatory prison" to "reformatory for boys," jail conditions and treatment continued to resemble that of local jails and penitentiaries (Hogeveen, 2005c).

The enthusiasm that surrounded the institution soon waned. W.L. Scott (1913: 71), who would later author the *JDA*, referred to reformatories as "schools for crime." For prison inspector J.W. Langmuir (1891: 87), the reformatory movement was a "great mistake." By the late 19th century, the public widely recognized that juveniles required *separate* institutions. Yet the conditions inside places like Pentanguishine were no different from local jails and the penitentiary. It was a reform institution in name only and finally closed in 1904. Pentanguishine fell short of reformers' expectations, yet they did not become discouraged.

In contrast to the United States, where reformatories for males and females flourished well into the 20th century, the reformatory movement was met with a modicum of success in Canada (Hannah-Rafter, 1983; Hogeveen and Minaker, 2005). Social reformers searched international developments for alternatives. The industrial school movement, concerned with preventing first-time and relatively non-serious youthful deviance from spiralling into careers, was next to enter the fray.

The Industrial School Movement The next panacea for juvenile delinquents was **industrial schools**, which were reform-style institutions designed to offer training rather than punishment not only to young people who had committed crimes but also to those deemed wayward or in danger of falling into criminality. The industrial school movement was a reaction to many things, including the demonstrated limitations of Pentanguishine, the reformatory movement in the United States and Europe, and the growing number of young people in local jails. In addition, many magistrates refused to send youth to Pentanguishine, arguing that it was a prison, that it was too far away from young people's homes, and that it was doing nothing to stem the rising tide of juvenile crime rates. By the 1860s, industrial schools modelled on the European and American experience had appeared. Provincial legislation passed in 1871 (*Act to Improve the Common and Grammar Schools of the Province of Ontario*) and 1874 (*Industrial Schools Act*) empowered school boards to establish such institutions.

The Halifax Protestant Industrial School was the first industrial school to open in Canada in 1864. It was designed primarily to provide a home for homeless and neglected young street youth. Other industrial schools followed, including Victoria Industrial School discussed below. Although the Halifax school purported to provide recreation, formal school instruction, training in trades, and religious guidance, the institution was hampered by limited resources. Carrigan argues (1998: 50) that "reformers began to campaign for new approaches that would attempt to counteract the results of a troubled background, rescue the children who were in circumstances that put them at risk, and turn young offenders into law-abiding, responsible citizens." Does this sound familiar? By 1894, approximately 200 children were housed in industrial schools throughout Ontario (Carrigan, 1998).

Proponents of industrial schools remained committed to the belief that well-ordered institutions provided the best environment for reforming delinquents. The view that children did not deserve harsh punishment but, given their stage of development, required love and protection was beginning to hold sway. The church played a key role. Religious authorities, philanthropists, judicial officials, correctional personnel, and other like-minded (i.e., privileged) individuals joined the campaign for institutions that could cure juvenile delinquency through reformative rather than punitive measures.

In 1884, legislators amended the *Industrial Schools Act* to allow any child under the age of 14 to be incarcerated in an industrial school if they had been "found guilty of petty crime, and who, in the opinion of the judge or magistrate before whom he has been convicted, should be sent to an industrial school instead of to a gaol or reformatory" (Report of the Commissioners to Enquire into the Prison and Reformatory System of Ontario, 1891). Major W.H. Howland, one of Toronto's political and business elite, was a staunch supporter of industrial schools. Howland had been police commissioner and had campaigned for temperance and prohibition. Between 1880 and 1885, his personal finances plummeted to near bankruptcy while he neglected his business interests in favour of humanitarian pursuits (Morton, 1973).

The industrial school movement spread into Quebec, Manitoba, and the Maritime provinces as it promised to create respectable working-class citizens out of errant boys and girls. The movement really took hold in Ontario during the 1880s. In the following section we briefly explore two of the first institutions in Ontario, the Victoria Industrial School for Boys and the Alexandra Industrial School for Girls, and the context surrounding their establishment and operations.

Turning "Bad Boys" into Good Men: Victoria Industrial School for Boys With no public funding, it took 12 years for the Victoria Industrial School for Boys (VIS) to open its doors on 20 hectares of land just outside Mimico, Ontario.[1] In 1887, with the financial and symbolic support of Howland, the VIS admitted its first inmates.

In contrast to reformatories, the VIS resembled a handsome residence rather than a prison. The industrial school differentiated itself from reformatories in its lessons in self-control and how to avoid potentially deviant situations—including schooling, training in the habits of industry, military drill, religious lessons, and participation in recreation and athletics. Proponents likened the institution to a home-like refuge or safe haven.

Industrial training for boys was aimed at creating breadwinners and encouraged the values of obedience, respect, and self-discipline (Hogeveen, 2003). In an attempt to transform wayward adolescents into good, wholesome, working-class youth, boys were trained in industrial pursuits, education, physical education, and religion. In theory, it was to have *none of the prison taint*. In practice, however, it was another story. The VIS housed only boys, who arrived at the school in the early years for myriad reasons, including unwillingness to obey the law, disobedience toward parents, lack of habits of industry, and truancy.

According to Kelso (1934), in these early years, editors, clergy, magistrates, and citizens generally "gave the School a good name." Soon after the VIS opened, one reporter passionately remarked:

> Success and the admiring gratitude of the people of Ontario are already theirs, but it is to be suspected that their brighter laurels will come in the future when the graduates of the Mimico school will have grown to men and be fully able to contrast the actual present with what "might have been" under the wrong handed system. (Mimico Boys' School, *The Globe*, March 14, 1891)

However, by the 1910s, few justice officials attached any hope that the VIS could reform bad boys. Kelso (1934), among others, thought "something new and better could

---

[1] If the VIS replaced the Pentanguishine Reformatory for Canada West, then the Brothers of Charity in Montreal was the successor to the Isle aux Noix Reformatory for Canada East.

be substituted with advantage." Finally, in 1930, the Ontario government released a scathing report condemning the VIS as an outmoded institution. The commissioners of the Royal Commission of Public Welfare concluded, "The condition at Mimico should no longer be tolerated" (Report of the Royal Commission on Public Welfare, 1930). The minister of Public Welfare shared this view and closed the school's doors in December 1934.

Making Good out of "Bad Girls": The Alexandra Industrial School for Girls In 1892, the Alexandra Industrial School for Girls (AIS), specifically for delinquent females, opened in Toronto. Similar institutions soon followed across the country. Although girls may have committed criminal-code infractions that warranted their incarceration in industrial schools (or refuges), they were primarily institutionalized *not* for criminal conduct but rather for offences related to sexuality. Errant female sexuality in the form of prostitution, promiscuity, being idle and dissolute, or illegitimate motherhood brought them to the attention of authorities and/or reformers. Before it closed in 1934, hundreds of girls were incarcerated at the AIS, both for criminal conduct and for defying appropriate standards for working-class girls. Thus, we see how delinquency and its governance were gendered. By the turn of the 20th century, although carceral institutions such as industrial schools were thought to contribute to the delinquency problem rather than curbing it, magistrates did not hesitate to continue to incarcerate girls.

As shown in this section, the emergence of reformatories and the creation of industrial schools for boys and girls provided increasing evidence that public perceptions were again shifting, and a new paradigm—that juveniles were indeed *different* from adults—was on the horizon.

III. Social Welfare

As the 20th century approached, a new rationality of government was beginning to take shape. As we have seen, the growth of separate state-run or state-funded institutions such as reformatories or industrial schools represented a different role for government. The long-standing *laissez faire* approach of a distanced state unwilling to intervene in the affairs of private families gave way to a **social-welfare** state. A plethora of interventionist policies and programs would emerge at the turn of the 20th century. As the Canadian government was establishing the country as a nation separate from Britain, it needed to demonstrate legitimacy and purpose.

In this context, a new legal doctrine called *parens patraie* came into dominance. *Parens patriae* requires the state to act "on behalf of the child's best interest" when parents are ill-equipped to care and control them. This doctrine originated in medieval England, where it ensured the king's right to control the property of orphaned heirs. Loosely translated, it means that the state is "parent of the country" and has a responsibility to deal with social problems. The doctrine was later expanded to include a "best interest" clause intended to safeguard children's well-being. This evolved over time to the state's practice of assuming legal guardianship over children in need of protection or those without parents. Concern for children's well-being and the belief that young lawbreakers are children first and offenders second formed the basis of this view. Therefore, juveniles should not be treated like adult offenders.

In 1891, the Ontario Prison Commission sought to devise public policy to rationalize the punishment of juveniles and secure reform. In so doing, it uncovered several limitations in its approach toward governing juveniles. The commission criticized the reformatory system and made several recommendations, among which were compulsory education, relocating the reformatory, controlling child immigration, after-care programs, and specific institutions for females (Langmuir, 1891). Another result was the enactment of the *Ontario Children's Protection Act* (1893), which helped the reformers' cause, although as a provincial statute it was limited in its application (Scott, 1931; McFarlane, Coughlan and Sumpter, 1966). Of note in such state initiatives and laws were changes in the way deviant children were regulated and adjudicated.

IV. Anti-Institutional Discourse

Growing dissatisfaction with institutional governance (an **anti-institutional discourse**) and a new enthusiasm for community-based strategies like probation were pivotal in shaping new, modern legal governance. Throughout the Western World, the public heard calls for deinstitutionalization on the grounds that institutional confinement 1) brought young people on the verge of a criminal career into contact with hardened and repeat offenders, 2) was unsuccessful at reforming, and 3) encouraged sexual relations. In particular, judges, lawyers, and politicians came to see that institutionalization had failed to deliver on its promise to reform.

In Canada, a discursive shift away from reform programs based in carceral settings was increasingly evident by the 20th century. However, the criticisms of institutionalization were more salient for boys than for girls. Key players like Kelso and Scott saw the incarceration of large numbers of deviant boys as outdated. Custodial facilities were not, however, entirely without purpose, nor were they eschewed with equal fervour for males and females.

Despite the passage of 50 years since the Brown Commission had encouraged the removal of all children from local jails and the penitentiary, boys were still assigned to these facilities for relatively minor crimes, and girls were being sentenced to spend indefinite periods either in industrial schools or refuges. The most recalcitrant boys were still being sent to places like the VIS, which became a dumping ground for the least reformable inmates. Reformers, like Kelso, saw that many offences committed by children were non-serious, but there were few alternative means of governance at their disposal. Late 19th century juvenile justice legislation remained a barrier to successful alternatives.

Scott and others promoted probation (a suspended sentence involving conditions) as a substitute to institutionalized discipline. It provided a seemingly natural alternative to the artificial environment of institutions as offenders remained in communities among their families. As the decade continued, probation gained more advocates as the *only* effective method of dealing with youthful offenders. To Scott and early 20th century American advocates, probation represented character building, reform of deviance, and a solution to the deleterious effects of industrial schools and fixed sentences.

Despite the proliferation of an anti-institutional discourse throughout the late 19th and early 20th centuries, carceral strategies remained a persistent element of the juvenile justice agenda. Although custodial facilities such as the VIS ceased to function the way their founders had intended, they nonetheless had a role to play in the emerging social-welfare continuum. Institutional incarceration was on the far end of the scale. In the case of boys, it was often reserved for the most recalcitrant, the most criminal, and those offenders diagnosed as "feeble-minded" or defective in mind. Recall from Chapter 2 that the eugenicists' solution to the boy problem advocated carceral isolation of the "feeble-minded" for the protection of society. In the absence of specialized institutions for the mentally deficient, officials used existing institutions. For girls (a much smaller proportion of juvenile delinquents), incarceration remained a fundamental element well into the 20th century of regulating those who flouted sexual norms, the few repeat offenders, and those diagnosed as feeble-minded (Sangster, 2001). Despite arguments in favour of community-based strategies for boys, when officials were confronted with evidence of sexually wayward conduct, they did not hesitate to incarcerate girls.

Refuges, reformatories, industrial schools, and probation represented a shift toward a new modern organization of law and the governance of young people, referred to as modern legal governance. Three main characteristics distinguish modern governance from its predecessor (Hogeveen, 2002: 45). It was

- **particularistic**—governance treats each case as unique;
- **knowledge based**—the offender is a subject of knowledge and is investigated;
- **a dense interlocking system of social controls**—the community, and not just the state, plays a key role in exercising control and surveillance over offenders.

In terms of being particularistic, legal governance is tailored to specific offenders. It focuses on individual circumstances and reasons for deviance rather than solely on criminal conduct. Second, modern governance relies on an accumulation of knowledge about the offender developed through a thorough investigation of their background, including interviews with parents, teachers, and other community members. Finally, the subject becomes an object of surveillance in the community by a dense interlocking system of social control agents and agencies. As demonstrated above, modern legal governance has its beginnings in both a *discursive turn* regarding the special status of juvenile delinquents and *practical shifts* toward establishing a distinct governance of juvenile delinquency.

ENTER THE *JUVENILE DELIQUENTS ACT*

The term "juvenile delinquent" did not come into widespread usage until the late 19th century. It was first used as a legal term to denote law violations by persons below the community's legal age of adulthood (Graeber, 1994). In 1892, parliament passed the *Criminal Code*, which included a section regarding juvenile delinquents entitled "Trial of Juvenile Offenders for Indictable Offences" (*The Criminal Code*, Ottawa: Edward Dawson Law Printer, 1892). On July 23, 1894, parliament passed the first official federal law relating to juvenile delinquents, the *Youthful Offenders Act*. It formalized the role of children's aid societies and brought together a series of enactments dating to 1857. These two legislative changes paved the way for Canada's first long-standing juvenile justice legislation. The *Juvenile Delinquents Act* formally changed the way the misdeeds of young people were to be handled in Canada. The JDA legislated a formal shift from classical to modernist governance, thereby ushering in a new era of juvenile justice that would last 76 years.

Despite the best efforts of W.L. Scott (author and proponent of the JDA) and shifts in the understanding and practice for juvenile delinquents, the JDA was far from a foregone conclusion. As Scott (1908: 6) explains,

> The juvenile court as we now know it cannot be said to have originated at any one place or time, still less to owe its existence to any one man. It has been the result of a slow growth extending back over many years and has borrowed features from many and various sources.

Several factors made Scott draft the first juvenile justice legislation in Canada. They included his attendance at the National Conference on Charities and Corrections in Philadelphia (May 9 to 16, 1906); his investigations into legislation and practice in Illinois, Colorado, and elsewhere; and his research of criminological literature.

Scott modelled the JDA after principles set out by American courts (Mack, 1909). In several public addresses he referred to the problems with Lombroso's biological determinism and the born criminal. He endorsed the American criminological paradigm that crime was the result of social influences and could be managed by intervening in a child's social environment. Finally, after extensive debate, dissent, and challenge (from inside and outside the Canadian Parliament), the JDA was passed in 1908 amid much political tension.

The JDA defined a **delinquent** as "any child who violates any provision of the Criminal Code or of any federal statute or provincial statute, or of any by-law or ordinance of any municipality or who is guilty of any similar form of vice, or who is liable by reason by any other act to be committed to an industrial school or juvenile reformatory under any federal or provincial statute" (Section 2(1)). This rather broad definition was accompanied by a similarly wide array of dispositions available to judges, including adjournment; fines; or placing the child in a foster home, reformatory, industrial school, in the care of CAS, or on probation.

With the introduction of the JDA, punishment was less **retributive** (based on retribution) and more reformative. It formalized some of the practices in which juvenile justice officials were already engaged. As Kelso (1907: 106) explained,

> To save the lad through human agencies, to awaken in him true repentance . . . is far nobler work, and more decidedly in the public interest than to send him to a felon's cell, with revenge in his heart.

A social-welfare orientation underpinned the JDA. Juvenile court officials were less concerned with criminal conduct than they were with the underlying social issues that manifested in youths' behaviour. Until the JDA was enacted, children were dealt with as "cases" to be adjudicated and accompanied by a set of facts to be deliberated. The JDA was based on awareness of the special status of children, and, more importantly, the accumulation of administrative knowledge about children's social environments and their "progress" while under supervision.

The inclusion of the term "parent" also characterized the social-welfare-inspired philosophy of the JDA and signalled that the state had a major role to play in intervening in the affairs of any family where a child was deemed delinquent or in need of protection. Section 38 (R.S., c. 160, s. 38) of the JDA states

> . . . that the care and custody and discipline of a juvenile delinquent shall approximate as nearly as may be *that which should be given by his* **parents**, and that as far as practicable every juvenile delinquent shall be treated, not as a criminal, but as a misdirected and misguided child, and one needing aid, encouragement, help and assistance. (emphasis added)

The JDA's philosophy can be understood in terms of three interconnected ideas: the doctrine of *parens patriae*, an interventionist state, and the best interests of the child.

Judges had wide discretionary powers and could sentence a child to a long term of incarceration "for their own good." As Section 20(5) states, "the action taken shall, in every case, be that which the court is of opinion the child's own good and the best interests of the community require" (R.S. c. 160, s. 20). One way such power was exercised was through **status offences**, which were introduced by the JDA and involved conduct that if undertaken by an adult would not incite legal action, such as drinking, gambling, truancy, and promiscuity. Such behaviours were only considered deviant because of the age (status) of the person engaged in the act. Proceedings were held in camera and the names of offenders could not be published. **Indeterminate sentencing** (rather than fixed) provided another means of discretion. Under the JDA, indeterminate sentences ensured that offenders were not released until they were no longer a threat to the public. Officials could return a young person to court to review his or her sentence at any time until they reached the age of 21 (R.S. c. 160, Section 20(3)).

The Juvenile Court

The JDA sanctioned the creation of juvenile courts and granted wide discretionary powers to judges and magistrates. The juvenile court sought to correct deviant children using a complex network of social agencies, knowledge, and actors—the cornerstone of the JDA. Juvenile courts did not exist to secure convictions and create criminals through legal sanction. Rather, they were social tribunals that signalled that deviant youth should be managed through non-institutional means. According to Toronto's first juvenile court judge, J.E. Starr (1913), the main purpose of the court was "to keep unruly children from being landed in the industrial school or reformatory and keep them under probation at home."

The accumulation of knowledge about deviant children and their social environments by means of surveillance distinguished the juvenile court from past practice. This knowledge, in turn, was used to normalize erring children. In this modern system of governance, law does not function as a generalized instrument of control. Instead, law is a point of access for what Foucault (1980, 1991) calls **"techniques of normalization."** Normalization is more than a form of state regulation; it is essentially an important dimension of *all* forms of governance (Hunt, 1995). The primary role of the juvenile court, according to then-Vancouver juvenile court judge Helen Gregory MacGill (1943: 11), was to function

> not only as legally constituted tribunals, but also as a social clinic, working as child welfare agencies in co-operation with mothers allowance boards, municipal relief bureaus, hospitals, children's aid societies, etc. Juvenile Courts are not intended to be operated for the detection and penalizing of crimes as such. Their duty is to bend every effort to discover and remove the cause of the wrong doing.

Before juvenile courts, the 1894 legislation *Respecting the Arrest, Trial, and Imprisonment of Youthful Offenders* had allowed for separate courts for children. Police magistrate G.T. Denison, with the assistance of the Toronto CAS, inaugurated the first separate court for children. Despite its name, the Children's Court was not really a separate court but rather a small room in the lower part of City Hall that Denison had set apart for this purpose. The development of the Toronto Juvenile Court in 1912 continued the move away from institutional responses to juvenile delinquency and is characteristic of social-welfare-oriented governance. Perhaps more significantly, the juvenile courts represented a significant shift in the administration of law.

The juvenile court was at the apex of the transition away from retributive legal governance. One of Jacques Donzelot's (1979: 111) most famous statements, the "juvenile court does not really pronounce judgment on crimes, it examines individuals," is significant to the transformation in juvenile justice. With the advent of the juvenile court, crimes were no longer evaluated and sanctioned according to criminal law, but instead the individual and his or her social milieu were subject to intense scrutiny from probation officers, social workers, and a whole range of justice officials. There was a **"dematerialization" of the offence**, which placed the juvenile delinquent, and not into the crime, at the heart of an investigation into his or her social condition, family life, and education. The individual's total existence came under scrutiny. Crimes and delinquencies became not an end in themselves to be judged in a court of law, but a starting point for the exploration of what led the individual to become delinquent and the search for appropriate treatment (Garland, 1981). In the spirit of the welfare sanction, crimes were considered a symptom of some underlying problem that required wide-ranging investigation and a tailor-made course of treatment.

The juvenile courts created as a result of the JDA moved juvenile justice in the direction of social meetings rather than courts of law. Although the Children's Court was said to consider the great value of the child and recognize that delinquency was the product of external causes, it amounted to little more than separate sessions of police court. Officials pondered legal questions consistent with the retributive mode of governance, such as, "What has this child done?" and "What punishment is suitable?" Juvenile court judges, by contrast, deliberated over rehabilitation-directed questions, such as, "In what ways do these children require help?" and "How can they be assisted?" Scott used the adjectives "paternal" and "salvatory" to describe juvenile court philosophy. Clearly, the social-welfare inspired juvenile court, with its emphasis on the reform of delinquency, its dematerialization of the offence, its individualized dispositions, and its community-based sanctions, was in marked contrast to the adult responsibility and retributive model of governance characteristic of adult police courts or the Children's Court. Indeed, by the early 1900s, the regulation of juvenile delinquents, stimulated by social-welfare developments throughout North America, Europe, and Australia, had moved in a completely different direction.

Central to the development of the JDA, welfare penality, and the move from adult governance was the desire of early 20th-century justice officials to add probation to the arsenal of a specialized court for young people. Scott's argument on behalf of the JDA was based on probation being the "the keystone of the arch." More significant than suspended sentences and not as contaminating as short-term detention, probation solved the dilemma of what to do with first-time and non-serious offenders. Recall that the Report of the Commissioners (1891: 216) recommended probation as a possible alternative to institutional confinement for bad boys. However, as a mode of managing deviance and reforming boys, probation had not yet found official backing, wide currency, or legislative authorization.

Increasingly, reformers favoured a move toward governance in the community over the artificial environment of industrial schools and reformatories. For many, like Scott, probation became the "crown jewel" because it was flexible and reflexive. It enabled a specific, tailor-made program particularly suited to the unique needs of every individual. Its greatest benefit, and evidence of its unique and flexible nature, was that conditions could be attached. In contrast, the generalized approach of incarceration housed many offenders together as a horde. A probation officer could investigate the home life, family background, peer influences, etc. of individual children. Ideally, the officer could then determine the most appropriate solution for each particular case. The task of the probation officer was to understand each offender's situation and pass along accumulated knowledge to the juvenile judge. According to Scott (1931: 72), the probation officer should

> ascertain what in this particular case is the cause of the trouble. The probation officer's duty is to go and see the child as a friend, to win its confidence and get its story on what has taken place. He then goes to the home, to the school . . . and anywhere else where information can be got.

The reflexive nature of probation meant that through weekly updates on progress reform, strategies could be altered to achieve desired ends. Through "friendly helpful influence," probation officers attempted to reform bad boys in relation to a masculine ideal (Hogeveen, 2001).

Individuals who came before the juvenile court were treated as separate cases. It was the personal touch and dynamic approach of probation officers, in contrast to the generalized and static strategy of institutions, that set probation apart as a novel strategy. Chadwick (1912: 333) argued that without provisions for community-based supervision, the juvenile court would have been "almost powerless as a factor for good." In contrast to industrial school programs of drill and group training, probation managed children individually according to their unique problems.

Like the industrial school program before it, probation was a gendered strategy. Tamara Myers (1999), in her study of the voluntary delinquent, argues that a fundamental part of probationary investigation of female cases involved examining their hymens for evidence of sexual conduct and gynaecological testing for venereal diseases. Mary Odem (1995), in her study of probation work in California, presents evidence that female probation officers subjected females appearing before Los Angeles and Alameda county courts to mandatory pelvic examinations and intense scrutiny of their sexual histories. If evidence of sexual immorality was found, the offending girls were incarcerated in reformatories and industrial schools. Even under the JDA, which emphasized probation, this process of incarcerating females continued unabated in Canada.

The JDA enshrined in law what Scott, Kelso, and others had been preaching for years—that institutionalization was unnatural and unsuited to turning bad boys into good citizens. Yet the JDA still allowed for incarceration (and was used, especially with females), given the wide discretionary power it granted to judges. Judges considered first-time and non-serious deviants (especially boys) who appeared in the juvenile court as the most "reformable" and often placed them on probation. Not coincidentally, these were the same offenders that industrial schools like the VIS were initially intended to manage. This meant institutions were increasingly becoming dumping grounds for the most hardened offenders, who were on their way to becoming a career criminals—the same boys who VIS officials anticipated little success in reforming.

By the 1920s, in some jurisdictions like Toronto, the Juvenile Court was at the centre of a carceral continuum that extended over the city's juvenile delinquents and boasted custodial institutions for recalcitrant boys and sexually errant girls and community-based options for others. The court drew on these organizations in order to intervene in the private sphere of families, whom probation officers investigated and often deemed responsible for juvenile delinquency. With the pervasiveness of **welfare penality**, the once-rigid division between public and private that epitomized the classical retributive rationality of state and government had been almost entirely eroded—at least for the working classes. The welfare penality manifested in Toronto's Juvenile Court promoted the rehabilitation of juvenile delinquents through an interwoven fabric of legal and extra-legal officials who intruded in the lives of what they perceived as derelict working-class families.

IMPLICATIONS

What was the most important consequence of all this? The focus of court investigation and governance moved from the *offence* to the *offender*. This transformation is akin to the shift in criminology from the classical school to the positivist school, where the punishment no longer fits the crime, but fits the criminal. In this way, it was not so much that "crimes" were investigated, guilt determined, and the offending party punished; instead, the "offender" (often presumed guilty) and what led to their wrongdoing garnered the most attention. The objective of modern legal governance was not to punish wayward children for *what* they had done, but to transform *who* they were (Foucault, 1980). In MacGill's (1943: 11) terms, this involved "learning what led the child to do wrong and how it can be taught to do better."

Recall that how a problem is socially constructed—the way it is understood, thought and talked about, and made sense of—has dramatic implications for how that problem is governed. With this shift in the image of the young person, now viewed as a "juvenile delinquent", the courts became less concerned with the crime itself and more interested in what led to it. The erring child was viewed as a product of their home, school, or community.

It was believed that only with this information about a child offender could a judge adequately make a decision on a case. The production of knowledge was essential. As Kelso (1907: 106) explains, "The youth would be carefully studied in advance of trial by earnest-minded Christian men and women, intent on one object—his restoration to good society." The knowledge produced informed the strategy enacted for each youth. In this way, wayward children were subject to a strategy of normalization and increasingly *expert* knowledge. In the few years after the JDA was enacted, psychologists and psychiatrists became involved in the treatment of deviant youth. In addition to the JDA's distinct knowledge function, there was increased regulatory control in the community. Normalizing erring children was not only a probation officer's task. For example, in 1934, Toronto had 137 private agencies, public welfare departments, and churches to assist in the surveillance of deviant children (Chunn, 1992).

Was the *JDA* quickly accepted and implemented across Canada evenly and expeditiously? Most definitely not! The juvenile court movement (and implementation of the *JDA*) developed slowly and unevenly (Oliver and Whittingham, 1987; Hatch and Griffiths, 1991). Winnipeg committed to the legislation almost immediately, bringing the *JDA* into effect in 1909. The impact of the *JDA* was felt early in large urban centres like Toronto, but elsewhere in Ontario, minor centres such as Guelph had neither a juvenile court nor probation until 1964. By 1933, 32 juvenile courts operated across the county, leaving many cities without a separate court. In contrast, in the United States, juvenile courts spread quickly (Platt, 1969).

Small rural communities like Tillsonburg, Ontario, and Magog, Quebec, continued to govern youth in much the same way as before. Many rural communities across the country combined informal governance and earlier forms of classical governance until well into the 20th century. Although the *JDA* was a federal statute, it was left up to the provinces to enact it. A province's lack of interest or refusal to provide funding had an impact on the statute's introduction.

The perceived promise of the *JDA* went unfulfilled in many communities in Canada. Oliver and Whittingham (1987) argue that juvenile offenders continued to be normalized outside the justice system by local priests and ministers. Although there is a need for more research in this area, we can speculate that informal governance, especially in rural communities, continued to play a predominant role long after some regions were operating under the principles and philosophies of the *JDA* (Hogeveen, 2001).

Probation marked the most important innovation in juvenile justice in the 20th century. Probation had the power to move surveillance, discipline, and expert knowledge from inside institutions out into communities. Proponents claimed that it was a more humane and cost-effective alternative to institutionalization. In theory, probation was the panacea. In practice, however, several complications unique to the Canadian context—including government bureaucracy, large caseloads, and the political-economic reality of small-town and rural communities—made its implementation less than ideal. As caseloads grew, the personal attention each officer could provide to each case soon became secondary to administrative demands, a problem still pervasive today.

Shifting conceptions about young people, specifically those in conflict with the law, are somewhat cyclical. As we will see in Chapter 4, by the time the *Young Offenders* Act (*YOA*) was enacted in 1982 and proclaimed law in 1984, focus had shifted away from causes of crime and societal influence back toward the offender and his or her behaviour. The view that the offender was hedonistic and responsible for his or her actions had returned.

Proponents of a separate juvenile justice system and the *JDA* were convinced that this new approach would both protect the public and eventually eradicate juvenile crime. What group was notably absent as authorized knowers? Juveniles themselves. Youth were not consulted about what the *JDA* would look like or how it would govern their conduct. Indeed, the exclusion of youth voices has long history.

CONCLUSION

We have seen, through a number of interconnected developments, how a generalized system of punishment (classical legal governance) changed into a specialized system of reform and punishment (modern legal governance) designed around the unique circumstances of—and assumptions about—youth. Recall the starting point of the chapter, which suggested two competing responses to juvenile delinquency. During the mid- to late 19th century, social reformers criticized the approach of simply punishing a child for his or her wrongdoing, and developed strategies for dealing with juvenile delinquency based on teaching, moulding, and guiding.

In this chapter, we have examined the origins of the first separate system for governing young people and the first separate legislation for youth, the *Juvenile Delinquents Act*. From 1857 onward, we saw a perceptible shift in the rhetoric surrounding juvenile delinquency. A transformation in legal governance turned children who were previously vulnerable to a system of punishments into manufactured deviants for whom the possibility of a cure depended on the investigation of their life and social environment. Investigation aimed to reveal the causes of deviance and help choose the correct path of reform. The introduction of the JDA represented an important departure from classical legal governance. No longer would punishment require the physical separation of the erring person from society in a jail, prison reformatory, or industrial school. The juvenile court and probation officers, as well as charitable agencies and community volunteers, operated as an interlocking network of surveillance and control that sought to normalize the behaviour of errant children. All this was made possible within the community. However, not all communities across Canada were quick to implement the JDA. Its impact was not even or uniform.

With change there is always continuity. Among the shifts in rhetoric and changing practice, classical legal governance was not altogether ruptured or forgotten. It continues to function along with, and as a supplement to, modern legal governance. At times, both forms of governance came up against (or worked in conjunction with) informal means of social control.

As we will see in the next chapter, although it would be almost 80 years before a different piece of legislation was enacted to govern young people, the JDA was widely criticized on several fronts soon after its adoption. Chapter 4 highlights the key events, players, and processes that characterized the second era of governance, from dissatisfaction with the JDA to the implementation of the YOA and the current *Youth Criminal Justice Act* (YCJA).

SUMMARY

- It is imperative to have an historical perspective on conceptions and the treatment of children in order to better understand current attitudes about how we should deal with young people who break the law.
- The distinction between youthful and adult deviance is only a relatively recent invention (late 17th century in Western Europe).
- There is nothing natural or inevitable about children committing crimes or adults punishing them, and the way the problem of juvenile delinquency is understood, thought about, and articulated is not a given.

- Juvenile delinquency first emerged as a social problem during the mid- to late 19th century in Canada. Previously, young people convicted of crimes were not treated in exactly the same way as adults, but were handled in much the same manner.
- Throughout the late 19th and early 20th centuries, a traditional, generalized system of punishment evolved into a modern, separate, juvenile justice system.
- During the 1800s, prisons, reformatories, and industrial schools came to be the dominant institutional response to juvenile delinquency; by the turn of the 20th century, officials viewed strategies such as probation as the solution to the problem.

DISCUSSION QUESTIONS

1. Why was a separate juvenile justice system established in Canada? Who were its main supporters?
2. What three types of governance are involved in juvenile justice? How does governance differ under each model?
3. What were the main claims made by authorized knowers in support of the JDA?

RECOMMENDED READINGS

Anand, S. (1998/1999) "Catalyst for change: The history of Canadian juvenile justice reform." *Queen's Law Journal, 24*, pp. 515-559.

Leon, J. (1977) "The development of Canadian juvenile justice: A background for reform." *Osgoode Hall Law Journal, 15*, pp. 71-106.

Platt, A. (1969) *The Child Savers: The Invention of Delinquency*. Chicago: University of Chicago Press.

Chapter 4

Legislating Youth Crime:
From the *YOA* to the *YCJA*

© Dick Hemingway

STARTING POINT

What comes to mind when you read the title of this chapter? What do you think of when you look at the image above? As you read Chapter 4, keep in mind the following questions:

- How do social problems such as youth crime become "legislated?"
- Where are the *youth* in youth crime legislation?
- Why did the *Youth Criminal Justice Act (YCJA)* replace the *Young Offenders Act (YOA)*?

LEARNING OBJECTIVES

After reading this chapter, you should be able to

- Highlight the main reasons for shifts in governmental and legislative thinking about youth crime.
- Compare and contrast the principles and legislative development of the YOA and the YCJA.
- Explore the factors that influenced changes in the practices governing youth crime.
- Explain what it means to "legislate" youth crime.
- Describe the key components of the YCJA.
- Identify the key players involved in the youth justice reform leading to the YCJA's passage into law.

INTRODUCTION

When the *Young Offenders Act* (YOA) was implemented in 1984, it signalled a new approach to governing juvenile deviance. The *Juvenile Delinquents Act (JDA)*, which was passed in 1908, managed wayward youth according to a belief in young offender rehabilitation. Juveniles who ran afoul of the law were perceived by experts and juvenile court officials not to be damaged goods, but to be the product of a defective social milieu. In the intervening 76 years, while society, criminological discourse, and law underwent significant changes, the *JDA* changed very little. Indeed, until the mid-1980s, Canadian juvenile justice largely reflected the original vision of W.L. Scott (the author of the *JDA*). This does not mean, however, that law makers and politicians were uninterested in changing youth justice legislation to reflect fundamental shifts in society. Unlike today, it was the public who were rather apathetic.

As the 1980s approached, mounting criticisms of the informality of day-to-day operations of the courts, the lack of due process guarantees, inconsistent age jurisdictions across the country, and a loss of faith in the rehabilitative ethic that underlay the juvenile court were all becoming particularly evident. In 1967, for example, the Department of Justice's Committee on Juvenile Delinquency submitted a report on the nature and extent of juvenile crime in Canada. Given the increase in the prison population and the impending maturation of the baby-boom generation, the report concluded that "Canadians knew that there was a problem of juvenile delinquency in Canada" (Department of Justice, 1967). In addition to the 1967 investigation, several other inquires were launched into the administration of juvenile justice in Canada. Finally, in 1981, a bill that would ultimately replace the *JDA* was introduced in Parliament.

This chapter examines not only the shifts in youth justice discourse and philosophy that gave rise to the YOA, but also the reports and examinations that called the *JDA* into question. We explore the process by which the YOA fell almost immediately out of favour for its rather heavy price tag and its dependence on incarceration and court interventions. You will also see how a vocal public, concerned about their safety from (socially constructed) "violent, gun-toting young offenders" helped compel the federal government to consider enacting new, more intrusive, less social-welfare driven legislation.

THE DEPARTMENT OF JUSTICE COMMITTEE ON JUVENILE DELINQUENCY

There is little evidence to suggest that between 1920 and the early 1960s politicians and citizens were overly concerned with the expedience or efficacy of Canada's juvenile court (see Hogeveen 2007 for exceptions). There seems to be no substantive proof that governments were overly dissatisfied with the existing legislative approach (Challen, 1996; Anand, 1999). Citizens during this period were not unconcerned with youth crime; rather, the federal government had little incentive to fundamentally alter the status quo.

The first indication of a heightened concern about youth crime among members of the federal government was the establishment of the Department of Justice Committee on Juvenile Delinquency (DJCJD). This committee was formed on November 6th, 1961, to investigate juvenile justice and suggest possible improvements. What prompted government officials to assemble such a committee? The public was not rallying against the

JDA, and academics, for the most part, were not criticizing it (Challen, 1996). Although historians have suggested numerous rationales, it seems evident from the DJCDJ report that politicians and government officials were becoming increasingly concerned about a potential increase in juvenile crime that would inevitably follow in the wake of the coming of age of the baby-boom generation. They speculated that any increase in the numbers of young people would invariably result in an increase in the juvenile crime rate and thus ignite a swelling of the costs associated with juvenile justice (Challen, 1996).

As such, it was not the *actual* crime rate that concerned the federal government when the DJCJD was created, but the *potential* for an escalation in juvenile crime. Anand (1999) gives three interrelated reasons why we should be sceptical of the view that high crime rates were on individuals' minds. First, his review of major Canadian newspapers from this period turned up very few editorials and articles dealing with or criticizing the government for its mismanagement of juvenile offenders. Second, the report of the DJCJD fully endorsed the rehabilitative underpinnings of the *JDA*. If the public had been disconcerted about the frequency of juvenile crime and had been demanding changes to the act, we could have legitimately expected the report to lay out a comprehensive framework for legislative change (Anand, 1999). Indeed, the DJCJD seemed to eschew a crime-control model in favour of the *JDA*'s treatment orientation. Third, no public uproar followed in the wake of the report. "If there was a perceived increase in juvenile crime under the welfare-inspired *JDA*, it would seem logical for the public, fearing for its safety, to advocate harsher punishment of juvenile offenders" (Anand, 1999: 539). Evidently, if the actual crime rate or mounting public pressure were not precipitating factors, the *potential* for these conditions prompted a proactive government response to the growing numbers of teenagers in Canada. By 1956, almost 40% of the population was under 19 (Challen, 1996; Anand, 1999). An expansion of the juvenile-offender population could have had dramatic implications for not only the YCJS, but for adult processes as well.

Perhaps this proactive step by the federal government was only half of the reason for the DJCJD. Corrado and Markwart (1992) maintain that another factor in the government's decision to create the committee was the Fauteux (1956) Commission's recommendation for a systematic study of the entire legislative framework underlying the Canadian correctional system, including juvenile justice institutions. Moreover, the senior departmental advisor to the Fauteux Commission—Allan MacLeod, a lawyer and bureaucrat—would later chair the Juvenile Delinquency Committee (Corrado and Markwart, 1992).

Although the report of the DJCJD seemed to support the existing medical model of correctional philosophy (the assumption that deviance had its root in mental illness or physical disturbance), cracks and fissures in this overarching strategy were becoming increasingly evident. Clearly, committee members were influenced by developments in criminology and social science. Specifically, labelling and societal reaction approaches were seeping into the youth justice consciousness. Labelling perspectives of crime and criminality had become increasingly popular in the period during which the report was commissioned, and had sparked the emergence of a discourse sanctioning **diversionary programs** (Lemert, 1951; Becker, 1963; Goffman, 1961; 1963). Diversionary programs channelled young people away from the formal YCJS to programs such as peer mediation for adolescents in conflict at school. Such strategies were based on the belief that removing a first-time and non-serious offender from the YCJS mitigated the stigmatizing effect that may accrue from criminal-justice processing (Hogeveen, 2001). Labelling discourse fundamentally criticized the "taken-for-grantedness" of crime categories and the state's criminal justice processes (Pavlich and Ratner, 1996). From this theoretical tradition emerged the perspective that "deviance is not a quality of the act the person commits, but rather a consequence of the application by others of rules and sanctions to an offender" (Becker, 1963: 11). Indeed, societal reactions to the label "criminal" or "young offender" stigmatize the individual as an *outsider*. As such, the label has the opposite effect to the YCJS's intentions. That is, instead of offering a solution, the form of social control becomes a "cause" of crime. Ironically, the YCJS was, by this account, criminogenic rather than rehabilitative (Hogeveen, 2001). A condition or structure that creates crime is criminogenic or crime-producing. In this way, the YCJS actually contributed to rather than decreased youth crime. By redirecting less serious deviance out of the formal court process, diversion programs promised to help young people avoid the stigma attached to deviant behaviour and to prevent future, and more serious, offending.

LABELLING THEORY, YOUTH, AND BILL C-192

Labelling and societal reaction theories of criminality conceptualize the deviant as "one to whom [a] label has successfully been applied" (Becker, 1963: 12). It follows that if a label is not applied to criminal actions, they remain "**primary deviance**"—the kind of wayward behaviour that the vast majority of the public have engaged in at one time or another. Primary deviance remains "symptomatic" and "situational" so long as it is justified as being a product of culturally situated roles (Lemert, 1951). By using the terms symptomatic and situational, Lemert (1951) drew attention to how minor infractions of laws and norms are part of the maturation process. So long as they remain within the realm of experience, deviant acts do not significantly alter the individual's concept of themselves. When the same behaviours become officially labelled, a shift in the individual's subjectivity into an active deviant status becomes increasingly evident. It follows that officially labelling as deviant those youth who commit trivial offences precipitates a subtle, yet significant, shift in their own and others' perceptions of themselves (Hogeveen, 2001). Here we encounter what Lemert (1951) described as "**secondary deviance**;" that is, when a young person comes to accept the label "criminal" and continues to engage in the behaviour that conditioned it.

The underlying logic of labelling theory maintains that wherever possible, diversion from formal intervention is the preferred course. In the 1960s and 1970s, labelling and societal reaction theories of criminality constituted a novel domain of youth crime and corresponding strategies of regulation (Hogeveen, 2001). These theoretical traditions singled out first-time trivial offenders as more adeptly managed (for both the offender and society) through community-based strategies that would leave the law-abiding self-concept intact. Although widespread recognition and implementation of diversionary strategies would have to wait until the YOA was passed in 1984, some evidence suggests that these programs were implemented on a smaller scale throughout the country beginning in the early 1970s. For example, Corrado and Markwart (1992: 154) suggest that during the "1970s British Columbia instituted a legislatively required scheme of universal consideration of all Criminal Code and federal statute offenders for diversion, while in 1977 Quebec's *Youth Protection Act* legislatively mandated an extensive system of diversion. More modest diversion schemes were also established in Manitoba and, to a lesser extent, other provinces."

In November 1970, the federal government introduced Bill C-192 into Parliament. The bill mirrored many of the DJCJD's concerns. Despite a modicum of support within the House of Commons, the bill ultimately died on the Order Paper (governmental agenda) two years later. It seems that widespread opposition from the provinces led the federal government to re-think their approach. Since the bill appeared to move a considerable distance away from the rehabilitative and medical bent of the *JDA*, Ontario, for example, was highly critical (Challen, 1996). The Ontario minister of Correctional Services, Allan Grossman, was convinced that the determinate sentencing scheme laid out in the bill was regressive and failed to take into account the needs of children undergoing care (Anand, 1999). For Grossman, forecasting the length of time required to fulfill the juvenile court's rehabilitative mandate was next to impossible.

Despite political posturing, Anand (1999) is certain that Ontario's fundamental opposition to Bill C-192 was not entirely about its philosophical antecedents. He argues that financial concerns precipitated Ontario's antagonism. Under the Canadian Assistance Plan (CAP), the federal government shared equally with the provinces the costs associated with health care and social services (if the individual service met CAP requirements). Thus, juvenile rehabilitation programs operating under the Attorney General were 50% funded by the federal government (Anand, 1999). However, in order for the provinces to continue to receive CAP funding, the federal government stipulated that only social-welfare departments were eligible for payments (Anand, 1999). Given that Ontario's organizational structure placed juvenile corrections under the correctional department of the Attorney General, they were confronted with an unpalatable choice: either move juvenile justice administration to a social welfare ministry (a very costly scheme), or be denied funding altogether (Anand, 1999; Challen, 1996). Since the inauguration of the CAP in 1966, the Ontario and federal governments had been unable to overcome their funding problems. Ultimately, given that this issue had not been resolved to Ontario's satisfaction, the province refused to back Bill C-192 (Anand, 1999). Indeed, when considering their support for new juvenile justice legislation, Ontario officials were justifiably uneasy about whether much-needed funding would be forthcoming.

Opposition to the bill emerged from not only the provinces, but also from special interests groups (Anand, 1999). The Canadian Psychiatric Association lamented the rejection of indeterminate sentences because they would unnecessarily forestall reformation. As we saw in Chapter 3, psychiatrists operating under the *JDA* had significant power and influence over correctional decision-making. This power would have been severely circumscribed under the determinate sentencing structure proposed by Bill C-192 (Anand, 1999). The Canadian Mental Health Association charged that the bill was "barbarously punitive in its measures." At that time, children's rights advocates were becoming increasingly active, and also objected to the bill, claiming it overlooked the importance of due process guarantees for young people and the importance of the availability of legal aid (Anand, 1999). Confronted with tension and opposition, the federal government allowed the bill to die on the Order Paper before its third reading. Table 4.1 outlines some criticisms of the *Juvenile Delinquents Act*.

Table 4.1 Criticisms of the *Juvenile Delinquents Act*

The *Juvenile Delinquents Act* was widely criticized for the following reasons:

- informality of the court process
- reliance on indeterminate sentences
- provincial variation in age jurisdictions
- too "soft" on some offenders, too "hard" on others
- inclusion of status offences
- inconsistent application of law across the country
- tensions between social/child welfare concerns and legal principles
- little protection of juvenile offenders' rights

Moving Toward the *YOA*

Bill C-192 was not simply an interesting yet unrelated side note on the path to the YOA. In many ways it was the impetus (Anand, 1999; Challen, 1996). Following the dissolution of Bill C-192, the Federal Solicitor General assembled a group of nine senior bureaucrats to investigate developments in juvenile justice. After surveying the international landscape, the committee issued draft legislation, which they dubbed "Young Persons in Conflict with the Law" (YPICL) (Corrado and Markwart, 1992). According to Corrado and Markwart (1992: 149), "While the YPICL was similar in thrust to its predecessor proposals—i.e., a legal rights orientation—the draft's Preamble, which was statement of philosophy and principles intended to guide the interpretation and operation of the proposed Act, marked a substantial turn in direction." The preamble was noteworthy because, for perhaps the first time, the residues of social-welfare and medical-model corrections were being submerged in a philosophical orientation stressing the importance of legal rights and young offender accountability. Whereas in a previous time, the offender's social, economic, and political milieu was considered blameworthy; now, responsibility for criminality was slowly coming to be considered as embedded in young people themselves.

This understanding of juvenile responsibility was increasingly evident throughout the 1970s and finally realized in Bill C-61, *An Act Respecting Young Offenders and to Repeal the Juvenile Delinquents Act*. Indeed, the proposed legislation almost completely abandoned the welfarist tack of the *JDA*. Surprisingly, opposition to the abrogation of rehabilitative philosophy was muted when compared to the CMHA's and CPA's protests to Bill C-192. This relative silence can be directly attributed to social-science research, which called the efficacy and effectiveness of rehabilitation and reformation into question (Anand, 1999). American sociologist Robert Martinson entered the debate in 1974 with an article titled, "What Works? Questions and Answers About Prison Reform." To evaluate the effectiveness of rehabilitation programs, Martinson and his colleagues performed a meta-analysis of 231 therapeutic programs operating between 1945 and 1967. His famous conclusion that "[w]ith few and isolated exceptions, the rehabilitative efforts that have been reported so far have had no appreciable effect on recidivism," had a considerable effect on juvenile justice worldwide (Martinson, 1974: 25). Martinson's findings have been whittled down to the trite phrase "nothing works." Evidently, if rehabilitation was ineffective, then "the treatment administered to delinquents, especially in custodial settings, really amounted to a kind of misguided benevolence that masked real punishment" (Anand, 1999: 549). This conclusion rocked the very foundation on which juvenile justice was administered.

As result of Martinson's conclusion, a new brand of child saver emerged, dedicated to rescuing juvenile offenders from a system that, under the banner of benevolence, could potentially do them great harm (Corrado and Markwart, 1992). Stanley Cohen maintains that the liberal left "capitulated," thinking that if the state could not be trusted to do good and if doing good had ambiguous results anyway, then we should at least let the system be fair, just, open, and safe from abuse. And so came the birth of the "Justice Model" or "back to justice movement" (see Cohen, 1985: 288 cited in Corrado and Markwark, 1992). Given the monumental shift in juvenile justice philosophy, in part precipitated by Martinson's conclusions, the almost total abandonment of social-welfare and medical-model interventions should come as no surprise.

Principles of justice and offender responsibility were inserted in place of these philosophical antecedents. When introducing the YOA, Solicitor General Bob Kaplan echoed the growing disillusionment with the social-welfare mentality invested in the JDA when he stated, "many are now of the opinion that treatment and rehabilitation can no longer stand on their own" (Debates, Kaplan, 1981: 9307 as cited in Challen, 1996). Criminological discourse that portrayed rehabilitation efforts as causing more harm than good also inspired shifts to an economy of regulation whereby legal judgements concerning young offenders should avoid unnecessary intrusions and instead highlight the criminal behaviour of young people. From care to offence, from ailment to responsibility, the youth court now began thinking about juvenile offending through a focus not who the offenders *are* but what they have *done* (Challen, 1996; Anand, 1999; Hogeveen, 2005).

Although opposition to the dearth of rehabilitative principles included in Bill C-61 was subdued, criticism of other elements was more vociferous. Perhaps the most significant debate centred on the rights granted to young offenders. During this period, many previously disenfranchised groups rallied for legal and procedural recognition, and during the 1960s, governments began to take notice. Ontario established the McRuer Royal Commission (1968) to investigate the province's legal framework and procedures for recognizing and protecting citizen's rights (Challen, 1996). The commission released a five-volume report with over 300 recommendations. Juvenile justice was briefly spotlighted in the 1968 edition. McRuer and his colleagues pointed to the potential abuse of young offenders' rights under the JDA and recommended increased procedural safeguards for youth (Challen, 1996). Clearly aware of recent civil-rights cases involving juvenile offenders in the United States, McRuer was adamant that such abuses of young people's civil liberties should not be tolerated in Canada (Challen, 1996). Indeed, under the JDA, lawyers were initially discouraged from representing their young "clients" at all. Moreover, sentences often lacked fairness and proportionately. To cite one example, young girls were routinely sentenced to indefinite periods of detention for holding hands with boys. Further abuses of youths' rights highlighted by McRuer included detaining young people without following proper legal procedures and holding a young person in custody without in due course informing a parent (Challen, 1996). The Report urged the provincial government to undertake a systematic study of the current legal procedures intended to protect the rights of young people—if there were any (Challen, 1996).

It seems almost intuitive that children, because of their age and level of maturity, require greater due process safeguards than adults (Anand, 1999; Bala, 2003; Hogeveen, 2005). In fact, this was the primary and most convincing argument made by children's rights advocates in the 1960s and 1970s. It follows that young people require more, not fewer, rights than adults. This rights discourse significantly impacted the DJCJD, whose recommendations included replacing indefinite sentencing schemes with definite ones of a maximum of three-year terms, safeguards to protect young people giving police statements, and broadened appeal rights (Anand, 1999). Pierre Elliot Trudeau's political mission to develop a Canadian constitution fully equipped with a Charter of Rights and Freedoms was a significant feature in this movement toward establishing rights for young people (Challen, 1996). This process did not begin when Trudeau first took office in 1968; rights for young people had been embedded in the doomed Bill C-192.

Clearly, the issue of children's rights was significant throughout the period leading to the introduction of the YOA. A related issue concerned the maximum age limit. Under the JDA, provinces were free to set the upper age limit as they saw fit. The variable upper age limit was in contradiction with principle of fairness and equality. A young person who committed a robbery in Ontario at 17 would be governed according to adult laws and procedures, but the same youth committing the same crime in Manitoba would be treated as a juvenile. On the eve of the YOA's passage into law, the federal government mandated that the Charter set a uniform upper age limit throughout the country (Challen, 1996). Not surprisingly, this decision created a great deal of friction between some provinces (particularly Ontario) and the federal government.

Robert Kaplan, the solicitor general of Canada, acting on advice from the Standing Commission on Justice and Legal Affairs, ultimately made the decision about the maximum age limit (Challen, 1996). But, according to Anand (1999), this decision was not inspired only by a pervasive rights discourse. He notes that the work of developmental psychologists such as Piaget and Kohlberg carried considerable weight with the federal justice officials. For these scholars, lack of maturity and understanding of responsibility severely circumscribed young people's ability to fully engage in and comprehend the court process. As a result of these scholarly influences, the age jurisdiction under the YOA was set at 12–17 years (Anand, 1999; Challen, 1996).

THE *YOA* BECOMES LAW: TROUBLE ALREADY?

After 14 years of debate, consultations, committee hearings, and minor revisions, the YOA was passed on May 17, 1982—the same year as the *Charter of Rights and Freedoms*. Nicholas Bala maintains that the act was received in the "midst of optimistic hopes that it would usher in a 'new era' of juvenile justice" (Bala, 1994a: 647). One of the unique features of the YOA was the Declaration of Principles, which was intended to guide implementation and provide advice on how to interpret the act's spirit and philosophy. The principles around which juvenile justice officials were to navigate included

- crime prevention (s.3(1)(a))
- accountability and responsibility of young persons (s.3(1)(a.1))
- protection of society (s.3(1)(b))

- limited maturity and special needs of young people (s.3(1)(c))
- the rehabilitation of young offenders (s.3(1)(c.1))
- restraint in the application of the law
- least possible interference with children's freedom (ss.3(1)(d, f))
- special guarantees of the rights and freedoms of the young person (s.3(1)(e))
- the primary responsibility of parents for their children (s.3(1)(h)).

(*Young Offenders Act*, Declaration of Principle, R.S., 1985, c. Y-1, s.3; 1995, c.19, s.1)

Many commentators have pointed out that these "principles are broad, diverse, and potentially conflicting, and that the YOA provided practically no guidance to decision-makers as to how to choose among them or to balance them" (Carrington and Schulenberg, 2005; Bala, 1997; Doob and Beaulieu, 1992). It seems equally true that those who framed the legislation were reflecting the complicated history of juvenile crime. Clearly, governing the youth crime problem requires a complex resolution rather than "facile solutions" (Bala, 1994b).

Justice officials and politicians debated over how such seemingly different and competing principles could possibly coexist within a single piece of legislation. Thus, a question of *balance* beset the negotiations and final outcome. That is, balancing the needs of young people and the need to protect the public from an excess of youth crime. Reid and Reitsma-Street (1984) highlight the difficulty involved in such an enterprise:

> This 'balance' is to be implemented in light of the resolution of virtually dichotomous issues: youth's accountability for their actions with society's responsibility for crime prevention; society's protection from crime with the least possible interference with an individual's freedom; and the needs and rights of youth being equally addressed. Furthermore, the YOA states that in the implementation of the Act, the provisions shall be 'liberally construed' so that 'young people will be dealt with in accordance with the principles'.

Whatever the case, while debates on the YOA were being held in parliament, the public and media appeared to be rather disinterested observers—at least until shortly after the act was introduced (Bala, 1994).

By the late 1980s, the optimism surrounding the YOA had faded. By far the greatest concern raised by interested observers was that (and this should sound familiar) the YOA was not sufficiently tough on juvenile crime (Corrado and Markwart, 1992). Much of the rhetoric surrounding the perceived inadequacy of the YOA centred on the public's belief that sentences were too short, that young offenders were being shielded by their rights, and that too few young people were being transferred to adult court where they could experience the full force of the justice system. In addition, many individuals were convinced that children under 12 were committing a large number of crimes and laughing at a justice system that was legally unable to do anything—these cases were and are handled under the child-welfare system. Fundamentally, then, much of the public's criticism revolved around the act's apparent lack of deterrence. Although the public had anticipated that the new act would have a favourable impact on crime, because of its perceived inadequacy and lack of deterrent effect, the opposite seemed the case.

The YOA's history is one characterized by amendment. In 1986, shortly after it was made into law, the act was augmented to allow for easier implementation and simpler record-keeping, along with permission to publish identifying information to assist in the apprehension of particularly dangerous offenders (Bala, 1994). By the late 1980s, public opposition to the act was increasing, especially related to the act's perceived inability to effectively manage violent crime and protect the public. In response, the Progressive Conservatives proposed several amendments. These changes were intended to increase the penalties for violent crime and facilitate transfer to adult court. Bala (1994a) maintains that the amendments proceeded quite slowly through Parliament because of a lack of a real sense of urgency and concern from the Liberals and New Democrats about what they perceived to be an unwarranted toughening of Canada's approach to juvenile justice.

Despite relative public apathy and a dearth of opposition in the House of Commons, the amendments were put into place in 1992. Once passed, the government used the occasion to remind the public that the new measures were for their protection (Bala, 1994a). Indeed, it seems that the amendments were intended to toughen up the law, especially as it related to violent juvenile offenders. The maximum sentence that youth court could impose for murder was increased from three to five years less a day (Bala, 1994). To reduce court reluctance to transfer juvenile cases to adult court, parole eligibility was cut from 10–25 years to 5–10 years (Bala, 1994a). Provisions were added to allow juvenile offenders serving adult sentences to serve time in juvenile detention until they reached the maximum age jurisdiction of the YOA (Bala, 1994a). These measures were clearly intended to "toughen" the YOA by cracking down on violent and serious young offenders.

Confronted with hardening public sentiment and intense political criticism, the ruling Liberal party attempted to placate concerns by introducing Bill C-37 in June 1994 (Bala, 1994a). Once again, the changes to the legislation were intended to toughen Canada's approach to juvenile justice. It became clear that when Minister of Justice Allan Rock introduced the bill, he was playing to Canada's law and order lobby. He maintained that "[t]he government is sending a strong message—we are dedicated to ensuring that Canadians can continue to live . . . in communities that are safe and free from fear . . . public protection must be our primary objective in dealing with young offenders" (Rock, 1994, as cited in Bala, 1994: 654). The strengthening of the system was most clearly reflected in provisions for transfers to adult court as well as longer sentences for murder.

Bala (1994a: 654) maintains that the bill was very much a "compromise, containing provisions that [were] intended to satisfy the progressive wing of the Liberal party as well as the law and order advocates within the Party." It must also be considered a response to the public demand that something be done about youth crime. Moreover, the Liberals had promised in their 1993 *Red Book* (their campaign promises document) that they were prepared to meet the public's demand for safety and protection from violent crime (Bala, 1994). Bill C-37 seemed to fulfill this election promise (Bala, 1994).

THE *YOUTH CRIMINAL JUSTICE ACT:* A STRATEGY FOR THE RENEWAL OF YOUTH JUSTICE

Bill C-37 represented the government's final attempt to fine-tune the YOA. By 1997, public and political opposition to the act had reached a fever pitch. Fear of violent youth crime was palpable. Fuelled by media reports of particularly heinous and senseless murders (e.g., Barb Danelesko), citizens grew increasingly impatient with a YCJS that seemingly failed to protect them from violent youth crime. For many, the YOA became a symbol for all that was wrong with "youth today." It failed to adequately deter young people from crime and did not allow for appropriate punishments. Perhaps more importantly, youth rights that had been granted under the *Charter* and enmeshed within the act seemingly shielded young offenders from feeling the sting of the YCJS. As such, the YOA became profaned. It was no longer revered—if it ever was—by politicians and a public who were demanding redress for victims and protection from ostensibly pervasive, violent, gun-toting young offenders.

The Violent Young Offender under the Failing *YOA*

Despite stabilizing and even declining rates of youth crime and an embarrassingly high rate of incarceration for young people, the media created a perception that youth crime was out of control and young offenders were becoming more dangerous (Smandych, 2005). As we saw in Chapter 1, citizens derive the vast majority of their knowledge and understanding of youth crime from the news and entertainment media. Armed with representations like these, it is no wonder that they were increasingly concerned with youth crime and demanded a rather vengeful solution.

In the wake of such media accounts and a perception that the YOA was ineffective, the public, media, and politicians became increasingly agitated and demanded redress in the form of a tougher, more intrusive approach to youth crime. Calls for a crackdown on youth crime centred not on first-time, non-serious offenders, but on violent, calculating criminals. This image drove public demand for new youth justice legislation and, in the minds of many, justified a surge in punitiveness that was reflected in high incarceration rates during the mid-1990s.

Public fear was not aberrant. It was not disconnected from the way many citizens encountered reality. For Guy Debord (1970: 6), our media-driven society is one of the "spectacle," where media events structure our perception of what counts as youth crime and youth justice. The "spectacle" is not exclusively a collection of images (Hogeveen, 2006). It is, as Debord (1970) writes, "[a] worldview that has actually been materialized, a view of the world that has become objective." Canadians more or less implicitly live according to notions they receive from the media concerning what is "real." Images from newspapers, television, and movies structure what has become known as "the face of youth crime" (the violent young offender) and what counts for effective control (incarceration). Who can blame citizens for the spectral images of youth crime that haunt their consciousness when we consider the headlines and images with which they are confronted? Indeed, it was rare in the 1990s for a violent young offender *not* to be featured on the front pages, prompting the public to demand punitive legislative change.

Related to this point, victims and families of victims of youth crime were the focus of debates around how to efficiently strengthen Canadian responses to the youth crime problem (Hogeveen, 2005). Victims became politicians. A notable example is Chuck Cadman, whose son Jesse was stabbed and killed at the age of 16 by a young offender. Following the tragic 1992 murder, Chuck Cadman ran for federal office and was eventually appointed justice critic for the official opposition (Hogeveen, 2005). Victims also lobbied the federal government for changes to the YOA. During the 1990s, the names of Joe Wamback and his son Jonathan, who was brutally maimed by a group of young offenders, became synonymous with the need to change the act. In the ultimate act of valourization, a feature on the story appeared in *Maclean's* magazine and a movie of the week aired on CTV (*Tagged: The Jonathan Wamback Story*) (Hogeveen, 2005). The plight of victims, their injuries, and the incident's broader social effects were held up in the House of Commons as evidence that the YOA was ineffective at protecting the public and that something needed to be done (Hogeveen and Smandych, 2001). Indeed, the names of victims and their injuries helped politicians make a case for more intrusive and punitive legislation. For example, Sharon Hayes, MP in the House of Commons, said:

> Yes, there is a shocking, tangible anger against the system. The rallying cry of the Jesse Cadmans, the Graham Nivens, the Melanie Carpenters, all tragic victims of this system, has served as the catalyst for a too long silent and threatened majority. Their concerns are real and widespread. And they, the people of Canada, must be heard. (Debates, Sharon Hayes, February 24, 1995)

Victims' names, when they centred in debate in this way, establish evidence that a problem exists (a violent young offender) and that more punitive legislative change is necessary (Hogeveen, 2005; Hogeveen and Smandych, 2001). It signals a desire to hold young offenders more responsible for their contraventions and to punish them more severely (Hogeveen, 2005).

Toward New Legislation

The 1990s saw the creation of the "punishable young offender," who was manifest in media reports (Hogeveeen, 2005). This young offender provided the impetus for the Liberals to announce their intention to enact new, tougher young-offender legislation. As such, the Liberal government demonstrated—in a dramatic, tangible, and convincing, fashion—that they were tough, resourceful, determined, and, above all, "doing something" about the recalcitrant and punishable young offender (Hogeveen, 2006). Advancing a "get tough" aesthetic as the keystone of youth justice allowed politicians to address the issue in contemporary vernacular. Significant here was a widely held belief that the most recalcitrant and violent young offenders were slipping through the cracks in youth justice. In creating and establishing new youth justice legislation, whether the federal Liberal Party "wanted to be tough on youths" is not the point; they wanted to *appear* to the "society of the spectacle" as such. (Hogeveen, 2006: 469).

How did new youth justice emerge? In response to public demand for a tougher and more intrusive governmental response to the punishable young offender, the federal Liberals signalled their intention to create new young-offender legislation. To this end, the federal and provincial governments created a task force of senior bureaucrats to study the YOA and submit recommendations for change. In June 1995, the committee released their mandate and set out the terms of reference for review. This document was widely circulated and interested groups were invited to make submissions (Bala, 2003). Over 300 witnesses and 166 groups appeared before the committee, attesting to their interest in this very public issue (Bala, 2003). In addition to working in Ottawa, the committee travelled throughout the country. They held hearings and round tables and visited various institutions and programs (Bala, 2003). A National Forum on Youth Crime and Justice was held, and the committee heard from additional individuals concerned and/or involved in Canadian youth justice (Bala, 2003).

The committee released their final report in 1997. It was voluminous and reflected regional variations in the administration and philosophical underpinnings of youth justice in Canada. Bala (2003) maintains that the Liberal majority on the committee attempted to write a report that stressed the importance of preventative programming while toughening certain provisions of the YOA. The committee's recommendations included increased federal spending on prevention, greater use of alternatives to the YCJS, greater recognition of public protection as the primary goal of youth justice, lowering the minimum age from 12 to 10 years, easier transfer to adult court, and publishing names of young offenders released from detention who pose a serious threat to the community (Bala, 2003). Despite the Liberals' efforts to pen a balanced report, criticism from both the Bloc and Reform parties was registered. The Bloc Québécois complained that the report did not reflect a nuanced understanding of youth crime (Bala, 2003). The Reform Party criticized the government for not going nearly far enough in toughening the legislation (Bala, 2003). Reflecting its desire for a tougher and more intrusive YCJS, the Reform Party recommended its own series of amendments to the YOA. These included forging an age jurisdiction from 10 to 16 years, longer sentences, automatic transfer to adult court for youth who are 14 and charged with violent offences, and public identification of all violent young offenders (Bala, 2003). Rather than placating the public and politicians, the report revealed the deep-seated tensions, both partisan and otherwise, that were at the very heart of the juvenile justice debate in this country.

Following closely on the heals of the report and in response to its recommendations, the Liberal government made public its *Strategy for the Renewal of Youth Justice* for the first time on May 12, 1998 (Bala, 2003). The strategy document made clear the federal Liberals' intention to repeal the much maligned YOA and replace it with new youth justice legislation (the *Youth Criminal Justice Act*) that would more adequately protect the public from youth crime (Hogeveen and Smandych, 2001). Part of the background information disseminated along with the strategy document suggested that

> A key part of the Youth Justice Strategy is the new *Youth Criminal Justice Act*, which replaces the *Young Offenders Act*. The Act signals a new approach to youth justice and a major re-structuring of the youth justice system.
>
> The *Youth Criminal Justice Act* is based on an accountability framework that promotes consequences for crime that are proportionate to the seriousness of the offence. More serious offenders could receive adult sentences or sentences of custody. Less serious offenders will be dealt with through measures outside the court process or be subject to constructive community-based sentences or alternatives. The Act emphasizes that, in all cases, youth should face consequences that promote responsibility and accountability to the victim and the community and teach good values by helping the young person understand the effect of his or her actions. (Department of Justice, 1999)

The Liberals were promoting a **bifurcated system**—a two-pronged approach to youth crime wherein petty and non-serious offenders would be handled through community-based and diversionary programs while serious and violent offenders would be subject to more carceral and punitive interventions. Indeed, it appeared as though government officials were unconcerned about minor and first-time offenders and had passed them off as too trivial to be of ultimate concern. MP Derek Lee stated, "[m]ost of us here have not directed much of our attention to the petty crimes of young offenders. They have been a problem and always will be, but we have petty crime problems with adults too. It is the more serious crimes that disturb us" (Canada, Hansard Debates, 12 May 1994). The Liberals marked a strict line of disjuncture between first-time and non-serious offenders and violent, punishable young offenders.

> Despite innovations and a willingness on the part of the Federal government to exper-
> iment with programming for minor offenders, the sentencing amendments contained
> in the YCJA for dangerous and repeat young offenders rarely venture much beyond the
> carceral. That is, special sentencing options for violent offenders that include long
> periods of supervised control, the addition of a serious violent offender category that
> mirrors American three strikes legislation and the easing of transfer provisions, signals
> the Canadian government is prepared to come down tougher on serious young offenders.
> (Hogeveen, 2005: 76-77)

At the same time, the federal Liberals built provisions into the YCJA that supported community-based interventions for first-time offenders, which ran under the rubric of **extra judicial measures**. Community solutions were not unique to the *Strategy for the Renewal of Youth Justice* or the proposed YCJA. They were part of a larger community-safety and crime-prevention blueprint initiated (not by coincidence) in 1998, the same year the strategy document was released (Hogeveen and Smandych, 2001). During the reading of Bill C-68 (the YCJA), Justice Minister Anne MacLellan noted the connection:

> Last June the Solicitor General and I launched the government's national crime pre-
> vention program. Since then millions of dollars have been invested in community-
> based crime prevention initiatives across our country dealing at the front end with the
> root causes of crime, with a special focus on youth at risk. (Canada, Hansard Debates,
> 22 March 1999)

In addition to the $32 million per year that the federal government promised to make available to support community-based crime-prevention programs, they pledged a further $206 million over three years to aid in the development and establishment of extrajudicial measures promised under the YCJA (Hogeveen and Smandych, 2001).

Indeed, while the idea of the punishable young offender may have established evident grounds for legislative change, it did not dictate the direction and flavour of the renewed approach to juvenile justice. The act certainly contains provisions to toughen up youth justice. At the same time, however, it advocates the creation and dissemination of creative community-based programs. Evidently, the "community" would be saddled with greater responsibility for the administration and governance of crime (Hogeveen, 2005). In the debates in the House of Commons leading up to the YCJA's passage, this sentiment became increasingly evident. For example, Mac Harb (Canada, Hansard, 21 October 1999, cited in Hogeveen, 2005: 290) stated clearly, "We do not have to always rely on the government to provide and come up with the solution. We as a community and as a society have a responsibility to put forward initiatives that could help, could improve the quality of life of our youth, and could ensure that we have a safer community and a better community."

Communities and Responsibilities

Why did the federal government, in the context of a promise to provide more meaningful consequences and tougher sentences for young offenders, turn to the "community" as a partner in crime prevention and governance? There are many reasons, but foremost among them was cost. Paradoxically, as Nicholas Bala (2003) notes, while government officials were demanding measures to crack down on crime, they were becoming keenly aware of the high cost such an approach to youth crime demands. As we saw in Chapter 1, the numbers of young people sentenced to custody rose sharply after the YOA was implemented. However, three quarters of young people sentenced had not committed a violent crime, but were being detained for administrative breaches and property-related crimes (Bala, 2003). Justice officials were convinced that resources could be deployed more wisely. Indeed, in comparison to countries like New Zealand, Canada seemed to be heading in the wrong direction (Bala, 2003). In the late 1980s and early 1990s, New Zealand was dedicated to reducing custody rates, court appearances, and, as a result, the criminal justice budget (Bala, 2003). In 1986, over 4000 young people served custodial sentences at a cost of $206 million; in 1991 this number was cut by 75% and costs were almost halved (Bala, 2003). New Zealand justice officials relied heavily on community-based and inspired restorative justice initiatives such as family group conferencing.

In light of the international experience, we can see that Canada was overly reliant on the courts and custody as solutions to the juvenile crime problem. Other countries were diverting many of their non-violent and less-serious cases out of the justice system and into relatively less expensive community-based alternatives (Bala, 2003). Even the United States seemed to make more productive use of non-custodial interventions. Bala (2003: 19) explains that "the United States has a much more serious youth crime problem than Canada—a youth homicide rate that is six times higher than that in Canada. But under the YOA, Canada was sending youth into custody at twice the rate of American courts" (Bala, 2006; Harnich, Bala, and Hudson, 1995). In light of the international experience and Canada's seemingly regressive attitude, the *Strategy for the Renewal of Youth Justice* maintained that "the system relies too heavily on custody as a response to the vast majority of non-violent youth when alternative, community-based approaches can do a better a job of instilling social values such as responsibility and accountability, helping to right wrongs and ensuring that valuable resources are targeted where they are most needed" (Department of Justice, 1998; www.justice.gc.ca/en/ps/yj/aboutus/yoas3.html).

Affording community groups an increasingly central place in the crime-control matrix allowed the state to begin a complex process of outwardly devolving its responsibility. On the surface, the state appears to be allowing community groups to manage local issues themselves. A deeper, more critical analysis reveals that community-based governance of first-time and non-serious offenders is indicative of government *through* community rather than community control of crime (Ratner, 1999; Cohen, 1985; Hogeveen, 2005). This suggests a de-governmentalization of the state. The state governs not by placing itself at the centre of a regulatory net threaded through the social fabric, but by seemingly seceding power to community groups. John Braithwaite (2000) suggests that the ideal mode of neo-liberal governance would see the state steering and civil society rowing. Through managerialist strategies, the state, while appearing to relinquish responsibility for crime control to community partners, continues to govern juvenile deviance and its administration "at a distance." This is a relationship in which the state "steers" by mandating the ends of youth justice, monopolizing resources and controlling the distribution of "clients." The neo-liberal managerial state leaves the "rowing," or the practical carrying out of the state's goals, to others (Crawford, 2001). It is a case of "less government but more governance" (Osborne and Gaebler, 1992, as cited in Crawford, 2003: 480). Shifting responsibility for first-time and minor forms of deviance to the community requires new forms of surveillance and control. Funding decisions, audits, performance evaluations, contracts, and inspections are means of ensuring community partners are committed to the state's mandate. Interaction between government and communities suggests a situation where the former "asserts a form of control through the setting of norms and the correction of deviations from them" (Crawford, 2001: 63). While appearing to recede and allow communities to manage local issues themselves, the neo-liberal state continues to invade youth crime policy at every turn, albeit in a much more latent manner than in the past.

Despite the important role that state officials offered to community groups, a definition or understanding of what community means is entirely absent from the legislation and supporting documentation (Hogeveen, 2005). Thus, given the prominent place community is afforded in the YCJA, it becomes particularly imperative that we question its meaning. This task, which will be discussed more fully in Chapter 10, becomes particularly important when we are aware that the term "community" begins in exclusion. That is, not everyone can, or does, belong to a community. The existence of a community means an inclusive group has defined itself against or in opposition to the excluded. As we will see in Chapter 10 and 11, this has particular significance for youth justice when we consider that young people are subject to legal interventions without having any meaningful input into a system that delivers pain to its members. Moreover, we will see that it is invariably disadvantaged populations that are routinely excluded from communities.

DISSENTING VOICES

After seven years of strategizing, hundreds of hours of debate in the House of Commons, 160 amendments, three separate drafts, a filibuster, and one year of planning and training sessions for youth justice practitioners, the YCJA replaced the much maligned YOA (Hogeveen, 2005). While justice and community groups across Canada seemed to (at least outwardly) embrace the YCJA's spirit, things were different in Quebec. The obvious division between Quebec and the rest of Canada was evident in debates in the House of Commons. In large part, the differences drawn along French/Anglo lines pertained to Quebec's opposition to the punitive climate that seemed to infect the rest of the country. Quebec MPs were vehemently opposed to the coercive spirit that apparently underpinned the legislation (Hogeveen, 2005). In response to what they perceived to be regressive legislation, some requested that Quebec be allowed to continue with its current approach. Hélène Alarie, for example, maintained that

> this Bill [C-68] be withdrawn or, if the minister does not comply with that request, that [it] be amended by adding after clause 3 a clause 3.1, which would read as follows: 3.1. This act is not applicable to Quebec. We also wish clause 196 to be replaced by the following: 196. This act replaces the YOA, except in Quebec, where it remains in effect. (Canada, Hansard Debates, Hélène Alarie, 5 May 1999 as cited in Hogeveen 2005: 79)

"What was it that Quebec did not want?" asked Jean Trépanier (2004). He argues that for many in Quebec justice circles, "the law that was to replace the YOA was an attempt to impose a criminal justice model that was viewed as step backwards that would threaten the educative and rehabilitation approach that had inspired the YCJS build over the year in Quebec" (Trépanier, 2004: 273-274) Indeed, a coalition of lawyers, social workers, and some academics openly opposed the new act. In the House of Commons, Bloc members were steadfast in their opposition to the proposed YCJA. Madelaine Dalphond-Guiral stated that the Bloc would resist implementing the new youth legislation "because it threatens the preventive approach developed by Quebec and because the Quebec model, with its focus on rehabilitation, might be forced unwillingly into becoming as repressive as the prevailing legislation in Canada" (Canada, Hansard Debates, 23 April 1999 as cited in Hogeveen 2005: 70-80).

Why was Quebec so vehement in its opposition? Fundamentally, because officials foresaw their rehabilitation-focused system transformed into a criminal justice institution where the primary emphasis traditionally placed on reformation and education would be unceremoniously ejected. This was in direct opposition to what Quebec had patiently and effectively fashioned. Indeed, Trépanier lists several factors that conditioned support for the YOA:

- "a deep rooted rehabilitation approach in the services for young offenders, with staff trained accordingly; diversion programs that were already in existence prior to the YOA;

- legal aid services and an acknowledgement of children's rights in provincial legislation, which had already contributed to creating a culture of protecting the rights of young people;

- an earlier transformation of perceptions of 16 and 17 year old youths as young offenders;

- a possibly lesser Americanization of perceptions than in English Canada;

- and a perception that the review of the act responded to political rather than policy needs" (Trépanier, 2004: 294)

Many in Quebec saw the YCJA as retrogressive (Trépanier, 2004). They argued that many of the suggested changes could be easily accomplished under the YOA rubric.

Critics outside Quebec argued that the province should not be too critical because the "new" legislation was eerily reminiscent of the YOA. Ontario Attorney General David Young complained, "Let there be no mistake: The federal government has just slapped a new coat of paint on an old barn that is rotten down to its foundations" (Benzie, 2001: A8). However, such statements and sentiments obscured the fundamental revisions to juvenile justice inspired by the YCJA, particularly in the area of community-based sentencing. After boasting one of the highest rates of youth incarceration among Western nations throughout the 1990s (Hogeveen, 2005, 2006), it seems that judges and justice officials had embraced the underlying spirit of community advocated in the act. During the first 365 days of the new legislation, several custodial institutions were closed, while others continued to limp along at a fraction of their capacity (Bala and Anand, 2004; Hogeveen, 2005).

Nevertheless, not everyone is entirely excited that judges are taking seriously the YCJA's instruction to use custody as a last resort (Hogeveen, 2005). Chuck Cadman, the official opposition's justice critic, argued that "the judges have been basically instructed that incarceration is a no-no except in the most extreme cases. So there's Crowns saying they can't get jail time for anything" (Trichur, 2004: B2; Hogeveen, 2005). Bob Eaton, a probation officer for young offenders, similarly suggested, "We've raised the bar so high for what it takes to get into custody that it's ridiculous" (Blackwell, 2003: A1). Justice officials and news reporters caustically referred to the YCJA's acronym as <u>Y</u>ou <u>C</u>an't <u>J</u>ail <u>A</u>nyone (CBC, 2006).

CONCLUSION

Information disseminated in advance and support of the introduction of the YCJA claimed, in contrast to Quebec's position, that "the *Young Offenders Act* (YOA) was not working as well as it should for Canadians. Too many young people were charged and often incarcerated with questionable results. Procedural protection for young people was not adequate and too many youth ended up serving custodial sentences with adults" (Department of Justice, 2005: 1). Thus, when the YCJA came into force on April 1, 2003, it attempted to address these and other flaws by doing the following:

- targeting responses to the seriousness of individual offences
- clarifying the principles of the YCJS
- ensuring fairness and proportionality in sentencing
- respecting and protecting rights
- enabling meaningful consequences aimed at rehabilitation
- supporting reintegration after custody

Whether it will ultimately be able to accomplish or, indeed, partially meet these commendable goals will not be known for several years. Nevertheless, the political push has been to legislate youth crime—to deal with the problem by altering the legislation. When law becomes the focal point of reform, the social conditions under which law is embedded remain hidden. In the next chapter, you will read how legislators and law makers attempted to put the YCJA's philosophical foundations into operation.

SUMMARY

- The YOA signalled a new approach to dealing with youth crime primarily through legislation—a political push to legislate youth crime, which was a departure from the social welfarist JDA. This approach tends to obscure the social conditions under which law is embedded.
- Another shift in rationality and practice was evident in the years leading up to the replacement of the YOA by the YCJA. Various factors influenced changes in youth justice, including a growing dissatisfaction with the YOA's ability to rehabilitate and the overuse of custody.
- Members of the public, politicians, and victims rights groups were all key players in youth justice reform prior to the passage of the YCJA. Unlike the YOA, the YCJA came about largely in response to a vocal public demand that something (read: punishment) be done about youth crime.

- Amendments to the YOA (e.g., lengthening sentences for murder and provisions for transfer to adult court) were intended to "toughen" the law by cracking down on violent and serious young offenders.
- The 1990s witnessed the creation of a "punishable young offender," manifest in media reports and victims discourse, that provided the impetus for new, "tougher" legislation.
- The YCJA is aimed at holding youth accountable for their crimes through meaningful consequences, which are to be achieved by proportionate sentencing, rehabilitation, and reintegration after custody. While more serious offenders can receive adult or long custodial sentences, less serious offenders are to be handled outside the court process and/or through community-based sentences or extrajudicial measures.

DISCUSSION QUESTIONS

1. What main issues or criticisms about the YOA led to the creation of the YCJA?
2. Why is reforming law such a dominant response to youth crime?
3. What makes a consequence (sentence) meaningful?

RECOMMENDED READINGS

Anand, S. (1999). "Catalyst for change: The history of Canadian juvenile justice reform," *Queen's Law Journal*, 24: 515–559.

Bala, N. (1997). *Young Offenders Law*. Concord, ON: Irwin Law.

A Strategy for the Renewal of Youth Justice, Government of Canada. http://www.justice.gc.ca/en/ps/yj/aboutus/ YOAs1.html

Hogeveen, B. (2005). "If we are tough on crime, if we punish crime, then people get the message: Constructing and governing the punishable young offender in Canada during the late 1990s." *Punishment and Society*, January 1; 7(1): 73–89.

Chapter 5

The Operation of the Youth Criminal Justice System

STARTING POINT

We asked professionals who work in the YCJS, "What are the biggest obstacles in youth justice system?" (Minaker and Hogeveen, forthcoming). One of the professionals, Brad, put it this way:

The youth justice system. That's it. The YCJS is the biggest obstacle. It's just a machine, it's a process, and it has a lot of strength, and if there is a reason why there's a lot of processes in place, one of them is to ensure that we're not convicting and sentencing these kids for offences they didn't do, but the biggest obstacle is the system itself. It's so cumbersome; it's so large! Just as an example, the YOA was only 1½ inches thick, while the YCJA is twice, three times the size. So, we keep putting those kinds of adjectives, sections, subsections, and we keep amending things and amending, and layering, and layering . . . at the legislative end and at the delivery end. Probation officers are gutted with it. They don't counsel and assist, they document and write, document and write. They are writing pre-sentence reports, writing and writing. The institutions are based on security, not so much rehabilitative . . . more bureaucratic, more paperwork . . . . Because a lot of my job is advocacy, where you're trying to punch the kid through the system. So, you're sharpening the kid, pointing that kid like a wedge, and then you cut, as an advocate! You ram the kids through the system, and the system has to tear, the system has to give . . .

[The system] dehumanizes kids, starts calling them using words like processes, natural consequences, and sharing circles and these institutional sorts of terminologies to deal with kids' lives. And they—these kids—get turned into machines, they become institutionalized, and then, if that happens, they're more inclined to just roll with the punches, and adapt . . . peer association. Youth get involved in the system and they're with some very victimized children, who act differently, and that rubs off and that affects the way you look at life in general, and you start changing your values and behaviours to fit the mould.

(Brad, Youth Professionals Study, Minaker and Hogeveen, forthcoming, emphasis added).

Both quotations use the metaphor of a machine to describe youth and the system called upon to respond to their criminal behaviour. What metaphor comes to mind when you think of the YCJS? Finish the following sentence: The youth criminal justice system is . . .

As you read this chapter, we encourage you to pause occasionally to critically reflect on your initial response and consider the following questions:

- What happens to a young person as she or he is processed through the system?
- Should the focus of the YCJS be on the offender, the offence, or the victim?
- What salient issues are related to police, the Crown, and judicial discretion?
- What position do young people occupy in the YCJS?
- What impact does criminal justice processing have on youth and on youth crime?
- What role should the adult community play in responding to youth and crime?

LEARNING OBJECTIVES

After reading this chapter, you should be able to

- Distinguish between two different readings of law as they relate to the operation of the YCJS.
- Describe factors related to police, the Crown, and judicial discretion in dealing with young people.
- Outline the key principles and uses of extrajudicial measures (EJM) and extrajudicial sanctions (EJS) under the YCJA.
- Identify how rights, a voice, and inclusion in a "community" are important as young people are processed through the YCJS.
- Examine the ways in which considerations of race, class, and gender may be significant in the processing of young persons through the YCJS.

INTRODUCTION

The contemporary Canadian youth criminal justice system deals with individuals between the ages of 12 and 17 when they have contravened the Criminal Code of Canada. It is currently governed by federal legislation (*Youth Criminal Justice Act*) and operates in conjunction with provincial ordinances and regulatory laws (e.g., Alberta's *Enhancement of Family and Children Act*). The existence of a separate justice system for young people is grounded in the assumption that young people have diminished capacity to understand the consequences of their behaviour, have increased dependence, and are less mature than adults.

The YCJS processes young people accused of breaking the law, and also does much more. It operates against a backdrop of social inequality and powerful discourses of risk and governance and dramatically affects countless lives every day. The socio-political climate of youthful offending and victimization is volatile. The socio-political climate refers to the "institutions, practices, and discourses" underlying particular modes of governance and control (Kellner, 1989, as cited in Comack and Balfour, 2004: 39). The preceding chapters examined the way legislation and policy formally governs youth crime. Our main focus in Chapters 3 and 4 was the law "on the books," historically and in contemporary society. Our discussion will now shift to what we understand about how the law governing young offenders operates in practice.

In this chapter, we outline significant features of the YCJS. We examine formal criminal justice processing for youth as well as alternatives currently being used in lieu of, and in conjunction with, the YCJS. The YCJS does not, however, operate in isolation from other "systems"—child welfare, group homes, foster care, social services, health, and education. Therefore, our discussion is artificially truncated, as the real-life experiences of youth going through the YCJS are intimately tied to their encounters with other social systems. Some of you may have already come up against the YCJS: as a young person accused of a crime, a volunteer in a criminal justice or social service agency, or in another capacity. Understanding what the system looks like, how it operates, and what kinds of processes are typical in youth justice courts across Canada can best be achieved by supplementing your reading of the chapter with a visit to your local youth court. We strongly encourage you to compare the ideas on these pages with your own observations of how the system operates in practice.

We begin the chapter by highlighting various key features of the YCJA and then discuss law's power to criminalize and the factors guiding the implementation of social policy for young offenders. Much of the chapter is devoted to youth involvement in the YCJS, and we explore the encounters young offenders have with key players in the system, including police, Crown attorneys, lawyers, judges, and probation officers. Our goal is to provide a context for the chapters that follow, which give particular consideration to issues of gender, race/ethnicity, and class. Diversity, as we shall see, *matters* in the operation of youth justice. Finally, we conclude with a discussion of future directions for the YCJS as they relate to investment, scarce resources, and the position of youth in the process.

LAW ON THE BOOKS/LAW IN PRACTICE

A specific piece of legislation is only one factor involved in the criminal justice processing of young people who have broken the law. There are limits to what the law can be reasonably called upon to do in response to youth crime. Susan Reid MacNevin (1991, as cited in Smandych, 2001a: 131) identifies three levels of guiding assumptions regarding the implementation of social policy affecting young persons:

1. philosophy (as declared) in legislation (what)
2. (the translation of philosophy into) program goals and objectives (how)
3. ideological orientation of the professionals responsible for delivering service to young people (who)

Attending to "what, how, and who" shows that the law on the books plays only a partial role in shaping what happens in practice as youths encounter the YCJS. For any young person involved in the system, the people (who) who implement legislation (what) and the procedures that govern the operation of the law (how) play a significant role in conditioning both the process and outcome of the experience. Several cases from our research demonstrate that how professionals view the youth with whom they work or their "ideological orientation" makes a big difference. As Brad put it, "I really have a lot of respect for them (kids). I enjoy their company, I enjoy interacting with them. I don't have a problem with them" (Youth Professionals Study, Minaker and Hogeveen, forthcoming). For this professional, respecting young people is essential. Alternatively, a view of youth as troublesome and beyond hope of rehabilitation will shape the relationships between system professionals and youth in a very different way.

The YCJS does not operate in a vacuum, and neither do the individuals who work within it. As we saw in Chapter 3 in our discussion of neo-liberalism, the state has downloaded considerable responsibility for dealing with crime and the conditions underlying criminal behaviour to members of the general public in the name of "community involvement." In the YCJA and the publicity material accompanying it, the government explicitly celebrates the role of communities in the youth justice process. *The Strategy for Justice Renewal* purports to achieve community safety through crime prevention and consequences that fit crimes. To what extent, however, are communities equipped with the skills, training, resources, knowledge, and funding that would enable them to engage in this work? In the current socio-political climate, where neo-liberalism operates, the state has been devolving responsibility for social problems. In addition to cutting or drastically reducing funding for social programs and essential services, the state has, in effect, downloaded responsibility for handling social issues to communities.

It is one thing to encourage alternatives to the YCJS, but quite another to support and encourage their implementation. This involves allowing adequate time for employees to do the work required of them, providing financial support to sustain necessary programs and services, and access to resources for developing and implementing creative strategies to deal with the root problems and systemic issues facing youth. The extent to which "youth"—and in particular, criminalized youth—are included in "the community" is an important question, which we will revisit later in Chapter 11.

Two Readings of Law

In their book *The Power to Criminalize: Violence, Inequality and the Law*, Elizabeth Comack and Gillian Balfour (2004: 20) differentiate between two key readings of law—"as a fair and impartial arbiter of social conflicts, or as a site in society for the reproduction of gender, race [age] and class inequalities." What form or structure does law such as the YCJA take? Ngaire Naffine (1997: 24) argues that the "official version of law" is "what the legal world would have us believe about itself . . . is that it is an impartial, neutral and objective system for resolving social conflicts." The modern legal system is based on this assumption. Consider the iconic figure of Justice, a blindfolded woman holding balanced scales. Elements of due process, professional codes of conduct, procedural requirements, and so on are all "evidence" of how just *blind* youth justice is. Or are they? Does law in practice live up to its image of itself as neutral, objective, and just?

James Messerschmidt's (1997: 3) concept of **structured action** is one way to explore how and where law in practice is going, and the extent to which inequality intersects with law's claim to be "fair, equal and just" in the YCJS. This refers to what professionals in the system "do to construct social relations and social structures, and how these social structures constrain and channel behavior in specific ways." As Comack and Balfour (2004: 20) argue, race/class/gender intersections can be found between individual action or actions on the part of police, defence lawyers, Crown attorneys, and judges, and the social structure and system in which they operate (i.e., capitalism, colonialism patriarchy). What's more, "[t]he capacity to exercise power is, for the most part, a reflection of one's position in social relationships" (Messerschmidt, 1997: 9). Ask yourself what role you think youth play in the YCJS. Is it a process enacted *upon* them by others? What choices do youth have for exercising their own autonomy or making decisions in matters that affect their lives? We will return to this topic in Chapter 11.

Like adult justice, the YCJS is adversarial. Crown attorneys, defence lawyers, and judges are granted what Comack and Balfour call a "power to criminalize." In exercising this state-sanctioned power, youth justice professionals deal with law not only "in formal rules and procedures, but also in *ideology and discourse*" (Comack and Balfour, 2004: 31, emphasis in original). Comack and Balfour (2004: 31) explain that

> law is not simply a formalized structure through which criminal cases are processed, but a contested terrain on which various discourses operate to produce and reproduce certain claims to 'truth.' And it is here where we can begin to locate law's role in the making of gender, race [age] and class inequalities.

Discourses shape practice, and in turn, practices shape discourse (Foucault, 1979). Carol Smart (1989) was one of the first to demonstrate law's ability to impose its own definition of events onto everyday life. Comack and Balfour argue (2004: 9) that

> [e]xtracting the legally relevant facts of a case from the messiness of people's lives involves a deciphering or translation. It also involves making judgments on the legal subjects themselves, in terms not only of what they have done, but also of who they are, and on the social settings and spaces in which they move.

The 1971 murder of Helen Betty Osborne illustrates how legal professionals make judgments about who legal subjects are. Osborne was a young Aboriginal student from The Pas, Manitoba. On the night of her death, she was walking home when four young white men forced her into their car. After driving to an isolated spot on the outskirts of town they brutally beat and stabbed her to death using a screwdriver. Following the discovery of her body, police attention focused on Osborne's Aboriginal friends. "Police questioned Aboriginal youth without the consent of parents, brought numerous people to the morgue to view Helen's battered body and widely distributed photos of her for the purpose of identification. Although police were made aware of the suspicious activities of four white men following Helen's murder, the officers failed to follow up on that information. Instead, they arrested, stripped-searched and detained two Aboriginal youth for questioning" (Comack and Balfour, 2004: 36).

Another example of the kinds of judgments professionals make—this time also about the spaces occupied by legal subjects—can be found in the case of Pamela George. A young Aboriginal woman working as a prostitute in Regina, Saskatchewan, Pamela George "was considered to belong to a space in which violence routinely occurs, and to have a body that is routinely violated, whereas her killers were presumed to be far removed from this zone" (Razack, 2000: 15). In both cases, Razack (2000: 115) continues, "[w]hite men forcibly and fatally removed Aboriginal bodies from the city space, a literal cleansing of the white zone" (Razack, 2000: 6). In the Report of the Aboriginal Justice Inquiry, Justices A.C. Hamilton and C.M. Sinclair wrote (1991: 96):

> To the people of The Pas, Osborne was not the girl next door; she was Aboriginal in a white town. Even though she had lived in The Pas for two years by the time she was murdered, she was a stranger to the community, a person almost without identity. She

was unknown to those who heard the rumours. Because of the racial separation of The Pas, those who cared about Betty Osborne, her Aboriginal friends, were not privy to the rumours about those who took her life.

Razack (2000) demonstrates that the identities of George and the young men responsible for her murder were differentially constructed. Whereas George was "a hooker" and the "Indian," the accused men were characterized as "boys who did pretty darn stupid things" (Razack, 2000: 117). Following these scholars, we encourage students to be mindful of the ways in which class privilege, economic marginalization, and racism may enter into legal practice in the YCJS. In other words, there are macro-level (social structures like race, class, and gender) and micro-level (social relationships and interaction) forces at work in the operation of the YCJS, all of which influence how individual youth are processed.

Before exploring how the philosophy enshrined in the act is put into practice, the following section will highlight several important elements of the YCJA.

Examining the *Youth Criminal Justice Act*

The YCJA outlines overarching principles and appears to be a more coherent and consistent law than the YOA. The YOA (Section 3 Declaration) had general guidelines, but no underlying philosophy. Consequently, judges adopted differing practices and philosophies (Roberts, 2003). The YCJA's Declaration of Principle formally outlines the philosophical approach of the current legislation (Section 3, YCJA) (see Box 5.1).

Box 5.1

Description of the *YCJA* Declaration of Principle Section 3 (1)

■ Purpose of YJSA
(a) (i) prevent crime (underlying circumstances); (ii) rehabilitate (and reintegrate); (iii) ensure *meaningful consequences* (to promote long-term public protection)

■ Separation from adult system that emphasizes
(b) (i) rehabilitation and reintegration; (ii) fair/proportionate accountability consistent with greater dependency and reduced maturity; (iii) enhanced procedural protection, fairness, rights; (iv) ensure timely intervention reinforces link between offence and consequences; (v) promptness and speed with which persons responsible for this Act must act, "given young persons' perception of time"

■ Within limits of *fair and proportionate accountability* measures should
(c) (i) reinforce respect for societal values; (ii) encourage repair of harm done to victims and community; (iii) "be meaningful for the individual young person given his or her needs and level of development, where appropriate, involve the parents, the extended family, the community, and social or other agencies in the young person's

rehabilitation and reintegration"; (iv) respect gender, ethnic, cultural, and linguistic differences and respond to the needs of aboriginal young persons and of young persons with special requirements

■ Special considerations
(d) (i) *rights and freedoms*, "such as a right to be heard in the course of and to participate in the processes, other than the decision to prosecute, that lead to decisions that affect them, and young persons have special guarantees of their rights and freedoms"; (ii) *victims* should be treated with courtesy, compassion, and respect for their dignity and privacy, and should suffer the minimum degree of inconvenience as a result of their involvement with the YCJS; (iii) victims should be provided with information about proceedings and given opportunity to participate and be heard; (iv) parents should be informed of measures or proceedings involving their children and encouraged to support them in addressing their offending behaviour.

Source: Department of Justice, *YCJA* Declaration of Principle Section 3 (1)

According to political discourse, the emergence of the YCJS was expected to signify a radical departure in youth justice in Canada, as Chapter 4 explained. However, as other authors have suggested (Moyer and Basic, 2005; Bala, 2005), the YCJA leaves much of the mechanisms, institutions, and system intact.[1] Specifically, the YCJA maintains several key elements of operation from the YOA:

- applies to youth from ages 12 to 17
- separate court
- youth have right to counsel
- parents receive notice
- two levels of custody (secure and open)
- youth held separately from adults
- most YOA sentences maintained

The YCJA purports to address youth crime through a three-pronged approach: 1) **crime prevention**; 2) **meaningful consequences**; and 3) **reintegration**. The act presumes that crime prevention and community can be best achieved through meaningful consequences, which are sanctions that reinforce respect for societal values and help offenders repair harm done to victims. Reintegration involves assisting a young offender to adjust back into his or her community (YCJA). Through several processes, the YCJA attempts to achieve three key outcomes, which are, namely, rehabilitation/reintegration, promoting long-term public safety, and preventing crime. These are described in Table 5.1.

As we can see from Table 5.1, consequences become "meaningful" if they contribute positively to a young person's rehabilitation and reintegration, and if they achieve community safety. Youth justice professionals working under the YCJA are supposed to recognize *both* the **offence**—the young person's offending behaviour—and the **offender**—the circumstances under which the youth's choice was made. For example,

Table 5.1 Process/Outcome of the *YCJA*

Process	Outcome
■ give a young person meaningful consequences	■ to rehabilitate and reintegrate youth
■ respect differences of young people	■ to promote long-term public protection
■ proportionate accountability, enhanced procedural protection,	■ to prevent crime
■ timely intervention	
■ reinforce societal values	
■ provide greater role for victims	

[1] Some minor changes in terminology have occurred between the YOA and YCJA, the most substantial of which is the shift from the Young Offender System to the Youth Justice System (YJS) or Youth Criminal Justice System (YCJS). In addition, "pre-sentence report" replaced "pre-disposition report" and "youth court" has become (at least officially) the "youth justice court."

judges must weigh long-term public protection with rehabilitation and reintegration of the young offender (Tustin and Lutes, 2005).

We have identified at least seven assumptions underlying the YCJA:

1. *Accountability* Young persons should be held accountable and be made to take responsibility for their crimes.

2. *Proportionality* Any response to youthful offending should be "fair and proportionate;" that is, it should match the seriousness of the offence and recognize the offender's level of maturity.

3. *Bifurcation* Violent and non-violent crimes are differentiated.

4. *Discretion* There is discretion at the police, Crown, and judicial levels guided by explicit principles; extra-judicial measures are encouraged and judges have more sentencing options.

5. *Community participation* There are more opportunities for parent and community involvement (i.e., extra-judicial sanctions).

6. *Role of victims* There is more emphasis on harm to victims, repairing harm, and victims' rights.

7. *Special needs of Aboriginal youth* There is a greater recognition of unique circumstances for Aboriginal youth.

With respect to the special needs of Aboriginal youth, Part 4 of the YCJA states that "With particular attention to the circumstances of Aboriginal young persons, all available sanctions other than custody should be considered" (s.38 (2)(d), YCJA). Does this mean differences will be respected? Or that racialized stereotypes will be reinforced, as they were in the cases of Pamela George and Helen Betty Osborne?

What about the **systemic issues**—poverty, racism, discrimination—that are inherent to the life experiences of many disenfranchised Aboriginal youth? Are these mitigating factors at sentencing? Do they provide context for offending behaviours? How appropriate is it for these factors to influence the manner in which a young person is processed through the system? In light of these controversial questions, to what extent can youth justice professionals under the YCJA appreciate the "special needs of Aboriginal youth"? We will return to these questions in Chapter 7. Sufficed to say, the act, on paper at least, recognizes that the structural conditions are distinct for Aboriginal youth, and that special protections should be afforded. In practice, however, it remains to be seen how the "special case" provision will affect Aboriginal youth. In *R. v. Gladue* (1999) the Supreme Court of Canada recognized and attempted to respond to the overrepresentation of Aboriginal people in the justice system (see Box 5.2 on p. 93).

The YCJA made two additional changes that impact how youth are processed through the system: 1) the expansion of sentencing options and inclusion of principles to guide judicial discretion; and 2) the elimination of transfer of youth to adult court. Under the YOA, a youth accused of a violent crime could be transferred to adult court. Currently, youths may still receive what is called an "adult sentence" but are sentenced in youth court. In this way, transfer hearings were replaced with access to adult sentencing hearings under the YCJA (Section 62 outlines the conditions under which the youth court has the power to impose an adult sentence on a young person). The Crown must give notice to seek an adult sentence before a plea and, if granted, it is imposed after

Box 5.2

The Supreme Court and the Special Needs of Aboriginal Offenders

Supreme Court Case of JJM

In the 1993 case of JJM, the Supreme Court of Canada affirmed a two-year open custody sentence for an Aboriginal male youth on three counts of break-and-enter and one breach of probation. The court called JJM's home life "abusive" and characterized him as "intolerable." For the original sentencing judge, child-welfare concerns justified a long custodial sentence. The Supreme Court decision presumed that rehabilitation and reformation *should* be the ultimate aim of all dispositions. This case occurred under the *YOA*, which was criticized for its overuse of custody. The decision, however, at least for a time, gave the direction to judges that taking into account non-criminal needs was acceptable in determining sentences.

Why is this case significant now?

The case raises issues regarding proportionality (i.e., the sentence fitting the crime), child-welfare needs, and the circumstances in which terms in custody are justified on the basis of social issues or the "needs" of a youth.

Moyer and Basic (2005: 53) found that the mental status of a young person may affect decisions. In one case, the Crown asked for more probation for a male drug addict who panhandled and often lived on the street— "He is not all there." The Crown recommended a period of intensive supervision and support for a young person with FASD, a sentence described as "purely rehabilitative."

Using detention for social-welfare purposes (i.e., to meet a social or child-welfare need rather than dealing with a criminal behaviour) is prohibited under subsection 29(1) of the *YCJA*.

Supreme Court Case of Gladue

In this case, the accused was an Aboriginal woman who pled guilty to manslaughter for killing her common-law husband. Gladue was sentenced to three years imprisonment. The Supreme Court argued that systemic and background factors did not appear to have been adequately considered by the initial sentencing judge. In dismissing her appeal, the Court of Appeal also erroneously neglected s. 718.2(3). The Superior Court held that judges have a duty, according to section s. 718.2 (3) of the CCC, to look at background factors bringing Aboriginal peoples before the court to "consider alternatives to incarceration" (*Gladue v. Her Majesty The Queen* (1999). 23 C.C.R. (5th) 197).

Why is this case significant now?

Taking the special needs of Aboriginal youth into consideration is built into the *YCJA*. How judicial discretion will be exercised in this regard remains to be seen. The extent to which the socio-economic circumstances of Aboriginal youth as a group are or should be taken into account remains a controversial issue.

Source: CanLII. R. v. M. (J.J.), [1993] 2 S.C.R. 421; and R. v. Gladue, [1999] 1 S.C.R. 688.

conviction. See Section 72 (1) for the factors the court must consider in determining the applicability of an adult sentence.

With this brief overview of the current legislation governing youthful offenders in mind, we turn our attention to how they are processed through the YCJS.

CRIMINAL JUSTICE PROCESSING

What happens when a young person breaks the law? For many children and youth, minor deviance often goes unnoticed (e.g., stealing a CD or getting caught on transit without paying), unreported, or is dealt with informally by parents, school authorities, or other adult members of the community. However, if a young person's crime comes to the official attention of the police, he or she enters the formal criminal justice process.

As we will see in the following chapters, encounters with the justice system impact youths in very dramatic ways, conditioning their choices and life chances and affecting their sense of self. This section explains the legal process for youth who break the law, taking into account the key players a young person may encounter in the YCJS. As a guide, review Figure 5.1.

Encounters with the Police

Historically, parents were often a young person's entry into more formal mechanisms of care and control. Parents routinely called on police for assistance with their recalcitrant boys and girls. Today, parents, school officials, and other community members

Figure 5.1 Processing a Young Person through the YCJS

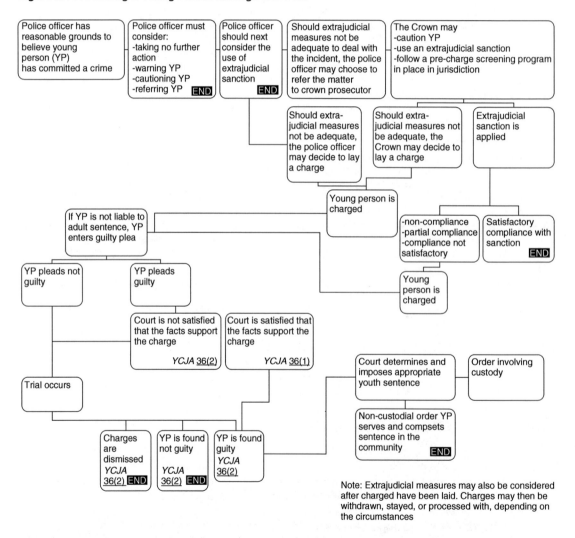

Note: Extrajudicial measures may also be considered after charged have been laid. Charges may then be withdrawn, stayed, or processed with, depending on the circumstances

Source: Adapted from Department of Justice Canada, *YCJA Explained,* Extrajudicial measures, YCJA, Section 6, Flowcharts 1-3. Reproduced with the permission of the Minister of Public Works and Government Services Canada, 2007.

Figure 5.2 Charging Rates Pre-*YCJA*

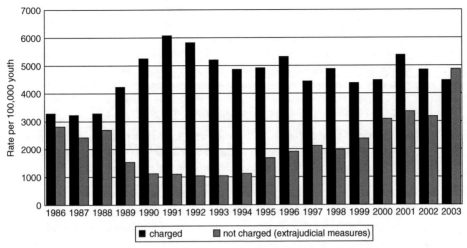

Source: Department of Justice Canada. Carrington, Peter J. & Jennifer L. Schulenberg (2005). *The Impact of the Youth Criminal Justice Act on Police Charging Practices with Young Persons: A Preliminary Statistical Assessment.* Reproduced with the permission of the Minister of Public Works and Government Services Canada, 2007.

may invoke the justice system on behalf of youth, but the police are the first formal contact youth have the YCJS. As Figure 5.2 shows, from 1986–2002, many of the youths who encountered police never made it further into the system (i.e., they were never charged).

In 2003, the charge rate for youth decreased by 16% from the previous year—the most significant annual decrease since 1977 (Department of Justice, 2005). Although the arrest rate was down for all offence categories, the reduction was more pronounced for less serious offences. The more serious the offences, the smaller decrease in the arrest rate (Centre for Justice Statistics, 2003). The graph in Figure 5.2 shows that between 1986 and 1999, more youth were charged than not charged. After 1999 this gradually changed, and in 2003, more youth were not charged than charged. It is too early to tell whether this represents a new pattern. Perhaps it reflects the aim of the *YCJA* to pursue alternatives to formal criminal justice processing as often as possible, or maybe it indicates police officers' increased use of extrajudicial measures.

As the systems' gatekeepers, police officers have incredible power in enforcing and implementing the *YCJA*. The police have the ultimate power to use discretion in determining whether or not a charge will be laid. Discretion refers to an individual officer's judgment and beliefs regarding a young person, the evidence, and his or her assessment of the situation. The police may give a warning, a caution, or take no further action, which often happens in cases of minor conflict (e.g., a scuffle between friends, an inexpensive item taken from a store). Alternatively, police may refer the young person to a program or agency with their consent (*YCJA*, Section 6). Police officers routinely attempt to call the youth offender's parents or guardians to inform them of the situation. Although the police have the power to make a referral (e.g., to a community program), they cannot force attendance.

Recent evidence released by the Department of Justice suggests that the police are more likely to detain a young person if they have had prior contact with the system

(Carrington and Schulenberg, 2005a). Police officers consider a number of situational factors (including legal and extra-legal factors) to determine whether to make an arrest. These are listed in Figure 5.3. An officer may investigate and find that no charge is warranted because there is insufficient evidence that the suspect committed a crime. In cases where they have reason to believe the young person is, in fact, responsible for the crime, discretion plays a key role. Many factors mitigate (reducing the chances of charges being laid) or aggravate (increasing the chances of charges being laid) the officer's construction of the event, the most significant of which are the seriousness of the offence, harm, or presence of a weapon, and by offender history.

Extra-Judicial Measures and Sanctions While informal action was permissible under the YOA, the YCJA formalized and more clearly structured police discretion and encouraged extra-judicial measures. It is worth noting that immediately after the YOA was put into force, discretionary police decisions *not to charge* apprehended youth declined, and the resulting increase in charges persisted relatively unabated (Carrington and Moyer, 1994; Carrington, 1998, 1999; Carrington and Schulenberg, 2004a; Federal-Provincial-Territorial Task Force on Youth Justice, 1996). Carrington and Schulenberg (2005b) recently undertook an assessment of the extent to which police practices (i.e., charging) were consistent with the directives outlined in the YCJA, based on national statistical data for 1986 to 2003 (uniform crime rates). They argue that "[t]he data indicate

Figure 5.3 Overall ranking of situational factors affecting police decision-making

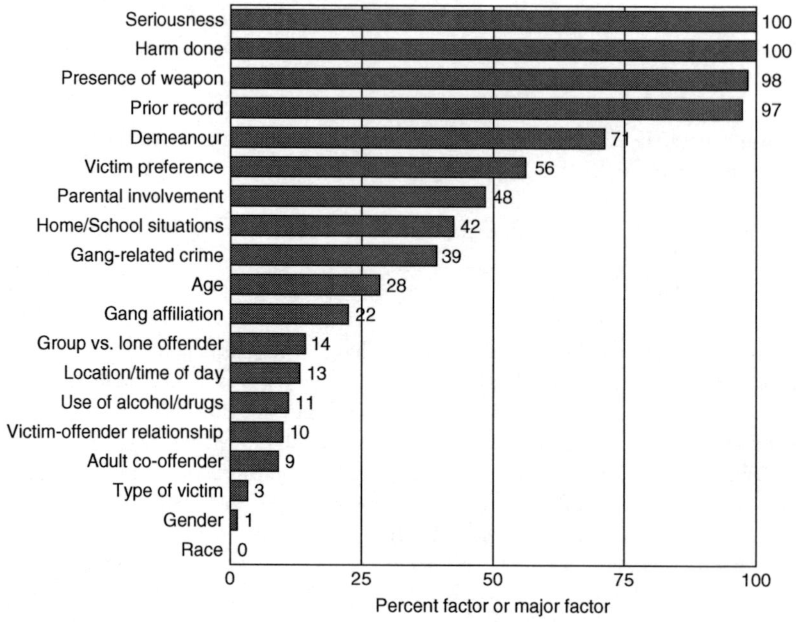

Source: Department of Justice Canada. Carrington, Peter J., and Jennifer L. Schulenberg (2003). *Police Discretion with Young Offenders.* Reproduced with the permission of the Minister of Public Works and Government Services, 2007.

that the YCJA has been remarkably successful in bringing about changes in police charging practices" (Carrington and Schulenberg, 2005b: 1). In short, they found that nationally, fewer youth were being charged and more young people were being given extra-judicial measures. Numbers of youths charged were reduced in 2003 by more than one-third for minor offences (e.g., theft under $5000 and drug-related offences), and decreased slightly for serious property and violent offences (other than common assault) (Carrington and Schulenberg, 2005b).

The initial impact of the YCJA on police charging practices against young persons is "remarkably strong, immediate, and consistent with its objectives, principles, and provisions" (Carrington and Schulenberg, 2005b: 2). The authors note, however, that in three provinces the levels of youths charged began to decrease before 2003, so the decline cannot be solely attributed to the impact of the YCJA. (Three other provinces saw no reduction in charges in 2003.)

The YCJA gives legislative direction for police to rely less on the formal court system and to use alternatives more often (YCJA). What the YOA referred to as "alternative measures" are refashioned under the YCJA as "extra judicial measures" (police or Crown-initiated alternatives to formal criminal justice processing) and **extra-judicial sanctions** (judge-initiated alternatives). Section 6(1) establishes the significant requirement:

> A police officer shall, before starting judicial proceedings [i.e., before laying a charge] or taking any other measures under this Act against a young person alleged to have committed an offence, consider whether it would be sufficient, having regard to the principles set out in section 4, to take no further action, warn the young person, administer a caution, if a program has been established under section 7, or, with the consent of the young person, refer the young person to a program or agency in the community that may assist the young person not to commit offences.

Subsections (b), (c), and (d) indicate that extra-judicial measures should encourage young persons to repair harm done, involve the family and community, and provide victims with an opportunity to participate. Repairing of the harm, though, must be accomplished within "the limits of a fair and proportionate response" (YCJA, Sections 4–12).

For example, community justice conferencing allows youths to be participants in a process with victims, family members, and others to come up with a strategy that will repair harm and help reintegrate young offenders back into society. Here, youths learn about the consequences of their behaviour and develop ways to make amends. Unlike the traditional justice system, victims can play an active role in a process that usually excludes them. It appears, however, that judges are not currently making extensive use of conferences at sentencing (Department of Justice, 2005).

Several advantages of extra-judicial measures have been documented widely in research literature, including 1) lower cost; 2) highly successful outcomes[2]; 3) less intrusive; 4) avoiding

---

[2] Involvement of community could be mutually beneficial. Through extra-judicial measures, offenders can gain insight into the causes and effects of their behaviour, and have the potential to take responsibility in a more meaningful way. There is much potential for reintegration into the community, the place where the process began. Victims have a much greater role than is available in the traditional adversarial justice system. In the process, victims can ask questions, receive answers, gain understandings, explain the impact of crimes, hopefully feel safe, and seek closure.

stigma of CJS; and 5) involving victims. The two main disadvantages of extra-judicial measures are widely recognized as 1) widening social control; and 2) eroding due process.

The first concern relates to regulating, controlling, or otherwise adjudicating a young person whose behaviour would have likely been dealt with informally or outside the youth justice process. An increase in the number of young persons dealt with by extra-judicial measures that exceeds a decrease in the number of youth charged may actually result in a net increase in the number of young persons apprehended and dealt with by police and an increase in the level of intrusiveness of extra-judicial measures. Because offenders must accept responsibility (i.e., confess to guilt) before proceeding, there is a concern about young people's right to fair judicial proceedings. Provincial variation exists in the use of these measures as it is up to the provinces to determine the measures or sanctions they will implement under the act.

Notably, Carrington and Schulenberg's (2005b) study of police officers indicated that race, gender, and age were of minimal importance. These findings, however, are insufficient evidence that these factors are not important at the level of police discretion (Carrington and Schulenberg, 2005b).

Carrington (1998), for example, examined over 94 000 incidents reported by police in various jurisdictions across Canada between 1992 and 1993. He found that charge rate differentials remained steady when other legal and extra-legal factors were controlled. Other scholars suggest that extra-legal factors such as race, class, age, family, and community actually *do* influence police discretion in dealing with youth. Older girls are less likely to be charged and end up in court than older boys, but younger girls are more likely to be charged and appear court than younger boys (Sauve, 2005; Thomas, 2005). As we will see in Chapter 8, research indicates higher rates of criminal activity for street-involved youth than for youth living at home (Gaetz, 2004; Hagan and McCarthy, 1997; Tanner and Wortley, 2002). Race and class are intertwined for Aboriginal youth, a large proportion of whom live in the downtown cores of cities such as Winnipeg, Regina, and Saskatoon—areas that are heavily policed (Schissel, 1993). Some authors have pointed to the way that impoverished urban areas in Canada have been mapped as "racialized spaces" where Aboriginality is contained (Blomley, 2003; Razack, 2002; Mawani, 2005). As we will explore further in Chapter 7, Aboriginal youth have more charges laid against them, are more likely to be held in detention prior to court, and are more likely to be denied bail (Hamilton and Sinclair, 1999). Aboriginal youth experience "**hyper-visibility**" (an amplified presence), as evident in recent research conducted by Bonar Buffam (2006) at a centre in Edmonton, Alberta. Three Aboriginal youth explained that as they walked across a major downtown street, a car full of white teenagers drove by and yelled to them, "Go back to the reserve!" Buffam (2006: 59) argues, "[o]nce their bodies were marked with stereotyped aboriginality these young men were made to feel 'out of place' by a group of White people who regarded the downtown area of Edmonton as a (settler) space of Whiteness. Told to return to the reserve, the space to which they were thought to *naturally* belong, these young men experienced their signs of racial difference as qualities that anchor them to certain racialized spaces" (Appadurai, 1998; Razack, 2002).

According to Bell (2007: 219), "[y]outh who fit a stereotypical image of delinquents—that is, who exhibit a disrespectful, uncooperative, or defiant manner—are more likely to be arrested." This is what happened to Mike, a participant in Buffam's study. Buffam (2006: 66) explains:

> Two patrol officers stopped Mike and another (aboriginal) friend as they walked down a strip of 118th Avenue [an urban, impoverished street in Edmonton's downtown core] . . . Upon request from one of the White officers, Mike *routinely* provided his Indian Status card as identification, which was run through the police scanner for a criminal record. When the White officers discovered that he did not have a criminal record Mike was accused of providing fake identification, instructed, '[y]ou're telling me you're not the right person. You can get charged with fraud!' Only upon insisting that he had in fact provided the correct identification did Mike receive an apology from the White officer who explained, 'Oh, you just don't seem like the type that would have a clean record. You seem like the ruffian type of the jail type.'

Underlying this encounter is a colonial stereotype of the Indian as criminal, a racialized discourse that individual officers, like the one in Mike's case, may draw upon, especially as they police inner city streets (Buffam, 2006).

In other ways, the judgments police make about a young person as "threatening" or "troublesome" dramatically impact police/youth encounters. The way an officer perceives a youth's demeanor influences the likelihood that they will be charged or directed to extra-judicial measures or another diversionary program. As Canadian researchers have recently found, this variable was evident in 71% of the police surveyed (Carrington and Schulenberg, 2005b: 166–9).

If a young person is arrested, one of two things happens: the youth either is released or is sent to (pre-court) custody. It remains unclear whether detention by police has increased or decreased under the YCJA. According to Moyer and Basic (2005), a breach of probation and having previously had three or more guilty findings makes a young person less likely to be released, which is consistent with YOA processing. Using 1999–2000 as a baseline, police have been more likely since then to impose or give more conditions on young persons who are released (Moyer and Basic, 2005). Notably, how long a young person is detained has not changed under the YCJA. While police are more likely to impose conditions of release, the average number of court-imposed release conditions under the YCJA remains the same as under the YOA (Moyer and Basic, 2005).

Remanding a youth to custody is more common when the crime is violent and/or the youth has a history of violent crime. In cases not involving violent crime, the youth typically signs a statement promising to show up in court or gets a summons for court (i.e., released on their own recognizance). After the arrest, the police send a report to the Crown counsel with a recommendation to charge the young person. This ends the police's role in the justice processing of a young person, unless they are later called to testify at trial.

Encounters with the Court System

> Arguably, there is a real philosophical incongruity. The adult system is replicated in youth court but there is still the paternal model there in the youth system. The two schools of thought make for difficulties. (B.C. defence counsel, as cited in Moyer and Basic, 2005: 22)

The next stage of criminal youth justice processing involves the courts. The defence lawyer above implicitly refers to what Reid-MacNevin (1999) calls the "philosophy as stated in legislation." Youth justice personnel struggle on a daily basis with considerations such as meaningful consequences, rehabilitation, proportionality, and the rights of the accused. Depending on his or her particular ideological orientation, any judge or lawyer may act idiosyncratically. However, as with police discretion, the YCJA has attempted to circumscribe their ability to inflict their own views by prescribing when custody can be used.

The Role of the Crown The Crown counsel, who acts as a lawyer for the state, has considerable discretion in terms of whether to go ahead with a criminal charge, use an extra-judicial sanction, or drop a case entirely. Crown attorneys "screen" cases to determine if there is enough evidence to substantiate charges, the likelihood of a guilty finding, and whether it is in the public interest to continue. The Crown has several options at this stage, including taking no further action, issuing a caution or warning to the youth, or recommending participation in a community-based agency program. If the Crown decides that the youth can be held accountable through extra-judicial measures, then a community-based strategy begins outside the formal YCJS. Otherwise, a formal charge is laid, followed by the youth making his or her first court appearance.

The Crown may choose to use alternatives to court in the following circumstances (YCJA, Section 10):

■ substantial evidence exists to prove guilt as charged

■ youth is advised of right to legal advice before agreeing to participate

■ the youth accepts responsibility for criminal actions and voluntarily agrees to participate

A youth's involvement in a community-based program may entail giving an apology; community service; providing compensation to the victim or charity; participating in counselling, cultural activities, reconciliation, or a mediation program; and being placed under the supervision of a youth justice committee member.

Some situations represent special challenges to the YCJS, as we will see in Chapter 8. For example, what do Crown counsels and judges do when the youth before the court is homeless and cannot be returned to his or her home or placement? In Saskatchewan, for instance, the upper age limit for child protection intervention is 16, so referral to child welfare authorities is usually not an option. In such cases, a bail hearing would be adjourned until child welfare, probation, or the defence counsel can make a plan. A Crown counsel in B.C. from Moyer and Basic's study explains, "I find that the YCJA is very clear on when it is or isn't appropriate to seek the detention of the youth. There is not a lot of negotiation with defence because by the time you're seeking detention you're on a solid ground . . . Infrequently, I say I am going for detention and then defence says 'I have this person who will sign for the kid'. Then I *might* sign over" (Moyer and Basic, 2005: 45).

In another case, a 17-year-old Aboriginal youth was charged with failure to attend court and assault with a weapon against his sister. The two had fought over a pair of pants and the accused tried to cut the pants off, resulting in a very small cut. He had no prior record, although he did have an outstanding charge of uttering threats. The Crown recommended detention because the offence was violent (as cited in Moyer and Basic, 2005: 47).

Many youth plead guilty and move on to be sentenced. The Crown provides a sentencing recommendation to the judge after a guilty plea, or acts on behalf of the state at trial if the youth pleads not guilty. If a trial is necessary, either a not-guilty verdict will be rendered and the youth will be released or a guilty verdict will be rendered and a judge will impose a sentence.

How are youth cases being prosecuted? Using case files, observations, and interviews, Moyer and Basic (2005) examined Crown decision-making in five youth justice courts in Saskatchewan and British Columbia in 2003, three to four months after the *YCJA* was proclaimed. Their work is one of few studies, as prosecutorial discretion remains almost invisible in the literature.

Moyer and Basic (2005) found that common assaults (assault level one) were diverted when extenuating circumstances (e.g., youthful age of the alleged offender) were present. Crown attorneys were concerned that young offenders should be "held accountable." Moyer and Basic (2005) conducted a multivariate analysis of the factors affecting the use of diversion by Crown counsel. They found that if a youth had no previous findings of guilt, no current property charge, or few to no outstanding charges, the Crown was more likely to refer the case to extra-judicial sanctions. It appears that offence and prior record play a greater role than social circumstances (Moyer and Basic, 2005).

The Role of the Defence All youth have the right to legal representation (see Box 5.3). The *Canadian Charter of Rights and Freedoms* and the *YCJA* both hold that youth should be provided ample opportunity for legal advocacy and advice prior to and during the court process. If they can afford it, the youth's family may retain outside council. Rather than hiring a lawyer, many youths use representation assigned through local legal aid offices, which occurs frequently with disenfranchised youth and "wards" in the child-welfare system.

Young people are represented either by retained or duty counsel at every stage of youth court proceedings, which includes bail hearings, sentencing, and trials. In Saskatchewan, for example, most youth are represented by legal aid staff acting as duty counsel (Moyer and Basic, 2005). In Alberta, the Youth Criminal Defence Office provides legal advice and advocacy to youth and works with many legal aid clients.

Defence lawyers in Moyer and Basic's (2005) research in Saskatchewan and B.C. commented that extra-judicial policies were overly restrictive. One defence lawyer explained:

Box 5.3
Legal Rights for Youth

When a young person is arrested, they should be afforded legal protections, including the right to

- know the charge
- remain silent
- talk with a lawyer and an adult
- have a parent, guardian, or other responsible adult person present during all police questioning
- have a lawyer in court (provided through legal aid if he is or she unable to afford one)

More generally, youth have human rights that should be protected. In addition, they should be given extra protections, including

- age considerations (i.e., young people have different needs, problems, and experiences then adults)
- right to privacy
- fair treatment before the law
- recognition of circumstances for Aboriginal youth

> Schoolyard assaults should be able to be able to go to EJS [extra-judicial sanctions] and
> also robbery, which is really bullying, that could go. For whatever reason, the police are
> honing in on them and they're going through court. If they don't have a record or very
> much of a record, they could learn a lot more from a mediation type of method. (Moyer
> and Basic, 2005: 33).

Ideological orientation and individual differences definitely play a role. There is ongoing debate over what is the most appropriate role for lawyers to play with young clients. Bala (2003) argues that this question revolves around two themes: Who is the client, and what are his or her instructions to counsel? Tension exists between what parents, institutional guardians, and the state consider in the "best interests" of youth. What about what a young person believes to be in his or her best interest? With young clients, many lawyers typically fall somewhere between the role of legal advocate and that of guardian (Milne, Linden and Kueneman, 1992). As an advocate, a defence lawyer takes the client's instruction or advice and attempts to raise legal challenges (if possible) and emphasize legal rights. Other lawyers take a more paternalistic approach. Taking on a guardian (or parent-like) role, these lawyers are not as adversarial and focus more on the child's welfare (i.e., the best interests of the child). In practice, the defence may employ various strategies that mirror either the advocate or guardian role, depending on the facts of the case, the age of the offender, and the stage of proceedings (Milne, Linden and Kueneman, 1992; Bloomenfeld and Cole, 2005). For example, a hybrid approach is possible where the lawyer is an advocate at trial, but a guardian at sentencing. "My attitude to the practice of law is not adversarial. I am aware of the legal issues and the fact that I am a lawyer, but I am concerned with rehabilitation. I do take the role of stern parent," explains one Manitoba lawyer (Milne, Linden and Kueneman, 1992: 333).

The Role of Judges When a young person stands before a court, the judge is ultimately responsible for what happens to them in terms of consequences. First, a judge must ensure that the young person understands the charge(s). The judge will then accept a plea of guilty or not guilty (although this often occurs at a later date, after remand). After a guilty plea, if there is sufficient evidence, the judge may hand out a sentence immediately. When a youth enters a not-guilty plea, an adjournment takes place until the trial date.

A special court called the "Youth Justice Court" hears all cases involving youths 12–17 years of age (YCJA). In most jurisdictions, one to three courtrooms hear only youth justice cases and some judges only appear in youth court. Youths encounter various other professionals, such as probation officers, court workers, and social workers, during their youth court involvement.

The most important change for judges in the YCJA has to do with the goal of youth sentences. Their purpose, as laid out in the act, is to *hold the youth accountable* and promote the young person's *rehabilitation and reintegration*. How a judge attempts to accomplish this goal varies. The extent to which individual judges favour accountability over rehabilitation and reintegration may also differ. Accountability is not defined in the act, other than with the phrase "meaningful consequences." Accountability is a subjective concept, depending upon individual judges' ideological orientations. The same could be said for whether a consequence is meaningful and what it means to take responsibility for one's actions. Judicial discretion is significant, as judges may consider a host of factors in determining a sentence, including the seriousness of the offence, the circumstances involved, and injury and/or harm caused—all factors similar to those for police and Crown discretion. For property crimes, this might include the extent of the damage (e.g., dollar value). Recall that the *YCJA* obligates judges to make special considerations for Aboriginal youth in determining sentences.

Incarcerating Youth

Up until 2004, Canada's incarceration rate for young offenders far surpassed the American rate (see Figure 5.4). The YCJS was highly criticized for its overuse of custody.

Why are youth being sentenced? According to the Canadian Centre for Justice Statistics, over 40% of youth court cases fell into four categories of less serious offences, including theft under $5000 (e.g., shoplifting), possess of stolen property, failure to appear (i.e., not showing up in court), and failure to comply with a disposition (e.g., breaching a condition of probation) (Statistics Canada, 2000). See Figure 5.5 on p. 104 for a breakdown of the types of cases in youth court.

In 2002–03, Canada's youth incarceration rate declined to its lowest point in eight years ("Youth custody and community services in Canada," Statistics Canada, *Juristat*, 2002/03, Vol. 24, no. 9). This is not altogether surprising, given that officially recorded crime rates fell in by 6% in 2005. The youth crime rate, which had declined throughout the 1990s, was generally on the rise between 1999 and 2003 ("Crime Statistics in Canada," Statistics Canada, *Juristat*, 2005, Vol. 26, no. 4).

From 2004 to 2005, 39 000 youth were admitted to youth custody or community correctional services in Canada, excluding Prince Edward Island, Saskatchewan, Yukon Territory, Nunavut, and the Northwest Territories. Of the total admissions, probation accounted for 41%, followed by remand (36%), sentenced to custody (14%), serving the community portion of custody and community supervision orders (6%), and deferred custody and supervision (3%).

Figure 5.4 Overall Rate of Youth Court Judges Imposing Custody

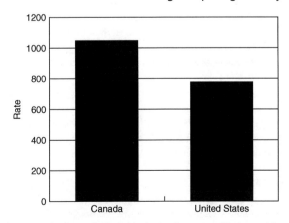

Source: Department of Justice Canada. *The Youth Criminal Justice Act: Summary and Background*. Reproduced with the permission of the Minister of Public Works and Government Services Canada, 2007. Youth Court Statistics 1997–98. Ottawa: Canadian Centre for Justice Statistics. Snyder, H., Finnegan, T., Stahl, A. and Poole, R. (1999). Easy Access to Juvenile Court Statistics (1988–97). Pittsburgh, PA: National Center for Juvenile Justice.

Figure 5.5 Types of Cases in Youth Court in Canada (1998–1999) (organized by principal charge)

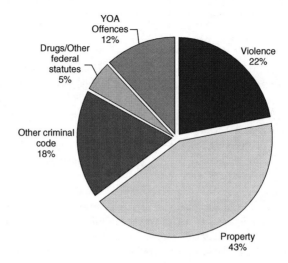

Source: Department of Justice Canada. Sprott, Jane B (2001). Background for YCJA. Reproduced with the permission of the Minister of Public Works and Government Services Canada, 2007.

Statistics Canada's *Juristat* documented that after the introduction of the YCJA, admissions to youth custody and community correctional services declined by 33%, admissions to probation declined by 54%, custody admissions by 50%, and remand by 22%. Aboriginal youth accounted for approximately 25% of custody admissions, but only 15% of admissions to probation ("Youth Custody and Community Services in Canada", Statistics Canada, *Juristat*, 2004/05, Vol. 27, no. 2).

The YCJA was aimed, in part, at reducing the number of youths being incarcerated, especially for property and non-violent offences. In light of rising incarceration rates during the 1990s and international criticism of the Canadian government, the federal government placed strict guidelines on custody and circumstances under which a youth could receive a custodial sentence.

Custody is meant to be reserved for repeat and violent offenders. The data thus far lend support to the idea that this philosophy is being observed in practice. Cases that result in custodial sentences under the YCJA involve significantly more charges than custodial sentence cases did under the YOA. Judges have the option of imposing adult sentences in cases of very serious violence. An adult sentence is presumed appropriate if a youth is 14 years or older and charged with serious violent crimes (YCJA, Section 62). There were four **"presumptive offences"** under the YOA: murder, attempted murder, manslaughter, and aggravated sexual assault; repeat violent crimes have been added under the YCJA. A **serious violent offence** is an "offence in the commission of which a young person causes or attempts to cause serious bodily harm" (Section 1(b), YCJA). A serious violent offence designation occurs when there have been at least two previous judicial determinations. After a young person is found guilty of an offence, the Crown may make an application to the youth justice court for a judicial determination that the offence is "a serious violent offence." A national age limit of 14 has been set, although the age of the presumption of an adult sentence for the most serious offences varies provincially (14, 15, or 16).

With this, a new category of offence (and consequently a label for offenders) was ushered in with the YCJA—the **violent repeat offender**. Courts can give a youth of at least 14 years an adult sentence if he or she is convicted of a serious offence or displays a "pattern of conviction for serious, violent offences" (there is a provincial variation in age). An adult sentence will be given if a youth is older than 14 and convicted of serious offence. In these cases, a judge can decide whether or not to allow the publication of the name of the youth after conviction. (Section 61 of the YJCA allows provinces to determine the age at which this presumption should apply: 14, 15, or 16.)

The YCJA also increased the range of sentencing options by adding the following non-custodial sentences: reprimand; intensive support and supervision; non-residential program or attendance order; and deferred custody and supervision. Under the act, all custody sentences have a period of supervision in the community (see Figure 5.6 on p. 106). The community supervision portion can be up to half as long as the custodial period, and the periods combined must not exceed the maximum sentence length specified in the YCJA. A **deferred custody and supervision sentence** "allows a young person, who would otherwise be sentenced to custody, to serve his/her sentence in the community. A deferred custody and supervision order is similar to a conditional sentence of imprisonment for adults" (Calverley, 2006). An **intensive support and supervision program (ISSP)** can be described as "similar to probation, the intensive support and supervision order is served in the community under conditions, but an ISSP provides closer monitoring and support than probation. Almost one-fifth of sentences imposed under the YCJA include one or more of the new sentencing options" (Calverley, 2006).

The trend since the passage of the YCJA appears to be a reduction in the number of youths in custody. The use of custodial sentences has decreased in all major offence categories under the YCJA, though only slightly (Carrington and Schulenberg, 2005a). In the year following the 2003 implementation of the YCJA, the number of young persons aged 12 to 17 who were admitted into some form of custody declined by nearly 50%. Overall, there were 17 113 admissions to custody in 2003–04, well below the 22 743 admissions in the previous year. Of the 17 113 young persons admitted to custody, 4651 were had been sentenced to custody, a 44% decline, and the remaining 12 462 were admitted to remand, down 13% (Statistics Canada, 2006) (see Figure 5.7 on p. 107). What do these numbers mean? Under the YCJA, youth are being incarcerated far less than under the YOA.

On closer analysis, there has been a marked increase in the proportion of Aboriginal youth admitted to custody since the implementation of the YCJA. This is especially disconcerting given that the YCJA draws attention to the needs of Aboriginal young people. Although approximately 1000 Aboriginal young people were admitted to sentenced custody in 2003–04 (down from 1500 in 2002–03), they represented 29% of admissions that year (see Figure 5.8 on p. 108), an increase from 22%. Put another way, almost a third of all females and just over one in five males admitted to sentenced custody were Aboriginal in 2004–05 (Calverley, 2006). Remember that Aboriginal youth comprise only about 5% of the population aged 12 to 17 years. Overall, Aboriginal youth made up a quarter of all sentenced custody admissions in 2004–05. Interestingly, the proportion of Aboriginal youth

Figure 5.6 Custody and Supervision Explained

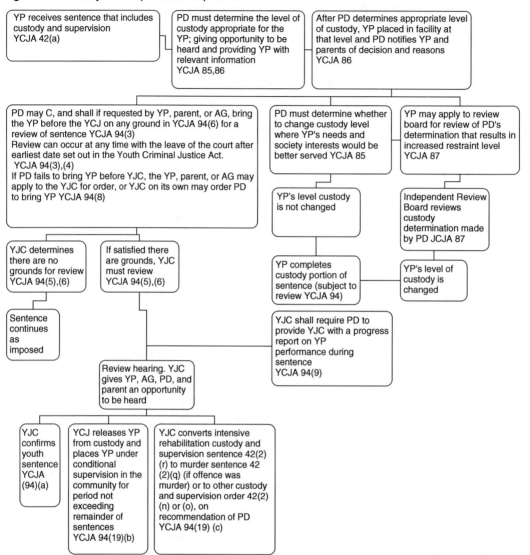

Source: Adapted from Department of Justice Canada. "Youth Sentencing, YCJA, Sections 38–56: Flow Chart 1, Imposing a Sentence" & "Custody and Supervision, YCJA, Sections 85-87: Flow Chart 1 - Determination of Custody Level by Provincial Director." *YCJA Explained*. Reproduced with the permission of the Minister of Public Works and Government Services Canada, 2007.

admitted to sentenced custody was on the decline before the YCJA was passed (Calverley, 2006). How is this explained? What we have seen is a much more substantial decrease in the number of admissions to sentenced custody for non-Aboriginal youth. A similar pattern can be seen with respect to remands. Before the YCJA, the proportion of Aboriginal young people among remand admissions was also decreasing gradually. In 2003–04, the percentage of Aboriginal youth on remand was 27% of all remand admissions (an increase from 23%

Figure 5.7 Use of Custody Prior to the *YCJA*

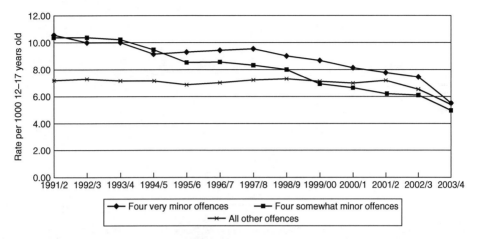

Source: Department of Justice Canada. Doob, Anthony N. & Jane B. Sprott (2005). *The Use of Custody under the Youth Criminal Justice Act.* Reproduced with the permission of the Minister of Public Works and Government Services Canada, 2007.

in 2002–03). In other words, 3000 Aboriginal young persons were admitted to remand, 3% more than in the previous year. In British Columbia, six times as many Aboriginal youth were sentenced to custody than their representation in the province (Calverley, 2006). An oft cited explanation, the disproportionate number of repeat contacts within the YCJS must be viewed in the context of systemic issues like the depressed socio-economic conditions in the lives of many Aboriginal youth and discrimination on the part of the YCJS.

The late 1990s saw an increase in the proportion of females aged 12 to 17 admitted to custody, but this trend changed with the new legislation. About 20% of all young persons sentenced to custody were young women in 2002–03 ("Youth custody and community services in Canada," Statistics Canada, *Juristat*, 2003/04, Vol. 26, no. 2). This number dropped to 13% in 2003–04. One explanation is that since females tend to be incarcerated for less serious offences, and *YCJA* sentencing principles encourage non-custodial sentences for minor law-breaking, then in practice more females are being diverted away from custody. A similar pattern has emerged for remands. From 20% in 2002–03 to 18% in 2003–2004, the proportion of females admitted to remand has gone down under the *YCJA* ("Youth custody and community services in Canada," Statistics Canada, *Juristat*, 2003/04, Vol. 26, no. 2.) Since remands are not recommended for less serious offences, the same reason for the decline is plausible.

Race and gender connections are significant, as we can see from the over-representation of Aboriginal females in the YCJS. In 2004–05, female Aboriginal youth represented 35% of all female youth admissions to secure custody and 29% of all female admissions to open custody. Aboriginal male youth represented 24% of all male admissions to both secure and open custody (Calverley, 2006: 8).

Under the new sentencing regime for young people, sentences must be *proportional* to the harm done and within the limits of proportionality, *and* must be as rehabilitative and re-integrative as possible. Sentences, then, should be *the least restrictive* possible (i.e., the least interference with freedom). The act assumes that if just and proportionate sanctions

Figure 5.8 Increase in Proportion of Aboriginal Youth Admitted to Custody, 2003–04

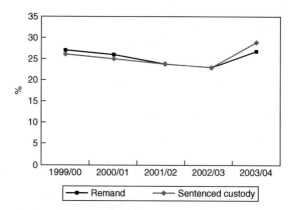

Note: Excludes data from Prince Edward Island, New Brunswick, Quebec, Ontario 12 to 15 year olds, Saskatchewan and Nunavut.

Source: Adapted from "Youth Custody and Community Services," *The Daily*, March 28, 2006. http://www.statcan.ca/Daily/English/060328/d060328a.htm; Youth Custody and Community Services in Canada, *Juristat*, 2003/04, Vol. 26, no. 2, Catalogue number 85-002-XIE, Released March 28, 2006.

are employed, the long-term protection of society will be achieved. In this way, courts take into account the social context of young people but, in theory, personal background characteristics do not become grounds for determining the severity of sanctions. Various factors, including time spent in pre-trial detention, previous convictions, and any reparations made, are among the aggravating or mitigating circumstances that influence outcomes for youths in court (YCJA, Section 38–42). What is the relationship between personal background characteristics and social context? We will explore the interconnections further in Chapters 6, 7, and 8.

ISSUES OF GENDER, RACE, AND CLASS: SPECIAL CONSIDERATIONS

[A]ge, race, class and gender still play a large role in how the YJS processes youth . . . being locked up for your own good is not justice, that is discrimination . . . true justice would require that some people give up privileges and put the needs of others ahead of their own . . . " (student: Youth, Crime, and Society class, 2007)

Do the gender, race, and class of a youth matter? Research suggests than one's gender, race, and class position does affect what happens in and outside of the YCJS. For instance, Moyer and Basic (2005: 35) found the following cases:

The behaviour of a 17-year-old female found intoxicated on the street and in possession of 16 grams of crystal methamphetamine was explained by "her father states that she's been having difficulty since the death of her mother." The Crown in this case had not wanted to divert her before the charge was laid because "it's important that she goes to court." In this case, involvement in drugs was an aggravating factor.

A 16-year-old girl who assaulted her mother was diverted after the Crown spoke to the mother: the accused had been sexually abused when younger and had been hospitalized for psychiatric problems. In the conversation, the Crown asked questions relating to her stability, associates, and drug use. The Crown commented, "I don't want to criminalize children who need support, not more problems" (the Crown had involved a youth worker because of concerns about the young person). In this case, past abuse and mental health issues were mitigating factors.

To the extent that a young person's personal characteristics and social background become part of the judgments made by different players at various levels of the YCJA, gender, class, and race *matter*. As we will elaborate in the following chapters, this is potentially disconcerting. It raises important legal, social, ethical, and moral issues. Given that social circumstances play a role in conditioning youths' choices, we will pay close attention to structural and systemic issues., We devote special consideration to Aboriginal youth, girls, and street-involved youth in the next section of the book (Chapters 6, 7, and 8). When we examine these "special populations" individually and attempt to make interconnections across gender, race, and class, we will see clearly how the YCJS serves to further marginalize already disenfranchised "others." We will explore the extent to which the YCJS perpetuates injustice and how a different future that aims for *justice for youth* is possible.

CONCLUSION

The YCJA and the government's larger *Strategy For Youth Justice Renewal* underscore the importance of alternatives to formal criminal justice processing, specifically calling upon "the community." An overriding issue with respect to community-based alternatives to criminal justice processing has to do with access: *who* controls and *who* participates. There is considerable provincial variation in terms of implementation, support, and resources for community-based programming. Of particular concern is accessibility and availability of resources for Aboriginal youth, the most disadvantaged group to encounter the YCJS.

On the Department of Justice website, under the "Youth Justice Initiative," you will see phrases like "a collaborative, multidisciplinary approach to youth justice," "enable greater citizen/community participation in the youth justice system," "improve public protection by reducing youth crime," and "increase the use of measures outside the formal court process" (Department of Justice website, www.justice.gc.ca/en/ps/yj/funding/funding.html). The federal government has developed a "Youth Justice Renewal Fund" for assisting projects that contribute to these aforementioned goals. It is left to the provinces and territories to apply to the fund for grants. Monies are also available to "test" innovative features of the YCJA (e.g., extra-judicial measures, custody, and reintegration). What will come of all these initiatives remains to be seen.

To returning to our starting point—to what extent is the system humane? What would it mean for the YCJS to operate with more *humanity* and less *machinery*? Can we envision more appealing metaphors than a machine?

SUMMARY

- The contemporary Canadian youth criminal justice system (YCJS) responds to law-breaking by individuals between the ages of 12 and 17 and operates according to the *Youth Criminal Justice Act* (YCJA). Three levels guide this process: the philosophy as declared in the legislation, how that philosophy is translated into goals and objectives, and the ideological orientation of professionals.

- Two main readings of law include 1) law as neutral arbiter of social conflicts; 2) law as reproducing social inequality. As such, the *law on the books*—what the legislation actually says—does not always mirror the *law in practice*—what actually happens when a young person in processed through the YCJS.

- Race, class, and gender are significant factors in understanding the processing of young people through the YCJS, given that, to varying degrees, a youth's personal characteristics and social background influence the judgments professionals make about criminalized youth.

  - Aboriginal youth account for approximately 25% of all custody admissions, a number that has risen since the implementation of the YCJA. To address the over-representation of Aboriginal youth, their special needs are to be recognized.

- The Declaration of Principle explains that youth crime will be addressed through 1) crime prevention, 2) meaningful consequences, and 3) reintegration. The YCJA encourages the use of extra-judicial measures, community participation, and the role of victims.

  - Youth justice professionals are supposed to recognize *both* the offence and the offender.

- A youth sentence is to *hold the youth accountable* and promote the young person's *rehabilitation and reintegration*. Sentences must be *proportional* to harm and within the limits of proportionality (i.e., the least restrictive), *and* must be as rehabilitative and re-integrative as possible.

  - The YCJA increased sentencing options (i.e., deferred custody and supervision) and allowed for a third of every custodial sentence to be served in the community.

- The extent to which the system is less punitive under the YCJA is debatable. The charge rate for youth is on the decline and fewer young people are being sentenced to custody since the passage of the YCJA. However, for "presumptive offences"— those for which an adult sentence is presumed (murder, attempted murder, manslaughter, aggravated sexual assault)—another category, repeat and serious violent offences, was added under the YCJA.

DISCUSSION QUESTIONS

1. How are scarce resources (money, time, etc.) allocated to developing community-based responses to youth crime?

2. What are the implications of criminal justice processing in terms of achieving social justice, in particular *for youth*?

3. What is the role of the YCJS in dealing with the problem of youth crime?

RECOMMENDED READINGS

Bala, Nicholas. (2003). *Youth Criminal Justice Law*. Toronto, ON: Irwin Law.

Chartrand, Larry. (2005). "Aboriginal youth and the criminal justice system" In Campbell, K. (ed) *Understanding Youth Justice in Canada*, Prentice Hall, Toronto, Ontario.

Moyer, Sharon and Maryanna Basic. (2005). *Crown Decision-Making Under the Youth Criminal Justice Act*. Ottawa: Department of Justice.

Chapter 6

Criminalized Girls

STARTING POINT

"Only a change in social attitudes will give girls any real chance at justice" (Hudson, 2002: 307).

"Criminalizing young women only makes them more vulnerable" (Justice For Girls, www.justiceforgirls.org).

Acts labelled criminal, deviant, or delinquent take place in a world where gender shapes our lives in very powerful ways. Consider how gender contours our everyday lives. Reflect on how girls are treated when they don't "act like girls." What kinds of behaviours are you thinking of? Think about what it means for young females to deviate from socio-cultural expectations. What are common reactions when girls act *differently*? What do the typical responses suggest about gendered expectations? What are the consequences of violating gender norms? What does this say about wider cultural values and the society in which we live? How does gender shape girls' possibilities?

When females commit crime, they violate not only the law, but also socio-cultural scripts (Sundow, 1968; Comack and Balfour, 2004). To fully appreciate the complex relationships between being female, victimization, and offending, we suggest that as you read this chapter, you should keep in mind the following important questions:

- What are the discourses that frame historical and contemporary understandings of criminalized girls?
- Why are "bad girls" viewed as *more* problematic than boys who engage in criminal behaviour?
- Do official statistics support the claim that girls' behaviour is getting worse?
- What unique problems do girls who come in conflict with the law experience?
- How do the processes of criminalizing girls reveal race/class/gender interconnections?
- How does the Canadian YCJS respond to girls and how does it deal with their troubles?

LEARNING OBJECTIVES

After reading this chapter, you should be able to

- Describe the prevailing themes and omissions in criminological theories of female crime and delinquency.
- Identify the nature and extent of female youth crime in Canada.

- Identify the individual and structural level pathways associated with girls' crime.

- Outline how the YCJS responds to female youth crime.

- Demonstrate the intersection of race, class, age, and gender in the study of and responses to female youth crime.

- Illustrate alternative ways of understanding and responding to criminalized girls and young women.

INTRODUCTION: MEDIA REPRESENTATION AND PUBLIC PERCEPTIONS

"Violent crime by females on the increase"

"Crime rate falls again, except among teen girls"

"Teenage Girls and Violence"

"Girls Fighting Marked by Insults, Rumours, Gangs"

"Equality with a Vengeance: Violent Crimes and Gang Activity by Girls Skyrocket"

Do these headlines sound familiar? In *The Vancouver Sun* on July 23, 1998, the front-page headline read, "Violent crime by females on the increase" and was only later followed by, "[d]espite the increase, the rate of female youths committing violent crime . . . is still only one-third the rate for their male counterparts." So the story goes . . . Girls are as aggressive as boys, or, as one headline put it: "Sugar and Spice and Veins as Cold as Ice: Teenage Girls are Closing the Gender Gap in Violent Crime" (Pearson, 1998). Pearson's play on the traditional nursery rhyme that girls are made of "sugar and spice and everything nice" reinforces a double standard for male and female conduct—one that is being simultaneously supported and challenged in 21st century North America. Often, girls who defy gender norms by being "naughty" are viewed more negatively than boys who engage in violence. A strong tendency persists to view boys' law-breaking as a part of growing up male—as the adage *boys just being boys* implies. When girls break rules, public perceptions and societal responses are not as benign. The barrage of media coverage of girls' violence represents a trend toward vilifying women and girls, the consequence of which is that, according to Kim Pate (2002: 1), "Women are the fastest growing prison population worldwide. Recent global trends are seeing the increased criminalization of women and girls, especially those who are poor and racialized."

On November 14, 1997, near Victoria, B.C. seven teenage girls and one boy attacked 14-year-old Reena Virk. Her beating and eventual death left her family and community grieving and searching for answers. Two young people, Warren Glowatski and Kelly Ellard, were tried for second-degree murder and convicted as adults. Both are serving life sentences, while the other six teens involved were sentenced in youth court to various periods of custody for assault causing bodily harm. In the wake of Virk's death, newspaper reports presented graphic stories about teenage girl violence, repeatedly stressing that girls were out of control. Headlines exclaimed, "Bad Girls: A Brutal B.C. Murder Sounds an Alarm About Teenage Violence" (Chisholm, 1997).

Watershed events like Virk's tragic murder reify claims about the "rise" in female delinquency as well as concentrate public attention upon, and fuel fears about, a new wave of violent teenage girls. Indeed, there are egregious examples of girl violence. The Medicine Hat case of a 13-year-old girl convicted in July 2007 for the murders of her mother, father, and 8-year-old brother no doubt incited a fear in some, especially in their small Alberta community, that girl violence is insidious and pervasive. Yasmin Jiwani (1997: 1) explains, however, that rather than a new breed of female transgressors, "existing research clearly links the issue of teen girl violence to the internalization of a dominant, patriarchal culture which values sex and power." Patriarchal culture is based on the ideology of familial patriarchy, which "supports the abuse of women who violate the ideals of male power and control over women" (DeKeseredy, 2000: 46). **Patriarchy** is "a system of male authority that oppresses women and girls through its social, political, and economic institutions whereby men as a group have greater access to, and mediation of, the resources and rewards of authority structures inside and outside the home" (Humm, 1995: 200). When we went to print, the 23-year-old co-accused of the teen (who could not be named under the YCJA), Jeremy Allan Steinke, had not yet been to trial. The convicted girl received 10 years incarceration, the maximum sentence under the YCJA. At the girl's trial, the judge refused to believe that her responsibility in the crime was mitigated by her relationship with Steinke, her then boyfriend. At the time of the murders, the girl was 12 years old. Feminists have long ascribed male violence against women to the unequal power and dominance that males exercise in society. Questions about power, dominance, and inequality are left out of media discourse, and were altogether absent from public consciousness in the Medicine Hat case. They were also peripheral to the Virk case.

The purpose of this chapter is to encourage students to develop a critical understanding of girls, their troubles, and the role of the YCJS in resolving or intensifying the problems that bring girls in conflict with the law. We encourage you to explore alternative ways of responding to female youth crime. In this way, we can better understand not "criminal girls," but *criminalized* girls" (Laberge, 1991). We examine girls' involvement in youth crime and the processes by which they are criminalized. Girls' troubles with the law and the profile of the "female young offender" are markedly different from boys' behaviours and social circumstances.

The chapter is organized as follows. First, we examine trends in female youth crime, including its nature, extent, and how it compares to male youth crime. Next, we explore the social context of girls' lives and choices, which involves a discussion of girls' pathways to criminalization. Finally, we examine girls' encounters with the YCJS, experiences of criminalization, and alternative ways of responding to girls and their troubles.

Indeed, there is a problem when it comes to girls and crime. The real issue, however, is *not* the girls themselves, but rather the injustices they face *outside* in the larger society— sexism, racism, poverty etc.—and *inside* the YCJS—from denial of rights to violence and abuse to harsh paternalism. As we will see, there has been a systemic failure on the part of the YCJS and most other social institutions to understand and attend to the unique circumstances of girls' lives. Consequently, their problems persist while the YCJS continues its long, paternalistic history of punishing girls in the name of protection.

CONSTRUCTION OF THE CRIMINALIZED GIRL

Media discourse presents "female violence as irrational, the product of an individual pathology capable of rearing its ugly head over petty reasons, such as slights about appearance, likeability and intelligence" (Barron and Lacombe, 2005: 57). Newspaper reports direct attention to a group of "bad girls" and subsume "any reference to unequal power relations . . . within a frame of 'the girl who tried desperately to fit in' but could not" (Jiwani, 1997: 1). Girls' involvement in criminality is far more complex than the simple view that Reena Virk was a "victim" and Kelly Ellard was the "offender."

Highly sensationalized, horrific events give the impression not only that more girls are involved in crime today, but that young females have become increasingly violent. The 1997 CBC documentary *Nasty Girls*, which examined high-school girls' experiences of violence and incarceration (*Nasty Girls*, CBC, 5 March 1997), and the 2004 film *Mean Girls*, starring Lindsay Lohan, reflect an overall impression that girls have "gone bad." Cultural images of underdressed teen pop stars like actress-turned-singer Lindsay Lohan and celebrity heiress Paris Hilton and their raunchy lyrics do little to contest the assumption that girls have "gone wild." Barron and Lacombe (2005: 52) refer to anxiety over girl violence as the "Nasty Girl phenomenon." The CBC documentary begins, as Barron and Lacombe (2005: 52) indicate, with a voice-over stating "Some things are at the heart of every little girl." The next scene features a young girl ironing with her mother and the comment that "mother's little helper is learning to become a homemaker." Viewers then see a black screen and hear an authoritative, female voice announce the dawning of a new age: "things have changed in the 1990s." As the film goes on, Barron and Lacombe explain (2005: 52), "we learn just how bad things have become." The documentary continues:

> In the late 1990s almost everything your mother taught you about polite society has disappeared from popular culture and nowhere is this more apparent than in what is happening to our teenage girls. Once the repository of sugar and spice and everything nice, today young women celebrate materialism, aggressive sexuality, and nasty behaviour. . . . Canada's teenage girls are committing more violent crimes than ever before and *girl crime is growing at an even faster rate than boy crime* (emphasis added).

It is not surprising that when the Virk case made headlines, the Canadian public was sensitized to the threat of the "Nasty Girl." According to Barron and Lacombe (2005), the Virk case provided evidence that girl violence was a significant problem for Canadians. Yet girl violence is not new. What *is* new is how it is constructed and what is being done about it.

Media discourse, and consequently popular consciousness, fails to contextualize girls' criminality. Contextualizing the behaviours of girls means placing them in the social, economic, cultural, and political context in which they are found. Girls commit approximately one fifth to one quarter of all youth crime. That means that adolescent males are responsible for about 75–80% of it. Given this, academic study has largely focused on, and youth justice practices have been directed toward, male (youthful) offenders. Before we visit the literature on explanations for female youth crime, we turn our attention to the official rates of female delinquency.

"IT'S ALL IN THE DENOMINATOR": FEMALE DELINQUENCY TRENDS[1]

Empirical evidence challenges media claims and public perceptions that girls are becoming more criminal and more violent. In other words, the panic over out-of-control girl violence is a social construction (Barron and Lacombe, 2005: 51). That said, this does not suggest that official rates of female delinquency are not today much higher than they were in, say, the 1940s or even the 1980s. However, although the numbers have gone up, the gender gap is far from closing (Doob and Cessaroni, 2004). Violent female delinquency remains remarkably rare, even among incarcerated girls. Media accounts of girl crime emphasize the *size* of the increase rather than the small *number* of incidents involved. Bernard Schissel (1997: 30) reminds us how easy it is "for average citizens to become embroiled in the alarm and to call for harsh justice."

As the following discussion will show, there are many reasons to be skeptical of claims about the rise of female delinquency and girl violence. First, we briefly explore the main differences between male and female delinquency. Next, we consider the extent (or quantity) of female youth crime—how much is there? Finally, we examine the nature (or quality) of female youthful offending—what does it look like?

Differences in Male and Female Delinquency

Is female delinquency that different from male delinquency? The answer is yes and no. First, the most frequent charge for males and females is theft under $5000, with theft accounting for proportionately more of female charges. This phenomenon has changed very little over the past several decades. Second, girls are much *less likely* to be arrested for crimes of violence (e.g., homicide, assault, or robbery) and more serious property crimes. Boys are responsible for far more violent crime than girls. Third, charges related to prostitution (and in the United States, running away from home) are more prevalent for girls. Gendered involvement in the sex trade (girls and women as prostitutes and males as johns) has a long history. Fourth, girls are charged with more administrative offences such as breach of probation than boys. Fifth, involvement in youth crime decreases at different ages, with girls less likely to extend delinquency into adulthood. Male involvement in crime peaks at age 17; female involvement peaks at 14–15 years (Savoie, 1999). The main gender difference is one of volume, followed by seriousness. In short, boys commit more crime than girls *and* are overwhelmingly responsible for violent youth crimes. For a quick review of these points, see Table 6.1 on p. 117.

The use of violence among male and female youth differs not only quantitatively, but also qualitatively. Violent activity peaks at a younger age for females than males—14 to 15 years for girls versus 17 years for boys (Saskatoon Police, 2003). The contexts of male and female violence are strikingly different. For example, in her book *Sex, Power, and the Violent School Girl*, Sybile Artz (1998) explains that girls, who had learned at home that "might makes right," engaged in "horizontal violence" often directed at other powerless females. Here, girls' violent actions toward other girls are an extension of relational aggression. In contrast, boys' use of aggression usually has more instrumental ends

---

[1] Title credited to Sprott and Doob (2003).

Table 6.1 Differences in Male and Female Delinquency: Volume and Seriousness

Compared to their male counterparts, girls . . .

- are engaging in property-related crime (theft under $5000) to a higher degree
- are much less likely to be involved in crimes of violence and more serious property crimes
- are more likely to incur charges related to prostitution
- are charged with more administrative offences
- are less likely to extend delinquency into adulthood

(e.g., robbery). According to Mark Totten (2002: 51), in contrast to male violence, which tends to be more frequent, serious, and utilitarian, female violence is "contextualized in significant factors related to self-defence, anticipation of an upcoming physical or sexual assault, or prior victimization by physical and sexual abuse." In this way, girls' expressions of aggression can be located in the socio-cultural context of abuse, sexism, and inequality (Artz, 1998).

The Extent of Female Delinquency

In the early 1980s, one in 10 youth court charges was laid against girls. By the mid-1990s girls were being charged at a rate of one in five. The official extent of female delinquency has increased over the past several decades. Yet 75% of the youth charged with criminal code offences in 2002 were male (Statistics Canada, *Juristat*, 2002, Vol. 23, no.5). After female youth crime rates increased in the 1980s, yearly fluctuation characterized the 1990s. Between 1992 and 1997 there was a small *decrease* in the number of females charged (Dell and Boe, 1998). In that period, the only significant, albeit small, increase occurred in violent and YOA offences (Dell, 2001). While the official rates of violent crime among young women increased during the 1980s and 1990s, this increase was only for *minor* offences such as common assault (Artz, 1998; Corrado and Markwart, 1994; Doob and Sprott, 1998).

Over the past 20 years, the number of young women charged with the most serious forms of violence—murder and attempted murder—has been constant and infrequent (Reitsma-Street, 1999). In contrast to the 1990s climb, however, the violent crime rate for female youth dropped by 6.5% in 1999 (Statistics Canada, 2000). In 2001, out of 485 people charged with murder, manslaughter, and infanticide, five (only 1%) were young women (Statistics Canada, CASIM Table 253-0003). Moreover, changes in the official record of girls' delinquency may reflect a heightened sensitivity and a different societal response rather than changes in actual conduct.

Of all Canadians charged with criminal incidents in 1997, only 5% were female youth (65% were adult males, 17% were male youth, 13% were adult females). Yet statistics—such as between 1986 and 1988, crime among young girls increased 200%—appear to capture the public's ire (Statistics Canada, 1999; Canadian Centre for Justice Statistics, 1998: 32). Totten and Reed (2000) argue that arrests for violent crime by young women (mostly minor assault) have risen twice as fast as those of young men over the past decade (+127% compared to +65%). Indeed, police departments across Canada are arresting more girls.

Table 6.2 Changing Female Youth Crime Rates

Year	Female youth (rate per 10 000)	Male youth (rate per 10 000)
1991	114 (16%)	575 (84%)
2000	113 (20%)	435 (80%)

Source: Sprott, Jane B. & Anthony N. Doob (2003). "It's all in the denominator: Trends in the processing of girls in Canada's youth courts." *Canadian Journal of Criminology*, 45(1), 73–80.

The data, however, obscures more than it illustrates. Given that the overall *number* of young women charged with violent offences remains relatively low, any increase in that number will create a much more substantial percentage increase than the increase in male rates, which are already considerably higher to begin with.

According to Jane Sprott and Anthony Doob (2003), when we consider the nature and extent of female delinquency using official statistics it is "all in the denominator." That is, to understand how much female youth crime exists we need to move beyond media headlines and percentage increases. We need to look at absolute numbers and contextualize the charge rates for girls in relation to the patterns for boys. Thus, while boys' arrest rates began to decline in the mid 1990s, girls' arrest rates did not.

Based on youth court data between 1991 and 2000, Sprott and Doob (2003) demonstrate that there was a *decrease* in guilty findings for boys (from 575 per 10 000 in 1991 to 435 in 2000), whereas guilty findings for girls remained stable (114 per 10 000 in 1991 to 113 in 2000). This indicates that boys are being found guilty at lower rates, while the rates for girls are about the same. Of all cases with guilty findings, girls accounted for approximately 16% in 1991 and 20% in 2000. This change can be described as a 25% *increase*. Alternatively, if we look only at the rate of guilty findings involving girls, the change is a slight *decrease* (114.5 per 10 000 in 1991–92 to 112.9 in 1999–00). Therefore, changes in female crime appear more or less striking depending on the denominator used. Table 6.2 provides a graph of the above statistics.

Although considerably more females are being processed through youth courts than they were in the past, the absolute numbers of Canadian girls involved in youth crime generally, and violent crimes specifically, remains disproportionately low (Reitsma-Street, 1999; DeKeseredy, 2000).

The Nature of Female Delinquency

The nature of girls' criminality is not as serious as media discourse suggests. Self-report surveys provide a glimpse into patterns of violent crime among girls that challenges the Nasty Girl phenomenon. Self-report data from the U.S. Centers for Disease Control (1992–02), taken from the Youth Risk Behaviour Survey, reveal that while 34.4% of the girls surveyed in 1991 said they had been in a physical fight in the previous year, the figure dropped to 23.9% in 2001 (U.S. Center for Disease Control, 1994-2002). While girls may be charged with more violent crimes than in the past, very few of the crimes of violence committed by girls are the horrifying acts of terror we hear about on the news.

Most youth crime among females is relatively minor. Young females are most likely to be arrested for shoplifting, cheque fraud, and prostitution-related offences. In both 1980 and 1995, 80% of the cases heard in Canadian youth courts against girls were for property offences or offences of non-compliance.

Corrado, Odgers, and Cohen (2000) found that the majority of female youth in custody in British Columbia were incarcerated for relatively minor offences such as theft under $5000. Gaarder and Belknap (2002) also found that the majority of girls tried and convicted as adults in the United States (presumably the most serious offenders) had committed relatively minor offences.

Placing girls and their behaviour within the context of youth culture, and "female culture" in particular, is illustrative. Consider the charge of theft under $5000, which for most female youth amounts to "shoplifting." Given that theft typically accounts for at least a quarter of all girls' delinquency, we can see a relationship between girls' troubles and their crimes. North American consumer culture encourages adolescents to buy goods to make themselves look, feel, and be "better." Watch an evening of prime-time television and count the number of commercials directed at girls for body wash, perfume, and make-up, or flip through teen magazines like *Teen People* and *CosmoGirl* to see how marketing heavily targets girls. What message does it send to girls when not only are the shrinking waistlines and cosmetic surgeries of young female celebrities featured in print and visuals across several magazines and on the web, but these young women are presented as role models?

The beauty industry—through print, magazine, television, and web advertisements—begins to indoctrinate young girls at an early age. Socialized to associate identity and popularity with appearance, fashion trends, and body image, girls are particularly sensitive to consequences like eating disorders (Smolak and Hayden, 1994) (see http://www.mediaawareness.ca/english/resources/educational/classroom_exercises/body_image/portrayal_girls.cfm for a look at the portrayal of teenage girls in magazines.)

How does this relate to shoplifting? Gender differences are reflected in the types of items that teens steal. Girls tend to take cosmetics and clothes, whereas boys view electronics as hot commodities (Campbell, 1981; Saraslo, Bergman and Toth, 1998). Living in this teenage subculture of consumption and a society that values material wealth is particularly difficult for girls of colour (African American and Latino females in the US and Aboriginal girls in Canada in particular) and girls from impoverished communities. Without money to purchase the "look" dictated by pop culture, some young women resort to illegal means of acquiring the products.

The criminalization of girls is not simply about criminal conduct, nor is it limited to the YCJS. Arrests for non-criminal conduct are largely responsible for the criminalization of girls (e.g., YOA and YCJA offences such as breach of probation). In Canada, there has been a striking increase in the number and rate of charges for failure to comply (with judicial orders)—from 6.1% of the total female cases in 1985–86 to 27.3% in 1995–96 (Reitsma-Street, 1999). This trend continues and is replicated across the globe in Australia (Hancock and Chesney-Lind, 1982; Adler, 1998), Great Britain (Smith, 1978; Cain, 1989), Belgium (Cain, 1989), and the United States (Chesney-Lind and Shelden, 2004). In the United States, curfew violations and running away constitute about a quarter of all arrests for girls. Research on American detention centres reveals that in 1999 only 2% of boys were incarcerated for status offences, while 8% of girls were held on non-criminal charges (Chesney-Lind and Shelden, 2004).

Under the YCJA (and the previous YOA) youth cannot be charged with status offences. However, Reitsma-Street (1991) argues that while the YOA abolished status offences (in 1984), failure-to-comply charges have become "status-like" offences because they have similar consequences. In other words, girls are being incarcerated not for their *criminal* behaviour, but for breaching conditions of judicial orders. Moreover, regulatory legislation in various Canadian provinces has contributed to an increase in the number of girls processed through the child-welfare system. For example, under Alberta's *Protection of Sexually Exploited Children Act* (PCEC) (formerly the *Protection for Children Involved in Prostitution Act*, PCHIP), females aged 17 and under who are suspected of involvement in the sex trade are locked up under the jurisdiction of child welfare for being sexually exploited children (similar legislation is in the works in British Columbia, Manitoba, and Ontario). This is most pronounced for Aboriginal young women, who are grossly over-represented in both youth detention and secure care facilities, and are now finding themselves locked up in safe houses in Alberta.

IGNORING AND MISREPRESENTING THE FEMALE DELINQUENT

Criminology has always been predominantly **androcentric**: based on male behaviour, written from a male perspective, and judged by a male standard. Until recently, men were the only authorized knowers deemed qualified to speak, and boys and men were the only subjects deemed worthy of knowledge claims. Female criminality was considered secondary to men's: a sidebar, afterthought, or footnote. Consequently, female juvenile delinquency has historically been "ignored, trivialized or denied" (Chesney-Lind and Okamoto, 2001: 3). Most theory and research throughout the early to mid-20th century was preoccupied with boys and men. A case in point is Frederick Thrasher's 1937 "The Gang," which was over 500 pages in length and devoted less than one full page to girls and gangs. Like their adult counterparts considered "too few to count," girls who engaged in delinquency were the "forgotten few" (Geller, 1987).

Early literature on female crime and the gender gap can be divided into three types, based on

1. *biological* differences, where female deviance is understood in terms of sexual dysfunction;
2. female deviance as the *masculinization* of women brought about through feminism and women's liberation, which minimize the gender gap;
3. *gender-role socialization*, where female deviance reflects gender roles and changes to them.

Not until the 1980s did a shift away from theories uncritically presuming a male standard begin. In the following pages we outline the dominant paradigms for understanding criminalized girls, which largely misrepresent female crime and delinquency.

The "Criminal Girl" and Biology

Traditionally, when girls appeared in criminological literature, they were misrepresented as "pathological" or "sexual delinquents" and understood as "other." Early criminologists **mythologized** the girl delinquent, assuming that because she was rare she must be profoundly different (from males and other females). Influenced by social Darwinism, they believed that biology was destiny. Cesare Lombroso argued that all criminals were biological throwbacks (atavists). The discourse held that females—biologically destined to bear and raise children—were not as evolved or intelligent as men, and therefore had little ability to engage in challenging, independent activities like crime. According to Lombroso, biology rendered females more passive and nurturing than males, so when they engaged in crime, they misrepresented their nature. Lombroso and Ferrero (1895: 150–2) argued, "Women are big children; their evil tendencies more numerous and more varied, but generally remain latent . . . The criminal woman is consequently a monster." It followed that "criminal women" and their adolescent counterparts were degenerate, unwomanly, and lacked maternal instinct (Lombroso and Ferrero, 1895).

Locating female criminality in physiology and sexuality continued in the work of Otto Pollack in the 1950s and Cowie, Cowie, and Slater in the 1960s. Otto Pollack, for example, (1950: 51) argued:

> One of the outstanding [issues relating to] the existing inequality between the sexes is chivalry and the general protective attitude of man towards woman . . . Men hate to accuse women and thus indirectly to send them to their punishment, police officers dislike to arrest them, district attorneys to prosecute them, judges and juries to find them guilty and so on.

In other words, relatively low rates of female crime were a facade. Instead, women and young girls committed a great deal of crime, which Pollack attributed to hormonal imbalances (e.g., during menstruation, pregnancy, and menopause). Females, he argued, were naturally more deceitful than men and were more likely to get away with their deviance. Why? For Pollack, a woman's ability to "fake" an orgasm, along with her sexual passivity, enabled her to conceal her crimes. Similar assumptions can be found in Cowie, Cowie, and Slater's (1968) work, which argued that an excess of male chromosomes explained female criminality. Anatomy, they believed, and particularly biological, somatic, and hormonal differences, explained differential criminality among male and females.

Historically, dominant responses to female crime and deviance reflected these views. Recall from Chapter 2 that 19th and early 20th century philanthropists and positivists presumed delinquent girls were wayward, incorrigible, idle, and dissolute, with a predilection for sex. While they viewed male misbehaviour as a threat to public order—a social problem—they understood female delinquency to be a sexual problem (Murdock, 1982; Frith, 1985; Pilkington, 1994). From early Lombrosian ideas about the normally passive woman who becomes a "femme fatale" to more contemporary arguments that PMS (premenstrual syndrome) causes female crime (Dalton, 1961), androcentric criminological theory has typically ignored the social context in which girls' and women's deviance occurs.

Masculinization of the "Criminal Girl"

The **masculinization** argument holds that females have become more like males. As women's participation in social and economic life raises their status relative to men, proponents reason, so too will their participation in crime rise. In other words, girls and women will have "equality" in criminality. Freda Adler (1975) is best known for proposing what is widely known as the **"women's liberation thesis."** Adler argued that in the same way that women are demanding equal opportunity in legitimate institutions, other determined women are calling for the same in the area of criminal activity. She posited that as the position of women "approximates" that of men, we will see a growth in the frequency and type of their criminal activity.

Rita Simon (1975) supported these claims, noting that more women were being arrested for white-collar crimes, which she connected to women's greater participation in the paid workforce. Widely citing Adler's book *Sisters in Crime* (1975), the media interpreted her claims as directly linking the women's movement with rising female crime rates. The recent case of affluent business executive Martha Stewart notwithstanding, these claims were based on false assumptions. First, most female crime is committed by those women who are *most* economically marginalized, not the advantaged. As Chesney-Lind and Shelden (1998: 77–87) point out,

> It seems peculiar . . . that so many academics would be willing to consider a hypothesis that assumed improving girls' and women's economic conditions would lead to an increase in female crime when almost all existing criminological literature stresses the role played by discrimination and poverty (and unemployment and underemployment) in the creation of crime.

Second, the assumption that women have gained parity in all social institutions does not have empirical support. However, these suppositions appear to be accurate and resonate with some members of the general public. Official statistics have shown dramatic changes in female crime rates since the 1960s (when the second wave of the feminist movement surfaced). However, the masculinization hypothesis has been contradicted on several fronts. Gioradano and Cernkovich (1979) found that delinquent girls typically hold not a positive attitude toward feminism, but more traditional attitudes about the women's roles. Similarly, the "violent" girls in Artz's study (1998) were not typically liberated, emancipated young women challenging traditional gender norms, but were more likely to support patriarchal ideologies. According to Artz (1998: 59), girls' policing of other girls' behaviour serve(d) to "preserve the status quo, including their own continued oppression." Artz, Blais, and Nicholson (2000: 124) found in case studies of girls' experiences of custody in British Columbia that the majority were male-focused (e.g., wanting boyfriends) and used derogatory terms to describe other girls (e.g., "pretty power hierarchy"). Reinforcing gender stereotypes, they targeted other girls for being "dirty," "ugly," or otherwise not fitting into the image of acceptable femininity.

The idea that females who offend are emulating males and rejecting their feminine role nevertheless remains dominant. Like the pervasiveness of Lombrosian ideas, masculinization theories have not disappeared. In *When She Was Bad*, journalist Patricia Pearson (1997: 32) asserts that girls have "gotten hip" to their capacity for violence and warns that women's equality comes with a price. Patriarchy, the context within which women's violence occurs, is conspicuously absent from her discussion. Chesney-Lind (1999: 117–118) argues that Pearson "minimizes and dismisses women's victimization and its clear connection to women's violence, and then argues that such violence should be punished without regard to gender." Another case in point is Celeste McGovern (1995: 28), who agrees that "new masculinized attitudes" permeate girls' attitudes today. She continues, "[p]rodded by feminism, today's teenage girls embrace antisocial behaviour." In a climate of anti-feminist backlash (the undermining of women's safety and feminist "victories"), many pundits find these claim appealing (Minaker and Snider, 2006).

Indeed, female aggression is being "rediscovered" and societal responses are changing. Until the 1970s, the police, media, and the general public largely ignored occasional violent acts by females. Parents, law enforcement officials, teachers, and social workers concentrated their attention on controlling girls' sexuality, not their "violent" behaviour. Consequently, girls' aggression, which has always existed to some extent, was trivialized rather than criminalized. More recently in North America, a resurgence of interest in girls' criminality has accompanied a change in societal reactions to girls' actions—what Chesney-Lind and Joan Belknap (2004) refer to as "rediscovery."

Recent studies on girlhood aggression that claim girls are as likely as boys to be bullies (they just use different, less physical, more verbal tactics—we are told) have fuelled the rediscovery of girls' "violent" behaviour (Pepler, 1998). Debra Pepler's (1998) research helped foster a new definition of bullying that includes teasing, gossiping, and quarrelling as intolerable acts of aggression. That Wendy Craig, one of Peplar's collaborators, was featured on *Oprah* to make a case for girl-on-girl violence lends support to the social problem of girls' bullying.

In a similar vein, in her book *Odd Girl Out: The Hidden Culture of Aggression in Girls*, Rachel Simmons (2002) argues that girls are just as aggressive as boys. She calls the kind of aggression girls do "alternative aggression." Notably, this kind of research is directed toward early detection and creating individualized, school-based violence prevention programs. These may have positive results and the best of intentions, but are likely to have unintended consequences. On one hand, books like Simmons's can amplify fears of the "Nasty Girl," ostracizing already disadvantaged girls who act out violently and labelling them as "bad girls." On the other hand, to ignore and invalidate the experiences of girls who have been victimized by other girls re-victimizes them. To what extent is girl-to-girl violence a systemic social problem in the way that male violence is? Research from a feminist-informed perspective is needed to answer this question. Girls may be ridiculed, ostracized, and otherwise emotionally abused by fellow girls, but their risk of being physically and/or sexually abused by their male classmates is far greater, as is the severity (Mercer, 1987).

The growing emphasis on "bullying" in the schoolyard and girls' aggression obscures the reality that male physical and sexual abuse accounts for most violence against girls. A Canadian Federation of University Women's report revealed that more than half (54%) of girls under the age of 16 have experienced some form of unwanted sexual attention (cited in Jiwani, 1998). Official statistics show that over 60% of sexual assaults reported to police involve girls under the age of 18. Aboriginal girls are more vulnerable. In Canada, 75% of Aboriginal females under age 18 have been sexually abused (Jiwani, 1998).

That girls' victimization is gender-based and linked to patriarchal power and authority is obscured under the banner of "bullying." Currie and Kelly (2006: 1) argue, however, that scholars must understand "day-to-day aggression" in girls and suggest that naming girls' aggression "complicates our understanding of their agency." Indeed, it moves away from rendering girls as only victimized by patriarchal culture and views them as subjects, not merely objects. We can take girls' victimization by other girls seriously by locating it within the larger context of patriarchy, rather than viewing it as a reflection of a "Nasty Girl" phenomenon or as an expression of their innate capacity for aggression (Pearson, 1997).

Thus, the masculinization hypothesis is misdirected, especially when it presumes that girls' aggression reflects their empowerment. The concept of hegemonic masculinity has been influential in theorizing about the relationship among masculinities and the over-representation of boys and men in crime (Messerschmidt, 1993). This approach does not focus on the culture of violence endorsed by the dominant contemporary masculinity (which will be discussed at greater length in Chapter 9). The connections between power, control, and *growing up male* are lost in favour of oversensitivity to violence by predominantly economically and racially marginalized girls and women. The masculinization hypothesis fails to place masculinity (or femininity) in its socio-cultural context and ignores the socio-economic circumstances of girls' criminalization. The portrait of the masculinist criminalized girl is problematic, but the claims therein raise important questions about girls' agency.

Girls' Criminality and Gender Roles

Hagan, Simpson, and Gillis (1987) and Hagan (1990) proposed power control theory to explain females' greater conformity to social mores. They argue that females experience more social control in traditional, patriarchal families than males or than females in egalitarian families. Power control theory holds that in reproducing the gender divisions they model, patriarchal families enforce less risk-taking behaviour among daughters (e.g., staying close to home, baking, cleaning, etc.), whereas boys are encouraged to roam more widely (e.g., staying out late, skateboarding, etc.). Thus, differential socialization accounts for females' lower rates of delinquency. In other words, with greater male control over women and girls in families, the risk for female adolescent deviance decreases. Particularly problematic is how the approach inadvertently suggests that mothers who work outside the home contribute to higher delinquency among their daughters. There is, however, no evidence to suggest that girls' delinquency increases with women's participation in the labour force (Chesney-Lind, 1988). Despite the way such claims have been (and can be) taken up in opposition to feminism, power control theory is more critical in scope than the previous two approaches in that it acknowledges the importance of gender and patriarchy in shaping male and female behaviour. Socialization patterns may help us understand differences in growing up male and growing up female. However, they alone cannot explain motivation or why females engage in crime and violent crime.

Gender roles must be located in a particular social context, where young women negotiate with dominant cultural representations of girlhood and femininity. Contemporary society presents young females with a variety of images and messages about growing up female, yet a dominant socio-cultural script for girls and young women continues to encourage a narrow version of femininity that prioritizes emotion, physical appearance, dependence, domesticity, caring, and family over more masculine-associated qualities like competition, aggression, independence, strength, and control. Addressing the ways that females negotiate these scripts is beyond the scope of power control theory.

Theoretical, Empirical, and Practical Issues

In making sense of female youth crime, contemporary approaches must address key theoretical, empirical, and practical issues. First, the **generalizability problem** asks: why do girls commit fewer delinquent and criminal acts than boys? If girls had the same opportunities, character traits, and experiences as boys, would their rate of delinquency be similar? After critics like Carol Smart (1976) called criminology out on its failure to explain female delinquency, various attempts to adapt theories about boys to reflect girls' lives followed. Many contemporary mainstream delinquency theorists typically take an "add women and stir" approach, which assumes that girls can be understood using research done by males on boys. Reitsma-Street (1999: 173) argues that delinquency theories anticipate the most crime from "those most abused, marginalized, and devalued by adults and societal institutions." Paradoxically, this characterizes girls' lives better than boys! However, the development, opportunities, and experiences of male and female youth are markedly different, such that theories based on boys can never hope to adequately explain female criminality, she argues. Male-centred theories fail to understand the gendered nature of girls' lives and overlook their victimization, particularly for young women of colour and those on the economic margins. Research demonstrates that "girls' unique situations in communities deeply divided by race, class, and gender have a definite impact on the character of girls' crime, whether trivial or serious" (Chesney-Lind and Shelden, 2004: 63). In Canada, this is most pronounced for young Aboriginal women.

Second, the **gender-ratio problem** asks: why do girls commit fewer delinquent acts than boys? In other words, what is it about girls' lives that produces less delinquency? Early attempts, such as the women's liberation thesis, to explain the uniqueness of female crime were met with confusion and criticism. It is ironic that the argument suggests that *greater* economic and social opportunities for girls and women will result in *more* crime and delinquency among females when these same conditions are assumed to reduce crime among males! Early intervention and programming for boys is typically aimed at expanding, not reducing, educational and employment options.

Finally, in practical terms, to what extent does and should the juvenile justice system take into account girls' distinct needs and experiences? What role does the YCJS play in perpetuating inequalities? We will return to these practical concerns at the end of the chapter.

THEORIZING CRIMINALIZED GIRLS: UNDERSTANDING GIRLS *AS GIRLS*

As the previous section demonstrated, criminology has systemically failed to understand girls *as* girls. Understanding girls *as girls* means putting their lives, experiences, and behaviours in a socio-cultural and political context, one largely structured by privilege or inequality along race, class, and gender lines. Feminist scholars have attempted to address gender insensitivity by exploring girls' conformity and criminality in the context of the unique problems and circumstances of girls' lives. Paralleling this mode of inquiry, a small contingent of male and female researchers is also examining the connection between masculinity and crime, looking for a better explanation for boys' disproportionate involvement in delinquency (Messerschmidt, 1999; Hogeveen, 2003).

The variables in the theories about boys (poverty, relationships with peers, family problems, racism, and school experiences) are not unimportant to the lives of girls. However, as Chesney-Lind and Shelden (2004) argue, importing androcentric theories uncritically onto girls' lives ignores a fundamental problem: that is, they were developed without awareness of or concern for gender or gender stratification. A **gender-sensitive analysis** is not simply about recognizing distinct gender identity (masculinity or femininity) or pointing to different gender roles (socialization). It is an approach that acknowledges that structural context is stratified by gender. Overt and subtle forms of patriarchy—its institutional manifestations, psychological dimensions, and social-context—figure prominently in gender-sensitive studies of girls and crime. In other words, theorizing about criminalized girls *as girls* takes into account not simply what girls do, but the context in which their lives and behaviours are embedded. Here are some questions to ask:

- How do agencies of social control (e.g., police, courts, prisons) reinforce girls' subordinate place in society?
- What impact does their structural position have on girls' development and ways of thinking and acting (e.g., agency)?
- What violations of traditional gender scripts typically attract the most attention?
- To what extent is victimization related to offending?

To understand girls *as girls*, we need to recognize the normative expectations of what a "good girl" ought to be (as our society constructs it): a standard for "appropriate" femininity, one that is white, Western, and middle-class. It also means exploring the consequences of not living up to this image. Patriarchy pushes women to be obedient, dependent, submissive, sexually accessible, and under male control. Patriarchal ideologies are still at work in the two main institutions that girls routinely find themselves in— school and family. For example, literature reviews on parental and teacher behaviour consistently find that girls are encouraged to be passive, verbal in orientation, and dependent, while boys are encouraged to be independent, to explore, and to learn how things work (Ehrhart and Sandler, 1987; Thorne, 1994).

Parental commitment to differential standards of adolescent behaviour reinforces a wider culture of gender difference and inequality. Recent studies seem to confirm these findings, suggesting that while the culture of girlhood in schools is undergoing change, implicit "rules" for a gendered order are still being reinforced. According to Currie and Kelly (2006: 4), girls today must navigate precarious standards of conduct:

> Girls must be pretty but not "self absorbed"; they must be attractive to boys but not seen as "slutty"; they must be popular among the "right people" but not a social "snob"; independent but not a "loner"; and so on.

Girlhood today appears a contradictory terrain! Currie and Kelly refer to this as the "double standard of womanhood." Few of the girls in Currie and Kelly's (2006: 4) study questioned the notion that today "girls can be anything," but "most were also acutely aware that girls, unlike boys, are judged by their looks, are emotionally rather than physically expressive, are not physically adept, and can be 'ruined' by sexually-demeaning labels." In this way, a contradiction exists between the rhetoric of equality and "the everyday reality of how girls are labelled, classified and—on that basis—achieve 'success.'" (Currie and Kelly, 2006: 4). Although many parents may be concerned about sex-role equality, few depart significantly from traditional socialization practices (Steinem, 1992; also see Katz, 1979: 24). Doing so is particularly difficult given strong cultural messages and institutions that celebrate, reinforce, and extol limited ways of being male and being female. The pervasiveness of sex-typing in textbooks, on television, in magazines, and in video games (among other places), the persistence of tired ideologies (from "good daughterhood to good motherhood,"), and the accompanying gendered practices (employment hierarchies, wage differentials, etc.,) all suggest that gender stratification is being reproduced in the next generation of adolescents.

Gender is not the only salient factor here. Racism and class inequality also figure prominently in the lives of criminalized girls. Take, for example, the fact that violence among Aboriginal girls, a majority of whom live in poverty, is alarming. Critical questions are important here:

- How is gender related to other social structures such as class and race?
- What does it mean to grow up female in a particular social location?
- What are the racial differences?
- What are the class differences?
- How do multiple forms of oppression intersect in the lives of criminalized girls?

Above all else, a gender-sensitive approach involves listening to girls' voices and attempting to understand criminalized girls on their own terms (Gilligan, 1982; Gilligan and Attanucci, 1988).

PATHWAYS TOWARD CRIMINALIZATION

> Girls' involvement in delinquency and crime arises out of a complex set of psycho-social [processes] that seem to draw in most of those who are marginalized and especially those who suffer from sexual abuse. (Artz, Nicholson & Rodriguez, 2005: 305)

Although adolescent boys and girls may experience similar problems (i.e., family circumstances, school and peer relations), they experience them differently because "they take on special dimensions as a result of the way gender works in the lives of young women" (Chesney-Lind, 2001: 38). In this section we examine **individual-level pathways** (e.g., psycho-social factors) and **structural-level pathways** (e.g., societal factors) to girls' criminalization. Following this, we illustrate the relationship between individual and structural pathways by exploring the sexual double standard and girls' victimization. See Box 6.1, *The Story of K*, told by Kim Pate, the Executive Director of the Elizabeth Fry Societies, for a compelling illustration of the complexity of factors involved in the lives of criminalized girls.

Box 6.1
The Story of K (by Kim Pate)

In an effort to encourage the Parliamentary Standing Committee to seriously examine the disastrous impact and untold human costs of jettisoning more young people into the adult system, the Canadian Association of Elizabeth Fry Societies facilitated a presentation by a young woman who had first-hand experience in and with the system. A summary of her story follows:

A Young Woman's Nightmare: K's Story

K is a young Aboriginal woman from Manitoba—the province that has the highest rate of transferring young people from the juvenile into the adult system. K was arrested when she was 16 years old. She was driving in a car from which a young man shot another youth. She was taken into custody and immediately sent to the Portage Jail, a provincial jail for women. As a result of her age, as well as the high profile nature of her case in the province, K was segregated in one of the worst segregation units in the country for almost the entire time that she was remanded in custody awaiting her transfer.

K was initially charged with first degree murder. It is common that the police usually charge with the most serious offence supported by their version of the facts those young people whom they wish to see transferred up to the ordinary of adult court. Evidence that is presented at a transfer hearing is not subject to the same rigorous examination as when it is raised at trial. K was transferred up essentially on the basis of that charge. She was one of seven youths who were involved, and, ultimately, the only young woman charged. Two young men were also charged, and the remaining four youth gave evidence against their "friends" in exchange for their freedom.

Once K was transferred to the adult court, the Crown Prosecutor immediately offered her a deal: a recommendation for three to four years in prison if she entered a guilty plea to a reduced charge of manslaughter. As is too often the case, although K's lawyer felt that she had a chance of acquittal, she was not willing to risk going to trial on the first degree murder charge because of the potential that she might end up convicted and therefore subject to a mandatory minimum sentence of life in prison with no parole eligibility for 25 years.

K consequently pleaded guilty and was convicted of manslaughter. Although the Crown argued that K should be sentenced to three to four years in prison, the judge decided to give her a sentence of one year. When K realized this meant she would have to return to the same prison in which she had spent the previous two years of remand, her lawyer was instructed to try to get her sent elsewhere. The result was a request for a prison sentence of two years so that she might be incarcerated in the new regional women's prison in Edmonton or the Okimaw Ochi Healing Lodge for Aboriginal women prisoners.

Unfortunately, the Correctional Service of Canada (CSC) classified K as a maximum security prisoner and shipped her off to the segregated maximum security unit in the Saskatchewan Penitentiary. I met K there, just after she had tried, for the second time, to kill herself. She was 18 years old. She was later transferred to the Regional Psychiatric Centre. CSC staff also recommended that she be detained in prison until the expiration of her warrant of committal thereto.

When K's grandfather died, her request for a compassionate temporary leave of absence pass to allow her to attend his funeral was denied. When a Winnipeg police officer exaggerated and misstated the reality of the risk posed by K, CSC and the Solicitor General refused to allow her to pay her respects to the man who had raised her and whom she had known more as a father than as a grandfather.

At her age of 19 years, K was released on statutory release. Although her grandmother requested that K be permitted to live with her, CSC chose instead to force her to go to a men's halfway house. K was the only woman in the house and she became the focal point of more than one resident's advances. Consequently, it was not surprising that she tried to use any means available to avoid being at the house. As a result, she was deemed to have breached the conditions of her parole and was twice put back into the Portage Jail.

When K's two-year-old jail sentence expired, she was still not free to move on with her life. She is now subject to a sentence which we consider excessive. When her prison sentence expired, K commenced three years of probation, the conditions of which are more stringent than her parole conditions. In addition to a 7:00 p.m. to 7:00 a.m. curfew, she has to complete 400 hours of community service work. These conditions preclude her being able to continue the work she was doing in the evenings while on parole—which means she cannot afford to support herself—nor is she able to continue in her educational endeavours. After spending time at her mother's beyond curfew, as well as because of difficulties she is experiencing in trying to complete her community service work hours, K has also now been charged with breaches of her probation order.

As K has so articulately challenged us and the members of the Parliamentary Standing Committee On Justice and Human Rights, where does she go for help and support now? K was in the care of the child welfare authorities at the time of her arrest. The state was therefore her "parents." Five years later, however, at the age of 21 years, K is "released to freedom" without resources or familial support. She feels beaten down by the system. K learned to slash and self-medicate as a means of coping with life in prison. It is all she has left when she is overcome by the bleak reality of her life—no family, no money, and no job. But, when she finds she cannot cope and fails to adhere to all of her conditions of probation, quick action is taken to charge and jail her. Where is the justice in this? And who should be responsible?

Source: Kim Pate, "The Jettisoning of Juvenile Justice? The Story of K." *Canadian Woman Studies Journal*, Vol. 20, No. 3, Fall 2000.

Individual-Level Pathways Individual-level pathways include the personal characteristics and problems that condition a young woman's choices, making her more vulnerable to criminalization. Research has identified a multiple-problem profile of the young female offender (Corrado, Odgers, and Cohen, 2000), which includes the following individual-level factors:

- physical and sexual abuse (Chesney-Lind and Shelden, 2004; Miller and Trapani, 1995)
  - family violence
  - child abuse
- home leaving or "running away from home" (Chesney-Lind and Shelden, 1998; Artz, 1998)
  - problematic family dynamics
  - dysfunctional home and abuse
  - neglect and mistreatment
- substance and drug abuse and untreated addictions (Crawford, 1988; Sondheimer, 2001)
- school problems (Figueria-McDonough, 1993; Sherman, 2002)
  - high drop-out rates
  - low levels of academic achievement
- negative experiences with adults (Acoca, 1999)
  - parents
  - trusted authorities
  - foster care or YCJS
- medical and mental-health concerns (Prescott, 1997; Hernandez, 1995)
  - eating disorders
- negative self-representations (Gilfus, 2002)
  - low self esteem
  - suicidal thoughts
  - self-harming tendencies

The personal context of girls' delinquency is often plagued by problems such as low self-esteem, the absence of relationships with trusted adults, mental-health issues, and witnessing or experiencing family violence. Adolescent girls are three times more likely than boys to suffer from depression (often associated with low self esteem, negative body image, etc.) (Leschied *et al.*, 2000). Nowhere are these personal problems more pronounced than for Aboriginal females, who have a suicide rate that is eight times the national average for non-Aboriginal adolescent girls (National Forum on Health, 1997). If these problems originate primarily at the psychological level, we risk pathologizing girls and viewing their collective troubles in isolation. Each of the above individual-level factors is related to the larger societal context of girls' lives.

Structural-Level Pathways Indeed, the individual circumstances of a young woman's life (i.e., personal characteristics such as family life and relationships) figure prominently in her decision-making. Overemphasizing a psychological profile negates the significant impact of structural factors on the lives of female young offenders. Structural-level pathways are those life circumstances largely beyond one's control that structure possibilities, constraints, and life chances. In K's case (Box 6.1), seemingly "personal characteristics"—being Aboriginal, a ward of the state, young, and living in Winnipeg's North End—were the structural conditions or context in which she made her choices. At the structural level, criminalized girls as a group are marginalized—by gender, class, race, and other forms of systemic oppression (see Figure 6.1 for a visual of how structural conditions are interrelated). Structural constraints play a significant role in female delinquency. The feminization and criminalization of poverty co-mingle to create a social context of girls' delinquency characterized by a) economic instability; b) continued gender inequality and male dominance; c) violence and racism.

As a group, girls who find themselves in trouble with the law typically have the following in common:

- experiences of gender-based oppression and victimization, which includes but is not limited to
    - abuse in families, relationships, state institutions
    - enforcement of discriminatory and coercive welfare, immigration, and corrections policies and drug laws
- living on the street and involvement in prostitution, which is associated with
    - poverty
    - drug use
    - homelessness
    - control by pimps
- participation in economic-related crimes, such as
    - theft under $5000
    - fraud

The demographic characteristics and social circumstances listed above reflect the social marginalization of criminalized girls. Criminalized girls, like their adult counterparts,

Figure 6.1 Structural Conditions Influencing Female Delinquency

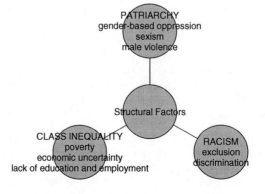

are likely poor, undereducated, unemployed, or under-housed, with untreated addictions and few employment skills. Canada's YCJS also over-represents low-income, ethno-racial minority females among its female population. The over-representation of Aboriginal females in the YCJS is proportionally greater than that for Aboriginal young males.

For many women, survival strategies, especially in the context of a shrinking welfare net, result in criminalization (e.g., fraud, soliciting for purposes of prostitution, importation charges, and shoplifting). Furthermore, many criminalized girls live in impoverished communities without the social supports necessary to accomplish pro-social goals or reintegrate upon release from custody. A scarcity of appropriate and effective prevention or reintegration options in their communities contributes to a cycle of poverty, poverty, and criminalization. Gilfus (2002: 6) argues that "[w]omen and girls are among the most impoverished and violated populations but they have few resources, services, or rights that can be reasonably exercised."

THE SEXUAL DOUBLE STANDARD AND GIRLS' VICTIMIZATION

Girls' experiences of physical and sexual abuse and their subsequent criminal behaviour are not merely personal circumstances but reflect the wider patriarchal context of girls' lives; that is, the pervasiveness of male violence against females and the subordinate position of women as a group in Canadian society. This is particularly evident in the **sexual double standard**—tacitly encouraging male sexual exploration and promiscuity and punishing female sexuality; and the violence against women that reflects, reinforces, and reproduces it.

Recall the starting point activity at the beginning of the chapter. North America has a long history of adjudicating females based on their physical appearance and their (presumed or actual) sexual history. Barbara Hudson (1989) explains in her study of late 19th century "troublesome girls" that girls were criminalized not because of their offence but because of their perceived sexual behaviour or for going against social codes of adolescent femininity. Research documents the role of romance culture here (Adler, Kless, and Adler, 1992; Thorne, 1994). Today, the **good girl/bad girl dichotomy** is at work when people and institutions respond to females on the basis of what kind of girl they are presumed to be. Girls who are too overtly sexual are labelled "sluts." Indeed, girls' subculture is rife with examples of punishing females for being "bad girls."

We can see the sexual double standard, its manifestations, and its reinforcement most clearly in violence inflicted against girls and women at the hands of men. One graphic example of gendered violence is the case of disappearing women—most of them young, poor, Aboriginal, and involved in the sex trade—from Vancouver's Downtown Eastside during the 1990s, some of whom were later found dead at Robert Pickton's pig farm. Aboriginal women experience condemnably high rates of violence (see *The Stolen Sisters: A Human Rights Response to Discrimination and Violence Against Indigenous Women in Canda*, Amnesty International, 2004). Men still use violence as a powerful patriarchal weapon to keep girls and women in their place, as can be seen in the growing numbers of women who access women's shelters. Physical and sexual victimization, inside and outside the family, play a significant role in reproducing patriarchy. Pimps coerce and directly recruit girls, some as young as 10, into prostitution during adolescence (Miller, 1986). DeKeseredy (2000: 25) argues that prostitution is a survival strategy, a "means of survival in a gender-stratified society" where adolescent females are valued more for their sexuality and as such get "involved in criminal activities that exploit their sexual object status."

In this context it is not surprising that *the most significant pathway to criminalization for females is victimization*. Female teens between 15 and 19 experience the most personal victimization of all age groups (McClelland, 2003). According to the Feminist Research, Education, Development, and Action (FREDA) Centre, 54% of girls under age 16 have experienced some form of unwanted sexual attention; 24% have experienced rape or coercive sex; and 17% have experienced incest (also see Holmes and Silverman 1992; Russell 1996). In addition, girls are much more likely to experience childhood sexual abuse; some experts estimate 70% of child abuse victims are girls (Finkelhor and Baron, 1986; Bagley, 1988). In a survey of three major Canadian hospitals, 75% of children admitted for sexual assault were female, as were 48% of children admitted for physical abuse (Canadian Centre for Justice Statistics, 1994). In 8 out of 10 family-related sexual assaults committed against children and youth, the victims are girls (Canadian Centre for Justice Statistics, Statistics Canada, 2005). These figures are significant because research evidence demonstrates a strong correlation between victimization and offending.

Like their adult counterparts, most girls who come in conflict with the law have abuse histories (Comack, 1996). Reported rates of physical and sexual abuse among delinquent girls range from 40 to 73%. According to Gilfus (2002), the majority of criminalized girls have experienced physical violence (61%) and sexual abuse (54%). Race plays a significant role. In Canada, the incidence of child sexual abuse in some Aboriginal communities is as high as 75 to 80% for girls under eight years old (McEvoy and Daniluk, 1995). The Ontario Native Women's study on violence against women in Aboriginal communities reports that 80% of women and 40% of children are abused and assaulted (Lynn and O'Neill, 1995). Among federally sentenced Aboriginal women (23% of population), 90% have backgrounds of physical abuse and 61% have experienced sexual abuse (Canadian Task Force on Federally Sentenced Women, 1991, cited in Comack, 1996).

Being victimized has significant long-term consequences that are directly or indirectly related to criminalization. In other words, trauma from physical and sexual abuse has a profound impact on the development of female juvenile delinquency. The consequences of sexual abuse include, but are not limited to, psychological stress, mental-health issues, disruptive conduct in school, running away from home, and early marriage (Tanner, 2001). One effect of intense family conflict—which may involve overly strict discipline, child abuse, or witnessing family violence—is running away from home (which will be further explored in Chapter 8).

For some girls, running away is the beginning of time spent in and out of foster and group care. Many continue to flee from foster and group home placements (Sullivan, 1988). Almost half (43%) of children in foster care have experienced violence within the foster home setting (Kufeldt et al., 1998: 21). Through in-depth interviews, Totten (2002) found that for a group of girls with violent convictions their first encounter with the YCJS was on child-welfare matters. From child welfare, many became involved with prostitution, ran away, and/or engaged in violent behaviour while in care and subsequently found themselves in the YCJS. Many girls in Totten's study did not use violence until after they had been institutionalized in child-welfare and young offender facilities, suggesting there is more at work in girls' use of violence. More research is needed to better understand the extent to which child welfare is a pathway to crime.

Box 6.2
Putting Girls' Violence in a Patriarchal Context

This article by Artz found the following:

1. Violent girls reported significantly higher rates of victimization and abuse than their non-violent counterparts.

2. 20% of violent girls stated that they were physically abused at home, compared to 10% of violent males and 6.3% of non-violent girls.

3. One in four violent girls, compared to one in ten non-violent girls, had been sexually abused.

4. Most of the violence was horizontal—directed at other powerless girls, with boys as the audience.

5. Girls who were violent reported fears of sexual assault, especially from boyfriends.

Source: Artz, 1998.

In Dohrn's (2004) study, over 80% of those incarcerated in British Columbia were "runaways," whose main reason for leaving was sexual abuse. Typically, girls leave feeling unwanted, abused, neglected, or rejected. This can lead or contribute to other personal problems such as negative self-evaluations, mental health issues, and drug use. Janus, Burgess, and McCormack (1987) found that Canadian girls are far more likely than boys to cite physical and sexual abuse as the main reason for running away. Specifically, the first time they ran away, almost half of the girls (49%) but only a third of the boys cited physical abuse as the reason, whereas the girls were six times more likely to cite sexual abuse as the reason for running away (24% versus 4%).

For most girls, life on the street is *as abusive*, if not more abusive, than their previous environment. A particularly troubling example is involvement in prostitution, where the mortality rates for girls and women is 40 times the national average (Davis, 1994; Fraser Committee, 1985). For many young women on the street, running away was a prelude to prostitution. Boyer and James (1982: 77) found that running away is the most common method of entering into prostitution (followed by being abandoned). Other girls use their bodies as weapons for survival, known as "survival sex," where they exchange sexual favours for shelter, drugs, or food.

Positing a more direct relationship, Totten (2002) found in his focus groups that young women claimed that men were the primary reason why they committed crime. In his focus groups, Totten (2002) found that young women claimed that men were the primary reason why they committed crime. For example, some pointed to prostitution and taking blame for their boyfriends' crimes, while others directed attention to their fathers, from whom they turned away and left for the streets to avoid rape (see Box 6.2).

THE (DE)GENDERED YOUTH CRIMINAL JUSTICE SYSTEM

Young women's experiences with criminalization demonstrate that the YCJS is both gendered and de-gendered as it offers little in the way of gender-specific attention to girls' troubles, yet relies on stereotypical assumptions about women in its management and operation. Girls' secondary status is reinforced through the YCJS. In a classic essay, Reitsma-Street (1999) argued that 1) the YCJS continues to be unequal despite the discourse of equality under the law; 2) girls continue to hold a devalued status, while societal expectations promote their "pro-social behaviour;" 3) girls conform despite the high socioeconomic costs (i.e., dependency); 4) there is a high public fear of girl crime despite actual low rates; 5) unjust variations in practice continue despite a national law; and 6) a profound but invisible racism exists whereby a disproportionate number of Aboriginal girls and girls of colour are in the YCJS.

We argue that these six key themes resonate today. In Reitsma-Street's view, justice for Canadian girls remains elusive. After reading this section, do you think there is justice for Canadian girls?

In Canada, female young offenders are routinely detained in mixed gender facilities. This often means that they are housed in juvenile detention centres intended for more serious offenders or are isolated in segregated units in adult jails (Pate, 2001). Given that only a small proportion of violent crimes are committed by young women, there seems little rationale for detaining them in highly punitive carceral settings (Jiwani, 1998). When young women are jailed in mixed youth centres, such as the Manitoba Youth Centre or the Edmonton Young Offender Centre, even if they have separate cottages, conditions are ripe for incidents of sexual harassment and sexual assault. However, many young women are reluctant to define their experiences (of inappropriate touching, sexism, sexual advances, derogatory comments, etc.) as abuse and, fearing repercussions, are unlikely to report it. See the Canadian Association of Elizabeth Fry Societies for more information (www.elizabethfry.ca/vilifica/Contents.htm). Pate (2001) explains the circumstances this way:

> When a young woman reports a rape or has suddenly ended up impregnated while in custody, the institutional response is rarely to address the issues. Instead, what generally happens is that the young women are subjected to more restrictive and isolated conditions of confinement. This reinforces the adage that women, especially racialized young women, are too few to count.

Without female-only secure custody facilities (only one exists) in Canadian cities, young females who are sentenced open custody dispositions will continue to serve their sentences in secure correctional facilities or group homes with males. The experiences of both of the authors working in Manitoba youth detention bear this out. That is, without placements, girls sentenced to open custody were routinely housed in secure custody facilities. The result is increased surveillance, more limits, and greater control. Although boys are sent to the facility best suited to deal with their particular needs, girls are sent to the facility with an open female bed.

Since the late 1990s, we have witnessed an erosion of resources and support for community-based support systems for young people generally. Nowhere is this felt more than for young women and girls. As Pate (1997: 5) explains: "[T]he relatively small numbers of young women who are criminalized and enter the system, as compared to young men, result in even fewer services for young [female] offenders in any community." She continues: "[Y]oung women are disproportionately disadvantaged as a result of a lack of gender-focused community and institutional programming and services, and extremely limited access to open custody settings." Criminalized girls are more isolated and have more limited access to services and programs than their male counterparts (see www.elizabethfry.ca/vilifica/Contents.htm). Other glaring omissions from the YCJS's approach to female young offenders include a lack of provisions for pregnant teens in institutions or daycare for teenage mothers and few parenting programs or life skills resources in the form of education and training.

Locking Them Up To Keep Them Safe

As we have demonstrated, most girls do not engage in the kinds of serious offences that warrant being locked up. Corrado, Odgers, and Cohen (2000), in their extensive study of incarcerated female offenders, found that girls usually present more of a danger to themselves than others. However, a lower tolerance for disobedient females can be seen in the fact that the rate of incarceration for girls charged with non-compliance is triple the rate for boys. Conditions intended to control behaviour and limit freedom often accompany these charges, such as no-go zones, no contact orders, no alcohol or drugs, or curfews. The proportion of female young persons being admitted to custody rose steadily until the implementation of the YCJA. In 2002–03, 20% of all young persons sentenced to custody were female, but this number dropped to 13% in 2003–04 (Statistics Canada, *The Daily*, March 28, 2006). What was/is happening?

In "Locking Them Up to Keep Them 'Safe': Criminalized Girls in British Columbia," Amber Richelle Dean (2005), along with four young criminalized women, writes of the challenges, firsthand experiences, and transformative potential of the YCJS for females. According to Dean (2005), girls are being locked up in Canada in order to "keep them safe." Criminalization of girls in the name of their "safety" is based on a discourse of protection that holds that controls must be put in place (regardless of how punitive) in order to "help" girls; that is, for their own good. Ostensibly, the response is focused on controlling girls rather than confronting men who commit the violence or the social inequalities that put women in danger in first place. Chesney-Lind and Shelden (2004: 7) summarize the system as follows:

> [T]he judicial system that was established to 'protect' them has not really been interested in their physical or emotional safety. Instead, it has served to shore up the boundaries of girlhood that shaped and forced young women into being future second-class citizens.

The response on the part of the YCJS to "protect" female youth from drugs, street life, and forms of abuse has created a host of additional problems.[2] One of the most damaging is that abuse continues in carceral settings. Evidence of this includes not being allowed to shower or use feminine hygiene products; harassment from male guards, strip searches, pat downs and inappropriate touching; and inappropriate conversations about sex and relationships. Dean (2005) argues that given that 63% of young women in custody have a history of abuse, routine strip searches and "pat-downs" can potentially re-victimize girls and should be prohibited. Likewise, in his study "The Special Needs of Females in Canada's Youth Justice System: An Account of Some Young Women's Experiences and Views,"

---

[2] The situation is even more compelling for Aboriginal girls. The case of *R vs. David William Ramsay*, a former B.C. judge who pled guilty in May 2004 to charges of sexual assault and exploitation of four young Aboriginal women who had appeared before him is demonstrative of judicial abuses that unfairly punish girls. He used his power and influence to rape, rob, and beat the young women, then threatened them with reprisals. In June 2004 he was sentenced to seven years in prison (the maximum is 14). Such cases reflect a failure to respond adequately to male violence against women who do not fit the typical victim role (non-white, criminalized).

Totten (2002) found that young women were not heard, had been assaulted and harassed by young men in custody, were falsely accused, and were harassed by staff. Participants shared similar experiences in child welfare, including abuse reports being ignored, multiple placements, unsafe group homes, feeling like a "target" for life, and unrealistic expectations. To summarize, research on girls' experiences in detention reveals a degrading, disempowering experience.

One Size Fits No One: Toward Gender Responsiveness

Paternalism continues to override the Canadian YCJS's response to girls' criminal behaviour. In most cases, programs were designed for boys, have been implemented by men, and have not proven to be effective for girls. Not surprisingly academics, practitioners, and lobbyists have argued that the YCJS does not effectively meet the needs of females across North America.

Dean (2005) found that imprisonment overwhelmingly impacts girls and young women in negative ways. This is especially true for girls who find no institutional support to help them change their lives, have difficulty reintegrating upon release, and have not developed meaningful relationships with caring adults. Others who describe their experience in detention as "not that bad" illustrate the conditions of marginalized females in society, which involve homelessness, hunger, poverty, racism, sexism, sexual exploitation, and drug addictions, etc.

While the problem requires attention beyond the confines of the YCJS, it is important to examine what can be done at the level of carceral facilities, programs, and supports to better meet the (unique) needs of female offenders. More research is required, including case studies, surveys, and qualitative analyses of the context of criminalized girls' lives. For example, much of the literature on the use of violence relies on a male model. Consequently, much youth justice programming is similarly modelled after young men. If young women have different pathways, a different context for their use of violence, and a shared experience of victimization, then gender-sensitive programming is essential. Can this be accomplished when most custody and community-based interventions serve young men and women together? Lack of attention to the differential needs of female young offenders reflects the YCJS's inability and resistance to approach correctional programming with gender sensitivity. Gender sensitivity does not mean relying on gender stereotyping (e.g., girls' facilities need more beauty schools).

The policy "buzzword" for a gender-sensitive approach is "gender responsive," which means addressing "the particular issues, problems, and assets of girls" (Totten, 2004:1). The meaning and application of gender-sensitive or responsive programming or practices cannot be taken for granted. What does it mean for an approach to attend to girls' "particular issues" or problems? Some authors advocate an environment that focuses on girls' sense of connection with others (in contrast to a focus for boys on independence and separation) (Covington, 2001). However, taking for granted gendered stereotypes (e.g. that girls are relational, boys instrumental) may exacerbate girls' troubles. For example, given that the majority of girls in custody have histories of abuse and negative experiences with male partners, emphasizing only relationships (e.g., boyfriends) over independence (e.g., self sufficiency) may be detrimental. We are skeptical as to how "gender responsiveness" could be integrated into a system never intended for females and whose primary responsibility is punishment. Similar strategies for adult females—*Creating Choices*—intended to make federal imprisonment more women-centred were co-opted by Corrections Canada (Hannah-Moffat, 2001), resulting in more punitive intrusions for some groups of women. Instead, we argue that a more useful approach would be based on the lived socio-structural realities of girls' lives. Take, for example, the experiential realities and knowledge claims surrounding young women, such as the fact that they are more likely to experience depression, negative self-concept, negative body image, and eating problems than young males. As a consequence of these circumstances, many young females internalize their distress and cope through self-harm. Attending to this *difference* at the level of programming need *not* mean assuming that girls are more inwardly focused and therefore need one-on-one counselling for psychological problems. The benefits of individualized treatment notwithstanding, the *differences* between girls' and boys' troubles and how they manifest themselves in criminal behaviour are not innate, but are socially constructed and structured. Alternatively, recognizing the differential needs of females could mean gender-sensitive strategies such as speaker sessions on unrealistic and dangerous cultural scripts for girls that portray sexualized—and in many cases, emaciated—bodies as desirable, or counselling sessions that emphasize the development of positive coping mechanisms for abuse survivors. These strategies attend to the social and cultural context of girls' law-breaking behaviours. Girls may benefit from family resources, peer counselling, mentoring, and better follow-up counselling and aftercare. Several authors have suggested that the gender of staff is a key determinant of success (Bloom, 2003; Bloom, Owen and Covington, and Raeder, 2003; Bloom and Covington, 2001; Bloom et al., 2002). Having female staff, however, will not necessarily meet girls' needs effectively. Again, experience from the adult system tells us that attempts to incorporate a woman-centred approach in the correctional system are fraught with difficulties (some perhaps insurmountable). Box 6.3 describes a gender-responsive program in Southern California.

Box 6.3
Children of the Night

One example of a gender-responsive program is Children of the Night, which began in 1979 in southern California to assist young women in the sex trade. Current director Lois Lee started the program while at UCLA as a graduate student in sociology studying the relationship between prostitutes and their pimps. She asked, "Why would a girl stand on a street corner and do something deplorable, then give all the money she earned to a pimp?" Before long, she was offering her apartment as a temporary shelter to adolescents who wanted to escape this life.

The program involves 1) a 24-hour hotline; 2) a walk-in centre that provides medical aid, clothing, crisis intervention, referrals, etc.; 3) free professional counselling by volunteer professionals; 4) an outreach component—volunteers walk the streets distributing information to potential clients and do on-the-spot counselling; and 5) "turn in a pimp"—entails cooperation among youth, agencies, police, and the court system.

Since its inception, approximately 10 000 adolescents (60% females) have gone through the program, with about 80% not returning to the streets. The majority were under 16 (all were under 18) and virtually all had a history of abuse. According to Chesney-Lind and Shelden (2004: 290), "[t]he most positive feature of the program is its provision of direct, emergency services."

Source: www.childrenofthenight.org

Individual-level interventions must deal with the issues facing girls today. These include, but are not limited to

- the effects of physical and sexual violence (e.g., counselling)
- the risk of HIV/AIDS (e.g., education, safe sex)
- pregnancy and motherhood (e.g., support groups for young mothers)
- family problems (e.g., support groups, counselling)
- education (e.g., courses and classes)
- employment and training (e.g., reintegration into the community)
- safe and affordable housing (e.g., finding a place to live)
- stress management (e.g., coping mechanisms) and development of self efficacy (e.g., empowerment)
- drug and alcohol dependency/addictions (e.g., counselling)—see Box 6.4

Chesney-Lind argues that a potentially successful program must be well designed, gender-specific, of sufficient length, and linked to aftercare in the community (in order to reduce post-release recidivism). One example of such a program is the Ma Mawi Wi Chi Itata Centre in Winnipeg, Manitoba, that operates a support program for urban Aboriginal teenage mothers (as well as a 10-week parenting program for young fathers). However, programs, especially when they take place in carceral settings, are short-term, time-limited, and narrowly focused. The gains made through an isolated program cannot be sustained without long-term intervention in the form of aftercare, community-based services, and the like.

Box 6.4
Substance Abuse

One troubling issue faced by many criminalized girls is drug abuse and untreated addictions. For all adolescents, a substance-abuse problem is the result of a compilation of difficulties that cannot be addressed through a traditional disease framework (Bukstein, 1995). Yet little is known to date about the needs of female youth offenders with substance abuse problems (Molidor, Nissen and Watkins, 2002). In recent years, however, there has been an increase in the number of women entering substance-abuse treatment programs (McCarty, Caspi, Panas, Krakow and Mulligan, 2000). Shearer (2003) argues that more substance abuse centres for girls are needed.

Predominantly male-based, traditional substance-abuse programming is unlikely to address the gender-specific treatment needs of females (Uziel-Miller and Lyons, 2000), which may include social, psycho-social, and physiological differences (Shelton, 2000). For example, hormonal differences and body fat percentage affect the ingestion of psychotropic substances (Davis and DiNitto, 1998; Gordis, 1990).

Women are stigmatized, according to Molidor, Nissen, and Watkins (2002), in three ways: as substance abusers, as females, and as presumably promiscuous. The 12-step approach (i.e., Alcoholics Anonymous) has been criticized for women. Feminists have raised concerns that it reinforces the concept of powerlessness on women whose fundamental problems arise from relative powerlessness (Kasl, 1992). For example, submission to a higher power may re-inscribe women's dependence on men.

As part of its Youth Justice Renewal Fund, the Government of Canada is financially supporting the development of programs aimed at young people in conflict with the law. Notably, of 17 pilot projects funded up until July 2004, only one was for female young offenders. Enviros Wilderness School Association's Reintegration Support Program in Calgary offers young girls in conflict with the law support services from the beginning of their involvement in custody through to release and community reintegration. It provides an individual reintegration plan and a reintegration worker who provides support and guidance.

We cannot overemphasize that interventions must not remain only or primarily at the individual level. Chesney-Lind (1997: 57) cautions, "As girls are demonized by the media, their genuine problems can be marginalized and ignored. Indeed, the girls have *become the problem*" (emphasis added). By attending only to personal consequences (e.g., eating disorders, self-harming behaviour), the structural conditions in which such problems emerge are obscured from view. The societal conditions—poverty, racism, sexism—that reproduce and reinforce the problems that girls experience in their lives must become central to societal responses to girls and crime. Not only was the YCJS designed by and for males, but it also has a Western, white, justice administrative bias. As we will see in Chapter 7, this is particularly troubling for Aboriginal youth. The injustices of the YCJS are very apparent for Aboriginal females. Recall the case of Helen Betty Osborne examined in Chapter 5. In the *Aboriginal Justice Inquiry of Manitoba: The Deaths of Helen Better Osborne and John Joseph Harper*, co-commissioners A.C. Hamilton and C.M. Sinclair stated: "There is one fundamental fact: her murder was a racist and sexist act. Betty Osborne would be alive today had she not been an Aboriginal woman" (Hamilton and Sinclair, 1991, as cited in Amnesty International, 2004: 38). The inquiry went on to implicate police inaction in relation to Aboriginal women's safety. "We know that cruising for sex was a common practice in The Pas in 1971. We know too that young Aboriginal women, often underage, were the usual objects of the practice. And we know that the RCMP did not feel that the practice necessitated any particular vigilance on its part" (Hamilton and Sinclair, 1991, as cited in Amnesty International, 2004: 40). It is particularly telling that in 2001 (10 years after the Aboriginal Justice Inquiry), A.C. Hamilton argued that of the 150 recommendations made, few have been acted upon. He explains, "[t]here is either the inability to understand the need for improvements or the same century-long governmental inertia. The result is clear; Aboriginal people continue to suffer at the hands of an inappropriate justice system" (Hamilton, 2001, as cited in Amnesty International, 2004: 42).

To adequately address girls' troubles, changes must occur simultaneously at individual and structural levels. It requires a fundamental change in the YCJS, which, like its adult counterpart, reinforces systemic inequality. To what extent can policy makers, program analysts, government officials, youth advocates, and academics resist the tendency to individualize and pathologize structural issues that emanate from inequalities of race, class, and gender in the wider society? In Table 6.3 on p. 140, you will notice that the individual-level interventions listed above have been reframed in terms of the structural conditions that need attention if they are to be addressed.

Much of the logic of girls' detention is explained by the paternalistic ideology of the juvenile justice system. However, both historically and today, for many criminalized girls, conditions in detention are not characterized by a protective atmosphere. Programs, services,

Table 6.3 Interventions

Individual-Level Interventions	Structural Conditions
Responding to these personal troubles:	*Requires attention to systemic issues:*
■ physical and sexual violence	■ social problem of violence against women
■ risk of HIV/AIDS	■ feminization of poverty, drug (ab)use, prostitution, sexual double standard
■ pregnancy and motherhood	■ differential socialization, lack of support for and discrimination against young mothers
■ drug and alcohol dependency/addictions	■ coping mechanisms for problems associated with marginalization (e.g., homelessness, discrimination, violence)
	■ systemic barriers to accessing treatment (e.g., age, status discrimination)
■ education	■ differential socialization and sexism in schools, barriers to completion (e.g., no childcare)
■ family problems	■ abuse, maltreatment, and conflict
■ employment and training	■ wage-gap, female job ghettos, glass ceiling, limited options for advancement, work/family responsibilities
■ safe and affordable housing	■ social assistance, lack of services and discrimination against single parents, women who leave abusive partners
■ development of self efficacy	■ structural barriers to choice and agency

and resources must respond to the compounding effects of multiple forms of oppression—male violence and marginalization through poverty, systemic racism, and homophobia. The challenge is to resist the tendency to criminalize teenage girls instead of developing and supporting services in the community that offer real help. To date, there are no comprehensive, standardized evaluations or outcome measures for youth justice interventions for females. Youth justice and community-based services that are accessible, culturally appropriate, respectful, and directed at the specific contexts of girls'/women's lives are likely to have the most positive results (Gilfus, 2002; Pate, 1997; Graydon, 1999; Chesney-Lind, 1998; Owen and Bloom, 1998; Alliance of Five Research Centres on Violence, 1999). As we have seen, in the name of protection, the YCJS removes girls from high-risk environments and street-entrenched lifestyles by incarcerating them, but does little to address what it is about those contexts that keeps girls there.

The first standalone young offender facility for girls in Canada—the Arctic Tern Young Women's Facility—opened in Inuvik, NWT, in 2002. Artic Tern was designed to meet the needs of girls. It could be a step in the right direction, or it could potentially exacerbate the situation for Canadian girls. The facility can hold up to 19 girls in two living units, with rooms designed for young mothers and equipped with handicapped access.

The mothering program provides young mothers the opportunity to bond in a structured and supervised setting and is unique to the facility. Operating costs for one year are 2 million dollars, of which 60% is currently subsidized by the federal government. Before the YCJA came into effect, Arctic Tern was operating at or near capacity (at least 8 to 11 inmates) with a staff of 20. Since April 2003, on average two women are detained there. Currently, the board is debating the economic costs of keeping the facility open and the human costs of closing its doors (e.g., girls would be sent out of the territory) (15th Legislative Assembly of the Northwest Territories, Standing Committee on Social Programs, Report on Review of Draft 2004–05 Main Estimates, Chair Sandy Lee). Are more female-only, gender-sensitive facilities advisable? Do such facilities need to be under the jurisdiction of the YCJS? We suspect that the consequence of building more jails will likely be an even greater push to incarcerate girls to fill those jails.

If the answer is not building female-only prisons or adding more female-only programming, then what role should the YCJS play? Making a change for the better requires difficult questions such as: How do girls define their choices, situations, and actions? How does poverty and racism contour girls' lives? How do the social settings girls find themselves in shape their choices and actions? More importantly, we need to question assumptions about the meaning of justice for girls and to unlearn some of our "taken-for-granted" beliefs. The justice system is an unlikely place to address these complex issues. What is the relationship between girls' vulnerabilities and social injustice? Alternatively, what is the relationship between social justice and making girls less vulnerable?

JUSTICE FOR GIRLS? TOWARD MAKING ALTERNATIVE CHOICES

If we recognize that the pathways for girls' and boys' entry into the YCJS are distinct (in terms of the process of charging, context of criminality, and offence type), then is it reasonable to expect the YCJS to respond accordingly? There are two key contradictions between the YCJS's response to girls and the behaviours called into question: girls are less likely to engage in serious, violent crimes and are more likely to enter the YCJS from the child-welfare system or for administrative reasons. There are "many ways in which young women's encounters with the justice system only serve to further their marginalization on the basis of gender, race, class, and sexual orientation by punishing them largely for their failure to conform to social norms that dictate 'appropriate' white, middle-class femininity" (Dean, 2005: 3).

The complex realities of girls' lives require special attention; something that cannot be addressed by simply grouping girls together. However, we cannot assume that all girls share the same experiences and social location or have the same needs. As the preceding discussion demonstrates, there are several institutional, structural, and personal barriers that impede girls' access to justice. Justice *for* girls means offering more meaningful choices—options that are not limited to a longer list of treatment programs available in custody. Instead, we define more meaningful options as contributing positively to criminalized girls' life chances and reducing their experiences of victimization and criminalization. As stated above, this can only be achieved at individual and structural levels.

The previous section explored possible ways of making the YCJS more amenable to, or less of an obstacle for, making meaningful change in girls' lives. We recommend a greater emphasis on attending to young women's troubles outside the YCJS. In the next section we move beyond the YCJS toward the social changes needed in order to achieve justice for girls.

Outside the YCJS

> It would be folly of the most profound and irresponsible proportions to focus on the development of institutionally based services alone. (Pate, 2001)

Female youth, like their male counterparts, are better served by supportive and proactive interventions directed at the context of girls' lives in their own communities or within child-welfare, medical, education, and mental-health systems rather than under the punitive and reactive YCJS. Developing, supporting, and enhancing high-quality supportive community-based services, programs, and resources is a far more cost-effective and humane strategy than incarceration. Initiatives can include enriched health care; addressing the problems of quality and quantity of child-care programs and funding; more educational opportunities for young people; and anti-poverty, anti-racism and anti-sexism campaigns or programs.

Based on your reading of this chapter, we encourage you to evaluate the strengths and drawbacks of the following program designed specifically for girls. Earlscourt Child and Family Centre established the Earlscourt Girls Connection in 1996. It offers to girls between three and twelve years old with behaviour problems a gender-specific, multifaceted intervention program. It accepts referrals from police, social workers, and schools, and according to Isabel Teotonio it is "busting at the seams and has a waiting list" (*Toronto Star*, "Steering Girls Away from Violence", March 23, 2002). It has offered about 300 girls and their families a 12-week anger-management group for the girls and a 12-week parenting-management training group for the parents. After completing these groups, together families attend a program called "Girls Growing Up Healthy," which aims to promote girls' sexual health and the bond between them and their mothers. The program focuses on teaching girls to think about consequences and family dynamics. The girls are encouraged to stay with the Girls Connection until they turn 18. During this time they may be involved in support groups, leader-in-training groups, tutoring, individual befriending, in-class school support, teacher consultation, and individual and family counselling. The program costs approximately $2000 a year per girl. In 1998, Earlscourt Girls Connection won the Children's Advocate Best Practices Award, City of Toronto.

The challenge becomes making changes to our culture and wider society that will expand girls' opportunities, support less damaging choices, and help girls lead more fulfilling lives. Above all else, it is essential to deal with marginalization and the structural inequalities of race, class, and gender.

Recall K's story (Box 6.1 on pp. 127–28). Based on this case study, consider the following questions:

- What key factors influence criminalized girls' lives?
- How might K's life chances have been different?
- What would assist young women like K make the transition from poverty, homelessness, and violence to a safe, healthy, and stable life?
- What do you think became of K?

CONCLUSION: WHO IS LISTENING TO GIRLS?

> Until our focus shifts from controlling young women to a broad-based, serious confrontation of male violence and of social iInequalities, we will be left with more and more girls suffering the inequalities of imprisonment "'for their own good." (Dean, 2005: 8–9)

We began the chapter with two quotations that reflected two related themes—justice and vulnerability. Criminalized girls comprise a vulnerable group, whose access to justice is questionable. This chapter has exposed many of the issues, problems, and potential opportunities in dealing with female youth in conflict with the law. If the YCJS and Canadian society more generally is going to better address girls and their troubles, we must listen to girls and hear their stories. Young women must play a central role in initiatives aimed at justice for girls. Girls need a voice in program design, implementation, and evaluation. A novel example of this strategy is the BC based group "Justice For Girls" (JFG). JFG is an organization created out of the reality that young women living in poverty need age-specific services that respond to conditions of violence, homelessness, and oppression, a need not met by mixed gender or adult women's groups. As a way to conclude our discussion of young female offenders, take a few minutes to check out their website at www.justiceforgirls.org.

SUMMARY

- Criminalized girls have different needs and experiences than male youth in conflict with the law. The social context and pathways related to law-breaking among female youth share some commonalities to male offending but are unique.
- Media representations of female youth crime grossly distort the nature (quality) and extent (quantity) of youth crime, especially in relation to male offending.
- The criminalized girl is constructed as "other," which has historically justified ignoring, misrepresenting, and otherwise discriminating against her.
- Processes of criminalizing girls reveal race/class/gender interconnections that must be recognized in terms of theorizing but also with respect to interventions. Sexism, racism, and class inequality figure prominently in the lives of criminalized girls.
- Attempts on the part of the YCJS to respond differently to female youth crime have failed by being paternalistic and punishing girls "for their own good." This is largely attributed to the simultaneously gendered and de-gendered nature of the system. At times the system recognizes girls' unique needs, but at other times it uses difference to justify harsher, less gender-sensitive treatment.
- Alternative ways of understanding criminalized girls *as girls* encourage a response to girls and young women that acknowledges their experiences and pays close attention to the ir voices.

DISCUSSION QUESTIONS

1. How are victimization and offending related for girls and young women?
2. Despite evidence to the contrary, why are concerns about girls' violence so pervasive and widespread today?
3. What does the phrase "justice for girls" mean?

RECOMMENDED READINGS

Chesney-Lind, M. and S. Okamoto. (2001). "Gender matters: Patterns in girls' delinquency and gender responsive programming." *Journal of Forensic Psychology Practice*, 1(3), 1–28.

Dean, A. R. (2005). "Locking Them Up to Keep Them 'Safe': Criminalized Girls in British Columbia." Vancouver, BC: Justice for Girls.

Yasmin, J. (2002). "Erasing Race: The Story of Reena Virk." In Katherine McKenna and June Larkin, Inanna, (Eds.). *Violence Against Women: New Canadian Perspectives.* Toronto, Inanna Publications, pp. 441–453.

Chapter 7

Marginalized: The Case of Aboriginal Youth

STARTING POINT

If you accept our assertion that much of the root cause of Indian peoples' disproportionate conflict with the justice system lies in their poverty and marginal position in Canadian society, then what do you think is going to happen in the next 10 or 20 years, if radical changes do not occur? (Ovide Mercredi, Manitoba Justice Inquiry, 1991).

Ovide Mercredi, former chief of the National Assembly of First Nations (1991–97), made the above statement at the Manitoba Justice Inquiry in 1991. Mercredi's long-time involvement in Aboriginal rights issues includes constitutional reform and legal and advocacy work on behalf of First Nations peoples. He is currently on the Faculty of Native Studies at Laurentian University. Mercredi uttered these words 16 years ago—so we are currently in the middle of what he referred to as "the next 10 or 20 years." Before you read this chapter, consider what comes to mind when you hear the words *poverty* and *marginal position*. Do you think of youth, who are over-represented among the poor? Do you think of Aboriginal youth specifically?

Marginality is a theme running throughout this chapter. Recall from Chapter 1 that we define marginalization as exclusion: the social inequalities that condition youth's involvement in crime. As you read the chapter we encourage you to consider the following questions:

- Where is marginalization visible?
- Why are Aboriginal youth marginalized?
- What can be done about the over-representation of Aboriginal youth in the YCJS?
- What is the role of non-Aboriginal Canadians in responding to the troubles facing Aboriginal youth, and especially criminalized youth?
- What "radical changes" are required?

LEARNING OBJECTIVES

After reading this chapter, you should be able to

- Explain how race and ethnicity are socially constructed.
- Discuss the complex and interconnected ways that race underscores our understanding of youth and crime.

- Identify how the socio-political and personal realities for Aboriginal youth are interrelated by describing the *historical* processes of colonialism and explaining the role their legacy plays in *present*-day problems in Aboriginal communities.

- Describe the nature and extent of Aboriginal youth crime in Canada.

- Outline the factors that contribute to the over-representation of Aboriginal youth in the YCJS.

- Identify alternative ways of responding to Aboriginal youth that are supportive rather than punitive.

INTRODUCTION

Youth involved in the YCJS are typically Canada's poorest and most marginalized; they face pervasive discrimination, victimization, and silencing. These young people find themselves caught up in a system that perpetuates, reinforces, and sustains established hierarchies. From the emergence of separate juvenile justice institutions to the present, racial minorities have disproportionately been on the receiving end of punishment. But different groups have historically received more harsh treatment. By the 1910s, Canada had a firmly established and widely accepted racial hierarchy (Valverde, 1991: 29). This ordering was not structured solely through skin colour, but also by degrees of "whiteness." Recall from Chapter 2 that Anglo-Celtic elite reformers believed that the Italian and Irish were not "white" in the same way as they were (Stone, 2001: 397). The Anglo-Celtic upper-middle-class professionals who inspired early juvenile justice campaigns positioned themselves in opposition to Irish and Italian immigrants and their ways of life. Juvenile justice in its infancy was influenced by, and helped to create and uphold, a common-sense racial logic that associated whiteness with the "clean and the good, the pure and the pleasing" (Jackson 2000: 641). This meant purging the nation of anti-social or/and "degenerative" influences, which, reformers argued, were predominantly concentrated in the immigrant working-class.

Today, it is primarily the indigenous "other"—Aboriginal people, First Nations, Natives, and minorities such as Blacks and Hispanics—that has replaced Irish and Italians as the most punishable or most subject to youth justice processing. In the 2001 census, 1.3 million Canadians reported some Aboriginal ancestry, making up 3.3% of the country's population (Statistics Canada, 2001). Aboriginal youth are not a homogeneous group, but include diverse cultural identities such as Cree, Ojibway, Mohawk, Inuit, and Métis, to name a few. Tragically, as this chapter will illustrate, we are witness to devastating consequences for another generation of young people. Intolerance for the "other" is built into the Canadian YCJS. Nevertheless, until recently, government and police officials abdicated responsibility for historical and contemporary injustices (Wortley and Tanner, 2003). Besides, they claimed, most minorities held state officials in esteem and were confident that the police and courts were egalitarian. This (now anachronistic) bubble has been popped. Subsequent research has produced ample evidence of the pervasiveness of discrimination in the CJS and the YCJS. If any doubts remained, the 1994 Commission on Systemic Racism in the Ontario Criminal Justice System put them to bed. Among the commission's findings were that three out of four black Torontonians were certain that the police treat blacks worse than they do whites. Furthermore, 56% of white respondents indicated that they thought visible minorities were treated worse by the police—a telling statistic indeed (Wortley and Tanner, 2003; Wortley, 1996). The long and tragic history of systemic discrimination is more pronounced for Aboriginal peoples than any other group in Canada, and it has been central to policy and practice since confederation. Accordingly, while we acknowledge that other minority groups are also disenfranchised and subject to harsh treatment by the YCJS, we use Aboriginal youth as our focal point in this chapter.

The chapter is organized as follows. First, we outline key concepts and make a case for our discussion of Aboriginal young offenders. Next, we explore the historical underpinnings of contemporary youth justice practices as they relate to Aboriginal young offenders. This discussion is followed by an examination of the over-representation of Aboriginal youth in the YCJS. We explore the various ways in which Aboriginal youth are made "other." This sets the stage for a brief outline of other disadvantaged groups. Finally, we explore promising alternatives that attempt to do more than manage over-representation and can potentially offer means to social justice for Aboriginal youth—strategies that support rather than punish.

CONCEPTUALIZING RACE/ETHNICITY AND ABORIGINAL YOUTH

The terms race and ethnicity are often misused. *Race* refers to a group of people who share observable physical traits. In this case, we can speak of Chinese or Aboriginal people as distinct racial groups. *Ethnicity* refers to identity or the means by which a group of people distinguish themselves. Often race is presumed to be biological, because its origin is usually related to something unchangeable like skin colour, while ethnicity is deemed cultural. However, both categories are social constructions. It is not inevitable or natural that we recognize things like skin pigment, eye colour, tradition, or language as socially important. In Canadian society, racial hierarchies and ethnic divisions structure our lives in ways that *seem* more pronounced for groups marginalized by their race or ethnicity. What often disappears from view is that the other side of marginalization is **privilege**, or the way that racial hierarchies and ethnic divisions structure the lives of dominant groups to their benefit. Racial and ethnic distinctions are often produced and maintained by power differentials between dominant racialized and ethnic groups and subordinate ones. In a multitude of ways, Aboriginal peoples are marginalized from dominant social institutions—the exception being carceral ones—and are the quintessential "other" in Canadian society.

Why do we cast a spotlight on Aboriginal youth? It is not because Aboriginal youth are particularly unique in the offences they commit. In contrast to media images of violent gun-toting gang members, the most common offences for Aboriginal youth are theft under $5000, break and enter, and wilful damage (Shkilnyk, 1985: 30). Thus, the typical "bad kid" locked up is a 16-year-old property offender. Nor do we give special attention to Aboriginal youth because of their **over-representation** at all levels of the YCJS (i.e., they are disproportionately represented in arrests, convictions, and custody) (Department of Justice, 1991; LaPrairie, 1983; LaPrairie and Griffiths, 1982; Morin, 1990; Royal Commission on Aboriginal Peoples, 1993). Rather, the case of Aboriginal youth reveals important structural conditions and socio-psychological factors that must be considered if we are to understand how race/ethnicity informs and underlies the YCJS. Aboriginal youth are arguably the most disadvantaged, especially when one takes into account race, class, and gender dimensions. Imagine the following prospects:

- facing greater infant mortality and lower life expectancy rates
- having poorer health, higher incidences of preventable diseases and disabilities
- having a suicide rate that is approximately five to six times higher than other youth, and has been estimated as between 3–40 times the national average
- being faced with rampant substance abuse in your community
- being victimized by physical and/or sexual abuse
- being at least twice as likely to end up poor
- having a better chance of going to jail than graduating high school
- being significantly over-represented among youth prison populations

See Table 7.1 for more detailed information.

Table 7.1 Imagine the Prospects Examined

For Aboriginal peoples . . .

Higher infant mortality rate and lower life expectancy	■ Infant mortality rate (number of deaths per 1000 live births) dropped from 23.7 in 1980 to 12.3 in 1991 and to 6.4 in 2000, but remains higher than the overall Canadian rate of 5.2 (Health Canada, 2004).
	■ The average life expectancy at birth for Canadians increased from 77.8 in 1991 to 79.7 years in 2002 (82.1 for women and 77.2 for men). However, for Aboriginal men during the same period, life expectancy rose from 66.9 to 70.4 and for women from 74 to 75.5 (Government of Canada, Report of the President of the Treasury Board, 2005)
	■ Life expectancy was 66.9 (compared to 74.6) in 1991 and 74 for Aboriginal women (compared to 80.9) (Royal Commission on Aboriginal Peoples, 1994).
	■ The death rate (annual number of deaths for the total population) for Aboriginal peoples was 4.6 in 1996, compared to 7.2 for Canada (largely higher due to higher average age of Canadian population and younger age of Aboriginal peoples) (Elgersma, 2001, First Nations and Northern Statistics). However, for persons between 25 and 44, the death rate is five times higher for Aboriginal peoples. For men, the average age at death is 25 years younger than for non-Aboriginal men, and for women, it is 28 years younger (Hull, 1987: 37).

Poorer health, higher incidences of preventable diseases and disabilities than non-Aboriginal Canadians	■ 6.6 times greater incidence of tuberculosis, three times as likely to be diabetic, and two times as likely to report a long-term disability (MSB, Health Canada). ■ A greater likelihood of hearing, sight and speech difficulties (Stats Can, 1994). ■ Off-reserve Aboriginal population is 1.5 times more likely to experience a major depressive episode; 1.5 times more likely to report chronic condition like diabetes and high blood pressure; 1.5 times more likely to report fair or poor health (Tjepkema, Statistics Canada, 2002).
Over-represented among Fetal Alcohol Spectrum Disorder diagnoses	■ A greater likelihood of suffering from fetal alcohol spectrum disorder (FASD), one of the most common preventable forms of brain damage to infants in the Western world.[1] FASD is a non-diagnostic umbrella construct first introduced in 1973, which covers a range of related birth defects (craniofacial abnormality, growth deficiency, and central nervous system dysfunction) that result from prenatal exposure to alcohol. The present estimate of FASD is 1.9 cases per 1000, with a higher prevalence among Aboriginal groups.[2] On one reserve, 190 cases per 1000 births (Robinson et al., 1992)
Higher suicide rate	■ Suicide rates are five to seven times higher for First Nations youth than for non-Aboriginal youth. ■ Suicide rates among Inuit youth are among the highest in the world, at 11 times the national average (www.hc-sc.gc.ca/fnih-spni/promotion/suicide/index_e.html)
Rampant substance abuse	■ 62% of Aboriginal peoples aged 15 and over perceive alcohol abuse as a problem in their community; 48% say drug abuse is an issue (Aboriginal Peoples Survey, Statistics Canada, 1991). ■ Among youth, solvent abuse is particularly troubling, with 22% of Aboriginal youth who report using solvents indicating they are chronic users (Health Canada, 2000).
Disproportionately victimized by physical and sexual abuse	■ 25% of Aboriginal women reported having been assaulted by a current or ex-spouse in the five years prior to the 1999 General

Social Survey, compared to 8% of non-Aboriginal women.

■ The Thompson Crisis Centre found that while one in 10 women in Canada is abused by her partner, for Aboriginal women the figure is closer to one in three (Thompson Crisis Centre, 1988.)

■ The Ontario Native Women's Association survey in 1989 found that 80% of Aboriginal women had personally experienced family violence (Ontario Native Women's Association, 1989).

At least twice as likely to live in poverty

■ Aboriginal peoples in urban areas were more than twice as likely to live in poverty as non-Aboriginal people (Urban Poverty in Canada, CCSD, 2000).

■ 52.1% of all Aboriginal children were poor and four times more likely to be hungry (UN Special Session on Children, 2002; Statistics Canada, 1996).

Disproportionately undereducated and underemployed

■ Have a better chance of going to jail than graduating high school (First Nations Child and Family Caring Society of Canada, 2003).

Over-represented in the CJS and YCJS

■ Almost 30% of youth in detention across Canada were Aboriginal in 2006.

■ In the Prairies, the situation is most pervasive—58% of imprisoned youth aged 20 and younger are Aboriginal (Annual Report of the Correctional Investigator, 2006).

[1] A recent literature review placed the overall incidence rate for FAS between 0.05 to 2 per 1000 births in the United States (May and Gossage, 2001). Bray and Anderson's (1989) review of the epidemiology of FAS among Canadian native peoples illustrates high incidence rates through several studies.

[2] Diagnostic terms such as Fetal Alcohol Syndrome (FAS), Alcohol Related Birth Defects (ARBR) and Partial Fetal Alcohol Syndrome (PFAS) are clinically used.

Consider these circumstances and you will have some idea of the plight of many Aboriginal youth in Canada today. If you are reading this textbook and are of Aboriginal descent, you know that the odds of there being many other like-situated students in your class are slim. Given these predominantly harsh realities, the image of aimless Aboriginal youth is transfixed in the public imagination. This view reflects common stereotypes that hold Aboriginal youth as "poor," "lazy," "FAS," "suicidal" and/or "violent," and locate their problems at the individual level (see Box 7.1 on pp. 151–52). The aforementioned problems are more of a reflection of depressed social conditions and a failure of Canadian society to provide alternatives (Law Commission of Canada, National Association of Friendships Centres, 1999: 65). Of course this dismal picture does not reflect the reality of life for all youth of Aboriginal origin. As we will see later in the chapter, beside the troubles facing Aboriginal youth are triumphs—amazing stories of resiliency that give much encouragement and hope for the next generation.

HISTORICAL CONTEXT/CONTEMPORARY IMPLICATIONS

To make sense of the current situation facing Aboriginal peoples in Canada and to understand Aboriginal youth involvement in crime, we need to examine the historical context of colonialism or **colonization**. Colonization is the "intentional, long-term process of replacing the traditional, self-determinant lifestyle and culture of indigenous people with a dependent, subordinate status" (Yerbury and Griffiths, 1991: 321). Through practices of **assimilation**, the Canadian government's formal policy with respect to Aboriginal people, which sought to incorporate Aboriginal peoples into the body politic, forced state dependency, **systemic racism**, and societal prejudice, and discrimination emerged. In short, this legacy has led to cultural and social dislocation whereby the *social adjustment problems* of Aboriginal youth—including crime and delinquency—can be linked to their current *social, economic, and political circumstances* (see Table 7.2 on p. 153).

Box 7.1

Genetics Meets the Social: Fetal Exposure to Alcohol and Aboriginal Youth

The relationship between youth crime and fetal alcohol spectrum disorder (FASD, previously known as fetal alcohol syndrome) has been the subject of increased attention and controversy, especially as it relates to Aboriginal young offenders. The disorder can affect any developing fetus exposed to alcohol during pregnancy, but in Canada there is some indication of over-representation of Aboriginal people with FASD. Chartrand and Forbes-Chilibeck (2003) calculated that in Canada, 3177 infants with FASD have been born since July 1, 1997. Chartrand and Forbes-Chilibeck (2002) studied offenders in the justice system, identifying 39 cases of a sentenced offender with a diagnosis of FASD or suspected FASD. Twenty-five of 39 cases were confirmed to be Aboriginal offenders (four non-Aboriginal and 10 unknown). Other research has reported that individuals with FASD are over-represented among Aboriginal peoples— at a rate as high as 10 times (Phillips, 1999).

Individuals with FASD are thought to be at an increased risk of getting into trouble with the law. Streissguth et al. (1996) studied 415 individuals with FASD in British Columbia. Of those aged 12 and over, 60% had been in

conflict with the law. Affected youth will experience a host of difficulties, which have recently begun to be understood as equivalent to a mental disorder that puts them at greater risk of committing crime. For this reason, some argue that criminalized youth with FASD deserve treatment rather than punishment. The words of Judge Trueman in *R. v. C.J.M.* are illustrative of the frustration within the court system as to what to do:

> In all cases of brain injury, however caused, permanent or otherwise, there exists the proven advantage of early intervention, to maximize social skills and shape behaviour. To incarcerate an individual in a prison setting that fails to recognize FAS, and fails to accommodate those with the disability, is to further the development of socially maladaptive behaviours that occur from forcing those with compromised mental functions to respond daily in a hostile environment. This is not only detrimental to them, but to the rest of society when they are ultimately released. (para. 82, *R. v. C.J.M.*, 2000, as cited in Chartrand and McKay, 2006: 34)

Research also demonstrates that individuals with FASD are highly vulnerable to victimization. Yet as Chartrand and McKay (2006: 34) point out, "[t]here is *no* research that examines the extent of victimization of Aboriginal people with

FASD. This is a serious research gap given the extent of victimization by those most vulnerable in Aboriginal communities and the extent of this disability in the Aboriginal community."

In terms of symptoms, the social and behavioural characteristics of individuals with FASD almost mirror those found in children who witness violence in the family.

There are also a host of problems associated with FASD: for infants—primary disabilities, including irritability, tremors, weak suck, problems eating and sleeping, poor motor control; for preschoolers—hyperactivity, attention problems, poor motor coordination, language problems; for school age children—hyperactivity, attention deficits, learning disabilities, cognitive difficulties, language problems, poor impulse control; for adolescents—memory impairments, problems with judgment, being unfocused and distracted, problems learning from experience, mental health problems, trouble with the law (see Streissguth and Kanter, 1997). It is believed that common risks that increase secondary disabilities include a poor home environment, abuse and neglect, and familial upheaval. As adolescents, these problems can be exacerbated.

Diagnosis of FASD is very difficult. No standardized diagnostic approach has been accepted in the medical community. "False diagnosis" and the consequent over-diagnosis of FASD among Aboriginal youth, especially given the prevalence of domestic violence in Aboriginal communities and the commonalities in symptoms between FASD offenders and those who have experienced or been exposed to violence, is a potential danger (Tait, 2002). Reviews of case law have found abuse as a child to be a common factor among those diagnosed with FASD or suspected of it (Chartrand and Forbes-Chilibeck, 2002).

How is this "genetic" problem a matter of social forces? What are the potential implications of FASD becoming another explanation for the over-representation of Aboriginal people in the criminal justice system? How should the YCJS handle criminalized youth affected by FASD?

Source: Department of Justice Canada. Chartrand, Larry & Celeste McKay (2006). "Fetal Alcohol Spectrum Disorder (FASD)." *A Review of Research on Criminal Victimization and First Nations, Métis and Inuit Peoples, 1990 to 2001*. Reproduced with the permission of the Minister of Public Works and Government Services Canada, 2007.

We cannot understand the offending patterns or criminalization of Aboriginal youth without directly looking at the situation of Aboriginal people as a group within the dominant non-Aboriginal Canadian society. Aboriginal people are much more likely than non-Aboriginal Canadians to find themselves isolated in welfare ghettos (on and off reserves) with a status of social, political, and economic marginality. LaPrairie (1988: 164) explains:

> The available research clearly shows that in relation to mainstream society aboriginal society has been relegated to a status of socio-economic marginality. Aboriginal communities have weak or non-existent economies, poorly developed utility structures, large number of dependent children and single parents, few opportunities to work, limited recreational and social service resources and high rates of alcohol and drug abuse.

Table 7.2 on p. 153 provides evidence of the social exclusion, marginality, and intolerance faced by Aboriginal peoples generally, and Aboriginal youth in particular.

Not only are Aboriginal youth more likely to be offenders, but they are also disproportionately victims, especially of violent crimes. Aboriginal women and children are the most vulnerable. Another form of victimization is dependency. Aboriginal peoples have a higher rate of state dependency than any other group in Canada. It is no wonder that Aboriginal youth in contact with the child-welfare system have a higher probability of ending up in the YCJS than any other group. Along with racism, Aboriginal youth face additional challenges related to social exclusion and innumerable barriers to improving their life chances. Given their socio-political reality, Aboriginal youth are more vulnerable to justice processing and suffer harsher effects than non-Aboriginal youth. For example, LaPrairie (1997) argues that geographic isolation leads to a poor quality of social services and limited access to justice services. Many northern and remote Aboriginal communities are overlooked, ignored, and excluded. This further perpetuates socio-economic

Table 7.2 Individual and Social Context of Aboriginal Youth Delinquency

Personal Reality/Individual Context	Socio-Political Realities/Social Context
child-welfare involvement	historical legacy of colonialism
poor, substandard living conditions	state dependency
sexual and physical abuse	poverty
suicide attempts	racism
alcohol and drug use/abuse	urban population
individual and systemic discrimination	birth rate and mortality rate
poor health	health status
poor educational attainment	education and unemployment
low employment rate	over-representation in YCJS as victims and offenders
psycho-social: stress, anger, frustration, desperation, hopelessness	social disorganization and community breakdown
= increased vulnerability	**= social exclusion and marginalization**

marginality, which is visible in fewer educational and employment opportunities or community-based activities for young people and adults on reserves and in isolated communities. Environmental factors like geographic isolation, however, reflect a wider problem: structural inequalities related to race, class, and gender. In turn, these inequalities create, reinforce, and sustain imbalances between Aboriginal youth and non-Aboriginal youth such as over-representation in the YCJS and systemic discrimination. For example, law makes illegal those acts that are directly related to poverty, such as vagrancy, public intoxication, and stealing. Subsequently, the most economically marginalized—those who cannot pay fines and are unable to post bail—are held in custody. Moreover, Aboriginal young people lack the means to fight the oppressive conditions imposed on them. The irony is that non-custodial sentences assume the availability of supportive services and resources, which are conspicuously absent in many Aboriginal communities and neighbourhoods. Conditions have been created in many Aboriginal communities such that young people respond in deviant and criminal ways.

Marginalization manifests itself in various ways, including poverty, high rates of unemployment, suicide, alcohol abuse, illness, etc. Aboriginal communities are also more vulnerable to family violence, sexual abuse, and the breakdown of social relations; largely attributed to a history of colonization and forced dependency (Boe, 2002). Chief Dennis Shorting gave the following statement to the Manitoba Justice Inquiry:

> So we find ourselves in the fertile breeding grounds of crime: high unemployment, lack of educational opportunities, substandard housing, inadequate health care, tradition, hunting, fishing and trapping rights being violated, a shortage of recreation facilities, and being subject to the law and which many times we don't understand, laws which do not fit with our culture, values and traditions. (Chief Dennis Shorting, Little Saskatchewan Band, Aboriginal Justice Inquiry of Manitoba, 1991)

Poverty among urban Aboriginal youth is unrivalled. While almost 25% of children in Canada live in poverty, 52.1% of Aboriginal children do (Canadian Council on Social Development, 2003). In a regional investigation of indigenous over-representation in Canadian corrections, Carol LaPrairie (2002) found that while demographic trends and history contribute, poverty is an almost insurmountable precursor. LaPrairie (2002: 202) claims that "if one is aboriginal and living in a city, the degree of advantage or disadvantage one experiences relates to the geographic location of that city. But it is not necessarily living on or off reserve, thereby increasing one's vulnerability to involvement in the criminal justice system, that is the real issue." Rather, La Prairie argues, the key concern is the "concentration of poor, single parent and poorly educated aboriginal people in the inner core of their large cities" (La Prairie, 2002: 202).

Aboriginal people are less likely to be employed (see Figure 7.1 for employment patterns). Unemployment is much greater for Aboriginal peoples, especially for urban Aboriginal youth aged 15–24, who are twice as likely as their non-Aboriginal counterparts to be unemployed (Anderson, 2003). In 1996, almost one in four Aboriginal people (defined as labour force participants actively searching for work) were unemployed. The figure was higher for on-reserve Aboriginals (29%). This was almost three times the national rate of 10% (Statistics Canada, 1999a). The Canadian Council on Social Development study of urban poverty found that in 1995, Aboriginal people living in cities were more than twice as likely to live in poverty as non-Aboriginal people (Lee and Engler, 2000). In major western cities, more than four times as many Aboriginal people as other citizens live below the poverty line (Indian and Northern Affairs Canada, 2001). In 2000, the median income for Aboriginal individuals was $13 593, up slightly from $12 010 in 1995. Compare this to the median income for non-Aboriginal Canadians, which climbed from $20 844 in 1996 to $22 431 in 2001 (Statistics Canada, 1996 census and 2001 census). Low incomes are most problematic in major urban areas. In Saskatoon,

Figure 7.1 Employed Aboriginal and Non-Aboriginal People

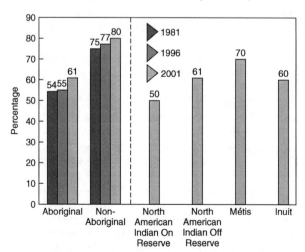

Source: Canada's Performance 2004, http://www.tbs-sct.gc.ca/report/govrev/04/cp-rc5_e.aps, Treasury Board of Canada Secretariat, 2004. Reproduced with permission of the Minister of Public Works and Government Services, 2007.

51%, in Regina, 48%, and in Winnipeg, 46% of Aboriginal people had incomes below
$10 000 in 1995 (Statistics Canada, 1999a).

Conditions of life both on and off reserve remain poor. Although 2% more *people* on-
reserve lived in inadequate housing in 2001 (37%) than in 1996 (35%), the percentage
of *households* living in unsuitable dwellings decreased in 2001 (from 27% in 1996 to 22%)
(Canada Mortgage and Housing Corporation, 2004). To some degree, off-reserve housing
improved between 1996 and 2001, such that about 25% of Aboriginal households off-
reserve were in core housing need, which is down from almost 32% in 1996 (Canada
Mortgage and Housing Corporation, 2004).

Education can provide a means of escape from appalling social conditions. The percentage of students remaining in school to grade 12 is increasing (from 31% in 1981–82 to
71% in 1996–97), but education for Aboriginal people lags behind other Canadians.
According to "Our Children: Keepers of the Sacred Knowledge" (Department of Indian
Affairs and Northern Development, 2002), 7 out of 10 Aboriginal youth will drop out of
school (see Figure 7.2). The situation is particularly troubling at the post-secondary level,
where just 3% of Aboriginal people aged 15 and over had a university degree in 1996, compared to 13% of the non-Aboriginal population (Statistics Canada, 1999a). According to
the Canada West Foundation (2003), the unemployment rate for Aboriginal people without an education (i.e., less than high school) is over 25%, but with an education (i.e., a
university degree) it drops to 5%. Yet compared to 53.4% of non-Aboriginal youth (up
from 33% in 1996), only 38% of Aboriginal youth have some post-secondary education

Figure 7.2 Educational Attainment

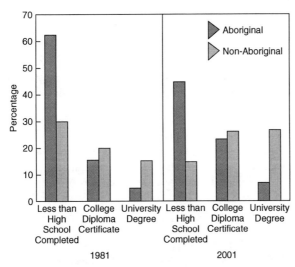

Note (1): Some of the improvement in educational attainment between 1981 and 2001 may be attributed to
some people changing their identity on their census forms from non-Aboriginal to Aboriginal, and already
having a high level of education.
(2) For the category "Less than High School Completed," the population age group is 20–24 years. For the
categories "College Diploma Certificate" and "University Degree," the population age group is 25–34.

Source: Canada's Performance 2004, http://www.tbs-sct.gc.ca/report/govrev/04/cp-rc5_e.aps, Treasury Board of Canada Secretariat,
2004. Reproduced with permission of the Minister of Public Works and Government Services, 2007.

(Canada West Foundation, 2003). Given that post-secondary education is essential to improving the economic and social outcome of Aboriginal youth, the link between education and employment is concerning (Chalifoux and Johnson, 2003). Higher education may be a means by which Aboriginal youth can combat historic social and economic exclusion and their silence as decision-makers in matters that affect them.

Despite these circumstances, there was no research on Aboriginal delinquency in Canada before 1981. In the first study of its kind, LaPrairie and Griffiths (1982) made four main claims:

1. There are no major differences in the offences committed by Aboriginal youth and non-Aboriginal youth.
2. Aboriginal youth were over-represented as offenders in the YCJS and in custody.
3. Aboriginal conflict with the law occurred at younger ages than for non-Aboriginals.
4. Structural differences in terms of income, education, and family background between Aboriginal and non-Aboriginal groups were striking and still hold true.

Today there is a growing body of literature on Aboriginal peoples generally and Aboriginal young offenders in particular. Nevertheless, a shortage of primary data remains, specifically regarding Aboriginal victimization. To date no comprehensive youth survey of Aboriginal victimization has been conducted.

As we will see, the failure of the YCJS to attend to the needs and circumstances of Aboriginal youth is not merely about a lack of recognition of cultural difference, to be fixed with cultural awareness training and anti-discrimination workshops. It is not simply about gaps in understanding, a gulf that can be filled with better communication between Aboriginal and white culture. It is most directly related to issues of power, privilege/marginalization, and social inclusion/exclusion. Disadvantages such as being under-educated, unemployed, and living in poverty make Aboriginal youth more vulnerable to involvement in crime. The 1996 Royal Commission on Aboriginal Peoples linked poor educational attainment, unemployment, and low income to subsequent criminal activity (Royal Commission on Aboriginal Peoples: Bridging the Cultural Divide: A Report on Aboriginal People and Criminal Justice in Canada, 1996).

Aboriginal social, economic, and political circumstances provide a context for understanding the high rates of involvement of Aboriginal youth in the child-welfare and youth justice systems. In contrast to other Canadian children, Aboriginal children and youth are much more highly represented in the child-welfare system. The relationship between child-welfare involvement and criminal justice requires careful attention. In 1996–97, 4% of First Nations children were in the custody of Child and Family Service agencies (McDonald and Ladd, 2000). The Department of Indian Affairs and Northern Development confirms that between 1995 and 2001, the number of registered Indian children who entered care rose by 71.2% (McKenzie, 2002). Residential schools have closed and various Reports and Commissions into the state of Aboriginal peoples in Canada have been conducted, yet the numbers of Aboriginal youth in the state's care continue to rise. The First Nations Child and Family Society (2003) estimates that between 22 500 and 28 000 Aboriginal children are currently in the child-welfare system—three times the enrolment figures of residential schools in the 1940s (United Nations Committee on the Rights of the Children, Non-Discrimination and Diversity, First Nations Child and Family Caring Society of Canada, 2003; Child Welfare League of Canada, 2003). Notably, almost

40% of the Aboriginal youth detained in facilities across Canada in June/July 2004 had some involvement with child protection agencies (Latimer and Casey Foss, 2004).

Historical and contemporary inequities have left Aboriginal children without much needed supports and services. According to a witness from the Urban Native Youth Association, the lives of Aboriginal youth "are profoundly influenced by both historical injustices and current inequities. Issues facing youth are rooted in a history of colonization, dislocation from their traditional territories, communities and cultural traditions, and the inter-generational impacts of the **residential school system**" (Chalifoux and Johnson, 2003: 2).

Aboriginal peoples have been historically and continuously subjected to intrusive and invasive state control aimed at reform, assimilation, and subjugation (Anderson 1999, Hogeveen 1999). Early encounters with indigenous people saw the Euro-Canadian state take away native land title to make way for white settlement and capitalist expansion. The tools of colonialism that the Canadian state employed to regulate Aboriginal men, women, and children—and establish the Anglo vision of the country's founders—included the North-West Mounted Police (the forerunner of the RCMP), laws, reserves, a pass system, forced adoption into white families, and the residential school system. Government officials and religious authorities removed Aboriginal children from their families and sent them away to be "civilized" in residential schools from the early 1800s through the 1960s. Children were forbidden to speak their traditional languages or practice traditions and were taught to disavow their spiritual beliefs (Bull, 1991; Haig-Brown, 1998). Emotional, psychological, physical, and sexual abuses suffered by hundreds of children have left inter-generational effects, not the least of which is the disintegration of familial relationships. With the closure of residential schools and many Aboriginal people living off-reserve, institutions of detention are now at the front lines of controlling the indigenous "other." As Hogeveen (2007a:217) has argued

> Penal practices are applied to Aboriginal people with special diligence and severity. Ceaselessly denied entry into Euro-Canadian institutional life, facilities that deliver unpleasantness being the obvious exception, driven back to the margins of society with tremendous zeal, the state has pushed increasing numbers of native youth through the justice process to the point that it is now, I think, possible to talk about the criminalization of indigenousness.

When there is a breakdown in social cohesion, leadership structures, and internal social controls that were once maintained by peace and community organization, **social disorganization** results. Shaw and McKay (1942) referred to areas, especially those in transition characterized by urban decay, poverty, high crime rates and a high dependency on social welfare as "socially disorganized." In a socially disorganized community, the social controls to prevent delinquency are absent (e.g., there is minimal parental control) and there are many more opportunities to engage in delinquency than there are to find gainful employment. As we will see, social-structural deprivation is directly related to psycho-social realities of self-worth and emotional well-being. The personal welfare of individuals in socially disorganized communities and impoverished neighbourhoods is compromised at best, and in jeopardy at worst. Deviant and criminal activity is more common in areas of social disorganization simply because inhabitants have little to lose. Crime can become a means of survival in, or escape from, the harsh realities of life. A prime example is the downtown core and North End of Winnipeg, Manitoba, which are heavily populated by poor, disenfranchised Aboriginal youth, many of whom are affected by and involved in prostitution, gang activity, drugs, and violence in their communities.

UNDERSTANDING OVER-REPRESENTATION OF ABORIGINAL YOUTH

Clearly, no group has been touched by Canada's appetite for youth incarceration more than Aboriginal youth. Government reports and investigations consistently demonstrate a gross *over*-representation of Aboriginal youth at the most punitive end of the system (Royal Commission on Aboriginal Peoples, 1993 and 1996). Conversely, Aboriginal people are *under*-represented as professionals in the YCJS.

A Canadian Bar Association report suitably titled "Locking Up Natives in Canada" put the dismal reality this way: a 16-year-old Aboriginal male has a 70% chance of serving at least one prison stint before turning 25. The report explains, "[p]rison has become for young native men, the promise of a just society which high school and college represents for the rest of us" (Jackson 1989: 216). Situated in the context of the historical assimilation policies of the Canadian state, centres of detention are the "contemporary equivalent of what the Indian residential school represented for their parents" (Jackson 1989: 216). Consequently, as more Aboriginal youth go into and out of custody, the Euro-Canadian social order that treats them as "other" is left unquestioned, and the group remains separate and unequal.

Aboriginal youth, incarcerated at a rate of 64.5 per 10 000, are vastly over-represented in the YCJS compared to non-Aboriginal youth, whose rate of incarceration is 8.2 per 10 000 (Latimer and Casey Foss, 2004). Canada's overall incarceration rate is 11.5 per 10 000, and Aboriginal youth are eight times more likely to be sent to custody than non-Aboriginal youth (Latimer and Casey Foss, 2004).

Although Aboriginal youth accounted for 5% of the total youth population in 1999, they occupied 24% of the beds in detention centres across the country. By 2004, this number had climbed to 33%. More tragic is the situation confronting indigenous youth in Canada's Prairie provinces, where indigenous youth were 30 times more likely to be detained in Saskatchewan and almost 20% more likely to be detained in Manitoba than their counterparts. In Saskatchewan and Manitoba, three-quarters of youth sentenced to custody were identified as Aboriginal, though they make up less than 10% of the youth population (Statistics Canada, 2000).

Peter Carrington and Jennifer Schulenburg (2004) argue that indigenous adolescents are 20% more likely to be charged when apprehended than non-Aboriginal youth. Moreover, Aboriginal youth are more likely to be denied bail, to spend more time in pre-trial detention, and to be charged with multiple offences (often for administrative violations) (Carrington and Schulenberg, 2004). They are also less likely to have legal representation in court proceedings (Roberts and Melchers, 2003; Statistics Canada, 2000; Schissel, 1993). Jeff Latimer and Lara Casey Foss (2005) found that Aboriginal youth disproportionately receive longer custodial sentences, regardless of criminal history or offence severity (Latimer and Casey Foss, 2005). For example, the median stay for an Aboriginal young person in custody is 212 days versus 182 for non-Aboriginal youth (Latimer and Casey Foss, 2004).

The experience of an Aboriginal young person in the YCJS differs starkly from that of non-Aboriginal youth. According to the Manitoba Justice Inquiry Implementation Commission (1999), compared to non-Aboriginal young people, Aboriginal youth

■ have more charges laid against them

■ are less likely to benefit from legal representation

■ are more often detained before trial

■ are detained for longer periods

■ are more likely to be denied bail

■ experience longer delays before cases are disposed

■ are more likely to be sentenced to custody

■ serve longer sentences

In addition, Aboriginal youth's involvement in the YCJS tends to occur at an earlier age than for other youth (LaPrairie, 1983: 343). These circumstances testify to the fact that the YCJS treats Aboriginal offenders differently than non-Aboriginal youth. The Canadian Research Institution for Law and the Family summarizes the situation this way:

> It is apparent that for these youths the extensive use of police, courts, and a corrections system operated and controlled by white society, has been a failure. It has failed to meet the special needs of native young offenders, many of whom continue to commit further offences after their involvement in the system. The system has also failed to meet the needs of native communities: first, by failing to give them responsibility for and involvement in helping their youth; and second, by failing to rehabilitate young offenders, it has also failed to protect their communities from recurrent patterns of offences. (Canadian Research Institution for Law and the Family, 1990: 1)

The YCJS is also more likely to interfere with or disrupt the lives of Aboriginal youth (Manitoba Justice Inquiry, 1991). For example, without support programs and appropriate facilities in their own communities, many Aboriginal adolescents are removed from their families and homes in reserve and/or remote communities for pre-trial detention or custody hundreds of kilometres away. This means that they may not have anyone from their family or community present in court.

In the current neo-liberal context of dismantling the social welfare system, poverty is growing among indigenous peoples—especially children. Not only are Aboriginal people highly over-represented among the homeless population, they are also more likely to be living in urban poverty and to inhabit overcrowded living quarters than the general Canadian population (Canadian Council on Social Development, 2003). According to Cindy Blackstock (2003), an Aboriginal activist, although Canada consistently ranks high on the United Nations' Human Development Index (HDI)—which measures poverty, literacy, education, and life expectancy—if only Canada's indigenous peoples are considered and not the rest of the population, Canada drops to 78th. The HDI has become the standardized means of measuring overall well-being and child welfare through three basic categories:

■ long and healthy life as indicated by life expectancy at birth

■ knowledge as measured by adult literacy rate

■ standard of living, derived from gross domestic product per capita

Compared to the rest of the world, "Canadians" are well-situated. Hidden among facts and figures is a long, silent, oppressed, and subjugated population—a group "other" to the social fabric of Canada. Is colonialism a long-forgotten, embarrassing period in Canada's past, or does it continue to rear its ugly head?

Several authors attribute the over-representation of indigenous peoples in prisons, in part, to population demographics; that is, the growth of this population has outpaced non-Aboriginal growth (Boe, 2002). While overall population growth in Canada has declined for most groups, Aboriginal people are currently experiencing a "baby boom," as evidenced by their relatively high birth rate (2.7 children per woman versus 1.6 for non-Aboriginals) (Boe, 2002). Demographically speaking, Aboriginal peoples are the youngest and fastest growing population group in Canada.

As of 2001, the median age of the Aboriginal population was 23.5 years (compared to 38 for the median Canadian), meaning that half of Aboriginal peoples were young adults, youth, or children (Chalifoux and Johnson, 2003; Statistics Canada, Children and Youth in Canada, 2001: 3). Given that almost 50% of the registered population is under age 25, the problems facing Aboriginal youth are particularly acute (Royal Commission, Department of Indian Affairs, 1995). Moreover, children 14 and under comprise 33% of the Aboriginal population, compared to just 19% for non-indigenous peoples (Chalifoux and Johnson, 2003). Stated differently, in 1995, almost 20% of the Aboriginal population was aged 15–24 years, compared to 13% of the non-Aboriginal population (Statistics Canada, 1999a). Like the non-Aboriginal population of the 1960s and 1970s, the indigenous population is much younger and at an age where their risk for committing crime is at its peak. That is, there are greater numbers of Aboriginal people in high-risk age categories—typically the population between the ages of 14 and 32 accounts for the bulk of crime reported to police each year (Boe, 2002).

The socio-economic reality of Aboriginal youth should be of concern to more than Aboriginal people, as it will shape the future of the country in very dramatic ways. Canada's overall rate of child poverty is an abysmal 15.6%, which means one in six children are poor (a rate higher than in 1989, when the House of Commons declared that by 2000 child poverty in Canada would be eliminated). Those most dramatically affected and who have the most to lose from the Canadian government's failed promise are Aboriginal children, who predominantly live in conditions similar to those in the developing world (Rae, 2003). As the gap between rich and poor continues to expand, the effects are more visible in urban centres like Vancouver, Regina, Winnipeg, and Toronto. The Canadian Council on Social Development (2003) estimates that 80% of Aboriginal children under six years of age in Canadian cities live in poverty. Aboriginal children are more likely to be members of one-parent families. For example, in Winnipeg, Regina, and Saskatoon, almost half of all Aboriginal children live with a single parent, who as a group are more likely to be poor (Statistics Canada, 1999a).

Recent years have witnessed a demographic shift of another kind involving Aboriginal peoples. Aboriginal peoples live in cities, which generates new discursive images, necessitates new research frameworks, and begs policy changes (Newhouse and Peters, 2003). Whereas in 1951 only 6.7% of the Aboriginal population called urban centres home, by 2001 this number had increased to 49% (Graham and Peters, 2002; Hanselmann, 2001, 2003). A quarter of urban Aboriginal peoples reside in ten cities, with the largest concentrations in Winnipeg and Saskatoon. For example, 56 000 Aboriginal people make up 8% of Winnipeg's population (Chalifoux and Johnson, 2003).

The Aboriginal population as a group is more mobile, which has several implications, including cultural isolation, family instability and dissolution, a high proportion of female one-parent families, economic marginalization and low incomes, high victimization and crime rates, and difficulty accessing vital programs and services (Chalifoux and Johnson, 2003). As the urbanization trend among Aboriginal peoples continues, a growing concentration of the young Aboriginal population will live in the core of larger cities (Boe, 2002). LaPrairie (1995) identified those who live in the inner core of large cities (such as Winnipeg's North End or Edmonton's 118th Ave) as the most vulnerable to involvement in crime and criminal justice processing.

To summarize, Aboriginal youth as a group are disproportionately poor, urban, young, undereducated, unemployed, and involved in the YCJS compared to their non-Aboriginal counterparts. What about the individual level? How do these circumstances impact their lives? Next, we shift our focus to socio-psychological processes.

Socio-Psychological Processes

> There is in much native crime a terrible element of self-destruction, a certitude of punishment to follow, a hopeless despair, and a loathing of self. No one who felt his or her life was worth living would act in this way. (Birnie, 1990: 205)

While many Aboriginal youth are dynamic, healthy, and contribute to their communities, others hold themselves in such low regard that they believe they are inferior and inadequate. Lisa Hobbs Birnie, a former member of the National Parole Board, offers the above description of the socio-psychological background of Aboriginal crime. Living in a society that continually devalues them, it is little wonder that many Aboriginal youth turn to destructive ways of coping with their troubles—both inwardly (e.g., self-harm and suicide) and outwardly (e.g., property destruction and violence) (see Figure 7.3). Self-destructive behaviours and confrontational violence are, for some, the end result of a lack of identity and the loss of hope. Before killing oneself or harming others, disenfranchised youth experience feelings that no one cares, loves them, or is there to help (Seventh Generation Helping to Heal, 2006). The Davis Inlet case of child gasoline sniffing provides a graphic example of what can happen when a group of young people lack guidance, love, and attention and feel that no one cares for them (Gorham, 1993). On this remote Innu island off the coast of Labrador, six youth high on gas fumes attempted suicide in

Figure 7.3 Personal and Socio-Political Realities

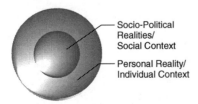

Individual lives are always embedded in a wider social context. In other words, personal realities (individual level) are always connected to socio-political realities (group level).

January 1992. Gorham (1993) explains, "The lives here are filled with contradictions. Ramshackle, frigid houses with little furniture and no running water or toilets contain large television sets with cable." The federal government moved the hunting community to the north coast of Labrador in 1949, but after two years they disappeared back into the interior and frequented a trading post at Davis Inlet. Here they became increasingly dependent on a community of Roman Catholic missionaries who had started a church in 1945. By 1967 the community had grown to 150 people living in four houses and 31 tents on the mainland. The government again moved the community to their present site and promised improved living conditions. They did not deliver. The community is now comprised of approximately 500 people. With little respect for themselves and faced with a YCJS that perpetuates disrespect, how can we expect young people like those from Davis Inlet to respect others?

In terms of self-image and identity, Aboriginal youth as a group are not faring well. According to Chalifoux and Johnson (2003), "[t]he projection of an inferior self-image has perhaps been one of the most powerful weapons of the colonizer in its 'conquest' of the New World. The human costs of this assault on the personal dignity of other human beings we reckon to be inestimable. It has carried enormous social costs and continues to do so today." Negative portrayals of Aboriginal people in mainstream media do little to change this image. The stereotype of Aboriginal people as inferior, uncivilized, and "savage" continues. Consider the demeaning image of Aboriginal women that is rampant in North American culture. School textbooks have portrayed them as ill-treated at the hands of Aboriginal men, almost like a "beast of burden." These images are more than symbolic and have helped facilitate the physical and sexual abuse of Aboriginal women in contemporary society. Emma LaRocque, a Metis woman and professor of Native Studies at the University of Manitoba, submitted the following to the Manitoba Aboriginal Justice Inquiry about such demeaning images:

> The portrayal of the squaw is one of the most degraded, most despised, and most dehumanized anywhere in the world. The 'squaw' is the female counterpart to the Indian male 'savage' and as such she has no human face; she is lustful, immoral, unfeeling, and dirty. Such grotesque dehumanization has rendered all Native women and girls vulnerable to gross physical, psychological and sexual violence . . . . (Emma LaRocque, written presentation to Aboriginal Justice Inquiry hearings, February 5, 1990)

Economic and social vulnerability is often compounded by feelings of isolation, dislocation, and hopelessness. Bob Ratner (1996) argues that when situated not only within a city, but also immersed in a cultural milieu disrespectful of identity and oppressive to their ways of life, Aboriginal youth find themselves in **cultural limbo**. That is, in the city, many indigenous young people are alienated from both white culture and their Aboriginal heritage (see Box 7.2 on p. 163 for an elaboration of Ratner's conception of cultural limbo). Ratner argues that Aboriginals' plight can be understood in terms of the impoverishment of their *life worlds* (everyday ways of being in the world), on one hand, and their chronic inability to access *system* processes (e.g., education, employment, etc), on the other. Thus, urban Aboriginal young people are caught in a double bind, one with dubious outcomes.

Box 7.2

Cultural Limbo Explained

Ratner's (1996) notion of "cultural limbo" was developed from Jürgen Habermas's (1987) concepts of "life world" and "system." For Habermas, the life world is the everyday perspective of people, or what he calls the "context forming background" or micro-interactional world. The system includes macro-institutions—structures like the state or the economy. In his terms, it is the "functional inter-connectedness of actions." Ratner argues that, ideally, the "instrumental" rationality of the system or its imperatives (i.e., how the system works) complement the "communicative" rationality of the life world (i.e., what people do and think). In the case of Aboriginal youth, their life worlds have been "colonized." This leaves many in a purgatory, where they are forced to either "endure the degradation of living on in the city without credible cultural roots (white or native); or to return to the reserves and experience the trauma of reverse cultural shock" (Ratner, 1996: 198). The instrumental rationality (e.g., means/ends) of the system has come to dominate, distort, and misrepresent their own needs and expectations, thereby colonizing their life worlds. While Ratner's research was done over a decade ago, his ideas have much to offer in understanding the identity problems faced by Aboriginal youth today.

Shkilnyk (1985) found among the Grassy Narrows people in Ontario that relocation to a new reserve close to an urban centre led to a loss of traditional lifestyle and "anomie." Recall that anomie refers to normlessness—when rules and expectations are no longer widely accepted. Consequently, crime became a means of escape for youth from their poor life conditions. Self-destructive behaviours are another common coping mechanism. Living in a society that devalues them, with few role models and even fewer supports or positive coping mechanisms, many young people turn to violence—inward (self-harm, suicide attempts) or outward (assault).

This section has offered a glimpse into the kind of "justice" Canadian society offers Aboriginal peoples, specifically youth. Colonialism's legacy has created a situation in which indigenous youth are subjected not to hospitality, inclusion, and respect, but to racism, exclusion, and inequality at almost every turn. To what extent do Aboriginal people perceive the avenues through which they might escape from their current social conditions—such as the justice system, the education system, economic development in their communities, and the institutions of local government—as viable options? So many Aboriginal children and adolescents are poor, hungry, excluded, and criminalized. As social-welfare programs disappear, social supports shrink, and needed dollars are taken away, these conditions and outcomes will continue. In response, the state and concerned citizens mobilize the **carceral complex** (including various forms of control along a punitive, not supportive, continuum) to regulate the excesses and the "others" deemed responsible. While we witness downsizing in social-welfare institutions, there is a movement to upsize the state's penal sector across North America. Caught most tightly within its net of surveillance, governance, and control are recalcitrant Aboriginal youth who live outside dominant Euro-Canadian mores on the economic, political, and cultural margins of society. While the gross over-representation of indigenous youth is the most glaring example of systemic racism evident in the YCJS, "other" ethnic groups are also disproportionately targeted by the long arm of the state. For a brief examination, see Box 7.3 on p. 164.

Box 7.3

"Other" Racialized Groups

On October 19, 2002, *The Toronto Star* began to publish a series on race and crime and claimed that black drivers in the city were unfairly targeted by police. The editors reviewed Canadian literature and analyzed data from the police service's criminal information processing system (CIPS) (Wortley and Tanner, 2003). The CIPS data contained information on 480 000 incidents where an individual was either charged with a crime or given a ticket for some moving violation (Wortley and Tanner, 2003). Analysis of the data suggested that black Torontonians were highly over-represented in drug possession charges, were treated more harshly after arrest, and were more likely to be detained and brought to the police station for processing than their white counterparts. On this evidence, the *Star* made such claims as "justice is different for blacks and whites," "blacks arrested by Toronto police are treated more harshly than whites," and that "police target black drivers." The paper raised the ire not only of the public, but also of the police (*The Toronto Star*, October 19, 2002; Melchers, 2003).

Predictably, police representatives responded swiftly, vehemently denying accusations of racism. Chief Julian Fantino argued that "[w]e do not do racial profiling . . . there is no racism . . . we don't look at, nor do we consider race or ethnicity, or any of that, as factors of how we dispose of cases, or individuals, or how we treat individuals" (cited in Wortley and Tanner, 2003). The Toronto Police Service commissioned its own report, which was subsequently undertaken by Alan Gold, a well-regarded criminal lawyer, and Edward Harvey, a University of Toronto sociology professor (Gold and Harvey, 2003; Harvey, 2003; cited in Melchers, 2003). In conclusion, Gold and Harvey (2003) stated that the *Star's* research amounted to little more than "junk science" and that the insinuations of racism were "completely unjustified, irresponsible and bogus slurs" to be "put down at once" (Gold and Harvey, 2003; as cited in Melchers, 2003: 347). Armed with this ammunition, the police union launched a $2.7 million class-action libel suit.

However, public and academic claims that black drivers are stopped by police on account of their skin colour alone is pervasive; it is known as DWB, or "driving while black" (Melchers, 2003). International and domestic evidence suggests there is genuine cause for concern. In England, for example, Bunyan (1999) and Brown (1997) have

demonstrated that during the period between 1997 and 1998, black people were stopped by police at a rate of 142 per 1000, compared to 45 per 1000 for Asians and 19 per 1000 for whites. Thus, black people in England were eight times more likely to be stopped and searched by police than their white counterparts (Wortley and Tanner, 2003). Although Canadian police forces are not, unlike their counterparts in the UK and the United States, obliged to record the race of individuals they stop, several ethnographies support the *Star's* claims. In an intensive study of 50 black youth in Ontario, James (1998) found that being stopped by police was a common occurrence.

Larger surveys reached the same conclusion. For example, a 1994 study of 1200 Torontonians found that almost half of the black male respondents had been stopped and questioned in the previous two years, while one third indicated they had been stopped more than once (Commission on Systemic Racism, 1995). Contrast this with the fact that only 12% of white and 7% of Asian males reported similar experiences. Nevertheless, differences in police interference cannot be accounted for in racial disparity in demographic variables (social class, education, income) (Wortley, 2003). Indeed, Wortley and Tanner (2003) conclude that while age and social class typically insulate white youth from contact with police, these demographic characteristics do not immunize black youth. In fact, affluence seems inversely related to being stopped by police. A respondent in Wortley's (2003) study concluded that "[i]f you are black and you drive something good, the police will pull you over and ask about drugs." These findings suggest Canada is not immune from racial profiling. Statistics from Corrections Services Canada confirm that black youth are not only over-represented in police stops, but in almost all areas of the YCJS. Blacks make up roughly 3% of the population in Ontario, but represent 12% of all admissions to federal prisons in the province (Wortley, 2003). These appalling statistics have lead Wortley (2003: 5), among others, to the conclusion that "racial disparities [in Canada] . . . are very similar to those found in the United States" (Tonry, 1995; Mauer, 1999).

Source: Adapted from Wortley, Scot and Julian Tanner. 2003. "Data, Denials and Confusion: The Racial Profiling Debate in Toronto." *Canadian Journal of Criminology and Criminal Justice* 45 (3): 367–389

ABORIGINAL YOUTH AS "OTHER"

Who Killed Garrett Campiou? asks writer Jeff Gailus. Garrett Campiou's tragic story is about "a young native boy who had come of age in a community rife with poverty and neglect and social injustice more often associated with the Third World. In Indian country" (Gailus, 2001: 2). On November 2, 2001, Garrett was killed by his peers. Gailus points to media attention on the case that blamed Garrett and his family. He also reveals a stark contrast between how the provincial government handled the case compared to the 1999 fatal Taber High School shooting. In the Taber High School case, the victim was a white middle-class teenager shot by another white student. In response, in the weeks following the incident, then-premier Ralph Klein launched a task force on children at risk of violence. In Garrett's case, the response was limited to children's services minister Iris Evans, who told *The Edmonton Journal* that "[t]he boy's tragic death demonstrates the importance of preventing fetal alcohol syndrome." In Gailus' (2001: 3) words

> [T]here was no mention, for instance, of the need to address the vicious cycle of poverty, addiction and despair that has, over the last 200 years, settled onto native culture. Nor was there acknowledgement of the colonial juggernaut of European settlement, captained by an indifferent political and economic system and imbued with anti-aboriginal racism.

The article can be seen at www.albertaviews.ab.ca/issues/2001/mayjun01/mayjun01social2.pdf. Indeed, Aboriginal youth like Garrett are the "other."

Think of the "other" as one who is not like you. They are other to you, but can only be understood in relation to your world view. Philosopher Merleau-Ponty (1962: 350) puts it like this:

> In so far as I constitute the world, I cannot conceive another consciousness, for it too would have to constitute the world . . . even if I succeeded in thinking of it as constituting the world, it would be I who would be constituting the consciousness.

Put simply, we think in terms we know. We respond to others according to our own particular view of the world. Thus, when we are confronted by difference, we tend to pursue one of two (equally disturbing) courses. First, we may think of the other as an extension of ourselves (merely the same as, or just not as good as) and overlook their uniqueness. Second, we may conceive of the other as an object alien to us, who is to be appropriated and/or manipulated for our advantage (Levinas, 1969). Arguably, justice through the criminal and youth justice systems has largely been directed toward the latter. In this way, the "other" (in this case, Aboriginal youth) is evaluated not just as *less than*, but as one who requires intervention. Indeed, wherever in the world "the other" has been constructed (or differences encountered), the "othered" group has been greeted with violence and anonymity (Dutta, 2005)—for instance, in South Africa, pre-WWII Nazi Germany, or Canadian cities. Criminological evidence overwhelmingly confirms that African American and Hispanic youth in the United States are over-represented at all stages of the juvenile justice process (Austin, 1995: 155). Moreover, discrimination tends to amplify as youth progress further through the system (Fagan et al., 1987). For example, James Austin (1995) reports that in California, like most other states, African Americans are highly over-represented in young offender detention centres. Of the 13 767 youth detained in California during 1992, 5309 (37%) were of African American heritage compared to a mere 8.7% of the youth population. The case is similar for Canadian Aboriginal youth, as we have seen.

Theorizing Race

> At every point, like all racisms, it [apartheid] tends to pass segregation off as natural—and as the very law of the origin. Such is the monstrosity of this political idiom. Surely, an idiom should never incline toward racism, (Derrida, 1985)

For nearly five centuries, Aboriginal peoples have been almost invariably been constituted symbolically and managed through Euro-Canadian institutions (i.e., law) not merely as barriers to civilization and the settlement of the country, but as authentic "anticitizens" standing in opposition to it (Roediger, 1991; Wacquant, 2005). In part, this accounts for perpetual attempts to strip them from the Canadian social body by moving their living spaces to make room for white settlement (e.g., to reserves), for taking children from their homes and placing them in residential schools, or for the "1960s scoop" whereby indigenous young people were sent to live with families of European descent. Pierre Boudieu (1989) refers to policies like these as guided by "the principle of social vision and division." Nowhere is this policy of "social vision and division" and the racism inherent to it more apparent than in the criminal justice system. Racism in the legal realm, according to Joanne St. Lewis (1994: 15), is

> [a]n attitude in the judicial decision making process which assumes the inherent superiority of the values of the dominant cultural/racial group and the concomitant inferiority of another cultural/racial group. The issue of racism is fundamentally about power of the mass and the shared belief system; the power to shape reality in accordance with one's values; the power to give voice to or to silence the diversity of others; the power to rewrite history and to develop legislation which meets the socioeconomic imperatives of the majority.

If this is the case, then why are *we* not fully aware of racism in our daily routines and institutional arrangements? If we are victimized by racism, then we are acutely aware of it; but if our social status grants us privilege, then racism remains largely invisible. It goes without saying because racism is deeply engrained in the social fabric. The idea of Canada as a tolerant nation, Mecca to the world's oppressed, is more facade than fact. As evidence of open-mindedness, we can point to the welcome that Canada extended to slaves who travelled north on the Underground Railroad or to the fact that Canada was the first nation to pass and implement a multiculturalism act (Aylward, 1999). Canada's multiculturalism may seem to be an opening to the "other" (e.g., refugees, immigrants) that welcomes and offers hospitality. But, as Nandana Dutta (2004) argues, this position has fostered a sense of complacency (even smugness) in social relations with such groups. Just because official policy is anti-racist does not mean that Canada as a country, the officials in the justice system, the members of your community, or the students in your classroom are immune from racism and intolerance, either at the giving or receiving end. Moreover, as James Walker (1997) argues, there is a vast discrepancy between Canada's national image as an "egalitarian society" and the material reality experienced by people of colour. A distorted image of Canada as egalitarian in practice, Walker (1997: 334) argues, can perpetuate inequality because it denies "the very existence of racial disadvantage." You will find support for this contention not only in Walker's work, but in the writings of Constance Backhouse, Franca Iacovetta, Sherene Razack, Patricia Monture, Renisa Mawani, Barrington Walker, Scot Wortley, and Carol Aylward. In 2005, the Government of Canada announced its action plan, *A Canada for All: Canada's Action Plan Against Racism*. This report and plan has received little coverage and has largely remained unheard of.

Recall from Chapter 5 that there are two ways to view law: as a neutral arbiter of social conflicts or as a reinforcer of the inequalities that exist outside of it. Justice, we are often told, is colour-blind, but leading Canadian scholars have called this common-sense notion into question. For example, Bernard Schissel (1993: 521) concluded that

> [I]t is apparent . . . that courts apply the law with discretion and prejudice . . . [and] [d]espite the fact that the *Young Offender's Act* was implemented to ensure equal treatment under the law, it is apparent that extralegal factors [like race] have a substantial impact on judicial decisions and certain categories of youth are targeted for especially harsh treatment.

Not only have scholars called the naturalness of "blind justice" into question, but several high-profile incidents are proof positive that racism is endemic to law and its practice (Comack, 1999). For example, a January 1990 provincial inquiry in Nova Scotia exonerated Donald Marshall, a person of Aboriginal descent from the Mi'kmaq nation, in the killing of a black woman (Sandy Seale). He had served 11 years in prison. The resulting inquiry determined that racial attitudes of police and judges plus systemic racism in the justice process were to blame for the injustice that had assailed Marshall. Similarly, the Aboriginal Justice Inquiry (AJI) of 1991 chips away at the vision of the justice system as fair to all and stands as an indictment of the law as a racist and racialized institution.

The AJI emerged in response to two cases involving gross injustices. We discussed the first case in Chapter 5; the killing of Helen Betty Osborne in The Pas, Manitoba, in 1971. A group of white boys had gone looking for a "squaw" one evening (Comack, 1999) and left her mutilated body in a bush. An autopsy determined that she had been stabbed 56 times with a screwdriver and raped. Even though one of the boys bragged about the incident at a party in 1972, the case was not heard until 1987. The second case involved the shooting of J.J. Harper, the executive director of the Island Lake Tribal Council, following an encounter with a Winnipeg police officer. Although the police service launched an internal investigation lasting only 36 hours, which exonerated the officer, many questions surrounding the incident remain unanswered—for example, why were the police still looking for a suspect when they already had someone in custody? Why did they stop Harper, who was 36, when they were looking for someone who was 22 (Comack, 1999)?

Injustices against racialized "others" by justice system officials raise important "questions about law's claims to be impartial, neutral and objective" (Comack, 1999: 56). Indeed, despite commissions of inquiry, these iniquities continue. For example, the case of Neil Stonechild in 1990 recently made headlines. Two Saskatoon police officers took Stonechild, only 17, for a "starlight tour"—an especially egregious practice of dumping "troublemakers" at the outskirts of town—on a particularly cold November night. He was found frozen to death in a field wearing only one shoe. The officers who took him into custody that evening have not been charged, despite testimony from Stonechild's friend,

Jason Roy, that he saw the youth in a police cruiser that night, handcuffed, bleeding, and screaming: "They're gonna kill me!"

Race, like gender and class, shapes justice and its administration. But how are we to understand this socially constructed category or the interconnections between race, class, and gender? First, we must understand that it is impossible to think about race without at the same time thinking about how racism delineates and interprets space (Mawani, 2005). Indeed, space, like law, is often defined in ways that make it seem free of racial bias. However, as Sherene Razack (2000: 5) explains

> [S]paces seem to us naturally occurring and we do not easily trace the long arm of the law in their creation, nor do we readily see the race, class and gender hierarchies such spaces (i.e., parks, slums, spaces of prostitutions, drinking establishments) enable.

Critical race theory (CRT) unpacks racist hierarchies and denaturalizes the assumptions that create and sustain law as racist. The emergence and development of CRT is closely tied, as its name suggests, to critical legal studies and the search for **counter hegemonic voices**—those intended to both question and undermine deep-seated ideologies about the nature of equality in society. To this end, CRT is informed by its subjects' life stories (Peters, 2004). Thus, CRT is both theory and activism. In the late 1960s a number of legal scholars and activists, bound by their belief that the gains achieved in the civil rights era were not only stalled but were being retrenched, gave birth to critical race scholarship (Delgado, 2003). CRT scholars such as Derek Bell and Richard Delgado indicated that new theories were needed to offset institutional racism. CRT scholarship has demonstrated how the greatest gains in African American civil rights have been achieved not through litigation in formal courts, but through "ordinary politics," including street protests, lobbying, and local elections (Delgado, 2003).

CRT scholars have diverged somewhat from the tradition's materialist roots (e.g., examining social structures) and have moved toward deconstructing racist constructions (Delgado, 2003). Instead of interrogating lived reality and social being through the eyes of the oppressed, the CRT tradition now examines discourse "and the language, terminology and mindsets with which society frames racial issues replaced the study of race and racism in the real world" (Delgado, 2003: 127). Despite Delgado's concern that CRT has become increasingly textual (to the detriment of material reality), contemporary scholars working within the earlier tradition are no less dedicated to meaningful social change. According to Matsuda (1996: 22), present-day scholarship consists of "criticism tempered by an underlying descriptive message of the possibility of human social progress" (Matsuda, 1996: 22, cited in Aylward). Following the path established by U.S. scholars, Canadian CRT emerged during the 1980s. During this turbulent time, students of colour articulated their dissatisfaction, claiming that Canadian and American legal scholarship had failed to analyze the role of race and racism in the political and legal structures of society (Aylward 1999: 39). Feminist CRT scholars have also drawn attention to racist and sexist logics embedded in Canadian law.

As we have seen, the "other" is routinely paraded in front of judges and put into cultural straitjackets that force them to comply with a particular social order. The media constructs the "other" as not like "us," yet fails to question *who* belongs in the "us" category and *who* is deemed dangerous. Thus, the us/other or we/them dichotomies seem fixed in popular discourses, the media, the justice system, and social interactions. Perhaps an alternative way of thinking and being can be envisioned. Alternative practices could include openness, welcoming, and respect rather than closure, hostility, and exclusion (Derrida, 1997; Pavlich, 2000). In sociological terms, Canada's official policy of respect for diversity and multiculturalism is more "ideal" than it is "real." Is it possible to really celebrate difference? To do so would mean having to accept difference and not treat Aboriginal youth as "other" (e.g., as *less than* or as an easy target for appropriation). Only when "the other" is no longer viewed as a social nuisance but is respected as a valued, contributing member of society can we confront the problems that face marginalized groups such as Aboriginal youth. Doing so, however, will require not only a change in *thinking*, but also different ways of *responding* to Aboriginal youth and their conflicts with the law. We will now turn to more innovative, supportive, and respecting alternatives.

BEYOND MANAGING OVER-REPRESENTATION: PROMISING ALTERNATIVES

> It is a tragic reality that too many Aboriginal people are finding themselves in conflict with the law. Canada must take the measures needed to significantly reduce the percentage of Aboriginal people entering the criminal justice system, so that within a generation it is no higher than the Canadian average. (Government of Canada, 2001)

> A well educated Aboriginal youth will be less vulnerable to a range of social and economic factors that erode their ability to be full, productive members of Canadian society, as well as to be able to contribute to the capacity of their own communities and institutions. (Chalifoux and Johnson, 2003: 37)

Recent research reveals that Aboriginal youth, especially those incarcerated for serious and/or violent offences, have multiple problems and varied experiences. It is only through a holistic intervention strategy that all the interrelated factors can be adequately addressed. According to Corrado and Cohen (2002), it is necessary to identify and target multi-problem needs for groups like female young offenders and Aboriginal young offenders. Corrado and Cohen (2002) contend that the needs of Aboriginal youth are characterized by a range of serious and entrenched issues, which include psychological, emotional, behavioural, family-related, abuse, substance-use, education, peer, and identity problems. These issues pose specific challenges for interventions, correctional programming, and reintegration. Effective programs, Corrado and Cohen (2002) argue, will incorporate and reflect Aboriginal traditions and culture (such as sweat lodges, Aboriginal healing circles, culturally-centred rehabilitation, and community members as mentors).

In the wake of the recommendations of numerous inquiries and in response to the claim that racial discrimination is intrinsic to criminal and youth justice institutions, officials have made some attempt to alter existing practices toward a less antagonistic relationship with the "other." Stenning (2003) argues that investigations of this type have forced police departments to make organizational changes to meet the needs of an ever-changing cultural mosaic. Police forces have diversified personnel, mandated cultural sensitivity training, created a police/minority community liaison, assembled hate crime units, implemented formal anti-racist policies, and encouraged minority representation on police governance boards (Stenning, 2003). In addition, programs attentive to indigenous culture are becoming more widespread across North America. This need was realized as early as 1991 when Justices Hamilton and Sinclair (1991: 589), in the final report of the Aboriginal Justice Inquiry of Manitoba, wrote:

> We believe the answer to dealing with the problems of young offenders is to provide services that take into account the culture, background and needs of an Aboriginal young person. The services must be *supportive*, rather than *punitive*. Finally, they must be provided by Aboriginal people where possible and, if that is not possible, by individuals educated to work with Aboriginal people and to apply culturally appropriate solutions. (emphasis added)

A key buzzword in criminal justice circles dealing with Aboriginal peoples is "cultural awareness." The notion recognizes a disjoint between the adversarial justice model and a restorative justice model presumed traditional to Aboriginal dispute resolution. We will discuss this at greater length in Chapter 10. Cultural awareness training typically involves such topics as the historical legacy of colonization; aboriginal values, traditions, and spirituality; and the unique problems faced by Aboriginal people. In theory, cultural awareness training for police, court personnel, and correctional staff would appear to deal with the mistrust, discrimination, and cultural divide between Aboriginal youth and the YCJS. In practice, however, careful attention must be paid to its authenticity; that is, the extent to which the content and delivery of the training reflects the lived realities of Aboriginal people. In much the same way, implementing cultural awareness programs for young offenders without recognizing that live by or understand Aboriginal customs, values, and traditions is doomed to fail. The most essential aspect of effective programming is **respect**—valuing of another for humanity's sake. All too often Aboriginal youth have no respect for themselves, and the YCJS perpetuates this.

Since the early 1990s, numerous programs inspired by indigenous culture and some run by Aboriginal peoples have emerged to tackle the problem of over-representation. Included among these initiatives are role-model programs, youth justice committees, rediscovery camps, Native youth court workers, and cultural-awareness training (Fisher and Jantti, 2000).

Given the large numbers of indigenous youth in prison, programs designed specifically *for* aboriginal youth have also been developed. These programs are intended to bolster self-esteem and deal with "identity" issues among inmates. Comprised of cultural awareness, spirituality, and the use of traditions, these strategies are supposed to aid youth in (re)discovering their native heritage (Fisher and Jantti, 2000). Numerous studies have documented how many Aboriginal youth have been socialized without regard for traditional ways (Ellerby and MacPherson, 2002; Heckbert and Turkington, 2001; Trevethan et al., 2001). Although, as we have seen above, socio-economic rather than cultural conditions may have precipitated involvement in the YCJS, encouraging youth to tap into their culture may have a positive effect on future offending rates (Trevethan, 2002). Trevethan (2002) makes the case that core elements of indigenous culture—language, culture, teaching, and ceremonies—are critical to the healing process. Thus, Trevethan (2002: 197) stresses the importance of providing

> Aboriginal offenders with the opportunity to participate in programs that introduce Aboriginal culture and spirituality or allow them to continue to develop their understanding.

She goes on to state that "[t]he ability of a program to aid Aboriginal offenders acquire the skills to manage their risk to re-offend may be heightened by a cultural approach" (Trevethan, 2002: 197). One such program that has received considerable attention is *In Search of Your Warrior*. Based on foundational teaching and ceremonies of Plains Aboriginals, the 12-session program is designed to assist the offender in breaking the cycle of violence (see Figure 7.4). Underlying the program is a holistic healing ethos that dictates that for an individual to attain any measure of wellness, all four parts of the self must be addressed and integrated. Furthermore, it is intended to uncover participants' experience with violence in an effort to assist them in coming to terms more effectively with how violence has shaped their lives and in developing empathy for their victims (the components are evident in the pie chart in Figure 7.4, reproduced from the Native Counselling Services of Alberta website at www.ncsa.ca/warrior.asp).

Thus, the *In Search of Your Warrior* program provides an opportunity for spiritual, physical, mental, and emotional growth. "Warrior" is a powerful metaphor that provides participants an ideal to strive for that includes such qualities as "self-possession, spiritual and psychic awareness/alertness/attentiveness, goodness and caring, endurance, patience, resilience, the capacity to fight for what must be defended and preserved in order to assure a Way of Life" (Couture, 1999).

A similar program involving young women is *Girl Power*, operated by NAN in Moose Factory, Kashechewan, and Sandy Lake First Nations communities. *Girl Power* targets girls and adolescents and works toward developing self-esteem and life skills. Traditional teachings are used to build rapport and support relationships between the youth and to develop positive role models.

The Supreme Court of Canada has attempted to resolve the troublesome over-representation of indigenous offenders in the justice system through law. The 1999 *Gladue* case provided them with an opportunity to interpret a controversial provision of sentencing reforms brought about by Bill C-41 (1996) (Roach and Rudin, 2000). Specifically, it involved a trial court's interpretation of Section 718.2(e), which instructs judges that all

Figure 7.4 In Search of Your Warrior

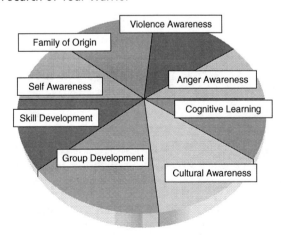

Source: http://www.ncsa.ca/warrior.asp © 2007 – Native Counselling Services of Alberta

available sanctions other than custody that are reasonable in the circumstances should be considered for all young persons, *with particular attention to the circumstances of Aboriginal persons*. In this case, the accused, an aboriginal woman, pled guilty to manslaughter for killing her common-law husband and was sentenced to three years' imprisonment. The facts of the case are as follows:

> On the night of the incident, the accused was celebrating her 19th birthday and drank beer with some friends and family members, including the victim. She suspected the victim was having an affair with her older sister and, when her sister left the party, followed by the victim, the accused told her friend, "He's going to get it. He's really going to get it this time." She later found the victim and her sister coming down the stairs together in her sister's home. She believed that they had been engaged in sexual activity. When the accused and the victim returned to their townhouse, they started to quarrel. During the argument, the accused confronted the victim with his infidelity and he told her that she was fat and ugly and not as good as the others. A few minutes later, the victim fled their home. The accused ran toward him with a large knife and stabbed him in the chest. When returning to her home, she was heard saying "I got you, you fucking bastard." There was also evidence indicating that she had stabbed the victim on the arm before he left the townhouse. At the time of the stabbing, the accused had a blood-alcohol content of between 155 and 165 milligrams of alcohol in 100 millilitres of blood. (*Gladue*, 1999)

When the accused appeared for sentencing, the judge considered the following as mitigating factors. She

- was a young mother with no criminal record, apart from an impaired driving conviction
- was from a supportive family
- had attended alcohol abuse counselling and upgraded her education while on bail
- was provoked by the victim's insulting behaviour and remarks
- suffered from a hyperthyroid condition that caused her to overreact to emotional situations.
- was remorseful when entering her plea.

In addition, the sentencing judge also considered several aggravating factors, including that she

- had stabbed the deceased twice, the second time after he had fled in an attempt to escape
- intended to harm the victim
- was not afraid of the victim; she was the aggressor.

Given these facts and the charge that no special circumstances arising from the Aboriginal status of the accused was evident—both accused and victim were living in an urban area and not within the Aboriginal community as such—the judge handed down a three-year jail term.

Canada's Supreme Court justices saw it differently. They overturned the lower court's decision by concluding in accordance with submissions by interveners and parties that aim of Section 718.2(e) was to reduce the over-representation of the indigenous other in carceral institutions (Roach, 1999; Roach and Rudin, 2000). In the Supreme Court's estimation, the lower courts must heed this laudable call as "they determine most directly whether an aboriginal offender will go to jail, or whether other sentencing options may be employed which will play perhaps a stronger role in restoring a sense of balance to the offender, victim, and community, and in preventing future crime" (Gladue, 1999: 65, as cited in Roach and Rudin, 2000). Thus, the Supreme Court not only acclaimed the importance of attending to indigenous differences in order to reduce over-incarceration, but also endorsed restorative justice for this purpose. The Court concluded that

> [i]n many instances, more restorative sentencing principles will gain primary relevance precisely because the prevention of crime as well as individual and social healing cannot occur through other means. (*Gladue*, 1999)

Accordingly, as we will again see in Chapter 10, the Supreme Court considered restorative justice the foundation for any attempt to reduce over-reliance on custody as a sentencing option.

The reverberations of the *Gladue* case have been felt throughout the justice process. Section 38(3)d of the YCJS mirrors Section 718.2(e) of Bill C-41 and makes clear that "all available sanctions other than custody that are reasonable in the circumstances should be considered for all young persons, *with particular attention to the circumstances of aboriginal young persons.*" In summary

> [t]he direction to consider these unique circumstances flows from the staggering injustice currently experienced by aboriginal peoples with the criminal justice system. The provision reflects the reality that many aboriginal people are alienated from this system which frequently does not reflect their needs or their understanding of an appropriate sentence. (*Gladue*, 1999: 89)

In the end, however, the Supreme Court did not reduce Jamie Gladue's sentence as they considered her the aggressor in the case. Nevertheless, commentators have heralded the SCC decision as a victory "in the bigger picture because the court confirmed aboriginals should be given special consideration because of their disadvantaged circumstances" and that "the court has said quite clearly that we have to find another way to deal with aboriginals" (Tibbetts, 1999: A1).

The federal government, too, has made strides to address indigenous over-representation. Justice Minister Anne McLellan set out the state's approach in 2000

> Our Aboriginal justice strategy has begun to address some of these issues through the design of community-based solutions to the problems faced by Aboriginal people in the mainstream justice system. The strategy actively administers 84 community-based justice initiatives serving over 280 communities across the country. Each of these programs is administered by the Aboriginal community and cost-shared, through joint contribution agreements, with the provinces and the territories. Programs have been developed that incorporate restorative justice principles derived from Aboriginal traditions and cultures while respecting basic legal principles and the charter. For example, a number of diversion projects have been developed that permit the community to be involved in resolving the issues surrounding the commission of an offence or in the sentencing process. (Canada, *Hansard Debates*, 10 May 2000: 1545)

MORE THAN JUST THE SUM OF THEIR PROBLEMS

> Whereas the vast majority of programming is geared to the social pathology of being urban and Aboriginal, we were told by youth that they wanted a supportive place to go where they could tap into their interests, develop their talents and nurture their leadership abilities: a place where they were more than just the sum of their problems. (Chalifoux and Johnson, 2003)

A common approach to the troubles facing Aboriginal youth is the "crisis intervention model," which focuses specifically on pathologies and/or individual problems (e.g., depression) or the provision of basic health and mental health services. Crisis intervention fails to attend to the social, educational, spiritual, and recreational needs of Aboriginal youth. An alternative strategy is to support and develop the aspirations and talents of Aboriginal youth. According to the Standing Committee of Urban Aboriginal Youth: An Action Plan for Change,

> The solution is provided by a weave of supports comprising education, recreation, urban transition services, labour market readiness, sound parenting skills, as well as strong community, cultural and family supports. Without these necessary supports, young Aboriginal people and their families can find it difficult to overcome the challenges they face and achieve a quality of life comparable to other Canadians. (Chalifoux and Johnson, 2003)

Urban Aboriginal youth centres can be "positive spaces" providing support and opportunities to meet with peers and elders that may counteract cultural and social dislocation. One such example is the Keewatin Winnipeg Youth Initiative (KWYI), a youth-driven, community-based centre established in 2001. KWYI provides a safe and positive environment for Aboriginal youth aged 15–19 who have been unemployed and out of school for a period of at least three months. Two on-site youth coordinators manage the project, which provides skills, resources, and opportunities for youth to become employable; gain an understanding and awareness with respect to recreation, health, and culture; do work placements and volunteering; train and participate in workshops; and build a career path. Kathleen McKay, AMC Youth Council, Assembly of Manitoba Chiefs, explains that the Keewatin Youth Initiative

> The Keewatin Youth Initiative is probably the best program I have seen implemented, because not only does it focus on the recreational aspect, it delivers on all four aspects of personal growth. For me that is a successful youth centre. And that is what we are encouraging in our communities to pursue as well as for their own communities, taking the holistic approach. It is more than just recreation, you have to instil values and create a sense of identity at the same time. (McKay, 2003)

Many of the youth at the centre had a history of involvement with gangs and street life, drugs, and alcohol abuse. According to one male participant,

> I was grateful for coming across the people that I met here . . . because at the age of 22 I decided to make a transition in my lifestyle. I was an active and recognized member of the streets here in the North End. I was grateful for the assistance I received and taking that opportunity to display to myself and to my family what I really can be. (Proceedings, 17 March 2003, Winnipeg Youth Round Table, youth participant, UAYAPC)

Another young woman shares her experience:

> I had to quit school when I was 17 because I had to start paying rent. So the program helped me to get back to high school . . . I plan to graduate and go to the University of Manitoba and pursue my long-term goal of being a social worker. Now I am confident I can do that. (Proceedings, 17 March 2003, Winnipeg Youth Round Table, Ms. Tracey Bradburn, UAYAPC)

The Report of the Royal Commission on Aboriginal Peoples (1996) also emphasized the need for developing and maintaining youth centres. Sustainable funding is required to keep these options viable. Some promising alternatives, however, are in jeopardy.

Role Models and Mentoring: Recreation Centres Closing?

On January 24, 2007, the Winnipeg city council voted in favour of closing Kelvin Community Centre. This facility was located in the city's Elmwood community—one of the poorest in Winnipeg. The decision was made in spite of the organized opposition of Elwood residents. "Mayor Katz frequently talks about the need to keep and attract young people to Winnipeg. But closing a recreation centre in a high-needs neighbourhood would suggest that the Mayor has a narrow vision when it comes to meeting the needs of youth. As a young person about to finish university, this concerns me," said Amy Reinink, a Manitoba social work student, writing on behalf of *Youth Voice*, a bulletin for the Canadian Centre for Policy Alternatives (Reinink, 2007: 1). In the same city, Forsyth (1998) found that children who participated in recreation programs had higher self-esteem, which she attributed to the positive role models in neighbourhoods where the lure of gangs is significant. Christian Smith (1991) found that participating in organized recreation helped youth develop skills to manage free time and actually reduces the need for government and social services. Another study in Fort Worth, Texas (1996), demonstrated that in a one-mile radius of community centres that offered a midnight basketball program, crime statistics dropped 28%. The centres that did not offer the program say crime increased by an average of 39% (Witt and Crompton, 1996). There is a contradiction apparent in the way the City of Winnipeg is investing in community centres. Reinink explains that $43 million is now being directed toward renewing community centres and recreation facilities in Winnipeg, but less than 25% of the money is going toward facilities in Winnipeg's inner city. The inner city is undoubtedly the area in most desperate need of recreational opportunities for young people. Seven million dollars is planned for the construction of a new recreation and leisure facility in the North End, $2.7 million for the redevelopment of Sargent Park (central), and another $400 000 for a spray park in Point Douglas. Yet such investments must be viewed in relation to the Kelvin Community Centre closure, other facilities that are drastically in need of attention (e.g., Sherbrook Pool, in danger of being shut down), and the resources directed toward facilities in Winnipeg's more affluent neighbourhoods. What does it say about priorities when the city spends the majority of its investments in the suburbs and eliminates small, essential centres in areas with a higher concentration of disenfranchised youth? "In areas with a high concentration of poverty, such as the Inner City and Elmwood, facilities that provide recreational opportunities for children and youth can have a positive impact that has far reaching benefits for us all" (Reinink, 2007: 2).

Urban transition programs are another potentially promising alternative for addressing the cultural dislocation and sense of powerlessness that many Aboriginal youth experience, especially when they move to the city. Lack of sufficient personal resources or community supports have led many youth to find a sense of belonging in gangs. In Winnipeg, an estimated 2000 Aboriginal youth are involved in gangs, the largest of which are the Manitoba Warriors and the Indian Posse. The Edmonton Youth Gang Task Force reported that there were 12 Aboriginal gangs with more than 400 members in Edmonton in 2003. Across the country, there are few agencies that provide support, referrals, advocacy, or programming related to intervention or prevention. Youth most susceptible to joining gangs are those who live in the inner core of large cities. Seeking a sense of belonging, safety, and refuge, they could benefit from more positive places for community, connectedness, and identity. Although there are mainstream programs in Canadian cities to help smooth the transition from a rural to urban lifestyle, racism and discrimination (whether real or perceived) are barriers for Aboriginal youth. In a submission to the UAYAPC, one participant explained, "The effects of discrimination are internalized and manifest themselves in feelings of isolation, leading to low self-esteem which may never go away" (Manitoba Education Submission, p. 6, UAYAPC). Key transition services include housing supports and referrals, employment and training services, English literacy skills, counselling services, advocacy and liaison, education and career planning, and information on available programs and services.

Sports, arts, and recreation are important for directing young people (particularly Aboriginal youth) toward positive alternatives to drinking, drug use, and criminal activity. There is a lack of affordable recreation in most Aboriginal communities. According to the UAYAPC, "[s]ustained efforts to make sport and recreational facilities available must be made in order to lessen the continued vulnerability of growing numbers of Aboriginal youth to social and physical dysfunction." A witness from Vancouver for the UAYAPC put it this way:

> Our young kids, the little pre-teens and the teenagers would jump off the school bus, pick up a smoke, a hit of some kind of dope or hand on the streets and get into trouble. There was nothing reaching them and occupying them in a constructive, positive way. (Proceedings, 19 March 2003, Gail Sparrow, Musqueam First Nation, UAYAPC)

In addition, the arts—theatre, music, dance—can provide positive outlets and can be a vehicle for fostering self-esteem. Another participant in UAYAPC related her experience:

> I am a Metis dancer; that is what kept me out of trouble. Even when I did get into addiction issues or trouble with the law, I always had my dancing to go to. It brought me to Ottawa a lot of times, and I think coming here has changed my life a lot. I think what we need are more recreational programs out there for youth, whether they be cultural or sports-related. They need something to be proud of themselves, and I think we need to encourage that. (Proceedings, 11 February 2003, Mr. John Potskin, UAYAPC)

The "Awareness Through Art" holistic program offered by the Native Canadian Centre of Toronto targets youth who are seeking to make positive change in their lives, particularly youth in transition. It uses theatre and other artistic media to provide opportunities for positive risk-taking and reintegration into the Aboriginal community of Toronto, as well as for developing peer networks and building self-esteem.

Given the poverty faced by many Aboriginal youth, their participation in organized mainstream sports is limited by their inability to pay for equipment, fees, and transportation. The Night Hoops Basketball Program in Musqueam, BC, was designed to meet a community-identified need to connect youth to the community. In response to a large increase in breaches of probation, Night Hoops, a basketball program for at-risk youth aged 13–18, began as a pilot project in 1996, and since then approximately 3000 teens have been involved. It has grown from 12 teams operating out of six facilities to over 40 teams at almost 30 sites (Chalifoux and Johnson, 2003: 62).

Youth are referred to the program by probation officers, police, schools, youth workers, or other social service professionals. The idea behind the program is simple: make playing basketball with friends more fun than doing anything else available late on the weekends. Such opportunities can only exist, however, with adequate and sustainable funding.

The above approaches are all directed toward building a sense of community, belonging, and self-esteem—responding to the personal realities that Aboriginal youth face today. They are each designed to build capacity and strengthen identity in Aboriginal youth, not to simply address a "problem." In addition to these programs, more far-reaching structural changes are needed in areas of social, economic, physical, and political life—which means responding to the socio-political realities. Above all, an effective anti-poverty strategy is necessary: one that would involve such things as national day care, raising the minimum wage above the poverty line, raising the national welfare standard above the poverty line, a national child-tax benefit that includes families on social assistance, a coordinated strategy for building low-income housing, and a specific urban Aboriginal anti-poverty strategy involving partnerships between federal, provincial, municipal, and territorial governments and native organizations.

More sustainable funding on reserve and urban Aboriginal needs is essential. A promising example is the Health Canada, Human Resources Development Canada, and the Department of Indian Affairs' commitment of $161 million to Aboriginal children in 2001 and 2002 (of this, $138 million was dedicated to on-reserve activities). This funding must be long-term.

The final report of the Minister's National Working Group on Education, "Our Children: Keepers of the Sacred Knowledge" (December 2002) concluded that Aboriginal education was in crisis. Much more needs to be done to address the high rates of truancy, drop-outs, and poor academic performance, which compromise the futures of many Aboriginal youth. Addressing this pressing issue requires attention to the complex reasons behind why so few Aboriginal youth finish school, including racism, lack of parental involvement, instability, isolation, cultural insensitivity, sexism, and poverty. Alternative schools are providing innovative ways to support quality education for Aboriginal students. In addition to the provincial curriculum, the academic program is enriched by courses reflecting Aboriginal knowledge, traditions, and values. By incorporating Aboriginal liaison workers into mainstream schools such as St. Joseph's High School in Edmonton, retention rates of 88% have been achieved (Chalifoux and Johnson, 2003. Notably, in 2002, Ben Calf Robe School, Edmonton, had a retention rate of 93% (Proceedings, 21 March 2003, Sean McGuiness, Principal, Ben Calf Robe School). At the post-secondary level, the Northern Alberta Institute of Technology (NAIT) increased its retention rates from 50% in 1999 to 70% in 2003 after the introduction of Aboriginal student support services (Proceedings, 21 March 2003, Eva Stang, NAIT). Long-term strategies directed at employment and training are also required. The federal government specifically targets Aboriginal youth through initiatives like the Youth Employment Strategy ($51 million to assist youth in making a successful transition to the labour market) and the Youth Entrepreneurship Program (designed to help Aboriginal youth become better entrepreneurs).

Of particular concern is how the problems facing Aboriginal peoples today will be reproduced in the next generation if nothing is done to address systemic issues. Attention must be directed toward the high socio-economic needs of young single mothers (including housing, parenting, child-care support, social assistance, and education and employment assistance). To this end, the Ma Mawi Chi Iata Centre, a non-profit Aboriginal-controlled organization in Winnipeg, offers culturally relevant preventative and support services to Aboriginal children and their families. The Positive Adolescent Sexuality Support is one such program. Two facilitators run workshops in the Manitoba Youth Centre (a detention facility) and visit schools to discuss issues of birth control, sexuality, HIV/AIDS[1], and fetal alcohol spectrum disorder.

Given the pervasiveness of drug and alcohol abuse, the federal government's National Native Alcohol and Drug Abuse Program (NNADAP) is a potentially good strategy. It supports First Nations and Inuit people and their communities in establishing and operating programs aimed at offsetting the high levels of drug, alcohol, and solvent abuse among target populations living on reserves. In its fifteenth year, the NNADAP is comprised of 54 treatment centres, 96% of which are managed directly by Aboriginal peoples. This program, however, does not extent to urban Aboriginal youth.

Dealing with the issue of gang membership, which is particularly acute in the Prairie provinces, is a delicate task. Gangs emerge out of stark social, cultural, and economic stratification. Attempts to eradicate poverty and racism will go a long way toward dealing with the reality of gang life among Aboriginal youth. Addressing the lack of identity, acceptance, and purpose felt by many Aboriginal young people will reduce the prevalence of gang membership. Consider that only 24% of Aboriginal peoples under 25 report an ability to converse in an Aboriginal language, thought by many to be integral to culture (Anderson, 2003, Canadian Council on Social Development). As Rob Papin, founder of the Edmonton Native Alliance puts it: "[T]he kids on the street are trying to find their identity, and they are doing it the wrong way" (UAYAPC, 2003). At Winnipeg's Circle of Life Thunderbird House, several programs came into being as a result of recommendations from gang-involved youth, including a safe house for gang members wanting out, a gang tattoo cover-up/removal project called "Clean Start," and an intervention program addressing criminal thinking and behaviours. The Wood Buffalo Native Youth Movement started in 1999 when a few Aboriginal youth were discussing ways of preventing Aboriginal youth gangs from moving from Edmonton to Fort McMurray. The project's mandate is to empower the youth to make positive lifestyle choices by promoting Native strength and unity through cultural identity, self-respect, honour, and self-esteem. Check out their website at mcaonline.ca/nativeyouth/index.html.

---

[1]The literature on Aboriginal people with HIV/AIDS indicates that there are serious concerns about an increased risk of victimization, particularly the result of increased risk of sexual assault and discrimination against people with HIV/AIDS. This is most troubling for Aboriginal young women (Neron and Roffey, 2000; Matiation, 1995, 19991, 1999b). Given the higher rates of violence in Aboriginal as compared to non-Aboriginal communities and the depressed health status of Aboriginal peoples (among other factors), Aboriginal girls and women are at increased risk of HIV infection. Matiation (1995) explains that high rates of sexual and physical abuse—rampant in some Aboriginal communities—are risk factors for the transmission of HIV/AIDS. Victim-blaming of individuals with HIVS/AIDS continues, which no doubt silences people from involving health professionals and others in their lives. Neron and Roffey (2000) also make a connection between HIV and sexual violence among Aboriginal women, particularly through rape, abuse, and incest.

Aboriginal Youth Network

The Aboriginal Youth Network (AYN) is building "community" among Aboriginal youth in Canada over the Internet. A volunteer Aboriginal Youth Steering Committee, along with MicroWorks Inc., was established in 1995. AYN is operated for and by Aboriginal youth. It received initial funding from Health Canada to develop a solvent abuse module, which Health Canada has sustained since 2003. AYN provides a forum for Aboriginal youth to express themselves and share their stories—a voice. Check out www.ayn.ca.

Most importantly, the participation of Aboriginal youth and communities is essential for making positive changes. The more difficult question is how to meaningfully involve youth in these matters that so directly affect them. This must involve more than a token Aboriginal representative; there must be a sustained attempt to listen to Aboriginal young people and to take their experiences, ideas, and visions seriously. Box 7.4 explains how a community for Aboriginal youth has been established on the Internet.

CONCLUSION: HOSPITALITY, INCLUSION, AND RESPECT

To appreciate the unique problems associated with Aboriginal youth and the YCJS, we must understand its *historical underpinnings* as well as the *socio-economic context* and *cultural environment* in which Aboriginal young peoples are situated. The life chances of Aboriginal youth as a group are bleak compared to non-Aboriginal adolescents. These prospects are not inevitable, nor are they representative of all Aboriginal youth. Although vulnerable to the problems discussed in this chapter, many Aboriginal young people are coming together to work for a better tomorrow. Hopelessness, alienation, poverty, violence, and racism—there is no single answer to the problems faced by Aboriginal young people. As the chapter demonstrated, a historical legacy of colonization, forced assimilation practices, and state dependency has contributed to cultural and social dislocation among many Aboriginal youth. Instead of viewing their involvement in crime and delinquency as symptomatic of personal pathologies, the personal circumstances of Aboriginal youth's lives and the social adjustment problems they face must be located in social, economic, and political terms.

> The Anishawbe have an ancient prophecy that tells of seven prophets foretelling the future. The seventh prophet—or the seventh fire—told them of a time when a younger generation would regain the people's pride and greatness after a period of loss, tragedy, and alienation. Many believe that this seventh generation has now been born. We are part of that seventh generation. We have a voice. We hope you will listen to our story. (Cheechoo, Spence et al., 2006: 1)

To find out more, visit the *Voice for Children* website at www.voicesforchildren.ca. Also see ayn.ca/FirstTruths-Stories-Seventhgen.aspx, where you will find an amazing story of resilience, hope, and one young man's triumph over obstacles written by Conrad Ritchie from Barrie, Ontario, and titled "Seventh Generation."

SUMMARY

■ Aboriginal youth, especially criminalized youth, are the most marginalized group in Canada and the quintessential criminalized "other." The current situation facing Aboriginal peoples in Canada and Aboriginal youth involvement in crime and their over-representation in the YCJS must be located in the historical context of colonialism, assimilation, residential schools, forced state dependency, and continued systemic racism.

■ Aboriginal youth crime largely stems from cultural and social dislocation, indicative of their marginalized place in Canadian society. Stated differently, Aboriginal youth's social adjustment problems (including crime and delinquency) are linked to their current social, economic, and political circumstances.

■ Conditions in many Aboriginal communities—poverty, unemployment, lack of educational opportunities, inadequate housing, gangs and prostitution, limited recreational options, limited social service resources, high rates of alcohol and drug abuse, and violence—influence the "choices" young people make to respond in deviant and criminal ways.

■ Aboriginal youth

■ are more likely to be offenders and are disproportionately victimized

■ have a higher likelihood of being involved in the child-welfare system, which in turn increases the probability that they will end up in the YCJS

■ are more vulnerable to harsh justice processing

■ face additional challenges such as social exclusion and economic and social barriers to improving their life chances.

■ Historical inequities have left Aboriginal children today without much-needed supports, resources, and services. However promising alternatives to a criminal justice response offer hope when they are supportive rather than punitive and when they respect youth.

■ "Cultural awareness" programming must not only attend to the social, educational, spiritual, and recreational needs of Aboriginal youth, but it must also involve them as decision-makers.

DISCUSSION QUESTIONS

1. How are the personal worlds of Aboriginal youth related to the social circumstances of Aboriginal peoples as a group in Canada?

2. How do racism, poverty, and systemic discrimination contribute to the over-representation of Aboriginal youth in the YCJS?

3. In what ways can we envision a different, more positive future for Aboriginal youth and what changes to Canadian society would be necessary to make this vision a reality?

RECOMMENDED READINGS

Brown, J.N. Higgitt, S. Wingert, C. Miller, and L. Morrissette. (2005). "Challenges faced by Aboriginal Youth in the Inner city," *Canadian Journal of Urban Research*, 14 (1): 81–106.

Hogeveen, B. (2005). "Toward 'Safer' and 'Better' Communities: Canada's youth Criminal Justice Act, Aboriginal youth and processes of exclusion." *Critical Criminology* 13 (3): 287–305.

Shkilnyk, A.M. (1985). *A Poison Stronger Than Love: The Destruction of an Ojibway Community.* New Haven, CT: Yale University Press.

Chapter 8

Street-Involved Youth: Conditions, Consequences, and Interventions

STARTING POINT

Brianna's Story

My name is Brianna Olson and I am 22 years old. I live in Edmonton, Alberta and for a living, I am a registered social worker. My background is that I grew up in Edmonton and I am Métis. I am Ojibway, my father is Irish and Norwegian and my Mom came from a reserve in Ontario. Basically I grew up my entire life living in the inner city. I had my eyes opened very quickly to a lot of stuff that went on in my neighbourhood— prostitution and a lot of crazy stuff . . . I was just always looking for a reason to escape or a way to escape, then I found downtown and I found drugs. I got involved in that at 15 . . . drinking and marijuana . . . from there I really went into the underground, the subculture of drugs . . . started smoking meth, [crystal methamphetamine] heavily and was basically living downtown . . . selling drugs . . . I looked up one day and I was in a parking lot with some older guys and my young friend and I said 'this is disgusting! I am way better than this" (Brianna Olson, personal communication, 2007).

Brianna's story is one of resilience, determination, and hope for street-involved youth. At 15, Brianna was living on the streets and addicted to drugs, not unlike a number of lost young people of her generation. Brianna sought assistance from an emergency youth shelter, where she stayed for one month. By 17, she had become her own guardian and had decided to return to school, but admits she was still using drugs, even when she graduated as valedictorian of her class. It wasn't until a close friend was murdered over money owed for drugs that she vowed to never touch them again. Later, she made the decision to go into social work. Over the next several years, Brianna made it from a life on the streets as a young person struggling with violence, drugs, and alienation to a career as a registered social worker. Critical in her journey, recovery, and struggle to make a better life were the relationships she developed and the support and guidance she received from iHuman Youth Society. iHuman is a non-profit charitable organization that works intimately with high-risk youth to promote their reintegration into the community through a program involving crisis intervention, mentoring in the arts, and life-skills development. The main premise of iHuman is to work with disenfranchised youth "where they are at" and to "build a person" through visual arts, drama, music, dance and writing, which cultivates self-esteem and empowers youth to have a "voice."

"I want to spread this message that drugs are killing people. I just want people to get through it and move on with their lives" (Brianna Olson, personal communication, 2007). Brianna is now a community leader, a speaker, a multi-disciplinary artist, and a mentor for disenfranchised youth facing similar challenges. Through painting, dance, poetry, and song, she relates to the youth she connects with as a social worker at iHuman. In 2006, Brianna Olson received a National Harm Reduction Award for her work.

There are several issues addressed in this chapter. We encourage you to use the following questions to guide your reading:

- What does the term "street-involved" youth mean?
- Why do some young people take to the streets?
- What are the social characteristics and lifestyles of street-involved youth?
- What economic survival strategies do street-involved youth employ?
- In what ways are street-involved youth an economically and socially marginalized group?
- How does the criminalization of poverty impact street-involved youth?
- How does homelessness complicate the study of youth and crime?

LEARNING OBJECTIVES

After reading this chapter, you should be able to

- Define "street-involved" youth.
- Illustrate how the plight of street-involved youth is compounded by class, race, and gender inequalities, which must be recognized in responding to the problem.
- Compare and contrast the risks of family/home life and those associated with the street, and identify the processes by which a young person becomes entrenched in street life.
- Discuss the reasons for the increase in the number of street youth in Canada.
- Discuss the various ways in which homelessness is a *youth* problem.
- Identify how various intervention strategies and services for street-involved youth could potentially address the troubles facing them and youth homelessness.

INTRODUCTION

Young people like Brianna, whose social, emotional, spiritual, and human needs are not met, face almost insurmountable challenges that may lead them to take to the streets. This chapter explores the circumstances and complexities of one of the most stigmatized and marginalized groups in our society. We broadly define this hard-to-reach population as **street-involved youth**, a group of young people working and/or living on or about the streets. There are an estimated 150 000 youth living on Canada's streets on any given day (DeMatteo et al., 1999). In Edmonton, for example, youth aged 15 to 18 years comprise about 10% of the homeless population (Edmonton Joint Planning Committee, 2000). These young people are "out-of-the-mainstream youth" (Anderson, 1993).

Stories like Brianna's offer hope, a reminder that street-involved youth can overcome **street entrenchment**—forced economic survival, the (ab)use of drugs, violence, and the denial of human dignity that comes with being immersed in street life. Resilient young adults like Brianna defy stereotypes, change their life chances, and persevere on their own paths to social mobility and political engagement. Some youth figure out not only how to survive the challenges associated with street life but also how to transcend circumstances of adversity and marginalization. Unfortunately, more is understood about the negative experiences that condition life on the streets than the processes through which adolescents have overcome them. In many ways, street-involved youth have had far more life experiences and challenges than many middle-aged, middle-class adults. Yet we must remember that the subjects of this chapter are youth, which by definition means individuals who have not reached adulthood in terms of cognitive development and emotional maturity. Though they share an age grouping, street-involved youth are heterogeneous, with experiences conditioned and contoured by race, class, and gender relations. Our attempts to theoretically understand this group and respond to their troubles through intervention must recognize these differences.

Some members of the public and politicians are increasingly alarmed about these youth and the perceived threat they represent. Consequently, street-involved youth have become an easy target for public vengeance. People in this marginalized and relatively powerless group face considerable obstacles in their attempts to create sustainable futures, not the least of which is government retrenchment in the area of social services. Other obstacles include increased criminalization, regulation, and control.

As Hogeveen (2007a: 211) argues, "A different rendering of justice [other than justice as vengeance] would view criminalized youth as requiring protection in the form of systems and a populace that respects their heritage, age, condition of life, and situation." Through the lens of street-involved youth we can see **politics of exclusion**—social isolation reinforced by relations of power. At its core is **neo-conservatism**, a discourse that holds accountable and targets vulnerable and marginalized groups, in this case young people living on and about the street. As Diane Martin (2002: 91) explains, we are "dominated by an ethos [neo-conservatism] that blames poverty on the poor and assumes that a life of privilege is the right of those fortunate enough to be born to it." Here lies the paradox:

> [I]n a time and in a nation of plenty, thousands of adults, children, and youth live on the streets and are reduced to begging, marginal efforts at work, and petty crime. Hundreds of thousands more live in shelters or are a step away from shelters. The response of legislators to the failure of current policies to provide food and shelter for all is punishment and prison for the poor. Thus we now have legislation designed to imprison the children driven to prostitution and the adults and youth reduced to begging, squeegeing and sleeping rough. *What is going on?* (Martin, 2002: 91, emphasis added)

WHO ARE STREET-INVOLVED YOUTH?

In contrast to prevailing stereotypes, which typically present an image of a homogeneous group, street-involved youth come from different backgrounds and have a unique range of characteristics (Caputo et al., 1997). **Chronic instability**—defined in terms of housing, relationships, income, and health—characterizes and unites street-involved youth. Actual living conditions of people in this group vary from temporarily staying in hostels or rooming with friends to living in "squats" or sleeping "rough" on the streets. Youth typically engage in various survival strategies (e.g., staying with friends, engaging in prostitution, committing petty offences) to meet the daily challenges of life. The longer an adolescent

A Socio-Demographic Snapshot of Street-Involved Youth: Key Findings

- **Sex and Age**
  - greater proportion were males: **2:1** ratio between 15 and 24 years old
  - average age **19**
- **Ethnicity and Citizenship**
  - less than **10**% born outside of Canada
  - **60**% reported Caucasian background
  - **12**% African, Asian, Middle Eastern, or other ethnicities
  - Aboriginal youth over-represented: only **3**% of Canadian population but **33**% of street-involved youth
  - majority born in Canada
- **Personal history**
  - conflict with parents is primary reason for leaving home
  - **70**% reported having had a social worker
  - nearly **25**% experienced homelessness while living with their family
  - more than half reported emotional abuse or neglect
  - almost **50**% reported either verbally or physically abusive parents
- **Education and Income**
  - **35**% reported dropping out of school (more common for females) or being expelled (more common for males)
  - only **35**% of those over 18 had completed grade 12
  - **25**% reported social assistance as their primary source of income
  - also reported occasional work, panhandling, prostitution, etc.
- **Health**
  - very sexually active population
    - average age of sexual activity is low at 14 years (compared to 16.8 in general youth population)
    - rates of chlamydia and gonorrhoea more than 10 times those in general youth population
    - many report multiple sex partners and low condom use
  - substance (ab)use
    - **80**% reported smoking daily
    - **40**% reported recent alcohol intoxication
    - **95**% reported non-injection drug use and 20% reported using injection drugs
    - poly-drug use common

Source: Snapshot from E-SYS, Enhanced Surveillance of Canadian Street Youth, Quick Facts. (Public Health Agency of Canada, 2006. "Street Youth in Canada: Findings from Enhanced Surveillance of Canadian Street Youth, 1999–2003.") [E-SYS is a sentinel surveillance system that monitors rates of sexually transmitted infections and blood-borne infections, risk behaviours and health determinants in the Canadian street youth population, developed to provide data on infection prevalence in a hard to reach population through the Public Health Agency of Canada's Surveillance and Epidemiology Section]

remains homeless, the more likely he or she is to commit offences in order to survive. Not surprisingly, membership in this population is in constant fluctuation. Take a few minutes now to review Box 8.1.

Street-involved youth are young people between the ages of 12 and 24 who are homeless or under-housed (i.e., living in temporary or inadequate housing). The general age ceiling is 25, because young people in Canada are no longer eligible to receive adolescent social services after their 25th birthday. There are more males recorded on the street than females, at a ratio of about 2:1. Most street-involved youth are between the ages of 15 and 24, with an average age of 19 (Public Health Agency of Canada, 2006). Older youth are likely to have been street-involved for longer periods and have the greatest likelihood of being entrenched.

Females comprise about a third of the homeless and street-youth population in Toronto (Hagan and McCarthy, 1998; Gaetz et al., 1999; Janus et al., 1987) and almost half in Vancouver (Hagan and McCarthy, 1998). In Calgary and Winnipeg, over 50% of street youth are female, with an over-representation of Aboriginal girls (SPCW, 1990; Kufeldt and Nimmo, 1987). Some females, however, are over-represented among street-involved youth, including Aboriginal girls, young women in public care, lesbians, and refugees. The age trend for females involved in street life tends to be younger. As age decreases, the proportion of homeless females increases. In a survey of shelters across Quebec, Bisson (1987) found that of 1538 youth served by youth shelters during 1987–88, 46% of the legal minors were female, compared to 17% of youth 18 and over who were female.

Street-involved youth are more likely than their housed counterparts to have dropped out of school and/or been expelled (Public Health Agency of Canada, 2006). In their Calgary study, Kufeldt et al. (1992) reported that almost half of homeless youth had dropped out of school. Novac et al. (2002) found that half of the homeless females aged 18 to 25 in Montreal had not completed high-school. What's more, 80% of all participants were not enrolled in school at the time of the interview. Other findings confirm that most street-involved youth do not have a high-school diploma (Public Health Agency of Canada, 2006). Notably, in a British Columbia study, two-thirds of the sample remained in school (McCreary Centre Society, 2001). Recall how Brianna completed high school while engaged in a street lifestyle and using drugs.

Increasing poverty is a significant factor related to youth homelessness. Poverty is reflected in economic pressures and a lack of sufficient resources. According to the E-SYS Snapshot of Street-Involved Youth, nearly a quarter had experienced homelessness while living with their families (Public Health Agency of Canada, 2006). However, while social marginalization makes it more likely that racialized youth and those from lower socio-economic backgrounds will end up on the streets, street-involved youth come from all social classes and ethnic origins, including middle- and upper-class households and economically disadvantaged families.

Family poverty alone is not strongly associated with homelessness among youth, but is related to more chronic or repeated homelessness (Robertson and Toro, 1999). Karabanow (2005) found that many street-involved youth lived in families that relied on social assistance and came from single-parent households. However, in Novac et al.'s (2002) Montreal study, 60% of the participants said that their family did not have financial problems, suggesting that implicating "family poverty" as primary is misleading.

CONDITIONS, DEFINITIONS, AND PREVALENCE OF HOMELESSNESS

North America is experiencing a vast increase in the number of recorded individuals who are living on the street or "homeless." Conceptualizing homelessness is fraught with debate over everything from its definition and research methodologies to intervention and policy goals. The concept is "fluid and elusive" (Daly, 1996: 1). More certain is what homelessness is not—secure and safe living conditions. The United Nations (UN) broadly defines two categories of homelessness: **absolute homelessness**—sleeping in places unfit for human habitation (e.g., abandoned buildings, vehicles, doorways, parks, and tents)—and **relative homelessness**—situations where basic standards are not met (Charette, 1991) (e.g., unsafe rooming houses or temporarily sleeping on a friend's couch). When a person's living situation does not meet the UN's basic standards—affordable, secure, and safe, with protection from the elements, clean water, and sanitation—that person can be characterized as homeless (Cox, 1986, as cited in Fallis and Murray, 1990: 3). This broad definition includes individuals who are housed but do not have safe and secure living arrangements.

On any given night, approximately 33 000 Canadians are homeless, including between 8333 and 11 000 youth (CBC News, *Fifth Estate*, March 10, 2004). People working with the homeless population estimate that between 250 000 and 500 000 people comprise this group, of which youth are a considerable proportion (Government of Canada, 1999). Estimating the number of street-involved youth in Canada is difficult because of definitional issues (i.e., how the group is defined, such as "runaway"), unique differences within the population (e.g., age, gender, etc.), access (i.e., no fixed address), and tracking issues (i.e., only some individuals seek out services and can be recorded).

No systematic measurement exists across Canada, nor is there a national database to help accurately determine the number and proportion of young homeless people. In the 1980s, between 50 000 and 60 000 young people were estimated to be reported missing across Canada (Appathurai, 1987). One source of information on the numbers of street youth comes from service agencies, but this is misleading. Although shelters provide a better source of data, many youth do not access the services, and therefore shelter counts dramatically underestimate the number of homeless youth. However, the statistics provided by shelters do capture important data such as the following: in 1999, about 6000 youth (or 21% of all users) stayed in Toronto's emergency shelters (Toronto, shelter use database, 2001). The problem is growing, as can be seen in the significant increase in shelter services in Toronto over the last 25 years—from two shelters with 95 beds in 1979 to 12 shelters with 522 beds in 2004 (Youth Services Network, 1979)—a 450% increase. In economic terms, a rough estimate suggests that Canadians are spending $1 billion a year in taxes to deal with homelessness.

Springer et al., (1998) offer significant insight into shelter use. They analyzed nine years of administrative data from Toronto shelters to track users. Of the 133 000 individuals or families who stayed at least one night between 1988 and 1996, almost 30% were youth. In other words, 37 000 different youth aged 15–24 used a shelter during this eight year period (Springer et al., 1998).

YOUTH, CHILD POVERTY, AND THE 'NEW' WELFARE STATE

Over the past two decades, youth homelessness has emerged as a significant social issue in Canada and many Western countries (Avramov, 1998; van der Ploeg and Scholte, 1997). By the late 1990s, the fastest growing group using shelters was youth and families (Springer et al., 1998). Homelessness among youth is particularly unique in that it occurs during a period of transition from childhood to adulthood, a time that usually entails establishing a household separate from one's parents no sooner than the age of 18 or 20.

In contrast to adolescents today who are staying in (or returning to) the parental home, many others are leaving long before the traditional period of dependency ends (Lemay, 1999). The situation of homeless youth is at odds with the extended reliance on parents for accommodation and other support. Homelessness cuts across class, gender, and race lines and must be understood as reflecting the social inequalities of the larger society from which it emanates.

Homelessness is a particularly acute problem among Aboriginal youth, especially in Vancouver, Edmonton, Prince Albert, Saskatoon, Winnipeg, Toronto, and Ottawa. Although Aboriginal people constitute only 4% of Edmonton's population, approximately 40% of the total number of homeless people is Aboriginal (1996 Census). In Ottawa, 18% of the population of homeless youth are Aboriginal males and 19% are Aboriginal females. These numbers are compared to only 1.5% of the general population in Ottawa. Similarly, the E-SYS Snapshot found an over-representation of Aboriginal street youth (Public Health Agency of Canada, 2006). One third of participants were Aboriginal, compared to 3% of the Canadian population (see Box 8.1 on p. 185). These numbers may actually be higher, given that a strict boundary between home and street (as is presumed in traditional concepts of homeless youth) is uncharacteristic among Aboriginal youth (Caputo et al., 1994). According to Lee (2002), Aboriginal people in urban areas are two times as likely as their non-Aboriginal counterparts to live in poverty. Recall from Chapter 7 that more than half of Aboriginal children across Canada are poor (CCSA, 2003).

Several systemic factors contribute to this problem, which must be understood before we investigate what conditions are like for street-involved youth. It is within this context that we locate youth homelessness. Hutson and Liddiard (1994: 23) argue that three main structural factors account for why youth comprise such a significant percentage of the homeless population:

1. reduction in affordable housing that is accessible to young people
2. youth unemployment
3. reduction in state benefits

These interrelated factors have all contributed to greater inequality and an unequal distribution of scare resources (Wacquant, 2001). Structural disparities intensify as resources are distributed such that "the most affluent benefit while the poor and visibly different spiral into desolation and misery" (Hogeveen, 2007a: 212).

Unstable Living Situations

There exists a prevailing misconception that the primary cause of youth homelessness is individual deficits. The increasing presence and visibility of homeless and disenfranchised youth reinforces the neo-liberal argument that these "social failures" should be made "responsible" for themselves or face the consequences (Fraser and Gordon, 2002). This understanding does not take into account the complex interconnections between systemic, societal, and individual-specific factors. Unstable living situations are seen as a characteristic of the individual rather than the context in which street-involved youth frame their decisions or the conditions that structure their choices. We must make connections between choices (individual) and conditions (structural).

Many Canadian cities are experiencing a housing crisis.[1] Between 1997 and 2001, rents in Toronto increased by 31% (more than double the 14% inflation rate). In the same period, 34% of Toronto children 17 years and under lived in low-income families. Poverty and homelessness are intertwined social problems. Homelessness as a societal issue must be understood not simply as a question of poverty per se, but also in relation to recent changes in labour trends, family composition, and government policies, all of which impact the redistribution of wealth in our society. Each of these has very real consequences in the lives of youth.

When vacancy rates are low, access to affordable housing for low-income tenants, especially those on social assistance and lone parents with children, is significantly harder to come by. With almost guaranteed certainly of finding tenants, landlords exercise considerable discretion in finding "suitable" ones, sometimes refusing to rent to certain groups (e.g., single mothers, visible minorities, young adults), which makes the situation even worse, especially for Aboriginal females and young mothers (Fallis and Murray, 1990). This has become particularly problematic in Edmonton, Alberta. Edmonton is in the throes of an economic boom. More people are moving to the city, rooming houses are being demolished, and vacancy rates are plummeting—from 10% in 1995 to 1.2% in 2007. Social assistance rates are not enough to cover the skyrocketing rental costs, and some families wait up to three years for subsidized housing (Edmonton Joint Planning Comittee, 2000).

Many young people are caught in what has been referred to as the "Catch 22 of homelessness"—the argument that a homeless person needs an address to get a job, but needs a job to get an address/home. Young people trying to leave the streets no doubt have difficulty finding and keeping a job or staying with an education program without the stability of safe and affordable housing. In turn, they need an income and education in order to afford a home.

Unstable Youth Employment

Although commonly believed to be the answer to poverty, obtaining work does not necessarily change one's homeless status. The youth unemployment rate currently sits at 16%, but those who are employed are not guaranteed an escape from poverty. Since 2000, the labour market, with its plethora of part-time, low-wage jobs with minimal benefits, has become insecure and more inequitable. The heads of more than half of low-income families worked in 1996, yet their families remained poor because they earned low wages and/or could find only seasonal or part-time work (Battle, 1996). Since the late 1990s, Canada has witnessed a rise in the working poor. The McCreary Centre Society's profile on street youth found that 40% of the youth surveyed said they had had a legal part-time or full-time job in the last three months (The McCreary Centre Society, 2001). When

---

[1]In Canada, housing risk is assessed using a two-step process. The first step examines whether at least one of three problems relating to suitability, adequacy, and/or affordability exist. Suitability compares the number of bedrooms relative to family composition with national occupancy standards of sufficiency. Adequacy assesses housing conditions in terms of safety, state of repair, and availability of basic amenities such as plumbing, an indoor toilet, bath, and shower. The ratio of rental cost to household income is used to calculate affordability. Households with shelter cost-to-income ratios greater than 30% are considered "in need" (Pomeroy, 2001; Fallis and Murray, 1990; Arnold and Skaburskis, 1989).

street youth obtain work it tends to be at the margins of the formal economy and largely in jobs that are informally organized (i.e., falling outside regulated employment and safety standards). Exploitation is rife in this context, where many youth are "hired" temporarily and paid "under the table."

Some "entrepreneurial" youth, with buckets and squeegees in hand, have taken to "squeegeing" (cleaning cars windshields for a few dollars or spare change) at urban intersections in Canadian cities. Hence, the popular term "squeegee kids" was born. Newspaper reports contributed to a moral panic around the problem of squeegee kids, emphasizing the nuisance and risk of theft they posed to citizens. In response, a number of municipal governments, such as London, Oshawa, Halifax, and Winnipeg, have passed anti-begging and anti-loitering legislation. For example, in 2000 the Ontario government introduced the *Safe Streets Act*. It helped relieve fears of aggressive panhandling, but critics argue it is another example of the law working in the politics of exclusion (Hermer and Mosher, 2002). Anti-panhandling legislation was challenged in Winnipeg. The National Anti-Poverty Organization convinced Winnipeg's city council to repeal the legislation, but only after a five-year battle. Focusing on panhandling and targeting street-involved youth deals with a symptom of the much larger problem of homelessness. It is worth noting that Grady et al. (1998) found that youth who squeegee were less likely to engage in criminal activities. Criminalizing their "squeegee-conduct" further marginalizes them and increases the likelihood they will resort to criminal means to survive on the streets. In O'Grady and Bright's (2002: 39) terms, "The reaction to squeegee cleaning in Ontario is a clear example of how a marginalized and relatively powerless group is being squeezed to the point of exclusion."

Changes in household structures and demographics have also contributed to growing poverty. Single-parent families, most of which are headed by women, face a higher risk of poverty (Johnson et al., 1995). Almost 61% of families headed by single-parent women were poor in 1996, compared with less than 12% of two-parent families (Pomeroy, 2001). Gender inequality further exacerbates the situation, since women earn only 71% of what men do. In 2003, for example, the female/male earnings ratio for all full-time workers in Canada was 71% ($36 500) (Statistics Canada, 2006). In 2003, the average pre-tax income for women over 16 was 62% of men's—$24 400, compared to $39 300. The gap was largest in Alberta, where women's income was only 56% of men's. Despite the public perception about the gains that women have made in the work force through affirmative action and pay equity legislation, gender inequality still persists.

Unstable Support: Reduction in State Benefits

As income inequality grows, the gulf between Canada's wealthiest and poorest families widens literally and figuratively. A case in point is the mid-1990s "Common Sense Revolution," the Ontario Conservative government's program of deficit and tax reduction and cuts to government programs and spending, and its aftermath. When the government came to power in 1995, one of its first moves was to introduce welfare reform in the form of "Ontario Works" (popularly known as "workfare"). It dramatically decreased social assistance benefits by approximately 22% while narrowing eligibility. Young people aged 16 and 17 cannot receive Ontario Works assistance in their own name; they can only receive assistance through a guardian, and they are ineligible unless they prove that they are attending school or a training program daily. Add to this a program called Learning Earning Parenting Program, which aims to encourage young parents to complete high school, develop parenting skills, and become financially independent. The program is mandatory for 16- and 17-year-old parents without high-school graduation, but most directly impacts females. It requires a mother to return to school when her infant is 18 weeks old. In contrast, adult mothers with a history of paid employment are eligible for employment insurance and have seen benefits extended from 25 to 35 weeks. Furthermore, adult education programs have been cut, and there is minimal, if any, support for school programs for these young people. No money has been put in place for day care, and parents pursuing post-secondary education are ineligible for social assistance. As the cost of living increases without a corresponding increase in social assistance benefits and as jobs become less secure and increasingly unstable, more individuals and families cannot bring in sufficient income to meet even their basic needs. Poverty is exacerbated, as are its effects.

Alberta has a similar strategy with its new income support program, "Alberta Works." In 1993, the provincial government of Alberta terminated a program that helped 16- and 17-year-old youth live independently while continuing with school or part-time work. What happened to the young people who lost assistance? It is reported that they were forced underground and are living with friends or on the streets, and that most dropped out of school (Novack et al., 2002). Central to the current economic, social, and political structures that shape young people's lives is a shift away from social welfarism to neo-liberal and neo-conservative rationalities and policies. Widespread funding cuts and government retrenchment from social services (characteristic of neo-liberalism) has led to the elimination of Alberta's social housing program. The effect of these policies has been exceptionally hard on youth, making it increasingly hard for marginalized young people to survive (Martin, 2002: 93). With its booming economy and a plethora of jobs, it would at first appear that the "would be" street-involved youth could simply trade "the streets" for lucrative employment on the oil rigs. Yet this ignores the instability of such positions and the housing situation (i.e., low vacancy rate, no rent control and discriminatory hiring practices). While the economy "booms" in some areas, social services have seen a "bust"—shelters have seen their funding cut or disappear (e.g., City Centre Mission). As Martin (2002: 94) puts it, "The totality of these policies is that the least fortunate among a generation of youth receive little or no support from the social welfare regime, from child welfare authorities or from the school system. Left to their own devices, usually on the street, they are also demonized as dangerous and lawless and bear the brunt of campaigns that have politicized criminal justice in unprecedented ways."

Social Exclusion: The Case for Female Youth

The case for female youth is particularly distressing. The Canadian Housing and Renewal Association recently investigated the causes, demographics, and patterns of homelessness among young women aged 12 to 24 in Montreal, Vancouver, and Toronto (Novac et al., 2002). Novac et al. explored how young street-involved females survive— including their characteristics as well as the gaps in service delivery and the challenges related to diversity (Novac et al., 2002). Based on interviews with more than 100 young women, they identified several age- and gender-related issues. Most significant to our mind is the backgrounds of sexual violence among females. Violence against girls and young women plays a significant role in their becoming homeless. Researchers also suggest there is a link between child abuse, pregnancy, and homelessness among young women (Novac et al., 2002). Pregnancy rates among street-involved females are high— at least double those of their housed counterparts. In Toronto, for example, it is estimated that half of the young women on the streets become pregnant (CMHO, Research Highlights, 2001). Moreover, young women who have histories of abuse and trauma are more vulnerable to re-victimization. Recruitment of young women into the sex trade is very common in large urban centres like Vancouver and Toronto. Contentious legislation with the expressed purpose of rescuing young prostitutes or minors engaged in high-risk activities is being adopted in several provinces, including Alberta, British Columbia, and Ontario. According to rhetoric, "at-risk youth" present a unique risk both to themselves and to the larger society. Within risk discourse, there is a move away from "causes" (of homelessness, youth crime, etc.) toward "risks" to be managed. Various examples of risk management can be seen across the country, including the aforementioned Ontario's *Safe Streets Act* (2000), which legally prohibits "aggressive solicitation of persons in certain places," and Alberta's *Protection of Sexually Exploited Children and Youth Act* (previously *Protection of Children Involved in Prostitution Act* (1999), aimed at the coerced removal of young prostitutes from the streets to protective safe houses.

Shifting the discourse from "villain" to "victim," youth prostitution has been reconceptualized as a form of sexual abuse and exploitation (Bittle, 2006). Critics such as Minaker (2006) and Bittle (2006) charge that mandatory treatment not only violates children's rights, but also discriminately criminalizes young females in the name of protection. Young women, many of whom are racialized, are being detained against their will, held on non-criminal charges, and otherwise punished for conditions that are not of their own choosing (Minaker, 2006). Bittle (2006) argues that although on the surface, secure care represents a decisive move by the state to take responsibility for combating the youth sex trade with the ultimate goal of returning young women to their families, the state has, in effect, rescinded its responsibility. It ignores the reality that many young women have left home environments characterized by violence, neglect, and mistreatment. This approach will funnel services to particular youth, extend social control strategies, and thereby drive some youth underground where young women are even more vulnerable to exploitation and violence (Busby, 2003). The focus becomes the presumed "errant sexuality" of young, disenfranchised females rather than their marginalization. It blames young girls and women for their victimization. It individualizes the problem, encouraging young women to adopt healthy lifestyle choices, thereby deflecting attention away from the social circumstances that make the sex trade a "choice" in the first place. Put another way, "[r]elations of power—or the conditions that make prostitution a 'choice' for some young women—remain unchallenged" (Bittle, 2006: 196). What are the alternatives? To search for alternatives, we need to look beyond the limits of the law to address complex social issues. Legislation such as Alberta's *Protection of Children Involved in Prostitution Act* (1999) obscures the underlying social structural constraints (race, class, and gender inequalities) in the lives of criminalized girls (Minaker, 2006).

Social Exclusion: The Case for Aboriginal Youth

The most flagrant instance of social exclusion and numerical over-representation on the streets is of Aboriginal youth, whose situation is unique in many ways. As we saw in Chapter 7, Aboriginal peoples have historically been subjected to intrusive, repressive, and invasive state control. Aboriginal youth, on and off reserves, who have witnessed and/or experienced violence, cultural disintegration, alcoholism, and the effects of residential school histories on their parents' generation are particularly vulnerable. The impact of colonialism is not a thing of the past; the lingering effects are omnipresent and dramatically apparent. On Prairie streets, 58% of the girls and women working in the sex trade are Aboriginal (Busby, 2002: 94). In some areas, such as Lord Selkirk Park in Winnipeg, Manitoba, almost 100% of the sex-trade workers are Aboriginal, and most are children, some as young as eleven (Gilchrist, 1995). A clear reminder of contemporary colonialism is the fact that the majority of clients in the same neighbourhood are white middle-class men.

Aboriginal people are not only highly over-represented in the street population, but they are also more likely than the general population to be living in urban poverty and in places deemed overcrowded (Canadian Council on Social Development, 2003). As Hogeveen (2007a: 219) puts it, "The upsizing of the state's penal sector, along with the downsizing of its social welfare institutions, has constituted a carceral complex directed toward surveilling, training, and neutralizing recalcitrant Aboriginal youth who exist outside Euro-Canadian mores." The case of other racial-minority youth and immigrant youth is similarly distressing, especially those in large urban centres where international trafficking in women for the sex trade brings in large numbers of immigrant women and girls.

In short, these circumstances have led many young people to experience alienation from mainstream institutions; a process with race, class, and gender dimensions. Alienation is depicted in Figure 8.1. Note the intersecting nature of the circles, which is meant to imply the exacerbating nature of each component; that is, they mutually reinforce one another. Kids need to cope with this, and some Aboriginal youth find the connection that they lack on the streets, specifically in the form of gangs. Fontaine explains this powerfully in her own words:

Figure 8.1 Alienation from Mainstream Institutions

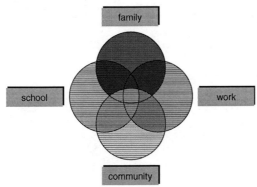

Anishiaabe Ikwe (Aboriginal girls and women) leaving poor socio-economic conditions in their home communities (First Nation reserves and Métis communities) often come to the city alone or with their families in search of equitable opportunities and a better standard of living, but instead find a dominant Euro-Canadian mainstream society culturally alien and the antithesis to their own experiences. Most, if not all, indigenous newcomers to the urban environment face myriad racist, alienating, and patronizing realities firmly entrenched within mainstream social institutions. (Fontaine, 2006: 117)

Gangs, as discussed in Chapter 9, appear to offer a means of surviving colonialism and its legacy.

PATHWAYS TO THE STREET: INDIVIDUAL HISTORIES AND MICRO-LEVEL CHARACTERISTICS

At an individual level, a young person's decision to leave home is complicated and multifaceted. What's more, choices are always made in a particular social context, which offers unappealing options for many youth. A constellation of micro-level and macro-level factors come into play in each case.

Let us turn our attention to individual histories. As we do, we encourage you to locate the multiple characteristics that play a role in a young person becoming involved in street life in a wider social context, keeping in mind that race, gender, and class relations provide pathways to the street. For an overview of the characteristics associated with street-involved youth as a group, see Table 8.1.

Children have always run away from home. Until the 1960s, the dominant paradigm for understanding runaways was pathology. This narrow concept gave way in the late 1960s and 1970s to the recognition of structural and environmental influences such as family and school. Finally, in the 1980s, studies began to connect abuse and maltreatment of children and subsequent running away (Kufeldt and Nimmo, 1987; McCormack, Janus, and Burgess, 1986). Viewing a young person's choice as connected to both individual personal characteristics and wider, social structures, we can explore four social/psychological pathways that have been demonstrated to lead some alienated and marginalized youth to the streets. These

Table 8.1 Multiple Characteristics: 10 Factors that Play a Role in a Young Person Becoming Involved in Street Life

Family dysfunction (violence, abuse, substance abuse)

Failure at and/or leaving school

Unemployment

Boredom

Mental health issues

Childhood behavioural problems

Poverty

Problems associated with non-heterosexual orientation

Unsatisfactory peer relations

Lack of opportunities and/or supports in community

include 1) parent–adolescent conflict; 2) family violence, child abuse, and maltreatment; 3) organizational dynamics, specifically child welfare; and 4) personal problems.

Parent–Adolescent Conflict

All teens have conflicts with their parents; that does not mean they will leave home. However, the most often cited, most significant pathway to the street is parent–adolescent conflict (see Table 8.1). Street-involved youth often share a background of strained and problematic relations with family and caregivers. Although the specific nature of family conflict varies—friction with step-parents, conflict over school, drug and alcohol problems, rejection over sexual orientation, or punishment for sexual activity—street-involved youth typically have had negative experiences with their primary caregivers, a fact that helps us understand why so many have so much difficulty trusting adults (Karabanow, 2004). Research suggests most youth typically run to escape a destructive home situation or family conflict (Jones, 1988). Although not always, child abuse, neglect, maltreatment, and family violence, which we will discuss next, are often at the root of the problem.

Family disruptions of some kind play a key role in creating instability. These include the death of a family member, divorce or separation, blending families, geographical moves, and abuse. A Toronto study of 563 housed high-school students and 386 homeless youth found that more of the homeless youth came from families with unemployed members and divorced parents (Hagan and McCarthy, 1998). In another study, almost two-thirds of 360 homeless youth reported that their parents had been separated during their childhood (Gaetz et al., 1999). More research is needed in this area. We can hypothesize that the nature of youth relationships with parents may be more important than whether their parents are married and/or unemployed.

Faced with such traumatic circumstances and limited alternatives, many youth "choose" to take to the streets (this becomes a structured choice with limited options that are conditioned by factors beyond their control).

Conflict over young women's sexuality and parental attempts to control daughters' sexual behaviour persists. Some female runaways express hurt and anger over being called "whores" by their parents (Schaffner, 1999). Whitbeck and Hoyt (1999) found that conflict with parents or caretakers about sexuality or sexual behaviour was twice as common among girls as boys as a reason for leaving—or being kicked out of—home. Another Calgary study (Kufeldt and Nimmo, 1997) reported that the majority of homeless youth left home because of family conflict or violence, which is the most studied aspect of the biographies of street-involved youth to date.

Family Violence, Child Abuse, and Maltreatment

> I left home because my father was abusive, physically, sexually, mentally. I went through it for years. I blamed my mother because she wasn't there to protect me . . . I was only a kid. That's why I started running. I was only twelve." (Homeless woman, aged 19, quoted in Gaetz, O'Grady, and Vaillancourt, 1999: 10)

The literature identifies physical abuse (Janus et al., 1995) and sexual abuse (Rotheram-Borus et al., 1996) as primary pathways to the street. Experiences of physical and sexual abuse are very common among street-involved youth—with reported rates ranging from 16 to 81% for physical abuse and between 5 and 50% for sexual abuse (Baron, 2003).

The familial context is especially salient and dangerous for females. Moreover, psychological distress experienced as a result of abuse likely differs for each gender. In one of the first studies of homeless youth in Canada in the late 1980s, Janus and colleagues found sexual abuse was pervasive among female street youth. According to their survey of 149 residents at a Toronto youth shelter aged 16 to 21, 75% of participants had been sexually abused (Janus et al., 1987). In addition, females were more likely than males to have histories of sexual abuse and to have been abused more severely. The caregiver was more likely to be the perpetrator for females.

Physical abuse appears to follow a similar pattern. Janus's findings are consistent with other research on youth on the streets. One Vancouver study, for example, found 71% of 110 homeless female teens reported a history of physical and sexual abuse, compared to only 13% of a larger sample of the province's students (Peters and Murphy, 1994). A Montreal project surveying 479 homeless youth reported that almost two-thirds (63%) of females had been sexually abused (Regie Regionale, 1998). Whitbeck and Hoyt (1999) found that young women who had been sexually abused by adults were two times as likely as young men to be re-victimized. Re-victimization and aggressive or coercive social networks (that many youth from troubled backgrounds gravitate toward) reinforce what they learned in their dysfunctional families, a process that is particularly damaging for young women. While street-involved youth as a group share histories of family conflict, females (Chapter 6) and Aboriginal youth (Chapter 7) are disproportionately victims of abuse.

Street-involved youth are likely to have been immersed in violent environments that go beyond their own victimization. Russell (1998) found that over half of her sample reported witnessing violence in their homes. Confirming these earlier studies, Karabanow (2004) found that street-involved youth had dysfunctional family settings and witnessed domestic violence. Not only did they have personal experiences of psychological, physical, emotional, and sexual abuse, their parents or guardians had high rates of substance abuse.

Organizational Dynamics: Child-Welfare Concerns

Studies in Canada and elsewhere have demonstrated that youth in public care, especially Aboriginal youth and females, are especially vulnerable. Homeless youth have high rates of current or previous involvement with the child-welfare system (Clarke and Cooper, 2000; Leslie and Hare, 2000; McCarthy, 1995). One Calgary study found that more than half of the participants had gone through the child-welfare system (Begin et al., 1999). Although in Canada no data exist on how many youth within the child-welfare system become homeless, one American study found that 12% of youth formerly in public care were living on the streets or in shelters within 12–18 months of their discharge (Coutney and Piliavin, 1998). Moreover, young people who run from child-welfare placements are also more likely to run farther away, to stay away for longer periods (Rees, 1993), and to be repeat runners (Fisher, 1989).

Being under the care in child welfare, and the state control and dependency that go along with it, is often generational. That is, it is a cycle that is perpetuated from one generation to the next. In a large sample of foster children who had experienced home-lessness, almost half of the birth parents had been homeless. In addition, those children whose parents had experienced homelessness were more likely than other foster children to have siblings in foster care and to be placed in the care of non-family members (Zlotnick et al., 1998). Compared to only 4% of their age cohort in the general population, more than half of the young women in a study of youth formerly in care were parenting a child on their own (Martin, 1996).

A pervasive problem concerns homeless minors who are not or are no longer involved in the child-welfare system but are ineligible to use shelters or receive income support. This "aging out" process is a tragic case of kids "falling through the cracks." After eligibility for child-welfare services ends, youth are not able to access adult income-support programs. The most comprehensive analysis of homeless youth and the child-welfare system comes from Fitzgerald (1995), who found that child-welfare services in Canada are inadequate for youth between 16 and 19. Depending on the jurisdiction, eligibility for child-welfare services generally ends at 16, 18, or 19. However, only in very particular circumstances are such youth eligible for adult income support. There exists a huge service gap for 16–17 year olds (and 18 in British Columbia) who receive no support from the child-welfare system but are ineligible to collect social assistance. The fact that community-based organizations provide inadequate resources may contribute to a young person's move to the streets. These circumstances make them highly vulnerable to exploitation. Being "aged out" of the child-welfare system presents particular disadvantages for young women, especially mothers. In addition, young adults aged 18 through 24 are ineligible for children's services systems, yet many of their needs are not adequately served by adult programs (Robertson and Toro, 1999).

Youth need stable, trusting, long-term, positive relationships, which are not present in the current system. It is little wonder that many run from foster care or group homes. Resources for children's services have declined across the country. Working with fewer dollars, agencies have narrowed their target populations, made services more residual, and reduced early intervention and preventive services (Williams, 1991).

Personal Problems

Psychological issues such as low self-esteem, depression, and addictions also appear to play an important role for many street-involved youth, especially young females. These personal problems must be understood in the context of a young person's family background and home life. An adolescent crisis brought on by one or more of a variety of problems may precipitate a flight from home and/or family. For many youth, the escape is either a call for help or a sign of an acute personal crisis or problem (i.e., pregnancy, drug addiction). Although there is evidence to suggest that personal problems are related to a young person's move from home, causal relationships between alcohol and drug use, mental illness, and criminal behaviour (on the part of youth or parents) have not been clearly established (Hutson and Liddiard, 1994). However, the literature does clearly indicate that drug use is a significant risk factor for homelessness and a subsequent barrier to getting off the street.

Homophobia and its negative effects for gay, lesbian, and bisexual street-involved youth have received media attention. Hunter (1990: 299) reported that of the American youth who reported violent physical assaults, 46% claimed they were related to homophobia. Kruks (1991: 515-517) states that "[a]nti-gay prejudice, discrimination, and homophobia are 'rampant' in modern American society and contribute to a multiplicity of problems for homeless and runaway gay males and lesbians, including increased incidence of attempted suicide and a sense of isolation." It is often on the streets that gay and lesbian youth first experience peer acceptance and support, and these very experiences make it more difficult for them to leave street life (Kruks, 1991).

Although depression or other mental illnesses are not directly linked to homelessness, these issues are more prevalent among street-involved youth, especially females. Hagan and McCarthy (1998) found over half of the female Toronto street-involved youth they interviewed had attempted suicide and suffered from clinical depression. Most women interviewed by Novac et al. (2002) had low self-esteem and felt "worthless," and some young women had attempted suicide and engaged in self-mutilation. Suicide among street youth has become a major problem in North America, especially among Aboriginal youth (Kidd, 2003). Depression in street-involved youth has been linked to low self-esteem and stressors such as insecure and potentially violent sleeping places and the lack of a stable support network (Ayerst, 1990; Smart and Walsh, 1993). As we will see, strategies to deal with depression, such as drugs, drinking, or engaging in self-harm, are not necessarily *mal*adaptive when put in the context of street culture (Ayerst, 1999).

Substance (Ab)use There is much to want to escape from on the streets. Drugs provide an immediate coping mechanism and/or thrill:

> More than typical adolescents, street kids are beset with oppressive problems, both those they bring from home and those they acquire on the street. They have more than the average need to escape. Killing the pain of their existence . . . is the most compelling lure drugs offer. Addictions develop naturally out of the vulgar business of living in the street because some kids can cope with what is being done to their bodies only be being out of their minds. Drugs offer . . . illusion. (Webber, 1991: 225)

For Brianna, escape took the form of crystal meth. Substance abuse is part of a cluster of interrelated factors that contribute to health problems and criminal involvement among street-involved youth. Research suggests that substance use is very common in this population. According to the McCreary Centre, a non-profit organization for youth in British Columbia, 51% of the youth who participated in their study reported having an addiction problem and 65% admitted that they thought they were addicted to two or more substances (The McCreary Centre Society, 2001). A Montreal study similarly revealed that almost half (46.8%) of street-involved youth had injected drugs and were 11 times more likely to die of a drug overdose or suicide (Roy et al., 1998).

Baron (1999) interviewed 200 male youths to determine the effects of a street lifestyle on drug and alcohol use. According to Baron (1999: 18), unstable labour market histories and prolonged unemployment can leave street-involved youth "alienated from conventional society or frustrated with their failure, both of which serve to increase the risk of drug and alcohol use." Drug use, rather than simply being a problem in itself, is a reflection of the inherent instability in the lives of street-involved youth (Gaetz et al., 1999).

CONSEQUENCES: DAILY CHALLENGES OF LIFE ON THE STREETS

Life on the streets is wrought with challenges, given the harshness, chaos, and instability that characterize street life. How street life impacts a young person varies, especially by gender, sexual orientation, ethnicity, and age. However, there is very little research that critically examines these factors, Family mistreatment is often cited as a factor contributing to youth homelessness, yet as many young people learn the hard way, the street is often a violent environment filled with multiple risks. Table 8.2 outlines the risks associated with street life.

What are the challenges that street-involved youth face in their attempts to survive? They experience obstacles to meeting basic needs and barriers to accessing services on account of their age and status, appearance, and lack of money or resources. Given the hazards of living in marginal circumstances, it is not surprising that many youth report that their experiences on the street were appalling at worst and mediocre at best. A cross-Canada study found that homeless youth are five times as likely to be victims of assault than domiciled youth, and 10 times more likely to be victims of sexual assault (Gaetz, 2004). Further, Gaetz (2004) found that despite increased vulnerability, few youth tend to

Table 8.2 Risks Associated with Street Life

Risks	Examples
Basic Personal Needs	■ survival needs (e.g., food, shelter, health care)
Mental Health Issues	■ depression, low self-esteem,
	■ suicidal thinking and attempts
	■ limited resources, restrictive access criteria
	■ unassessed mental health issues
Prostitution	■ involved in street prostitution for social support and "survival sex"
HIV/AIDS and Other Diseases	■ high risk of HIV infection (e.g., drugs and unprotected sexual intercourse)
Criminal Involvement and/or Violence	■ involvement usually based on survival (e.g., "squeegee" cleaners, prostitution)
Drug and Substance Use/Abuse	■ alcohol and drug problems and untreated addictions (e.g., crystal methamphetamine)
Street Entrenchment	■ length on streets is key—the longer on the street, the more likely to be involved with drugs, crime, prostitution, etc., and the more difficult it becomes to leave street life

Source: Table is based on the following literature: basic needs (Antoniades and Tarasuk, 1998); health risks (Hwang, 2001; Busen and Beech, 1997; Haley et al.,1998; Hwang, 2001; Roy, Lemire, et al., 1998); mental health (Ayerst, 1990; Smart and Walsh, 1993); criminal involvement (McCarthy and Hagan, 1992; Baron and Hartnagel, 1999); substance abuse (Baron and Hartnagel 1998; Brannigan and Caputo 1993; Caputo, Weiler, and Kelly 1994b, 1994c; Fitzgerald 1995; Hwang 2001; Webber 1991).

go to the police for help. Street youth face many challenges during their time on the streets, which are compounded by social and economic issues or "barriers" to leaving the lifestyle. Koeller (2005) summarizes eight salient issues facing street-involved youth, as identified by Jeff Karabanow (2004) and other:

- public perceptions
    - i.e., street youth report that the general public views them negatively as all criminals/delinquents (Karabanow, 2004; Higgit, Wingert and Ristock, 2003; Novac et al., 2002)
- housing and shelter strategies
    - i.e., youth have limited access to safe, affordable housing; they opt for different non-permanent housing strategies. Among them:
        - *sleeping rough*—staying outside (e.g., parks, alley, cemetery) or residing in a place *not* designed for human habitation (e.g., landing of an unlocked apartment building, entrance to instant bank machines)
        - *squatting*—groups occupying an empty or abandoned space or building without permission
- safety
    - i.e., criminal victimization from other youth and adults, though this is under-reported (Karabanow, 2004, Baron, 1997, 2003; Gaetz, 2004)
- health and well-being
    - i.e., transience, instability, risks associated with street lifestyle (i.e., drugs, violence, prostitution) pose multiple health problems, which are exacerbated by "cold, hunger, poor housing, poor diets, high risk behaviours they engage in to survive" (Karabanow, 2004)
    - health problems include but are not limited to depression, anxiety, suicidal tendencies, low self-esteem, substance misuse, untreated addictions, and sexually transmitted diseases
    - being homeless can complicate other health problems
    - barriers to accessing health services complicate these problems (e.g., identification and/or health card required, no coverage, etc.)
- education
    - i.e., at odds with street lifestyle—lack of access due to homeless status (no address, transcripts), no stability for studying, attendance, etc.
- goals, dreams, and aspirations
    - i.e., many street-involved youth have future plans (e.g., the film *Inside Boystown*)
    - many street-involved youth interviewed by Karabanow (2004) longed for "conventional" families and lifestyles, such as returning to school, pursuing a trade, getting stable work, finding own place, getting married, having children

- trust
    - i.e., mistrust among youth of the social service system
    - could be related to dysfunctional family backgrounds and/or negative experiences with service provision systems such as child welfare or juvenile justice (Karabanow, 2004)
- economic survival strategies
    - i.e., lack training, homeless status, and age make securing/maintaining employment difficult
    - involvement in criminal activities like theft, panhandling, dealing drugs, and prostitution to survive and reliance on welfare and other forms of social assistance. (Halifax Regional Municipality, 2005)

Indeed, the boundaries between victimization and offending are blurred on the street.

Criminalization and Victimization

Involvement in the street lifestyle may include participation in illegal activities and criminal victimization. Brannigan and Caputo (1993) developed a model for understanding runaways and street youth based on the intersection of 1) involvement in the street lifestyle and 2) time spent on the street. Involvement in the street lifestyle includes participation in illegal activities (i.e., stealing, shoplifting, or breaking and entering) largely to acquire the resources needed to meet basic needs; alcohol and other drug use; high-risk sexual activities; and facing the dangers associated with living in marginal circumstances (no food, no money, no place to stay, violence, victimization, and other threats to one's physical or emotional well-being). Figure 8.2 on p. 202 depicts a model for understanding runaways and street youth (Brannigan and Caputo, 1993).

Precarious and potentially traumatic conditions on the street make youth increasingly vulnerable and likely to find other ways to survive and/or cope, such as using drugs and/or prostituting themselves, which pose significant risks to their health, well-being, and safety. Hagan and McCarthy (1997) link females involved on the street to the sex trade and male street youth to theft. This does not mean that female youth do not engage in criminal activities or that males are not involved in prostitution. In the McCreary Centre Society's British Columbia (2001) study, almost a quarter—including 27% of females and 21% of males—reported having engaged in sexual activities in exchange for money or goods.

Studying youth in four Canadian cities, Fisher (1989) found that 80% were involved in criminal activities. McCarthy and Hagan (1992) reported that out of 500 subjects, over 75% were involved in serious delinquency (e.g., theft, drug dealing, and breaking and entering). Involvement in criminal activity among street youth is largely a form of survival. In *Mean Streets: Youth Crime and Homelessness*, the first Canadian study of its kind, Hagan and McCarthy (1997) compared youth on Vancouver streets and in schools to identify adverse situational conditions that contribute to deliquency:

- hunger (often related to theft of food)
- inadequate shelter (often related to serious theft)
- problems of unemployment and shelter (often related to prostitution)

Figure 8.2 Model for Understanding Runaways and Street Youth

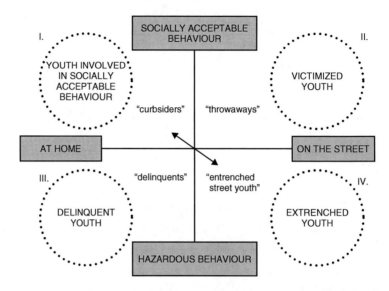

Source: Figure 1, "Studying Runaways and Street Youth in Canada: Conceptual and Research Design Issues." *User Report Responding to Violence and Abuse*, pg 216, No. 1993-05, ISBN 0-662-20386-0.

The authors found that "compared with adolescents still at home, street youths are disproportionately drawn from families characterized by no control and 'aversive strain.'" Hagan and McCarthy (1997: 625) conclude: "[M]any of the most serious problems of the street derive from the conditions of street life itself" (i.e., problems of sustenance and security).

Recall that statistics show crime is more clearly a male activity and that males are more likely to be arrested than females. One study (Novac et al., 2002) showed that more females than males begged (75% against 61%) and prostituted themselves (25% against 9%), whereas more males than females dealt drugs (49% against 36%) and stole (36% against 27%). O'Grady and Gaetz (2004) found that 55% of males and 67% of females indicated they had never been involved in property crimes. Moreover, the researchers found that for panhandling, male and female youth earned the same amount, $27/day. Males out-earned females in drug dealing and in squeegeeing (for every $1 males made females took in 75 cents). Only in sex trade work did females report that they earned more money than males. In short, males are involved in the more financially lucrative sectors of the street economy (O'Grady and Gaetz, 2004). One important aspect of this context concerns its gendered nature and how a male street culture exploits young women. This is where we will now turn.

Gendered Streets and Subsistence Strategies

> The gendered nature of the streets means that the various spaces that street youth colonize—to sleep, to occupy at night, to walk alone within, to eat, to meet friends, to drink or take drugs, to rest in, or to otherwise exist within—carry different risks for males and females. (O'Grady and Gaetz, 2004: 410)

Like the larger society, the streets that youth live on and about are gendered. Gendered streets provide male street-involved youth with considerably *more* power and control than their female counterparts (O'Grady and Gaetz, 2004). In this gendered space, wider cultural notions of masculinity and femininity are shaped and reproduced (O'Grady and Gaetz, 2004). Despite real dangers on the streets for males and females, according to Wardhaugh (2000) "[m]en can claim a place on the streets in ways that women seldom can, and their survival strategies differ accordingly." Moreover, females are more vulnerable to certain types of violent and sexual crimes (Simons and Whitbeck, 1991). Consequently, women perceive and experience personal safety and danger differently, which affects their choices. As Novac et al. (2002: 18) put it, "Women must 'disappear' in order to survive, while men have the option of seeking safety in numbers and thereby asserting 'ownership' of some public places . . . women maintain at best an ambivalent relationship with the street, never as comfortable as men, even if they are streetwise."

Gender inequality is manifest in many contexts. For example, in San Francisco, young men organize most squats, assigning room and sleeping arrangements on the basis of a sexist hierarchy. Pfeffer (1997) found that females acted out traditional feminine roles of nursing others, finding new squats, and helping men through hard times. Gender dynamics in co-ed youth shelters, drop-in centres, and on the street are traditional or "patriarchal" and thereby oppressive for young women, making them more vulnerable to sexual exploitation and violence.

Subsistence strategies are similarly gendered. Youth engage in the informal economic activities associated with homelessness, such as begging, squeegee cleaning, sex-trade work, and illegal criminal activities (and, to a lesser extent, paid jobs on a short-term basis in the formal economy), differentially by gender. Young women typically report lower incomes, largely a function of their involvement in different economic activities than their male counterparts. In addition, males and females report different living conditions, which influence their opportunities for income generation.

O'Grady and Gaetz (2004) found the following:

- Females (17%) more than males (12%) were more likely to report engaging in daily panhandling (or asking people for money, also referred to as panning or begging).

- More males (22%) than females (13%) reported squeegee cleaning, which usually occurs in small groups of 2 or 3. Proceeds are typically shared and used to purchase goods consumed collectively (e.g., food).

As stated earlier, in exchange for money or other goods like food, shelter, or drugs, some youth offer sex (Webber, 1991).

The sex trade offers another avenue, albeit dangerous and illicit, for generating income for homeless youth. It involves a broad range of activities from escort services and strip clubs to street prostitution. Surprisingly, males and females report similar numbers of involvement in the sex trade. However, differences emerge relating to street prostitution. Typically females (unlike males) work under the control of pimps, which restricts personal freedom and their ability to keep money they earn. The trade provides few opportunities for females to operate alone. According to the McCreary Centre Society (2001) study, 46% of girls and 18% of boys reported that they have been forced or coerced to have sex, compared to only 3% of students in a provincial survey comprised of non-street involved youth.

Gender disparity in terms of subsistence strategies has a lot to do with how males and females negotiate their gendered identities in the context of the streets. As O'Grady and Gaetz (2004: 409) would put it,

> As space is negotiated with the public and other street youth, economic opportunities become structured in particular ways that reflect both the youth and the general public's understanding of gender and homelessness.

That fewer young women than men turn to the streets to begin with can be explained by the fact that "the streets" and activities associated with them have historically been colonized by men and defined as a male space. Consequently, many young women have no choice but to endure family difficulties or seek alternative living arrangements.

In summary, the gendered nature of male and female experiences on the street cannot be explained simply by background characteristics, but must be understood in relation to structural factors of street life that differentially shape the experiences of homelessness for males and females. Street-involved youth are often at risk not only of direct violence, but also of many other types of victimization, including homophobia, harassment, racism, and intolerance. Some scholars suggest that homelessness "may erode street youth's ties to conventional society and destroy inhibitions restricting violent behaviour while placing them in locations and situations in which violence is more likely" (Baron, 2003: 28). Other research emphasizes how criminal victimization has an impact on health and well-being. For instance, research indicates that the rate of criminal victimization among homeless youth in Toronto is much higher than among the general population (Tanner and Wortley, 2002; Gaetz, 2004).

Pregnancy and Motherhood   A salient feature of life on the streets for young women is pregnancy and motherhood.

> I became pregnant while I was living on the street and it was a pretty, pretty hard thing. I was doing a lot of drugs, a lot of chemicals like acid and glue, and I really didn't care about myself so it was kind of impossible to care about anything else in life. When I had my son, no one came to see me in the hospital. I gave him up for adoption—and left alone. (Homeless teen, quoted in Bernstein et al., 2000: 25)

According to Greene and Ringwalt's (1998) examination of three national samples of runaway and homeless youth, youth living on the street had the highest lifetime rates of pregnancy; 48% compared to 10% for youth living in stable households with and without recent homeless experiences.

Pregnancy inevitably has young women considering shelter options, relationships, independence, and safety in profoundly different ways than young men. Bernstein and Lee (1998) estimate that up to 300 babies are born annually to homeless women in Toronto alone, and almost a third of these are to teenagers. For some, pregnancy exacerbates homelessness; for others, like some immigrant women, it is the catalyst for it (Novac et al., 2002). Some young women "are chronically homeless and live in a round of incarceration, pregnancy, and hospitalization for addictions and deteriorating mental health" (Novac et al., 2002: 43), while for others, pregnancy is an opportunity to make a change and get off the streets (Minaker and Hogeveen, forthcoming). In many cases, pregnancy increases dependence, on boyfriends in particular. The majority of babies born to homeless young mothers are not kept by their birth mothers or adopted, but are apprehended by the child-welfare system within a couple of years. For serious drug users, babies are taken away at the hospital. They are also routinely removed from women with severe mental illness. Novac et al. (2002: 50) argue, "For young women who have been wards of the child welfare system themselves, the cycle is completed when their babies are apprehended and taken into public care." Young mothers' experiences and situations are particularly unique. Modern maternity homes offer more comprehensive services for young mothers-to-be, but are only supportive if accessible. Pregnant women who stay in shelters are required to leave before the birth, forcing young women out when they are most frightened and require stability and support.

Despite these challenges and risks, there are youth like Brianna who make it off the streets. How do they do it?

OVERCOMING BARRIERS: TOWARD GETTING OFF THE STREETS

The problems associated with and obstacles to leaving the streets mirror many of the reasons youth end up homeless in the first place. According to the Street Lifestyle Survey (Caputo, Weiler, and Anderson, 1997), three significant factors associated with transitioning away from the street include,

1. a decent place to live—*housing*
2. a decent job—*employment*
3. access to appropriate services and supportive individuals—*social supports*.

To the above three factors we would add a sense of and belief in their own capacity to change their lives. With a lack of income and limited education and job opportunities, many youth are caught in a cycle, able only to meet their short-term immediate needs. Schooling is extremely important, especially for young women who see it as a means out of social, political, and economic forms of deprivation (Dhillon, 2005). Novac et al. (2002) found that a lack of economic support is a prime condition of instability and marginality in the lives of participants. Without access to affordable and safe housing, youth remain under-housed. Discrimination, especially for mothers and Aboriginal youth, further limits the potential to get off the streets. Untreated addictions, general poor health, and low self-image make it almost impossible to change the direction of one's life. With a lack of appropriate and responsive services, many youth feel there is nowhere to turn. They often rely on peers in their survival strategies and come to see other street youth as a surrogate family; this is often a more supportive, accepting, and safe environment than their original family circumstances. Novac et al. (2002) found in their Montreal study that more females than males stayed with friends and acquaintances (90% against 83%), family members (32% against 25%), and the families of friends (46% against 32%), revealing that young women are more likely to use their personal networks to cope with homelessness and avoid visible homelessness.

A very significant barrier to getting off the streets is overcoming the extreme isolation that comes along with street life. It is also difficult to find personal support. Building personal motivation and self-confidence to change one's situation is a necessary but insufficient requirement for getting out of the street lifestyle.

In the context of addictions, homelessness, mental illness, abuse and violence, prostitution, intergenerational impacts, loss of identity, and involvement in criminal activity, the "decision" to leave the streets is complicated.

The process of exiting street life is not linear or simple. Based on his analysis of 128 street-involved youth across Canada, Karabanow (2005) argues that successful services for one youth might not be successful for another. Diversity and heterogeneity within the Canadian street-youth population is served by a continuum of organizations, each with different characteristics and philosophies. Keeping in mind that the steps are not linear or mutually exclusive but are layers or dimensions of various activities, Karabanow (2005) identified the following stages or characteristics commonly experienced by those who have attempted to move out of homelessness:

- precipitating factors
  - a traumatic event, boredom, or disenchantment with street culture starts youth thinking about getting off the street
- developing the courage to change
  - gaining courage with more responsibility, support of family/friends, and awareness that someone cares for them builds "personal motivations"
- seeking support
  - initial stages involve using available services, searching for formal employment, stable housing, formal institutional involvement such as school and/or supportive housing program
- transitioning away from the street
  - *street disengagement*—physically leaving the downtown core, breaking ties to street culture and friends, and making new relationships outside of the street—is complex and difficult
- restructuring of one's routines
  - changing patterns of behaviour involves youth shifting their thinking about future aspirations, allowing a renewed sense of self but still requiring social assistance to support transitioning
- final stage: "successful exiting"
  - defined as a sense of "being in control" and "having direction" in one's life
  - participants in Karabanow's (2005) study spoke of feeling *proud* of moving on from street life, of living *on their own terms*, and, importantly, stability in terms of housing, security, and wellness

Source: Jeff Karabanow (2005), *Getting Off The Street: Exploring Strategies Used by Canadian Youth to Exit Street Life*; and Halifax Regional Municipality (2005), *Background Report, Homelessness and Street-Involved Youth in HRM, Summary of Local Findings*.

IMPLICATIONS FOR INTERVENTIONS

Street-involved youth need basic care and compassion, ongoing support, and assistance in making the transition from the streets to mainstream society. This can only be accomplished if provincial and federal governments provide monetary and other support. A survey of 387 agencies in 1996 showed that 40% of programs serving youth had lost paid staff as a result of government funding reductions (CSPA, 2000). One huge difficulty faced by youth and those interested in helping them is overcoming alienation from mainstream institutions and rebuilding trust with adults. Without professionals whose positions are valued enough to be kept and adequately remunerated, and who have the time, patience, and resources to develop relationships with youth, interventions will be ineffectual. Many street-involved youth need to learn to trust adults again. Any disenfranchised youth wants to be cared for and treated as a person worthy of dignity and respect. Stable support services and trusting, long-term relationships with caregivers work best, but they are the least available (Raychaba, 1993).

There are no rigorous studies of interventions for street-involved youth (Robertson and Toro, 1999). It makes intuitive sense, however, that the greater the extent to which pathways to the streets are addressed and the more that barriers to getting off the street are removed, the easier it will become for problems faced by street-involved youth to be alleviated.

Typically, there are two main ways to approach intervention or treatment. The first step is to help a young person with basic survival aspects of their life. This involves providing essentials (e.g., shampoo, shaving cream), doing crisis intervention work (e.g., for suicide attempts), giving information, counselling about prevention (e.g., STD awareness), harm reduction (e.g., safe needle exchanges), and coping strategies for street life (e.g., self-defence workshops). The next level is a more complicated process of helping the young person move away from street life. Trained professionals and outreach workers with personal experience work with youth toward more long-term goals. This step includes programs that offer training in social skills, literacy, employment and leadership, and access to transitional housing.

At present, there are four main levels (and one additional approach) of service delivery for street-involved youth in Canada:

1. *public agencies*: funded and operated by the government's social service department. The focus is on the family as a whole, with the aim of returning youth to their families

2. *private agencies*: include residential treatment centres. The focus is on youth who agree to return home or to alternative care facilities.

3. *diversion agencies*: residential and outpatient counselling programs, including those at hospitals.

4. *counter-cultural agencies*: specifically for homeless youth and runaway children; voluntary and confidential

5. *not-for-profit alternative approaches*: include, but are not limited to, harm reduction and innovative, unconventional programs targeted at the specific needs of street-involved youth.

However, there are huge gaps in services (e.g., those under 16 are ineligible for youth shelters) for this hard-to-reach and at times reluctant population. Many academics and practitioners recommend a continuum of youth-targeted services (employment, health, shelter, education, addiction) that include structured and less-programmed options—youth-driven, flexible, and varied services are key (Karabanow, 2005). Some youth with drug problems will benefit from harm reduction programs, while others with mental-health issues may benefit from mental-health outreach workers. At a minimum, to overcome the traumatic effects of the street and to transform their lives, street-involved youth need long-term, affordable, accessible, and safe housing. A recent assessment in Edmonton determined that an additional 5000 units of affordable housing are required (Edmonton Joint Planning Committee, 2000). Making meaningful change also requires employment, income maintenance, and tax policies that allow people to break the cycle of destitution, poverty, and homelessness (Shinn and Baumohl, 1999). As this discussion has suggested, the problem can begin to be addressed only through a continuum of services that emphasize before/on the street/transitional services/off the street. Given the heterogeneity of this population, it follows that a variety of services are required to respond to unique differences. Programs and initiatives—whether in terms of health services, housing, employment training and placement, and support programs—must be designed taking into account race, class, and gender diversity (O'Grady and Gaetz, 2004: 413); for example, female-only services like STOP 86 and culturally specific programming like that found at Bissell Centre (discussed below).

Given Toronto's large homeless youth population, it is promising to see several successful Toronto-based initiatives dealing directly with street-involved youth:

- *Sketch:* a working arts program for street-involved and homeless youth; youth are key to the development of all programs

- *Beatrice House:* opened in May 1999 as a privately funded transitional housing project for homeless mothers. Beatrice House is open to up to 30 single mothers and their children. Early childhood intervention programs are a key component of the program, and the development of parenting skills is integrated into the nursery and day care.

- *STOP 86:* the only shelter exclusively for homeless female youth aged 16 to 25. Run by the YWCA since 1970, the shelter is woman-centred, lesbian-positive, and anti-racist (Fraser, 2000).

Other initiatives across the country include

- *Foyer de Jeunes et Travailleuses de Montreal,* founded in 1993, offers a successful attempt to address the need for supportive, transitional housing. Foyer de Jeunes et Travailleuses accommodates youth who have been homeless (Rose et al., 1998), and is distinct from transitional housing because it offers training and employment, not simply accommodation (Quilgars and Anderson, 1997).

- *The Bissell Centre* in Edmonton offers services for young mothers and provides healing sessions based on traditional Aboriginal practices as well as a fetal alcohol syndrome prevention program. It allows no-cost care for young mothers with children under six for up to six days a month or longer.

- *Ndinawe Outreach Program* in Winnipeg offers outreach services to street-involved youth aged 11–25 (provides food, free condoms, referrals, and counselling). Their goal is to reach out to high-risk youth, develop relationships, and connect them to helpful services. A youth board governs all services offered and the program operates in Cree, Sautaux, and English.

- *Urban Native Youth Association—Aboriginal Youth Safe House* in Vancouver, British Columbia. A self-referral program for street-involved youth aged 16–18, Aboriginal Youth Safe House offers a "non-judgmental place" for youth to use as a resource and a place to stay for up to seven days. Youth are offered three meals a day, a resource centre and library, a television room, arts and crafts, and a cultural area, as well as cultural reunification (see www.unya.bc.ca/psresprog.htm for more information).

On a broader level, intervention must not attend only to the specific problems faced by street involved youth—including barriers to legitimate educational and employment opportunities, youth-related housing initiatives that address the lack of low-cost housing, and discrimination against youth and sub-groups of youth. It must also attend to the underlying socio-political context in which these situations arise (Rose et al., 1998).

iHuman Youth Society played a key role in Brianna Olson's journey away from the streets. She gives a lot of credit to the people who helped her on her way, and quickly recounts those who posed obstacles. iHuman, which derives its name from an Inuit term identifying the sympathetic relationship of an individual within a collective community, is not a typical intervention strategy, nor is its model replicated anywhere. The organization's approach to youth is certainly imaginative. The programs aim to create workable pathways—a support system to meet the basic needs of a safe shelter, food, and mental and physical health care—for youth to live healthy lives. This involves support and guidance for young people as they work on kicking a drug habit and/or getting out of prostitution. According to their mission statement, iHuman Youth Society is "a non-profit, charitable organization whose mission is to work with high-risk youth and to promote their reintegration into the community through a process involving crisis intervention, arts mentorship and career development program." Most importantly, iHuman does not give up on youth. Rather, the professionals and "senior" youth (previous street-involved youth who act as mentors) at iHuman treat each young person as unique with specific needs and talents. iHuman nurtures, guides and provides opportunities for youth to develop their creative abilities so that they can build identities and re-connect with their communities. In addition, iHuman offers support for

- a safe and secure environment with shelter, food, and health care that meets essential needs while advocating on behalf of youth to address more chronic issues such as addictions and mental health
- academic achievement, literacy, computer competency, résumé writing, and job-finding
- creative pursuits such as music instruction (e.g., lessons in CD production); theatre; designing and producing clothing; guidance on diary and literary development (e.g., poetry, spoken word); hip-hop workshops; and visual arts, silk-screening, and dry painting.

These programs aim to support youth making the transition to independent living. In 2006, Wallis Kendal, one of the founders of iHuman, received a University of Alberta Honorary Alumni Award for his long-recognized humanitarian work with high-risk youth. Most recently iHuman organized an afternoon and evening event entitled "Relabelled," with three forum discussions on the alienation and marginalization of Edmonton's high-risk youth, a fashion show, an art exhibit, and a performance. Check out the link at www.ihuman.org. These youth-involved and youth-driven initiatives make real differences in the life of marginalized youth. What is most amazing is how "graduates" like Brianna *give back* to other similarly situated youth at iHuman and in the wider community through various advocacy, education, and social justice activities.

CONCLUSION

Making changes for street-involved youth in neo-liberal times is not difficult. To borrow from Snider, "[w]hat *is* difficult is making change that matters to disempowered, marginalized people, change that provides tools they can use to lessen oppression, challenge repression, and change the relations of power" (Snider, 2006: 323–324). The YCJS is ill-equipped to deliver empowerment or social justice for youth—we must be careful, however, not to let the YCJS go unchecked. At the same time, other systems—education, social service, health—must be called upon to respond to the varied social, emotional, psychological, and physical needs of street-involved youth.

Making change that matters—that is, meaningful in the lives of youth—involves concentrating on changing the social conditions and underlying social structures that make children and youth vulnerable to exploitation and violence and make them legitimate targets of policies that criminalize, exclude, and punish. The voices of youth must be central to this process.

SUMMARY

- Street-involved youth comprise a diverse group of young people (12–24 years) who live and/or work on or about the streets. As an economically and socially marginalized group, street-involved youth are subjected to criminalization, victimization, and experiences compounded by race, class, and gender inequalities.

- Youth take to the streets through individual pathways such as 1) parent–adolescent conflict; 2) family violence, child abuse, and maltreatment; 3) organizational dynamics, specifically child welfare; and 4) personal problems.

- While on the street, youth employ economic survival strategies (e.g., petty crime and prostitution) and are vulnerable to victimization. Therefore, some of the risks associated with leaving homes and families are similar to the risks associated with the street.

- Street-involved youth are at risk of street entrenchment, yet stories of resilience and determination (like Brianna's) offer hope for youth plagued by problems associated with disenfranchisement and street life. There are tensions between the politics of exclusion, inequality, and silence and the agency and sheer will of street-involved youth.

- Systemic conditions that contribute to youth homelessness revolve around instability (e.g., unstable youth employment and housing, reduction in state benefits, and social exclusion). These contribute to the chronic instability that characterizes street life (e.g., in terms of housing, relationships, income, and health). Housing, employment, and access to appropriate and supportive services and individuals are integral to a move away from the street. In addition, youth must overcome social isolation, a very significant barrier.

- Making meaningful changes involves altering the social conditions and sociopolitical contexts that make children and youth vulnerable to exploitation and violence and makes them legitimate targets for policies that criminalize, exclude, and punish. It also means interventions aimed at the specific, individualized problems experienced by street youth.

DISCUSSION QUESTIONS

1. To what extent is youth homelessness a gendered and racialized problem?
2. In what ways can street-involved youth become actively involved in dealing with the problems that so dramatically affect them?
3. What would meaningful systemic change for street-involved youth look like?

RECOMMENDED READINGS

Dhillon, J. (2005). *Struggles for Access: Examining the Educational Experiences of Homeless Young Women and Girls in Canada*. A Research Report by Jaskiran Dhillon in Partnership with Justice for Girls. Vancouver: Justice for Girls

Hagan, J., and B. McCarthy. (1997). *Mean Streets: Youth Crime and Homelessness*. Cambridge: Cambridge Univ. Press.

Higgert, N. S.Wingert, and J.Ristock. (2003). *Voices from the Margins: Experiences of Street-Involved Youth in Winnipeg*. Winnipeg, MB: Winnipeg Inner-city Research Alliance.

Chapter 9
Violence and Youth

STARTING POINT

Gang violence, school violence. Are youth today becoming more violent? It appears that our schools and streets are no longer safe. Try typing the term "youth violence" into a search engine on the internet. In seconds, you will see almost 2 million sites. The sponsored links on the side read something like: "Stop the Violence," "Eliminate Youth Violence," and "Tools to Fight Hate." This is telling, but of what? Now try modifying your search to Canada. Thousands of sites are sure to appear. Somewhere you will find a link to the Public Health Agency of Canada's Violence and Youth Fact Sheet. A 1993 Environics poll revealed that Canadians believed "school-based youth violence is the single most important issue facing public education" (cited in Saskatchewan Schools Trustees Association, 1994).

According to 80% of survey respondents in Gabor's (1995) study, violence is more prevalent in schools than it was 10 years ago. Moreover, the solicitor general (2000) indicates that the present level of public concern for youth violence has not declined. Solutions like increased discipline—"bring back corporal punishment"—and a **zero-tolerance** approach (get-tough policies and codes of conduct that punish infractions rapidly and inexorably) are being proposed and/or implemented across North America. Outside the school system, there is alarm about youth gangs despite evidence that most youth crime is not violent and much violent youth crime is *not* gang-related. News media is replete with examples, such as "City wide gang violence linked to economic boom" (a recent Edmonton Examiner headline, *Edmonton Examiner*, May 23, 2007).

As you read through this chapter, ask yourself the following questions:

- What is violence?
- Why is there a growing concern over youth violence?
- How is school violence understood today?
- How are youth gangs perceived?
- What is the relationship between youth and violence?

LEARNING OBJECTIVES

After reading this chapter, you should be able to

- Define violence—as a social construct, psychological construct, and biological construct.

- Describe how various authorized knowers understand violence—biological, psychological, and sociological.

- Explain how perceptions of violence have changed over time.

- Identify the relationship between youth and violence.

- Explain the role of media in youth violence.

- Articulate the role of youth in responding to youth violence.

INTRODUCTION[1]

Would you say that youth violence is a major concern? We hear, see, and talk about school shootings, stabbings at house parties, and random gun violence; and young people are usually at the centre of our awareness. Youth violence captures the public imagination. These narratives do more than "entertain;" they fundamentally alter how we come to understand our world. But should they? Are our fears warranted? Youth violence shapes the way we view and interact with our world.

In this chapter, we examine the connections in North American society between violence and young people. This requires that we first ask the question, "What is violence?" We intuitively *think* that we *know* what violence is, or that we can at least point to it when we *see* it. But it is not that simple. Our account of the causes or conditions of violence is informed by a variety of authorized knowers, including biologists, psychologists, sociologists, criminologists, and philosophers. The main focus, as we examine their claims, will be the relationship between youth and violence as opposed to quantifying the amount of violence (e.g., "violence is on the rise") or qualifying the nature of violence (e.g., "violence is getting worse"). We will uncover the various ways that youths are victimized by violence, and how they come to be the perpetrators of violent acts.

We begin by looking at how our culture represents violence through the lens of a "spectacle." Next, we discuss shifts and changes in violence through time. Subsequently, we delve into theoretical efforts to deconstruct and problematize youth violence. Finally, we will explore the meaning and definition of violence from the perspective of respect and reverence for all life.

---

[1] Portions of Chapter 9 first appeared in *Sociology Compass* (2007) Volume 7, Issue 2. This content has been used with permission from Blackwell Publishing.

VIOLENCE AND THE SPECTACLE

Concerns over violence are inconsistent and contradictory in North American society. We eschew it as unpalatable and dream of a time free of "violence," but at the same time rise to cheer a hockey fight. We stand in line for tickets to watch graphic displays of violence in the cinema and routinely rent or buy the DVDs for our home entertainment. Consider how often young children play violent-themed video games, which whet an appetite (whether natural or socially-constructed) for blood, agony and destruction. Consider, however, why kids laugh when cartoon characters are violently dismembered, or how celebrated violently postured musicians are in videos. A recent example is the way rapper 50 Cent was glamorized in trailers and on websites advertising the 2006 movie *Get Rich or Die Trying* (www.getrichordietryinmovie.com/home.html). Examples of the pervasiveness of violence in media culture are numerous. A fascination seems to hold for many of us, so long as it is not done to *us* or anyone close to us. However, violence—both entertainment and real-life versions—affects all of us. Our fears of violence, whether absurd or authentic, shape our lives in very definite ways. This means that our movements, understandings of law and governance strategies, and relations with others are all conditioned by violence, whether experienced directly or indirectly.

Violence has become spatially diffused. In our global age of continuous communication, violent images and messages constantly circulate and bombard us from every angle. From state-sponsored armed combat in Iraq to bullying in schoolyards, no one (youth included) is immune from the effects of violence, especially when a violent event halfway across the world (e.g., bombing in Baghdad) is almost instantaneously broadcast on Canadian television screens and webcasts. With the advent of *YouTube*, a violent act performed three minutes ago in a place you have never heard of can be viewed on your computer screen and witnessed almost firsthand.

Violence is omnipresent. It appears as such an obvious, widespread, and persistent phenomenon that many come to consider it *natural*. Carl Goldberg (2003: 1) maintains that violence "has become a dominant force in contemporary life [and] according to public opinion polls 2 out of every 5 Americans living in large cities are afraid to leave their homes at night." Violence alters our way of life, where we choose to live, and how we conduct ourselves. Just think about your own decisions about your weekend plans—where you will go, who you will be with, and why. Will you be going to a local bar or after-hours club? Yes, shootings occasionally take place in bars and on the street. Yes, young women are accosted or date raped. In fact, young people are disproportionately victimized by interpersonal crimes, especially those involving violence. Yet it is the elderly (not youth) who have the greatest fear of crime, despite having one of the lowest victimization rates. Goldberg (2003: 1) points out that "[m]any go hungry rather than chance an assault on city streets on their way to the market." Even more tragic is that during the summer heatwave of 1995 in Chicago. some older people may have perished in stifling apartments because they refused to "risk" opening their windows in case they allowed intruders to breach the security of their homes.

Media discourse grossly distorts the prevalence and risks associated with youth crime while accentuating young people as perpetrators of violence and underplaying their victimization. According to Guy Debord (1970), our society is one of a "spectacle" in which media events structure our perception of (in this case) what *counts* as youth violence. The **spectacle** is not exclusively a collection of images. It is, as Debord (1970) writes, "[a] worldview that has actually been materialized, a view of the world that has become objective." We come to believe that broadcast versions represent what is really going on, which structures how we understand the relationship between youth and violence. In a socio-cultural context where violence is *made to seem* so widespread and frightening in all aspects and at all levels of today's life, from *CSI* to *Law & Order* to *Cold Case*, what violence *is* gets left largely un-problematically assumed.

Iconic murders (Barb Danelesko, Reena Virk, Jesse Cadman, and Jordan Manners in Canada) and school shootings (Dawson, Taber, Columbine, Virginia Tech, and, most recently, C.W. Jeffreys Collegiate) are indeed tragic. However, these events are hardly representative of the everyday and mundane reality of youth crime, or of youthful violence. Comments posted online after death of Jordan Manners are indicative of the moral panic that quickly ensues after such events. For example: "We [must] toughen up our handgun laws and hold parents accountable" . . . "I'm so confused about why in the world someone would do that" . . . "This is just the latest in a rash of youth related violent incidents seeping across our country." The focus on victims like Jason Lang, whose young life was cut short in Taber, is obscured when terms like "school shootings" and "youth violence" are bandied about (see Box 9.1).

It is significant that in a society where television franchises like *Law & Order* and *CSI* stream into our living rooms and children and youth routinely play violent video games and listen to graphic lyrics in music, the exceptional cases mentioned above confirm the spectacle. The implications are huge. In such a cultural context, citizens take steps to protect themselves from the seemingly pervasive threat by installing burglar alarms, hiding away in gated communities, and demanding more intensive state punishment. To argue against these measures becomes problematic. A common retort would sound something like, "What? You *want* to see another school shooting, more gang-related murders?" Soon people fear that *their* schools will be turned into shooting galleries and *their* neighbours

Box 9.1
Responses to School Shootings

The following is a partial excerpt from www.cbc.ca/news/background/taber/yourletters.html, accessed on May 24, 2007.

In this letter I am hoping that not only can it help, but have people see what I have to say and think about the many things that are going on in this world as we know it . . .

I am a student who is 16 years of age. I feel that not only has our media blown this thing out of proportion but that these events should not have ever been covered on national news. The reason that I say this is because I come from a small town in Alberta. Much similar to Taber. Maybe even smaller. But as I see it every person in my hometown in which I have known all my life has come to know mostly every aspect of these shootings. The thing that is a concern are people in my school are saying extremely rude things such as "What would you do if I came into school tomorrow and did the same thing?" Many of

our teachers here are beginning to become paranoid of the things that this is bringing about. These events that have happened in Colorado and Taber are tragic events. All I ask is that the media should not get so involved into this. My main concern is that children are watching the news with their parents are getting more than they bargain for . . .

It is amazing that it takes the death of teens before anyone expresses some sorrow for those killed. Many people view teens as a wild bunch of yahoos. Until someone dies everyone's perspectives change. And for those that see people my own age as humans also. I give them my thanks. Now as I am going to do right now is take another moment to end this short message that might help people see that what has happened is a extremely sad thing and needs time to heal.

Source: Brent Hoff. Letter originally published on www.cbc.ca.

will be used as target practice by local youth gangs. These images and the perceptions accompanying them unnerve a restless public and arouse the sentiment that *something* needs to be done about youth violence (Huffine, 2003). Consider the Ontario provincial government's attempt to combat gun and gang violence by announcing a $51 million package of initiatives in January 2006. This involved expanding the Guns and Gangs Task Force; hiring more police officers, Crown attorneys, probation officers, and parole officers; and opening an operations centre to provide coordinated investigation and prosecution of gang and gun-related crimes. For the Liberal government, this task required being "tough on crime," using "strong enforcement," and taking aim at the "causes of crime" (Ministry of the Attorney General, Ontario, 2006). The assumption behind this approach is that coming down harder, stronger, and more punitively on the problem of guns and gangs will make communities safer. Although some attention has been paid to after-school activities, programs for disenfranchised youth and their families, and better housing, the main thrust of the government's plan involves a criminal justice response.

An ethos of fear exists in Canada fuelled by the "spectacle," a condition that has been seen in Western nations since the mid-1990s. It is characterized by concerned citizens (rallying in largely middle-class neighbourhoods) demanding that governments impose the most austere punishments on violent youth and enact increasingly intrusive legislation. Misguided reactions born of frustration and fear can turn upon themselves, thereby contributing to rather than dealing with the problem. Despite scant proof of their effectiveness (as we will see in Chapter 10), many proponents of law and order continue to support boot camps, chain gangs, corporal punishment, and incarceration. These "solutions" appear to satisfy the public, at least for a while. By contrast, relatively few "resources have been allocated to understanding the phenomena of youth violence or to understanding etiology or changes in prevalence, the meanings of violence to the youth involved, or the appropriate societal response when tragic incidents occur" (Huffine 2003: 361). People appear to be more willing to accept a quick and easy fix such as incarceration (e.g., adding more beds to the local detention centre) instead of being willing to spend their money, offer their time, and devote sustained attention to long-term responses and prevention—which would involve research into the underlying conditions of youth crime and developing effective, youth-centred interventions. Do people want the easy solution because they are afraid? Perhaps there is more at stake. When we look more critically at the systemic issues that underlie the choices that youth make, we are confronted with questions of privilege and power. In short, who is willing to listen to youth?

VIOLENCE THROUGHOUT TIME

Violence Then

The normative grounds or the accepted cultural understandings of violence have undergone considerable shifts. How has violence changed? The answer takes us back to antiquity. Any reading of traditional history books, religious discourses, or period literature will confirm an omnipresence of violence. In the Bible (II Chronicles 20: 23-24), for example, the following scene appears:

> The men of Ammon and Moab rose up against the men from Mount Seir to destroy
> and annihilate them. After they finished slaughtering the men from Seir, they helped

to destroy one another. When the men of Judah came to the place that overlooks the desert and looked toward the vast army, they saw only dead bodies lying on the ground; no one had escaped.

This is hardly the only biblical event where the blood of God's enemies is spilled. Countless other references to violence dot human history. Homer's epic, *The Iliad*, is dominated by scenes of annihilation. Indeed, Homer is not reticent to share the gory nuances of violence. For example, he writes:

> First, Ajax son of Telamon killed brave Epicles, a comrade of Sarpedon, hitting him with a jagged stone that lay by the battlements at the very top of the wall. As men now are, even one who is in the bloom of youth could hardly lift it with his two hands, but Ajax raised it high aloft and flung it down, smashing Epicles' four-crested helmet so that the bones of his head were crushed to pieces, and he fell from the high wall as though he were diving, with no more life left in him. (Homer Iliad, Book 12: 435–443)

Consider, for example, the spectacle put on by Roman Gladiators and the thousands who packed the amphitheatres to cheer as their favourites maimed, battered, and disfigured animals, criminals, and each other. Historically, violence has been persistent and widespread, but its meaning is not obvious. A complex mixture of biological, cultural, psychological, and social forces interact to produce what we refer to as "violence."

Violence Now

Today violence continues to shape how we view and interact with our social world. The tools of violence have changed—from jagged stones to Mach10 pistols, from four-crested helmets to Kevlar vests. But what really differentiates the nature of violence today from that of Homer's time is how it is *perceived* and the way it is *evaluated*. Telecommunications, the internet, air travel, etc. have transformed the globe into a seemly *continuous* and *inseparable* space. Sergio Cotta (1991: 10) reminds us that "messages of violence arrive from everywhere and circulate constantly." Twenty-four-hour news channels and continuous media internet feeds circulate an almost endless supply of violent encounters (i.e., school shootings, war, homicide, torture, etc.). A spectacle of violence in one place can almost immediately be reproduced to form another spectacle elsewhere. The bombardment of images and stories flooding our consciousness gives no time for sombre reflection before our senses are assaulted by the next one. To the public it matters little which government is *not* invading another country, which youth are *not* involved in gang swarming, or which buildings have *not* (yet) been blown up. That the great preponderance of violence is sporadic and will probably never touch the lives of most people matters little. As we stated earlier, violent events seem usual rather than exceptional. A cultural attitude infused with the universality and omnipresence of violence has spread, in Cotta's terms, "like an endemic disease" (Cotta 1991: 10). Taking the analogy of "disease" one step further, the question becomes, "Do we treat the symptoms or the underlying condition?"

So, the great novelty in violence lies in our subjective sensitivity to it. Perhaps, then, it is more significant to explore not how *violence* has changed over time, but how *we* have changed (Cotta, 1991). This is an important shift in our thinking about the problem. It allows us to focus on our attitudes about violence and those engaged in violent acts.

Because violence, and especially youth violence, plays a formative role in human experience, it is paramount that we openly examine it as critically as possible.

WHAT IS "VIOLENCE"?

The problems of violence still remain most obscure. (Sorel, 1906)

Take a break from your reading to consider the word "violence." What is violence? What does this word mean to you? How do you define it? When going about our daily lives, we are certain we *know* what violence is, but when asked to reflect on it more carefully our definition becomes elusive. John Keane (2004) claims that although constructing concepts and defining terms like violence can be dangerous, these constructs are still fundamentally necessary. Keane (2004: 30) is certain that "they can be fatal for the imagination in that they lull their users into a false sense of certainty about the world, seducing them into thinking that they 'know' it like the backs of their hands." However, "without such categories thinking is swamped, sometimes drowned, by the world's otherwise unintelligible tides and waves and storms of events, people and things."

Let us consider an example to illustrate this idea. If we see a husband push his wife, we may intuit that he was acting violently. However, we cannot immediately objectify and quantify the force and power involved to provide a foundational checklist with criteria to determine if the event was violent or not. What is it about this event that made it *violent*? Clearly, we can agree that all pushing is not violence. Indeed, what if the man was pushing the woman on a swing? It would not be violent. What is it about a push that can render it violent?

The point is that the word "violence" is typically used without serious reflection on its meaning or essence—even in academic and legal circles. Consider the following examples of appropriate cultural deployments of the term: a violent sneeze; violent pain; violent storm; a threat of violence; crimes of violence; violent words; a violent death; violent punishment (Wade, 1971). Do these phrases all refer to the same phenomenon? If so, what is constant? What is the link between crimes of violence and a violent storm? This list is not intended to be exhaustive, but may help focus attention on the differential and expansive meanings surrounding violence.

Perhaps the origin of the word violence—its etymology—will shed some light on its underlying essence. According to Francis Wade (1971), "violence" and "violent" descend from two Latin words: *violentus* and *violare*. The first is an adjective meaning forcible, vehement, impetuous, and boisterous, and emphasizes the manner through which an action is conducted. The second, *violare*, is a verb meaning to treat with violence, to injure, to dishonour, to outrage, or to violate, which reflects the end to which an action is put (Lewis and Short, 1879). Wade (1971) argues that *violentus* is primarily a *descriptive* term because it concerns itself with describing an agent's action, whereas *violare* considers the effect of one action on another and is primarily a *normative* word expressing condemnation (Wade, 1971). Thus, for an action to be considered violent, it must be descriptively and normatively violent. Returning to our example of the man pushing his wife on the swing, the reason we cannot definitely say this was an instance of violence is because although the action of pushing is normatively violent, the description of pushing a person on a swing is certainly not. His action cannot constitute violence if no one is injured, nothing is damaged, nothing is destroyed, and there is no infringement (Wade, 1971).

The corollary, then, suggests that violence is when someone or something is damaged, destroyed, or infringed upon. Is a classmate engaging in violence when he or she drops your laptop computer and it crashes to the ground with a thump? If we determine meaning by result—a broken computer that no longer works—then the answer is yes. Suppose, however, that the laptop is dropped on a carpeted floor and shows no sign of damage when you successfully log on. If we determine meaning by intent—a malicious student retaliates against your A-grade paper by pushing your computer off the desk and onto the floor—then regardless of whether or not the thing is actually damaged, isn't she or he inflicting violence? Descriptive criteria offer an alternative to a purely normative understanding of violence that at least allows our interpretation to be context specific.

Although the addition of *normative* and *descriptive* criteria is somewhat helpful, still we are in no position to clearly articulate what violence *is*. That is, we cannot definitively state what makes an action descriptively or normatively violent other than *what we intuit or understand as such*. This is why our subjective sensitivity to violence is significant; it directs us to the criteria to be employed (i.e., motivation, outcome, etc.).

Perhaps our definitional advantage will come from juxtaposing violence with two phenomena that have traditionally been closely aligned with, but not identical to, violence—force and aggression. First, let us consider force. Allan Back (2004) argues that force is that "which is capable of producing . . . change in motion, in shape, in quality, or in all these aspects." Important to note here is that force is defined by the *effects* it has on the object of its intention, rather than by its own intrinsic characteristic. That is, to fill a balloon, air is forced into it. An act, then, is forceful in relation to the effects it has on its recipients—not in terms of its own "rapidity, effort, quantity or force exerted or etc." (Wolff, 1969: 602). Thus, Robert Wolff (1969) claims that force can be seen as the ability to render some change through physical effort. We could drive a screw into a piece of wood, push a child on a swing, or twist a lid off a jar by employing force without being violent. Force, then, is not morally objectionable, whereas some forms of violence certainly have become so. Indeed, there may be little distinction between the amount of force required by a medical doctor to reposition a dislocated collarbone and the force applied to dislocate it in the first place.

Force seems to lead us further from understanding violence. Is aggression more helpful? It is often employed as a synonym for violence and is certainly of similar ilk. Aggression is a particular form or type of forcefulness that is directed to a *particular* object. That is, it is not generalized like wind, but is a force applied within a specific context. Thus, we do not speak of an aggressive storm or an aggressive wind since these entities do not pick out particular targets. Aggression, then, is an intentional forceful action (Wilson, 1975). Many scholars seem to follow E.O. Wilson (1975), who defines "aggression" as "a physical threat or threat of action by one individual that reduces the freedom or genetic fitness of another."

But aggression and violence do not contain the same essence. For Colin Sumner (1996), aggression is an action that the majority considers to be largely acceptable, whereas violence is typically not morally condoned. Jane Snyder (2003: 262) agrees when she argues:

> Violence *is* destructive. Aggression is the forceful pursuit of tension discharge and can be constructive in aim and consequence; aggression is involved in pursuing life sustaining and social aims. The need to discharge and eliminate tension is a primary need; violent action is more commonly the result of a drive fusion or diffusion, in the sense that the life drive may be subverted to destructive ends.

Aggression is not only acceptable, but, according to Snyder (2003), is indeed integral to our continued co-existence. But where is the line drawn between aggression (acceptable) and violence (repugnant)? Who decides? Sumner concludes that the difference between violence and aggression is less in kind than in how it is constructed in discourse. Sumner (1996: 5) claims that if violence is a social construct rather than something ordained by nature, it might be "best understood as the censure of some forms of human practice as unacceptable forms or levels of aggression."

Is this all there is to violence? A social and moral censure of aggressive actions we find abhorrent? There is something *more*, some qualitative difference between a group of protestors who lie on a pavement in an *aggressive* attempt to block traffic while making a political or social statement and a group of dissenters who shoot a police officer to make the same point. This must be where we need to locate the behaviour in question—in the social context in which it takes place (e.g., a sanctioned sporting event like a boxing match versus a fistfight in a nightclub). We have been attempting to ascertain what violence *is*, but perhaps it is an impossible task because whenever we approach it and attempt a definition, it disappears into something *other* (force, power, aggression, etc.). Perhaps, with our working definition of violence as a social censure, we can now focus on the victims of violence.

What sets violence apart is its destructive quality as it is related to the other. Accordingly, violence is a *relational* act in which its target is not deemed worthy of respect. Instead, the "other" goes unrecognized and, as such, is rendered suitable for harm and destruction. It follows, then, as Emmanuel Levinas (1969: 198) articulates, "The Other is the sole being I can wish to kill." Using Levinas's rationale, it is much easier to kill those who are at distance from us and those who we determine to be mere objects blocking us from attaining a desired end. In violence there is no reverence for life, no respect for another who is like us but unlike us. We do not esteem and honour those to whom we do violence. It is human- and world-destroying.

From this argument, we can see that pushing a child on a swing, body-checking in hockey, or even sneezing, for that matter, are not *necessarily* violent. They are part of our expected horizon of experience. This is not to say, however, that a push on a swing or a body-check cannot *be* violent, only that they are not in and of themselves violent. When the force of a push, the intensity of a check, or the motivation behind these acts transgresses normative bounds (or exists outside a normative social context), then we come to know the meaning of violence. Violence only has an effect because it is unexpected and, moreover, considers others "as mere objects, as bodies deemed worthy of a kick and a punch, or a knife, a bullet or a bomb" (Bar On, 2002: 38).

Following this line of thinking, the more saturated our culture becomes with that-which-is-believed-to-be violence, the less objectionable society finds harm against others. The question becomes, "To what extent are youth generally and specific groups of young people deemed unworthy of respect and viewed as appropriate objects of denigration?" As we saw in Chapters 6, 7, and 8, young females, Aboriginal youth, and street-involved youth are excessively objects of othering and violence. To sum up, violence is a relational, context-specific censure that works as an othering process—that is, it disrespects another.

Prevalence

With a reasonable grasp on the meaning of "violence," we now turn our attention to how much of it we can expect to find in North American society. Official statistics—arrest rates gathered by local police forces and nationally aggregated—paint a picture that is quite at odds with the perception of those living in the "society of the spectacle," where exceptional crime events are broadcast by media outlets as if they are representative. In fact, while violent youth crime rates escalated from the mid-1980s to the mid-1990s, they have subsequently declined. Gregg Barak (2006) maintains that one of the best kept "secrets" in the United States at the turn of the 21st century was that youth and school violence was abating throughout the late 1990s.

Whereas violent crime rates have declined in recent years, far too many citizens are in pain and hurting because of it. It warrants our attention. Indeed, even with recent declines, contemporary rates are substantially higher than the 1970s and 1980s.[2] With this in mind, Prothrow-Smith and Weissman (1991) make a convincing argument that social violence is endemic to North American society and that its spike in the 1990s was an epidemic on top of an epidemic.

Although the United States experienced more than a decade of decline in youth violence rates, this trend reversed in 2005 (FBI, 2006). In Canada, violent youth crime rates continued the downward trend evident since the mid 1990s. This has been even more pronounced since the *Youth Criminal Justice Act* (YCJA) was passed in 2002 and implemented a year later. Statistics Canada reported that the rate of violent youth crime declined from 947 charged per 100 000 in 2001 to 782.4 per 100 000 in 2005 (Statistics Canada, 2006b), a rather substantial and impressive reduction. For example, Edmonton made headlines across the country for its "gang problem" and its thriving economy—and has been awarded the moniker "Alberta Advantage." In Edmonton, police arrest statistics reveal a similar, rather striking trend. In comparison to 2004, 2005 youth charges for criminal code offences declined 15% (see Figure 9.1). Decreases in violent crime were similarly significant (see Figure 9.2 on p. 212).

Figure 9.1 Adult and Youth Charges for Violent Crime

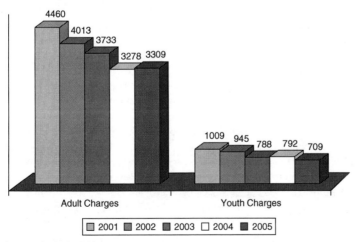

Source: Edmonton Police Service, 2006,

---

[2] Making such comparisons in a Canadian context is complicated by the shift in legislation from the social-welfare inspired JDA to the YOA, which is based on justice and crime control models.

Figure 9.2 Adult and Youth Charges for Criminal Code Offences

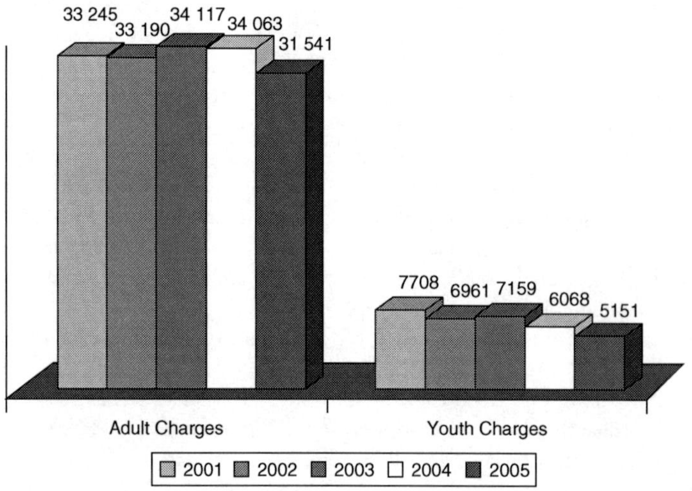

Source: Edmonton Police Service, 2006,

To what do we attribute these impressive reductions? While any hypotheses would move little beyond conjecture, there is some scholarly support to suggest that a healthy economy invariably contributes to declining crime rates. With its abundant oil and natural gas reserves, Alberta is Canada's most resource-rich province. While oil production increased, violent crime decreased. In light of work by Franklin Zimring (1999) and others, this trend is not altogether unexpected. Zimring concludes that economic difficulties are positively correlated with rates of violent crime. While this striking correlation is significant as far as both youth and adults are concerned, the range of the fluctuation is greater for youth.

A caveat must be entered at this point: scholars can never be absolutely certain of just how much violence exists in any given society. Official statistics reveal only those cases that have come to police attention or, more specifically, where police have arrested a suspect for committing what the criminal code determines to be a violent offence. Criminologists refer to undetected and unreported incidents as the dark figure of crime. That is, crime scholars and statisticians can never be certain they have captured all the crime, violent or otherwise, that exists in a society. There are many reasons why violence may not be reported to police. First, the violent incident may not be viewed as a crime, but as a normative element of a social scene. For example, in an effort to clear an obstructed view of the puck, a hockey goalie may repeatedly slash an opposing player's ankles. Hockey players consider this part of "paying the price" for screening a goaltender's view. However, hitting a fellow bus-rider in the shins with a stick because they are blocking your view is likely to bring about retaliation, legal or otherwise. Second, victims may feel that their story would not be believed. This rationale is often employed by women who have been raped. Convinced that no one will listen, feeling too embarrassed to talk about it, or fearing ridicule in court, many victims opt for silence.

Closely related, another reason for under-reporting is victim blaming, which is particularly relevant for youth who are disproportionately victimized by other youth. Some people refuse to come forward in order to avoid the risk of being blamed. In such a case, the victim believes (or is said to believe) that he or she was in the "wrong" part of town (i.e., the inner city), wearing the "wrong" attire (a short skirt, an expensive watch), or engaged in the "wrong" activity (drinking, taking money out of an ATM, being in a gang). The belief is that if they hadn't been in that end of town, wearing those clothes, and or doing that, they could have avoided the incident. Nothing is said about the perpetrator. Other reasons for not reporting violence include not wanting the offender to get into trouble, fear of reprisal, believing the incident was far too minor to justify police intervention, or believing that the police will do nothing about it. Official statistics obscure a lot of harm and victimization.

TOWARD AN EXPLANATION

Why do youth act violently? The answer will largely depend on to whom the question is posed. This section surveys a variety of experts, including biologists, psychologists, sociologists, criminologists, and philosophers. First, however, we will consider scholars who attempt to find causal links to violence in our biology.

The Biological Approach

Seeking biological derivations of violence is hardly a novel enterprise. Indeed, the father of modern criminology, Cesare Lombroso, was certain that criminal behaviour was marked on the body. He was convinced that an official trained to recognize distinguishing physical features (e.g., long canine teeth, long arm span, raised forehead, or the presence of tattoos) could predict criminality. Phrenologists also believed that aggressive character could be "read" on the skull through the arrangement of bumps and depressions. Contemporary researchers attempt slightly more radical means of determining violent personalities by examining human DNA. Indeed, scientific knowledge about how genes influence behaviour, gained through gene mapping and brain scans, has exploded under the influence of the Human Genome Project (Desai, 2005). The idea that violence may be hard-wired into our genes has re-emerged, but not without considerable controversy.

In recent years, highlighted by sensational court cases, the brave new world of biological science has begun to infiltrate criminal justice proceedings and procedures. DNA testing has had undeniable implications for court proceedings in determining guilt or innocence. It has also been usefully employed to overturn wrongful convictions. A particularly important case where DNA evidence was employed involved David Milgaard. At the age of 16, Milgaard was convicted of the murder of Gail Miller on January 31, 1970. He declared his innocence throughout the ordeal, but to no avail. Not until 1991, 21 years after his conviction, did his case receive recognition. Despite pleading by Winnipeg Liberal member of parliament Lloyd Axworthy, parliament initially rejected Milgaard's appeal for a review of his case. Finally, after a new trial in 1997, he was cleared of the murder through DNA evidence. Not, however, before he had spent 27 years in prison. This is certainly among the least controversial ways DNA can be deployed in criminal justice matters.

In recent years, under the influence of rapid advances in bio-chemistry, researchers have attempted to identify genetic markers of aggressiveness and, in some cases, violence. During the late 1980s and early 1990s, scientists identified what they thought were genetic markers and, in a few notable cases, genetic variants associated with diseases long suspected of being inherited (e.g., diabetes, breast cancer). Once aware that some diseases and inheritance patterns could be successfully linked to DNA, behavioural researchers took notice. They sought to determine whether genetic variants of societal-level problems like violence were genetically linked. Adapting methods and techniques from the natural sciences led to what seemed to be immediate breakthroughs in the study of schizophrenia, bipolar disorder, and alcoholism. Researchers were ecstatic. However, the euphoria was short-lived. Wasserman (2004) reports that early findings linking the first two mental disorders with genetic markers had to be retracted for lack of reliability, while the third still remains mired in controversy. Unfortunately for research scientists, the first application of molecular genetics techniques to psychiatric and behavioural disorders could not be replicated. In fact, in the early years, no one discovered a single finding to link genetic markers with behavioural patterns.

In the early 1990s, researchers studying a Dutch family discovered a gene associated with male violence, and the future of genetic science was promising once again. Scientists were convinced that they may have inadvertently found the "crime gene"—no doubt a major discovery (Wasserman, 2004). Although the family under study was not representative, what the scientists uncovered was not easily dismissed. Indeed, the researchers successfully linked the gene in question to the production of the serotonin-metabolizing protein monoamine oxidase A or MAOA. Because serotonin is implicated in numerous psychological conditions, varying from depression to impulsive violence, this was an important finding (Wasserman, 2004). Nevertheless, it is problematic to draw conclusions from such a small sample. Were the males studied indeed more aggressive or simply less intelligent, with less creative and more destructive coping mechanisms?

Despite the controversy, research on MAOA continued, and by 2002 researchers were reasonably confident they had found a reliable, albeit indirect, link between violence and genetics (Rowe, 2001). Caspi and his colleagues (2002) were involved in a long-term longitudinal study of New Zealand youth. They found that the only variable that contained a reliable causal relationship with violence was childhood maltreatment. Caspi et al. (2002: 851) write: "[B]oys who experience abuse—and, more generally, those exposed to erratic, coercive, and punitive parenting—are at risk of developing conduct disorder, antisocial personality symptoms, and of becoming violent offenders . . . [and] the earlier children experience maltreatment, the more likely they are to develop these problems." The problem for behavioural researchers, however, has been that although maltreatment increases a subject's risk for becoming violent, not everyone affected becomes violent. Thus, there must be some intervening explanatory variable (e.g., low MAOA). Caspi et al. (2002) concluded that although only measuring levels of MAOA did little to improve their ability to predict violent outcomes, this changed when combined with childhood maltreatment. High levels of MAOA seemed to render children more resilient to the effects of abusive parental treatment, whereas children with lower levels showed signs of being far less resilient.

Such research results strike a chord, as they are reminiscent of how genetic "findings" were misappropriated in the early 20th century. Hitler and the Nazi party employed "scientific" assessments of inferiority to first segregate and then exterminate six million Jews. North Americans employed the same eugenics discourse in their efforts to sterilize and incapacitate "the criminal," "the prostitute," and "the feeble-minded" in the interests of purifying the race. Hard lessons learned from WWII have exposed the xenophobia that such science can be fuel. We must ask whether data concerning "defective" or "mutant" genes outweigh the potential harm that is certain to follow. Consider what would happen if scientists isolated a gene that they were convinced was connected to violent outcomes. What would we, as a society, conclude should be done with these individuals? Would you want youths with the violent crime gene at your child's school? What if you were a youth identified as such?

Many studies linking genes with behaviour have typically been found to be spurious (Beecher-Monas and Garcia-Rill, 2006, Lucentini, 2004). Such evidence is cold comfort for policy makers and citizens who think that behavioural genetics represents the future of criminal justice. There seems to be little sound reason to—and a myriad of compelling reasons not to—venture into this "brave new world" of behavioural genetics.

Psychological Constructions of Violence

If genes are not the underlying rationale for violence, what is? Is there a psychological root? Hundreds of academic and popular psychology books suggest that there is. Psychoanalyst Phyllis Meadow (2003) maintains that because of the nature and extent of human cruelty (e.g., genocide, rape, torture, and exploitation), we would be remiss not to "at least entertain the idea of a biological level aggressive drive." Psychoanalytic theory, following the influence and direction of Sigmund Freud, groups instinctive urges into two broad headings: sex and aggression. Those drives gathered under sex, or *Eros*, are concerned with and directed toward preservation, propagation, and unification. Those instincts gathered under aggression, or *Thanatos*, serve to destroy and annihilate life (Pashmna, 1974). *Eros* and *Thanatos*, like many of Freud's concepts (e.g., Oedipus), derive their meaning from Greek mythology. The modern concept of eroticism finds its roots in *Eros*, the god of lust and fertility. *Thanatos*, on the other hand, was the incarnation of death. Freud maintained that instinctual energy in the service of *Eros* is dedicated to the preservation and creation of life as it co-joins and co-mingles human beings. By contrast, *Thanatos* energy or the death drive, as the name and Greek mythology suggest, moves callously toward the destruction of one human by another. This is where violence, or destruction of the other, comes into play.

Albert Einstein was particularly taken by Freud's dual drive theory of aggression and the impetus to violence. He sent a letter to Freud informing him about and inviting him to participate in an organization of intellectual leaders who were concerned about how best to manage or control the problem of human aggression, put vividly on display in WWI (Einstein and Freud, 1960). Einstein wrote, "You have shown with irresistible lucidity how inseparably the aggressive and destructive instincts are bound up in the human psyche with those of love and the lust for life." Bolstered by Einstein's invitation and support, Freud offered the following theory as to why humans are so intent on destroying each other: "Only one answer is possible; because man has within him a lust for hatred and destruction. In normal times this passion exists in a latent state, it emerges only in unusual circumstances; but it is a comparatively easy task to call it into play and raise it to the power of a collective psychosis. Here lies, perhaps, the crux of all the complex factors we are considering, an enigma that only the expert in the lore of human instincts can resolve." Freud viewed human beings as a projection of instinctual forces; instincts far more powerful than the conscious ego.

Thus, Freud was convinced that physical and mental prerequisites for violence are intrinsic to our very essence. But how does violence become manifest? We are not always likely to lash out in every situation. What occurs within an individual to produce this manifestation of drive energy? According to Freud (1920: 36), "An instinct is an urge inherent in organic life to restore an earlier state of things. Thus in the interests of equilibrium, tension beyond a certain threshold will activate *Thanatos*." That is, the collection of this energy will at some point demand discharge. In this way, energy—aggression and destruction—is released on an object outside the individual. Freud was quite reticent and reluctant to offer solutions to the problem of violence, in part because he did not consider aggression to be independent of human existence. In correspondence with Einstein he despondently concludes, "To me this hope seems vain. . . . In any case, as you too have observed, complete suppression of man's aggressive tendencies is not in issue; what we may try is to divert it into a channel other than that of warfare." For Freud (1960), human beings are *naturally* violent and what was required were more positive, productive, and acceptable avenues for the release of tension.

Although psychoanalytic thought and practice has been at the centre of thinking about and managing youth violence, it is not without criticism. What should we make of this approach to explaining youth violence? The most significant barrier to discerning the general efficacy of Freud's theorizing is the lack of empirical support for even the existence of *Thanatos* and *Eros*; never mind how these drives operate within any one individual in different social contexts. Even Freud later "resisted" the actuality of *Thanatos*. In 1929, he stated, "It might be assumed that the death instinct operated silently within the organism toward its dissolution, that, of course, was no proof. A more fruitful idea was that a portion of the instinct is diverted towards the external world and comes to light as an instinct of aggressiveness and destructiveness" (Freud, 1920: 119). Following this logic, evidence of *Thanatos* is located in its outward expression of aggression. But Freud's argument is circular: it claims that violence is a manifestation of *Thanatos* energy but the only evidence of *Thanatos* is violence.

Criticism of Freud's "death instinct" has been unabated since he first introduced the concept in the early 20th century. René Girard, for his part, was particularly dismissive of Freud's idea that *Thanatos* propels humans toward death. "No more that a last surrender to mythological thinking," he argued, "a final manifestation of that ancient belief that human violence can be attributed to some outside influence [such as] to gods, to fate, to some force men can hardly be expected to control" (Girard, 1977: 145). Freud's theory provides humans with a means to avoid directly confronting the underlying rationality for violence, Girard contends. Attributing violence to a "mythical" drive fails to engage in the difficult and painful work of exploring how violence is embedded in social and cultural artifacts. This is where social forces become significant.

Girard understood violence as emerging out of desire and mimicry or imitation. In any violent encounter, he maintains, there are three elements available or present: the subject, the object, and the rival. This testifies to the nuances of violence absent from much prior theorizing. The rival "desires the same object as the subject, and to assert the primacy of the rival can lead to only one conclusion. Rivalry does not arise because of the fortuitous convergence of two desires on a single object; rather, '*the subject desires the object because* the rival desires it'" (Girard 1977: 145, emphasis added). By demonstrating an interest in a particular object, the rival signals to the subject that the object she or he possesses is infinitely covetable. Such mimicry of childhood desire is universally recognized. A young child sees a sibling playing with a toy (e.g., building bricks) and immediately wants *that* specific toy even though there are numerous others (e.g., cars, blocks) to choose from nearby. The child does not want something else because he or she sees the other child having fun and aspires to the same. According to Girard (1977), the child's attraction to the toy has little to do with its intrinsic attraction; it has more to do with a desire to mimic. Adult desire, according to Girard (1977), "is virtually identical, except that (most strikingly in our own culture) the adult is generally ashamed to imitate others for revealing his lack of being." Girard is convinced that two desires converging on the same object will invariably clash. Thus, mimicry coupled with desire invariably leads to violence.

Other psychological accounts focus on the developmental stage of adolescence and how it relates to youth violence (Elliot and Tolan, 1999; Pepler and Slaby, 1994, as cited in *Youth Violence: A Report of the Surgeon General*, US, 2001). Various explanations—from young people exerting their independence to gain respect among peers or responding to restricted opportunities at school or in their community—mirror criminological theories of juvenile delinquency such as strain (e.g., blocked opportunities), social disorganization (e.g., disorganized communities), and differential association (e.g., delinquent peer associations). Some psychologists are concerned with identifying risk factors and domains of intervention for "at risk" children and youth.

Psychological textbooks continue to cite Albert Bandura's (1977) powerful social learning theory, which argues that humans begin imitating others at a very early age and that young children learn motor and social skills by observing the behaviour of others. Most social-psychological researchers agree that observational learning is the major psychological process underlying the effects of media violence on aggressive behaviour, many pointing to how social interaction shapes the behavioural scripts acquired by children and youth (Huesman, 1998).

The role of media, and particularly violent imagery and messages, is particularly controversial. Vast interdisciplinary literature examines questions relating to media and violence. Psychologists today argue that "[t]he interactive nature of many of these new media may affect children's behavior more powerfully that passive media such as television. Research to test this assumption is not well developed, and accurate measurement is needed to determine how much violence children are actually exposed to through various media—and how patterns of exposure vary" (Surgeon General, 2001). Psychological constructions emphasize the individual level, whereas sociological theorizing attempts to connect personal troubles with political issues; that is, to link individual biographies with history (Mills, 1959). In the next section we explore sociological constructions of violence, including the role of media.

Social Constructions of Violence

David Burgos was a runaway, a petty thief and a fighter diagnosed with bipolar disorder and attention deficit disorder. The most serious crime for which he'd been convicted, however, was breach of the peace for carrying a dangerous weapon. That alone might have raised questions about why he was in an adult prison in Connecticut at age 17. When he was found hanged from a prison bed sheet in his cell on Sunday morning two summers ago, those questions were raised statewide. Now, questions about the way the U.S. treats its juvenile offenders are being asked nationwide, questions that could echo in Canada, where the Conservative government is promising to get tougher on youth crime." (Harper, 2007)

Sociologists affirm that human beings are necessarily *social* beings, which implies that we must locate the causes or conditions that bring about our attitudes, behaviours, and identities in social terms. If violence is not adequately explained by DNA, drives, or even desires, then perhaps we need to look beyond any one individual's acting out in violence to see how violence operates as a socio-cultural construct. In this section and for the remainder of the chapter, we examine the Western social and cultural ethos. Violence and aggression are *social* acts, which mean they exist within a particular socio-cultural context. They are not, as we noted earlier, disparaged equally or systematically. Rather, our society reinforces various forms of socially acceptable violence daily through media, public discourse, and in schools (West, 1993). Zero tolerance policies and anti-gang legislation cannot eradicate the violent attitudes and behaviours of individuals who are conditioned by social and cultural contexts (Jull, 2000).

Toward this end, we first look at social theory. A tremendous amount of sociological theorizing on youth violence has materialized from macro or generalized theories. These traditional theories, such as strain theory, emerged through the testing of hypotheses about crime in general, with no specific attention paid to violence. Only later would a theory be tested against violent youth crime in order to determine its validity. This method seemed to "add violence and stir." By contrast, Wolfgang and Ferracuti's (1967) theory of violence is grounded in their analysis of youth violence endemic to certain subcultures. According to their theory, subcultural behavioural norms demand that violence be used and be ready at hand in a variety of settings and contexts.

It is important, Wolfgang (1978: 8) maintains, that "there is no society that does not contain in its normative system some elements of acceptable limits to violent aggression in some form." The difference is that while a modicum of violence is tolerated within a broader cultural context, there remains a subset of the population "characterized by residential propinquity and shared commitment to the use of physical aggression as major mode of personal interaction and a device for solving problems." Wolfgang claims that these subcultures are most likely to be found in working-class or disadvantaged pockets of a city where violence is not only permitted, but specifically encouraged. Thus, in every element of life, from child-rearing to adolescent play to domestic conflict, violence is not merely condoned, it is expected. Individuals socialized within such a subculture find their repertoire of responses to frustration, threat, or embarrassment severely limited.

The relationship between media violence and social violence is complex and contradictory. North Americans get heavy doses of media violence. A recent content analysis of more than 8000 hours of programming on cable and broadcast television in the United States found that 60% of programs contained violence (National Television Violence Study, 1996, 1997, 1998). It is estimated that by the time the average child leaves elementary

Try the following experiment with a child who is verbally able to communicate (approximately age two-and-a-half to five years old).

Ask the child where Elmo lives or where Dora the Explorer's house is. Better yet, watch an episode of Franklin, Little Bear, or Thomas the Tank Engine with the child. After the episode, talk with the child about what happened. You will likely notice that he or she does not clearly distinguish fantasy (their fictitious friend Dora) from reality (their brother or sister). Think of how they refer to locations in the programs as actual places. Until a child reaches approximately five or six, they are not able to cognitively understand where information is coming from (i.e., television, a place of make-believe that does not actually exist, or from their own backyard playing with their own sibling).

When young children see Franklin kicking a soccer ball to his friend Bear or Dora opening her backpack, they understand it as if it is really happening, even if they have some conception of it being "make-believe," or "imaginary." A child of three, four, or five years relates to characters and makes friends with them. Suppose, then, that they watch those friends being hunted or brutally murdered. Some argue that this is the moral equivalent of introducing a child to a new friend, allowing them to play, and then butchering the friend in front of their eyes

Source: Lieutenant Colonel Dave Grossman. Killology Research Group. www. killology.com. Trained to Kill, 1998: 4.

school, he or she will have seen more than 8000 murders and more than 100 000 acts of violence on television (Huston et al., 1992). Hammerman (1990:79) claims that violent media is becoming America's "most exportable commodity." Decades-old debates about the medium and the message continue: Is the media a mirror that reflects society? There is, indeed, more "reel" violence than "real" violence (Bushman and Anderson, 2001) (see Box 9.2).

Content analyses over the past 30 years have systematically examined violence on television (Gerbner et al., 1980; Potter et al., 1995; Signorielli, 1990; Wilson et al., 1997, 1998) and reveal the complexity of the relationship between media violence and actual violence. Paik and Comstock's (1994) study, the most recent and comprehensive meta-analysis of media violence, indicates that brief exposure to violent dramatic presentations on television or in film leads to short-term increases in aggressive behaviour of youth. These studies were largely based, however, on experimental methods, which may not be applicable to real-world settings. One thing is for certain: not all youth are equally affected by media violence. What is not certain is whether aggressive youth are attracted to media violence or if media violence strongly influences youth to be more aggressive. Longitudinal studies (Huesmann and Eron, 1986) demonstrate a small but statistically significant long-term relationship between television violence in childhood and aggression later in life. There is little to no systematic research on the role of other media, such as music videos, video games, and the internet, in youth violence. Clearly much more work needs to be done in this area.

Nevertheless, much support for the view that violence on television *does* influence behaviour comes from the continued use of commercials that advertise products. "If a sitcom can sell soap, salsa and cereal, then who could argue that TV violence cannot affect to some degree some viewers, particularly impressionable children," remarked former federal communications commission chairperson Reed Hundt (Eggerton, 1994: 10) (see Box 9.3 on p. 230).

Box 9.3

Parallels between Smoking and Violence?

Hundreds of psychology studies have been conducted on the topic of the effects of media violence, most coming to the same conclusion: viewing violence increases aggression (Hearold, 1986; Hogben, 1982, Wood, Wong, and Chachere, 1991). Bushman and Anderson (2001) use a smoking and media violence analogy to demonstrate the current understanding of the impact of media violence.

1. Not everyone who smokes gets cancer and not everyone who gets lung cancer is a smoker.

   → Not everyone who watches violent media becomes aggressive, and not everyone who is aggressive watches violent media.

2. Smoking is not the only factor that causes lung cancer, but it is important.

   → Watching violent media is not the only factor that causes aggression, but it is important.

3. The first cigarette can nauseate a person. Repeated exposure reduces these sickening effects, and the person begins to crave more cigarettes.

   → The first exposure to violent media can make a person (especially a child) anxious and fearful (Cantor, 2000). Repeated exposure reduces these effects and leaves the viewer wanting stronger doses of violence.

4. The short-term effects of smoking are relatively innocuous in most cases and dissipate fairly rapidly. Smoking one cigarette has numerous physiological effects that are rarely serious and that dissipate within an hour or so.

   → Watching one violent television program or film increases aggressive thoughts, feelings, and behaviours, but these effects usually dissipate within an hour or so (Bushman and Huesman, 2001).

5. The long-term, cumulative effects of smoking are relatively severe. One cigarette has little impact on lung cancer. However, repeated exposure to tobacco smoke—for example, smoking one pack of cigarettes a day for 15 years—seriously increases the likelihood of a person contracting lung cancer (and other diseases).

   → Watching one film or television show has little impact on the likelihood of a child becoming a habitual violent offender, but empirical evidence now clearly shows that repeated exposure to violent media—for example, a couple of hours a day for 15 years—causes a serious increase in the likelihood of a person becoming habitually aggressive and, occasionally, a violent offender (Huesmann, Moise, Podolski and Eron, 2000).

6. In the long fight of medical science against the tobacco industry, the big money interests of the tobacco industry apparently led them to deny publicity that there was any scientific evidence supporting the claim the tobacco products cause lung cancer.

   → Many of the same arguments used in this "war of deception" have been and continue to be made by the entertainment industry regarding reports that exposure to violent media causes aggression.

Source: Bushman, B. J., & Anderson, C. A. (2001). "Media violence and the American public: Scientific facts versus media misinformation." *American Psychologist, 56,* 477-489.

Children raised in an environment where violence is conventional, if not expected, are aware of few other "acceptable" options for handling disputes (or, in the case of our earlier example, acquiring a desired object) beyond physical aggression. Conflicts that seem trivial can quickly escalate into all-out violence. Criminologists have found that most homicides are not usually planned, methodical, and deliberate acts; murder is the end result of a character contest. Although violence is not used in every situation, "it is frequently an expected response. The appearance of a weapon, a slight shove or push, a derogatory remark, or the opportunity to wield power undetected may very well evoke an aggressive reaction that seems uncalled for to middle class people" (Adler, Mueller, and Laufer, 2007). Think of how a skirmish is likely to result whenever a boy's manliness is questioned through such taunts as "bitch" or "pussy." Indeed, should the offended party *not* respond with violence there is sure to be reprimand from those witnessing the scene: the subculture of youth.

Many sociologists have argued that what is important in this scenario is not the values advocated and adopted by the subculture, but the larger cultural manifestations of violent masculinity. One thing should be clear: violence is a man's game. The claim that men commit most acts of physical violence is possibly the nearest that criminology has to an indisputable fact (Hall, 2002). According to the FBI Uniform Crime Report, in 2005, 82.1% of persons arrested for violent crime were male (Federal Bureau of Investigation, 2006). Steven Hall (2002: 35) maintains that "[w]orking from this platform, criminology has made a major contribution to the placement of masculinity under the scrutiny of a number of critical standpoints, many of which have been influenced by varieties of feminism and pro-feminism." While gender—specifically maleness—as an important category in explaining crime has entered the criminological landscape, many studies (especially quantitative replications of mainstream criminological theories like strain and control) fail to question masculinity.

Violent Masculinity

What is it about being a man that conditions violent outcomes? Until very recently, when scholars considered gender they were referring to females. For James Messershmidt, the dearth of attention paid to gender is lamentable. In an effort to move beyond this silence in the literature, Messershmidt (2000: 5) employs a "life-history method," which involves "appreciating how adolescent male violent offenders construct and make sense of their particular world, and to comprehend the ways in which they interpret their own lives and the world around them." How is it possible to understand *why* males commit the preponderance of violent crime if we fail to appreciate *what it means* to be a male within this subculture and the wider society?

Indeed, young children are bombarded with scenes of what is projected as appropriate masculinity through music videos, video games, movies, etc. These images and messages present a limited socio-cultural script that narrowly defines manhood through power, control, and dominance, as well as the acceptable use of violence—especially when one's manliness is called into question. This **hegemonic masculinity** subordinates other more humane, sensitive, and respectful male ways of being. Typically, the epistle is of a tough and violent masculinity characterized by physical strength and size, independence, and tremendous sexual prowess. Young boys are fed a steady diet of this, making violent masculinity the cultural norm.

In an effort to understand the meaning of violence to boys, Messershmidt (1999: 198) "tried to walk in the shoes of violent boys—talk to them in depth about their experiences—and learn what they actually did and experienced and how their lives resulted in violence." His life-history method is intended to detail personal experiences and alterations in life courses over time rather than at a set point in time (which is characteristic of much criminological theorizing). Researchers engaged in such research must carefully scrutinize the meaning of social life to those immersed in it by documenting their horizons of meaning. Agnew (1990: 271) maintains that hearing the voices of those involved in crime "may be the only way of obtaining accurate information on the individual's internal states and those aspects of the external situation that the individual is attending to." To this end, Messershmidt conducted detailed interviews in an effort to discern how boys "accomplished" masculinity in situations they confronted in their personal histories. His research suggests that most boys are convinced that physical violence is the most expedient avenue through which to settle interpersonal conflict. In short, a real man is obliged to respond to threat with violence. No wonder so many male youths today engage in violence. Put another way, no wonder so many male youths—especially the racialized and economically disadvantaged—are victimized by violence.

YOUTHS AS VICTIMS OF VIOLENCE

It is particularly troubling that the victimization of young people remains obscured when official statistics and media reports are the only means employed to construct the public face of youth crime. In light of the number of school shootings and high-profile stabbings, the public forgets that youth are the most likely victims of violence. Indeed, when the focus of public ire is set against youth, their victimization becomes a seemingly irrelevant sidebar to the larger issue. But this is the very issue that should concern us. A national survey of American adolescents by the National Institute of Justice (2003) examined the prevalence of sexual assault, physical assault, physically abusive punishment, and witnessing an act of violence. The survey looked at the subsequent effects that violence had on mental health, substance use, and delinquent behaviour. The researchers concluded that "[r]ates of interpersonal violence and victimization of youths in are extremely high in the United States. As of 1995, approximately 1.8 million adolescents ages 12 to 17 had been sexually assaulted and 3.9 million had been severely physically assaulted. Another 2.1 million had been punished by physical abuse" (National Institute of Justice, 2003; 1) (see Table 9.1).

Perhaps what is most important and overlooked is how racial minorities, especially Black and Aboriginal groups, are the most likely to be victimized. These groups are the most likely to be physically assaulted, and they also have the largest prevalence of sexual assault victimization. Although there seems to be a lack of academic literature in Canada focusing on indigenous groups, a recent report for the Department of Justice by Larry Chartrand and Celeste McKay (2006) confirms these conclusions.

Victimization is a serious problem among Aboriginal youth, and has been largely ignored by the media, academics, and the wider society (Kingsley and Mark, 2000). Dion (1999) remarked almost a decade ago that no comprehensive survey of Aboriginal youth victimization existed in Canada and it is still true today. Public and academic discourse continues to emphasize the offending behaviours of Aboriginal youth rather than the various ways in which social systems and individuals victimize them. A case in point is the treatment of the topic of Aboriginal involvement in gangs. No chapter on violence and youth would be complete without a discussion of gangs or the experiences of Aboriginal youth. Most discussions look at the problem in terms of the offending behaviours. We offer a different account, one that explores how the choice to engage in violence and/or participate in organized gang activities such as drug trafficking and prostitution is conditioned by social factors beyond the control of Aboriginal youth. By putting this discussion in the context of victimization, we attempt to highlight the importance of the marginal social, political, economic, and historical circumstances that condition the involvement of Aboriginal youth in violence and gangs.

Table 9.1 Prevalence of Violence

Exhibit 1 Prevalence of violence types in the NSA sample and estimates for U.S. ages 12 to 17 and across racial/ethnic groups

	Sexual Assault	Physical Assault	Physically Abusive Punishment	Witnessed Violence
Number of adolescents in sample (N=4023)	326	701	376	1586
Percent of total sample	8.1	17.4	9.4	39.4
Estimated number of victims in U.S. adolescent population (in millions)	6.7	3.9	2.1	8.8
White (%)	6.7	15.6	7.9	34.3
Black (%)	13.1	24.2	15.4	57.2
Hispanic (%)	10.0	20.9	8.4	50.5
Native Americans (%)	15.7	27.3	15.1	55.7
Asian (%)	6.5	6.5	6.5	26.1

Note: Percentages do not equal 100 because not all respondents experienced or witnessed a type of violence.

Note: Population estimates are based on 1995 U.S. Census data indicating that there are 22.3 million adolescents in the U.S. population.

Source: National Survey of Adolescents, 1995

Source: National Institute of Justice (2003). *Youth Victimization: Prevalence and Implications.*

Child abuse in Aboriginal communities is staggering (Royal Commission on Aboriginal Peoples, 1996d). Numerous studies have documented the epidemic proportions of family violence in Aboriginal communities (Cohen, 2002; Thomlinson, et al., 2000; Trocmé et al., 2001). La Prairie, (1995), for instance, found a disturbing rate of domestic violence: in 621 interviews, 74% had experienced family violence and 49% had experienced child sexual abuse. La Prairie concluded that child abuse and sexual abuse were more likely to occur in non-biological or extended family contact situations. Kingsley and Mark (2000) studied 150 Aboriginal youth and children from 22 communities across Canada. They confirm that many Aboriginal youth are being victimized by family, friends, neighbours, and/or peers.

Family victimization is also linked to subsequent victimization and criminal activity later in life (La Prairie, 1995; Fattah, 1991b). Boys who have been severely abused as children are at a higher risk of repeating the cycle of violence with their future spouses (McGillivray and Comaskey, 1996). In contrast, in their study of commercial sexual exploitation of Aboriginal children and youth, Kingsley and Mark (2000) found a link between childhood abuse and involvement in the sex trade, but not for violent crimes towards others. Eighty percent of the Aboriginal youth in Kingsley and Mark's (2000) study reported having been a victim of sexual abuse. Abuse of children under the age of 11 has been found to increase their likelihood of adult criminality and violent behaviour, particularly for female victims (Widom, 1989). Clearly, much more research is needed to better understand the impact that various types of abuse in childhood have on subsequent behaviour, and the role of age and gender in the process.

Aboriginal identity may exacerbate the ability to cope with victimization. Participants in the 1994 Royal Commission on Aboriginal Peoples talked about "surviving" the residential schools and the child-welfare system. They reported "stories about multiple foster homes, shaming of anything Aboriginal and all forms of abuse. The men in the inmates circle were testimony to this pattern as most were the children of residential school students and were graduates of the child welfare system. These men expressed the anger and rage of their victimization with great frankness" (Absolon and Winchester, 1994). The generational perpetuation of violence is a learned social behaviour fuelled by frustration due to identity conflicts and turmoil (Chartrand and McKay, 2006).

Youths do not have to be direct targets of violence, but they are victimized and traumatized through exposure to violence during childhood (Aboriginal Nurses Association of Canada, 2001). Walker (1979, 1984) argues that female children who have witnessed spousal assault learn that such violence is part of life and that they cannot do anything about it, which may predispose them to becoming victims themselves. In this way, abuse is normalized. However, this theory, referred to as learned helplessness, is controversial and requires further empirical support. Suffice to say, children exposed to violence are 10 to 17 times more likely to have serious "emotional and behavioural problems when compared to children who are raised in a non-violent home environment" (Aboriginal Nurses Association of Canada, 2001: 11).

A disproportionate percentage of commercially sexually exploited youth in Canada, particularly in some western cities, are Aboriginal females (Kingsley and Mark, 2000). They explain: "In some communities, the visible sex trade is 90 per cent Aboriginal . . . While Aboriginal peoples make up only two to three per cent of Canada's population, in many places they form the majority of sex trade workers. In Winnipeg, for example, virtually all streetinvolved youth are Aboriginal" (Kingsley and Mark, 2000: 8, 12). These findings are consistent with a case study by Elliot (1997), who examined the sex trade in the small urban setting of Kamloops, B.C. Elliot's conclusion still holds true today: Aboriginal girls and women involved in the sex trade lack access to various support services because of a lack of cultural relevance. Participants in both studies confirm that this negative stereotyping leaves many Aboriginal children and youth feeling worthless and undeserving of help.

The historical, cultural, and economic circumstances of Aboriginal children and youth in Canada are unique. There are parallels between the factors that lead Aboriginal youth, especially young Aboriginal women, to become involved in the sex trade and the factors that lead Aboriginal youth, especially males, to become involved in gangs.

Aboriginal Youth, Gangs, and Violence

Jails awash in Gangs, Drugs, Inquest Told (Rocky Bird Inquest, February 26, 2003)

News media reports accentuate incidents of youth violence attributed to "youth gangs," depicting the problem as having reached epidemic proportions. Paradoxically, entertainment media glamorize gangs by bolstering the "cool factor" of gang membership and enhancing the value of the label. A youth subculture of gangs and violence is portrayed in music and videos, on television, and in movies. These constructions are distorted and misleading, as they ignore the hidden personal and social realities of gang-involved youth. The images are also racial and racist in nature, which racializes and marginalizes already disadvantaged youth even further. The hyperawareness of youth violence generally and gangs specifically reinforces the notion that youth are armed and dangerous and that the problem is spiralling out of control.

The term "gang" conjures up images of crime, violence, and disregard for life—its cultural definition is neither positive nor desirable. Popular discourse understands gangs as anything from small, loosely organized groups of youth to highly organized hierarchical power structures. Gangs use violence in the form of retaliation, intimidation, or more lethally, but gang members are not continually "out on a rampage" as media discourse suggests.

There is no consistent, agreed-upon definition of gangs and many people erroneously associate youths in groups with gangs and criminal activity. According to the Criminal Intelligence Service of Canada (CISC), a gang is a "group of persons consorting together to engage in unlawful activity." This broad definition means that five kids who together concoct a plan to get into a movie theatre without paying to see the latest blockbuster "are a 'gang,'" but if one backs out and only four actually go then the "gang" dissolves. The definition of a criminal organization such as a gang in Bill C-24 (CCC, section 467.1 (1), declared law in February 2002) is: "composed of three or more persons in or outside Canada; and, has as one of its main purposes or main activities the facilitation or commission of one or more serious offences, that, if committed, would likely result in the direct or indirect receipt of a material benefit, including a financial benefit, by the group or by any one of the persons who constitute the group. It does not include a group of persons that forms randomly for the immediate commission of a single offence." By this definition, our movie-night-for-free group would constitute a gang so long as they continued this activity weekend after weekend. Regardless, members of a panicked general public seeing youth en mass routinely refer to them as gangs, or will use a pejorative euphemism (e.g, hoodlums).

"Youth" gang discourse also hides the overestimation of youth gang activity insofar as most street gang members are adults. Totten (1999: 2) explains:

> Less than one per cent of youth in Canada belong to hard-core criminal youth gangs . . . A youth gang is a group of three or more youth whose members routinely commit serious crimes and regularly engage in severe acts of violence. The media's inaccurate usage of the term gang does real harm to all youth, in particular visible minority youth. More often than not, the media present black youth as being representative of all gang members. Although racial origin is an important factor in gang analysis, the media do not offer any thought of analysis as to why this may be the case. For example, visible minority youth face discrimination in many areas of their lives and as a result, experience blocked opportunities in the areas of schooling and employment. In the face of this, gangs have more appeal.

The stereotypical image of Aboriginal youths as dangerous and violent criminals is reinforced by the label "gang member." As the police, courts, and general public rush to judge Aboriginal youths who are involved in gangs, their experiences, their voice, and their humanity is lost. The general public's "fear of gangs," especially in cities like

Winnipeg and Edmonton, is part of a wider moral panic around youth and youth crime. The fear is not totally unwarranted. Research into the gang lifestyle reveals pervasive violence, drug addictions, health problems, a culture of control over others, and inflicting fear. Despite the small number of young people who engage in violent crime, and the even smaller number of individuals involved in gangs, many Canadian communities are struggling with the question, "What do we do about youth, gangs, and violence?"

A plethora of reports and committees have tackled this issue. In 1999, a National Forum on Youth Gangs was undertaken by the solicitor general and Justice Canada. Aboriginal-based organized crime is one of the intelligence priorities of Criminal Intelligence Canada (CISC). In 2003, the Federation of Saskatchewan Indian Nations (FSIN) released a report titled *Alter-Natives to Non-Violence Report: Aboriginal Youth Gangs Exploration: A Community Development Process*. The report documented a two-year study of the conditions underlying gangs in Saskatchewan's urban communities. It found that Aboriginal youth in the Prairies join gangs for money, power, and excitement. For many, it is a question of sheer survival. The group collectively experienced feelings of disenfranchisement from their families and communities and had no attachment to school. The report states that of the 98 000 youth aged 12 to 17 in Saskatchewan, approximately 15 000 are Aboriginal. Known risk factors for gang involvement, including poverty, lack of opportunity for education and employment, racism, and discrimination, coupled with a sense of hopelessness and despair, make these youth especially vulnerable to recruitment.

Criminologists have opted to define gangs using a more specific definition of organized crime; that is, ongoing activity involving a continuing criminal conspiracy, with a structure greater than any single member, with the potential for violence facilitating the criminal process. By this definition, a group of young people are simply a group of young people. Gangs today are much like early street gangs, which banded together for support and emerged out of economic necessity. However, two features more clearly define today's gangs: the heightened use of lethal weapons and drug use and trade. Drugs are used in recruitment and are a main source of revenue. They support gang activity. With drugs and weapons, gang mentality (respect, retaliation, and reputation) can be summed up in one word—fear. Young offender facilities, correctional centres, and federal institutions are breeding grounds for gang recruitment (Federation of Saskatchewan Nations, 2003).

Over the past several decades, street-gang activity has changed qualitatively and quantitatively in Canada, especially in the Prairie provinces (Report of the Royal Canadian Mounted Police, "D" Division, Manitoba, 2004). While no gang is strictly "Aboriginal," aboriginal membership is predominant in several gangs, including the Manitoba Warriors, Native Syndicate, Indian Posse, Duece, and Red Alert.

Historical Perspective and Contemporary Issues

> There is no beautiful high-rise that you live in. There are no beautiful clothes that you wear. Nobody has their own space. Nobody has personal belongings . . . it's just a crappy place with crappy stuff. (Roberta C., *Illusions*, Bear Paw Productions, 2005)

Traditional discourse offered to account for gangs mistakes the involvement of Aboriginal youth in gangs as "a malignant and deviant thorn in the side of a so-called upstanding, productive, middle-class, Christian civilization" (Fontaine, 2006: 114). Rather,

Aboriginal gang involvement is the result of the colonial experience and the current socio-economic and political context in Canada. As Fontaine (2006: 116) puts it, "Aboriginal gangs surfaced, developed, and organized in response to the reality and experience of colonialism and its perpetual legacy in our daily lives. Aboriginal gangs are the product of our colonized and oppressed space within Canada—a space fraught with inequity, racism, dislocation, marginalization, and cultural and spiritual alienation."

Recall from Chapter 7 how colonialism virtually destroyed indigenous cultures and institutions and dislocated the original societies of the First Peoples of Canada. In removing Aboriginal peoples from their lands and territories through reserves and residential schooling, the Canadian government broke down Aboriginal economies and self-sufficient institutions as well as the people within them. In particular, hundreds of Aboriginal children growing up in the 1950s and 1960s suffered physical and sexual abuse, racism, and other ill effects of the assimilation efforts of Canada's residential school era. Ross (1996: 46–48) insightfully summarizes the impact of colonization and its connection to domestic violence when he explains that

> residential schools were not the solitary cause of social breakdown amongst Aboriginal people. Rather, they were the closing punctuation mark in a loud, long declaration saying that nothing Aboriginal could possibly be of value to anyone. That message had been delivered in almost every way imaginable, and it touched every aspect of traditional social organization. Nothing was exempt, whether it was spiritual beliefs and practices, child-raising techniques, pharmacology, psychology, dispute resolution, decision-making, clan organization or community governance . . . . And what happens when you are told, from every direction and in every way, that you and all your people have no value to anyone, no purpose to your lives, no positive impact on the world around you? No one can stand believing those things of themselves . . . . At some point people brought to this position stand up and demand to be noticed, to be recognized as being alive, as having influence and power. And the easiest way to assert power, to prove that you exist, is to demonstrate power over people who are weaker still, primarily by making them do things they don't want to do. The more those things shame and diminish the weaker person, the more the abuser feels, within the twisted logic of victimization, that they have been empowered and restored themselves.

Today we are witness to a continued legacy of colonialism in the prevalence of social issues and problems facing Aboriginal children, and particularly youth. Derek Powder, former gang member, explains:

> I was embarrassed to be who I was . . . seeing my Mom and step-Dad fighting a lot. That's how they handled their problems, by yelling, swearing, physically assaulting each other. So I thought this is the way to deal with things. I enjoyed that, you know? Being a 'tough guy,' that's what I was called in school. I enjoyed that—getting that title at a young age. It gave me power, you know, over people. (Derek Powder, *Illusions*, Bear Paw Productions, 2005)

Lewis Cardinal, Aboriginal relations consultant, narrated a video called *Illusions*, produced by Bear Paw Productions in Edmonton, Alberta. It presents a revealing and candid look at gang involvement. Cardinal explains that Powder, ashamed of growing up in poverty and violence, was pushed away from his family and onto the street. There he found what he describes as "the community league for the hood," where the street was his *home* and the gang became his *family*.

The residual effects of colonialism provide a context for the social unrest and unease about Aboriginal youth gang involvement. According to former Assembly of First Nations national chief Ovide Mercredi (2000: 4), colonialism weakened "the inherent capacity of the Aboriginal Peoples to deal effectively with their problem, needs and development." In many ways, Aboriginal youth is in a "state of crisis," being the most disadvantaged, marginalized, and excluded group in Canada. Tammy A. explains, "I had no sense of belonging. I had no role models" (*Illusions*, Bear Paw Productions, 2005).

In Winnipeg, almost two-thirds of all Aboriginal households have incomes below the poverty line, and in the inner city, this rate is as high as 80% (Lezubski, Silver, and Black, 2000: 39). This partial view, however, distorts reality as it fails to recognize the resiliency, hope, and triumph of numerous Aboriginal youth across Canada. We need look no further than the vast over-representation of Aboriginal men and women in adult prisons to see where the next generation is headed if something dramatic is not done to instil a sense of pride and identity in this generation of young Aboriginal peoples at a personal level, and to make real structural changes to the society in which they live at a political level.

Mercredi conducted an initial examination of gangs for Correctional Services of Canada (CSC), which resulted in 23 strategy options included in his report *Aboriginal Gangs: A Report on Aboriginal Youth Gang Members in the Federal Corrections System* (Mercredi, 2000). One of these was "[t]hat a new program be developed with the participation of Aboriginal leaders and members of the 'Aboriginal youth gangs' aimed at transforming the 'gang' organizations into groups whose new aims and objectives no longer involve criminal activity but seek solutions to the issues and problems in society that led them to crime such as poverty, racism and lack of equal opportunity" (Mercredi, 2000: 23). Herein lay the impetus for the Aboriginal Gang Initiative (AGI), launched in 2001 by CSC in Winnipeg.

A team of five aboriginal facilitators, guided by elders, worked with youth involved in or affected by gangs. The initiative was recently renamed "Bimosewin," which in Ojibway means *walk your path in life in a good way*.

> No matter what you go through growing up, no matter what choices you make when you're younger, even if they're wrong ones, you can still lift yourself up and go in a better direction. (Roberta C., on hope, *Illusions*, Bear Paw Productions, 2005)

The goal of AGI is to "assist in the disengagement of Aboriginal Gang members from organized crime activities and in their safe reintegration into the community as law-abiding citizens" (Yates, 2004). Yates (2004) found that "there were no significant differences for those offenders exposed to the Initiative." In addition, in a follow-up, student AGI participants were more likely to return with new offences. The report recommended a reconfiguration of the program and its management to more specifically address incarcerated offenders and their needs.

Alter-Natives to Non-Violence Report, Aboriginal Youth Gangs Exploration: a Community Development Process (Federation of Saskatchewan Indian Nations, 2003: 12) suggests that "[g]angs are the presenting problem; in other words, gangs are what we observe. It's what we are not seeing that must be further studied to provide clear connections to the presenting problem of gangs. Hence, gangs are an expression of our collective social ills." Their approach eschews the tendency to take for granted recognizable labels and the compulsion to identify the number of youth gang members, and views the problem not as one of "gangs," but as "complete youth disenfranchisement from family and society . . . [Youth gangs are] one of the many symptoms of the social crisis experienced by Aboriginal youth in our neighbourhoods and communities . . . [expose] the underlying causes of youth at-risk and re-evaluate the language that shapes our views and further labels youth as gangs" (2003: 4).

The initiative is compelled to respond to the shallow analysis of "youth gangs" as the problem by articulating a preferable alternative that describes it as complete youth disenfranchisement from family and society. This precondition leads to malfunctioning youth living in poverty, exposed to multiple at-risk factors observed and labeled as the social phenomena known as "youth gangs." This is only one of the many symptoms of the social crisis experienced by Aboriginal youth in our neighbourhoods and communities. The initiative is determined to expose the underlying causes of at-risk youth and re-evaluate the language that shapes our views and further labels youth as "gangs."

As its name suggests, *Alter-Natives to Non-Violence* is aimed at redirecting Native youth behaviour toward non-violent activities. One component was the Alter-Natives to Non-violence Youth Cultural Camp, held in August 2002, which involved 100 participants, including 65 at-risk Aboriginal youth.

A significant lingering element of the effects of colonialism is the altered power relations between men and women. The roles and responsibilities of Aboriginal females encompassed every aspect of communal life, and a reverence and respect for life and care-giving was bestowed on women before contact with Europeans. The introduction of Christianity, incorporation into a wage economy based on a private/public divide, residential schools, and the introduction of alcohol, among other things, dramatically changed Aboriginal men's and women's roles. As a consequence, Aboriginal girls and women are doubly victimized—disempowered and oppressed within Euro-Canadian institutions and the Aboriginal community. A high percentage of the girls and women involved in prostitution on the streets of Canada's Prairie cities like Regina and Winnipeg are Aboriginal (58%) (Busby, 2003: 94). In one almost predominantly Aboriginal community in Winnipeg, "[t]he majority of the sex trade workers on the low track, as this area is referred to, are mostly Aboriginal children, some as young as eleven years. The majority of the men who come to this area are white and middle class" (Gilchrist, 1995).

A key area of concern is the future of Aboriginal women involved in gangs. Gang affiliation gives alienated, marginalized, and disenfranchised young women a sense of power (Nimmo, 2001). The illusion of power is contrasted with their actual experience of danger and abuse. Peer relationships appear to be the most significant determinant of female gang membership. In the film *Gang Aftermath*, Rob W. explains: "There is no woman in the group. There's a bunch of women who gang around the guys. I'll tell you straight up, they say 'you're nothing but a mattress.'" Tammy A., former gang associate agrees: "In a gang you have to satisfy your man."

Systemic Racism Today

Aboriginal peoples have been struggling for years. Back in the day we were fighting extinctions, identity. Years later, fighting addictions. Nowadays fighting each other. (Rob W., maximum security inmate, *Illusions*, Bear Paw Productions, 2005)

Reparation, healing, and respect are being shown toward the First Nations peoples of Canada in the form of the Indian Residential Schools Class Action Settlement (see the Indian Residential Schools Class Action Settlement website, www.residentialschoolsettlement.ca, for information about the approved settlement between the Assembly of First Nations and the General Synod of the Anglican Church of Canada, the Presbyterian Church of Canada, the United Church of Canada and the Roman Catholic Church). However, contact with the justice system for Aboriginal peoples continues to involve pervasive, endemic, systemic discrimination. Various Aboriginal justice inquiries confirm this, but by and large have focused on the impact on offenders, not victims. The Manitoba Justice Inquiry Report (Hamilton and Sinclair, 1991) is still the most comprehensive review. Despite all the reports and their long lists of recommendations, very little has changed. To see how racism and systemic discrimination continue to exist, we need look no further than the case of the Saskatoon police practice of dropping off Aboriginal "troublemakers" like 16-year-old Neil Stonechild at the edge of town on what have come to be known as "starlight tours." A brief police investigation in 1991 concluded that the Aboriginal teen died in the cold during his attempt to walk to an adult jail to turn himself in for leaving a youth home and that there was no foul play involved. An autopsy revealed that Stonechild died of hypothermia. The case received little attention until 2000, when two Aboriginal men were found frozen to death in a field outside Saskatoon. A third man (who had survived) explained that Saskatoon police officers drove them to a field and left them to find their own way back to the city. On February 20, 2003, the Saskatchewan government appointed Honourable Justice D.H. Wright to conduct an inquiry into the death of Neil Stonechild and the circumstances of the original investigation of his death. The resulting "Commission of Inquiry Into Matters Relating to the Death of Neil Stonechild," which lasted 43 days, heard testimony from 64 witnesses and cost close to $2 million. To view the final report, go to www.stonechildinquiry.ca/finalreport/default.shtml A different reading on the case can be found at www.injusticebusters.com/2003/Stonechild_Inquiry2.htm.

If systemic discrimination contributes to Aboriginal victimization and our existing social systems do not address it, then the underlying causes of Aboriginal criminality will continue and we will see growing numbers of Aboriginal youth spending their lives in and out of Canadian prisons. According to the Hollow Water First Nation Community Holistic Circle Healing (1994), jail only makes young people better criminals, and more bitter and angry when they return to their communities. Aboriginal children, youth, and adults are also discriminately targeted as worthy of direct personal attacks simply because they are "different." The violence inflicted against Aboriginal boys and men by institutions of Euro-Canadian society is now being turned against Aboriginal women and children. Moreover, non-Aboriginal men continue to exercise their gendered racial privilege by victimizing Aboriginal women (Razack, 2002). This gendered racism is manifested in the violence targeted at female Aboriginal sex trade workers by non-Aboriginal men. Sherene Razack's powerful case study of Pamela George (2002) reveals how racism and gender contributed to her death at the hands of two white men. George, who was working as a prostitute in Regina, was raped and murdered by two middle-class university athletes. The courts deemed "race" to be irrelevant, but, as Razack demonstrates, race was a key factor in George's victimization. Razack explains:

> Two white men who buy the services of an Aboriginal woman in prostitution, and who then beat her to death, are enacting a quite specific violence perpetrated on Aboriginal bodies throughout Canada's history, a colonial violence that has not only enabled white settlers to secure the land *but to come to know themselves as entitled to it.* In the men's encounter with Pamela George, these material (theft of the land) and symbolic (who is entitled to it) processes shaped both what brought Pamela George to the Stroll and what white men from middle-class homes thought they were doing in a downtown area of prostitution on the night of the murder, (Razack, 2002: 128)

Despite Canada's rhetoric of tolerance and respect of difference, factors such as alcohol abuse are still pointed to as personal failings of Aboriginal people rather than as indicative of the broader impact of colonization. The commonly accepted response to Aboriginal offenders and their troubles—youth and adult—remains intricately limited to criminal justice. In other words, individuals are institutionalized in prisons and other institutions, thereby individualizing social problems (Johnson, 1997).

Research by Sugar and Fox (1990) and LaPrairie (1996) found that most of the female inmates in prisons were victims of violence themselves. In the words of Sugar and Fox (1990: 3), "As our stories show, aboriginal women who are in prison grow up in prison, though the prisons they grow up in are not the ones to which they are sentenced under law."

Why Youths Join Gangs

> Kids join gangs because they're hopeless. It's a sense of hopelessness. And they don't really care what's going to happen to them, because they can't see anything for themselves in the future. You know? So, there's just a sense of utter hopelessness. (R10, Nimmo, 2001: 22)

Youths who become involved in gangs are no different from other adolescents in many respects. All adolescents are involved in varying degrees in three important negotiations: 1) identity exploration; 2) peer group acceptance; and 3) the need for family/parental attachments. For most of us, our key life decisions are rooted in our sense of self—who we are and how we view our place in the world. Take Sarah, for instance, who planned to become a veterinarian. She *decided* to volunteer at a local animal shelter during her adolescence. After graduating from high school, she made the *choice* to enrol at a local college to begin her training. Let us look more closely at the social and material circumstances in which Sarah made her choices. For Derek Powder, getting into the gang lifestyle was about power: "I wanted to be in power. I wanted to have that control over people. I wanted to have respect and inflict fear in people and I wanted people to back me" (*Illusions*, Bear Paw Productions, 2005).

Youth are involved in relationships with adults and other youth. The nature of these relationships is a primary factor in determining whether young people will join a gang. Whether or not any one youth *chooses* to associate with a gang reflects his or her own subjective interests and external pressures—namely **gang pushes** and **gang pulls**. When asked about their early gang involvement, members indicate the following reasons (*Gang Aftermath*, Bear Paw Productions, 2005):

- poverty
- shame
- violence
- alcohol
- need for power, respect, to inflict fear
- few legitimate opportunities
- home life
- communities
- place to be oneself
- material culture
- belonging, acceptance
- no attachment to school
- recruitment
- sense of community

The film *Gang Aftermath* exposes the power of constructive and supporting relationships, as viewers witness the pivotal role Rob Papin played in Derek Powder's life. Rob showed Derek that there are alternatives to gang life. A connection was made between the two. Derek explains how Rob met him "where I was at." Rob reached out, provided guidance and support, and saw Derek as worthy of respect. Above all else, Rob cared.

For Aboriginal youth, gangs offer much of what was taken from their peoples—a sense of ritual, tradition, community, belonging, and dispute resolution. The gang lifestyle, for the most part, offers the same elements (in more destructive forms). For a young, marginalized group of Aboriginal males who are searching for *something* and struggling for an *identity*, the allure of gangs is strong. Loss or dislocation of traditional Aboriginal culture is a significant reason for youth gang membership (Royal Commission on Aboriginal Peoples, 1996).

Think about what kids who join gangs are looking for. Many have been kicked out of their homes, are on the street, or are living poor home lives. They are without money, without a place to stay, without love, and are approached by charismatic recruiters who tell them, "We'll support you, we're behind you." This offer seems appealing. It may even appear "cool." The gang, especially at first, may fill needs not being met elsewhere—providing support and psychological belonging. Even when young people are treated poorly in a gang (e.g., at the bottom of the hierarchy), it might still be better than the conditions from which they came. Involvement carries many risks: HIV and other STDs, prison, drugs, and violence. Gang violence becomes commonplace. Table 9.2 on p. 243 outlines the pushes and pulls of gang life. Table 9.3 on p. 244 shows how gangs meet individual needs.

Gangs recruit insecure, disassociated teens and exploit their naiveté for personal gain (Barnsley, 2000). "Ghetto-like," impoverished living conditions also contribute to gang membership. Larose (2001) makes a link between Aboriginal street gangs and the sex trade of young Aboriginal girls insofar as their involvement in *criminal* activity is often a component of their continued victimization. From a position of powerlessness, the *gang* offers (an illusion of) power. One novel approach to responding to gang involvement is the *Spirit Keeper Youth Society* (SKYS), which works primarily with Aboriginal youth to

Table 9.2 Gang Pushes and Pulls

Gang Pushes

Colonialism
- racism and discrimination
- economic deprivation and abject poverty—socioeconomic conditions in reserves and rural areas lead to many youth to move to cities

Culture/Community
- loss, interruption of, or lack of cultural identity

Family
- parental disengagement
- socialization, expectations, and controls
- child welfare involvement

Peers
- "proxy" family
- meet social needs for support
- risk taking, especially in male–male groups
- alleviate boredom—big gap in service is recreational activities that meet needs/interests of children and youth—when boredom meets lack of activities, an antecedent to youth gang involvement

Individual
- personal problems and victimization

Gang Pulls

Status—i.e., recognition and identity

Belonging—i.e., group membership and respect

Protection—i.e., "watch your back"

Peer pressure—i.e., no mentors to intervene

Excitement—i.e., "rush"

Recruitment—i.e., enticement, allure of above

disassociate gang members and prevent gang involvement. The organization offers workshops, training, learning centres, and early intervention and prevention programs. With the assistance of former gang members, SKYS deals with a host of issues facing the young Aboriginal population of Edmonton and surrounding areas, including drug use, mental health, and violence. Alternatives to gang activity include

- structured activities
- asking youth what they want or need
- traditional teachings and activities
- employment opportunities
- role models

Personal Safety and basic security	Peers Peer pressure and peer models	Family Escape abuse and/or neglect	Systemic Limited educational options	Societal Ageism and exclusion
Power and control	Group dynamics	Modeling of anti-social sibling behaviour	Limited employment opportunities	Sexism and gendering
Affection, affirmation, understanding	Support—place to go, people to turn to	Inadequate parental controls	Legal impediments	Racism and racialization
Fun, thrills, excitement in response to boredom	Sub-culture, group affiliation, and shared identity	Parental indifference	Influence of media—violence, images of gangs	Poverty and economic disadvantages
Capacity building = experience of "success"	Camaraderie and friendship ties	Family problems	School problems	Financial needs such as money for food and shelter
Reputation, recognition, respect = identity	Bonding, "bros" and support	= Surrogate Family	Negative experiences with social systems = Distrust	Money, glamor, "lifestyle" = victimization and offending

Table 9.3 How Gangs Fulfill Young People's Needs

- affordable recreation and sports activities
- art classes, music lessons

CONCLUSION: RESPECT FOR OTHERS

[T]here can be no true cohesion between the parts that violence has welded. (Freud 1932)

It is no coincidence that the term *respect* appears 22 times in this chapter (although *violence* is used 317 times). Just as in society, violence casts a shadow over this text. Violence is a complex, nuanced, and multifaceted phenomenon. This is perhaps why a concise, all-encompassing definition escapes students and scholars alike. Moreover, because of this labyrinth, it is impossible to devise an absolute, irrefutable theory on the relationship between youth and violence.

Although much remains masked when it comes to youth violence, we have made several claims. First, violence has a tragically long history. Violent encounters pervade the historical record, and war, genocide, fighting, and torture permeate the current landscape. Whether nor not violence is endemic to human culture, our fascination and celebration of it continues.

Second, boys are enmeshed in a culture of violent masculinity and are more likely than girls to employ violence to service their ends. Although girls do engage in violence, our culture is still far less permissive when females are the perpetrators.

Third, violence shapes the life choices and experiences of young people today in very significant ways. By listening to youth and hearing about their experiences of violence, we could move closer to a better understanding of the problem. If youth are heard and respected, and if their input is acted upon, it "may be possible to create a future that focuses on respect and dignity, and not violence" (Ma, 2004: 2). Last, and perhaps most important, violence causes pain, pain that could be eradicated, we argue, when an ethos of respect overpowers a culture of punishment.

Current punitive responses such as "zero tolerance," as we will see in Chapter 10, do not address culturally acceptable violence resulting from the reinforcement of hegemonic heterosexual masculinity through sports and other social and cultural constructs (see Frank, 1987). Nor does zero tolerance identify the subtle and insidious elements of heterosexism most often observable in systemic gender reinforcement and homophobia in schools. School disciplinary policies based on the principle of zero tolerance reinforce Euro-Canadian sensibilities of right and wrong and the authoritative structures of public education (see Epp, 1997; Jull, 2000: 3).

We are left now with many more questions than answers. These questions, however, involve critical engagement with significant, practical concerns for young offenders and young victims. For instance, what about police tracking and monitoring systems that place increased surveillance on *some* youth? Who are the stakeholders? What creative, counter discourses can challenge dominant discourse? What is the role of Correctional Services Canada and the prison system in dealing with gangs? What is the role of the school system in responding to and curbing violence? What is the role of young people themselves?

Several challenges will surely arise in our attempts to grapple with these issues. First, political and public will is necessary to advocate on behalf of, rather than against, youth in our responses to violence. But how can this be accomplished? Another key challenge involves convincing government departments and funding partners that these issues are critical and require the undivided, sustained attention of an organization that can concentrate its efforts on the needs of youth in relation to issues of violence.

Many anti-violence programs are now in operation. Some attempt to prevent violence before it occurs, while others intend to reduce or eliminate the risk of recurrence. These are indeed laudable goals. On the whole, however, these strategies do not address the root conditions that reflect and reinforce violence and make it a readily available tool that youth with few legitimate opportunities and alternative coping mechanisms use to respond to their conflicts. "Risk management" techniques and law-and-order reform strategies engage the symptom and individualize the "violent offender" while leaving untouched the cultural influences and social forces that are precursors to violence. More challenging still is how to address the violent masculinity so fundamentally embedded in our culture, being, and identities. Are boys being taught that *not* being tough is okay? To what extent are alternative forms of masculinity put forward as acceptable? One only has to turn on the television, walk through a video store, or browse the hiphop section of a local music store to find an answer. So, youth violence, as we argued at the outset, only *appears* inevitable; it can be challenged.

Something else is always possible. Because youth violence is firmly entrenched in Western discourses, media, entertainment, and being, we require a radical reorientation of strategies to annihilate it. Our efforts should thus be directed toward prying open the (seemingly) naturalized order of things. To break out beyond the current limits of the human violent condition commands problematization and denouncement of silent, arbitrary, and taken-for-granted assumptions. One place to begin would be to expose the shortcomings of stolid cultural artifacts (e.g., a "real man," "being solid") that cause pain; for instance, violent masculinity. This requires a new ethic; a novel way of being with others that demands respect and reverence for all life. We conclude with youthful voices, as articulated in *Just Listen to Me* (Ma, 2004: 2):

- involve and engage us in all levels of decision-making
- treat us as people/citizens
- teach relationship and living skills
- promote sensitivity to multiculturalism and diversity
- create a system that cares
- support good parenting and care initiatives
- celebrate us

SUMMARY

- The present heightened level of public concern about youth violence (gangs, school violence, etc.) is not just a reflection of rising rates of violent crime, it has a lot to do with the spectacle of violence in North American culture.

- What is violence? Meanings of violence have changed historically, but violence itself has been a pervasive component of human history. Violence is a discursive construction, a social construct that is not ordained by nature, but as a censure of some forms of human aggression as "unacceptable."

  - *Violent Masculinity* as a cultural norm is connected to hegemonic masculinity. There is something about masculinity or "being a man" that conditions violent outcomes.

- A complex mixture of biological, cultural, psychic, and social forces interact to produce what we refer to as "violence." Various authorized knowers (biological, psychological, sociological) conceptualize violence differently.

- Given that our society is a "spectacle," where media events structure our perception of what *counts* as youth violence, it continues to shape how we view and interact with our social world.

- Youth are disproportionate victims of violence (including institutional violence) and the perpetrators of violent acts, primarily against other young people. A case in point is the involvement of Aboriginal youth in gangs.

  - Youth join gangs for numerous reasons, reflecting their own personal experiences and social locations. Various gang pushes and pulls have been identified, such as violence, home life, lack of options in communities, a struggle for acceptance, and sense of belonging.

- There are no simple answers to the problems of youth and violence, but a place to start would be respect and tolerance for all, including young people. Youth must play a key role in dealing with the violence that influences their lives. This would involve their engagement as decision-makers, a system that cares, and an adult community that celebrates (rather than condemns) youth. It is paramount to hear youthful voices.

DISCUSSION QUESTIONS

1. Where do the limits of our efforts lie? That is, what are we willing to give up to fight poverty, racism, and sexism?
2. How is it possible to revere all life in our own daily lives?
3. What is the role of youth in understanding and dealing with violence?

RECOMMENDED READINGS

Kerr, J. H. (2005). *Rethinking Aggression and Violence in Sport*. London: Routledge.
Kirsh, S. (2006). *Children, Adolescents and Media Violence: A critical look at the research*. Thousand Oaks, Calif.: Sage Publications.
Messerschmidt. J. W. (2004). *Flesh and Blood: Adolescent Gender Diversity and Violence*. Lanham, MD: Rowman and Littlefield Publishers.

Chapter 10

What To Do about Youth Crime?

STARTING POINT

Never doubt that a small group of thoughtful citizens can change the world. Indeed, it is the only thing that ever has. (Margaret Mead)

Ubuntu ngumuntu ngabantu (a person is a person through persons)—Xhosa proverb (Lionel Abrahams, "Ubuntu or not to?" Sidelines, June 1997).

Underlying much of our discussion of the issues relating to youth, crime, and society has been the role of social relationships. The above proverb explains the African concept of "ubuntu," which, loosely translated, suggests that *my humanity is tied up with your humanity.* As such, what makes others worse off also brings harm to oneself. After the European colonization of Africa, much of the customary law was replaced with a Western retributive system. But the restorative approach embodied in traditional practice has not been completely lost. In the Canadian context, restorative ideas intrinsic to Aboriginal understandings of and approaches to justice, sometimes called "sacred justice," have recently gained acceptance. "Sacred justice is found when the importance of restoring understanding and balance of relationships has been acknowledged" (LeResche, as cited in Ross, 1996: 7). This focus on relationships as a starting point can potentially transform the common picture of justice. How, then, can we restore relationships among youth to reflect dignity, compassion, and respect? Before reading further, consider the following questions:

- How is it possible to shift public focus away from the individual toward the collective?
- What would rebuilding negative relationships or establishing more positive ones mean to and/or for the young people most likely to be criminalized?
- Where are the seeds of change in the dominant value system of North American society already visible (for example, toward compassion, respect, and the importance of relationships)?

LEARNING OBJECTIVES

After reading this chapter, you should be able to

- Examine the limitations of system-based responses to youth crime.
- Distinguish between retributive justice and restorative justice through examples of programs that fit each model.
- Identify the advantages and disadvantages of restorative justice.
- Develop a critical, informed understanding of justice for youth based on relationships, lived experience, and social context.
- Demonstrate how systemic issues are related to responses to youth crime.
- Identify what a restorative justice as "ethics" might look like.

INTRODUCTION

Have you ever been hurt by youth crime? Has the effect of crime in your community become an important concern for you or your family? If so, you may be interested to know that a resolution to crime need not always come from the criminal justice system. Crime and justice are sensationalized; television bombards us with images of police officers "fighting crime" and lawyers bringing offenders "to justice." But behind this spectacle are important questions: Is the criminal justice system the only way to deal with crime? Who should be responsible for dealing with the problem of youth crime?

Decades ago, Norwegian criminologist Nils Christie (1977) argued that ownership of crime and the responsibility for determining how to deal with it should be transferred from the state and defence lawyers to victims, offenders, and their communities. Community programs such as Neighbourhood Watch and Crime Stoppers may come to mind, but restorative justice involves much more than having members of the community involved. It fundamentally challenges the underlying philosophy and day-to-day practices of the criminal justice system, which are largely based on a retributive model.

Recall from Chapter 2 that the juvenile court emerged in order to deal with young offenders *differently* than their adult counterparts. It must be thought of in the context of individualized treatment in the best interests of the child. Notwithstanding the idea that many of the early practices in juvenile justice were punishment disguised as treatment, a separate justice system was developed based on the assumption that young people require a qualitatively different response. So now when we ask what should be done about youth crime, reconsider who we are talking about. What does the *youth* in youth crime mean for how we as a society handle its associated problems? Definitions of justice are both intimately personal and inherently political. Different conceptions of justice resonate with different moral concerns and political interests. In this chapter, we will explore a different idea of justice (for youth) based less on behaviour *per se* and more on relationships, lived experience, and social context. As you read this chapter, keep in mind its title: What to do about youth crime? As you consider answers, ask yourself what the role of the young person is in the process. To what extent does this approach recognize the conditions under which youth make choices?

DEBATES IN THE LITERATURE

What is the *solution* to the problem of youth crime? A common response is, "Lock them up!" But how can society best respond to youth crime? "The perception that an imminent crisis in youth crime calls for a 'tougher' juvenile justice system backed by improved legislation is widely held by some juvenile justice officials, politicians, and members of the general public" (Hogeveen and Minaker, 2005: 516). Recall that pressure for a more punitive YJS came from a vocal public who blamed the YOA for juvenile offending. Canada witnessed political determination to "get tough" with young offenders when the government declared its intention to repeal the YOA. Interestingly, the *cause* of the problem—law—becomes the *solution*—a new law. This is not the only voice, however. Debates in the House of Commons around changing youth justice legislation demonstrate a bifurcated approach—a two-way process—to youth justice. Proponents of alternatives to custody have also entered the fray. Labelling theory argues that a young person's self-concept changes to be consistent with a label, making delinquent behaviour more likely.

Literature from both perspectives shows that criminal justice processing does not invariably reduce the likelihood of recidivism. Doob (1995) found that being caught, apprehended by the police, charged or given short, sharp shocks produced no real differences in recidivism. In other words, "More is certainly not always 'good,' but it may not always be 'bad.'" In some cases, however, "contact with the system often *increases* the likelihood of subsequent offending" (Doob, 1995: 87).

Nowhere is the thrust to come down harder on youth crime more apparent than in the United States, where most states have enacted statutes dealing with juvenile violence (e.g., three strikes, anti-gun ordinances, and curfews) that allow for more intrusive sanctions. However, as we noted in Chapter 4, Canada's incarceration rate for young people was much higher than that of the United States until the passage of the YCJA in 2003. This common position, based largely on a retributive model of justice, argues that society must deal more harshly with recalcitrant youth. It also assumes that the more severe the processing, the less likely future delinquencies will be—individual deterrence. The solution offered here is to come down harder in the way of more custodial sentences for longer periods. Indeed, there is considerable support in Canada for youth crime remedies that focus not on punishment but on the root conditions that bring about youth crime. Why is incarceration so popular? Think about our previous discussion of the media's role in influencing moral panics around the problem of youth crime. Recall that under the YCJA, it is more difficult for judges to sentence youth to custody. The notable exception, however, is in cases of serious violence offences.

DETENTION CENTRES: RESPONDING TO CRIME WITH INCARCERATION

A young person has committed a crime and the police are called. An officer takes the perpetrator away in a squad car. It is a familiar scene on television. We have learned to understand a crime as breaking the law, and we have also been socialized to expect that justice is retributive; that is, if you have caused hurt/harm, you too should be hurt/harmed. The idea of deterrence, discussed above, also comes into play here. Underlying the retributive paradigm of justice is the idea that punishment should send a message or warning that those who cause hurt and harm will also suffer.

"Do the crime, do the time," the story often goes. As we saw in Chapter 4, until the YCJA was passed in 2003, Canada frequently relied upon custodial sentencing as a response to young offenders. Throughout the 1990s, sentencing youths to custody was publicly and politically popular. The image of the gun-toting gang member captured public disdain and became a main focus of political campaigns. Indeed, the young offender—especially the Aboriginal, disenfranchised young person—became the punishable young offender (Hogeveen, 2005b). More recently, however, the discourse of intrusive punishment has been challenged. According to Campbell (2005: 272), "Youth custodial facilities are generally quite harsh, sterile environments serving large numbers of young persons institutionalized for a variety of crimes . . . surrounded by other delinquent youth, and are thus exposed to peers and role models who have engaged in much illegal activity, increasing opportunities for further delinquency . . . unlikely gains [made] in highly structured, highly supervised facilities are easily transferred to less structured, home environments." Nevertheless, calls for intrusive punishment are still being made, heard, and acted upon. One such example is **boot camps**—facilities or programs that emphasize military-style discipline, physical conditioning, and teamwork in their attempt to both punish and rehabilitate offenders.

Boot Camps

Custody is not the only intrusive measure taken against young offenders. Boot camps in the United States have received much publicity and academic attention. Also referred to as "shock incarceration," the movement began in Oklahoma and Georgia in 1983 as a sentencing option for adult offenders and a way to reduce prison overcrowding and correctional control costs. By the late 1980s, boot camps had been established for young people. There are over 40 facilities in at least 29 states (Begin, 1996). Boot camp programs are characterized by a strong militaristic regime that involves physical labour, military drills, and a highly structured daily schedule. The subject is fraught with controversy.

The 1960s and 1970s were a time of great social change. Recall from Chapter 4 that rehabilitation discourse was called into question under the banner of "nothing works." The development of boot camps can be attributed to a loss of faith in rehabilitation and a shift toward a focus on preventing recidivism and protecting the public. As rehabilitation lost sway, the idea of "just deserts," with its concern for proportionality, regained wide appeal. The therapeutic needs of individual offenders should not, it was argued, supplant the gravity of the offender's offence. As criminal justice issues became more highly politicized, law-and-order proponents married public safety to harsher sentences. Law-and-order campaigns continue to promise community safety through a crackdown on crime. With probation criticized as "too soft," more and more judges in adult and youth courts relied on custodial sanctions. At all levels, America witnessed unprecedented growth in correctional populations (Begin, 1996).

By its definition, boot camps involve detention, so it is necessarily more intrusive than probation, but non-conventional prisons and shorter sentences may make it less intrusive than a typical secure custodial institution. One argument suggests that kids can leave boot camps with a positive, pro-social attitude, as long as rehabilitation is also included in the program. Another argument challenges the belief that anything positive and productive can come from exposing vulnerable youth to overt, militaristic punishment techniques.

During the 1990s, conservative right-wing groups in Canada heralded boot camps as a cure-all. Boot camp strategies in Canada are generally perceived as more intrusive and accepted as part of a wider "get tough" approach to young offenders. Individuals who believe that youth today lack discipline and respect for authority often find boot camps attractive. According to Doob (2003), boot camps serve different, contradictory purposes. They wear down young offenders and attempt to "build them back up." Doob argues that the popularity of boot camps is more dramatic than their impact. In other words, boot camps are typically adopted for political, financial, and ideological reasons rather than for demonstrated success or effectiveness. This was the case in Canada with Project Turnaround, which opened in 1997. In 1995, the Ontario government established the Task Force on Strict Discipline for Young Offenders, with the objective of developing a strict discipline program. The task force defined strict discipline as "an orientation that uses a structured and consistent learning environment to teach high-risk, repeat young offenders the advantages of socially acceptable behaviour." Amid media attention and public controversy, Project Turnaround opened in July 1997 as Ontario's first private-sector, strict-discipline secure-custody program. Table 10.1 on p. 252 shows a typical daily schedule.

Table 10.1 Project Turnaround Program

Daily Schedule for Squad 1 (Entry-Level) Cadets

Weekday		Weekend	
Time	**Activity**	**Time**	**Activity**
06:00	Reveille	06:00	Reveille
			Washroom parade
06:05	Prep. for inspection	06:15	Prep. for inspection
06:45	Washroom/inspection parade	06:45	Shower parade
07:15	Breakfast	07:15	Breakfast parade
07:45	Hygiene parade	08:00	Inspection parade
07:50	Inspection parade	08:15	Deep cleaning parade, incl. kitchen, laundry, gym, rotunda
08:00	Mess hall cleanup parade	09:30	Movie/discussion
08:10	Drill & ceremony parade	11:30	Performance guide
09:15	Phys. ed. (Mon, Wed, Fri)	12:30	Lunch parade Vocational (Tue, Thu)
10:45	PPS groups/core program	13:00	Sports parade
11:30	PPC groups/core program	15:00	PPC
12:30	Prep. for lunch	16:00	Drill
12:30	Lunch parade	17:00	Supper parade
12:55	Hygiene parade	17:30	Dorm time—reading, homework
13:00	School parade & physical ed.	18:10	Telephone calls, privilege incentives—guitar, radios, games, magazines
	13:00 English classroom B		
	15:50 Math classroom A		
	15:40 Break		
	15:50 Personal Life Managment Health (Wed)		
17:00	Supper parade	19:10	Sport parade
17:25	Hygiene parade	20:00	Area cleanup: showers
			Last laundry
17:30	Dorm time: reading, homework	20:30	Evening snack parade
18:15	Telephone calls	20:45	Bunk area parade: medication Performance guide, prep for next day, cleaning
19:15	Sports parade	22:00	Lights out parade
20:15	Dorm time		
20:30	Evening snack parade		
20:45	Hygiene parade		
21:00	Mess hall, rotunda, bathroom cleanup		
21:45	Lights out—kit lockup		

Source: © Correctional Service Canada. 1999. Reproduced with the permission of the Minister of Public Works and Government Services Canada, 2007.

Proponents argue that a military environment in boot camps like Project Turnaround provides a structure—previously absent—where a young person can focus his or her attention on positive activities. Their progress can be evaluated and their behaviour rewarded by promotion. For example, a behaviour-based reward style was implemented to encourage compliance. The military model was evident by the dress and titles assigned to staff and youth (i.e., sergeants and cadets). Each day was highly structured with military precision and little free time (i.e., reveille, washroom, breakfast, and inspection parades, etc.), as is evident in Table 10.1. Project Turnaround offered academic, vocational, and recreational programs (similar to many young offender facilities) and specialized treatment in cognitive skills, substance abuse, anger management, and moral reasoning.

Evaluation studies of boot camps in the United States reveal several problems, including community resistance to location; inadequate aftercare facilities/programs; inappropriate placements; and tensions between rehabilitation and military discipline. As with any program, how it is implemented depends on the staff, the program's integrity and delivery, and the group involved. There is no substantial evidence to indicate that boot camps reliably impact recidivism rates. In four states (Texas, Oklahoma, Florida, and South Carolina) there were no significant differences in recidivism between youth who had completed boot camps and those in comparison groups. Researchers found no evidence that boot camps decrease re-offending. In Georgia, youth released from boot camps actually re-offended at higher rates than their counterparts in the comparison sample (Begin, 1996).

The Ministry of Correctional Services of Ontario undertook evaluations in conjunction with private, external organizations. It conducted independent process (internal program feedback) and outcome (recidivism) reviews of Project Turnaround, as well as its own internal program review. These analyses revealed that Project Turnaround cases and comparison cases were very similar on most factors investigated (T3 Associates, 2001). The Ontario government closed Project Turnaround in January 2004, arguing that its decision was operationally and fiscally responsible.

Other intrusive measures based on a deterrence model include "Scared Straight" programs, which attempt to frighten youth into behaving in conventional ways in society—to be "scared" into being "straight" or law-abiding. "Scared Straight" programs aim to invoke fear in young persons who have not yet committed crimes or have only minor law violations in order to convince them that the potential punishment far outweighs the any pleasure they may accrue in breaking the law. In New Jersey, a group of inmates serving life sentences started a program to "scare" at-risk youth from going down the path they did. The main component of the program was an aggressive presentation to juveniles held at the prison. Underlying the program is the theory of deterrence. Advocates believe that realistically depicted adult prisons will deter adolescents from further involvement in crime. Arnold Shapiro directed a documentary film, *Scared Straight!* (1978), narrated by Peter Falk, which inspired the movement. The film followed a group of young offenders through a trip to Rathway State Prison, where they met a group of "lifers" who screamed at, berated, terrified, and otherwise attempted to "scare them straight." In other words, to demonstrate the harsh realities of prison life would be enough to convince young offenders to choose a legitimate path in life. The youth decided at the end that they didn't want to end up in jail. Later films included *Scared Straight! Another Story* (1980), *Scared Straight! 10 Years Later* (1987), and the latest sequel, *Scared Straight! 20 Years Later* (1999). Hosted by Danny Glover, the final documentary showed that most of the teenagers from the original program had been "scared straight" and were living happy, productive lives. During the 1980s, many states introduced "Scared Straight" programs.

The effectiveness of these programs has been called into question. The film won awards (1978 Academy Award for Documentary Feature, and Emmy Awards for Outstanding Individual Achievement–Informational Program and Outstanding Informational Program), but the extent to which the visit itself actually impacted future choices cannot be determined. Anthony Petrosino et al. (2000, 2003) conducted a meta-analysis of seven programs and concluded that "Scared Straight" programs failed to deter crime and actually led to more offending behaviour. It should be noted that the youth in the films had been involved in minor forms of deviance and crime, which often decrease after adolescence with or without intervention.

Despite early evidence of its failure, a belief in the program's effectiveness caught on. Finckenauer (1982) reported that participants in the experimental program were more likely to be arrested. He described this belief the "panacea phenomenon," as policymakers, practitioners, and lay people continue to latch on to quick, short-term, and inexpensive cures for difficult social problems (Finckenauer et al., 1999). Since the early study, research on the effects of crime prevention programs has not found deterrence-oriented documentaries like Scared Straight to be effective (Sherman et al., 1997; Lipsey, 1992). Positive perceptions persist, and were reinforced by the 1999 television program.

Underlying much of the argument for a "tougher, stronger youth justice system"—one that provides secure custodial facilities, boot camp facilities, and Scared Straight and other deterrence-based programs—is a "just deserts" philosophy. Such a framework focuses on individual behaviour, determining guilt, and then delivering appropriate punishment through an adversarial process. For example, a purely retributive sanction message (focusing on punishment) would be: "Jeff, you are a bad person who wilfully chose to steal a car. Your punishment should be swift, severe, and proportionate to the seriousness of your crime. It was a Lexus, brand new . . . " In contrast, a purely restorative view (focusing on accountability), would be: "Jess, your actions (stealing the car) have consequences (Bob has no transportation to work and you have wronged him and his family). You are responsible for your behaviour and capable of repaying the damages (i.e., cost recovery of vehicle, lost wages, etc.)."

A damaging effect of the retributive paradigm is the tendency for non-punitive "alternative sanctions" to appear weak and less adequate than incarceration, thereby obscuring inexpensive, less-intrusive responses to youth crime (Garland, 1990; Wilkins, 1991; Bazemore and Umbreit, 1995: 299). Box 10.1 on p. 255 compares the costs of responses to youth crime. In the following section, we discuss a different understanding of crime that encourages a rethinking of system-based responses.

Box 10.1

How Can We Use Scarce Resources?

Consider the long-term impact of our use of scarce resources.

Costs

Secure custody = $126 000 per youth, per year

Open custody = $93 000 per youth, per year

Community-based sentence = from $600–700 to $6000–7000 per youth, per year

From a critical social justice perspective, the question becomes: Are the social and financial costs of intrusive measures justifiable? What if only $1 million usually put toward an incarceration strategy was diverted elsewhere? How could those dollars translate to safety, security, and protection?

RE-THINKING SYSTEM-BASED RESPONSES

When a young person commits a crime, what should happen? Naturally, the public and many youth justice officials think it will likely be handled by the country's courts and the YCJS. But is their behaviour—the crime—simply breaking the law? Is youth crime merely about the deviant behaviours of recalcitrant youth? The relationship between youth, crime, and society is far more complex. However, in most industrialized nations, this narrow concept of crime as law-breaking is widely understood and accepted.

If crimes are those behaviours that are prohibited by law and have a penal sanction attached, then to what extent is the interplay of events that bring about a crime legally relevant? In legal terms, a crime is a localized event—something easily put into a category (e.g., theft, arson, assault). For example, if someone takes a DVD player from an electronics store, that person could be charged with "theft under $5000." What came before and after, though perhaps very important for the store and our hypothetical thief, is irrelevant in the legal arena. The thief is not charged with harming the store or for the loss suffered by the owner; he or she is charged with breaking the law or, more accurately, committing a crime against the state. From this perspective, it is not surprising that the victim has no place in the process. If the store's employees want to sit in court at trial (if the case went that far), no one will stop them, but their presence is not encouraged or required. Once the case enters the criminal justice system, the "crime" is no longer between the thief and the store, but is between the accused and the state. That an offender is "caught" and that she or he is "punished" may do very little for the victims and their communities. It is ironic that many public criticisms of responses to adult and youth crime focus on the *failure* of the justice system, but also argue in favour of strengthening the system and adopting more (not less) law and criminal justice. This understanding leaves much of the real suffering and long-term consequences of crime obscured. It fails to appreciate the consequences of crime for victims, and also does little to recognize the conditions under which offenders make their choices. Circumstances for many disenfranchised youth are characterized by sexism, racism, poverty, and neglect (systemic issues that often remain unchecked).

The young offender typically does not have an opportunity to face the victim(s) and hear how his or her action caused harm or hurt. According to Susan Sharpe (1998: 5)

[T]hinking in terms of harms done rather than rules broken can free community members to respond to crime with wider-ranging questions, more penetrating discernments, and a more *innovative* search for options. They can focus on what makes a criminal incident unique, not on whether it fits a category. Understanding the full effects of an incident and its aftermath allows a *richer enactment of justice*—one that recognizes what is needed by whom, assigns responsibility in right proportion, and hold people directly accountable for what they have done. (emphasis added)

Before we consider more innovative options and explore what a richer enactment of justice may look like, have you or has anyone you know been accused of committing a crime? What happened? Were you, like many, confused by the rules and rituals of the criminal justice system? A process that excludes victims and is done "to" rather than "with" offenders can leave victims and offenders feeling that justice cannot be served. Those working within the system—judges, lawyers, and Crown attorneys—have also expressed frustration about the backlog of cases. Imagine you are going through the current system of criminal justice. Perhaps you have been the victim of a crime, or maybe you are an offender. Most often, victims and offenders find their encounters with the criminal justice system less than satisfactory. For example, in her study of abused women's experiences, Minaker (2001) found than the criminal justice system hindered the women's healing journey more than it facilitated it. One of the main obstacles was the isolation and exclusion of victims. Critics also point to a lack of accountability on the apart of offenders, especially if a defence lawyer argues an offender's "innocence." One way to approach these problems is to deal with the current system. This assumes that if more police, court, and corrections officials worked more efficiently, things would get better. Or, if we toughened the system and made it stronger, harsher, and more punitive, then fewer individuals would end up there. An alternative path is to move beyond the current system and reconsider how resources are allocated. **Restorative justice** may offer an alternative, one that attempts to involve victims and engage offenders and hold them accountable for their actions and for repairing harm. Restorative justice is a non-adversarial, non-retributive approach that emphasizes healing for victims, meaningful accountability of offenders, and the involvement of citizens in creating healthier, safer communities. Putting restorative justice ideals into practice requires a rethinking of how we understand crime, define accountability, and respond to crime in a community-building, life respecting way.

Restorative Justice and Community

Is a different orientation needed? A growing international movement based on a restorative justice framework or paradigm and developed in John Braithwaite's (1989) theory of reintegrative shaming has spread throughout New Zealand, Australia, the United Kingdom, the United States, and Canada since the early 1990s. Restorative justice is a buzzword in youth justice circles today, but it is certainly not new. Restorative justice has also been referred to as "satisfying justice" or "transformative justice." It echoes traditional justice in Aboriginal cultures and is engaged in reconciling two seemingly contradictory aims: 1) sending a message that an act is unacceptable (e.g., punishment) and 2) supporting the offender (e.g., rehabilitation). You can find numerous references to restorative justice on the Canadian Department of Justice website (www.justice.gc.ca/en/ps/voc/rest_just.html). In some ways, it has become fashionable in legal and social policy discourse. Yet to a large extent, despite the widespread use of terms associated with restorative justice, its philosophy, process, and practices are on the periphery of youth and adult criminal justice systems. According to Elliot (2005: 259), "[r]estorative justice under the YCJA, despite its structural limitations, still offers greater potential for strengthening social development capacities and yielding greater crime prevention."

The label "restorative justice" is routinely applied to any practice that takes place outside a courtroom without two lawyers and a judge or jury. Restorative justice is difficult to define. The term has as many meanings and contexts in which it is applied. Many program models, approaches, and practices fall under the rubric of restorative justice. There has been far more written about its pros and cons and philosophy than there is empirical research or records of what is happening around the world. One of the reasons why a definitive definition of restorative justice remains so elusive is that it encompasses a variety of practices at different stages of the criminal justice process, including diversion away from courts, action taken within the courts, and connecting victims and offenders at various stages throughout the process. Restorative concepts of justice can be found in ancient times and throughout human history (Llewellyn and Howse, 1999). Three principles guide most restorative justice approaches (Law Commission of Canada, 1999):

- Crime is a violation of a relationship among victims, offenders, and the community.
- Responses to crime should encourage the active involvement of victim, offender, and community.
- A consensus approach to justice is the most effective response to crime.

Is restorative justice a program, practice, philosophy, or model? Is it inherently transformative? John Braithwaite (2003) describes the intellectual tradition and political practice of restorative justice as radically transformative. Other authors similarly view it as a holistic change in the way we do justice in the world (Zehr, 1995; Van Ness and Strong, 2000). For Braithwaite (2003: 1), "Restorative justice is about struggling against injustice in the most restorative way we can manage." We approach restorative justice as one framework for justice rather than a unified theory or set of practices for responding to youth crime. There are many different types of restorative justice programs, usually falling into one of five categories, explained in Table 10.2.

Table 10.2 Restorative Justice Conflict Resolutions

TYPE OF PROGRAM	EXAMPLES
Victim–offender mediation	Youth Mediation Program, John Howard Society in Vancouver, British Columbia
Family group conferencing	Dena Keh in Watson Lake, Yukon, Liard First Nation
Sentencing circles	Youth Circles Preventative Program, Saskatoon, Saskatchewan
Victim–offender reconciliation programs (VORP)	Fraser Region Community Justice Initiatives Association (closed after 20 years of operation but still runs victim–offender mediation programs for serious offending)
(Youth) justice committee	Youth Restorative Action Project, Edmonton, Alberta (see Chapter 11)

The history of restorative justice in Canada can be traced to a 1974 experiment conducted in Ontario. **Victim–Offender Reconciliation Programs (VORP)** were initially developed in Kitchener in the late 1970s, later transplanted to Elkhart, Indiana, and continuing to crop up across North America. Canadians Mark Yantzi and Dave Worth asked a judge in Kitchener to allow them to deal in a different way with two young offenders arrested for vandalism. In this approach, the victim and the offender come together to discuss an event and are mediated by a trained facilitator in a closed setting. The approach allows victims and offenders to play key roles in determining the most appropriate method of responding to the conflict. VORP began as offender-centred, getting the victim involved in order to help the offender take responsibility and make things "right." During the 1980s, as the victims' movement gained momentum, VORP began to view the victim as more important. Emphasis is placed on volunteers as mediators, facilitators, and circle keepers. In VORP, offenders meet with their victims, prepare a report detailing the psychological and material damage they caused, and make amends for their deeds (i.e., provide some compensation). One former young offender who was involved in the early program shares his story on the website for The Centre of Restorative Justice at Simon Fraser University, at www.sfu.ca/crj/kelly.html (also see www.sfu.ca/empower/sruss1.html).

Restorative justice advocates explain that VORPs can be unsatisfactory if they are "individualized and private" (Johnstone, 2002), but can be open and involve the community. Umbreit (1994) undertook a four-site, two-year study of victim–offender mediation programs with young offenders and found 95% of mediation sessions resulted in a successfully negotiated restitution agreement to restore the victim's financial losses. Victims who had a trained mediator present in their meetings with offenders were more likely to be satisfied with the justice system than similar victims who went through the standard court process (79% against 57%). Victims were also significantly less fearful of being re-victimized after the meetings. In terms of offenders, those who met with victims were far more likely to successfully complete their restitution obligation than similar offenders who did not participate in mediation (81% against 58%). Finally, recidivism rates were lower (18%) for offenders who participated in mediation than for offenders who did not participate (27 %).

Some scholars opt for a continuum between an ideal form of restorative justice and more "real" or actual articulation of it in practice. The most common way to define, deconstruct, or otherwise dissect restorative justice is by contrast; that is, in reference to what is it not: namely, retributive justice. Common statements suggest that restorative justice focuses on *repairing harm* whereas retributive justice *punishes an offence*. *Dialogue* and *negotiation* in restorative justice replace the *adversarial relations* involved in retributive justice. Daly (2002: 59) argues, "To make the sales pitch simple, definite boundaries need to be marked between the *good* (restorative) justice and the *bad* (retributive) justice, to which one might add the *ugly* (rehabilitative) justice." In theory, many advocates frame justice aims in opposition. In practice, however, Daly found that participants engaged in a flexible incorporation of multiple justice aims; for example, elements of retributive justice (e.g., censure for past offences), rehabilitative justice (e.g., how to encourage law-abiding behaviour in the future), and restorative justice (i.e., how the offender can make up for what he or she has done).

Holding offenders accountable—a traditionally retributive element of justice—is central to the *YCJA*. This step in the restorative justice process, Daly argues, must not be taken too quickly in the name of repairing harm. Based on her research on youth justice conferencing in Australia and New Zealand, Daly reveals what she calls the four myths of restorative justice:

1. Restorative justice is the opposite of retributive justice.
2. Restorative justice uses indigenous practices and was the dominant form of pre-modern justice.
3. Restorative justice is a "care" (or feminine) response to crime in comparison to a "justice" (or masculine) response.
4. Restorative justice can be expected to produce major changes in people.

Daly has observed conferences since 1995, having seen approximately 60 of them as well as 89 youth justice conferences, and has done interviews with 170 young people and their associated victims. She acknowledges that the more she saw, the more perplexed she became. There were considerable gaps between what advocates, critics, and researchers were saying about restorative justice. A common erroneous claim is that the modern idea of conferencing has "roots in Maori culture" (Shearing, 2001: 138). Daly (2001) argues that in the 1980s, conferencing emerged in the context of a Maori political challenge to white New Zealanders and their welfare and criminal justice systems.

Restorative Justice as "Ethics"

The other is in us. (Pavlich, 2002:10)

George Pavlich prefers to view restorative justice in terms of "restoring harms and hurt, reflecting a commitment to such normative values as individual empowerment, responsibility, peace, community strength, respect, compassion, agreement, and so on." Pavlich (2002: 1) asks, "How might the ethics of restorative justice be formulated under the historical conditions facing us nowadays?" In a similar vein, we resist the tendency to find one absolute moral maxim under which certain principles guarantee no evil, terror, or danger. For Pavlich, restorative ethics may be guided as *hospitality*. This offers a different frame for youth justice. Restorative ethics is about envisioning new ways for subjects to be with others; such as when a host opens up his or her home to a "guest" and welcomes them. If we take as given that "there are no ethics in general. There are only—eventually—ethics of processes by which we treat the possibilities of a situation," then we can begin to consider what kinds of hospitable ethics youth deserve (Badiou, 2001: 16). What if we sat around together to think, talk about, and name injustices and harms? Any actual, practical approach is not necessarily going to be harm-reducing, community-centred, life-respecting, or transformative. It could equally be harmful, exclusionary, disrespectful, and destructive (or at least normative). What if we critically imagined new ways to be with others?

Umberto Eco underscores how ethics is about being *with others*. He and Martini write:

This is not a vague sentimental propensity, but rather a basic condition. As we are told by the most secular of the social sciences, it is the other, his gaze, that defines us and determines us. Just as we couldn't live without eating or sleeping, we cannot understand who we are without the gaze and reaction of the other. Even those who kill, rape, rob, and violate do so in exceptional moments, and the rest of the time beg love, respect, praise from others. And even from those they humiliate, they seek recognition in the form of fear and submission . . . We might die or go insane if we lived in a community in which everyone had systematically decided never to look at us and to behave as if we didn't exist. (Eco and Martini, 1997: 94)

What kinds of just patterns of being with others can we imagine? "A hospitable restorative justice will keep discussing and challenging the ways in which it professes to welcome, deferring to the promise of a future justice and imagining new ways to be with others" (Pavlich, 2002: 13).

According to critical criminologist David Garland, the time may be ripe for shifts in public perceptions about what to do about youth crime:

> The perceived normality of high crime rates, together with the widely acknowledged limitations of criminal justice agencies, have begun to erode one of the foundational myths of modern societies: namely, the myth that the sovereign state is capable of providing security, law and order, and crime control, within its territorial boundaries. (Garland, 1996: 445–448)

In her oft-quoted book *Restorative Justice: A Vision for Healing and Change*, Susan Sharpe (1998) explains that restorative justice reflects the belief that "justice" should accomplish five key objectives:

1. invite full participation and consensus
2. heal what has been broken
3. seek full and direct accountability
4. reunite what has been divided
5. strengthen the community to prevent further harm

Participation and Consensus Restorative justice requires the youthful offender to accept responsibility for his or her actions. At this point, dialogue can begin that examines what happened and why. The participation of all those affected by an offender's actions is key to this process. The question moves away from guilt or innocence toward a collective solution, one that reflects everybody's needs. Ideally, through collective participation, a consensus is reached that is believed to be fair by everyone involved.

Healing Rather than using the illegal act as a starting point, restorative justice begins with the harm caused. Harm could include physical or emotional damage—from breaking a window or vandalizing a car to more intangible things like damaging a sense of trust or safety (e.g., by breaking into a house). The victim is central here; what will help her or him heal? The process usually takes place in a face-to-face setting. The victim is given the opportunity to explain how the offender's actions have caused harm, and the short- or long-term consequences. Healing, however, is not confined to victims. Healing from fear, guilt, or other problems is also an important element for the offender. Community members may get involved, as other relationships may require healing. This type of justice attempts to address all kinds of harm that result from a criminal act.

Accountability Accountability is a central component of the YCJA. Critics of retributive approaches argue that during sentencing in the mainstream criminal justice system, the offender is not usually called upon to account for his or her behaviour. The end point of punishment for wrongdoing takes precedence over the process. Restorative justice requires that the person responsible for a crime be held accountable. Accountability usually involves having to "face" the victim, explain actions, and acknowledge consequences. Coming face to face with the people one has injured necessitates accountability. But restorative justice is concerned not only with explanations, but also with ways to repair the harm caused. This is usually more complicated than a bicycle thief simply returning it to the owner and saying, "I should not have taken it." Reparation must be that which is determined to be meaningful to a particular victim.

Reintegration The mainstream YCJS process is adversarial. In contrast, restorative justice attempts to bring together victims and offenders and reintegrate them back into their community. Often the victims and offenders come from the same community. A restorative approach presumes "victim" and "offender" are not identities but temporary roles. Closure is about restoring victims and offenders to their communities so they are no longer primarily defined by the harm they have suffered or caused.

Community Restorative justice is future-oriented in comparison to the mainstream criminal justice system. At its core, it is about people working together to solve problems related to all aspects of crime. It changes the distribution of power (LaPrairie, 1998).

Table 10.3 Retributive and Restorative Justice

Retributive	Restorative
Crime is: an act against the state, violation of a law, an abstract idea.	Crime is: an act against another person and the community, practical.
■ punishment is effective: deters crime and changes behaviour	■ retributive punishment is not necessarily effective
■ YCJS is responsible for controlling youth crime	■ community is partly responsible for controlling youth crime
■ adversarial relationships (between lawyers, offender and lawyer, offender and judge)	■ non-adversarial process: parties affected are involved, dialogue between offender and community
■ focus on offender, victims are process, victims are central	■ focus on community facilitating peripheral
■ goal: establishing guilt, punishing offender	■ goal: reconciliation, restoration, reintegration
■ accountability = punishment	■ accountability = meaningful outcomes
■ harm to: state, not individual	■ harm to: victim, community, offender
■ little encouragement of repentance, forgiveness	■ possibility of forgiveness and healing

Source: Adapted from H. Zehr (1990), *Changing Lenses: A New Focus for Crime and Justice.* Waterloo: Herald Press; and from L. Elliot, "Restorative Justice in Canadian Approaches to Youth Crime: Origins, Practices, and Retributive Frameworks." In K. Campbell (2005) *Understanding Youth Justice in Canada.* Toronto: Pearson Education Canada.

The philosophy of restorative justice reflects many widely held beliefs and attitudes. Move one step further into the *practice* of restorative justice, however, and the consensus about its benefits disappears. Critics have said, "It is just not realistic," "It cannot be done," or "It's too much work." A retributive focus on punishing offenders quickly creeps back in.

Restorative justice is not a universal solution. It is not about replacing courtrooms or jails altogether. Restorative justice has much potential for offering a way for communities to play a powerful role in redefining "justice." If most crime committed by young persons is relatively minor, then our task is to find an appropriate way of dealing with specific offences in a way that has an integrative effect on the young offender and is acceptable to the victim and the community. Should we not be concerned with reintegrating young offenders into the community? What about the role of the victim in the process?

Community-based initiatives have more potential (than those offered in institutional settings) to include the victim and to reintegrate the young offender into the community. Table 10.3 compares restorative and retributive justice, and Table 10.4 looks at its advantages and disadvantages.

Table 10.4 Advantages and Disadvantages of Restorative Justice

Advantages:	Disadvantages
■ community and youth involved in how best to respond to offending	■ all parties may not reach agreement
■ avoids court backlog	■ difficult to define "community" integrated into traditional CJS
■ returns crime to the community	
■ refocuses offender accountability or debt from the state to the victim	■ developed by Maori people years ago, put in context of less integrated, cohesive society
■ diversion, deinstitutionalization, making young people accountable	■ difficulty developing effective practice
■ can meet needs of communities to provide meaningful consequences, confront offenders, denounce delinquent behaviour, relay message such behaviour is unacceptable	■ may increase punitiveness, impose more severe punishments
	■ few published evaluations of initiatives
■ opens space for "community" involvement	■ inadequate resources
	■ may widen the net of social control
	■ deals (primarily) with minor deviance
	■ not taken seriously; often called "amateur justice system"

Source: Adapted from L. Elliot, "Restorative Justice in Canadian Approaches to Youth Crime: Origins, Practices, and Retributive Frameworks." In K. Campbell (2005) *Understanding Youth Justice in Canada*. Toronto: Pearson Education Canada.

Greater and more secure, intensive responses to youthful offending do not completely characterize youth justice in Canada. A bifurcation, or two-way process, exists. Serious offenders are managed through more traditional, intrusive, and carceral responses (retributive), while first-time offenders are often governed using innovative, community-based approaches (restorative). There is much potential, then, for both kinds of responses to proliferate.

SYSTEM VERSUS SYSTEMIC RESPONSES

System-based approaches do not address the structural inequalities that condition crime and deviance. Restorative justice has the potential to deal more directly with an individual youth, but still responds after the fact and deals with the behaviour in question rather than the context in which it took place. A serious discussion of what to do about youth crime raises an important issue: what is role of civil society—individuals and communities—in reinforcing and/or rectifying social problems? To strive for, promote, and ultimately achieve real change, advocates for social justice need to influence public opinion and work toward altering the conditions that foster injustice and keep young people living in conditions with few legitimate opportunities or appealing choices. Box 10.2 on p. 264 discusses the employment situation for youth in Edmonton.

The YMCA and YWCA have a long humanitarian history. Their core values are simple: care, honesty, respect, and responsibility (see Figure 10.2 on p. 265). These values reflect humanity, respect for life, and dignity. What if young people were routinely approached in this way? We hear in public discourse how young people should "care" more, "be honest," "respect their elders," and take "responsibility for their actions." These values are relational; they imply reciprocity, community, and working together. Caring relationships are essential for young people.

Conducting an honest appraisal of the situation facing many disenfranchised youth, especially girls, Aboriginal youth, and street-involved kids is a huge step forward in really dealing with the problem of youth crime. As a society, we have a responsibility to youth and the children of the next generation. Robert Fox, executive director of Oxfam Canada, wrote the following in his 2005 annual report:

> Ending poverty and injustice. An ambitious objective. Not only must we achieve it, we can. To do it we need to look at power—who has it, who is denied it, how those with power use and abuse it, how those with little power can build it and share it, (Oxfam Canada, 2005: 3)

Who is advocating for youth? Changes to our society (to the way individuals treat youth, the way systems manage youth and their needs, and the way youth as a group are understood and governed) that will have a lasting impact are those that deal with root issues and systemic problems. Short-term solutions (or the "panacea problem") that focus only on behavioural outcomes or philosophize youths' troubles ignore much larger underlying factors. Looking critically at the problem of youth crime as a societal issue rather than a personal issue does not equal failing to recognize individual problems. On the contrary, if we put youth, their troubles, and their choices in the correct social contexts (rather than pathologizing and individualizing social structural issues), we will be better able to respond in more just ways. Relationships are central in responding to youth involved in

Box 10.2

Case Study: Youth and Work in Edmonton

Youth comprise almost 25% (23.6) of the overall population in Edmonton, a number significantly higher than the national average (20.3%). According to the 2001 census, 155 195 youths live in the city of Edmonton. Moreover, Edmonton's youth experience higher rates of unemployment than the adult population. For youth aged 15-24, the unemployment rate is 11.4%, as compared to 4.7% for those 25 years and older (Statistics Canada, 2001).

Another factor that makes Edmonton an important site to investigate youth and employment is the Aboriginal youth population, which is younger than the overall population in the city. Twenty-nine percent of Edmonton's Aboriginal population falls between the ages of 15 and 29; that is, 7.5% of the total Edmonton youth population. For Aboriginal youth, the unemployment rate is 17.3% (ages 15-24), compared to 9.8% for Aboriginal people 25 years and older.

Youth advocates are critical of government cutbacks to social programs and the lack of full reinstatement of funding to pre-1990s recession levels.

The Edmonton Youth Community Engagement Steering Committee, comprised of federal, provincial, and municipal government representatives and members of Aboriginal organizations delivering youth programming under Aboriginal Human Resources Development Agreements, conducted a review of service gaps and best practices among other goals in 2004 and developed a region plan for the coordination of youth services. Thirty-eight stakeholders participated in roundtables. The following major barriers to

and issues affecting youth employment in Edmonton were evident: 1) unreliable or inconvenient transportation; 2) lack of experiences; 3) lack of education or appropriate skills; 4) employer attitudes and behaviours; 5) lack of housing or permanent address; 6) lack of information on career planning or job searching; 7) difficulty accessing or using available employment resources; 8) low self-esteem and unrealistic expectations of youth; 9) funding difficulties for service providers; 10) coordination of youth services (see Figure 10.1).

As we discussed in Chapter 8, youth are disproportionately represented among the homeless population. According to Baron (2001), street-involved youth with past negative experiences in their jobs are alienated from the labour market. This situation is made worse by their long-term unemployment. Subsequently, they lose motivation and look for other material opportunities. As Baron explains, when youth view the social system as unfair, they see "themselves as unemployable, making it more likely they will become involved in criminal activities." Similarly, one participant in the Edmonton Youth Community Engagement Steering Committee Study explained, "I am homeless so it is hard to get hired, which makes it hard to get a place to live" (Malatest and Associates, 2004). The same study found that Aboriginal youth who come to the city from reserves express feeling vulnerable to the lack of permanent housing. Malatest and Associates (2004) concluded that subsidized housing in Edmonton was insufficient, plagued by long waitlists and strict eligibility criteria. Youth participants signalled out iHuman as an organization that worked well to support traditionally marginalized youth. Additional barriers to youth (re)entering the labour force include inadequate jobs (i.e., no livable or sustainable wages); unique barriers for youth with criminal records; severe barriers to finding and holding jobs, especially for youth with addictions; barriers to youth self-employment (i.e., hindered from seeking entrepreneurial avenues); barriers to youth employment in the trades; and significant barriers for recent immigrants and refugees.

Figure 10.1 Basic Needs Issues Related to Youth (Un)Employment

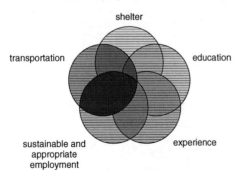

Source: Statistics Canada, 2001, Census. Chart 2-1 Youth Unemployment Rates in Edmonton. Diagram based on Malatest and Associates (2004) data. *Edmonton Regional Plan for Coordination of Youth Servises.* Edmonton, AB.

Figure 10.2 Core Values of the YMCA/YWCA

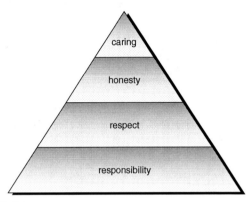

caring

honesty

respect

responsibility

Source: YMCA Canada and YMCA of Edmonton.

crime. As citizens, what are we willing to give in order to better meet the needs of youth in trouble?

We do not present a proposal for change; we encourage continual reflection on the issue. What kinds of sustainable approaches can we develop to ensure long-term futures for young people? What is the role of youth in the process?

CONCLUSION

We must be the change we wish to see in the world. (Ghandi)

One of the complaints of many citizens about the YOA was that it "had no teeth," or that young people received only a "slap on the wrist," which did little to deter them from criminal activity. There were loud calls to strengthen the youth criminal justice system: to make it more punitive, charge more kids, and hand out more and longer custodial sentences. These are not the only voices heard in the debate about what to do about youth crime. Restorative justice acknowledges that coming down harder and stronger on youthful offenders does very little for accountability or satisfying victims. Restorative justice attempts to make justice more humane, focusing on healing rather than punishment. It shifts the focus from degradation to reintegration. Moving past reintegrating youth into communities where they were previously excluded, strategies could address inequalities that stand in the way of making meaningful, positive choices. Social, economic, political, and cultural discrimination on the grounds of gender, race, class, and age are very much related to the question of what to do about youth crime.

The resources put into the YCJS are necessary, but they divert attention and support away from responses that deal with systemic issues of sexism, racism, and poverty. When all the eggs are placed in the criminal justice basket, *less* support, money, etc. exists for other systems, i.e., education, mental health, child welfare, and the larger community.

We received some thoughtful, critical, and innovative ideas from our students in our Youth, Crime, and Society courses. We end this chapter focusing on these ideas for positive change:

- using restorative justice methods (e.g., sentencing circles), especially for Aboriginal youth, to reduce breach of probation charges and help in cultural awareness
- developing programs targeting females and their unique needs in order to support their healing process, deal with the mistreatment of girls in prison, and eliminate sexism
- ensuring more effective rehabilitation programs are available in all youth facilities and that there are adequate resources to meet the needs of youth
- moving toward "community" in a way that gives victims a chance to be heard and enables offenders to appreciate the harm they have caused
- emphasizing meaningful consequences by building a stronger sense of community rather than putting more financial resources into incarceration
- soliciting sustainable government funding of organizations and programs
- providing opportunities for youth to build positive relationships that encourage them in the right direction
- soliciting funding from the government to keep programs afloat, positive role models to detach the youth from the street, and positive relationships to encourage them in the right direction.

Finally, as one student explained, "The youth justice system has become the 'catch-all' cure for dealing with the problems created in part by underfunding in all other systems—health care, education, mental health, and child welfare . . . Ameliorative change will never occur by dealing with the aftermath of youth crime! It will only occur by strengthening our social support network so that the structural factors that contribute to youth crime are reduced or eliminated."

Few researchers would suggest that the "best" method—or even *an effective* way—to reduce the amount of youth crime is to look to the laws that govern it. Yet not only is the immediate resource usually the law, but the primary focus of initiatives tends to be the justice system. Will officials continue to build more secure young offender facilities? Will authorities invest in new innovative strategies, prevention programs, and restorative approaches with the same zeal as they have for intrusive measures? To what extent can transformative ideals and humanitarian quests for social justice coexist amid fiscal restraint, risk management, public security, and law-and-order campaigns? In the next chapter, we explore the role of youth in youth justice and youth crime issues. We examine the extent to which youth voices are heard and acted upon. We argue that there is a connection between the choices youth make (that end with conflicts with the law) and the lack of respect, care, and trust afforded them by the larger society. Whose responsibility is it to deal with youth crime?

SUMMARY

- This chapter asks two related questions: What should be done about youth crime? Who should be responsible for dealing with the problem of youth crime?
- A retributive ("eye for an eye" or "just deserts") model of justice is still a widely accepted response to youth crime. This approach involves boot camps, intrusive measures such as secure custody, non-rehabilitative sentences, and longer terms.

- In contrast, restorative justice is a non-adversarial approach to justice that places emphasis on healing victims, offender accountability, and community involvement. Some elements of restorative justice are currently being incorporated in the YCJS in Canada in the form of youth justice committees, circle sentencing, and victim–offender reconciliation programs.

- System-based responses to youth crime are limited because they centre "youth crime" as the problem, rather than the systemic issues underlying youthful offending. Working both within and outside of the YCJS, restorative justice potentially removes the stigmatizing effects of incarceration. However, the potential disadvantages include the possibility of more control exercised over many (i.e., "net widening").

- A critical, informed understanding of justice for youth recognizes that definitions of justice are political. One such example is restorative justice as "ethics;" that is, "justice" is about restoring harm, raising questions of empowerment, responsibility, and respect.

- Social relationships are one key link between youth, crime, and society. As such, relationships are a starting point for social justice. To this end, we may ask: Who is advocating for youth? What is the role of youth in the process of responding to youth crime?

DISCUSSION QUESTIONS

1. To what extent are criminalized youth engaged in the quest to answer the question: What should be done about youth crime?
2. What are the limitations of a deterrence-based, retribution-focused model of corrections for youth?
3. What would it mean to take a systemic approach to responding to the problem of youth crime?

RECOMMENDED READINGS

Braithwaite, J. (1989). *Crime, Shame and Reintegration.* Cambridge, UK: Cambridge University Press.

Department of Justice Canada. (1998). *A Strategy for the Renewal of Youth Justice.* Ottawa. Department of Justice Canada.

Prashaw, R. (2001). Restorative Justice: Lessons in empathy and connecting people. *Canadian Journal of Mental Health,* 20(2), 23–27.

Chapter 11

Youth Voices and Youth-Centred Innovations

STARTING POINT

The one thing I that I wanted that I never got, and that no one was giving me, that I wanted more than anything, was someone to listen. I didn't want someone to talk to me, I wanted someone to just sit there, be an empty vessel and just listen to everything I said without any advice, without any response, just listen. (Participant, Ontario Youth Roundtable Discussions on Violence, 2004)

Do we listen to youth? Do we respect young people and value their contributions? A professional who works with youths gave this explanation: "I think we make our youth very vulnerable in a lot of ways. I think that we take away . . . we don't empower them enough, we DON'T EMPOWER THEM! We don't say 'gee, that was really good, you did really well,' it's 'you got to do more, you've GOT TO DO BETTER. You've got to!'" (Grace, Youth Professionals Study, Minaker and Hogeveen, forthcoming). Whose responsibility is it to empower youth? Before you begin this chapter, we encourage you to reflect on the following important questions that frame our analysis:

■ Where are the voices of young people today?

■ Who is listening to what youth have to say about their own experiences and the problems that affect their lives?

■ To what extent does the community have an obligation to not only hear from young people, but to also act on their claims?

LEARNING OBJECTIVES

After reading this chapter, you should be able to

■ Describe the meaning and potential impact of **youth-centred innovations**.

■ Define respect as it relates to youth, otherness, and voice.

■ Identify youth-inspired strategies for change.

■ Outline what makes *Just Listen to Me* an innovative report.

■ Outline what makes YRAP innovative.

INTRODUCTION

There has been much attention paid to *responding* to the problem of youth crime and far less interest in *relating* to youth involved in crime. The quotation in the Starting Point is a reminder that perhaps in the quest to come up with the most effective way to deal with youth crime, young people themselves have become lost. The voices of youth are missing from professional, academic, public, and media discourses. Youth are more often the *object* of social regulation than the *subject* of social discourse. Criminalized youth have become the "other," inseparable yet excluded from the social order (Acland, 1995). Youth who find themselves involved in crime, like the participants in the Ontario Youth Roundtable Discussions on Violence (Ma, 2004), are first and foremost human beings—people who deserve to be respected, loved, cared for, and cared about. There are a host of complex problems that need attention (as examined in previous chapters), but what should not be forgotten and what matters most of all, is the people involved—all of us. There is little opportunity for most of us to have a meaningful, truly valuable conversation with these youth, and even less opportunity to gain a better understanding of who they are. So we warehouse them or write them off and let them go to waste. We rarely, if ever, ask ourselves what would it take to make a difference and, perhaps, more important, what we would risk in trying to connect with them. In the foreword to Kirsten Sikora's book of poems entitled "Sundry" (2005), Ken Chapman writes:

> Kirsten Sikora has been one of those street kids and her poetry is but one of her gifts . . . She is a personal success-in-the-making . . . her journey is not yet complete but she is well on her way. This volume of her work is an experiment. It is intended to beg the question: "Can art and self expression be the bridge which will allow troubled youth to be better understood by the rest of us?" As you encounter her perspectives and experiences, be open to your insights and ideas. And, just as I was asked to do, consider how you, as a citizen, can become engaged in a common cause to help our vulnerable and at-risk young citizens. We have to do better. (Sikora, 2005, foreword)

Sikora (2005) introduces herself to her readers this way:

> I could start by telling you that I was born in Edmonton, AB, a place where, if flowers are going to grow they have to be hearty. Still, it pays to remember that despite the cold winters and dry conditions, wildflowers can be found in alleyways and sidewalk cracks. The people here grow like that too—irrepressible.

> I could paint you a stereotypical portrait of an angry, tough teenage street kid, but that wasn't really me. At 14, I was more like a paper boat on the North Saskatchewan, perilous and fragile. I slipped through all the cracks, was tossed by the waves and still somehow miraculously managed to dock one day.

> Instead, I could shock you, revealing how I lost my mind and subsequently became a heroin addict.

> I could try to explain how all these events led to my landing at iHuman, whereby I discovered my passion for art, and, with their help, salvaged my life and fashioned it into something I had never believed possible.

But . . .

> . . . what I really want you to know is the journey through these experiences has taught me compassion and understanding. (Sikora 2005)

"Children are rarely seen as competent articulators of their own experiences" (Jenks, 1982, as cited in James and Jenks, 1996: 329). Siroka's poignant words dramatically call this assumption into question. Playing a very small active role, the words of children and youth "carry no effective power" in the social world (James, 1993: 7). Almost 15 years ago, a youth delegate explained at the 1994 Conference on the UN Convention on the Rights of the Child: "Probably the biggest issue for most of the youth I spent time with, was finding a voice and being 'heard' by the experts and the professionals. A strong sense of the people 'in power' not understanding the real issues" (cited in National Crime Prevention Strategy, 1997). This young person was pointing to the fact that youth have historically been the *subjects* of processes that directly affect their lives, such as the YCJS, but not the authors. Youth are continually denied an authorized voice; they are not given the status of authorized knowers.

Not until recently has the traditional power imbalance between youth and society been challenged. This chapter examines two groups of enterprising, innovative young people who are actively engaged in dealing with complex issues related to youth and crime. Novel in their assumptions, approach, and impact, the Ontario Youth Roundtable Discussions on Violence (and the resulting report *Just Listen to Me*) and the Youth Restorative Action Project (YRAP) serve as exemplar strategies on, by, and for youth. Through these two groups we can learn to listen, hear, and take seriously the claims of young people as a basis for working for real systemic changes that will deal with issues of marginalization, processes of disenfranchisement, and day-to-day adolescent struggles. In this way, our focus is not youth justice, but justice *for* youth. Possibilities for meaningful change are apparent when youth are respected—that is, recognized as valuable, contributing members of society, and not merely seen as a "problem" that adult society must manage. This chapter highlights the lessons that can be learned from these innovations in terms of identity, social relationships, community engagement, and making and sustaining meaningful change. Not only does listening to youth represent a departure from established academic and youth justice traditions, but it also broadens the array of strategies for responding to youth and crime. In North American, for example, where traditional age-based hierarchies remain relatively intact, a particular ethos—or order of things—appears self-evident and ordinary; almost natural. It is always the subordinate group who share an interest in challenging societal limits. The two groups of youth discussed in this chapter show that traditional norms are socially constructed and culturally created attitudes and behaviours. These ways of making sense of the world are not as static as they may at first appear; they are fluid and mutable. As one eloquent student recently put it, "Another possible outcome is attainable if we just listen to the voices of youth themselves; they know the problems better than anyone, perhaps, then, they also know the solutions."

YOUTH VOICES

Youthful inexperience, perceived immaturity, and chronological age have provided a rationale for youth's continued exclusion from social policies that dramatically affect their lives. The assumption is that something inherently differentiates youths from adults

(Jones 2000; Hogeveen, 2006b). Youth is ostensibly about "becoming an adult, becoming a citizen, becoming independent, becoming autonomous, becoming mature, becoming responsible" (Kelly, 2001: 30). *Becoming* an adult, it is presumed, signals that youth have normalized (i.e., they have been socialized to become productive citizens by schools, religious institutions, sports activities, etc.) and have undergone various legitimate rights of passage (e.g., graduation, first job). When hindered by troubles with the YCJS, youthful "becoming" becomes the subject of increasingly intrusive intervention. As we have demonstrated (especially in Chapters 6, 7, and 8), many young people have been forced to deal with life circumstances that far surpass what most adults have experienced in their lifetimes. Perhaps on some of these issues, it is adults—particularly members of society privileged by class, race, gender, and age—who are naive.

Penelope Leach (2000) calls for an unsettling of the traditional power imbalances between youth and society that underlie the devaluing of young people and their experiences. Following her lead, we argue that society, and youth justice officials in particular, must engage with young people as meaningful social actors. According to Owain Jones (2001), the otherness of youth must be "acknowledged, welcomed, and respected within society so as to bring them into various practices and policies" (as cited in Hogeveen, 2006b: 48; Jones, 2001; also see Holt, 2004; Matthews, 2001) Yet without being consulted, young people have been "subjected to adult inspired interventions" (Hogeveen, 2006b: 48). Western discourses with respect to family, school, and civil society typically constitute children as unique—so different and distinct from adults that their otherness justifies their absence from decision-making in institutional arrangements such as youth justice, child welfare, and education. This failure to recognize youth as significant contributors to youth justice practices has existed since the era of the JDA. Power dynamics are not only cultural; they have a systematic, structural basis. Bernard Schissel (1997: 10–11) explains:

> The panic that vilifies children is a coordinated and calculated attempt to nourish the
> ideology that supports a society stratified on the basis of race, class and gender, and . . .
> the war on kids is part of the state-capital mechanism that continually reproduces an
> oppressive social and economic order.

A "moral panic" around youth violence specifically and youth crime more generally is fuelled by what Schissel refers to as the current pastime of "blaming children" (Cohen, 1972; Schissel, 1997: 11). While the disadvantaged are the most sharply affected, all adolescents may suffer the consequences not only of social exclusion, but of being vilified just for being young. While a "search" for solutions to youth violence seems continual, with one-dimensional *causes* bandied about, the input, perspective, and voices of youths themselves have remained outside the debate; their knowledge claims disqualified. To have youths as authorized knowers would challenge taken-for-granted assumptions about knowledge and power in our society.

Do youth want to be heard on matters that affect them directly? Think about your own life. To what extent were you afforded the opportunity to voice your own concerns, ideas, and opinions during adolescence? What about now that you are attending a post-secondary institution? How much, if at all, does your institution *hear* the demands of its students? A young participant in a roundtable discussion on the future of youth justice stated emphatically, "I don't know if people are going to listen to me this week or not. But everyone who makes decisions about young offenders doesn't have to live with them. I do. If I have a chance to speak out and tell people how it is . . . I will" (Ontario Youth Roundtable on Violence, 2004, sponsored by the Department of Justice Canada).

Just Listen to Me

Between October 2003 and June 2004, 80 young Ontario citizens between the ages of 13 and 24 gathered in six regions (Kenora, London, Manitou Island, Ottawa, Thunder Bay, and Toronto) to engage in wide-ranging discussions about youth and violence—one of the most talked-about issues in contemporary North American society. Thirteen of the participants came together again for a final discussion and presentation of their issues and recommendations to government officials. This innovative youth-centred project was organized jointly by the Office of the Child and Family Service Advocacy and Voices for Children.

Stephanie J. Ma is credited with writing the final report, *Just Listen to Me: Youth Voices on Violence*, but it was very much a collective work. At the time of writing, Ma was a full-time university student at the University of Toronto, specializing in Political Science and Anthropology. Since the *Just Listen to Me* project, she has continued her involvement with Voices for Children and has undertaken more volunteer work with youth, including facilitating the Art Group, an organization with Toronto CAS. Ma describes herself as "a former Crown Ward of the Children's Aid Society of Metro Toronto." She first came into its purview at age eight and was placed into care at 12. She explains:

> I was very angry and misguided and I turned all my anger back onto myself. Eventually I realized with support from dear friends and surrogate 'parents' that I wanted to write, but with a purpose. I was always arguing with authoritarian figures and finally somebody suggested that I channel this anger in a positive way. I took the advice to heart and have never looked back . . . My experiences with violence have been many and that is my reason for being involved with projects like this one, to create awareness about violence and to help prevent it. I am most passionate about rights of children, youth, homeless people, underprivileged and marginalized groups. (Ma, 2004: 23)

The starting point of the roundtable was first-hand experiences with violence, something all participants shared in common. Their discussions were based on examples of violence from their own lives—what Barron (2000: 8) refers to as "experience-based ways of knowing." Eleven themes emanated from the young people's conversations with each other. We explain these themes below in their own words:

1. Violence is everywhere:
   - ■ "Violence is everywhere . . . it feels overwhelming, like we're destined to repeat it" (youth participant, as cited in Ma, 2004: 8).

2. Violence has many faces:
   - ■ "To me, violence is when you intend to harm or to hurt or to gain power" (youth participant, as cited in Ma, 2004: 9).

3. Certain groups are seen as more violent than others:
   - ■ "None of them see that they have a future because of the way the society treats

them and the stigma that they all walk with" (youth participant, as cited in Ma, 2004: 10).

4. "Broken parenting" can result in violence:
   - "Violence has pretty much been my life since the day I was born" (youth participant, as cited in Ma, 2004: 10).

5. Substance abuse is connected to violence:
   - "Drugs are no longer just a problem for teens, but are trickling down to an even younger generation, one that is being forced to grow up too quickly due to peer and societal pressures" (Ma, 2004: 12).

6. Peer-on-peer violence:
   - "I think, very much so, that youth violence and teenage issues etcetera, are kind of like a glamorized lifestyle that you know, it's you against the world type of thing, that it's almost like you have to go and be as violent as you can" (youth participant, as cited in Ma, 2004: 14).

7. Abuse of power within institutions:
   - "Oh, you're just street bums—nobody cares about you,' and then they'll [police] take them back [to a holding cell] and they beat on them some more and you see people coming out with . . . big bruises" (youth participant, as cited in Ma, 2004: 15).

8. No respect: youth as second-class citizens:
   - "[P]eople in authority should respect youth, because respect is learned and if you treat someone the way you want to be treated then they'll reciprocate that" (youth participant, as cited in Ma, 2004: 15).

9. The doors are closed to youth:
   - "How are these people supposed to change their lives if they have that record behind them and people keep on looking at it, and stereotyping them based on their past?" (youth participant, as cited in Ma, 2004: 16).

10. The "un-rehabilitative" system:
    - "kids need to stop being treated as textbook [cases] . . . I also think that kids should stop being referred to as case files. My name is not '01 something something" (youth participant, as cited in Ma, 2004: 17).

11. No accountability in the system or among youth:
    - "from my experience growing up, I always felt like the adults were not going to do anything for me. Like if I told them that someone was hurting me, or doing something, or saying something, they didn't protect me" (youth participant, as cited in Ma, 2004: 18).

The youth involved in the *Just Listen to Me* project agreed there is no *one* cause; instead they saw many factors contributing to youth violence. Moreover, they were emphatic that no "magic bullet" approach would deal with the problem. Rather, they maintained that the precursors to violence must be addressed and to do so requires asking "some hard questions," such as: Why are our children dying at the hands of institutions meant to protect them? Why are so many of us still being abused—systematically, publicly, emotionally, and physically, and why are we allowing it? They did not come up with answers, nor will we. "More than anything, what evolved from our discussions is that our voices must be heard on the issue of violence. The seeds of anger and violence are planted when individuals are ignored or belittled. We ask you to listen and learn" (Ma, 2004: 19).

The youth who participated in the *Voices* project talked about cultural exclusion and racism—about their being targeted by institutions, being ostracized, having fewer opportunities, being more susceptible to public scrutiny, and being increasingly isolated. Ma (2004: 10) explains: "[A]ll of this reduces our sense of belonging to a community, and perpetuates self-hatred and mistrust of oneself and society. This can trigger violence on an individual basis and perhaps on a larger community level."

The youth spoke of their experiences of violence at home. They did not describe "broken parenting" as individual aberrations, not solely as parents' use of violence. They attributed stress problems to things like inadequate governmental supports for parents; a lack of affordable, quality daycare; insufficient access to relief and support services; and financial difficulties (Ma, 2004: 11). For many youth participants, abuse and violence occurred at the hands of individuals in positions of power in the YCJS.

Voices for Youth questioned why specific groups, not exclusive to ethnicity, were being targeted for criminalization. In sharing their experiences, the youth discovered that police brutality, misuse of authority, and abuse of power were all too common, especially for First Nations youth, black teens and street-involved youth. Their experiences suggest that a youth is more likely to be perceived as a criminal and become a target of criminalization if he or she is 1) a young person; 2) a person living in care or on the streets; and/or 3) a member of a minority group. The case of a girl named Stephanie J. impressed upon us the seriousness of the issue. Stephanie was under the care of the Children's Aid Society and residing in a youth facility when she died from suffocation while being restrained. Children dying in institutions may *appear* to be a draconian part of our history not to be repeated, but it continues to happen today. Ma (2004:15) asserts: "[W]e need to be involved and included within the institutional hierarchy: we can help to make the system more caring, respectful and humane" (Ma, 2004: 15). It seems that abuse is the extreme end on a continuum of responses that follow the same assumption: youth are second-class citizens. Negative projection of attitudes and the stigma attached to youths, in their view, leads to a degeneration of services. Moreover, "youth stigmatize adults as being uncaring and 'out to get them.' This reciprocal treatment only helps to perpetuate negative stereotypes, creating an atmosphere of general mistrust, anxiety, and anger" (Ma, 2004: 16).

We agree with participants that there exists a need for real opportunities for youth to contribute to their communities. Ma (2004: 16) explains that when youth join committees or work for agencies, they usually are given positions with little or no authority. This reinforces the silencing of youth, as it allows adults in positions of power to ignore youthful voices or take their opinions as irrelevant, invalid, or unimportant. In this context, it is not surprising that youths who have attempted to create their own initiatives have difficulties finding resources like funding and a location, and also being accepted as legitimate in the community.

Finally, Ma explains how the institutional care system has an inability to rehabilitate and reintegrate youth. Ma (2004: 17) put it this way: "Service providers are failing to fight the roots and causes of violence by treating our behaviours." The group demonstrated the system's failures, including cutting off services for older youth (18–24 years); providing uneven service delivery; not teaching a variety of methods to deal with anger or aggression; employing verbally abusive staff; returning youth to violent situations; and doing little to raise awareness about where to go for help. The youths recognized the paradox in holding young people accountable for their actions when the system itself fails to demonstrate accountability. System accountability issues include abuse against youth in foster and group homes, detention centres, and schools; over-burdened staff and incessant paperwork; and no third party to oversee the police. More salient, though, was a belief on the part of many young people that left them feeling alienated and alone.

Just Listen to Me is particularly innovative in that a group of youth are telling adults to "listen and learn" (Ma, 2004: 19). How this actually translates into hearing youthful voices and respecting youth is a much more complicated undertaking. However, to this end, the group devised several creative approaches. These were listed in Chapter 9, but deserve repetition here:

■ Involve and engage us.

  ■ This means . . . "[i]nclude youth in committees, boards, and councils at decision-making levels," "make youth more aware of what's going on," "give more support to activities, drop-ins, programs, and services involving youth."

■ Treat us as people/citizens.

  ■ This means . . . "[m]ake sure [youth] voices are heard and taken seriously," "ensure more transparency in institutions," "create more opportunities for involvement."

■ Teach relationship and living skills.

  ■ This means . . . "[i]nitiate peer mediation," "make available social skills, anger management, self-help, and life-skills programs in schools, group homes, and other institutions."

■ Promote sensitivity to multiculturalism and diversity.

  ■ This means . . . "[p]rovide education and training for and about youth," "introduce more initiatives that bring youth together for multicultural experiences."

■ Create a system that cares.

  ■ This means . . . "[g]ear systems toward helping kids believe they are worth something," "ensure youth are involved in decision-making," "place a youth advocate in every correctional facility."

■ Support good parenting and care initiatives.

  ■ This means . . . "[m]ake youth and parents aware, educate the public about violence."

■ Celebrate us.

  ■ This means . . . "[r]ecognize the struggle *all* youth face," "see the potential of *all* youth," "stop seeing youth in a group as a gang," "provide opportunities for kids to be recognized as valuable and valued," and "encourage youth to believe in themselves even when no one else does."

Ma (2004: 16) eloquently reveals how connected the above strategies are when she states: "[I]nstitutions are designed to help, teach, support, and foster the development of youth, but these very institutions view us as being incapable of helping ourselves. If the general view is we are incapable of helping ourselves, then we may start to believe this or it may cause us to resent these institutions and only further intensify our lack of engagement and sense of exclusion."

Are youth involved, included, and respected? According to Ma (2004: 16), "[a]t times we feel that our contributions are paid lip service by the public, as though to placate and silence us" (Ma, 2004: 16). We strongly believe that a cultural shift is possible.

Ma was barely 20 when *Just Listen to Me* came out. She had had time to reflect on the process and acknowledges "flaws" in the report, including its lack of follow-up. For Ma, real meaningful youth engagement means having youth in every part of the process. She insists it is essential not to censor what youth have to say and to compensate them in the way adult consultants would be. She admits now that the recommendations were too vague. She learned that recommendations should be very specific and should each target a specific government ministry in order to cultivate accountability. She wrote to us in an email:

> As for real government action I am happy to say that there are some good outcomes.
>
> 1) The Office of Child and Family Services Advocacy—or the Child Advocates Office—is now autonomous from the Ministry of Child and Youth Services. The Bill 165 enacting this came into effect last week. This means that the provincial child advocate can now do her job more effectively and can speak more freely on behalf of children and youth in governmental and institutional care.
>
> 2) Voices for Children is reformatting to include more young people in its organization—formerly it was just me—we learned that in order to really say that we work for youth and want to help elevate their voices we have to be an exemplar of that. Adding more youth to the organization is part of that. Also we are working on being less academic and more inclusive . . . more accessible so we can reach a wider audience.
>
> 3) Right after *Just Listen to Me* was written it was shipped off to the UN and helped shape along with a number of other reports a similar document called *Canadian Youth and Children Condemn Violence in Society.*

Perhaps a positive change is forthcoming. We now turn our attention to a second youth-centred project, the **Youth Restorative Action Project (YRAP)** .

YRAP: The Youth Restorative Action Project

"Kids help kids in innovative programs." (*The Edmonton Journal*, January 19, 2004)

"Youth and Consequences" (*Ottawa Citizen*, September 13, 2004)

Youthful voices are too often silenced and invalidated in our current cultural milieu, which allows adult voices to dominate (Hogeveen, 2006b). Nowhere is the exclusion of youths as decision-makers in institutional arrangements that fundamentally influence their lives more apparent than in the YCJS. As we discussed in Chapters 4 and 10, under the YCJA, the Canadian government emphasizes community-based programming under the rubric of restorative justice. This call on "community" provides an opening to unsettle youth justice norms. Through Youth Justice Committees (YJC), established under section 18 of *YCJA*, an opportunity is open to challenge the long-standing exclusion of youth. Table 11.1 shows the number of Youth Justice Committees in Canada in 2003. Table 11.2 on p. 278 shows the recognition it has received.

Young people have become actively involved in youth justice decision-making processes. In Edmonton, the Youth Restorative Action Project (YRAP) is a grassroots youth organization that challenges the adult-dominated hegemony of the YCJS. In other words, the YRAP unsettles youth justice and cultural norms (Hogeveen, 2006b). Designed, fought for, implemented, and administered almost entirely by youths, the YRAP is made up young people (ages 14–24) from diverse ethnic, social, and economic backgrounds. Together, they share the goal of making a positive impact in their community.

In 1999, several young people had a novel idea—a restorative justice program run entirely by youth—and approached youth court worker Mark Cherrington. Sixteen-year-old

Table 11.1 Designated Youth Justice Committees by Province/Territory

Jurisdiction	Designated	Contacted	Comments
Yukon Territory	0	0	The Yukon has nine active Community Justice Committees, which are not designated.
Nunavut	24	6	All existing YJCs are designated.
Northwest Territories	23	15	All existing YJCs are designated.
British Columbia	2	2	British Columbia has 81 Community Accountability Programs and eight Youth and Family Court Committees, which are not designated.
Alberta	98	22	All existing YJCs are designated.
Saskatchewan	4	3	Saskatchewan has 50 Aboriginal initiatives that are similar to YJCs though not designated.
Manitoba	57	28	Manitoba has Aboriginal committees under the umbrella of the Manitoba Keewatinowi Okimakanak organization, which are not designated.
Ontario	22	20	All existing YJCs are designated.
Quebec	0	0	None of the existing YJCs are designated.
TOTAL	262	113	

Newly-created committees in the beginning stages of operation were included in the above counts while those that were inactive or disbanded were excluded.

Source: Department of Justice Canada. Adapted from "Table 1: Number of Designated Youth Justice Committees by Province/Territory," in Hann & Associates (2003). *A National Survey of Youth Justice Committees in Canada.* Reproduced with the permission of the Minister of Public Works and Government Services Canada, 2007.

Table 11.2 YRAP Recognized

YRAP, the first committee of its kind worldwide, has received several prominent awards, among which are:

- Government of Canada, Ron Wiebe Award—Restorative Justice (2004)
- Royal Commonwealth Award, Gold Medal Winner International, Georgetown, Guyana (2004)
- City of Edmonton Youth Council, Community Organization Promoting Youth Award (2004)
- Royal Commonwealth Award, Canadian Recipient, "Outstanding Youth Program" (2004)
- City of Edmonton Youth Council, Youth Investment Award "Growth Award"' (2003).

Jasmina Sumanac, after arriving in Edmonton from her native Serbia, experienced rampant racism. In her relationship with Cherrington, she found a positive outlet for her frustration, and together with several other youth helped create the YRAP. They developed the broad idea by drawing upon practices that mirror the fundamental tenets of restorative justice (described in Chapter 10).

In "a cultural milieu where youth are marginalized and their radical proposals nullified, possessing a rough outline for a programme involving justice by and for youth is one thing—finding it realized in practice in something altogether different" (Hogeveen, 2006b: 60). The two did not approach government officials with their "radical" idea, but subverted usual channels when (drawing on respect earned after years of service with youth justice professionals in Edmonton) Cherrington asked an area youth court lawyer to look out for an appropriate case. The case that would become YRAP's first was a serious violent offence connected to systemic issues like racism. The lawyer presented the idea to a judge, who, adjourning the case to receive more information about the YRAP's plans, then sent the youth to the YRAP for sentencing recommendations. The first YRAP "conference" demonstrated that the group could be responsible for sentencing youth involved in serious crimes. The first YRAP meeting took place at iHuman studio—an appropriate site since street-involved youth routinely congregated there—on October 7, 2002. The consequence for the youth involved was to produce an audio or visual project describing the negative effects of racism. Our research demonstrates that youth involved in the YRAP "have a radically different understanding of the *who* and *what* of justice which implores a thorough reassessment of Western discourses around youth and the underlining tenets of youth justice" (Hogeveen, 2006b: 64).

The YRAP began working with young people who caused harm as a result of racism, intolerance, and what they term "significant social issues." The YRAP meets with young offenders to discuss the harm that has been caused by criminal actions and to come up with creative, effective resolutions that address and repair their offences. The sanctions are intended to be educational not only for the youth involved, but also for society as a whole.

Since being sanctioned in Alberta in 2003, the YRAP has handled over 160 cases referred from police officers, judges, and lawyers. It now encompasses more than 50 youth members and roughly 30 adult advisors. The majority of cases referred are not minor criminal matters, but criminal actions often resulting from underlying social issues (i.e., racism, substance abuse, homelessness, prostitution). The process (although not linear) is depicted in Figure 11.1.

Typically, after a charge has been laid against a young person, the police or court refers the case to the YRAP. To qualify for a referral, the youth involved must accept that she or he is responsible for the offence committed. The referral takes the form of a disclosure package (i.e., a booklet containing information about the offence). The court process is usually adjourned for a few days to allow YRAP members to vote on the case. The voting process begins with members receiving an email summary of the disclosure. All youth members have seven days to vote yes or no and to give a brief rationale for their vote. Once the votes have been tallied, a final decision is made by the director. If the referral is accepted, the YRAP creates a file for the youth. The prosecutor is then made aware, the complainant is contacted with a letter and a follow-up call, and a meeting is set up with the youth.

The actual conference involves between three and five youth members, an adult advisor, the young person, and their support. Complainants occasionally become involved, but not usually. A conference typically runs for two to three hours. Panel members ask questions intended to elicit information about the young person's life circumstances, the offence, and possible resolutions. The conference ends with a contract, which includes a sanction to which the troubled young person agrees. It is important to note that at any time during the process, the young person is free to halt the proceedings and have his or her case referred back to the traditional court for adjudication. If a final decision is reached between the YRAP panel and the "accused," a mentor is assigned to guide the youth through the process of completing the agreed-upon conditions. A file is deemed "successful" when the youth has completed all the conditions, at which time a letter is sent to the court confirming that the case has been closed. If the file is unsuccessful—the youth has not completed all the conditions—a letter is sent to the Crown and the file is no longer the YRAP's responsibility.

The YRAP is innovative in the sanctions typically handed out. Creative consequences are found in such unconventional sentences as having troubled youth compose

Figure 11.1 YRAP Process

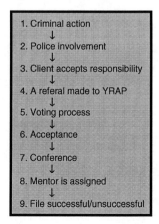

"The Youth Restorative Action Project is the World's first YJC mandated to work in youth court with young people who have caused harm as a result of hate crimes and significant social issues . . . . YRAP began in response to the concerns of a group of youth in Edmonton, Alberta, Canada, that young people were not properly equipped to act as advocates for their rights, especially in the criminal justice, child welfare, education and employment systems. In addition, they were interested in finding a way to resolve social issues which could cause or complicate these systemic problems.

Their vision was to form a program accessible to all youth to allow access to educational programs to promote advocacy, and a support network that would aid in resolving social challenges. In this spirit, YRAP was formed as a Youth Justice Committee, in order to reach young people at a time when these issues held greatest importance, in court, and provide the support and mentorship necessary to address their situation."

Source: Youth Restoration Action Project, www.yrap.org.

rap songs about their experiences, videos explaining the problem with shoplifting, CV documentaries on prostitution, and essays on how crystal methamphetamine helped a youth cope on the street. These are not simply hypothetical examples, but have all been successfully completed by YRAP youth.

The YRAP is the only youth justice committee governed by youth for youth, and, as such, is truly unique and innovative. The description in Box 11.1 is taken from the YRAP website (www.YRAP.org). As a Youth Justice Committee created and administered entirely by youth, the YRAP forces state actors to revisit how the YCJS should function. Youth participants in innovative strategies like the YRAP must continually engage in the process of reflexivity in order to guard against co-option by adult society (e.g. government) (Hogeveen, 2006b).

(DIS)CONNECTED YOUTH: SOCIAL RELATIONSHIPS AND ENGAGEMENT

I think they need to stop discriminating. I really do, I think that they, you know, we do too much we're so visual—I don't know—oriented and we look at a young person . . . my grandson comes to visit and my granddaughter, that's even worse because she's a female and she's got all her ears pierced, all her lips pierced and her nose and she's a gorgeous looking little girl, right? She's 19 and the first time I saw her with piercings, especially on her lips, I kept thinking 'oh, my why would you do that to yourself—you've disfigured yourself . . . I got over that! That's what we need to do; we need to stop discriminating because of the way someone dresses or the way they look, what colour they are, and it's easy for me to sit here and say that but you have to put it into practice. And youth are a viable, viable resource, so whether you're let's say 19 and sitting in a lecture at the university or you're 19 and walking the street, you know? You have the same aspirations, you have the same desires and it's maybe because of your education that you can verbalize it better than the 19-year-old on the street. But basically, yeah, there's a lot in common and that's what I'd say is probably you have a lot in common. You need to find out about it. (Grace, Youth Professionals Study, Minaker and Hogeveen, forthcoming)

When asked, "What would you want a group of college or university students taking a course on youth crime to know?" one professional who works with youth underscored the magnitude of humanity. Grace in the opening quotation refers to respect for the other, where, in our view, social justice begins. Another professional in the justice system, Brad, reiterated the importance of treating youth with respect: "You need to look at people as human beings and you need to treat them as human beings and you need to understand that they are equal to you in every aspect. There is always a story, behind a story, behind a story . . . You shouldn't forget what they've done, but what's wrong with forgiving what they have done?" (Brad, Youth Professionals Study, Minaker and Hogeveen, forthcoming).

You may be asking yourself, "What can I do?" Listen. Be open-minded. Think critically. Be willing to act upon the ideas for change that youth have and are developing. Be engaged. Celebrate youth. If you have had similar experiences, talk about them. If you have no experiential basis for understanding, you have the capacity for empathy and understanding. Respect youth—all youth. Given the importance of social relationships in a young person's life and the significance of identity, especially for marginalized youth, role models and mentors provide opportunities to connect disconnected youth with their community and to connect caring adults with disenfranchised children and youth. There is much we all *can* do.

CONCLUSION: BEYOND THE MAZE

> It seems like the very system that is meant to protect us and support us functions more like a maze of barriers and hurdles. This only inhibits us and leads us to be aggressive and violent, much like simmering water before it boils over from the pot. This breeds frustration and hopelessness, and perpetuates a sense of devaluation amongst us that can lead to further violent behaviours. (Ma, 2004: 16)

We are not the first to draw attention to the absence of youthful voices in the YCJS, nor are we the first to attempt to listen to their stories. Christie Barron (2000) argues that while Canadian scholars have a huge archive on and about juvenile offending, voices of youth remain noticeably absent. By foregrounding youthful experience and knowledge claims, her work attempts to counter the hegemonic discourse of youth justice professionals. More work of this type is necessary. Actually having those claims acted upon, heard, and integrated into a system designed and administered by adults is a different matter. The enterprising young people featured in this chapter challenge not only youth justice norms, but also cultural notions of what constitutes an "authorized knower." The quest—justice for youth—is not over, not by any means. Looking at the YRAP and the Ontario Youth Roundtable Discussions on Violence and its report *Just Listen to Me*, we can see new ways of thinking, acting, and being in the world with the *potential* to really make a difference. However, these processes require continual negotiation, critical reflection, and sustained engagement. We conclude with a poem, written by Kirsten Sikora, who was introduced at the beginning of this chapter.

Let me tell you a secret

There is no pot of gold
There are no heroes

Not all mothers love their children

And lots of daddies just aren't there

Drugs can be the breast milk you never got
And violence can be your best friend

But the well is poisoned
And the last one you should trust is the one who wants it the most

Nobody ever gets better
And we all die alone

Eulogies are designed to blow smoke up your rotting ass
And most kids cry on their birthday

Every war is killing somebody's baby
But they're just as invisible as the ones asking for change

Nobody cares about anything but themselves

Except you

Right at this moment
And if you hold onto that
There's hope

(Sikora 2005)

Compassion and understanding: isn't that what respect is all about?

SUMMARY

- While much attention has been paid to *responding* to the problem of youth crime, less emphasis has been given to relating to the youth involved in crime. In other words, voices of youth are largely silenced in societal discourses (i.e., youth are objects, not subjects).

- Innovative youthful initiatives are challenging the historical silence of youthful voices. The extent to which adult society (and those with the power to make change) will take their claims seriously is another issue.

- Youth-centred innovations begin from the premise that young people, and criminalized youth in particular, have experiences that position them well to play a central role in responding to the problems they face (individually and collectively) in their lives.

- Many youths are disconnected from their communities and caring adults. As such, building meaningful social relationships and engaging youths in their communities are important strategies in responding to youth crime.
- Respect means to approach the other as a valued member of society, deserving of recognition, dignity, and compassion. Respect for the other is where social justice begins.
- *Just Listen to Me* and the YRAP are two exemplary youth-inspired innovations because they represent real, meaningful, youth engagement aimed at dealing with systemic issues related to youth, crime, and society.

DISCUSSION QUESTIONS

1. As a student, what can I do?
2. What is the role of post-secondary institutions?
3. Youth do not speak with *one* voice—how do we make sense of their heterogeneous claims?

RECOMMENDED READINGS

Barron, C. L. (2000). *Giving Youth a Voice: A Basis for Rethinking Adolescent Violence*. Halifax: Fernwood Publishing.

Ma, Stephanie. (2004). *Just Listen to Me: Youth Voices on Violence*. Office of Child and Family Services Advocacy and Voices for Children. Toronto, Ontario.

Sikora, Kirsten. (2005). *sundry: a book of poems*. Edmonton: Sextant Publishing.

Chapter 12
Conclusion

STARTING POINT

Try Again?

Youthful offending
– it seems never ending!
What can be done?
Who should be doing it?

Victimization, Marginalization
Young people need real alternatives to alienation
Where can they find them?
Who should be responsible?

Violence, Despair
Aggression, Don't Care
Who counts?
Who cares?
Try again
Kochee Mena.

In the Cree language, *kochee mena* means "try again." It seems with each new era of youth justice, there is an attempt on the part of the federal government to "try again," to respond more *effectively* to the youth crime problem. How is it working? As we have seen, the law is only one avenue for dealing with social problems such as youth crime. Typically, legislation is seen as answer to the question, "What should be done about youth crime?" An alternative would be to ask, "What is the relationship between youth, crime, and society?" and, further, "What about issues of power and justice?" We are then positioned to respond in very different ways. Rather than relying on the law or on the YCJS to do *better*, the challenge becomes how to develop, implement, and sustain alternatives, interventions, and practices that occur outside the YCJS, while at the same time calling upon law to live up to its claim to be just, fair, and impartial.

As you read this final chapter, we encourage you to revisit the learning objectives of the other chapters. We began each with a Starting Point. In the introduction, we asked you to consider your own starting point. It makes sense now to evaluate how far you have come. Rather than an "ending point," think of your new outlook as a *new* point of departure.

LEARNING OBJECTIVES

After reading this chapter, you should be able to:

- Describe your new outlook and how, if at all, it relates to the authors' three main claims.

- List the book's 10 main themes (or learning outcomes).

- Explain and illustrate your own informed claim(s) about youth crime.

- Explain and illustrate your own informed claim(s) about youth justice.

- Explain and illustrate your own informed claim(s) about the relationships between youth, crime, and society.

- Create (or identify) a *try again* strategy for change aimed at justice for youth.

INTRODUCTION

Self-taught Mohawk artist Garrison Garrow created this illustration (Figure 12.1), which depicts a youth in the centre, surrounded by his or her community. The picture represents the hope that youth find positive relationships in their communities with caring people who guide and support them. The underlying assumption is that problems among youth are a reflection of problems within the community. We are each a part of a community affected by and reacting to youth and crime. Ask yourself, "What am I prepared to do?"

We posed this question at the outset of the book: Are youth troubled/troubling? Think back to your initial reaction to the poem at the start of Chapter 1. To what extent have your knowledge, understanding, and opinions about youth crime and youth justice changed?

Figure 12.1

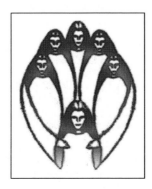

Source: Illustration by Garrison Garrow, provided courtesy of the Congress of Aboriginal Peoples.

In this concluding chapter, we briefly outline the key points in the text. We use this space to share some of our ideas, along with those from youth and youth professionals we have spoken to, about where we should go from here.

As we have seen—from the *JDA* to the *YOA* to the *YCJA*—significant shifts have taken place in the way the problems of youth crime and youth justice are constructed, in the individuals and groups who are deemed to be authorized knowers, and in the ways youthful offending has been handled. We have offered a critical perspective on the study of youth crime and youth justice and focused on issues of power and justice. As a guide for our final discussion, we draw on the three main arguments first presented in our introduction and developed throughout the book.

MAIN CLAIMS

In this section we briefly restate our main claims, which provided the basis for the themes running throughout the text.

Constructing Problems and Their Solutions: Discourse and Practice

Discourses concerning youth crime circulate continually; some are fresh and new, some old and tired. We have demonstrated that how youth crime (as with any other social problem) is defined and the discourses through which it is understood have powerful consequences for individuals, groups, and social institutions. Youth experience the effects most intimately. Along with particular ways of constructing youthful offenders and their criminality (rationalities) come policies, procedures, and processes (practices) that govern youth crime through the regulation, management, and control of criminalized youth. Media and popular discourses are open to change, negotiation, and contest. So too are political discourses that justify governance practices that prioritize punishment over support, harm over healing, and offence over offender.

Discourses do not circulate in isolation from their material contexts. Discourses related to youth crime and youth justice emerge, are employed, and shift in particular social conditions; that is, historical, political, cultural, and social contexts. The social structural conditions that frame our lives and experiences include, but are not limited to, age, race, class, and gender inequalities or privileges.

Youth Crime = Youth, Crime, and Society

We have argued that the time has come to move away from traditional concepts that direct attention primarily to "youth crime" toward more nuanced, intricate, and critical analyses of the interrelationships between youth, crime, and society. Youth crime is not primarily a *criminal* justice issue, it is social and political. Our discussions of the behaviour of youth who have broken the law are not limited to questions of individual motivation or psychology. Although psychological processes are at work, individualized factors such as self-esteem, identity, belonging, connection, etc. are integral to understanding a young person's decision to break the law, and are intimately connected to social forces, a part of a socio-political context that is much larger than any one individual. In other words, a young person's "choice" to be involved in crime is a reflection of their own agency and is their own responsibility, but it must be linked to their available alternative choices.

Thus, the problem is both political and theoretical; both concrete and abstract. Youth, crime, and society must be engaged at the level of ideas (the creation of knowledge claims or theorizing about the problem) and in a material context (intervention in social spheres or practice). Moving beyond the terrain of ideas (outside of the pages of this book) to the social situations, circumstances, and everyday lives of youth is no easy undertaking. Criminalized youth know most intimately the implications of governance practices.

Social Justice Praxis

We embrace a social justice praxis because it allows us an opportunity envision a more humane, respectful, and inclusive social system. Our approach is by no means the only alternative. Recall from Chapter 1 that social justice praxis is aimed at addressing the systemic conditions of marginalization, exclusion, and social inequalities that lead to young people's involvement in crime in the first place. Social justice praxis involves theorizing (i.e., processes of critical reflection) and social engagement (i.e., interventions in the social world).

Thinking outside the current socio-political climate—the context in which our lives are embedded—involves questioning the assumptions and ideologies we tend to take for granted. This is no easy task! But when we do, we can see a gendered, racialized, class-based, and adult-centred social order. Does to *"try again"* have to mean to continue with more of the same—to deal with the "youth crime" problem primarily through criminal-justice focused interventions? What if *try again* implied more creative alternatives, such as not giving up on disenfranchised youth, or giving up some of our own possessions, time, or money? What about respecting rather than demonizing the other?

This process of critical engagement, we believe, must be inclusive of all youth. Only in a culture of sensitivity toward youth, one based on respect and empathy, is a justice for youth possible.

IN THEIR OWN WORDS: "A STORY BEHIND A STORY, BEHIND A . . . "

Young people involved in the YCJS and the professionals who work with them have a unique vantage point from which to interpret the issues we have discussed. In this section, we weave the voices of the participants in our research (Minaker and Hogeveen, forthcoming) around the 10 themes of the book—the "learning outcomes." Throughout your reading of the text you have been encouraged to understand, integrate, and critically reflect on the following:

1. Youth crime is socially constructed.

> Kids don't look at the world the way I do (or you do), especially the ones who've been damaged. They look at the world as something that has failed them. And they feel that they need to take what they can get and the only way they can get it is to take, whether they, for instance, steal—everything is very tentative . . . they need an immediate satisfaction, the gratification is only as it is that moment. There is no gratification—they're missing a component within themselves. (youth professional)

2. Youth are disproportionately victimized; something media and popular discourse obscures by emphasizing youthful offending. Youth crime is primarily non-violent, yet atypical cases of youth crime involving violence are sensationalized and presented as the norm. Thus a moral panic around youth crime, and specifically "violent youth," instills public fear.

> Choices are made for you—the choices are there for you . . . I've never seen a kid that's wanted to be in despair. I've never met a kid that is not unhappy with who they are that is living in this kind of lifestyle. I just had one youth with me this morning and Sheila's very unhappy right now. She is back on crystal meth, she's put in a place that she can't live in, she's got no support. (youth professional)

3. The relationship between youth and violence is complex and significant. All violence (emotional, psychological, physical, and institutional) causes pain.

> My culture didn't come to me at all. I don't believe in the culture so it doesn't matter . . . In some communities all you have on a reserve is you have either, either you're going with a gang or you're going to the Native centre. You're going to the recreation centre or you're going out with this gang. You have to figure out the two, so yeah it is a difficult . . . between the criminal, the crime sprees or your culture. It's do you go to AA [alcoholics anonymous] if you have a problem or do you just keep drinking . . . do you go to the Native centre or do you just keep drinking . . . do you go to the Native centre or are you going to take that gun that's been handed to you, you know? It's just there. (youth)

4. The rationalities and practices governing youth crime have changed over time, beginning with classical legal governance. This was followed by modern legal governance and contemporary approaches.

> I hear from kids stories where they are at. There's always there's always another side . . . a side to them that's not okay with being violent. There's always a side of them not being okay with being disrespected. There's always a side that, you know, would like to be different or has been different but hasn't been that way for a while or would like to get back to that. That's often when you work with teenagers in trouble with the law . . . I've had situations where the kids came to the conclusion that 'this is just the way my parents are and that doesn't mean that I have to keep on acting the way I have been . . . I have other ways that I can cope so I can stop wanting to change them or expecting them to be any different because I can't make them be different or make them be the way I want them to be but I have within my power ways to make my life go the way I prefer.' . . . I'm talking about parents who drink, who abuse each other or are not available to the kids or not interested to listen to them or not prepared to look at themselves . . . so, ah, that's the other side the resiliency that comes up when kids that grow up in really difficult circumstances. (youth professional)

5. Race/class/gender intersections underlie youth crime and youth justice issues. This is evident when exploring specific populations: female youth, Aboriginal youth, and street-involved youth.

> I remember being called a dirty Indian and stuff when I was younger. It was always kids that said it, but I don't know I think it just stuck with me. I always felt like I was, like, out of place. I was Native and I always felt that I was less than all the other kids so then

I would just perpetuate that stigma. I always felt bad about myself inside and that's why I would always act like tougher than everybody . . . I think from the get go I kind of discriminated against myself in a way, like, I always hung out with the Native kids when I was in junior high. It would always be that way before I was involved in meth or E [ecstasy], like I was drinking when I was 13. I was drinking all the time and smoking weed. I was involved in gangs and stuff and that was mainly, I was mainly involved with the Aboriginal youth in my school and we would always like perpetuate that—I don't know, tough Native kid persona and just have our little gangs and stuff (youth).

6. Although any young person may be involved in crime and delinquency, disenfranchised youth with few appealing alternatives are over-represented in the YCJS. Therefore, it is essential to make connections between personal (i.e., individual context) and socio-political (i.e., social context) realties in order to better understand their choices.

I grew up on the streets of . . . foster homes and group homes and by the time I hit a group home when I was 13 I started learning about drugs and the street and stuff like that. I experimented with drugs when I was in junior high, probably when I was in grade seven and I started smoking weed. Then it grew to crystal meth and then drinking and by the time I graduated I had already experienced a lot of the streets and meth. I had actually graduated, which was amazing I passed all my courses, you know? But after that I hit rock bottom and, the streets took over and the drugs took over. I just went to the street and I finally got out when I got pregnant with my daughter when I was 18.

[describe rock bottom for me]

Pregnant, on the streets, nowhere to go, um, no food. I couldn't do drugs and that was really hard because everyone I hung around with did. For me family is really important and for LS [a caring adult] to say 'You're going to lose your kid,' that was it for me. I said 'Ok, I need help.' . . . So I just hit rock bottom—I had nowhere to go, nothing, nobody there for me, I was pregnant and I was all, like, 'Well, I see now if you're pregnant on the street it's your choice to smoke drugs, but, I mean, like, if you don't then who's going to be there to help you? On the streets I mean, you do drugs. It's all about doing drugs, right? (youth)

7. To think and act critically is to engage in a process of critical reflection and social engagement. It is about more than asking particular kinds of questions, it involves a way of being in the world that respects difference and questions social inequalities— not limited to race, class, gender, and age.

I think that everybody deserves a chance to be able to change their life, if they really want it. I don't think, like, I don't think people should be judgmental about youth on the streets. I mean yeah . . . there are people out there who really want to change their lives and who just get down and out and just steal. I . . . think people should be very open-minded and . . . should really listen to what people with my situation have to say . . . I got charged with robbery because these girls lied, like, I felt that sucks for me. I had to plead guilty to that because I felt like I couldn't tell the truth because I was going to get longer time . . . I got another 15 months added on to my probation on top of that so I'm on two different probation orders for something that I got charged for that I didn't do right and it sucks that I couldn't be able to be honest about it without getting myself in more trouble. (youth)

8. Respecting youth and building stable, caring relationships with young people, whatever their situation, is integral to resolving the personal troubles of criminalized youth.

> To help a systemic youth that becomes systemic at 13 years of age and then continues on until young adolescence or into their mid 20s you need four to five years of patience. I have a wonderful girl, Jessica. She's 14. We met her when she was 13. She'd been working on the Avenue [prostitution track]. Her mother's an alcoholic, she's got no father, she lives in a crack house with other kids because it's the only place to live . . . The only way to help Jessica is to try and work steadily through to her and provide her with what you can provide her with on the streets (food, safety, make sure she's not beaten up) . . . Who is going to stay in the "game" for Jessica? A lot of organizations and people only get money for projects with a limited time frame . . . there's no sustainability. (youth professional)

9. Dealing with youth crime not with simplistic, narrowly conceived "solutions," but through intelligent, creative YCJS programming *and* non-criminal justice interventions holds much promise. This means using multi-level strategies that include *both* individualized approaches that primarily address the needs of young people and wider, structural changes that tackle the root conditions underlying the choices of criminalized youth.

> Right now I am working with a lot of girls that are all pregnant and are in recovery, which is awesome, hopefully the thing that they need to be able to kick it forever, but who knows. I'm working with them to basically get off the streets, with their recovery, keep their housing, maintain housing, working with the system to get them enough money so they can live; advocate for them. I was working with one girl a couple of weeks ago. She is expecting a baby in two weeks. [Name of government program] gave her two cheques of $150 each—that's including rent (she just got a new place), damage deposit, baby stuff, food, electricity. $300 for the month! So I went with her and advocated for her. She asked me to come because she said, 'The worker is going to be nice to you if you come because he wasn't very nice to me.' So, I went in with her and she left there with $2500 in her account. (youth professional).

10. Social justice praxis is aimed at justice *for* youth through listening to youthful voices, taking seriously their claims and acting upon them, a long-term commitment to individual kids, and a long-term commitment to responding to the underlying systemic issues. Social justice praxis advocates for youth in order to help them toward a space where they can advocate for themselves.

> If you see an issue—don't ignore it! Don't just be like everyone else and be like it's not my life. It doesn't affect me because it does affect you. It affects everyone and I don't know how it all works, but it will affect everyone, whether people have to see it or whether they put blinders on and make themselves ignore it. It all affects everyone. (youth)

MOVING BEYOND

We need to ask challenging questions if we are to develop more effective, creative, and inclusive responses to youth crime. We hope the list below only begins your process of critical reflection about how we can best move beyond the current controversies.

- What are the conditions that contour and constrain the lives of criminalized youth?
- What practices, claims, discourses, and rationalities contribute to the problem?
- How are relations of age, race, class, and gender implicated in societal responses to youth crime?
- What meaningful changes would improve the life chances of young people generally and criminalized youth in particular?
- What would more just and humane social conditions look like?
- What practices, claims, discourses, and rationalities offer more just and humane alternatives?

We hope you have gained your own informed understanding regarding the complex problems we have outlined in the book. To help you to draw your own conclusions, develop claims on the issues, and create your own strategies for change, we have included Figure 12.1, Making Your Own Connections.

Figure 12.1 Making Your Own Connections

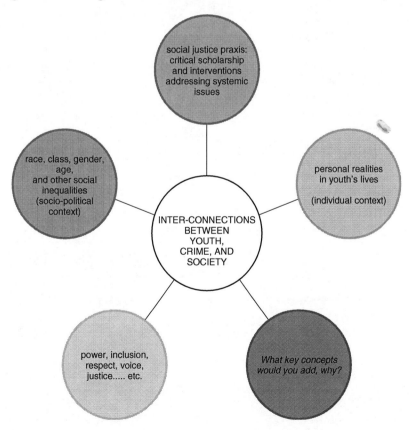

SUMMARY

- The current era of youth justice attempts to "try again," to respond more *effectively* to the youth crime problem. Law is only one avenue through which to deal with the issues and problems associated with youth crime. Youth crime is not primarily a *criminal* justice issue; it is also a social and political issue.

- Youth crime is socially constructed. Discourse and practice are interrelated and how the problems of youth crime and youthful offenders are understood has implications for responses.

- An alternative starting point would be to ask, "What is the relationship between youth, crime, and society?" From this perspective, we can see how youth are disproportionately victimized and tend to engage much more in property offences than in violent crimes.

- Simplistic, narrowly conceived "solutions" are far less effective than intelligent, creative YCJS programming *and* non-criminal justice interventions; that is, multilevel strategies that include *both* individualized approaches and systemic changes.

- *Social Justice Praxis* is aimed at addressing the systemic conditions of marginalization, exclusion, and social inequality that lead to youths' involvement in crime. This involves theorizing (i.e., processes of critical reflection) and social engagement (i.e., interventions in the social world).

- Criminalized youth know most intimately the implications of governance practices. All youths, especially those disenfranchised by race, class, and gender, deserve respect and stable, caring relationships with adults as well as more appealing alternatives to marginalization, exclusion, crime, and delinquency.

DISCUSSION QUESTIONS

1. How are the conditions that contour and constrain the lives of criminalized youth reinforced by the YCJS?

2. How is it possible to respond to the problem of youth crime in an individualized and systemic way?

3. How is it possible to work through the challenges and contradictions inherent in taking youthful claims seriously and acting upon them?

RECOMMENDED READINGS

Green, R. and K. Healy. (2003). *Tough on Kids: Rethinking Approaches to Youth Justice*. Saskatoon, SK: Purich.

Mann, R. M. (2000). "Struggles for Justice and Justice for Youth: A Canadian Example." In R. Mann (Ed). *Juvenile Crime and Delinquency: A Turn of the Century Reader*. pp.3–18. Toronto: Canadian Scholars Press.

Van Ness, D.W. and K.H. Strong. (2000). *Restoring Justice*. Cincinnati, OH: Anderson.

Glossary

absolute homelessness – sleeping in places unfit for human habitation (e.g., abandoned buildings, vehicles, doorways, parks, and tents)

accountability – holding young people accountable for their crime means having them take responsibility for their behaviour

adult-centred social order – how society is structured and operates according to age hierarchies; that age conditions and shapes life experiences

androcentric – (male-centredness) based on male behaviour, written from a male perspective, and/or judged by a male standard. Historically, androcentricism, which positions men exclusively as authorized knowers and subjects of knowledge, characterizes mainstream criminological scholarship and youth-justice practices.

anti-institutional discourse – growing dissatisfaction with institutional governance; calls for deinstitutionalization were accompanied by a new enthusiasm for community-based strategies (like probation) as modern legal governance expanded.

assimilation – practices and policies whereby the Canadian government sought to incorporate Aboriginal peoples into the body politic, coinciding with forced state dependency and systemic racism

assumptions – preconceived understandings (about how some aspect of the world works) that underlie knowledge claims

authorized knowers – those key individuals and groups granted the status of "expert," whose claims are heard and whose arguments are taken seriously and subsequently acted upon

bifurcated system – a two-pronged approach. Under the *Youth Criminal Justice Act*, petty and non-serious offenders are handled through community-based or diversionary programs, while serious and violent offenders are subject to more carceral and punitive interventions.

bifurcation – how violent and non-violent crimes are differentiated under the *Youth Criminal Justice Act*

boot camps – a sentencing option used in some North American jurisdictions; characterized by a strong militaristic regime that involves physical labour, military drills, and a highly structured daily schedule

Brown Commission (1849) – represented one of the first significant departures in the dominant way of thinking about the legal governance of deviant children in Canada; that is, a new conceptualization of young people and their crimes accompanied by a shift in how to respond to them (i.e., in separate institutions from adults)

carceral complex – various forms of control along a punitive, not supportive, continuum through which various institutions govern marginalized and disenfranchised groups

censure – more complex than social control, censures are categories of "denunciation or abuse lodged within very complex, historically loaded practical conflicts and moral debates" (Sumner, 1990a: 28–29)

chronic instability – defined in terms of unstable housing, relationships, income, and health; characterizes and joins the lives of a heterogeneous group of street-involved youth

class – in capitalist societies, class relates to relative economic positioning (i.e., wealth), although this division can be based on other valued resources such as power or prestige

class-based social order – how society is structured and operates along class lines; that socio-economic position conditions and contours life experiences

classical legal governance – a generalized system of adjudication and punishment that was largely based on deterrence and retribution. Also referred to as generalized justice, this approach was primarily concerned with establishing guilt or innocence and treated all offenders equally rather than separating adults from juveniles.

classical theory –considered the first formal school of criminology; based on the Enlightenment philosophies of liberalism and utilitarianism that dominated between 1600–1800. Making no distinction between adult or youthful offenders and viewing all criminals as rational, calculating actors, classical theory offered a simple explanation for crime and focused on finding ways to control it.

colonization or colonialism – describes historical and lingering processes whereby the traditions, lifestyle, and cultures of indigenous people were replaced with a dependent, subordinate status

community participation – the involvement of members of the public in matters relating to youth crime is encouraged under the *YJCA*; an example is greater opportunities for parents and communities to participate in extra-judicial sanctions

conflict approach – assumes that individuals and groups in society hold conflicting social, political, cultural, or economic interests, which often pit more powerful groups against marginalized ones.

consensus approach – assumes there is agreement stemming from shared beliefs, values, and goals among societal members on matters related to youth crime and justice

counter hegemonic voices – those intended to question and undermine deep-seated ideologies about the nature of (in)equality in society

counter-discourse – represents a challenge to dominant paradigms and traditional orthodoxies. Counter-discourses begin with the premise that society is hierarchically organized and, as such, the dominant (i.e., elite white men) produce dominant discourses that guide definitions of crime and practices of governance (often employed against racialized groups, the poor, and women).

crime prevention – to prevent crime or to "tackle crime in order to build stronger, healthier communities" (Public Safety Canada, www.publicsafety.gc.ca/prg/cp/index-en.asp)

criminalization – the processes of making a person "criminal." To criminalize is to turn a person into a criminal.

criminalized youth – young people who have been involved in the youth justice system and have been subject to processes of criminalization

criminogenic needs – factors that play a role in preventing offending. Practitioners use actuarial tools to classify prisoners in terms of security risks and criminogenic needs. These are divided into either *static* factors (e.g., age, offence history) or *dynamic* factors (e.g., things that treatment programs can modify, such as antisocial attitudes, personality traits, or substance abuse).

criminological knowledge(s) – those knowledge claims about youth and crime upon which forms of social control and/or punishment are based

critical approach – an examination of systemic issues vis-a-vis youth, crime, and society. Critical analyses direct attention to issues of power, justice, and structural inequalities and reject traditional assumptions of mainstream criminological theory.

cultural artifact – a socially constructed rather than biologically based phenomenon. For example, Aries argued that childhood was not a biological imperative, but a cultural one.

cultural limbo – a term coined by Bob Ratner (1996) to refer to the position of Aboriginal youth alienated from the dominant white culture and from their Aboriginal heritage. Ratner argues that this cultural milieu disrespects Aboriginal identities and is oppressive to their ways of life.

culture of sensitivity – an attitude and approach to youth that is rooted in respect for difference and an empathy toward their needs rather than hostility and disdain

debunking – moving beyond "common sense" and searching for deeper or hidden meaning; what Peter Berger (1963) described as looking beyond the obvious explanation and unpacking taken-for-granted assumptions

deferred custody and supervision sentence – under the YJCA, this sentencing option enables youth (otherwise given a custodial sentence) to serve their sentences in the community

delinquent – defined in the *Juvenile Delinquents Act* as "any child who violates any provision of the Criminal Code or of any federal statute or provincial statute, or of any by-law or ordinance of any municipality or who is guilty of any similar form of vice, or who is liable by reason by any other act to be committed to an industrial school or juvenile reformatory under any federal or provincial statute" (Section 2(1)). This term used to describe young people in conflict with the law began to lose sway during the 1980s as the discourse of the "young offender" became more prominent.

dematerialization of the offence – means that a juvenile delinquent is situated at the heart of an investigation not of a crime, but of his or her social condition, family life, and education. Jacques Donzelot (1979: 111), who coined the phrase, asserts that the "juvenile court does not really pronounce judgment on crimes, it examines individuals."

dense interlocking system of social control – describes a network of various forces (institutions, individuals, and/or ideas) that exercise surveillance over the subject; one of three features of modern legal governance

deterrence – the sentencing rationale that presumes crime prevention can be accomplished through threat or fear of punishment

discipline – found operating at the smallest level of detail, at the intricacies of human movements through surveillance; presumes that the everyday and the mundane are important for governing

discourse – a way of speaking about a particular social issue or problem (e.g., youth and crime). Discourses are ways of knowing and ideas representing "that which is believed to be reality" (Hamilton, 2005). Discourses have social consequences.

discretion – at the police, Crown, and judicial levels, professionals have the latitude to exercise their own judgment, guided by explicit principles. Under the YJCA this is translated into the encouragement of extra-judicial measures and the expansion of judicial sentencing options.

diversionary programs – programs that channel young people away from the formal youth justice system; such as peer mediation for adolescents in conflict at school

doli incapax – literally translated means "incapable of wrongdoing," which manifests a belief in children's lack of maturity (Bala, 1988). This English common-law doctrine held that since children under age seven were "too immature" to form the requisite intent for criminality, they were immune from prosecution, and that children between seven and 14 had a diminished ability to appreciate consequences. Unless the Crown could prove that a youth *could* form the necessary criminal intent, they could not be legally convicted.

emphasized femininity - contemporary society presents young females with a variety of images and messages about growing up female, yet a dominant socio-cultural script for girls and young women continues to encourage a narrow version of femininity that prioritizes emotion, physical appearance and beauty, dependence, domesticity, caring, and family over more masculine-associated qualities like competition, aggression, independence, strength, and control. This powerful discourse works to justify women's secondary status relative to men [see hegemonic masculinity].

environmental psychology or the third wave of positivism – a more benign mental hygiene perspective that entered the discipline of psychology in the 1930s; it inspired a concern with changing environmental causes of deviance. Environmental psychology viewed the offender as malleable and therefore treatable.

errant female sexuality – defying feminine prescriptions of domesticity, submissiveness, dependence, and piety. Errant females or "bad girls" were/are doubly deviant as offenders and as women. As such they were/are incarcerated for their "immorality" (a euphemism for errant female sexuality).

ethnicity – the social construction that refers to cultural identity based on factors that include language, nationality, or religion; the means by which a group of people distinguish themselves

eugenics discourse – translated as "well born" or "good genes." Eugenics assumes that like livestock, *some* (white Anglo-Saxon) humans possess "better" genes than *others* (non-white immigrants). In the post WWI economic boom and mood of social progress, second wave positivists were committed to progress through social and biological engineering.

eugenics-informed psychiatry or the second wave of positivism – influenced medical psychology and psychiatry during the late 1910s and early 1920s in Canadian juvenile justice. When the professional "expert" challenged the expertise of non-trained philanthropists, social scientific knowledge about causes and treatment justified new methods.

extra-judicial measures (EJM) – police- or Crown-initiated alternatives to formal criminal justice processing under the *Youth Criminal Justice Act*

extra-judicial sanctions (EJS) – judge-initiated alternatives to formal justice processing under the *Youth Criminal Justice Act*

feeble-minded, feeblemindedness – mentally defective or defective in mind. Eugenicists drew on Cesare Lombroso's "born criminal" to advocate deportation of feeble-minded immigrants (and their families), incapacitation of feeble-minded criminals (adult and juvenile), and (especially for females) sterilization to prevent those deemed mentally defective from reproducing.

feminist critique – the body of feminist writing that calls mainstream scholarship into question for its gender-blindness and disregard for female criminality, victimization, and criminalization

feminist perspectives – includes many variants, among these are radical, liberal, socialist, and anti-racist feminism, which share in common an attention to structural inequalities in women's lives

Foucaultian conception of power – a positive theory of power, not in terms of being good or beneficial, but as productive. For Foucault (1979: 194), "[p]ower produces; it produces reality; it produces domains of object and rituals of truth."

gang – there is no consistent agreed-upon definition of (youth) gangs and many people erroneously refer to youth in groups as a gang and associate criminal activity with them. According to the Criminal Intelligence Service of Canada, a gang is a group of persons consorting together to engage in unlawful activity.

gender – the socio-cultural ideas (beliefs, values, and attitudes) about sex differences and the accompanying practices (behaviours, expressions, and characteristics) associated with being male (masculinity or masculinities) and being female (femininity or femininities)

gendered – inextricably linked to particular conceptions of masculinity and/or femininity. Youthful misbehaviour during the era of juvenile delinquency was cast in large part as a "boy problem," but in contemporary times "girl problem" discourse is equally as pervasive.

gendered social order – how society is structured and operates along gendered lines; that gender conditions and contours life experiences

gender-ratio problem – part of the feminist critique that asks why girls commit fewer criminal and delinquent acts than boys. In other words, what is it about girls' lives that encourages greater conformity?

gender-sensitive analysis – more than recognizing distinct gender identity (masculinity or femininity) or pointing to different gender roles (socialization), gender sensitive analyses acknowledge how the structural context is stratified by gender. Overt and subtle forms of patriarchy, its institutional manifestations, psychological dimensions, and social-context figure prominently in a gender-sensitive study of youth, crime, and society. The policy buzzword for a gender sensitive approach is "gender responsive."

generalizability problem – part of the feminist critique that asks to what extent theories of delinquency generated to explain boys can adequately capture girls' offending. Stated differently, if girls had the same opportunities, character traits, and experiences as boys, would their rate of delinquency be similar?

good girl/bad girl dichotomy – the discursive and practical separation of girls and women into culturally laden and socially constructed categories either "good" or "bad"

governmentality – not merely parliamentary governance (i.e., state government), but more broadly defined by Foucault as the "conduct of conduct" (Gordon, 1991: 2). For Foucault (1982: 221), government is "the way in which the conduct of individuals or states might be directed; the government of children, of souls, of communities, of families, of the sick." The study of governmentality addresses broad questions regarding self-governance and the governance of others.

hegemonic masculinity – (first proposed by Kessler et al., 1982, and later developed by others including Bob Connell, James Messerschmidt, and Michael Kimmel) This cultural script for being a man in contemporary North American society is distinguished from other subordinated masculinities. Hegemonic masculinity is a glorified, extolled version of acting and being a "real man" that defines manhood through rigid characteristics, including dominance, control, toughness, and independence. The concept is evolving to include a relational practice (as opposed to emphasized femininity) that men negotiate in constructing their own identities. Ideologically, hegemonic masculinity legitimates the widespread subordination of women to men [see emphasized femininity].

hyper-visibility – an amplified presence in particular social spaces often accompanied by more intense surveillance; especially common for disenfranchised groups such as Aboriginal youth.

ideological orientation – the guiding ideology and/or sets of ideas and assumptions of professionals responsible for delivering service to young people. Ideological orientation relates to the *who* of youth justice.

ideology of separate spheres – the idea that men's and women's natures (their sensibilities, minds, souls, and hence their "proper" spheres) are distinct. This ideology was the logic behind the first special reformatory for women in Canada.

incapacitation – incarceration not for what people have done, but to prevent future harm. Incapacitation can be contrasted with retribution or deterrence as a rationale for sentencing.

indeterminate sentences – under the *Juvenile Delinquents Act* sentences were not fixed, but were indeterminate, which meant that offenders were not released until they were no longer a threat to the public or had been reformed. Officials could return a young person to court to review his or her sentence at any time until they reached 21 years of age (R.S. c. 160, Section 20(3)).

individual-level pathways – the path into crime and/or processes of criminalization that involve psycho-social factors

industrial schools – reform-style institutions designed to offer training rather than punishment not only to young people who had committed crimes but also to those deemed wayward or in danger of falling into criminality

informal governance – includes such forms of social control as church discipline, shaming, and other community-based strategies. Informal governance exerts control over youthful deviance at a distance, either from the city, the street, the rural countryside, the community, the state, or the formal legal system. It continues today, especially in rural areas.

intensive support and supervision program (ISSP) – under the *Youth Criminal Justice Act*, ISSP (like probation) is served in the community under specified conditions, although it involves more intense monitoring and support than probation.

interactionism – The Chicago School of Sociology was characterized by the tradition of symbolic interactionism (in its heyday during the 1930s and 1940s). Interactionism understands the criminal conduct of young people as reflective of their individual experiences and social circumstances.

intrusive punishment discourse – holds young people accountable for their criminal actions through more punitive sanctions and is epitomized in the phrase "if we are tough on crime, if we punish crime, then people get the message."

JDA's philosophy – three interconnected ideas: the doctrine of *parens patriae*, an interventionist state, and the best interest of the child

juvenile courts – specialized separate courts that hear only cases involving youth, now referred to as "youth court" or "youth justice court." The *JDA* sanctioned the creation of juvenile courts and granted wide discretionary powers to judges and magistrates. Early courts sought to correct deviant children using a complex network of social agencies, knowledge, and actors. Juvenile courts were social tribunals.

juvenile delinquency – how the wayward behaviour of recalcitrant young people came to be understood around the turn of the 20th century, and the rationality for a separate system to govern young people's misbehaviour.

Juvenile Delinquents Act (JDA) – the first piece of legislation to separately govern juveniles in Canada; in effect from 1908 to 1984.

knowledge-based – the offender is a subject of knowledge and is investigated; one of three features of modern legal governance

labelling theories –theories that criticized the negative impact of criminal justice processing on disenfranchised groups like African Americans, women, and youth. Howard Becker's (1963: 9) famous phrase, "[d]eviant behaviour is behaviour that people so label" is a classic representation of labelling theory. Labelling theory today examines criminal and deviant acts as emerging from the labelling of social groups and institutions.

little adults – how children were viewed until the 17th century in Western Europe. Society was characterized by few social and cultural distinctions on the basis of age, and children were integrated into work and recreation in family life (Aries, 1962).

marginalization – the partial exclusion of certain social groups from mainstream society and the social inequalities that contribute to a person's involvement in crime

Marxian praxis – the premise that knowledge should not simply exist for its own sake but rather that it should be used for social transformation. To paraphrase Karl Marx, knowledge of the social world should move beyond academia and be applied to make change in the world.

masculinization – the argument that females have become more like males. Proponents reason that as women's participation in social and economic life raises their status relative to men, their participation in crime will increase.

meaningful consequences – sanctions that reinforce respect for societal values and help an offender repair the harm done to victims. A consequence is "meaningful" if it positively contributes to a young person's rehabilitation and reintegration and/or achieves community safety (under the *Youth Criminal Justice Act*).

media discourse – (media "talk") how the media represents social problems or issues such as youth crime

modern legal governance – a particularized system based more on knowledge of the offender than on his or her criminal conduct. Modern legal governance was formally enshrined with the passage of the *Juvenile Delinquents Act*.

moral panic – a term coined by Stanley Cohen (1972: 31) in *Folk Devils and Moral Panics* to describe what happens when there is "exaggerated attention, exaggerated events, distortion, and stereotyping" about a particular group. Moral panics are overreactions to forms of deviance or wrongdoing whereby claims made about particular groups as threats to the moral order touch people's fears, gain momentum, and infiltrate public consciousness.

mythologize – to make mythical or rare; for instance, the girl delinquent was mythologized. It was assumed that because she was *rare* she must be profoundly *different* (from males and other females).

neo-conservatism – a discourse cloaked in moralism that provides the rationale for "law and order" and a crime control model that presumes that coming down harder on the recalcitrant is the best way to respond to crime and other social problems. Neo-conservatism holds accountable and targets vulnerable and marginalized groups, in this case young people living on and about the street.

neo-liberalism – a social, political, and economic regulatory system and discourse characterized by policies and programs around security, privatization, a strengthened penal state, and "risk." Since the mid 1980s, neo-liberal reforms have made it easier for capital to expand (i.e., corporations to make larger profits) and have contributed to a disappearance of the social welfare state (i.e., protections like employment insurance and social assistance have become more difficult to access or live on).

non-criminogenic needs – systemic factors that require intervention but are not related (according to actuarial statistics) to recidivism such as poverty and health. Corrections Canada ranks these lower than criminogenic needs.

normalize – to make deviant actions and actors "normal"

normalization – the process of normalizing actions and actors

objectivist approach – follows a traditional historical reading of juvenile delinquency as a problem simply because the anti-social behaviour and/or criminal behaviour of adolescents became dangerous at a particular historical moment

offence – a young person's offending behaviour (e.g., the criminal act or crime category)

offender – an individual young person as related to the circumstances under which a young person's choice was made

over-representation – when a group has a greater proportion of its members in some condition (e.g., in prison) than the proportion they occupy in the larger population

parens patraie – a legal doctrine customary in the *JDA* era that requires the state to act "on behalf of the child's best interest" when parents are ill-equipped to care and control them. The doctrine later expanded to include a "best interest" clause intended to safeguard children's well-being, which evolved into the state's practice of assuming legal guardianship over children in need of protection or those without parents.

particularistic – a way to govern that treats each case as unique; one of three features of modern legal governance; represents a kind of knowledge about and unique to an individual

patriarchy – a discourse and organized system of male domination whereby men as a group have the power to oppress women and girls through social, political, and economic institutions. Patriarchal culture is based on the ideology of familial patriarchy, a set of ideas that support and encourage violence against women.

Pentanguishene Reformatory – one of the first reformatories for boys in Canada

perfectibility – the belief that the human race can be perfected or made better through human attention, effort, and initiative; one of three characteristics of the elite reformers during the first wave of positivism

philanthropic elite or first wave of positivism – interested volunteers who became early Canadian reformers in the area of juvenile justice. They consisted largely of the white Anglo-Celtic political and business male elite.

philosophy in legislation – the model of juvenile justice that a particular law closely resembles (i.e., restorative, welfare, punishment). Philosophy as declared in the legislation that relates to the *what* of youth justice.

politics of exclusion – social isolation reinforced by relations of power, especially visible through the lens of street-involved youth, criminalized girls, and Aboriginal youth

popular consciousness on youth crime – ways of thinking and speaking about youth crime, comprised largely of media and public discourses

popular or public discourse – (popular "talk") refers to all that is said about a particular topic (e.g., youth crime) by members of a particular culture and society at any given historical moment; how the general public perceives a problem

Positivism – also known as the Positive School or Positivist Theories of Crime. It was the first scientific school of criminology, which predominated from the late 1800s to early 1900s. Positivism views criminality as determined (or the effect in a cause-and-effect sequence) and assumes that criminals can be distinguished from non-criminals. As such, positivism holds that investigation using methods of controlled observation will lead to the causes of crime.

power/knowledge – the operation of relations of power and knowledge claims, coined by Michel Foucault

PPP – progressive, perfectibility, and products of the environment; the three Ps of the elite reformers' philosophy during the first wave of positivism

practices of governance – *what* is done to respond to a social problem or issue such as youth crime

praxis of possibility – thinking through *what could be*, or as Hogeveen and Woolford (2007: 690) define it: attending "to the suffering of those about us and to open up worlds of the possible beyond human misery."

presumptive offences –include murder, attempted murder, manslaughter, aggravated sexual assault (as they did under the YOA) and repeat violent crimes (added in *YCJA* Section 1(b) as serious violent offence). A serious violent offence is an "offence in the commission of which a young person causes or attempts to cause serious bodily harm" (Section 1(b), *Youth Criminal Justice Act*).

primary deviance – the kind of wayward behaviour that the vast majority of the public have engaged in at one time or another. Deviance is "primary" or remains symptomatic and situational only so long as it is rationalized as a function of culturally situated roles (Lemert, 1951).

privilege – the way hierarchies or divisions (such as those of race, class, gender, age, etc.) structure the lives of dominant groups in ways that benefit them. Privilege (social inclusion) is the other side of marginalization (social exclusion).

problematize – to question embedded assumptions and ideologies usually taken for granted; to uncover what lies beneath knowledge claims

products of environment – the belief that a child's environment and social circumstances (positive or negative) impact the direction of his or her life and behaviour; one of three characteristics of the elite reformers during the first wave of positivism

program goals and objectives – how a philosophy as declared in legislation is translated into practice. Program goals and objectives relate to the *how* of youth justice.

proportionality – any response to youthful offending should be "fair and proportionate" under the *Youth Criminal Justice Act*. This means that sentences must match the seriousness of the offence and recognize the offender's level of maturity.

punishable young offender – a discursive construction of young offenders as those who require punishment first and foremost, leaving reform and rehabilitative interventions secondary. During the late 1990s, the young offender (especially the Aboriginal, disenfranchised young person) was discursively constructed as the "punishable young offender."

race – the social construction that refers to categorical divisions between groups of people based on physical characteristics that are deemed socially relevant, such as skin colour. Races are distinct groups of people who share observable physical traits.

racialized social order – how society is structured and operates along racial hierarchies; that race and/or ethnicity conditions and contours life experiences

rationalities of governance – *why* certain governance practices are employed (e.g., what policies, programs, or processes are justified)

reformable young offender – a discursive construction of young offenders as those who require intervention and can be rehabilitated

reformation – the belief that corrective and rehabilitation oriented practices (as opposed to punishment) are the best antidote to crime

reformatories – reform-oriented institutions used in the late 19th and early 20th century as a method of reversing the ill effects of a child's home environment. Reformatories were premised on a belief in reformation.

refuge – an institution organized to provide a "refuge" or place of safety. Proponents argued that refuges provided protection rather than punishment; that is, a safe, home-like atmosphere where working-class females could develop their moral character through lessons in femininity and domesticity offered *voluntarily* by upper-middle class Protestant women.

reintegration – involves assisting a young person to adjust safely and productively back into his or her community (under the *Youth Criminal Justice Act*)

relative homelessness – living in a situation where basic standards are not met (e.g., unsafe rooming houses or temporarily sleeping on a friend's couch)

residential school system (or residential schools) – Government officials and religious authorities removed Aboriginal children from their families and sent them away to be "civilized" in residential schools from the early 1800s through to the 1960s. In these schools, children were forbidden to speak their traditional language or practice their traditions and were ridiculed for and taught to reject their spirituality and Aboriginal identity.

respect – approaching the "other" as a valued member of society, deserving of recognition, dignity, and compassion. Respect for the other in the form of understanding is where social justice begins.

responsibilization – accompanying individualization in a neoliberal society are new forms of responsibility placed upon youth and their families to *manage* their risks (Burchell, 1996). Individual youth and their families are "responsibilized," which means they are held to account for their own riskiness and are themselves categorized as "at risk."

restorative justice – involves victims and engages offenders to hold themselves accountable for their actions and for repairing harm done. Restorative justice is a non-adversarial, non-retributive approach to justice that emphasizes healing for victims, meaningful accountability of offenders, and the involvement of citizens in creating healthier, safer communities.

retribution – the sentencing rationale that presumes punishment is deserved because of an offence (an eye for an eye)

retributive – based on retribution

rights discourse – social processes in the form of rights revolutions during the 1960s and 1970s altered state politics and juvenile justice, thereby changing academic theorizing on crime and criminality. Emergent rights discourse reflected a new respect for cultural, sexual, and other differences brought about through social protest and critique of the state.

risk society – credited to Ulrich Beck (1992: 9), who argues that since the new millennium a break with modernity has occurred whereby the contours of the classical, industrial (modern) society have begun to give way to a new (advanced modern) risk society. In a risk society, social production of wealth is "systematically accompanied by the social production of risks."

risk/need – combines two distinct elements: traditional security concerns (i.e., associated with danger and harm prevention) and an emphasis on need (i.e., what an offender is lacking or entitled to in terms of resources). Risk/need classification determines both security classification and treatment in Canadian correctional institutions.

role of victims – more emphasis on harm to victims, repairing harm, and victims' rights under the *Youth Criminal Justice Act*

secondary deviance – when the young person comes to accept the label "criminal" and continues to engage in the behaviour that conditioned it

serious violent offence – after a young person is found guilty of an offence and has had at least two previous judicial determinations, the Crown may make application to the youth justice court for a judicial determination that the offence is "a serious violent offence" under the *Youth Criminal Justice Act*

sexual double standard – a different standard of acceptable sexual behaviour and sexuality for boys/men than for girls/women. The sexual double standard tacitly encourages male sexual exploration and/or promiscuity and punishes female sexuality; violence against women reflects, reinforces, and reproduces it.

social conditions – cultural, historical, political, and social context under which youth make choices; includes, but is not limited to, age, race, class, and gender inequalities. These underlying social structures make children and youth vulnerable to exploitation, violence, and legitimate targets of policies that criminalize, exclude, and punish.

social construct or social construction – the label, name, and meaning given to a particular phenomenon in society

social constructionist perspective – holds that juvenile delinquency becomes a *problem* when it is defined as such by social reformers (be they prominent individuals or social groups); that is, when it has been labelled as problematic by authorized knowers

social control – various sociological definitions of social control circulate from a planned, conscious, and scientifically based form of regulation (Ross, 1969) to regulation that is "of the community by the community, of like-minded people by like-minded people" (Sumner, 2004: 10). Critical criminology has all but abandoned the concept in favour of terms like regulation, governance, and censure.

social disorganization – a breakdown in social cohesion, leadership structures, and internal social controls that were once maintained by peace and community organization. Shaw and McKay (1931, 1942) referred to areas—especially those in transition characterized by urban decay, poverty, high crime rates, high dependency on social welfare, etc.—as "socially disorganized."

social (in)justice – conditions of (dis)advantage and relations of power/privilege that underlie race, class, and gender inequalities. Inequalities of race/class/gender/age reinforce and perpetuate social *injustice* , but working to change the way power relations such as these condition peoples' lives is directed at *social justice*.

social justice praxis – a process of critical reflection and social engagement aimed at addressing the systemic conditions of marginalization, which would improve the life chances of the marginalized. It is one way to envision a more humane, respectful, and inclusive social system.

social progress (or progressive) – a forward-looking attitude toward social and personal betterment; one of the three P's of the elite reformers' philosophy during the first wave of positivism

social reformers – in the 19th century, reformers were primarily upper-middle class business, political, and legal elite males who began to question the wisdom of then-dominant governance practice, adjudicating young people through a generalized system of punishment. Many different groups occupy the position of social reformer in contemporary society.

social welfare – in contrast to a laissez faire approach or a distanced state unwilling to intervene in the affairs of private families, a social welfare oriented state is characterized by a plethora of policies and programs and an interventionist approach to individual, family, and community (also see welfare penality)

sociological imagination – C. Wright Mills (1959b) used this phrase to describe the ability to see the relationships between individual experiences (biography) and the larger society (history). Linking biography with history means recognizing that private or personal troubles are connected to larger public or social issues.

socio-political climate – the social, economic, and political context in which people live; institutions, practices, and discourses that underlie various methods of governing and influencing youthful offending and victimization

special needs of Aboriginal youth – greater recognition of unique circumstances for Aboriginal youth under the *Youth Criminal Justice Act*

spectacle – more than a collection of spectacular images; a world view that has seemingly become "objective" in such a way that the public believes the broadcasted representation to be what is *real*

statistical artifacts – unreal reflections of recidivism based on theoretical predictions and mathematical equations. Risk assessments are probabilistic calculations based on tools that output a score that is interpreted as predicting the likelihood of recidivism. O'Malley (1992) refers to "risk" (the output generated by the assessments) as a statistical artifact.

status offences – first introduced in the *Juvenile Delinquents Act*; involved conduct that if undertaken by an adult would not incite legal action, such as drinking, gambling, truancy, and promiscuity. Such behaviours were only considered deviant because of the age (status) of the person engaged in the act.

stigmatization – Goffman (1963) coined this term, which refers to a process of applying a stigma (negative evaluation of difference) to an individual or group (on behaviour and identity)

street entrenchment – forced economic survival, the (ab)use of drugs, violence, and the denial of human dignity that comes with being immersed in street life

street-involved youth – a group of young people working and/or living on the streets. Street-involved youth are one of the most stigmatized, marginalized, and hard-to-reach populations in our society.

structural and cultural barriers – conditions of inequality and disadvantage that influence a person's "choice" to engage in deviance or crime and/or impede their participation in legitimate activities. Having no recreational opportunities, being expelled from school, and growing up in an impoverished environment are *structural* barriers. *Cultural* barriers include feelings of hopelessness, lack of belonging, and lack of identity.

structural-level pathways – the paths to crime and/or processes of criminalization that involve the contribution of societal factors toward girls' criminalization

structured action – what professionals in the system "do to construct social relations and social structures, and how these social structures constrain and channel behavior in specific ways" (James Messerschmidt, 1997: 3)

systemic issues – system-based or societal-level problems such as poverty, racism, and discrimination. These are inherent to the life experiences of disenfranchised, marginalized groups.

systemic racism – beyond the individual level, this refers to societal prejudice and discrimination at the system or structural level

techniques of normalization – are possible through law, which operates not as a generalized instrument of control but as a point of access for what Michel Foucault (1980, 1991) calls "techniques of normalization." Accumulating knowledge about deviant children and their social environment through surveillance (e.g., as the Juvenile Court did), served to normalize erring children.

the "other" – the disenfranchised, marginalized (by race, class, gender, age, etc.) individual or group in society; the other is systematically excluded and often voiceless; those whose claims are silenced, not heard, ignored, and not taken seriously by authorized knowers

theoretical underpinnings – assumptions, discourses, concepts, and implications of various responses to social problems such as youth crime

theory – a set of knowledge claims that attempts to interpret a complex world and the events that take place within it. Theories about youth crime are used to make sense of how a problem should be understood and is thereby governed.

victimization – having been a victim is a significant pathway to criminalization, especially for female youth. Some groups (including youth, females, and Aboriginal peoples) are disproportionately victims of abuse, violence, and oppression.

victim-offender reconciliation programs (VORP) – an approach that allows victims and offenders to play key roles in determining the most appropriate method of responding to a conflict. Offenders meet with their victims, prepare a report detailing the psychological and material damage caused, and provide compensation for their misdeeds.

violence – a complex, nuanced, and multifaceted phenomenon without an agreed-upon, concise, all-encompassing definition. Violence is socially constructed, relational, and a censure. Our working definition of violence is a social and moral censure of aggressive actions that *we* find abhorrent.

violent masculinity – a crucial component of the socio-cultural script for being a boy/man in contemporary North American society or *what it means* to be a male within this

subculture and the wider society. Violent masculinity is the cultural norm such that a "real man" is obligated to respond to threat through violence.

violent repeat offender – reference to both a youth labelled as such for having been given the judicial determination that s/he has committed a "serious violence offence" and the discursive construction of violent recidivist youth

way of theorizing – a more integrative approach to understanding the relationships between youth, crime, and society than theory construction. A way of theorizing is an approach *to* theory, not the knowledge claims.

welfare penality – promotes the rehabilitation of youth through an interwoven fabric of legal and extra-legal officials who intrude into the lives of those they perceive to be ruined working class families

women's liberation thesis – initially proposed by Freda Adler (1975); argues that as women gain social and economic equality so too will they gain "equality" in crime; that is, gender parity in crime rates will result from women's emancipation.

Young Offenders Act (YOA) – the legislation that replaced the *Juvenile Delinquents Act* in 1984 and governed youthful offenders (aged 12–17) until 2003 when the *Youth Criminal Justice Act* came into effect

youth – the legal definition from the *Youth Criminal Justice Act* and *Young Offenders Act* is individuals between the ages of 12–17. Our definition is significantly broader than the legal one. Social definition: young people into their mid-twenties, many of whom are still serving youth sentences and/or are still impacted by their experiences in the youth justice system into adulthood.

youth-at-risk discourse – a powerful truth claim, the position holds that youth are *at risk* for and to everything. With this heightened concern about youth at risk, some youth are deemed "riskier" than others. In the context of risk discourse, the search for *causes* of youth crime shifts to a focus on *risks*. In practice, risk management techniques presume risk can be calculated according to (and also emerging from) *individual* decision-making, not structural location.

youth crime – a socially constructed problem that labels the misbehaviour and law violations of young people. Discourse and practice are interrelated such that how the problem of youth crime and youthful offenders is understood has implications for responses to it.

***Youth Criminal Justice Act* (YCJA)** – the current piece of legislation that governs young offenders (under the age of 18) in Canada; came into effect in 2003.

youth voices – involvement and engagement of young people in matters that affect them; respecting youth voices means taking their claims seriously

youth-centred innovation – begins from the premise that young people and criminalized youth in particular have experiences that position them well to play a more central role in responding to the problems they face (individually and collectively) in their lives. A youth-centred innovation represents real, meaningful youth engagement aimed at dealing with systemic issues related to youth, crime, and society and is novel in assumptions, approach, and impact.

YRAP (The Youth Restorative Action Project) – a grassroots youth organization based in Edmonton, Alberta, made up of youth (ages 14–24) who come from diverse ethnic, social, and economic backgrounds and collectively hand out sentences as a youth justice committee

zero tolerance – an approach to crime and other social problems characterized by "get tough" policies and codes of conduct that punish infractions rapidly and relentlessly

Bibliography and References

Aboriginal Justice Implementation Commission. (2001). *Final Report.*

Aboriginal Justice Inquiry of Manitoba. (1991). *Report of the Aboriginal Justice Inquiry of Manitoba.* Winnipeg: Queen's Printer.

Aboriginal Nurses Association of Canada. (2001). *Exposure to Violence in the Home: Effects on Aboriginal Children Discussion Paper.* Ottawa, ON: ANAC

Aboriginal Women's Council of Saskatchewan. (1989). "Child Sexual Abuse: Words from concerned women." [Electronic version]. *Canadian Woman Studies,* 10, 90–91.

Abrahams, Lionel. "U buntu or not to" *Sidelines,* June 1997.

Abramovitch, R., Higgins-Biss, K., and Biss, S. (1993). "Young persons' comprehension of waivers in criminal proceedings." *Canadian Journal of Criminology,* 34(3), 309–322.

Abramovitch, R., Peterson-Badali, M., and Rohan, M. (in press). "Young people's understanding and assertion of their rights to silence and legal counsel." *Canadian Journal of Criminology.*

Absolon, K., and Winchester, T. (1994). *Cultural Identity for Urban Aboriginal Peoples Learning Circles Synthesis Report.* In Royal Commission on Aboriginal Peoples, *Seven Generations* [CD-ROM]. Ottawa, ON: Libraxus.

Acland, C.R. (1995). *Youth Murder Spectacle: The Cultural Politics of "Youth in Crisis."* San Francisco: Westview.

Acoca, L. (1999). "Investing in girls: A 21st century challenge." *Juvenile Justice,* 6(1), 3–13.

Adelberg, E. and Currie, C. (1989). *Too Few to Count: Canadian Women in Conflict with the Law.* 2nd ed. Vancouver: Press Gang.

Adler, C. and Worrall, A. (2004). "A Contemporary Crisis?" In C. Adler and A. Worrall (Eds.), *Girls' Violence: Myths and Realities.* Albany: State University of New York Press.

Adler, F. (1975). *Sisters in Crime.* New York: McGraw-Hill.

Adler, F., Mueller. G., and Laufer, W. (2007). *Criminology.* 6th ed. New York: McGraw Hill.

Adler, P.A. (1998) *Peer Power: Pre-Adolescent Culture and Identity.* New Brunswick: Rutgers University Press.

Adler, P.A., Kless, S.J., and Adler, P. (1992). "Socialisation to gender roles: Popularity among elementary school boys and girls." *Sociology of Education,* 65, 172.

Agnew, R. (1990). "The origins of delinquent events: An examination of offender accounts." *Journal of Research in Crime and Delinquency* 27(3), 267–294.

Ainger, A. (1890). "Those bad boys." *Canadian Educational Monthly* (December).

Akers, R. (1977). *Deviant Behavior: A Social Learning Approach.* Belmont, CA: Wadsworth.

Akers, R. and Burgess, R. (1966). "A differential reinforcement theory of criminal behavior." *Social Problems* 14: 128–47.

Akers, R., et al. (1979). "Social learning and deviant behavior: A specific test on a general theory." American *Sociological Review,* 44 (4): 636–55.

Alberta Solicitor General. (1992). *Young offender daily population statistics report for April 30, 1992.* Edmonton, Alberta: Alberta Solicitor General.

Alberta Solicitor General. (1992a). *Annual report of the Department of the Solicitor General, 1991/92.* Edmonton, Alberta: Alberta Solicitor General.

Alexander, R. and Lynden Langford. (1992). "Throwing down: A social learning test of student fighting." *Social Work in Education* 14 (2): 114–24.

Allen, H. (1987). *Justice Unbalanced: Gender, Psychiatry and Judicial Decisions.* Milton Keynes: Open University Press.

American Bar Association. (2001). *Justice by Gender: The Lack of Appropriate Prevention, Diversion and Treatment Alternatives for Girls in the Justice System: A Report.* (May 1). Washington DC: American Bar Association and the National Bar Association.

Amnesty International. (2004). *Annual Report of the President.*

Amnesty International. (2004). *Stolen Sisters: Discrimination and Violence Against Indigenous Women in Canada.* AI Index: AMR 20/003/2004.

An Act Respecting Juvenile Delinquents (1908). Ottawa: King's Printer.

Anand, S. (1998/1999). "Catalyst for change: The history of Canadian juvenile justice reform." *Queen's Law Journal,* 24, 515–559.

Anand, S. (1999). "The good, the bad and the unaltered: An analysis of Bill C-68, the Youth Criminal Justice Act." *Canadian Criminal Law Review,* 4, 249–270.

Andersen, P and Telleen, S. (1992). "The relationship between social support and maternal behaviors and attitudes: a meta-analytic review." *American Journal of Community Psychology,* 20(6),753–774.

Anderson, C. (1999). "Governing Aboriginal justice in Canada: Constructing responsible individuals and communities through tradition." *Crime, Law and Social Change*, 31(2): 303–326.

Anderson, E. (1999). *The Code of the Street: Decency, Violence, and the Moral Life of the Inner City*. New York: W.W. Norton.

Anderson, G.L. (1993). *When Chemicals Come to School* (Rev. ed.). Greenfield, WI: Community Recovery Press.

Anderson, J. (2003). Canadian Council on Social Development, *Aboriginal Children in Poverty in Urban Communities: Social Exclusion and the Growing Racialization of Poverty in Canada*. Notes for Presentation to Subcommittee on Children and Youth at Risk of the Standing Committee on Human Resources Development and the Status of Persons with Disabilities. Retrieved from www.ccsd.ca/pr/2003/aboriginal.htm.

Anderson, M. and Gobeil, S. (2003). Child Welfare League of Canada. *Recruitment and Retention in Child Welfare Services: A Survey of Child Welfare League of Canada Member Agencies*.

Anderson, S. (1999). "Depression and stress in street youth." *Adolescence*, 34(135), 567–575.

Andrews, D.A. and Bonta, J. (1998). *The Psychology of Criminal Conduct*. 2nd ed. Cincinnati, OH: Anderson Publishing Co. Ann Arbor (MI): Rutgers University.

Andrews, D.A. et al. "Does correctional treatment work? A clinically relevant and psychologically informed meta-analysis." *Criminology*, 28(3), 369–404.

Antonowicz, D.H. and Ross, R.R. (1994). "Essential components of successful rehabilitation programs for young offenders." *International Journal of Offender Therapy and Comparative Criminology*, 38, 97–104.

Appadurai, A. (1998a). "Dead certainty: Ethnic violence in the era of globalization." *Public Culture*, Vol. 25. pp. 225–247.

Appadurai, A. (1998b). "The production of locality." In A. Appadurai (Ed.) *Modernity at Large. Cultural Dimensions of Globalization*. Minneapolis: University of Minnesota Press. pp. 178–199.

Appadurai, A. (1998c). *Modernity at Large*. Minneapolis: University of Minnesota Press.

Appathurai, C. (1987). *Runaway Behaviour: A Background Paper*. Toronto: Ministry of Community Services.

Archambault, R.O. (1986). "Young Offenders Act: Philosophy and principles." In R.A. Silverman, J.J. Teevan, and V.F. Sacco (Eds.), *Crime in Canadian Society*. 3rd ed. Toronto: Butterworths.

Archives of Ontario, Department of the Attorney General. (1930). *The Report of the Royal Commission on Public Welfare*, RG 29–138 Box 1. 1930.

Aries, P. (1962). *Centuries of Childhood: A Social History of Family Life*. New York: Vintage Books.

Arnold, E. and Skaburskis, A. (1989). "Measuring Ontario's increasing housing affordability problem." *Social Indicators Research*, 21, pp.501–515.

Artz, S. (1998). *Sex, Power, and the Violent School Girl*. Toronto: Trifolium Books.

Artz, S., Blais, M., and Nicholson, D. (2000). *Developing Girls' Custody Units*. Report to Justice Canada.

Artz, S. and Nicholson, D. (2002). *Aggressive Girls*. Ottawa: Family Violence Prevention Unit, Health Canada. Catalogue H72-22/24-2002E.

Artz, S., Nicholson, D., and Rodriguez, C. (2005). "Girl delinquency in Canada." In K. Campbell, (Ed.), *Understanding Youth Justice in Canada*. Toronto: Pearson Education Canada.

Austin, J. (1995). *The Overrepresentation of Minority Youth in the California Juvenile Justice System: Perceptions and Realities*. Thousand Oaks, CA: Sage Publications. Available at www.prevention.gc.ca/en/library/publications/youth/mobilize/advance.html (accessed 21 July 2004).

Avramov, D. (1998). *Youth, Homelessness in the European Union*. Brussels: FEANTSA.

Avramov. D. (1999). "Introduction: The state-of-the-art research of homelessness and the provision of services in Europe." *Coping with Homelessness: Issues to be Tackled and Best Practices in Europe*. Aldershot, England: Ashgate Publishing.

Ayerst, S. (1999). "Depression and stress in street youth." *Adolescence* 34(135), 567–575.

Aylward, C.A. (1999). *Canadian Critical Race Theory: Racism and the Law*. Halifax: Fernwood Publishing Company.

Back, A. (2004). "Thinking clearly about violence." *Philosophical Studies*, 117, 219–230.

Badiou, A. (2001) *Ethics: An Essay on the Understanding of Evil*, trans. Peter Hallward, New York: Verso.

Baehre, R. (1982). *The Prison System in Atlantic Canada before 1800*. Ottawa: Solicitor General of Canada.

Bagley, C. (1988). *Child Sexual Abuse in Canada: Further Analysis of the 1983 National Survey*. Calgary: University of Calgary, Family Violence Initiative Project.

Bala, N. (1988). "Young Offenders Act: A legal framework." In J. Hudson, J.B. Hornick, and B. Burrows (Eds.) *Justice and the young offender in Canada*. Toronto: Wall and Thompson.

Bala, N. (1994). *Ottawa Law Review*. Report to the Department of Justice Canada. Canada: Queen's Printer.

Bala, N. (1994). "What's wrong with YOA bashing? What's wrong with the YOA? Recognizing the limits of the law." *Canadian Journal of Criminology*, 36(3), 247–270.

Bala, N. (1997). *Young Offenders Law*. Concord, ON: Irwin Law.

Bala, N. (2002). *Diversion and Extrajudicial Measures*. National Judicial Institute, Conference on the *Youth Criminal Justice Act*, Toronto, September 2002. Available March 2004 http://www.nji.ca/postings/YJC/youthjustice.html.

Bala, N. (2003). *Youth Criminal Justice Law*. Toronto: Irwin Law.

Bala, N. (2005). "The development of Canada's youth justice law." In K. Campbell (Ed.) *Understanding Youth Justice in Canada*. Toronto: Pearson Education.

Bala, N. and Anand, S. (2004). "The first months under the *Youth Criminal Justice Act*: Survey and analysis of case law." *Canadian Journal of Criminology*, 46(Spring), 251–271.

Balfour, G. and Comack, E. (2005). *Criminalizing Women: Gender and (In)Justice in Neo-liberal Times*. Halifax: Fernwood Publishing.

Bandura, A. (1973). *Aggression: A Social Learning Analysis*. Upper Saddle River, NJ: Prentice Hall.

Bandura, A. (1977). *Social Learning Theory*. Englewood Cliffs, NJ: Prentice-Hall.

Bar On, B. (2002). *The Subject of Violence: Arendtean Exercises in Understanding*. Boston: Rowman and Littlefield.

Barak, G. (2003). *Violence and NonViolence: Pathways to Understanding*. Thousand Oaks, CA.: Sage.

Barak, G. (2006). "A Critical Perspective on Violence." *Advancing Critical Criminology: Theory and Application*. W. Dekeseredy and B. Perry (Eds.). Lanham: Lexington Books.

Barnhorst, R. (2004). "The Youth Criminal Justice Act: New directions and implementation issues." *Canadian Journal of Criminology and Criminal Justice 46(3)*, 231–250.

Barnsley, P. (2000). "Anti-gang program comes to Edmonton." *Windspeaker*, 18(1).

Baron, S. (2001). "Street youth labour market experiences and crime." *Canadian Review of Sociology and Anthropology*, Vol. 38, no. 2. pp. 189–215.

Baron, S. (2003). "Street youth violence and victimization." *Trauma, Violence and Abuse* 4(1), 22–44. January.

Barron, C.L. (2000). *Giving Youth a Voice: A Basis for Rethinking Adolescent Violence*. Halifax: Fernwood Publishing.

Barron, C. and Lacombe, D. (2005). "Moral panic and the nasty girl." *Canadian Review of Sociology and Anthropology*, 43 (1), 51–69.

Bastien, R. and Adelman, H. (1984). "Noncompulsory versus legally mandated placement, perceived choice and response to treatment among adolescents." *Journal of Consulting and Clinical Psychology*, 52(2), 171–179.

Batacharya, S. (2004) "Racism, 'girl violence' and the murder of Reena Virk," In Alder, C. and Worrall, A. (Eds.) *Girls' Violence: Myths and Realities*. New York: SUNY, pp. 61–80

Battle, K. (1996). *Persistent Poverty*. Caledon Institute of Social Policy. (December).

Bazemore, G. (1996). "Three paradigms for juvenile justice." In *Restorative Justice:International Perspectives*, Burt Galaway and Joe Hudson (Eds.). Monsey, NY: Criminal Justice Press.

Bazemore, G. (2001). "Young people, trouble and crime: Restorative justice as a normative theory of informal social control and social support." *Youth and Society*, 33(2), 199–227.

Bazemore, G. and Schiff, M. (Eds.) (2001). *Restorative Community Justice: Repairing Harm and Transforming Communities*. Cincinnati, OH: Anderson Publishing Co.

Bazemore, G. and Umbreit, M. (1995). "Rethinking the sanctioning function in juvenile court: retributive or restorative responses to youth crime." *Crime Delinquency*, 41, 296–316.

Bazemore, G. and Walgrave, L. (1997). *Restoring Juvenile Justice*. Monsey, NY: Criminal Justice Press.

Bazemore, G. and Walgrave, L. (1999). "Restorative juvenile justice: In search of fundamentals and an outline for systemic reform." In *Restorative Juvenile Justice: Repairing the Harm of Youth Crime*, G. Bazemore, and L. Walgrave (Eds.) Monsey, NY: Willow Tree Press.

Bear Paw Productions. (2005). *Illusions* (film).

Bear Paw Productions. (2005). *Gang Aftermath* (film).

Beattie, J. (1986). *The Cycle of Juvenile Justice*. New York: Oxford University Press.

Beaulieu, L. (1994). "Youth offences, adult consequences." *Canadian Journal of Criminology*, 36(3), 329–341.

Beccaria, C.B.M. (1819). *An Essay on Crimes and Punishments*. Philadelphia: Philip H. Nicklion.

Beck, U. (1992). *Risk Society*. London: Sage.

Becker, H. (1963). *The Outsiders: Studies in the Sociology of Deviance*. New York: Free Press.

Beecher-Monas, E. and Garcia-Rill, E. (2006). "Genetic predictions of future dangerousness: Is there a blueprint for violence?" *Law and Contemporary Problems*. 69(1/2), 301–341.

Begin, P. (1996, 1994). *Homelessness in Canada*. Ottawa: Minister of Supply and Services.

Beirne, P. and Messerschmidt, J. (1991). *Criminology*. San Diego: Harcourt Brace Jovanovich.

Bell, S. (2007). *Young Offenders and Youth Justice: a century after the fact*. 3rd ed. Toronto: Nelson Canada.

Benzie, (2001). "Changes to youth crime bill called weak-kneed: Ontario minister requests appearance at Senate hearing." *National Post*, 15 June 2001, A.8.

Berger, P. (1963). *Invitation to Sociology*. New York: Doubleday.

Berger, P. and Luckman, T. (1967). *The Social Construction of Reality: A Treatise in the Sociology of Knowledge*. Anchor.

Bernstein. J., Adlaf, E., and Paglia, A. (2000). *Drug use in Toronto*. Toronto: Research Drug Group on Drug Use.

Bernstein, J. and Lee, J. (1998). *Young Parents: No fixed address*. Toronto: Public Health Department. Report to City Council.

Best, J. (1989). *Images of issues: Typifying contemporary social problems*. H. Silverstein, (Ed.) New York: Macmillian.

Birnie, L.H. (1990) *A Rock and a Hard Place: Inside Canada's Parole Board*. Toronto: Macmillan.

Bisson, L. (1987). *Le salaire a-t-il un sexe?: Les inegalites de revenus entre les femmes et les hommes au Quebec*. Quebec: Government of Quebec.

Bisson, L. (1989). *Les Maisons d'Hébergement pour jeunes: État de la situation*. Quebec: Conseil permanent de la jeunesse, Government of Quebec.

Bittle, B. (2006). "From victim to villain: Secure care and young women in prostitution." In G. Balfour and E. Comack (Eds.) *Criminalizing Women: Gender and (In)Justice in Neo-Liberal Times*. Halifax: Fernwood.

Bittle, S. (2002). "When Protection is Punishment: Neo-liberalism and Secure Care Approaches to Youth Prostitution." *Canadian Journal of Criminology*, 44(3), 317–351.

Blackstock, C. (2003). "First Nations child and family services: Restoring peace and harmony in First Nations communities." In K. Kufeldt and B. McKenzie (Eds.), *Child welfare: Connecting research, policy, and practice* (pp. 331–342). Waterloo, ON: Wilfrid Laurier University Press.

Blackwell, T. (2003). "Few youths jailed under new law." *National Post*, 18 July 2003.

Blomley, N. (2003) "Law, property, and the geography of violence: The frontier, the survey. and the grid." *Annals of the Association of American Geographers*, 93 (1): 121–141.

Bloom, B. (Ed.). (2003). *Gendered Justice: Addressing Female Offenders*. Durham, NC: Carolina Academic Press.

Bloom, B. and Covington, S. (2001). *Effective gender-responsive intervention in juvenile justice: Addressing the lives of delinquent girls*. Paper presented at the 2001 Annual Meeting of the American Society of Criminology. Atlanta, Georgia, November 7-10, 2001. (Available at www.centerforgenderandjustice.org/girls/html).

Bloom, B., Owen, B., Covington, S., and Raeder, M. (2003) *National Institute of Corrections Gender-Responsive Strategies: Research, Practice, and Guiding Principles for Women Offenders*. www.nicic.org. June 2003.

Bloom, B., Owen, B., Deschenes, E.P., and Rosenbaum, J. (2002). "Improving juvenile justice for females: A statewide assessment of California." *Crime & Delinquency*, 50 (2).

Bloomenfeld, M. and Cole, D. (2005). "The roles of legal professionals in youth court." In K. Campbell (Ed.) *Understanding Youth Justice in Canada*. Toronto: Pearson Education.

Boe, R. (2002). "Future demographic trends may help Canada's Aboriginal youth." *Forum on Corrections Research*, 14(3), 13–16.

Boe, R. E. (2000). "Aboriginal inmates: demographic trends and projections." *Forum on Corrections Research*, 12 (1), 7–9.

Boland, F. J. et al. (1998). *Fetal Alcohol Syndrome: Implications for the Correctional Service*. Ottawa: Correctional Service of Canada.

Borum, R. (2000). "Assessing violence risk among youth." *Journal of Clinical Psychology*, 56(10): 1263–86.

Bosworth, M. (2004). "Gender, risk and recidivism." *Criminology and Public Policy*, 3(2): 181–4.

Bourdieu, P. (1989). "Toward a reflexive sociology: A workshop with Pierre Bourdieu." *Sociological Theory*, 7(1), 26–63.

Bourdieu, P. (1977). *Outline of a Theory of Practice*, Cambridge: Cambridge University Press.

Boyer, D., and James, J. (1982). "Easy money: Adolescent involvement in prostitution." In S. Davidson, (Ed.), *Justice for young women: Close-up on critical Issues New Directions for Young Women* (July 1982)

"Boys and the Police." *Toronto Daily Star*, August 20, 1900.

Bradley, Ann. (1994). "A Morality Play For Our Times." *Living Marxism*, 63.

Braithwaite, J. (1989). *Crime, Shame and Reintegration*. Cambridge, UK: Cambridge University Press.

Braithwaite, J. (2000). "The new regulatory state and the transformation of criminology," *British Journal of Criminology*, 40(2), 222–238.

Braithwaite, J. (2003). "Principles of Restorative Justice." In *Restorative Justice and Criminal Justice: Competing or Reconcilable Paradigms?* A. Von Hirsch, et al. (Eds.) Oxford; Portland: Hart.

Brannigan, A. and Caputo, T. (1993). *Studying Runaways and Street Youth in Canada: Conceptual and Research Design Issues*. Ottawa: Minister of Supply and Services.

Brener, N.D., Simon, T.R., Krug, E.G., and Lowry R. (1999). "Recent trends in violence related behaviors among high school students in the United States." *Journal of the American Medical Association*, 282(5), 330–446.

Brown Commission. (1849). "Appendix to the journals of the Legislative Assembly of the Province of Canada." *Second Report of the Royal Commission on the Provincial Penitentiary in Kingston*. Ottawa: King's Printer.

Brown, D. (1997). *PACE Ten Years On: A Review of the Research*. London: Home Office.

Brown, J.N. et al. (2005.) "Challenges Faced by Aboriginal Youth in the Inner City," *Canadian Journal of Urban Research*, 14 (1): 81–106.

Brown, S. (2005). *Understanding Youth and Crime: Listening to Youth?* 2nd ed. Milton Keynes: Open University Press.

Buffam, H.V.B. (2006). *Becoming Part of Inner City Space: A Critical Ethnography of Racialized Youth*. University of Alberta. unpublished Master's thesis.

Bukstein, O.G. (1995). *Adolescent Substance Abuse: Assessment, Prevention and Treatment*. New York: John Wiley and Sons.

Bull, L.R. (1991). "Indian residential school: The Native perspective." *Canadian Journal of Education*, 18:1–65.

Bullen, J. (1991). "J.J. Kelso and the—New Child Savers: The genesis of the Children's Aid Movement in Ontario." In R.

Smandych, G. Dodds, and A. Esau, eds. *Dimensions of Childhood: Essays on the History of Children and Youth in Canada*, 135–58. Winnipeg: University of Manitoba Legal Research Institute.

Bunyan, J. (1999). *The Pilgrim's Progress*.

Burchell, G. (1996). "Liberal government and technique of the self." In A. Barry, T. Osborne and N. Rose (Eds), *Foucault and Political Reason: Liberalism, Neo-Liberalism and Rationalities of Government*. London: Harvester Wheatsheaf.

Burwash, N. (1906). *Egerton Ryerson*. Toronto: Morang & Co.

Busby, K. (2003). "The protection confinement of girls involved in prostitution: Potential problems of current regimes." In K. Gorkoff and J. Runner (Eds.), *Being Heard: The Experiences of Young Women In Prostitution*. Black Point, NS: Fernwood.

Bushman B.J. and Anderson C.A. (2001). "Is it time to pull the plug on the hostile versus instrumental aggression dichotomy?" *Psychological Review* 108: 273–79.

Bushman B.J. and Huesmann L.R. (2001). "Effects of televised violence on aggression." In D. Singer (Ed.), *Handbook of Children and the Media*, 223–54. Thousand Oaks, CA: Sage

Butler, J.P. (1999). *Gender Trouble: Feminism and the Subversion of Identity*. New York: Routledge.

Cain, M. (Ed). (1989). *Growing Up Good: Policing the Behaviour of Girls in Europe*. London: Sage.

Calverley, D. (2006). Centre for Justice Statistics, *Juristat*. Statistics Canada. Catalogue no. 85-002-XIE, Vol. 27, no. 2 Youth custody and community services in Canada, 2004/2005.

Campbell, A. (1981). *Girl Delinquents*. Oxford: Basil, Blackwell.

Campbell, D.T. and Stanley, J. (1963). *Experimental and Quasi-Experimental Designs for Research*. Boston: Houghton Mifflin.

Campbell, K. (2005). *Understanding Youth Justice in Canada*. Toronto: Prentice Hall.

Canada. (1857). *An Act for Establishing Prisons for Young Offenders*. Consolidated Statutes of Upper Canada, 1857, Chapter 28.

Canada. (1857). Consolidated Statutes. *An Act for Establishing Prisons for Young Offenders, for the Better Government of Public Asylums, Hospitals and Prisons, and for the Better Construction of Common Gaols*.

Canada. *Hansard Debates*, 10 May 2000.

Canada Mortgage and Housing Corporation. (2001). *Research Highlights: Environmental Scan on Youth Homelessness*. July, Issue 86.

Canada Mortgage and Housing Corporation. (2004). *2001 Census Series: Aboriginal Households*. Ottawa: Queen's Printer.

Canada. National Archives. *J.J. Kelso Papers*. MG 30, C-97, vol. 1 (1890–95).

Canada. National Archives. *W.L. Scott Papers*. MG 30, C-27, vol. 1 (1905–10), vol 2 (1911–15).

Canada West Foundation. (2003). (Loleen Berdahl). April. *Looking West 2003. A Survey of Western Canadians*.

Canadian Centre for Justice Statistics. (1992). Youth Court Statistics 1991–92 Highlights. *Juristat Service Bulletin*, 12(16).

Canadian Centre for Justice Statistics. (1994) *Statistics Canada Report: Family Violence in Canada, Current National Data*. Ottawa, ON: Department of Justice, June 1994.

Canadian Centre for Justice Statistics. (1998). Statistics Canada. Cat. No. 85–205.

Canadian Centre for Justice Statistics. (2002). *Uniform Crime Reporting Incident-Based Survey Reporting Manual*. Version 2.0. Unpublished.

Canadian Centre for Justice Statistics. (2003). *Proposed National Data Requirement Changes to the UCR2 Survey due to the YCJA*. Unpublished working document, February 27, 2003.

Canadian Centre for Justice Statistics. (2004). Canadian Crime Statistics 2003. Ottawa: Department of Justice.

Canadian Council on Social Development (1996). *Putting Promises into Action, Campaign 2000*, May 2002, for the UN Special Session on Children. Statistics Canada Census 1996, custom tabulation.

Canadian Council on Social Development (1999). *Youth at Work in Canada: A Research Report*. Ottawa: Canadian Council on Social Development.

Canadian Council on Social Development. (2000). *Urban Poverty in Canada: A Statistical Profile*.

Canadian Council on Social Development (2003). *Aboriginal Children in Poverty in Urban Communities*. www.ccsdca/pr/2003/aboriginal.htm.

Canadian Federation of University Women. (1999). *Report on the Girl Child*.

Canadian Research Institution for Law and the Family (1990). *Alternative Programs for Native Youth*, Alberta.

Canadian Task Force on Federally Sentenced Women (1991). Shaw, M. K., K. Rodgers, J. Blanchette, T. Hattem, L. Seto Thomas and L. Tamarack (1990). *Survey of Federally Sentenced Women: Report to the Task Force on Federally Sentenced Women on the Prison Survey*. Ottawa: Ministry of the Solicitor General User Report No. 1991-4.

Cantor, J.A. (2000). *Higher Education Outside of the Academy*. ERIC. ERIC Clearinghouse on. Higher Education, Washington D.C.: Office of Educational Research

Caputo, D.O. (1991). *Crime and Punishment in Canada: A History*. Toronto: McClelland and Stewart.

Caputo, T. and Kelly, K. (1997). *Police Perceptions of Current Responses to Youth Crime*. Catalogue No. JS4-1/1997–3. Ottawa: Ministry of the Solicitor General of Canada.

Caputo, T. and Linden, R. (2005). "Early theories of criminology." In R. Linden (Ed.) *Criminology: A Canadian Perspective*. 5th ed. Toronto: Harcourt Canada.

Caputo, T., Weiler, R., and Anderson, J. (1997). *The Street Lifestyle Study*. Health Canada. Public Works and Government Services Canada. Cat. No. H39-382/1997E

Caputo, T., Weiler, R., and Kelly, K. (1994). *Phase II of the Runaways and Street Youth Project: The Saskatoon Case Study*. Ottawa: Minister of Supply and Services.

Careless, J.M.S. (1984). *Toronto to 1918: An Illustrated History*. Toronto.

Carlen, P. (1988). *Women, Crime and Poverty*. Milton Keynes: Open University Press.

Carlen, P. (1990). *Alternatives to Women's Imprisonment*. Milton Keynes: Open University Press.

Carlen, P. and Worrall, A. (Eds.) (1987). *Gender, Crime and Justice*. Milton Keynes: Open University Press.

Carrigan, D. (1991). *Crime and Punishment in Canada: A History*. Toronto: McClelland and Stewart.

Carrigan, D. (1998). *Juvenile Delinquency in Canada: A History*. Toronto: Irwin Publishing.

Carrington, K. (1997). "Postmodernism and feminist criminologies: Fragmenting the criminological subject." In P. Walton and J. Young (Eds.). *The New Criminology Revisited*. Macmillan.

Carrington, P. (2001). "Youth at risk: processes of individualization and responsibilization in the risk society." *Discourse: Studies in the Cultural Politics of Exclusion*, 22(1), 23–34.

Carrington, P.J. (1995). "Has violent youth crime increased? Comment on Corrado and Markwart." *Canadian Journal of Criminology* 37(1): 61–93.

Carrington, P.J. (1998). "Changes in police charging of young offenders in Ontario and Saskatchewan after 1984." *Canadian Journal of Criminology*, 40, 153–164.

Carrington, P.J. (1998). *Factors Affecting Police Diversion of Young Offenders: A Statistical Analysis*. Ottawa: Solicitor General of Canada at www.psepc-sppcc.gc.ca/Publications/Policing/199802_e.pdf

Carrington, P.J. (1999). "Trends in youth crime in Canada, 1977–1996." *Canadian Journal of Criminology*, 41(1), 1–32.

Carrington, P.J. and Moyer, S. (1994). "Trends in youth crime and police response, pre- and post- YOA." *Canadian Journal of Criminology*, 36(1), 1–28.

Carrington, P. J. and Schulenberg, J.L. (2003). *Police Discretion with Young Offenders*. Ottawa: Department of Justice Canada.

Carrington, P.J., and Schulenberg, J. (2004a). *Police Discretion with Young Offenders*. Ottawa: Department of Justice Canada. At: http://canada.justice.gc.ca/en/ps/yj/research/carrington-schulenberg/report.html. Accessed on March 23, 2005.

Carrington, P.J. and Schulenberg, J.L. (2004b). "Introduction: The Youth Criminal Justice Act–A New Era in Canadian Juvenile Justice?" *Canadian Journal of Criminology and Criminal Justice*, 46(3), 219–223.

Carrington, P.J. and Schulenberg, J.L. (2004c). *Prior Police Contacts and Police Discretion with Apprehended Youth*. Ottawa: Canadian Centre for Justice Statistics, Statistics Canada. Crime and Justice Research Paper Series. Cat. No. 85-561-MIE-003.

Carrington, P.J. and Schulenberg, J.L. (2005a). *The Impact of the Youth Criminal Justice Act on Police Charging Practices with Young Persons: A Preliminary Statistical Assessment*. Ottawa: Department of Justice.

Carrington, P.J. and Schulenberg, J.L. (2005b). "Police decision-making with young offenders: Arrest, questioning and dispositions." In K. Campbell (Ed.) *Understanding Youth Justice in Canada*. Toronto: Pearson Education.

Carter, T. (1999). "'Equality with a vengeance': Violent crimes and gang activity by girls skyrocket." *ABA Journal*. (November).

Caspi, A. et al. (2002). "Role of genotype in the cycle of violence in maltreated children." *Science*, 297(August): 853.

Cast, A., Schweingruber, D., and Berns, N. (2006). "Childhood physical punishment and problem solving in marriage." *Journal of Interpersonal Violence*, 21(2): 244–61.

Catherine Ford, *Calgary Herald*, 12 March 1992.

Canadian Broadcasting Corporation. (1997). *Nasty Girls*.March 5. Producer Maureen Palmer. Reporter Margo Harper.

Canadian Broadcasting Corporation. (2006). *You Can't Jail Anyone Act*.18 January 2006 www.cbc.ca/newsatsixns/archives/2006_jan_w3.html. Accessed on June 27, 2007.

CBC News. (2004). The Fifth Estate. *No Way Home*. Available from: http://www.cbc.ca/fifth/main_nowayhome_who.html.

CBC News. (2004). *Starlight Tours*. In-depth Aboriginal Canadians. July 2.

CBC News. (2005). *Police Stop More Blacks, Ont. Study Finds*.Friday, May 27.

Centers for Disease Control (1991–2005). *National Youth Risk Behavior Survey*.

Cernkovich, S.A. and Gioradano, P.C. (1979). "A comparative analysis of male and female delinquency." *Sociological Quarterly*, 20:131–145.

Cernkovich, S. A. and Giordano, P. (1987). "Family relationships and delinquency." *Criminology*, 25, 295–321.

Chadwick, R.B. (1912). Juvenile deliquents act of Canada. *American Prison Association*. Indianapolis: W.M. Burford.

Chalifoux, T., and Johnson, J.G. (2003). Urban Aboriginal youth: An action plan for change. (October). The Standing Senate Committee on Aboriginal Peoples.

Challen, R.D. (1996). "The reform of Canada's juvenile justice system, 1969–1982." Unpublished Ph.D. thesis, University of Toronto.

Charette, C. (1991). *Research Initiatives on homelessness: International Year of Shelter for the Homeless*. Occasional Paper No. 27. Institute of Urban Studies. University of Winnipeg.

Chartrand, L. (2005). "Aboriginal youth and the criminal justice system" In K. Campbell (Ed.) *Understanding youth justice in Canada, 2005*. Toronto: Pearson Education Canada.

Chartrand, L. (2006). "Youth custody and community services in Canada, 2003/2004." *Juristat* 26(2), Catalogue no. 85-002. Ottawa: Statistics Canada, Canadian Centre for Justice Statistics.

Chartrand, L. and McKay, C. (2006). *A Review of Research on Criminal Victimization and First Nations, Métis and Inuit Peoples 1990 to 2001*. Canada: Department of Justice.

Chartrand, L.N. and Forbes-Chilibeck, E. (2002). *The Sentencing of Offenders with Fetal Alcohol Syndrome: A Report for the Annual Joint Policy Forum*. Ottawa, ON: National Associations Active in Criminal Justice, Department of Justice Canada & Solicitor General Canada.

Chartrand, L.N. and E.M. Forbes-Chilibeck. (2003). "The sentencing of offenders with fetal alcohol syndrome" (2003) 11 *Health L. J*. 35–70: 37–38.

Cheechoo, C., Spence, S., and members of the Nishnawbe Aski Nation Decade Youth Council (2006). *The Seventh Generation Helping to Heal: Nishnawbe Aski Youth and the Suicide Epidemic*.

Chesney-Lind, M. (1988). "Girls in jail." *Crime and Delinquency*, 34, 151–168.

Chesney-Lind, M. (1997). *The Female Offender: Girls, Women, and Crime*. Thousand Oaks: Sage Publications Inc.

Chesney-Lind, M. (1998). *Girls, Delinquency, and Juvenile Justice*. Belmont, CA: Wadsworth.

Chesney-Lind, M. (1999). "When she was bad: Violent women and the myth of innocence." Book review. *Women and Criminal Justice*, 10(4), 113–118.

Chesney-Lind, M. (2001). "What about the girls? Delinquency programming as if gender mattered." *Corrections Today*, 38–45. February.

Chesney-Lind, M. (2004). "Beyond bad girls: Feminist perspectives on female offending." In C. Sumner (Ed.), *Blackwell Companion to Criminology*. Oxford: Blackwell Publishing, pp. 255–267.

Chesney-Lind, M. and Belknap, J. (2004). "Trends in delinquent girls' aggression and violent behavior: A review of the evidence." In M. Putallaz and P. Bierman (Eds.), *Aggression, Antisocial Behavior and Violence Among Girls: A Development Perspective*, New York: Guilford Press, pp. 203–220.

Chesney-Lind, M. and Irwin, K. (2004). "From badness to meanness: Popular constructions of contemporary girlhood." In A. Harris (Ed.), *All About the Girl Culture, Power, and Identity*. New York: Routledge, pp. 45–56.

Chesney-Lind, M. and Okamoto, S. (2001). "Gender matters: Patterns in girls' delinquency and gender responsive programming." *Journal of Forensic Psychology Practice*, 11(3), 1–28.

Chesney-Lind, M. and Paramore, V. (2001). "Are girls getting more violent? Exploring juvenile robbery trends." *Journal of Contemporary Criminal Justice*, 17(2), May, pp. 142–166.

Chesney-Lind, M. and Shelden, R. (1998). *Girls, Delinquency and Juvenile Justice*. Belmont, CA: West/Wadsworth.

Chesney-Lind, M. and Shelden, R. (2004). *Girls, Delinquency and Juvenile Justice*. 4th ed. Belmont, CA: Wadsworth.

Chisholm, P. (1997). "Bad girls: A brutal B.C. murder sounds an alarm about teenage violence." *Macleans*, 8 December, p.12.

Christie, N. (1977). "Conflicts as Property." *British Journal of Criminology*. 17. 1–26.

Chunn, D.E. (1992). *From Punishment to Doing Good: Family Courts and Socialized Justice in Ontario, 1880–1940*. Toronto: University of Toronto Press.

Chunn D.E. and Gavigan, S.A.M. (1988). "Social control: analytical tool or analytical quagmire?" *Crime, Law and Social Change*, 12(2), 107–124.

Chunn, D.E. and Menzies, R. (1990). "Gender, madness and crime: The reproduction of patriarchal and class relations in a psychiatric court clinic." *Critical Criminology*, 1(2) (March), 33–54.

Clark, B. and O'Reilly-Fleming, T. (1994) "Out of the carceral straightjacket: Under twelves and the law." *Canadian Journal of Criminology*, 36(3), 305–327.

Clarke, M. and Cooper, M. (2000). *Homeless youth: Falling between the cracks: An investigation of youth homelessness in Calgary*. Youth Alternative Housing Committee.

Cloward, R. and Ohlin, L. (1960). *Delinquency and Opportunity*. Glencoe, IL: Free Press.

Cohen, S. (1972) *Folk Devils and Moral Panics*, London: MacGibb and Kee.

Cohen, S. (1985). *Visions of Social Control: Crime, Punishment and Classification*. Cambridge: Polity Press.

Cohen, S. (2002). *Folk Devils and Moral Panics: The Creation of the Mods and Rockers*. 3rd edition. London: Routledge.

Cole, David. (1999). *No Equal Justice: Race and Class in the American Criminal Justice System*. New York: New Press.

Collier, R. (1993). *Masculinity, Law and Family*. London: Routledge.

Collier, Richard. (1997). *Masculinities, Crime, and Criminology: Men, Corporeality, and the Criminal(ized) Body*. Thousand Oaks, CA: Sage.

Collier, Richard. (2003). "Reflections on the Relationship Between Law and Masculinities: Rethinking the 'man question' in Legal Studies." *Current Legal Problems*, 56.

Comack, E. (1996). *Women in Trouble: Connecting Women's Law Violations to their History of Abuse.* Halifax, NS: Fernwood Publishing.

Comack, E. (1999). *Locating Law: Race/Class/Gender Connections.* Halifax: Fernwood Publishing.

Comack, E. (1999). "New Possibilities for a Feminism in Criminology? From Dualism to Diversity." *Canadian Journal of Criminology and Criminal Justice,* 41(2), 161–171.

Comack, E. and Balfour, G. (2004). *The Power to Criminalize: Violence, Inequality and Law.* Halifax: Fernwood Publishing.

Commission on Systemic Racism in the Ontario Criminal Justice System. (1994). *Racism behind bars: The treatment of black and other racial minorities in Ontario prisons (Interim report on the Commission on Systemic Racism in the Ontario Criminal Justice System).* Toronto: Queen's Printer for Ontario.

Commission on System Racism in the Ontario Criminal Justice System. (1995). *Report of the Commission on Systemic Racism in the Ontario Criminal Justice System.* Toronto: Queen's Printer for Ontario.

Commissioners Appointed to Enquire into the Prison and Reformatory System of Ontario. Toronto, 1891.

Community Social Planning Council of Toronto (1998). *Surviving the Street: Street Youth and Squeegeeing in Toronto.* Toronto: The Council.

Congar, J. (1975). *Adolescence and Youth.* New York: Harper and Row.

Congress of Aboriginal Peoples. (1998). *Canada's Youth Justice Renewal Initiative.* Accessed on July 9, 2007. www.abo-peoples.org/YouthPages/PLEI/PLEIthree.htm.

Congress of Aboriginal Peoples. (2004). Background Paper on Off-Reserve Aboriginal Housing Issues. In Government of Canada. *Canada Aboriginal Peoples Roundtable: Sectoral Follow-Up Sessions. Housing.* Ottawa, Canada.

Connell, R.W. (1987). *Gender and Power.* Sydney: Allen and Unwin.

Connell, R.W. (1990). "An iron man: The body and some contradictions of hegemonic masculinity." In M. Messner and D. Sabo, (Eds.) *Sport, Men and the Gender Order,* Champaign, IL: Human Kinetics Books.

Connell, R.W. (1995). *Masculinities.* Cambridge, UK: Polity Press.

Connell, R.W. (1998). "Masculinities and globalization." *Men and Masculinities* 1(1):3–23.

Connell, R.W. (2002). *Gender.* Cambridge, UK: Polity Press.

Connell, R.W. and Messerschmidt, J.W. (2005). "Rethinking the Concept." *Gender and Society,* 19(6): 829–859

"Continuing Crime Wave Convinces Langdon to Bring in Teen Curfew." *The Edmonton Journal,* September 3, 2002.

Corrado, R.R. and Cohen, I.M. (2002). "A Needs profile of serious and/or violent Aboriginal youth in prison." *Forum on Corrections Research.*

Corrado, R. and Markwart, A. (1992). "The evolution and implementation of a new era of juvenile justice in Canada." In R. Corrado et al. (Eds.). *Juvenile justice in Canada: A new theoretical and analytical assessment.* Toronto: Butterworths.

Corrado, R. and Markwart, A. (1994). "The Need to Reform the YOA in Response to Violent Young Offenders: Confusion, Reality or Myth?" *Canadian Journal of Criminology,* 36, 343–378.

Corrado, R.R., Odgers, C., and Cohen, I.M. (2000). "The Incarceration of Female Young Offenders: Protection for Whom?" *Canadian Journal of Criminology,* 42 (2) 189–207.

Corvo, K. (2006). "Violence, Separation and Loss in the Families of Origin of Domestically Violent Men." *Journal of Family Violence* 21: 117–25.

Cotta, S. (1985). *Why Violence? A Philosophical Interpretation.* Gainsville: University of Florida Press.

Cotta, S. (1991). "The Nihlistic significance of violence." In James Brady and Newton Garver (Eds.), *Justice, Law and Violence.* Philadelphia: Temple University Press.

Coughlan, D. (1963). "The History and Function of Probation." *Canadian Bar Journal.* 6: 103–27.

Courtney, M. and Piliavin, I. (1998). *Foster youth transition to adulthood: Outcomes 12 to 18 months after leaving out-of-home care.* School of Social Work and Institute for Research on Poverty. University of Wisconsin-Madison.

Couture, J. (1999). *Psychological Evaluation/Critique of the In Search of Your Warrior Program.* Native Counselling Services of Alberta, Unpublished Document.

Covington, S. (2001). "Creating Gender Specific Programs." *Corrections Today,* p. 85–89.

Covington, S. and Bloom, B. (2006). "Gender Responsive Treatment and Services in Correctional Settings." In E. Leeder (Ed.), *Women and Therapy.* Hawthorn Press.

Cowie, J., Cowie, V., and Slater, E. (1968). *Delinquency in Girls.* London, UK: Heinemann.

Crawford, A. (2001). "Joined up but fragmented: contradiction, ambiguity and ambivalence at the heart of New Labour's 'Third Way.'" In R. Mathews and J. Pitts (Eds.), *Crime, Disorder and Community Safety: A New Agenda?* London: Routledge, pp. 54-80.

Crawford, J. (1988). *Tabulation of a Nationwide Survey of Female Inmates.* Phoenix, AZ: Research Advisory Services.

Crowe, C. and Hardill, K. (1993). "Nursing research and political change: the street health report." *Canadian Nurse.* 89: 21–24.

Cullen, F. and Gendreau, P. (1989). "The effectiveness of correctional rehabilitation: Reconsidering the 'nothing works' debate." In L. Goodstein and D. MacKenzie (Eds.), *The American Prison.* New York: Plenum.

Currie, D.H. and Kelly, D.M. (2006). "'I'm going to crush you like a bug': understanding girls' agency and empowerment." In

Jiwani, Y., Steenbergen, C., and Mitchell, C. (Eds.), *Girlhood: Redefining the Limit*. Montreal: Black Rose Press, pp.155–172.

Currie, D. H., Kelly, D. M., and Pomerantz, S. (2007) "The Power to Squash People: Understanding Girls' Relational Aggression." British Journal of Sociology of Education, 28(1):23–37.

Curtis, B. (1988). *Building the Educational State: Canada West, 1836–1871* (London, ON: The Althouse Press).

Dalton, K. (1961). "Menstruation and crime." *British Medical Journal*, 2: 1752–53.

Daly, G. (1996). *Homeless: Policies, Strategies and Lives on the Street*. London: Routledge.

Daly, K. (2001). "Conferencing in Australia and New Zealand: variations, research findings, and prospects." In A. Morris and G. Maxwell (Eds.), *Restorative Justice for Juveniles: Conferencing, Mediation and Circles*. Oxford: Hart Publishing.

Daly, K. (2002). "Restorative justice: the real story." *Punishment & Society*, 4(1), 55–79.

Daly, M. (1999). "Regimes of social policy in Europe and the patterning of homelessness." In D. Avramov (Ed.), *Coping with homelessness: Issues to be Tackled and Best Practices in Europe*. Aldershot, England: Ashgate Publishing.

Danny Glover. (www.contrib.andrew.cmu.edu/aaron2/upn/upn-specials.html).

Davis, D. and DiNitto, D.M. (1998). "Gender and drugs: Fact, fiction, and unanswered questions." In C.A. McNeece and D.M. DiNitto (eds.), *Chemical dependency: A Systems Approach*. (pp.406–439). Needham Heights, MA: Allyn & Bacon.

Davis, S. (1994). *Prostitution in Canada: The Invisible Menace or the Menace of Invisibility?* www.walnet.org/csis/papers/sdavis.html.

Dean, A. (2005). *Locking Them Up to Keep Them 'Safe': Criminalized girls in British Columbia*. Vancouver, B: Justice for Girls.

Dean, M. (1999). *Governmentality: Power and Rule in Modern Society*. London: Routledge.

Debord, G. (1970). *Society of the Spectacle*. Detroit: Black and Red.

DeKeseredy, W. (2000). *Women, Crime and the Canadian Criminal Justice System*. Cincinnati, OH: Anderson.

Delgado, R. (2003). "Crossroads and Blind Alleys: A Critical Examination of Recent Writing About Race." *Texas Law Review*, 82 (1): 121–152.

Dell, C.A. (2001) "Female young offenders in Canada: Revised edition." In *Forum on Corrections Research*, 13(2). Ottawa: Correctional Service of Canada.

Dell, C. and Boe, R. (1998). *Female Young Offenders in Canada: Revised Edition*. [electronic version] Ottawa: Correctional Service of Canada. Retrieved February 3, 2003 from www.csc-scc.gc.ca/text/rsrch/reports/r8/r80e_e.shtml.

Dematteo, D., et al. (1999). "Toronto street youth and HIV/AIDS: prevalence, demographics and risks," *Journal of Adolescent Health*, 25(5), 358–366.

Denov, M.S. (2005). "Children's Rights, Juvenile Justice, and the UN Convention on the Rights of the Child: Implications for Canada." In K. Campbell (Ed.), *Understanding Youth Justice: History, Legislation and Reform*. Toronto: Harcourt Canada.

Denzin, N. (1984). "Toward a Phenomenology of Domestic, Family Violence." *American Journal of Sociology*. 90(3):483–513.

Department of Agriculture, *Census of Canada, 1871–1921*. Toronto: Wall and Thompson.

Department of Indian Affairs and Northern Development (2002). *Our Children, Keepers of the Sacred Knowledge*. Final Report of the Minister's National Working Group on Education.

Department of Justice Canada. (1967) *Juvenile Delinquency in Canada: The Report of the Department of Justice Committee on Juvenile Delinquency*. Canada: Queen's Printer.

Department of Justice Canada. (1991) *Aboriginal People and Justice Administration: A Discussion Paper*. Ottawa: Department of Justice.

Department of Justice Canada. (1998) *A Strategy for Youth Justice Renewal*. Ottawa: Ministry of Supply and Services. (available online at http://canada.justice.gc.ca).

Department of Justice Canada. (2001) *The Youth Criminal Justice Act: Summary and Background*. Ottawa: Youth Justice.

Department of Justice Canada. (2003a). *YCJA Explained*. Accessed on June 21 2007 at http://canada.justice.gc.ca/en/ps/yj/repository/index.html.

Department of Justice Canada. (2003b) *Youth Criminal Justice Act: Resource Manual for Police*. Ottawa: Department of Justice Canada.

Department of Justice Canada. (2004) *Youth Justice, Roundtable Discussions*, [Online] Available at: www.canadajustice.ca/en/ps/yj/partnership/partnership.html (accessed 10 July 2004).

Department of Justice Canada (2005). *Annual Statement, Executive Summary*.

Derrida, J. (1985). "Racisms' Last Word." In H.L. Gates Jr. (Ed.), Writing and Difference. Chicago: University of Chicago Press.

Derrida, J. (1997). *Politics of Friendship*. London: Verso. 271–307.

Derrida, J. (1998). "Hospitality, justice and responsibility." In M. Dooley and R. Kearney (Eds.), *Questioning Ethics: Contemporary Debates in Continental Philosophy*, pp. 65–83. London: Routledge.

Derrida, J. (1999) "Justice, law and philosophy." *South African Journal of Philosophy* 18(3): 279–86.

Derrida, J. (2002). *On Cosmopolitanism and Forgiveness*, trans. M. Dooley and M. Hughes. New York: Routledge.

Derrida, J. (2002) "Force of law." In G. Anidjar (Ed.), *Acts of Religion*, pp. 228–298. New York: Routledge.

Desai, J. (2005). "In the minds of men." *Science and Spirit*, 16(2), 36–39.

Dhillon, J. (2005). *Struggles for Access: Examining the Educational Experiences of Homeless Young Women and Girls in Canada. A Research Report by Jaskiran Dhillon in Partnership with Justice for Girls.* Vancouver: Justice for Girls.

Dion, T. (1999). *Aboriginal Children and Offending Behaviour: A Literature Review.* Ottawa: Department of Justice.

Dohrn, B. (2004). "All Ellas: Girls Locked Up." *Feminist Studies,* 30: 302–324.

Donzelot, J. (1979). *The Policing of Families.* New York: Pantheon Books.

Doob, A.N. (1995). "Criminal Justice Reform in a Hostile Climate." In J.M. Brisson and D. Greschner (Eds.), *Public Perceptions of the Administration of Justice* (pp. 277–298). Montreal: Les Editions Themis.

Doob, A.N. (1989). "Disposition under the Young Offenders Act: Issues Without Answers." In L. Beaulieu (Ed.), *Young Offender Dispositions: Perspectives on Principle and Practice.*

Doob, A.N. (2002). *An Overview of Sentencing in Seven Steps.* National Judicial Institute, Conference on the Youth Criminal Justice Act, Toronto, September 2002. Available at www.nji.ca/postings/YJC/youthjustice.html.

Doob, A.N. (2003). *Thinking About Police Resources.* Toronto: Centre of Criminology.

Doob, A.N. and Beaulieu, L.A. (1992). "Variation in the exercise of judicial discretion with young offenders." *Canadian Journal of Criminology, 34(1),*35–50.

Doob, A.N. and Cesaroni, C. (2004). *Responding to Youth Crime in Canada.* Toronto: University of Toronto Press.

Doob, A.N., Marinos, V., and Varma, K. (1995). "The Impact of Criminal Justice Processing." *Youth Crime and the Youth Justice System in Canada.* Toronto: Centre of Criminology Press.

Doob, A.N. and Sprott, J.B. (1996). "Interprovincial variation in the use of youth courts." *Canadian Journal of Criminology,* 38(4), 401–412.

Doob, A.N. and Sprott, J.B. (1998). "Is the "quality" of youth violence becoming more serious?" *Canadian Journal of Criminology,* 38(2), 185–194.

Doob, A.N. and Sprott, J.B., Marinos, V, and Varma, K. (1998). *An Exploration of Ontario Residents' Views of Crime and the Criminal Justice System.* Toronto: Centre of Criminology, University of Toronto.

Durkheim, Emile. (1893). *The Division of Labor in Society.* The Free Press (reprint), 1997.

Durkheim, Emile. (1987). *Suicide* (John A. Spaulding and George Simpson, Trans.) Reprinted 1933. London, UK: Free Press of Glencoe.

Dusenbury, L., et al. (2004). "Nine critical elements of promising violence prevention programs [review]." *American Journal of Preventive Medicine,* 26 (1 Suppl): 3–11.

Dutta, N. (2005). "The Face of the Other: Terror and the Return of the Binarisms." *Interventions* 6(3), 431–450.

Dyer, R. (1997). *White.* New York: Routledge.

Eco, U. and Martini, C.M. (1997). *Enque creuen els qui no creuen.* Barcelona: Empuries.

Edmonton Community and Family Services. (1990). *Alternative Measures Program: Helping Youth Take Responsibility.* (pamphlet). *Edmonton Examiner,* May 23, 2007.

Edmonton John Howard Society. (1993). *The Young Offenders Act: Issues and implementation.*

Edmonton Joint Planning Committee on Housing. (2000). *Edmonton community plan on homelessness 2000–2003.* November.

Eggerton, J. (1994). "Hundt hits television violence." *Broadcasting and Cable,* 124(5), 10–12.

Ehrhart, J.K. and Sandler, B.R. (1987). *Looking for More Than a Few Good Women in Traditionally Male Fields.* Washington: Association of American Colleges, Project on the Status and Education of Women.

Einstein, A. and Freud, S. (1960). "Einstein–Freud Correspondence (1931–1932)." In O. Nathan and H. Norden (Eds.), *Einstein on Peace.* New York: Schocken Books, 186–203.

Ellerby, L.A. and MacPherson, P. (2002). *Exploring the Profiles of Aboriginal Sex Offenders: Contrasting Aboriginal and Non-Aboriginal Sexual Offenders to Determine Unique Client Characteristics and Potential Implications for Sex Offender Assessment and Treatment Strategies Research Report R-122.* Ottawa: Research Branch, Correctional Service Canada.

Elliott, D. (1997). *Social and health-care pilot project for sex trade workers: Interim report.* Retrieved June 17, 2002, from www.city.kamloops.bc.ca/planning/pdf/shop.pdf.

Elliott, D.S. and Tolan, P.H. (1998). "Youth violence, prevention, intervention and social policy: An overview." In D. Flannery and R. Hoff (Eds.), *Youth Violence: A Volume in the Psychiatric Clinics of North America.* Washington, DC: American Psychiatric Association.

Elliot, L. (2005). "Restorative Justice in Canadian Approaches to Youth Crime: Origins, Practices, and Retributive Frameworks." In K. Campbell (Ed.), *Understanding Youth Justice in Canada.* Toronto: Pearson Canada.

Emblach, H. (1993). *A One-Way Street? A Report on Phase 1 of the Street Children Project.* Geneva: World Health Organization Programme on Substance Abuse.

Empey, L. (1982). *Juvenile Delinquency: Its Meaning and Construction.* Chicago: Dorsey Press.

Engler, C. and Crowe, S. (2000). Canadian Centre for Justice Statistics. Alternative Measures in Canada, 1998–99. *Juristat*, Vol. 20, no. 6.

Epp, J.R. (1997). "Authority, pedagogy, and violence." In J.R. Epp and A.M. Watkinson (Eds.), *Systemic Violence in Education: Promise Broken* (pp. 25–36). Albany, NY: State University of New York Press.

Ericson, R. and Haggerty, K. (1997). *Policing the Risk Society*. Toronto: University of Toronto Press and Oxford: Oxford University Press.

Ewald, F. (1991). "Insurance and Risk." In G. Burchell, C. Gordon and P. Miller, *The Foucault Effect: Studies in Governmentality*. London: Harvester Wheatsheaf.

Experiments in Rehabilitation, Deterrence and Delinquency Prevention [dissertation].

Fagan, J., Slaughter, E., and Hartstone, E. (1987). "Blind Justice? The Impact of Race on the Juvenile Justice Process." *Crime and Delinquency*, 33, 224–258.

Fallis, G. and Murray, A. (1990). *Housing the Homeless and the Poor*. Toronto: University of Toronto Press.

Fara-On, M. (2002). An investigation of the factors that contribute to the housing stability/instability of former clients of Massey Centre. Executive Summary. December.

Farrington, D. (1991). "Childhood Aggression and Adult Violence: Early Precusors and Later Life Outcomes." In Debra Pepler and Kenneth Rubin (eds.), *The Development and Treatment of Childhood Aggression*, Hillside, NJ: Erlbaum.

Farrington, D. (1998). "Predictors, Causes and Correlates of Male Youth Violence." *Crime and Justice* 24: 421–75.

Fattah E.A. (1991a). "From Crime to Victim Policy: The Need for a Fundamental Change." *International Annals of Criminology* 29.

Fattah, E. (1991b). *Understanding Criminal Victimization: An Introduction to Theoretical Victimology*. Scarborough, ON: Prentice-Hall Canada.

Fauteax Committee. (1956). *Report of a Committee Appointed to Inquire into the Principles and Procedures Followed in the Remission Service of the Department of Justice*.

Federal Bureau of Investigation. (2006). *Persons Arrested: Crime in the United States (2005)*. www.fbi.gov/ucr/05cius/arrests/index.html. (accessed September 2006).

Federal–Provincial–Territorial Task Force on Youth Justice. 1996. *A Review of the Young Offenders Act and the Youth Justice System in Canada*. Ottawa: Report of the Federal–Provincial–Territorial Task Force on Youth Justice for the Standing Committee on Justice and Legal Affairs of the House of Commons, Department of Justice Canada.

Federation of Saskatchewan Indian Nations. (2003). *Alter-Natives to Non-Violence Report. Aboriginal Youth Gangs Exploration: a Community Development Process*.

Feely, M. and Simon, J. (1992). The New Penology: Notes on the Emerging Strategy of Correction and Its Implication. *Criminology*, 30(4), 449–74.

Feeley, M. and Simon, J. (1994). "Actuarial Justice: The Emerging Criminal Law." In D. Nelken (Ed.), *The Futures of Criminology*. New York: Sage.

Feely, M. and Simon, J. (1997). "Actuarial Justice: The Emerging New Criminal Law." In D. Nelken (Ed.), *The Futures of Criminology*, 173–201. London: Sage.

Feld, B. (1999). *Bad Kids: Race and the Transformation of Juvenile Court*. New York.

Figueria-McDonough, J. (1993). "Residence, dropping out, and delinquency rates." *Youth and Society*, 25, 3–30.

Finckenauer, J.O. (1982). *Scared Straight and the Panacea Phenomenon*. Englewood Cliffs, NJ: Prentice-Hall.

Finckenauer, J.O., Gavin, P.W., Hovland, A., Storvoll, E. (1999). *Scared Straight: The Panacea Phenomenon Revisited*. Prospect Heights, Ill. USA: Waveland Press.

Finkelhor, D. and Baron, L. (1986). "High-risk children." In D. Finkelhor (ed.), *A Sourcebook on Child Sexual Abuse*. Beverly Hills, CA: Sage.

First Nations and Inuit Health Branch, Health Canada.

First Nations Child and Family Caring Society of Canada. (2003).

Fisher, J. (1989). Missing children research project, Volume 1: Findings of the study– a focus on runaways. (No. 1989-07). Ottawa: Solicitor General of Canada.

Fisher, L. and Jantti, H. (2000). "Aboriginal youth and the youth justice system." In J. Winterdyk (Ed.), *Issues and Perspectives on Young Offenders in Canada*. 2nd ed. Toronto: Harcourt.

Fitzgerald, M.D. (1995). "Homeless youths and the child welfare system: implications for policy and service." *Child Welfare* 74(3):717–730.

Fitzpatrick, S. (2000). *Young Homeless People*. London: Macmillan Press.

Fontaine, N. (2006). "Surviving Colonization: Anishinaabe Ikew Gang Participation." In G. Balfour and E. Comack, *Criminalizing Women*. Fernwood: Halifax.

Forsyth, S. (2001). *Mother's Health and Access to Recreation Activities for Children*.

Foshee, V. et al. (2005). 'The Association Between Family Violence and Adolescent Dating Violence Onset: Does It Vary by Race, Socioeconomic Status and Family Structure?' *Journal of Early Adolescence*, 25(3): 317–41.

Foucault, M. (1977). *Discipline and Punish: The Birth of the Prison*. New York: Vintage.

Foucault, M. (1980). *Power/Knowledge: Selected Interviews and Other Writing, 1972–1977*. New York: Pantheon Books.

Foucault, M. (1982). "The subject and power." In H.L. Dreyfus and P. Robinow, *Michel Foucault: beyond structuralism and hermeneutics*, Chicago: Chicago University Press.

Foucault, M. (1983). "Structuralism and poststructuralism: an interview with Michel Foucault." *Telos*, 55, pp.195–211.

Foucault, M. (1991). "Governmentality." In G. Burchell, C. Gordon, and P. Miller, (Eds.), *The Foucault Effect: Studies in Governmentality*, 87–104. Chicago: University of Chicago Press.

Frank, B. (1987). "Hegemonic heterosexual masculinity." *Studies in Political Economy*, 24, Autumn, 159-170.

Fraser Committee. (1985). Special Committee on Pornography and Prostitution (Ottawa: Department of Supply and Services, 1985).

Fraser, K. (2000). *Stop 86 - 1999 Annual Report*.

Fraser, N. and Gordon, L. (2002). "A Genealogy of Dependency. Tracing a Keyword of the U.S. Welfare State." In E.F. Kittay, and E.K. Feder, (Eds.), *The Subject of Care: Feminist Perspectives on Dependency*. Lanham, MD: Rowman & Littlefield.

(The) FREDA Centre for Research on Violence against Women and Children. www.harbour.sfu.ca/freda/.

Freud, Sigmund. (1920). *Beyond the Pleasure Principle*. Vienna: Psycho-Analytical Press.

Freud, Sigmund. (1930). "Civilization and its Discontents." *Standard Edition*, 21, 59–145.

Freud, Sigmund. (1932). *Civilization and its Discontents*. New York: W.W. Norton.

Freud, Sigmund. (1960). *Letters of Sigmund Freud* (E.L. Freud, Ed.; T. Stern and J. Stern, Trans.). New York: Basic Books.

Frith, S. (1985). "Sociology of Youth." In Michael Haralabos (Ed.), *Sociology: New Directions*. Ormskiek: Causeway Press.

Gaarder, E. and Belknap, J. (2002). "Tenuous borders: Girls transferred to adult court." *Criminology*, 40 (3), 481–517.

Gabor, T. (1995). *School Violence and the Zero Tolerance Alternative: Some Principles and Police Prescriptions*. Solicitor General Canada. Cat. No. JS 42–67.

Gabor, T. (1999). "Trends in Youth Crime: Some evidence pointing to increases in the severity and volume on the part of young people." *Canadian Journal of Criminology*, 41(3), 385–392.

Gaetz, S. (2004). "Safe Streets for Whom? Homeless Youth, Social Exclusion, and Criminal Victimization." *Canadian Journal of Criminology and Criminal Justice*, 423–455.

Gaetz, S., O'Grady, B., and Waillancourt, B. (1999). *Making Money: The Shout Clinic Report on Homeless Youth and Unemployment*. Toronto: Central Toronto Community Health Centres.

Galius, J. (2001). "Who Killed Garrett Campiou?" *Alberta Views*, May/June: 27–31

Garland, D. (1981). "The Birth of the Welfare Sanction." *British Journal of Law and Society*, 8, 29–42.

Garland, D. (1985). *Punishment and Welfare: A History of Penal Strategies*. Aldershot, UK: Ashgate.

Garland, D. (1990). *Punishment and Modern Society: A Study in Social Theory*. University of Chicago Press and Oxford University Press.

Garland, D. (1996) "The limits of the sovereign state: strategies of crime control in contemporary society." *British Journal of Criminology*, 36(4): 445–71.

Garland, D. (1997). "'Governmentality' and the Problem of Crime: Foucault, Criminology, Sociology." *Theoretical Criminology*, 40: 189–204.

Garland, D. (2001). *The Culture of Control: Crime and Social Order in Contemporary Society*. Chicago: University of Chicago Press.

Garland, D. and Sparks, R. (2000). "Criminology, Social Theory and the Change of Our Times." *British Journal of Criminology* 40(2), 189–204.

Garland, D. and Sparks, R. (2001). "Criminology, Sociology and the Challenge of our Times." In *Criminology and Social Theory*. London: Oxford.

Geller, G. (1987). "Young women in conflict with the law." In E. Adelberg and C. Currie (Eds.), *Too Few to Count: Canadian Women in Conflict with the Law*. Vancouver: Press Gang, 113–126.

Gelles, R. (1972). *The Violent Home: A Study of Physical Aggression Between Husbands and Wives*. Thousand Oaks, CA: Sage.

Gelsthorpe, L. and Morris, A. (Eds.) (1990). *Feminist Perspectives in Criminology*. Milton Keynes: Open University Press.

Gerbner, G., Gross, L., Morgan, M., and Signorielli, N. (1980). "The 'mainstreaming' of America: Violence profile no. 11." *Journal of Communication*, 30(3), 10–29.

Giddens, A. (1991). *Modernity and Self Identity*. Cambridge: Polity Press.

Gilchrist, L. (1995). *Urban Survivors, Aboriginal Street Youth: Vancouver, Winnipeg and Montreal*. Research Report presented to the Royal Commission on Aboriginal Peoples (January).

Gilfus, M. (2002). *Women's Experiences of Abuse as a Risk Factor for Incarceration*. VAW Net, National Resource Center on Domestic Violence.

Gilligan, C. (1982). *In a Different Voice: Psychological Theory and Women's Development*. Cambridge, MA: Harvard University Press.

Gilligan, C. and Attanucci, J. (1988). "Two moral orientations: Gender differences and similarities." *Merrill-Palmer Quarterly*, 33(3), 223–237.

Giordano, P.C. and Cernkovich, S.A. (1979). *Social Problems*, Vol. 26, No. 4, Theory and Evidence in Criminology: Correlations and Contradictions (Apr., 1979), pp. 467–481.

Girard, R. (1977). *Violence and the Sacred*. Baltimore: Johns Hopkins Press.

"Girl gang members on the rise; Six per cent are female, say police. Major change in the last five years." *The Toronto Star* May 17, 2006.

Gittens, M. and D. Cole (1995). *Report of the Commission on Systemic Racism in the Ontario Criminal Justice System*. Toronto: Queen's Printer for Ontario.

Goddard, H.H. (1912). *The Kallikak Family: A Study in the Heredity of Feeble-Mindedness*. New York: MacMillan.

Goffman, E. (1961). *Asylums: Essays on the Social Situation of Mental Patients and Other Inmates*.

Goffman, E. (1963). *Stigma: Notes on the Management of Spoiled Identity*. Toronto: Prentice Hall.

Gold, A. and Harvey, E. (2003). *Executive Summary of Presentation on Behalf of the Toronto Police Service*. Toronto: Toronto Police Service.

Goldberg, Carl. (2003). "The face of violence: hopeful signs among the frightening reflections." *Journal of Applied Psychoanalytic Studies* 5(1), 1–8.

Goldman, B. (1988). "Health of Toronto's street kids disturbing, study reveals." *Canadian Medical Association Journal*, 138, 1041–1043.

Gordis, E. (1990). *Alcohol Alert*, 10, 1–3.

Gordon, C. (1991). "Government Rationality: An Introduction." In G. Burchell, C. Gordon, and P. Miller (eds.), *The Foucault Effect: Studies in Governmentality*. Chicago: University of Chicago Press, pp. 1–51.

Gorham, B. (1993) February 7. Island of Despair. *Province* [Vancouver], A34.

Government of Canada. (2001). *Speech from the Throne to open the first session of the 37th Parliament of Canada*. Ottawa.

Government of Canada. (2005). *Canada's Action Plan Against Racism. A Canada for All*. Department of Canadian Heritage. Ottawa: Ministry of Public Works and Government Services Canada. Catalogue CJ34–7.

Graeber, W. (1994). *Growing up in America: Historical Experiences*. Detroit: Wayne State University Press.

Graham, K. and E.J. Peters. (2002). *Aboriginal Communities and Urban Sustainability*. Canadian Policy Research Networks, Family Network. Discussion Paper F/27.

Graydon, S. (1999) "Bad Girls." *Homemakers Magazine*, March 1999. Retrieved January 2003 from www.media-awareness.ca/english/resources/articles/stereotyping/bad_girls.cfm.

Green, R. and K. Healy. (2003). *Tough on Kids: Rethinking Approaches to Youth Justice*. Saskatoon, SK: Purich.

Greene, J, M. and Ringwalt, C.L. (1998). "Pregnancy among three national samples of runaway and homeless youth." *American Journal of Public Health* 89(9), 1406–1409.

Griffin, C. (1993). "Bad boys and invisible girls: Youth, crime and 'delinquency.'" In *Representations of Youth: The Study of Youth and Adolescence in Britain and America*. Cambridge: Polity Press.

Griffin, C. (2004) "Good girls, bad girls: Anglocentrism and diversity in the constitution of contemporary girlhood." In A. Harris (Ed.), *All About the Girl: Culture, Power and Identity*. New York: Routledge, pp. 43–57.

Griffiths, C. and Verdun-Jones, S.N. (1994). *Canadian Criminal Justice*, 2nd edition. Toronto: Harcourt Brace.

Grinberg, I., Dawkins, M., and Fullilove, C. (2005). "Adolescents at Risk for Violence: An Individual Validation of the Life Challenges Questionnaire and Risk Assessment Index." *Adolescence*, 40: 573–99.

Grossman, D. (2000). *Aggression and Violence*. Oxford Press.

Habermas, J. (1987). *Theory of Communicative Action*. Vol. 2. Boston: Beacon Press

Hackler, J. (2005). "How should we respond to youth crime?" *Canadian Journal of Law and Society*, 20(1), 193–208.

Hagan, J. (1990). *Structural Criminology*. New Brunswick: Rutgers University Press.

Hagan, J. and Leon, J. (1980). "The Rehabilitation of Law: A Socio-Historical Comparison of Probation in Canada and the United States." *Canadian Journal of Sociology*, 5: 235–51.

Hagan, J. and McCarthy, B. (1997). *Mean Streets: Youth Crime and Homelessness*. Cambridge: Cambridge University Press.

Hagan, J. and McCarthy, B. (1998). *Mean Streets: Youth Crime and Homelessness*. Cambridge: Cambridge University Press.

Hagan J., Simpson, J., and Gillis, A. (1987). "Class in the Household: A Power-Control Theory of Delinquency." *American Journal of Sociology*, 92, 788–816.

Haig-Brown, C. (1988). *Resistance and Renewal. Suriving the Indian Residential School*. Vancouver: Tillicum Library.

Haig-Brown, C. (1998). "Warrior Mothers." *Journal of Just and Caring Education* 4(1).

Halifax Regional Municipality. 00 (2005).

Hall, S. (2002) "Daubing the Drudges of fury: Men, violence and the piety of the 'hegemonic masculinity' thesis." *Theoretical Criminology*, 6.1 (2002): 35–61.

Hamilton, A.C. (2001). *A Feather Not a Gavel: Working Towards Aboriginal Justice*. Manitoba: Great Plains Publications.

Hamilton, A.C. and Sinclair, C.M. (1991). *The Justice System and Aboriginal People: Report of the Aboriginal Justice Enquiry of Manitoba*. Winnipeg: Queen's Printer.

Hamilton, A.C. and Sinclair, C.M. (1999). *Report of the Aboriginal Justice Inquiry of Manitoba. Volume 1: The System and Aboriginal People*. Winnipeg: Queen's Printer.

Hamilton, R. (2005). *Gendering the Vertical Mosaic: Feminist Perspectives on Canadian Society*. Toronto: Pearson Canada.

Hammerman, J.K. (1990) "Dead Men Don't Smirk." *Esquire* October 1990, p. 79.

Hancock, L. and Chesney-Lind, M. (1982). "Female status offenders and justice reforms: an international perspective." *Australian and New Zealand Journal of Criminology*, 15 (June), 109–122.

Hannah-Moffat, K. (1997). "From Christian Maternalism to Risk Technologies: Penal Powers and Women's Knowledge in the Governance of Female Prison." Unpublished PhD thesis. University of Toronto, Centre of Criminology.

Hannah-Moffat, K. (1999). "Moral Agent or Actuarial Subject: Risk and Canadian Women's Imprisonment." *Theoretical Criminology*, 3(1): 71–94.

Hannah-Moffat, K. (2000). "Prisons that empower: Neo-liberal governance in Canadian women's prisons." *British Journal of Criminology*, 40 (3), 510–531.

Hannah-Moffat, K. (2001). *Punishment in Disguise: Penal Governance and Federal Imprisonment of Women in Canada*. Toronto: University of Toronto Press.

Hannah-Moffat, K. (2002). *Criminogenic Need and the Transformative Risk Subject: The Hybridizations of Risk/Need in Penality*. Paper presented at the British Criminology Conference. UK: Keele University.

Hannah-Moffat, K. and Maurutto, P. (2005). *Youth Risk/Need Assessment: An Overview of Issues and Practices*. Ottawa: Department of Justice.

Hannah-Moffat, K. and Shaw, M. (Eds.) (2000). *Ideal Prison: Critical Essays of Women's Imprisonment in Canada*. Halifax: Fernwood Press.

Hannah-Moffat, K. and Shaw, M. (2001). *Taking Risks: Incorporating Gender and Culture into Classification and Assessment of Federally Sentenced Women*. Ottawa: Status of Women Canada.

Hannah-Rafter. (1983). "Chastising the Unchaste: Social Control Functions of the Women's Reformatory System." In S. Cohen and A. Scull (Eds.), *Social Control and the State*. Oxford: Martin Robertson, pp. 288–311.

Hansard Debates, Canada, 25 September 2000.

Hansard Debates. Canada. House of Commons. www2.parl.gc.ca/housechamberbusiness/Chamber Sittings.aspx?View=H&Language=E&Mode=1&Parl=37&Ses=2.

Hanselmann, C. (2001). *Urban Aboriginal People in Western Canada: Realities and Policies*. Calgary: Canada West Foundation.

Hanselmann, C. (2003). *Shared responsibility: Final Report and Recommendations of the Urban Aboriginal Initiative*. Calgary: Canada West Foundation.

Harper, Tim, "Youth Crime . . . and Punishment." *The Toronto Star*. March 25, 2007: A11.

Hartnagel, T. (2002). "Youth Crime and Justice in Alberta: Rhetoric and Reality." Report for the Parkland Institute, December 2002.

Hartnagel, T. (2004). "The rhetoric of youth justice in Canada." *Criminology and Criminal Justice*, 4(4), 355–374.

Hartnagel, T.F. and Baron, S.W. (1995). "It's Time to Get Serious: Public Attitudes toward Juvenile Justice in Canada." In J.H. Creechan and R.A. Silverman (eds.), *Canadian Delinquency*. Scarborough, ON: Prentice Hall Press.

Harvey, E. (2003). *An Independent Review of the Toronto Star Analysis of Criminal Information Processing System Data Provided by the Toronto Police Service: A Summary Report*. Toronto: Toronto Police Service.

Hatch, A. and C. Griffiths. (1991). "Child Saving Postponed: The Impact of the *Juvenile Delinquents Act* on the Processing of Young Offenders in Vancouver." In R. Smandych, G. Dodds, and A. Esau (Eds.), *Dimensions of Childhood: Essays on the History of Children and Youth in Canada*, 233–66. Winnipeg: University of Manitoba Legal Research Institute.

Hawkins, J.D. et al. (1998). "A Review of Predictors of Youth Violence." In Loeber, R. and Farrington, D. (Eds.), *Serious and Violent Juvenile Offenders: Risk Factors and Successful Interventions*. Thousand Oaks, CA: Sage: pp.106–46

Hay, D. (1975). Property, Authority and the Criminal Law. In D. Hay (Eds.), *Albion's Fatal Tree: Crime and Society in Eighteenth-Century England*, 17–63. New York: Pantheon Books.

Health Canada (2000). *A Statistical Profile on the Health of First Nations in Canada for the Year 2000*.

Hearold, S. (1986). "A synthesis of 1043 effects of television on social behaviour." In G. Comstock (Ed.), *Public Communications and Behavior: Volume I*. New York Academic Press.

Heckbert, D. and Turkington, D. (2001). Turning points: A *study of the factors related to the successful reintegration of Aboriginal offenders*. Research Report R-112. Ottawa: Research Branch, Correctional Service Canada.

Heidensohn, Frances. (1996). *Women and Crime*. (2nd edition) London: Macmillan.

Heidensohn, Frances. (2000). *Sexual Politics and Social Control*. Open University Press.

Henderson, Jean. (1994). "Masculinity and crime: The implications of a gender-conscious approach to working with young men involved in 'joyriding.'" *Social Action*, 2(2), pp. 19–26.

Henriques, J. et al. (1984). *Changing the Subject*. London: Methuen.

Hernandez, J. (1995). "The Concurrence of Eating Disorders with Histories of Child Abuse among Adolescents." *Journal of Child Sexual Abuse*, 4, 3, 73–85.

Higgitt, N., Wingert, S., and Ristock, J., (2003). *Voices from the Margins: Experiences of Street-Involved Youth in Winnipeg*. Winnipeg, MB: Winnipeg Inner-city Research Alliance.

Hirschi, T. (1969). *Causes of Delinquency*. Berkeley, CA: University of California Press.

Hobbs Birnie, L. (1990). *A Rock and a Hard Place: Inside Canada's Parole Board*. Toronto: Macmillan.

Hogeveen, B. (1999). "An Intrusive and Corrective Government: Political Rationalities and the Governance of Plains Aboriginals 1870–1890." In R. Smandych (Ed.), *Governable Places: Readings on Governmentality and Crime Control*, Aldershot, UK: Dartmouth Publishing.

Hogeveen, B. (2001). "Winning Deviant Youth Over by Friendly Helpfulness." In R. Smandych, (Ed.), *Youth Justice: History, Legislation, and Reform*. Toronto: Harcourt Canada.

Hogeveen, B. (2002). "Mentally Defective and Feeble-Minded Juvenile Offenders: Psychiatric Discourse and the Toronto Juvenile Court 1910– 1930." *Canadian Bulletin of Medical History*, 20(1), 43–74.

Hogeveen, B. (2003). "Can't you be a man? Rebuilding wayward masculinities and regulating juvenile deviance in Ontario, 1860–1930." Unpublished doctoral thesis, University of Toronto.

Hogeveen, B. (2004). "'The Evils with Which We are Called to Grapple': Elite Reformers, Eugenicists, Environmental Psychologists, and the Construction of Toronto's Working-Class Boy Problem, 1860–1930." *Labour/Le Travail*, 55 (Spring) pp. 37–68.

Hogeveen, B. (2005a), "Toward 'Safer' and 'Better' Communities: Canada's Youth Criminal Justice Act, Aboriginal Youth and the Processes of Exclusion." *Critical Criminology: An International Journal*, 13(3), 307–326.

Hogeveen, B. (2005b). "If we are tough on crime, if we punish crime, then people get the message: Constructing and governing the punishable young offender in Canada during the late 1990s." *Punishment and Society*, 7(1), 73–89.

Hogeveen, B. (2005c). "History, Development, and Transformations in Canadian Juvenile Justice, 1800–1984." In K. Campbell (Ed.), *Understanding Youth Justice: History, Legislation and Reform* (pp. 144–168). Toronto: Harcourt Canada.

Hogeveen, B. (2006a). "Memoir of a/the Blind." *Punishment and Society*, 8(4).

Hogeveen, B. (2006b). "Unsettling Youth Justice and Cultural Norms: The Youth Restorative Action Project." *Journal of Youth Studies*, 9(1), 47–66.

Hogeveen, B. (2007a). "Is there Justice for Youth?" In G. Pavlich and M. Hird (Eds.), *Questioning Sociology: Canadian Perspectives*. London: Oxford.

Hogeveen, B. (2007b), "Violence (and) Youth." *Sociology Compass*, 1(1): (forthcoming).

Hogeveen, B. and Smandych, R. (2001). "Origins of the Newly Proposed Youth Criminal Justice Act: Political Discourse and the Perceived Crisis in Youth Crime in the 1990s." In Russell Smandych (Ed.), *Youth Justice: History, Legislation and Reform*. Toronto: Harcourt, pp. 144–169.

Hogeveen, B. and Minaker, J. (2005). "Juvenile Justice System." In M. Bosworth (Ed.), *Encyclopedia of Prisons and Correctional Facilities*. Vol. 1. London: Sage.

Hogeveen, B. and Woolford, A. (2006). "Critical Criminology and Possibility in the Neo-Liberal Ethos." *Canadian Journal of Criminology and Criminal Justice*. September. 48(5), 681–701.

Holland, S. (2005). "The Last Word on Racism: New Directions for a Critical Race Theory." *South Atlantic Quarterly*, 104(3), pp. 403–423.

Hollow Water First Nation Community Holistic Circle Healing. (1994). Position paper on incarceration. Hollow Water First Nation, MB: Author.

Holmes, J. and Silverman, E.L. (1992). *We're Here, Listen to US! A Survey of Young Women in Canada*. Ottawa: Canadian Advisory Council on the Status of Women.

Holt, L. (2004). "The voices of children: de-centering empowering research relations." *Children's Geographies*, 2(1), 13–27.

Hornick, J.P., Bala, N., and Hudson, J. (1995). *The Response to Juvenile Crime in the United States: A Canadian Perspective*. Ottawa: Department of Justice Canada.

Houston, S. (1982). The "Waifs and Strays" of a late Victorian city: Juvenile Delinquents in Toronto. In J. Parr (Ed.), *Childhood and family in Canadian history*. Toronto: McClelland and Stewart.

Hudson, A. (2004). "Troublesome Girls? Towards alternative definitions and policies." In J. Muncie, G. Hughes, and E. McLaughlin (Eds.), *Youth Justice: Critical Readings*. London, UK: Sage Publications Ltd.

Hudson, B. (1989). *Justice through Punishment: A Critique of the 'Justice' Model*. Basingstroke: Macmillan.

Hudson, B. (1998). "Punishment and Governance." *Social and Legal Studies*, 7(4), 532–559.

Hudson, B. (2001). "Punishment, rights and difference: Defending justice in the risk society." In K. Stenson and R. Sullivan (Eds.), *Crime Risk and Justice: The Politics of Crime Control in Liberal Democracies*, pp. 144–72. Portland, OH: Willan Publishing.

Hudson, B. (2002). "Gender Issues in Penal Policy and Penal Theory." In P. Carlen (Ed.), *Women and Punishment: The Struggle for Justice*. Devon, UK: Willan.

Huesmann. L.R. (1998). "The role of social information processing and cognitive schema in the acquisition and maintenance of habitual aggressive behavior." See Geen and Donnerstein, pp. 73–109 in R.G. Geen and E. Donnerstein (Eds.), *Human Aggression: Theories, Research, and Implications for Policy*. New York: Academic Press.

Huesmann, L.R. and Eron, L.D. (1986). *Television and the Aggressive Child: A Cross-National Comparison*. Hillsdale, New Jersey: Lawrence Erlbaum Associates.

Huesmann, L.R., Moise, J., Podolski, C.P. and Eron, L.D. (2003). "Longitudinal relations between childhood exposure to media violence and adult aggression and violence: 1977–1992." *Developmental Psychology*, 39(2), 201–221.

Huffine, C. (2003). "Youth Violence: Its meanings to society in the 21st century." *Adolescent Psychiatry*, 27 (2003): 361–373.

Hughes, G. (1991). *Understanding Crime Prevention: Social Control, Risk and Late Modernity*. Maidenhead, UK: Open University Press.

Hull, J. (1987). *An Overview of Registered Indian Conditions in Manitoba*. Ottawa: Department of Indian and Northern Affairs.

Humm, M. (1995). *The Dictionary of Feminist Theory*. 2nd ed. Ohio State University Press.

Hunt, A. (1995). "Law, Politics, and the Social Sciences." In A. Hunt (Ed.), *Sociology after Postmodernism*, 103–23. New York: Blackwell.

Hunt, G.P. and Laidler KJ. (2001). "Alcohol and violence in the lives of gang members." *Alcohol Health and Research World*, 25(1): 66–71.

Hunter, J. (1990). "Violence against lesbian and gay male youths." *Journal of Interpersonal Violence*, 5: 295-300.

Huston, A.C. et al. *Big World, Small Screen: The Role of Television in American Society*. Lincoln: University of Nebraska Press.

Hutson, S. and Liddiard, M. (1994). *Youth Homelessness: The Construction of a Social Issue*. London: Macmillan.

Hylton, J. (1994). "Get Tough or Get Smart? Options for Canada's Youth Justice System in the Twenty-First Century." *Canadian Journal of Criminology*, 36, 229–246.

Hyde, J.S. (1985). *Half the Human Experience: The Psychology of Women* (3rd edition). Lexington, MA: Heath.

Indian and Northern Affairs Canada. (2001). *Basic Departmental Data*. Ottawa, ON: Minister of Public Works and Government Services Canada.

Institute, Conference on the *Youth Criminal Justice Act*, Toronto, September 2002. Available March 2004 www.nji.ca/postings/YJC/youthjustice.html.

Jackson, C. (2000) "Waste and Whiteness: Zora neale Hurston and the Politics of Eugenics." *African American Review*, 34. Winter 2000: 641.

Jackson, M. (1989). "Locking Up Natives in Canada." *University of British Columbia Law Review*, 23(2):215–300.

Jackson, S. (1999). "Family Group Conferences and Youth Justice: The New Panacea?" In B. Goldson (Ed.), *Youth Justice: Contemporary Policy and Practice*. 127–147. Aldershot, UK: Ashgate.

James, A. (1993). *Childhood Identities: Self and Social Relationships in the Experience of the Child*. Edinburgh University Press, Edinburgh.

James, A. and Jenks, C. (1996). "Public Perceptions of childhood criminality." *British Journal of Sociology*, 47(2), 315–331.

James, C. (1998). "'Up to no good': Black on the streets and encountering police." In V. Stazewich (Ed.), *Racism and Social Inequality in Canada*. Toronto: Thompson

Janus, M., Burgess, A.W., and McCormack, A. (1987). "Histories of sexual abuse in adolescent male runaways." *Adolescence*, 22: 405–417.

Janus, M., McCormack, A., Burgess, A., and Hartman, C. (1987). *Adolescent Runaways: Causes and Consequences*. Lexington, Mass.: D.C. Heath and Company.

Janus, M.D., Archambault, F.X., Brown, S.W., and Welsh, L.A. (1995). "Physical abuse in Canadian runaway adolescents." *Child Abuse and Neglect* 19(4), 433–447.

Jefferson, T. (1994). "Crime, criminology, masculinity and young men." In Coote, Anna (Ed.), *Families, Children and Crime*. London: Institute for Public Policy Research.

Jefferson, T. (1997). "Masculinities and crime." In M. Maguire, R. Morgan, and R. Reiner (Eds.), *The Oxford Handbook of Criminology*. 2nd ed. Oxford: Clarendon Press, 535–557.

Jenkins, J. (1994). *Men, Masculinity and Offending*. ILPS and London Action Trust, October.

Jewkes, Yvonne. (2005). "Men Behind Bars: 'Doing' Masculinity as an Adaptation to Imprisonment." *Men and Masculinities*, 8(1), July, pp. 44–63.

Jiwani, Y. (1998a). *Violence against Marginalized Girls: A Review of Current Literature*. Vancouver: The Feminist Research, Education, Development and Action Centre.

Jiwani, Y. (1998b). *The Girl Child: Having to "Fit"* (October). The FREDA Centre for Research on Violence against Women and Children.

Jiwani, Y. (1999). "Erasing Race: The story of Reena Virk." *Canadian Women's Studies*, 19(3), 178–184.

Jiwani, Y. et al. (1999). *Violence Prevention and the Girl Child. Phase One Report*. Alliance of Five Research Centres on Violence.

Joe, K. and Chesney-Lind, M. (1993). *Just Every Mother's Angel*. Paper presented at meetings of the American Society of Criminology, Phoenix, AZ: October.

John Howard Society of Ontario. (1994). Youth crime: Sorting fact from fiction. Fact Sheet #3. Toronto: John Howard Society of Ontario.

Johnson, A.K., McChesney, K.Y., and Butterfield, W.H. (1995). "Demographic differences between sheltered homeless families and housed poor families: Implications for policy and practice." *Journal of Sociology & Social Welfare*, 5–22.

Johnson, J. (1997). "Aboriginal offender survey: case filed and interview sample." Report prepared for the Correctional Service of Canada. Retrieved July 2, 2002, from www.csc-scc.gc.ca/text/rsrch/reports/r61/r61e_e.shtml.

Johnson, S. (2002). "Custodial remand in Canada, 1986/1987 to 2000/2001" *Juristat*. Catalogue no. 85-002, Vol.23, no.7. Ottawa, Statistics Canada, Canadian Centre for Justice Statistics.

Johnstone, G. (2002). *Restorative Justice: Ideas, Values, Debates.* Portland, Oregon: Willan Publishing.

Jones, A. (1978). "Closing Pentanguishene Reformatory: An attempt to deinstitutionalize treatment of juvenile offenders in early 20th-century Ontario." *Ontario History* 70, 227.

Jones, A. (1988). "Closing Pentanguishene Reformatory: An Attempt to Deinstitutionalize Treatment of Young Offenders in Early Twentieth-Century Ontario." In R.C. MacLeod (Ed.), *Lawful Authority in the History of Criminal Justice in Canada.* Toronto: Copp Clark Pitman.

Jones, A. and Rutman, L. (1981). *In the Children's Aid: J.J. Kelso and Child Welfare in Ontario.* Toronto: University of Toronto Press.

Jones, L.P. (1988). "A typology of adolescent runaways." *Child and Adolescent Social Work,* 5(1), 16–29.

Jones, O. (2000). "Melting geography: purity, disorder, childhood and space." In S. Holloway and G. Valentine (Eds.), *Children's Geographies: Playing, Living and Learning,* London: Routledge.

Jones, O. (2001). "Before the dark of reason: some ethical and epistemological considerations on the otherness of children." *Ethics, Place and Environment,* 4(2), 173–178.

Jull, S. (2000). "Youth Violence, Schools, and the Management Question: A Discussion of Zero Tolerance and Equity in Public Schooling." *Canadian Journal of Educational Administration and Policy,* 17. November 30.

Karabanow, J. (2004). *Exploring Salient Issues of Youth Homelessness in Halifax, Nova Scotia.* February.

Karabanow, J. (2005). *Getting Off the Street: Exploring Strategies Used by Canadian Youth to Exit Street Life.* Maritime School of Social Work.

Kasl, C.D. (1992). *Many Roads, One Journey, Moving Beyond the Twelve Steps.* New York: Harper Perennial.

Katz, M.B. (1990). *The Undeserving Poor: From the War on Poverty to the War on Welfare.* New York: Pantheon Books.

Katz, P.A. (1979). "The development of female identity." In *Becoming Female: Perspectives on Development.* New York: Plenum Press. pp. 3–28

Keane, J. (2004). *Violence and Democracy.* Cambridge: Cambridge University Press.

Kellough, G. and Wortley, S. (2002). "Remand for Plea: Bail Decisions and Plea Bargaining as Commensurate Decisions." *British Journal of Criminology,* 42, 186–210.

Kellough, G. and Wortley, S. (2003). "Quiet discretion: Racial profiling in the application of pre-trial release conditions." (Unpublished paper).

Kelly, P. (2000a). "Youth as an Artifact of Expertise: Problematizing the Practice of Youth Studies in an Age of Uncertainty." *Journal of Youth Studies,* 3 (4), 301–315.

Kelly, P. (2000b). The dangerousness of youth-at-risk: the possibilities of surveillance and intervention in uncertain times." *Journal of Adolescence,* 23(4), 463–476.

Kelly, P. (2001). Youth at Risk: processes of individualization and responsibilisation in the risk society. *Discourse: Studies in the Cultural Politics of Education,* 22(1). April: 23–33.

Kelso, J.J. (1907). "Delinquent Children: Some Improved Methods Whereby They May Be Prevented from Following a Criminal Career." *Canadian Bar Review* 6: 106–10.

Kelso, J.J. (1909). *Helping Erring Children.* Toronto: Warwick.

Kelso, J J. (1911). *Early History of the Humane and Children's Aid Movement in Ontario, 1863–1893.* Toronto: King's Printer.

Kelso, J.J. (1934). *History of the Victoria Industrial School.*

Kerns, S.E. and Prinz R.J. (2002). "Critical issues in the prevention of violence-related behaviour among youth [review]" *Clinical Child and Family Psychology Review* 5: 133–160.

Kerr, J.H. (2005). *Rethinking Aggression and Violence in Sport.* London: Routledge.

Kessler, S.J., Ashenden, D.J, Connell, R.W., and Dowsett, G.W. (1982). *Ockers and Disco-maniacs.* Sydney, Australia: Inner City Education Center.

Kidd, S. (2003). *Trapped: Street Youth Suicide.* June, unpublished MA thesis. University of Windsor.

Kimmel, M.S. (1987). "Rethinking 'masculinity': New directions in research." In Kimmel, M.S. (Ed.), *Changing Men: New Directions in Research on Men and Masculinity.* Newbury Park, CA: Sage.

Kingsley, S. and Mark, M. (2000). *Sacred lives: Canadian Aboriginal Children and Youth Speak Out about Sexual Exploitation.* Ottawa: Save the Children Canada.

Kipnis, A. (1999). *Angry Young Men: How Parents, Teachers, and Counselors Can Help 'Bad Boys' Become Good Men.* San Francisco: Jossey Bass.

Kirsh, S. (2006). *Children, Adolescents and Media Violence: A Critical Look at the Research.* Thousand Oaks, CAO: Sage Publications.

Koeller, R. (2005). *Background Report: Homeless and Street-Involved Youth in HRM, Summary of Local Research Findings.* Halifax: Halifax Regional Municipality.

Kowalski, M. (1999). Canadian Centre for Justice Statistics. Alternative Measures for Youth in Canada. *Juristat,* Vol 19, 8.

Kruks, G. (1991). "Gay and lesbian homeless/street youth: special issues and concerns." *Journal of Adolescent Health,* 12(7), 515–518.

Kufeldt, K. (1994). "Social Policy and Runaways." *Journal of Health and Social Policy,* 2(4), 37–49.

Kufeldt, K., Baker, J., Bennett, L., and Tite, R. (1998). *Looking After Children in Canada: Interim Draft Report.* St. John's, NF: Memorial University.

Kufeldt, K., Jarvis, S., and Kurtz, G. (1992). "Providing shelter for street youth: Are we reaching those in need?"

Kufeldt, K. and Nimmo, K. (1987). "Youth on the street: abuse and neglect in the eighties." *Child Abuse and Neglect*, 11, 531–543.

Kufeldt, K. and Nimmo, M. (1987). "Kids on the street, they have something to say: Survey of runaway and homeless youth." *Journal of Child Care*, 3: 53–61.

Laberge, D. (1991). "Women's Criminality, Criminal Women, Criminalized Women?: Questions in and for a Feminist Perspective." *Journal of Human Justice*, 2, 2.

Lahelma, E. and Gordon, T. (2003). "Home as a Physical, Social and Mental Space: Young People's Reflections on Leaving Home." *Journal of Youth Studies*, 6(4), 377–390.

Langbein, J. (1978). "The Criminal Trial before the Lawyers." *University of Chicago Law Review*, 45(2), 263–316.

Langmuir, J.W. (1891). *Ontario, Report of the Commissioners Appointed to Enquire into the Prison and Reformatory System of Ontario*. Toronto: Warwick and Sons.

LaPrairie, C. (1983a). *Native Juveniles in Court: Some Observations on Social Disparity*. Ottawa: Solicitor General of Canada.

LaPrairie, C. (1983b). "Native Juveniles in Court: Some Preliminary Observation." In T. Fleming and L.A. Visano (eds.), *Deviant Designations: Crime, Law and Deviants*. Toronto: Butterworths.

LaPrairie, C. (1988a). "The Young Offenders Act and Aboriginal Youth." In J. Hudson, J. Hornick, and B. Burrows (Eds.), *Justice and the Young Offender in Canada*. Toronto: Wall and Thompson.

LaPrairie, C. (1988b). *Native Juveniles in Court: Some Observations on Social Disparity*. Ottawa, ON: Solicitor General of Canada.

LaPrairie, C. (1988c). "Young Offenders Act and Aboriginal Youth." In J. Hudson et al. (Eds), *Justice and the Young Offender in Canada*, 1988, page 164; The Aboriginal Justice Implementation Commission 1999, Report of the Aboriginal Justice Inquiry of Manitoba, 1991.

LaPrairie, C. (1992). *Dimensions of Aboriginal Over-Representation in Correctional Institutions and Implications for Crime Prevention*. Aboriginal Peoples Collection, Ottawa: Ministry of the Solicitor General.

LaPrairie, C. (1995a). "Altering Course: New Directions in Criminal Justice Sentencing Circles and Family Group Conferences." *The Australian and New Zealand Journal of Criminology, Special Supplementary Issue* 78–99.

LaPrairie, C. (1995b). "Seen but not heard: Native people in four Canadian inner cities." *Critical Criminology*, 6(2): 30–45.

LaPrairie, C. (1996). *Examining Aboriginal Corrections in Canada*, Aboriginal Corrections Policy Unit. Ottawa: Ministry of the Solicitor General.

LaPrairie, C. (1997). *Seeking Change: Justice Development in LaLoche*. Saskatchewan: Saskatchewan Justice.

LaPrairie, C. (1998). "The 'new' justice: Some implications for Aboriginal communities." *Canadian Journal of Criminology*, 40, 61–79.

LaPrairie, C. (2002). "Aboriginal over-representation In the criminal justice system: A tale of nine cities." *Canadian Journal of Criminology*, 44, 181–208.

LaPrairie, C. and Griffiths, C.T. (1982). "Native Indian Delinquency: A Review of Recent Findings: Native People and Justice in Canada." *Canadian Legal Aid Bulletin*, 5 (1) (Special Issue, Part 1), 39–46.

LaPrairie, C. and Griffiths, C.T. (1984). "Native juvenile delinquency: A review of recent findings." *Canadian Legal Aid Bulletin*, 5(1):39–46.

LaRocque, E. (1990). Written presentation to Aboriginal Justice Inquiry hearings, 5 February 1990.

Larose, S. (2001). "Battling the child sex trade." *Windspeaker*, 18 (9).

Latimer, J. and Casey Foss, L. (2004). *A One-Day Snapshot of Aboriginal Youth in Custody Across Canada: Phase II*. Department of Justice Canada. Youth Justice Research.

Latimer, J. and Casey Foss, L. (2005). "The Sentencing of Aboriginal and Non Aboriginal Youth Under the Young Offenders Act: A Multivariate Analysis." *Canadian Journal of Criminology and Criminal Justice*, 47(3): 481–500.

Law Commission of Canada, (1999). National Association of Friendships Centres, *Urban Aboriginal Governance: Re-Fashioning the Dialogue*. 1999: 65.

Law Courts Education Society of BC. (2003). *On the Road to Justice: The Youth Criminal Justice Act and Aboriginal Communities*. Guide to the Posters for the Youth Criminal Justice Act, 2nd edition.

Leach, P., (2000). *Children First*. London: Vintage.

Lee, K. (2002) *Urban Poverty in Canada: A Statistical Profile*. Ottawa: Canadian Council on Social Development.

Leigh, A. (1996). "Youth and street racing." *Current Issues in Criminal Justice* (7)3, Mar: 388–393.

Lemay, R. (1999). "Pushed out of the nest . . . Another way in which the life experiences of youth in care are different from those of other Canadian youth." *Ontario Association of Children's Aid Societies* 43(3), 9–10.

Lemert, E. (1951). *Social Psychology*. New York: McGraw.

Lemert, E. (1951). *Social Pathology*. New York: McGraw-Hill.

Leon, J. (1977). "The Development of Canadian Juvenile Justice: A Background for Reform." *Osgoode Hall Law Journal* 15: 71–106.

Leschied, A. and Jaffe. P.G. (1986). "Implications of the Young Offenders Act in Modifying the Juvenile Justice System: Some Early Trends." *Young Offenders Act Update*. 450–459, Toronto, ON: Butterworths.

Leschied, A. et al. (2000). *Female Adolescent Aggression: A Review of the Literature and the Correlates of Aggression*.

(Ottawa: Solicitor General of Canada, 2000), User Report No. 2000-04.

Leslie, B. and Hare, F. (2000). *Improving the Outcomes for Youth in Transition from Care.* Toronto: Working Group of the Children's Aid Society of Toronto, Covenant House and Ryerson University Research Project, 1995–1999.

Lethwaite, S. (1994). "Violence, Law, and Community in Rural Upper Canada." In J. Phillips, T. Loo, and S. Lethwaite (Eds.), *Essays in the History of Upper Canada: Vol. 5, Crime and Criminal Justice.* 353–86. Toronto: University of Toronto Press.

Levinas, E. (1969). *Totality and Infinity: An Essay on Exteriority.* Pittsburgh: Duquenne Press.

Levit, Nancy. (1996). "Feminism for Men: Legal Ideology and the Construction of Maleness." *UCLA Law Review,* 43(4).

Lewis, C. and Short, C. (1879). *A Latin Dictionary,* Oxford: Clarendon Press.

Lezubski, J., Silver, J., and Black, E. (2000). "High and Rising: The Growth of Poverty in Winnipeg." In J. Silver (Ed.), *Solutions that Work: Fighting Poverty in Winnipeg.* Winnipeg, MB: Canadian Centre for Policy Alternatives (Manitoba) and Fernwood Publishing.

Linden, R. and Caputo, T. (2005). "Early Theories of Criminology." In R. Linden (Ed.), *Criminology: A Canadian Perspective.* Toronto: Nelson.

Lindsay, E.W. (1996). "Mothers' Perceptions of Factors Influencing the Restabilization of Homeless Families." *Families in Society: the Journal of Contemporary Human Services,* 203–214.

Lindsay, E.W. (1998). "Service providers' perception of factors that help or hinder homeless families." *Families in Society: The Journal of Contemporary Human Services,* 160–172.

Lipsey, M.W. (1992). *Juvenile Delinquency Treatment: A Meta-Analytic Inquiry into the Variability of Effects.* New York: Russell Sage Foundation.

Llewellyn, J. and Howse, R. (1999) *"Restorative Justice – A Conceptual Framework,"* Law Commission of Canada, Government of Canada. Available at www.lcc.gc/en/themes/sr/rj/howse/howse_main.asp.

Loeber, R. and Magda Stouthamer-Loeber. (1998). "Development of Juvenile Aggression and Violence: Some Common Misconceptions and Controversies." *American Psychologist* 53: 242–59.

Lombroso, C. (1972). "Criminal Man." In S.F. Sylvester (Ed.), *The Heritage of Modern Criminology.* Cambridge, MA: Schenkman.

Lombroso, C. and Ferrero, W. (1895/1959). *The Female Offender.* New York: Peter Owen.

Lucentini, J. (2004). "Gene Association Studies Typically Wrong: Reproducible Gene-Disease Associates Are Few and Far Between." *The Scientist,* 18(20): 20.

Lynn, M. and O'Neill, E. (1995). "Families, Power, and Violence." In Nancy Mandell and Ann Duffy (Eds.), *Canadian Families: Diversity, Conflict and Change,* 271–305. Toronto: Harcourt Brace Canada.

Ma, S. (2004). *Just Listen to Me: Youth Voices on Violence.* Office of Child and Family Services Advocacy and Voices for Children. Toronto, Ontario.

MacDonald, N.E. Fischer, W.A., and Wells, G.A., (1994). "Canadian street youth: correlates of sexual risk-taking activity." *Pediatric Infectious Disease Journal,* 13(8), 690–697.

Macey, D. (2004). *Michel Foucault.* London: Reaktion.

MacGill, H.G. (1919). "The relation of the Juvenile Court to the Community." *Canadian Journal of Mental Hygiene,* Vol. 1.

MacGill, H.G. (1943). *The Work of the Juvenile Court and How to Secure Such a Court in Your Canadian Community.* Vancouver.

Mack, J. (1909). "The Juvenile Court." *Harvard Law Review,* 23: pp. 104–122.

MacLean, M., Embry, L., and Cauce, A. (1999). "Homeless adolescents' paths to separation from family: Comparison of family characteristics, psychological adjustment, and victimization." *Journal of Community Psychology,* 27(2), 179–187.

Maguin, E. and Rolf Loeber. (1996). "Academic Performance and Delinquency." In M.Tonry (Ed.), *Crime and Justice: A Review of Research* (vol. 220), Chicago: University of Chicago Press, pp. 145–264.

Malatest, R. A. and Associates Ltd. (2004). *Edmonton Regional Plan for Coordination of Youth Services.* Edmonton, AB.

Manitoba. (1991). *Report of the Aboriginal Justice Inquiry of Manitoba.* Winnipeg: The Aboriginal Justice Inquiry.

Manitoba Justice Inquiry Implementation Commission, (1999). Winnipeg.

Mann, R. M. (2000). "Struggles for Justice and Justice for Youth: A Canadian example." In R. Mann (Ed.), *Juvenile Crime and Delinquency: A Turn of the Century Reader.* Toronto: Canadian Scholars Press, pp. 3–18.

Marks, L. (1998). "Christian Harmony: Family, Neighbours, and Community in Upper Canadian Church Disciplinary Records." In F. Iacovetta and W. Michinson (Eds.), *On the Case: Explorations in Social History,* 109–128. Toronto: University of Toronto Press.

Markwart, A. and Corrado. R.R. (1995). "A response to Carrington." *Canadian Journal of Criminology,* 37(1), 74–87.

Martin, L. (1998). "Domestic Violence Victim: Due Process and the Victim's Right to Counsel." *Gonzaga Law Review,* 34: 329.

Martin, D. (2002) "Demonizing Youth, Marketing Fear: The New Politics of Crime." In J. Hermer and J. Mosher (Eds.), *Disorderly People: Law and the Politics of Exclusion in Ontario,* Halifax: Fernwood, pp. 91–102.

Martinson, R. (1974). "What Works? Questions and Answers About Prison Reform." *The Public Interest*, 35: 22–54.

Massey, D. (1998). "The spatial construction of youth cultures." In T.L. Skelton and G. Valentine (Eds.), *Cool Places: Geographies of Youth Cultures*. London: Routledge.

Matsuda, M.J. (1996). *Where is your body? And Other Essays on Race, Gender, and the Law*. Boston: Beacon Press.

Matthews, H. (2001). "Participatory structures and the youth of today: engaging those who are hardest to reach." *Ethics, Place and Environment*, 4(2): 153–159.

Mauer, M. (1999). *Race to Incarcerate*. New York: New Press.

Mauer, M., Potler, C., and Wolf, R. (1999). *Gender and Justice: Women, Drugs and Sentencing Policy*. Washington: The Sentencing Project.

Mawani, R. (2005) "Genealogies of the Land: Aboriginality, Law, and Territory in Vancouver's Stanley Park." *Social and Legal Studies*, 14 (3): 315–339.

May, P.A. and Gossage, J.P. (2001). "Estimating the prevalence of fetal alcohol syndrome, A summary." *Alcohol Research and Health*. 25 (3).

Maynard, S. (1997). "'Horrible Temptations': Sex, Man, and Working-Class Male Youth in Urban Ontario, 1890–1935." *Canadian Historical Review*, 78 (2): 194–237.

Mayor's Homelessness Action Task Force. (1999). *Taking Responsibility for Homelessness: An Action Plan for Toronto*. Toronto: City of Toronto.

McCarthy, B. (1995). "Getting into crime: The structure and process of criminal embeddedness." *Social Science Research*, 7(4): 412–430.

McCarthy, B. and Hagan, J. (1992). "Mean Streets: the theoretical significance of situational delinquency among homeless youths." *American Journal of Sociology*, 3: 597–627.

McCarty D. et al. (2000). "Detoxification Centers: Who's in the Revolving Door?" *Journal of Behavioral Health Services and Research*, 27(3): 245–256.

McClelland, S. (2003a). "Institutional correction: A new youth crime act aims to fix a broken system." *Macleans*, June 9, 2003.

McClelland, S. (2003b) "Sugar and spice no more." *Macleans*, July 21, 2003.

McCormack, A., Janus, M.D., and Burgess, A.W. (1986). "Runaway youths and sexual victimization: Gender differences in an adolescent runaway population." *Child Abuse and Neglect*, 10, 387–395.

McCreary Centre Society. (2001). *No Place to Call Home: A Profile of Street Youth in British Columbia*.

McCullagh, J. and Greco, M. (1990). *Servicing Street Youth: A Feasibility Study*. Toronto: Children's Aid Society.

McDonald, R.J., and Ladd, P. (2000). *First Nations Child and Family Services Joint National Policy Review. Final report*. Ottawa: The Assembly of First Nations and Department of Indian and Northern Affairs Development.

McEvoy, M. and Daniluk, J. (1995). "Wounds to the Soul: The Experiences of Aboriginal Women Survivors of Sexual Abuse." *Canadian Psychology/Psychologie Canadienne*, 36(3) (August): 221–235.

McFarlane, G., Coughlan, D.F.W., and Sumpter, A.H. (1966). *The Development of Probation Services in Ontario*. Toronto: Queen's Printer.

McGillivray, A. and Comaskey, B. (1996). *Black Eyes All of the Time: Intimate Violence, Aboriginal Women, and the Justice System*. Toronto: University of Toronto Press.

McGovern, C. (1995). "You've come a long way baby." *Alberta Report*, 1(33): 24–7.

McIntyre, S. (2002). *Strolling Away*. Department of Justice, Canada.

McKay, K. (2003) *Proceedings, 17 March 2003, Winnipeg Youth Round Table, AMC Youth Council, Assembly of Manitoba Chiefs, UAYAPC*.

McKenzie, B. (2002). *Block funding child maintenance in First Nations child and family services: A policy review*. Report prepared for Kahnawake Shaktiia'takehnhas Community Services. (February) Winnipeg.

McLaren, A. (1990). *Our Own Master Race: Eugenics in Canada, 1885-1945*. Toronto: McLelland and Stewart.

McLellan, A. (1999) [Press Release] Remarks by (then) federal justice Minister, Department of Justice, 12 May.

Meadow, P. (2003). "Drives, Aggression, Destructivity." *Modern Psychoanalysis* 28(2), 199–205.

Melchers, R. (2003). "Do Toronto Police Engage in Racial Profiling?" *Canadian Journal of Criminology and Criminal Justice*, 45(3), 347–366.

Mercer, S.L. (1987). *Not a Pretty Picture: An Exploratory Study of Violence against Women in High School Dating Relationships*. Toronto: Education Wife Assault.

Mercredi, O.W. (2000). *Aboriginal Gangs: A Report to the Correctional Service of Canada on Aboriginal Youth Gang Members in the Federal Corrections System*. Ottawa: Corrections Canada.

Merleau-Ponty, M. (1962). *Phenomenology of Perception*. C. Smith (translator). Routledge & Kegan Paul.

Merton, R.K. (1938). "Social Structure and Anomie." *American Sociological Review*, 3, 672–682.

Messerschmidt, J. (1993). *Masculinities and Crime: Critique and Reconceptualization of Theory*. Lanham MD, Rowman and Littlefield.

Messerschmidt, J. (1997). *Crime as Structured Action: Gender, Race, Class and Crime in the Making*. Thousand Oaks, CA: Sage.

Messershmidt, J. (1999). "Making Bodies Matter: Adolescent Masculinities, the body and varieties of violence." *Theoretical Criminology*, 3(2), 197–220.

Messershmidt, J. (2000). *Nine Lives: Adolescent Masculinities, the Body and Violence*. Boulder: Westview.

Messerschmidt. J. W. (2004). *Flesh and Blood: Adolescent Gender Diversity and Violence*. Lanham, MD: Rowman and Littlefield.

Messerschmidt, J.W. (2005) *Men, Masculinities, and Crime*. In M. Kimmel, J. Hearn, and R.W. Connell (Eds.), *The Handbook of Studies on Men and Masculinities*. Thousand Oaks, CA: Sage.

Miller, D. and Trapani, C. (1995). "Adolescent female offenders: Unique considerations." *Adolescence*, 30 (118), 429–436.

Miller, E.M. (1986). *Street Women*. Philadelphia: Temple University Press.

Miller, Jerome G. (1996). *Search and Destroy: African-American Males in the Criminal Justice System*. Cambridge: Cambridge University Press.

Miller, K.J. (1996). "Prevalence and Process of Disclosure of Childhood Sexual Abuse among Eating-Disordered Women." In M.F. Schartz, and L. Cohn, (Eds.), *Sexual Abuse and Eating Disorders*, 36–51. New York: Brunner/Mazel.

Mills, C.W. (1959). *The Sociological Imagination*. London: Oxford University Press.

Milne, H., Linden, R., and Kueneman, R. (1992). "Advocate or Guardian: The Role of Defence Council in Youth Justice." In R. Corrado, N. Bala, R. Linden and M. LeBlanc (Eds.), *Juvenile Justice in Canada: A Theoretical and Analytical Assessment*. Toronto: Butterworths.

"Mimico Boys' School". *The Globe*, March 14, 1891.

Minaker, J. (2001). "Evaluating Criminal Justice Responses to Intimate Abuse through the Lens of Women's Needs, 13." *Canadian Journal of Women and the Law*, 74.

Minaker, J. (2003). "Censuring the Erring Female": Governing Female Sexuality at the Toronto Industrial Refuge. Unpublished PhD dissertation.

Minaker, J. (2006). "Sluts and Slags: The Censuring of the Erring Female." In G. Balfour and E. Comack (Eds.), *Criminalizing Women: Gender and (In)Justice in Neo-Liberal Times*. Halifax: Fernwood Publishing.

Minaker, J. and Snider, L. (2006). "Husband Abuse: Equality with a Vengeance?" *Canadian Journal of Criminology and Criminal Justice 48(5)*. September, 753-780.

Ministry of Children and Family Development of British Columbia, (2003). "Youth Justice Policy and Program Support, Community Youth Justice Programs." *Community Pre-trial Services and Remand Custody, Pre-bail Enquiries*.

Ministry of Social Development, Centre for Social Research and Evaluation. 2006. *From Wannabes to Youth Offenders: Youth Gangs in Counties Manukau*. Research Report.

Mohr, L.B. 1995. *Impact Analysis for Program Evaluation*. 2nd ed. Thousand Oaks, CA: Sage.Molidor, C.E., Nissen, L.B., and Watkins, T.R. (2002). *The Development of Theory and Treatment with Substance Abusing Female Juvenile Offenders*. Human Sciences Press, Inc.

Moore, E. and Skaburskis, A. (2002). "Canada's increasing housing affordability burdens." (Manuscript). In Fara-On, M. (Ed.), *An investigation of the factors that contribute to the housing stability/instability of former clients of Massey Centre*. Executive Summary. December.

Morin, B. (1990). "Native Youth and the Young Offenders Act." *Legal Perspectives*, 14 (4), 13–15.

Morris, R. (2002). *Stories of Transformative Justice*. Toronto: Canadian Scholars' Press.

Morrison, T. (1992). *Playing in the Dark: Whiteness and the Literary Imagination*, New York: Vintage.

Morton, D. (1973). *Mayor Howland*. (Toronto: Hakkert).

Mott, H. (1929). "Juvenile Court." *Annual Report*, Toronto 8.

Moyer, S. (1996). *A Profile of the Juvenile Justice System in Canada: Report to the Federal–Provincial–Territorial Task Force on Youth Justice*. Ottawa: Department of Justice.

Moyer, S. and Basic, M. (2005). *Crown Decision-Making Under the Youth Criminal Justice Act*. Ottawa: Department of Justice.

Muncie, J. and Hughes, G. (2002). "Modes of youth governance: Political rationalities, criminalization and resistance." In J. Muncie, G. Hughes, and E. McLaughlin (Eds.), *Youth Justice: Critical Readings*. London: Sage Publications.

Murdock, G. (1982). "Mass Communication and Social Violence." In P. Marsh and A. Campbell (Eds.), *Aggression and Violence*. Oxford: Blackwell.

Myers, T. (1999). "The Voluntary Delinquent" and "Qui t'debauchee? Family Adolescent Sexuality and the Juvenile Delinquent's Court in Early Twentieth Century Montreal." In L. Chambers and E. Montigny (Eds.), *Family Matters*. Toronto: Canadian Scholars' Press.

Naffine, N. (1997). *Feminism and Criminology*. St. Leonards, NSW: Allen & Unwin.

Nancy, Jean-Luc. *The Ground of the Image*. New York: Fordham, 2005.

National Crime Prevention Centre. (1998) *National strategy on Community Safety and Crime Prevention: Safer Communities*. Ottawa: National Crime Prevention Centre.

National Crime Prevention Centre. (1999). *National Forum on Youth Gangs*. (December). Ottawa: Solicitor General Canada, Department of Justice Canada.

National Crime Prevention Strategy. (1995). Mobilizing Political Will and Community Responsibility to Prevent Youth Crime www.prevention.gc.ca/en/library/publications/youth/say/ch3.html.

National Crime Prevention Strategy. (1997). Young People Say: Report of the National Youth in Care Network [online]. Available at www.prevention.gc.ca/en/library/publications/youth/say (accessed 12 July 2004).

National Forum on Health. (1997) "An Overview of Women's Health." *Canada Health Action: Building on the Legacy*. Ottawa: National Forum on Health.

National Institute of Corrections. available at www.nicic.org.

National Institute of Justice. (2003). *Youth Victimization: Prevalence and Implications* available at www.ncjrs.gov/pdffiles1/nij/194972.pdf.

National Post, March 30, 2006. "45 gangs plague York schools, malls: 'Know no boundaries': Police compiled database with gangsters' profiles."

National Resource Center on Domestic Violence. 2002. *In Brief: Women's Experiences of Abuse as a Risk Factor for Incarceration*. (December).

National Television Violence Study, 1996, 1997, 1998. The Center for Communication and Social Policy website. University of California, Santa Barbara.

Native Counselling Services of Alberta (1999). *The In Search of Your Warrior Program Manual*. Native Counselling Services of Alberta Publications.

Newburn, T. and Stanko, E.A. (Eds.). (1994). *Just Boys Doing Business? Men, Masculinities and Crime*. London: Routledge.

Newhouse, D. and Peters, E.J. (2003). *Not Strangers in These Parts: Aboriginal People in Urban Areas*. Ottawa: Privy Council Office.

Newton, Carolyn. (1994). "Gender theory and prison sociology: Using theories of masculinities to interpret the sociology of prisons for men." *Howard Journal of Criminal Justice*, 33(3), August, pp. 193–202.

Nimmo, M. (2001). *The "Invisible" Gang Members: A Report on Female Gang Association in Winnipeg*. Winnipeg, MB: Canadian Centre for Policy Alternatives.

Noble, J. (1979). "Classifying the Poor: Toronto Charities 1850–1880." *Studies in Political Economy*, 2 (Spring), 109–128.

Novac, S., Serge, L., Eberle, M., and Brown, J. (2002). *On Her Own: Young Women and Homelessness in Canada*. Ottawa: Canadian Housing and Renewal Association. Status of Women, Canada.

Odem, M. (1995). *Delinquent Daughters: Protecting and Policing Adolescent Female Sexuality in the United States, 1885–1920*. Chapel Hill: University of North Carolina Press.

Odem, M. (1991). "Single Mothers, Delinquent Daughters, and the Juvenile Court in Early 20th Century Los Angeles." *Journal of Social History*, 25 27–43.

Odem, M. and Schlossman, S. (1990). "Guardians of Virtue: the Juvenile Court and Female Delinquency in Early 20th century Los Angeles." *Crime and Delinquency*, 37, 186–203.

O'Grady, B. and Bright, R. (2002). "Squeezed to the point of exclusion: The case of Toronto squeegee cleaners." In J. Hermer and J. Mosher (eds), *Disorderly People: Law and the Politics of Exclusion in Ontario*. (pp. 23–40). Halifax: Fernwood Publishing.

O'Grady, B. and Gaetz, S. (2004). "Homelessness, Gender and Subsistence: The Case of Toronto Street Youth." *Journal of Youth Studies* 7(4), December, 397–416.

Oliver, P. and Wittingham, M. (1987). "Elitism, Localism, and the Emergence of Adult Probation Services in Ontario, 1890–1935." *Canadian Historical Review*, 78(2), 194–237.

O'Malley, P. (1992). "Risk, Power and Crime Prevention." *Economy and Society*, 21(2), 252–275.

O'Malley, P. (2002). "Globalizing Risk? Distinguishing Styles of Neo Liberal Criminal Justice in Australia and the USA." *Criminal Justice* 2(2), 205–22.

Ontario Legislative Assembly. (1883). Sessional Papers. *Fifteenth Annual Report of the Inspector of Prisons and Public Charities*.

Ontario Legislative Assembly. Sessional Papers. 1906–1907. *Report of the Superintendent of Neglected and Dependent Children of Ontario*, Annual Report. Toronto: L.K. Cameron.

Ontario Ministry of the Attorney General, (2001). No more free ride for the Young Offenders Act. June 12.

Ontario Native Women's Association. (1989). *Breaking Free: A Proposal for Change to Aboriginal Family Violence*. Thunder Bay.

Osborne, D. and Gaebler, T. (1992). *Reinventing Government: How the Entrepreneurial Spirit is Transforming the Public Sector*. Reading, MA: Addison-Wesley.

Ottawa Citizen. "Youth and Consequences." September 13, 2004.

Owen, B. and Bloom, B., (1998/1995). "Profiling women prisoners: Findings from national survey and California sample." *The Prison Journal*, 75(2), 165–185.

Owen, B. and Covington, S. (2003). *Gender Responsive Strategies: Research, Practice and Guiding Principles for Women Offenders*. U.S. Department of Corrections.

Oxfam Canada, (2005). Annual Report.

Palmer, B. (1978). "Discordant Music: Charivaris and Whitecapping in 19th Century North America." *Labour/Le Travail*, 3, 27–52.

Pashmna, J. (1974). "On the Learned Origin of Violence." *Revue Internationale de Philosophie*. 28. (1–2) 194–208.

Pate, K.(1997). *Justice for Battered Women—Denied, Delayed... Diminished: Jails are Not the Shelters Battered Women Need*, Elizabeth Fry Society, September 28, 1997. www.elizabethfry.ca/diminish.htm

Pate, K. (1999). "Young Women and Violent Offences: Myths and Realities." *Canadian Women's Studies*, 19(1 and 2), 39–44.

Pate, K. (2000). "The Jettisoning of Juvenile Justice? The Story of K." *Canadian Women's Studies*, 20 (3).

Pavlich, G. (2000). *Critique and Radical Discourses on Crime*. Aldershot: Ashgate.

Pavlich, G. (2002). "Towards an Ethics of Restorative Justice." In L. Walgrave (Ed.), *Restorative Justice and the Law*. Portland: Willan Publishing, pp.1–18.

Pavlich, G. (2006). *Governing Paradoxes of Restorative Justice*. London: Glasshouse Press.

Pavlich, G. and Ratner, R.S. (1996). "Omnes et Singulatim in Criminological Theory." In T. O'Reilly-Fleming (Ed.), *Post-Critical Criminology*, pp. 303-409. Ontario: Prentice Hall.

Payne, S. (1996). "Masculinity and the redundant male: Explaining the increasing incarceration of young men." *Social & Legal Studies*, 5(2).

Pearson, P. (1998a). *When She Was Bad: Violent Women and the Myth of Innocence*. New York: Viking.

Pearson, P. (1998b). *When She Was Bad: How and Why Women Get Away With Murder*. Random House.

Pepler, D. (1998). *Girls' Aggression in schools: Scenario and strategies*. Unpublished paper. Toronto: The Ministry of Training and Education, Government of Ontario.

Pepler, D.J. and Sedighdeilami, F. (1998). *Aggressive Girls in Canada*. Working Papers. Hull, Quebec: Applied Research Branch, Strategic Policy, Human Resources Development Canada.

Peters, E.J. (2004). "Urban Aboriginal People and Public Policy". *CAG Newsletter*, 11, 2:4, 6.

Peters, L. and Murphy, A. (1994). *Adolescent Health Survey: Street Youth in Vancouver*. Burnaby, BC: The McCreary Centre Society.

Peterson, M. (1988). "Children's understanding of the juvenile justice system: A cognitive-developmental perspective." *Canadian Journal of Criminology*, 30(4), 381–395.

Peterson-Badali, M. and Abramovitch, R. (1992). "Children's knowledge of the legal system: Are they competent to instruct legal counsel?" *Canadian Journal of Criminology*, 34(2), 139–160.

Petrosino, A.J. (1997). 'What Works?' Revisited Again: A Meta-Analysis of Randomized Experiments in Rehabilitation, Deterrence and Delinquency Prevention [dissertation]. Ann Arbor (MI): Rutgers University.

Petrosino, A. and Turpin-Petrosino, C. (2000). "'Scared Straight' and other prison tour programs for preventing juvenile delinquency" (Protocol for a Cochrane Review). In *The Cochrane Library*, Issue 4. Oxford: Update Software.

Petrosino, A., Turpin-Petrosino, C., and Buehler, J. (2003) Scared Straight and Other Juvenile Awareness Programs for Preventing Juvenile Delinquency. *Annals of the American Academy of Political and Social Science*. 589: 41–62.

Pfeffer, R. (1997). *Surviving the Streets: Girls Living on their Own*. New York: Garland Publishing.

Phillips, D. (1999). *Fetal Alcohol Syndrome/Effect (FAS/E) and Aboriginal People: Towards a Unified Strategy*, Issue 3. Ottawa: Correctional Services of Canada.

Pilkington, H. (1994). *Russia's Youth and its Culture : A Nation's Constructors and Constructed*. London; New York: Routledge.

Pinchbeck, I. and Hewitt. M. (1969). *Children in English Society*. Toronto: University of Toronto Press.

Pisciotta, A.W. (1981). "Theoretical Perspectives for Historical Analyses: A Selective Review of the Juvenile Justice Literature." *Criminology*, 19(1): 115–29.

Platt, A. (1969). *The Child Savers: The Invention of Delinquency*. Chicago: University of Chicago Press.

Platt, P. (1991). *A Police Guide to the Young Offenders Act*. Toronto: Butterworths.

Pollack, O. (1950). *The Criminality of Women*. New York: Barnes.

Pomerantz, S., Currie, D.H., and Kelly, D.M. (2004). "Sk8er girls: Skateboarders, girlhood, and feminism in motion." *Women's Studies International Forum*, 27, 547– 557.

Pomeroy, S. (2001). *Toward a Comprehensive Affordable Housing Strategy for Canada*. Caledon Institute of Social Policy, October.

Potter, W.J., et al. (1995). "How real is the portrayal of aggression in television entertainment programming?" *Journal of Broadcasting and Electronic Media*, 39, 496–516.

Prashaw, R. (2001). "Restorative Justice: Lessons in empathy and connecting people." *Canadian Journal of Mental Health*, 20(2), 23–27.

Prentice, A. (1977). *The School Promoters: Education and Social Class in Mid-19th Century Upper Canada*. (Toronto).

Prescott, L. (1997). *Adolescent Girls with Co-occurring Disorders in the Juvenile Justice System*. New York: Policy Research, Inc.

President of the Treasury Board of Canada. (2005). *Canada's Performance: The Government of Canada's Contribution*. Ottawa: Treasury Board of Canada Secretariat.

Prothrow-Smith, D. and Weissman, M. (1991). *Deadly Consequences: How Violence is Destroying our Population and a Plan to Begin Solving the Problem*. New York: Harper Collins.

Province of Canada. (1861). *Isle aux Noix Report for 1860*, Province of Canada, Sessional Papers, 1861, vol. 19, no. 4, paper no. 24.

Public Health Agency of Canada. (2006a). *Enhanced Surveillance of Canadian Street Youth in Canada*. Ottawa.

Public Health Agency of Canada. (2006b). E-SYS Quick Facts. *Who Are Canada's Street Youth: A Socio-Demographic Snapshot from E-SYS* (Enhanced Surveillance of Canadian Street Youth). Catalogue HP5-15.

Public Health Agency of Canada. (2006c). *Sexually Transmitted Infections in Canadian Street Youth*. Findings from Enhanced Surveillance of Canadian Street Youth, 1999–2003. March. Catalogue HP5-14.

Pulis, J.E. (2003). *A Critical Analysis of Probation for Young Offenders in Canada*. Unpublished MA thesis, University of Guelph.

Purdy, C. (2004). "Kids help kids in innovative program." *The Edmonton Journal*. Monday January 19.

Putting Promises into Action Campaign 2000. (May 2002). For the UN Special Session on Children. Statistics Canada

Census, 1996, custom tabulation for Canadian Council on Social Development. Queen's Printer.

Quilgars, D. and Anderson, I. (1997). "Addressing the problem of youth homelessness and unemployment: The contribution of foyers." In R. Burrows, N. Pleace and D. Quilgars (Eds.), Homelessness and Social Policy. London: Routledge.

R. v. Gladue[1999] 1 S.C.R. 688.

R. vs. JJM (1993). 19 WCB 2d. Supreme Court of Canada.

Rae, J. (2003) Indigenous Children: Rights and Reality: A Report on Indigenous Children and the UN Convention on the Rights of the Child. First Nations Child and Family Caring Society of Canada.

Rafter, N.H. (1983). "Chastizing the Unchaste: Social Control Functions of a Women's Reformatory, 1894–1931." In S. Cohen and A. Scull (eds.), Social Control and the State: Historical and Comparative Essays. Oxford: Martin Robertson.

Ratner, R.S. (1996). "In Cultural Limbo: Adolescent Aboriginals in the Urban Life-World." In G. O'Bireck, (Ed.), Not a Kid Anymore. Scarborough, ON: ITP Nelson.

Ratner, R.S. (1999). "Tracking Crime: A Professional Odyssey." In J. Hodgson (Ed.), The Criminal Justice System: Alternative Measures. Toronto: Canadian Scholars Press, pp. 101–134.

Raychaba, B. (1993). Pain, lots of pain: Family violence and abuse in the lives of 168 young people growing up in care. Ottawa: National Youth in Care Network, 607–251 Bank Street, Ottawa ON K2P 1X3.

Razack, S. (2000). "Gendered Racial Violence and Spatialized Justice: The Murder of Pamela George." Canadian Journal of Law and Society, 15(2), 5–8.

Razack, S. (2002). Race, Space and the Law: Unmapping a White Settler Society. Toronto: Between the Lines.

Rees, G. (1993). Hidden Truths: Young People's Experiences of Running Away. London: The Children's Society.

Regie Regionale de la Sante et des Services sociaux de Montreal-Centre. (1998). Defie de l'access: pour les jeunes de la rue. Montreal: Le Regie.

Reid, S. and Reitsma-Street, M. (1984). "Assumptions and implications of new Canadian legislation for young offenders." Canadian Criminology Forum, 7(1), 1–19.

Reid-MacNevin, S. (2001). "Toward a Theoretical Understanding of Canadian Juvenile Justice Policy." In R. Smandych (Ed.), Youth Justice: History, Legislation and Reform. Toronto: Harcourt Canada.

Reinink, Amy. (2007). "Closing Recreation Centres Won't Win Over Youth." Youth Voices. Winnipeg: Canadian Centre for Policy Alternatives.

Reitsma-Street, M. (1991). "Girls learn to care: Girls policed to care." In T. Baines, P. M. Evans and S.M. Neysmith (Eds.), Women's Caring: Feminist Perspectives on Welfare, Toronto: McClelland & Stewart, 106–38.

Reitsma-Street, M. (1999). "Justice for Canadian girls: A 1990s update." Canadian Journal of Criminology, 41, 335–364.

"Report Strongly Condemns Jails" The Bulletin: Official Organ of the Canadian National Committee for Mental Hygiene, 5 (1935), 5.

Report of the Commissioners Appointed to Enquire into the Prison and Reformatory System of Ontario. (1891). Toronto: Warwick & Sons. 98.

Report of the Aboriginal Justice Inquiry of Manitoba, Volume 1. (1999) Winnipeg.

Report of the Royal Canadian Mounted Police, "D" Division, Manitoba (2004).

Report of the Royal Commission on Public Welfare (1930).

Report of the Superintendent, Andrew Mercer Reformatory. (1883).

Ritchie, Conrad. Nd. Seventh Generation. Accessed on May 3, 2007 http://ayn.ca/FirstTruths-Stories-Seventhgen.aspx.

Roach, K. (1999). Due Process and Victims' Rights: The New Law and Politics of Criminal Justice. Toronto: University of Toronto Press.

Roach, K. (2000). "Changing punishment at the turn of the century: Restorative justice on the rise." Canadian Journal of Criminology 42: 249–280.

Roach, K. and Rudin, J. (2002). "Gladue: The judicial and political reception of a promising decision." Canadian Journal of Criminology, 42:355–388.

Roberts, J. (2003). "The Sentencing of Juvenile Offenders in Canada: An analysis of Recent Reform Legislation." Journal of Contemporary Criminal Justice 19 (4): 413.

Roberts, J. and Melchers, R. (2003). "The incarceration of Aboriginal offenders." Canadian Journal of Criminology 45 (2): 170–189.

Robertson, M. and Torro, P. (1999). "Homeless youth: Research, intervention, and policy." In L. Forburg and D. Dennis (Eds.), Practical Lessons: The 1998 National Symposium on Homelessness Research. U.S. Department of Housing and Urban Development and the U.S. Department of Health and Human Services.

Robertson, S. (2001). "Separating the men from the boys: Masculinity, psychosexual development, and sex crime in the United States, 1930s–1960s." Journal of the History of Medicine Allied Sciences, 56 (1): 3–35, Jan.

Robinson, G.C., Armstrong, R.W., Moczuk, I.B. and Loock, C.A. (1992). "Knowledge of Fetal Alcohol Syndrome among Native Indians." Canadian Journal of Public Health, 83: 337–338.

Rocky Bird Inquest, February 26, 2003. Government of Saskatchewan.

Roediger, R. (1991). Wages of Whiteness: Race and the Making of the American Working-Class. New York: Verso.

Rose, D., Mongeau, J, and Chicoine, N. (1998). Housing Canada's Youth. Ottawa: Canada Mortgage and Housing Corporation.

Rose, N. (1989). Governing the Soul. London: Routledge.

Rose, N. (1996). "Governing 'advanced' liberal democracies." In A. Barry, T. Osborne and N. Rose (Eds.), *Foucault and Political Reason: Liberalism, Neo-Liberalism and Rationalities of Government*. London: UCL Press.

Ross, E.A. (1969). *Social Control*. Cleveland: Case Western Reserve University Press.

Ross, R. (1996). *Returning to the Teachings, Exploring Aboriginal Justice*. Saskatoon, SK: Penguin Books.

Rotheram-Borus, M.J., Mahler, K.A., Koopman, C., and Langabeer, K. (1996). "Sexual abuse history and associated multiple risk behaviors in adolescent runaways." *American Journal of Orthopsychiatry*, 66, 390–400.

Rothman, D.J. (1980). *Conscience and Convenience: The Asylum and Its Alternatives in Progressive America*. Boston: Little Brown.

Rowe, D.C. (2001). "Problem Behavior Model with American Indian, Hispanic, and Caucasian Youth." *The Journal of Early Adolescence*, May, 21(2): 133

Rowe, D.C. (2002). *Biology and Crime*. Los Angeles: Roxbury.

Roy, E. et al. (2000). "Prevalence of HIV infection and risk behaviours among Montreal street youth." *International Journal of STD and AIDS* 11(4), 241–247.

Royal Commission on Aboriginal Peoples. (1993). *Aboriginal Peoples and the Criminal Justice System. Report of the National Round Table on Justice Issues*. Ottawa: Canada Communications Group.

Royal Commission on Aboriginal Peoples. (1995). *Choosing Life: Special Report On Suicide Among Aboriginal People*. Ottawa: Canada Communication Group Publishing.

Royal Commission on Aboriginal Peoples (1996a). *Report of the Royal Commission on Aboriginal Peoples, Vol. 1: Looking Forward, Looking Back; Vol.3: Gathering Strength; Vol.5: Renewal, A Twenty-Year Commitment*. Ottawa: Canada Communications Group.

Royal Commission on Aboriginal Peoples. (1996b). *Report of the Royal Commission on Aboriginal Peoples*. Ottawa: Department of Indian and Northern Affairs.

Royal Commission on Aboriginal Peoples. (1996c). People to people, nation to nation: *Highlights from the report of the Royal Commission on Aboriginal Peoples*. www.ainc-inac.gc.ca/ch/rcap/rpt/gs_e.html

Royal Commission on Aboriginal Peoples. (1996d). *Bridging the Cultural Divide: A Report on Aboriginal People and Criminal Justice in Canada*, 1996.

Russell, L.A. and Robertson, M. (1998). *Child maltreatment and psychological distress among urban homeless youth*. New York: Garland.

Russell, S. (1996). *Take Action for Equality, Development and Peace: A Canadian Follow-up Guide to Beijing '95*. L. Souter, and B. Bayless, (Eds.) Ottawa: CRIAW, Canadian Beijing Facilitating Committee.

Russell, S. (2003). *Factors Affecting Saskatoon's Crime Rates*. Report to the Saskatoon Board of Police Commissioners, 2003. See www.ojp.usdoj.gov/bjs/dcf/duc.htm.

Ruxton, S. (1996). "Boys won't be boys: Tackling the roots of male delinquency." In L. Trefor and T. Wood (Eds.), *What Next for Men?* London: Working With Men.

Sacco, V. (1995). "Media Constructions of Crime." *Annals of the American Academy of Political and Social Science*, 539. 141–154.

Safe Street Act, S.O. 1999. c.8.

Sangster, J. (2001). *Regulating Girls and Women; Sexuality, Family, and the Law in Ontario, 1920–1960*. Don Mills: Oxford University Press.

Santoni, R. (1993). "On the existential meaning of violence." *Dialogue and Humanism*, 4 (1993): 139–150.

Sarasalo, E., Bergman, B., and Toth, J. (1998). "Repetitive shoplifting in Stockholm, Sweden: a register study of 1802 cases." *Criminal Behaviour and Mental Health*, vol. 8, pp. 256–65.

Saskatchewan Schools Trustees Association. (1994). *One incident is too many: Policy guidelines for safe schools*. SSTA Research Report #94–05.

Saskatoon Police. (2003). *Factors Affecting Saskatoon's Crime Rates*.

Sauve, J. (2005). Crime Statistics in Canada–2004. *Juristat*, 25(5). Ottawa: Statistics Canada. Canadian Centre for Justice Statistics.

Savoie, J. (1999). Youth Violent Crime. *Juristat*, 19. (13) Ottawa: Statistics Canada, Canadian Centre for Justice Statistics.

Schaffer, L. (1999). *Teenage Runaways. Broken Hearts and "Bad Attitudes."* New York: Haworth Press.

Schinn, M. (1997). "Family homelessness: State or trait?" *American Journal of Community Psychology* 25(6), 755–769.

Schissel, B. (1993). *Social Dimensions of Canadian Youth Justice*. Toronto: Oxford University Press.

Schissel, B. (1997). *Blaming Children: Youth Crime, Moral Panics and the Politics of Hate*. Halifax: Fernwood Publishing.

Schissel, B. (2001). "Youth Crime, Moral Panics and the News: The Conspiracy against the Marginalized in Canada." In R. Smandych (Ed.), *Youth Justice: History, Legislation and Reform*. Toronto: Harcourt Canada.

Schissell, B. (2006). *Still Blaming Children: Youth Conduct and the Politics of Child Hating*. Halifax: Fernwood.

Schissel, B. and Fedec, K. (1999). "The Selling of Innocence: The Gestalt of Danger in the Lives of Youth Prostitutes." *Canadian Journal of Criminology*, 41(1).

Schulenberg, J.L. (2004). *Policing Young Offenders: A Multi-Method Analysis of Variations in Police Discretion*. Unpublished doctoral dissertation, University of Waterloo.

Schwartz, M.D. (1996). "Study of masculinities and crime." *Criminologist*, 21 1, January-February, pp. 1, 4–5.

Scott, K. (2007). *Presentation to Senate Committee on Social Affairs, Science, and Technology.* Canadian Council on Social Development.

Scott. W.L. (1908). *An Explanation of the Need for the Dominion Act Dealing with Juvenile Delinquency.* Ottawa: unpublished pamphlet.

Scott. W.L. (1913). *The Juvenile Court and Probation System for Children.* Ottawa: unpublished pamphlet.

Scott. W.L. (1931). "The Genesis of the Juvenile Delinquents Act." Unpublished notes and letters.

Standing Senate Committee on Aborigianl Peoples. (2003). Proceedings 18 February Mr. Randy Jackson, Aboriginal Persons Living with HIV/AIDS Coordination Programs, Canadian Aboriginal Aids Network.

Séguin, R.L. (1972). *La vie libertine en Nouvelle-France au XVIIe siècle.* Ottawa: Lemeac. 1:95.

Seventh Generation Helping to Heal, 2006. *The Seventh Generation Helping to Heal: Nishnawbe Aski Youth and the Suicide Epidemic.* www.nanseventhgeneration.ca/documents/Voices_for_Children_7th-Generation-Helping-to-Heal1.pdf (retrieved November 6, 2007).

Shapiro, A. (1978). *Scared Straight!* (film).

Sharpe, S. (1998). *Restorative Justice: A Vision for Healing and Change.* Edmonton: Edmonton Victim Offender Mediation Society.

Shaw, C.R. and MacKay, H.D. (1942), *Juvenile Delinquency and Urban Areas: A Study of Rates of Delinquency in Relation to Differential Characteristics of Local Communities in American Cities.* Chicago: University of Chicago Press.

Shaw, M. (1991). *Survey of Federally Sentenced Women: Report of the Task Force on Federally Sentenced Women.* User Report 1991–4. Ottawa: Corrections Branch, Ministry of Solicitor General of Canada.

Shaw, M. (1995). "Conceptualizing Violence by Women." In R. Emmerson Dobash, Russel P. Dobash, and Lesley Noaks (Eds.), *Gender and Crime.* Cardiff: University of Chicago Press.

Shearer, R. (2003). "Identifying the Special Needs of Female Offenders." *Federal Probation,* 67(1), 46–51.

Shearing, C. (2001). "Transforming Security: A South African Experiment." In H. Strand and J. Braithwaite (Eds.), *Restorative Justice and Civil Society.* Melbourne: Cambridge University Press.

Shelton, D.L. (2000). "New study highlights gender's impact on addiction." *American Medical News,* 43(7), 30.

Sherman, F. (2002). "Promising justice in an unjust system: Part one." *Women, Girls and Criminal Justice,* 3(4), 49–60.

Sherman, L. and Barnes G. (1997). *Restorative Justice and Offender's Respect for the Law.* RISE Working Papers: Paper No. 3. Available: http://ba048864.aic.gov.au/links/rise/risepap3.html. [20 June 1997].

Sherman, L. and Strang, H. (1997). *Restorative Justice and Deterring Crime.* RISE Working Papers: Paper No. 4.

Available: http://ba048864.aic.gov.au/links/rise/risepap4.html. [20 June 1997].

Sherman L.W., et al. (1997). *Preventing Crime: What Works, What Doesn't, What's Promising.* A Report to the United States Congress. College Pk, MD: University of Maryland, Department of Criminology and Criminal Justice.

Shinn, M. and Baumohl, J. (1999). "Rethinking the prevention of homelessness." In L. Forburg and D. Dennis (Eds.), *Practical Lessons: The 1998 National Symposium on Homelessness Research.* U.S. Department of Housing and Urban Development and the U.S. Department of Health and Human Services.

Shkilnyk, A.M. (1985). *A Poison Stronger than Love: The Destruction of an Ojibway Community.* New Haven, CT: Yale University Press.

Signorielli, N. (1990). "Children, television, and gender roles: Messages and impact." *Journal of Adolescent Health Care,* 11, 50–58.

Sikora, K. (2005). *sundry: a book of poems.* Edmonton: Sextant Publishing.

Simmons, R. (2002). *Odd Girl Out: The Hidden Culture of Aggression in Girls.* New York: Harcourt.

Simon, J. (1993). *Poor Discipline: Parole and the Social Control of the Underclass, 1890–1990.* Chicago: University of Chicago Press.

Simon, R. (1975). *Women and Crime.* Lexington, MA: Lexington Books.

Simons, R. and Whitbeck, L. (1991). "Sexual abuse as a precursor to prostitution and victimization among adolescent and adult homeless women." *Journal of Family Issues,* 13:361–379.

Smandych, R. (1991). "Tory Paternalism and the Politics of Penal Reform in Upper Canada, 1830–1834: A 'Neo-Revisionist' Account of the Kingston Penitentiary." *Criminal Justice History: An International Annual,* 12, 57–83.

Smandych, R. (2001a). (Ed.) *Youth Justice: History, Legislation and Reform.* Toronto: Harcourt Canada.

Smandych, R. (2001b). "Accounting for Changes in Canadian Youth Justice: From the Invention to Disappearance of Childhood." In R. Smandych (Ed.), *Youth Justice: History, Legislation and Reform.* Toronto: Harcourt Canada.

Smandych, R. and Linden, R. (2005). "Administering Justice without the State: A Study of the Private Justice System of the Hudson's Bay Company to 1800." In C. McCormick and L. Green (Eds.), *Crime and Deviance in Canada: Historical Perspectives.* 11–26. Toronto: Canadian Scholars Press. Edited version of article originally published in *Canadian Journal of Law and Society* (1996), Vol. 11: 21–61.

Smandych, R. and McGillvray, A. (1999). "Images of Aboriginal Childhood: Contested Governance in the Canadian West to 1850." In R. Halpern and M. Daunton, (Eds.), *Empire and Others: British Encounters with Indigenous Peoples, 1600–1850,* 238–59. London: University College London Press.

Smart, C. (1976). *Women, Crime and Criminology: A Feminist Critique*. London: Routledge and Kegan Paul.

Smart, C. (1989). *Feminism and the Power of Law*. London: Routledge.

Smart, C. (1995). *Law, Crime and Sexuality: Essays in Feminism*. London: Sage.

Smart, R.G. and Walsh, G.W. (1993). "Predictors of depression in street youth." *Adolescence*, 28(109), 41–53.

Smart, R.G., Adlaf, E.M. and Porterfield, K.M. (1990). *Drugs, Youth and the Street*. Toronto: Addiction Research Foundation.

Smith, C. (1991). *Overview of Youth Recreation Programs in the United States*. Washington: Carnegie Council on Adolescent Development.

Smith, D.E. (1978). "'K is Mentally Ill': the Anatomy of a Factual Account." *Sociology*, 12(1), 23–53.

Smolak, L. and Hayden, H. (1994). "The relation of sociocultural factors to eating attitudes and behaviors among middle school girls." *Journal of Early Adolescence*, 14(4), pp. 471–490.

Snider, L. (1998). "Towards safer societies: Punishment, masculinities and violence against women." *British Journal of Criminology*, 38(1), pp. 1–39.

Snider, L. (2003). "Constituting the punishable woman." *British Journal of Criminology*, 43(2), 354–378

Snider, L. (2006). "Making Change in Neo-Liberal Times." In G. Balfour and E. Comack (Eds.), *Criminalizing Women: Gender and (In)Justice in Neo-Liberal Times*. Halifax: Fernwood Publishing.

Snyder, Jane. (2003) "On Violence: Epilogue." *Modern Psychoanalysis*, 28 (2): 259–265.

Social Planning Council of Winnipeg. (1990). *Needs Assessment of Homeless Children and Youth*. Winnipeg: Social Planning Council of Winnipeg.

Sondheimer, D.L. (2001). "Young Female Offenders: Increasingly Visible Yet Poorly Understood." *Gender Issues* (Winter), 79–90.

Sorel, G. (1906). *Reflections on Violence*. London: Allen and Unwin.

Sparks, R.F. (1982). *Research on Victims of Crime*. Washington: Government Printing Office.

Splane, R. (1969). *Social Welfare in Ontario, 1791–1893*. Toronto: University of Toronto Press.

Springer, J., Mars, J., Dennison, M. (1998). "A profile of the Toronto homeless population." In A. Golden, W. Currie, E. Greaves and J. Latimer (Eds.), *Taking Responsibility for Homelessness: An Action Plan for Toronto*. Background Papers: Volume II. Toronto: Report of the Mayor's Homelessness Action Task Force.

Sprott, J.B. (2005). *Backgrounder for YCJA*. Department of Justice. Ottawa: Department of Justice.

Sprott, J.B. and Doob, A.N. (1996). "Understanding public views of youth crime and the youth justice system." *Canadian Journal of Criminology*, 38(3), 271–290.

Sprott, J.B. and Doob, A.N. (1997). "Fear, victimization and attitudes to sentencing, the courts and police." *Canadian Journal of Criminology*, 93(3), 275–291.

Sprott, J.B. and Doob, A.N. (2003). "It's all in the denominator: Trends in the processing of girls in Canada's youth courts." *Canadian Journal of Criminology and Criminal Justice*, 45(1): 73–80.

Sprott, J.B. and Doob. A.N. (2005). "Trends in Youth Crime in Canada." In K. Campbell (Ed.), *Understanding Youth Justice in Canada*. Toronto: Pearson Education.

Streissguth, A.P., Kanter, J. (Eds.). (1997). *The Challenge of Fetal Alcohol Syndrome–Overcoming Secondary Disabilities*. Seattle: University of Washington Press.

Starr, J.E. (1913). "First Annual Report of the Juvenile Court." *Public Health Journal*, 4, pp. 201–212.

Statistics Canada, Cansim Table 253-0003.

Statistics Canada. (1991). *Aboriginal Peoples Survey*. Ottawa: Health and Welfare Canada.

Statistics Canada. (1999a). *Aboriginal Peoples in Canada*. Ottawa: Canadian Centre for Justice Statistics.

Statistics Canada (1999b). *General Social Survey: Victimization Cycle 13*. Ottawa: Statistics Canada.

Statistics Canada. (1999c). "Labour force update: Youths and the labour market." *The Daily*. December 23.

Statistics Canada (2000). *Youth in Custody and Community Services in Canada, 1998/9*. Ottawa: Canadian Centre for Justice Statistics.

Statistics Canada. (2001a) *Children and Youth in Canada*. Canadian Centre for Justice Statistics Profile Series. Catalogue no. 85F0033MIE.

Statistics Canada. (2001b) *Aboriginal Peoples in Canada*. Canadian Centre for Justice Statistics Profile Series. Catalogue no. 85F0033MIE.

Statistics Canada. (2003). *Aboriginal Peoples of Canada: A Demographic Profile*.

Statistics Canada (2005). *Canadian Centre for Justice Statistics. Children and youth as victims of violent crime. Family Violence in Canada: A Statistical Profile, 2005*. Available at www.statcan.ca/Daily/English/050420/d050420a.htm.

Statistics Canada. (2006a). *Women in Canada: A Gender-Based Statistical Report*. 5th ed. Report 89-503 XIE.

Statistics Canada. (2006b) *Persons Charged by Type of Offence (Rate, Youths Charged)*. Cansim Table: 252-0014 modified 2006-07-20.

Statistics Canada. (2006c). *Crime Statistics in Canada*. Canadian Centre for Justice Statistics. (1994). Volume 27, (25).

Statistics Canada, *Juristat*. (2001/2002) *Youth Custody and Community Service in Canada*. Vol. (24)3.

Statistics Canada, *Juristat*. (2002/2003) *Youth Court Statistics*. Vol. 24(2).

Statistics Canada, *Juristat*. (2003) *Children and Youth as Victims of Violent Crime*. Vol. 25(1).

Statistics Canada, *Juristat*. (2003/2004) *Youth Court Statistics*. Vol. 25(4).

Statistics Canada, (2004/2005) *Juristat: Youth Custody and Community Services in Canada*. Vol. 27(2).

Statistics Canada, *The Daily*, July 18, 2000.

Statistics Canada, *The Daily*, July 19, 2001.

Statistics Canada, *The Daily*, July 17, 2002.

Statistics Canada, *The Daily*, July 24, 2003.

Statistics Canada, *The Daily*, July 28, 2004.

Statistics Canada, *The Daily*, July 21, 2005.

Statistics Canada, *The Daily*, July 20, 2006.

Statistics Canada, *The Daily*, July 18, 2007.

Statistics Canada, *The Daily*, "Youth Court Statistics," October 23, 2007.

"Steering Girls away from violence." *The Toronto Star*, March 23, 2002.

Steinem, G. (1992). *The revolution from Within*. Toronto: Little, Brown and Company.

Stenning, P. (2003). "Policing the Cultural Kaleidoscope: Recent Canadian Experience." *Police & Society*, 7(1): 21–87.

Stenning, P. and Roberts, J.V. (2001). *Empty Promises: Parliament, the Supreme Court, and the Sentencing of Aboriginal Offenders*, 64 Sask. L.Rev. 137.

St. Lewis, J. and Galloway, S. (1995). *Reform of the Defence of Provocation*. Toronto: Ontario Women's Directorate.

Stone, D. (2001) "Race in British Eugenics." *European History Quarterly*, 31, 397–400.

Strange, C. (1985). "The Criminal and Fallen of Their Sex: The Establishment of Canada's First Women's Prison, 1874–1901." *Canadian Journal of Women and the Law* 1(1).

Strange, C. (1995). *Toronto's Girl Problem: the Perils and Pleasures of the City, 1880–1930*. Toronto: University of Toronto Press.

Streissguth, A., Barr, H., Kogan, J. and Bookstein, F. (1996). *Understanding the occurrence of secondary disabilities in clients with fetal alcohol syndrome (FAS) and fetal alcohol effects (FAE)*. Unpublished manuscript, Center for Disease Control and Prevention.

Sugar, F. and Fox, L. (1990). *Survey of Federally Sentenced Aboriginal Women in the Community*. Ottawa: Native Women's Association of Canada.

Sullivan, T. (1988). "Juvenile prostitution: A critical perspective." In Hagan, F. and Sussman M.B. (Eds.), *Deviance and the Family, Marriage and Family Review*, 12, (1/2), New York: The Haworth Press.

Sumner, C. (1990). *Censure, Politics and Criminal Justice*. Philadelphia: Open University Press.

Sumner, C. (1996). "The Violence of Censure and the Censure of Violence." In C. Sumner (Ed.), *Violence, Culture and Censure*. London: Taylor and Francis.

Sumner, C. (2004). *Blackwell Companion to Criminology*. Malden: Blackwell.

Sudnow, D. (1965). "Normal Crimes." *Social Problems* 12: Winter, 255–76.

Sudnow, D. (1968). *Passing On: The Social Organisation of Dying*, Englewood Cliffs, N.J., Prentice-Hall.

Surgeon General (2001). Youth violence: A Report of the Surgeon General. Washington: Department of Health and Human Services, U.S. Public Health Service.

Sutherland, N. (1976). *Children in English–Canadian Society: Framing the 20th Century Consensus*. Toronto: University of Toronto Press.

T3 Associates of Ottawa. (2001). *Evaluation of Project Turnaround*. Ottawa: T3 Associates.

Taft, J. (2004) "Girl power politics: Pop-culture barriers and organizational resistance." In A. Harris (Ed.), *All About the Girl: Culture, Power and Identity*. New York: Routledge, pp. 69–78.

Tait, G. (1995). "Shaping the 'at-risk youth': risk, governmentality and the Finn Report." *Discourse*, 16(1), pp. 103–158.

Tait, H. (1999). *Educational Achievements of Young Aboriginal Adults*. Canadian Social Trends (Spring). Ottawa: Statistics Canada, Catalogue no. 11–008.

Tannenbaum, F. (1938). *Crime and the Community*. New York: Columbia University Press.

Tannenbaum, F. (1979). "The Dramatization of Evil." In J.E. Jacoby (Ed), *Classics of Criminology*. Prospect Heights, IL: Waveland Press.

Tanner, J. (2001). *Teenage Troubles: Youth and Deviance in Canada*. 2nd edition. Toronto: Nelson.

Tanner, J. and Wortley, S. (2002). *The Toronto Youth Leisure and Victimization Survey Final Report*. Toronto: University of Toronto.

"Teens Lead Anti-violence March." *The Edmonton Journal*, May 20, 2006.

Teotonio, I. (2002). "Steering Girls away from violence." *Toronto Star*, 2002, 361–79.

TheStar.com. "Youth crime . . . and punishment." March 25, 2007.

Thomas, J. (2005) *Youth Court Statistics, 2003/04, Juristat*. Statistics Canada. catalogue 85-002-XPE, Vol. 25 (4) Canadian Centre for Justice Statistics.

Thomas, W.I. (1923). *The Unadjusted Girl*. New York: Harper and Row.

Thomas, W.I. (1925). *The Laws of Psychology*. Chicago: University of Chicago Press.

Thomlinson, B., Stephens, M., Cunes, J.W., and Grinnell R.M. (2000). Reprint of: "Characteristics of Canadian Male and

Female Child Sexual Abuse Victims." *Journal of Child & Youth Care, Special Issue* (1991): 65–76.

Thompson Crisis Centre. *Presentation to Aboriginal Justice Inquiry hearings.* Thompson, Manitoba, 21 September 1988.

Thonre, B. (1994). *Gender Play: Girls and Boys in School.* New Brunswick, NJ: Rutgers University Press.

Thrasher, F. (1927). *The Gang: A Study of 1,313 Gangs in Chicago.* Chicago: University of Chicago Press.

Tibbetts, J. (1999). " Top court tells judges to use restraint in jailing aboriginals: Supreme Court justices are concerned by the high rate of incarceration for natives." *Vancouver Sun 24 April.*

Tjepkema, M. (2002). *The Health of the Off Reserve Aboriginal Population.* Supplement to Health Reports (Ottawa: Statistics Canada, Catalogue no. 82-003-XIE, Vol. 13), pp. 73–88.

"Toll keeps mounting as violent youth spawn an epidemic of violence." *Calgary Herald,* June 29, 1992.

Tomas, A. and Dittmar, H. (1995). "The experience of homeless women: An exploration of housing histories and the meaning of home." *Housing Studies* 10(4), 493–515.

Tomsen, S. (1996). "Ruling men? Some comments on masculinity and juvenile justice." *Australian and New Zealand Journal of Criminology,* 29.

Tomsen, S. (1997). "A top night: Social protest, masculinity and the culture of drinking violence." *British Journal of Criminology,* 37(1), Winter.

Toneguzzi, M. (2003). "Youth justice options backed." *Calgary Herald,* 1 July 2003, B5.

Tonry, M. (1995). *Malign neglect.* New York: Oxford University Press.

Tonry, M. (Ed.) (1994). "Racial disproportion in US prisons." *British Journal of Criminology,* 34:97–115.

Toronto, City of. (1999). *Taking Responsibility for Homelessness: An Action Plan for Toronto.* Toronto: Report of the Mayor's Homelessness Action Task Force. www.city.toronto.on.ca/pdf/homeless_action.pdf.

Toronto Metro Newspaper, November 25, 2002.

Toronto Metro Newspaper, November 27, 2002.

Toronto Metro Newspaper, Oct. 2, 2002, p. 13.

Toronto News, 19 March 1907.

The Toronto Star, October 19, 2002.

Totten, M. (1999) "Dispelling Myths about Youth Violence." The Ottawa Citizen, February 10, 1999. Republished with permission on the Media Awareness Network at www.media-awareness.ca/english/resources/articles/perceptions_of_crime/myth_youth.cfm.

Totten, M. (2002). *The Special Needs of Females in Canada's Youth Justice System: An Account of Some Young Women's Experiences and Views.* Ottawa: Department of Justice, Canada.

Totten, M. (2004). *Gender-responsive young offender services and the need for female staff.* (May 4). Ottawa: Youth

Services Bureau. www.ysb.on.ca/english/pdf/Gender_Responsive_Youth_Justice_Services.pdf.

Totten, M. and Reed, P. (2000). "Understanding Youth Violence." Ottawa: Department of Justice, Canada.

Trépanier, J. (1991). "The Origins of the Juvenile Delinquents Act of 1908: Controlling Delinquency Through Seeking Its Causes and through Youth Protection." *Dimensions of Childhood: Essays on the History of Children and Youth in Canada,* 205–32. Winnipeg: University of Manitoba Legal Research Institute.

Trépanier, J. (2004). "What Did Quebec Not Want? Opposition to the Adoption of the Youth Criminal Justice Act in Quebec." *Canadian Journal of Criminology and Criminal Justice,*46(3), 273–299.

Trevethan, S. (1993). Police-reported Aboriginal crime in Calgary, Regina and Saskatoon. Ottawa, ON: Canadian Centre for Justice Statistics, Statistics Canada.

Trevethan, S., et al. (2001). "The Effect of Family Disruption on Aboriginal and Non-Aboriginal Inmates." Research Report R-113. Ottawa, ON: Department of Justice.

Trevethan, S., Moore, J., and Allegri, N. (2005). The "In Search of your Warrior" Program for Aboriginal Offenders: A Preliminary Evaluation. (November). R-172.

Trevethan. S., Moore, J., and Rastin, C.J. (2002). "A profile of Aboriginal offenders in federal facilities and serving time in the community." *Forum on Corrections Research,* 14(3), 17–19.

Trichur. R. (2004). *Behind Bars.* London Free Press, 1 April 2004, B2.

Trocme, N. et al. (2001). *The Canadian Incidence Study of Reported Child Abuse and Neglect, M Final Report.* Retrieved October 14, 2005 from Health Canada website: www.phac-aspc.gc.ca/ncfv-cnivf/familyviolence/pdfs/cis_e.pdf

Tustin, L. and Lutes, R. (2005). *A Guide to the Youth Criminal Justice Act, M 2006 Edition.* Markham, Ontario: Lexis Nexis Canada Inc.

Umbreit, M.S. (1985). *Crime and Reconciliation: Creative Options for Victims and Offenders.* Nashville, TN: Abingdon Press.

Umbreit, M.S. (1986a). "Victim Offender Mediation and Judicial Leadership." *Judicature,* December.

Umbreit, M.S. (1988). "Mediation of Victim Offender Conflict." *Journal of Dispute Resolution.* University of Missouri School of Law, Columbia.

Umbreit, M.S. (1994). *Victim Meets Offender: The Impact of Restorative Justice & Mediation.* Monsey, NY: Criminal Justice Press.

United Nations Committee on the Rights of the Children (2003), *Non-Discrimination and Diversity.* First Nations Child and Family Caring Society of Canada.

UPN. (1999). *Scared Straight! 20 Years Later.* Television program on US television.

US Centers for Disease Control. (1992–2002). *Youth Risk Behavior Study.* Office of National Drug Control Policy. US Centres of Disease Control 1992–2002.

Uziel-Miller, N., and Lyons, J.S. (2000). "Specialized substance abuse treatment for women and their children: An analysis of program design." *Journal of Substance Abuse Treatment*, 19, (4), 355–367.

Valentine, G. (1996). "Children should be seen and not heard: the production and transgression of adults' public space." *Urban Geography*, 17(2), 205–220.

Valentine, G. (2000). "Exploring children and young people's narratives of identity." *Geoforum*, 31(2), 256–267.

Valverde, M. (1991). *The Age of Light, Soap, and Water: Moral Reform in English Canada, 1885–1925*. Toronto: McClelland and Stewart.

Van der Ploeg, J. and Scholte, E. (1997). *Homeless Youth*. London: Sage Publications.

Van Ness, D.W. and Strong, K.H. (2000). *Restoring Justice* (2nd ed.). Cincinnati, OH: Anderson.

Varma, K.N. (2002). "Exploring 'youth' in court: An analysis of decision-making in youth court bail hearings." *Canadian Journal of Criminology*, 44(2), 143–164.

Verbrugge, P. (2003). *Fetal Alcohol Spectrum Disorder and the Youth Criminal Justice System: A Discussion Paper*. Ottawa: Department of Justice.

Virtual Resource for Addiction Treatment System, Centre for Addiction and Mental Health, http://sano.camh.net/resource.street.htm.

Wacquant, L. (2000). "The New 'Peculiar Institution': On the Prison as Surrogate Ghetto." *Theoretical Criminology*, 4(3), pp. 377–389.

Wacquant, L. (2001). "Deadly Symbiosis: When Ghetto and Prison Meet and Mesh." in D. Garland (Ed.), *Mass Imprisonment: Social Causes and Consequences*, London: Sage. pp. 82–120.

Wacquant, L. (2005). *Pierre Bourdieu And Democratic Politics: The Mystery Of Ministry*. Oxford: Blackwell Publishing.

Wade, Francis. (1971) "On Violence." *The Journal of Philosophy*, 68 (12): 369–377.

Wade, J., Biehal, N., Clayden, J., and Stein, M. (1998). *Going Missing: Young People Missing from Care*. New York: John Wiley and Sons.

Walker, J.W. (1997). *Race, rights and the law in the Supreme Court of Canada*. Toronto: The Osgoode Society for Canadian Legal History and Wilfred Laurier University Press.

Wallace, M. (1950). The Origin of the Social Welfare State in Canada, 1867–1900. *Canadian Journal of Economy and Political Science*, 16, 383–93.

Wallace, M. (2002). Crime Statistics in Canada, 2002. *Juristat* (23:5).

Wallace, M. (2004). *Crime Statistics in Canada, 2003. Juristat* 26(6). Ottawa: Canadian Centre for Justice Statistics, Statistics Canada. Cat. No. 85-002-XIE.

Wang, E., King, S., and Goldberg, E. (1991). "Hepatitis B and human immunodeficiency virus infection in street youth in Toronto, Canada." *Pediatric Infectious Disease Journal* 10(2), 130–133.

Wardhaugh, J. (1999). "The unaccomodated woman: home, homelessness and identity." *The Sociological Review*, 47(1), 91–109.

Wardhaugh, J. (2000). *Sub City: Young People, Homelessness and Crime*. Aldershot, England: Ashgate Publishing Co.

Wasserman, D. (2004). "Is there value in identifying individual genetic predispositions to violence?" *Journal of Law, Medicine and Ethics*, 32(1), 24–33.

Watson, S., and Austerbery, H. (1986). *Housing and Homelessness: A Feminist Perspective*. London: Routledge and Kegan Paul.

Webber, M. (1991). *Street Kids: The Tragedy of Canada's Runaways*, Toronto: University of Toronto Press.

West, W.G. (1993). "Escalating problem or moral panic? A critical perspective." ORBIT, *24(1)*, 6–7.

Whitbeck, L. and Simons, R. (1993). "A comparison of adaptive strategies and patterns of victimization among homeless adolescents and adults." *Violence and Victims*, 8(2), 375–392.

Whitbeck, L., Hoyt, D., and Bao, W.N. (2000). "Depressive symptoms and co-occurring depressive symptoms, substance abuse, and conduct problems among runaway and homeless adolescents." *Child Development*, 71, 721–732.

Whitbeck, L. and Hoyt, D. (1999). *Nowhere to Go: Homeless and Runaway Adolescents and their Families*. New York: Aldine de Gruyer.

Widom, C.S. (1989). The cycle of violence. *Science*, 244: 160–166.

Williams, C. W. (1991). "Child welfare services and homelessness: Issues in policy, philosophy and programs." In J. Kryer-Coe, L. Salamon, and J. Molnar (Eds.), *Homeless Children and Youth: A New American Dilemma*. New Brunswick, NJ: Transaction.

Wilkins, L.T. (1991). *Punishment, Crime and Market Forces*. Brookfield, VT: Dartmouth.

Wilson, E.O. (1975). *Sociobiology: The New Synthesis*. Cambridge, MA: Harvard University Press.

Winterdyk, J.A. (2000). Explaining delinquent behaviour. In J.A. Winterdyk (Ed.), *Issues and Perspectives on Young Offenders in Canada*. 2nd ed. pp. 35–60. Toronto: Harcourt Canada.

Wither, G. and Batten, M. (1995). *Programs for At-Risk Youth: A Review of the American, Canadian and British Literature Since 1984*. Camberwell: Australian Council for Educational Research.

Witt, P.A. and Crompton, J.L. (1996). "The at-risk youth recreation project." *Journal of Park and Recreation Administration*, 14(3), 1–9.

Wolfe, J.M. (1998). Canadian Housing Policy in the Nineties. *Policy Review*, 13(1),121–133.

Wolff, Robert Paul. "On Violence." *Journal of Philosophy*, 66.19 (1969): 601–616.

Wolfgang, M. (1978) "The Sociology of Aggression: Crime and Violence." *Australian Journal of Forensic Sciences* (September): 3–32.

Wolfgang, M. and Ferracuti, F. (1967). *The Subculture of Violence.* London: Tavistock.

Wood, W., Wong, W.F., and Chachere, J.G. (1991). "Effects of media violence on viewers' aggression in unconstrained social interaction." *Psychological Bulletin*, 109(3), 371–83.

Wortley, S. (1996). "Justice for All? Race and Perceptions of bias in the Ontario criminal justice system—a Toronto survey." *Canadian Journal of Criminology* 38(4), 439–468.

Wortley, S. (2003). *The Illusion of Accountability: Civilian Governance of the Police in a Multi-cultural Society.* Ottawa: Ministry of Citizenship and Immigration, Heritage Canada.

Wortley, S. and Tanner, J. (2003). "Data, Denials and Confusion: The Racial Profiling Debate in Toronto." *Canadian Journal of Criminology and Criminal Justice* 45 (3): 367–390.

Yalnizyan, A. (1998). *The Growing Gap: A Report on Growing Inequality Between Rich and Poor in Canada.* Toronto: Centre for Social Justice.

Yasmin, J. (2002). "Erasing Race: The Story of Reena Virk." In Katherine McKenna and June Larkin, (Eds.) *Violence Against Women: New Canadian Perspectives.* Toronto, Inanna Publications, pp. 441–453.

Yates, P. (2004). *Citizens' Advisory Committees to the Correctional Service of Canada 2004–2005 Annual Report.* Correctional Service Canada.

Yerbury, J.C. and Griffiths, C.T. (1991). "Minorities, crime, and the law." In M.A. Jackson and C.T. Griffiths (Eds.), *Canadian Criminology. Perspectives on Crime and Criminality.* Toronto: Harcourt Brace.

York, G. (1990). *The Dispossessed: Life and Death in Native Canada.* London, UK: Vintage.

"Young and Bloodied." *The Edmonton Journal*, June 25, 2006.

Youth Criminal Justice Act: 2005 Annual Statement, Executive Summary. (June 22). Ottawa: Department of Justice.

Youth custody and community services, *The Daily*, Tuesday, March 28, 2006.

Youth Violence: A Report of the (US) Surgeon General, 2001 www.surgeongeneral.gov/library/youthviolence/chapter4/appendix4b/html.

Zehr, H. (1985). *Retributive Justice, Restorative Justice.* Elkhart, IN: Mennonite Central Committee, U.S. Office of Criminal Justice.

Zehr, H. (1995). *Changing Lenses: A New Focus for Criminal Justice.* Scotsdale, PA: Herald Press.

Zehr, H. (2002). *The Little Book of Restorative Justice.* Intercourse, PA: Good Books.

Zhang, S.X. (1998). "In Search of Hopeful Glimpses: A Critique of Research Strategies in Current Boot Camp Evaluations." *Crime and Delinquency,* 44(2), 314–334.

Zimring, F. (1999) *American Youth Violence.* New York: Oxford.

Zlotnick, C., Kronstadt, D., and Klee, L. (1998). "Foster care children and family homelessness." *American Journal of Public Health* 88(9), 1368–1370.

Index

Cadman, Jesse, 215
Campiou, Garrett, 165
Canada for All, A: Canada's Action Plan Against Racism (2005), 167
Canada,
    Aboriginal youth incarcerated in, 18
    FASD in, 151
    female crime rates in, 117–118, 118t
    HDI in, 159–160
    homelessness in, 187
    housing crisis in cities in, 189
    immigration to, 47
    racial hierarchy in, 146–147
    racism in, 166–169
    restorative justice in, 258
    sexual assault rates in, 132
    urbanization in, 47
    violent youth crime rate in, 221
    YJC in, 277t
    young women in custody in, 107
    youth crime rate in, 9
    youth custody rate in, 105
    youth incarceration rate in, 103, 104
    youth numbers in, 9
Canadian Assistance Plan (CAP), 70
Canadian Association of Elizabeth Fry Societies, 127, 134
Canadian Bar Association, 158, 193
Canadian Centre for Justice Statistics, 103
Canadian Centre for Policy Alternatives, 175
Canadian Charter of Rights and Freedoms, 73, 101
Canadian Council on Social Development, 154
Canadian Federation of University Women, 123
Canadian Housing and Renewal Association, 191
Canadian Mental Health Association (CMHA), 70
Canadian Psychiatric Association (CPA), 70, 71
Canadian Research Institution for Law and the Family (1990), 159
Canadian Sentencing Commission, 9
Canadian Youth and Children Condemn Violence in Society, 276
Caputo, T., 201
carceral complex, 163
Cardinal, Lewis, 237
Carrigan, D., 40, 41, 45, 53
Carrington, Peter J., 98, 158

CAS. *See* Children's Aid Society (CAS)
Caspi, A., 224
Centre of Restorative Justice, Simon Fraser University, 258
Centuries of Childhood, 43–44
Cernkovich, S. A., 122
Chadwick, R. B., 61
Chalifoux, T., 162
Chapman, Ken, 269
charivari (sliwaree) rituals, 42
Chartrand, Larry N., 151, 152, 232
Cherrington, Mark, 278
Chesney-Lind, M., 122, 125, 135, 137, 138, 139
Chicago School of Sociology, 29
child abuse, 196
    in Aboriginal communities, 233–234
child welfare, 49–50, 196–197
    Aboriginal youth and, 156–157
childhood,
    as cultural artifact, 44
    before Confederation in Canada, 45–46
    in 17th and 18th centuries Canada, 44
    juvenile delinquency and, 43–44
Children of the Night program, 137
Children's Aid Society (CAS), 50, 58, 272, 274
Cho, Seung-Hui, 13
Christie, Nils, 249
chronic instability, 184
CIPS. *See* criminal information processing system (CIPS)
Circle of Life Thunderbird House, Winnipeg, 178
CISC. *See* Criminal Intelligence Service of Canada (CISC)
Clarke, C. K., 27
class, 19, 20
    inequalities, 6
classical legal governance, 41, 45–46
classical theories, 24
Cloward, R., 22
CMHA. *See* Canadian Mental Health Association (CMHA)
Cohen, I. M., 119, 135, 169
Cohen, Stanley, 8, 43, 72
Cold Case (TV series), 215
colonialism. *See* colonization (colonialism)

assaults on, 199
causes of, 188–189
child welfare and, 196–197
definition of, 187
factors contributing to, 188
family conflict and, 195–196
personal problems and, 197–198
poverty and, 189
relative, 187
see also street-involved youth
shelters for, 187
stages to move out of, 206
substance abuse and, 198
unemployment and, 189–190
young women and, 191–192
Homer, 217
homicide,
    rate, 11
    see also murder
homophobia, 198
Howland, W. H., 25, 54
Hoyt, D., 195
Hudson, Barbara, 131
Human Genome Project, 223
human immunodeficiency virus (HIV), 31, 138, 178, 242
Human Resources Development Canada, 177
Hundt, Reed, 229
Hunter, J., 197
Hutson, S., 188
hyper-visibility, 98

I

Iacovetta, Franca, 167
iHuman Youth Society, 182–183, 209, 264, 278
Iliad, The, 217
Illusions, 237
In Search of Your Warrior program, 171
incapacitation, 48
incarceration,
    young women in, 134–136
indeterminate sentencing, 59
Indian Residential Schools Class Action Settlement, 240
individual-level pathways (toward criminalization), 127, 129
industrial school movement, 53–55
Industrial Schools Act (1874), 53
informal governance, 41–42

church in, 42
Inside Boystown, 200
institutionalized racial discrimination, 166–169
Integrated Criminal Court Survey, 11
intensive support and supervision program (ISSP), 105
interactionism, 29
intrusive punishment discourse, 17–18
Isle aux Noix, Quebec, 48, 52
ISSP. *See* intensive support and supervision program (ISSP)

J

James, J., 133
Janus, M., 133, 196
JDA. See Juvenile Delinquents Act (JDA)
Jiwani, Yasmin, 114
John Howard Society, 48
Johnson, J. G., 162
Jones, Owain, 271
judges, role of, 102
Juristat, 11, 104
Just Listen to Me: Youth Voices on Violence, 270, 272, 273, 274, 275, 276
justice, 255–256
    definition of, 249
    restorative, 248, 249, 256, 257, 261t, 262t
    retributive, 248, 250, 261t, 262t
    sacred, 248
juvenile courts, 40, 59–62
    JDA and, 59
juvenile delinquency,
    as male issue, 51
    childhood and, 43–44
    discourse of, 40
    gendered strategy of, 40
    historical perspectives of, 23, 24t
    in early Canada, 40
    JDA definition of, 58
    objectivist approach to, 42
    separate institutions for, 48
    social constructivist approach to, 42
Juvenile Delinquents Act (JDA), 40, 41–53, 57–59, 67, 72
    criticisms of, 71t
    DJCJD and, 67–69
    impact of, 62–63
    philosophy of, 59

P

PAA. *See* Prisoners' Aid Society (PAA)
Paik, H., 229
Papin, Rob, 178
parens patraie, 55, 59
parent-adolescent conflict, 195
partial fetal alcohol syndrome (PFAS), 150
particularistic knowledge, 47
Pate, Kim, 113, 127, 134
paternalism, 136, 139–140
patriarchy, 114, 126
Pavlich, George, 259
Pearson, Patricia, 122
peer mediation, 68, 137
Penetanguishene Reformatory, Ontario, 25, 48, 52–53
Peplar, Debra, 123
perfectibility, 26
Petrosino, A., 254
PFAS. *See* partial fetal alcohol syndrome (PFAS)
Pfeffer, R., 203
philanthropic elite, 25, 26
Piaget, Jean, 73
Pickton, Robert, 131
Platt, Anthony, 49
police, 95–96
    extra-judicial measures and, 96–99
politics of exclusion, 184
Pollack, Otto, 121
popular consciousness, 3, 6–7
Positive Adolescent Sexuality Support program, 178
Positive School, The, 25
positivism, 25
    characteristics of, 25
Powder, Derek, 237, 241
Power to Criminalize, The: Violence, Inequality and the Law, 88
PPP. *See* progressive, perfectibility, and products (PPP) of the environment
practices of governance, 4–5
praxis,
    Marxian, 5
    of possibility, 5
    social justice, 5, 6
presumptive offences, 104
primary deviance, 69
Prince Edward Island,

    unemployment in, 5
Prison Break (TV series), 7
Prisoners' Aid Society (PAA), 48
probation, 63
products of the environment, 26
progressive, perfectibility, and products (PPP) of the environment, 25
Project Turnaround, 251, 252t, 253
proportional sentencing, 107
prostitution, 133, 200, 241
    street youth and, 203
    youth, 192
Protection of Sexually Exploited Children Act (PCEC) (Alberta) (prev. *Protection for Children Involved in Prostitution Act* (PCHIP)), 120, 192
Prothrow-Smith, D., 221
psychoanalytic theory, 225, 226
psychological approach (to violence), 225–227
public (popular) discourse, 7, 8–9, 12
    see also discourses
    youth as victim, 17
    youth in need of discipline, 17
Public Health Agency of Canada's Violence and Youth Fact Sheet, 212
public school movement, 49–50
punishable young offender, 17
punishment, 4

Q

Quebec,
    YOA in, 81–82

R

R. v. C.J.M. (2000), 151
R. v. David William Ramsay (2004), 135
R. v. Gladue (1999), 92, 171, 172
    results of, 173
race, 19, 20
    definition of, 147
    inequalities, 6
    see also institutionalized racial discrimination
rationalities of governance, 5
Ratner, Bob, 162, 163
Razack, Sherene, 89, 90, 167, 168, 240
recidivism, 12, 250
Red Book (1993), 75

Thanatos, 225, 226
Thomas, W. I., 42
Thompson Crisis Centre, Thompson, Manitoba, 150
Thrasher, Frederick, 120
Toronto Industrial Refuge for Girls, 51
Toronto Juvenile Court, 60
Toronto Police Service, 164
Toronto School Board, 25
Toronto Star, The, 164
Toronto,
    displaced youth in, 5
Totten, Mark, 117, 132, 133, 136, 235
tough on crime, 17–18
Trépanier, Jean, 82
Trevethan, S., 170
Trudeau, Pierre Elliot, 73

U

U.S. Centers for Disease Control, 118
Umbreit, M. S., 258
UN Convention on the Rights of the Child Conference
    (1994), 270
UN. *See* United Nations (UN)
United Nations (UN), 186–187
United Nations Human Development Index
    (HDI), 159
University of Alberta, 209
University of Chicago, 28
University of Toronto, 164, 272
urban legend, 8
Urban Native Youth Association, 157, 208
urban transition programs, 176
utilitarianism, 24

V

Vancouver Sun, 113
Victim-Offender Reconciliation Programs (VORP), 258
victimization, 12, 13, 200, 232
    Aboriginal youth and women dependency, 152
    family, 233
    long-term effects of, 132
    of Aboriginal youth, 232
    of girls, 132–133
    street youth, 201, 202
Victoria Industrial School for Boys (VIS), 53, 54–56
violence,

biological approach, 223–225
contemporary, 217–218
definition of, 218–220
gender and, 231
genetics and, 224–225
history of, 216–217
in society, 214–215, 216
media and, 12, 76, 228, 230
on television, 229, 230
psychological approach to, 225–227
public belief about, 9
redefined, 11
school, 7, 13–212, 215
smoking and, 230
sociological approach to, 227–229, 230–231
youth crime and, 3, 4, 8, 12–13
youth crime rates and, 221
violent repeat offender, 105
Virginia Polytechnic Institute and State University
    (Virginia Tech), 13, 215
Virginia Tech. *See* Virginia Polytechnic Institute and
    State University (Virginia Tech)
Virk, Reena, 113–114, 115, 215
VIS. *See* Victoria Industrial School for Boys (VIS)
Voices for Children, 272, 276
VORP. *See* Victim-Offender Reconciliation Programs
    (VORP)

W

W.R. Myers High School, Taber, Alberta, 13
Wade, Francis, 218
Walker, Barrington, 167
Walker, James, 166–167
Wamback, Joe, 76
Wamback, Jonathan, 76–77
Wardhaugh, J., 203
Wasserman, D., 224
Watkins, T. R., 138
way of theorizing, 22–23
Weissman, M., 221
welfare penalty, 62
When She Was Bad, 122
Whitbeck, L., 195
Who Killed Garrett Campiou?, 165
Williams, John, 17
Wilson, E. O., 219